A HISTORY OF
THE CRUSADES

PLATE I

TEMPLAR KNIGHTS FIGHTING THE SARACENS

A HISTORY OF
THE CRUSADES

VOLUME II
THE KINGDOM OF JERUSALEM

BY
STEVEN RUNCIMAN

CAMBRIDGE
UNIVERSITY PRESS

PUBLISHED BY THE PRESS SYNDICATE OF THE UNIVERSITY OF CAMBRIDGE
The Pitt Building, Trumpington Street, Cambridge, United Kingdom

CAMBRIDGE UNIVERSITY PRESS
The Edinburgh Building, Cambridge CB2 2RU, UK   www.cup.cam.ac.uk
40 West 20th Street, New York, NY 10011-4211, USA   www.cup.org
10 Stamford Road, Oakleigh, Melbourne 3166, Australia
Ruiz de Alarcón 13, 28014 Madrid, Spain

First published in hardback 1951
First published in paperback by Cambridge University Press 1987
Reprinted 1951, 1953, 1954, 1957, 1962, 1968, 1975, 1980, 1987,
1988, 1989, 1990, 1992, 1994, 1995, 1996, 1997, 1999

Printed in the United States of America

Typeset in Bembo

Library of Congress Catalog card number: 75-10236

Volume I: ISBN 0 521 06161 X hardback
             ISBN 0 521 34770 X paperback
Volume II: ISBN 0 521 06162 8 hardback
             ISBN 0 521 34771 8 paperback
Volume III: ISBN 0 521 06163 6 hardback
             ISBN 0 521 34772 6 paperback
Set of three volumes: ISBN 0 521 20554 9 hardback
             ISBN 0 521 35997 X paperback

Paperback editions for sale in USA only

To
RUTH BOVILL

CONTENTS

Contents

viii

LIST OF PLATES

frontispiece

I Templar knights fighting the Saracens
(From the 12th century frescoes of Cressac, Charente.
Photograph by the Musée des Monuments français)

between pp. 276 and 277

II Jerusalem from the Mount of Olives
(From *Syria, Illustrated,* Vol. III by Bartlett, Allom, etc.,
London, 1838)

III Tripoli
(From *Syria, Illustrated,* Vol. I by Bartlett, Purser, etc.,
London, 1836)

IV The Emperor John Comnenus
(From a mosaic in Agia Sophia, Constantinople, reproduced in Whittemore: *The Mosaics of Haghia Sophia
at Istanbul,* Oxford, 1942)

V Damascus
(From *Syria, Illustrated,* Vol. I)

VI Seals of Baldwin III, King of Jerusalem;
Bohemond III, Prince of Antioch; Pons,
Count of Tripoli; William of Bures,
Prince of Galilee
(From designs by Amigo, published in Schlumberger:
Sigillographie de l'Orient Latin, Paris, 1943)

VII The Emperor Manuel Comnenus and his
wife, Maria of Antioch
(Codex Vaticanus Graecus, 1176)

VIII Aleppo
(From Maundrell: *A Journey from Aleppo to Jerusalem,*
Oxford, 1731)

ix

LIST OF MAPS

PREFACE

In this volume I have attempted to tell the story of the Frankish states of Outremer from the accession of King Baldwin I to the reconquest of Jerusalem by Saladin. It is a story that has been told before by European writers, notably with German thoroughness by Röhricht and with French elegance and ingenuity by René Grousset, and, too briefly, in English by W. B. Stevenson. I have covered the same ground and used the same principal sources as these writers, but have ventured to give to the evidence an interpretation that sometimes differs from my predecessors'. The narrative cannot always be simple. In particular, the politics of the Moslem world in the early twelfth century defy a straightforward analysis; but they must be understood if we are to understand the establishment of the Crusader states and the later causes of the recovery of Islam.

The twelfth century experienced none of the great racial migrations that characterized the eleventh century and were to recur in the thirteenth, to complicate the story of the later Crusades and the decline and fall of Outremer. For the moment we can concentrate our main attention on Outremer itself. But we must always keep in view the wider background of western European politics, of the religious wars of the Spanish and Sicilian rulers and of the preoccupation of Byzantium and of the eastern Caliphate. The preaching of Saint Bernard, the arrival of the English fleet at Lisbon, the palace-intrigues at Constantinople and Baghdad are all episodes in the drama, though its climax was reached on a bare hill in Galilee.

The main theme in this volume is warfare; and in dwelling on the many campaigns and raids I have followed the example of the old chroniclers, who knew their business; for war was the background to life in Outremer, and the hazards of the battlefield often decided its destiny. But I have included in this volume a chapter on the life and organization of the Frankish East. I hope to give an account of its artistic and economic developments in my next volume. Both of those aspects of the Crusading movement reached fuller importance in the thirteenth century.

In the Preface to my first volume I mentioned some of the great historians whose writings have helped me. Here I must pay special tribute to the work of John La Monte, whose early death has been a cruel blow to Crusading historiography. We owe to him, above all others, our specialized knowledge of the governmental system in the Frankish East. I wish also to acknowledge my debt to Professor Claude Cahen of Strasbourg, whose great monograph on Northern Syria and whose various articles are of supreme importance to our subject.

I owe gratitude to the many friends who have helped me on my journeys to the East and in particular to the Departments of Antiquities of Jordan and of Lebanon and to the Iraq Petroleum Company.

My thanks are again due to the Syndics of the Cambridge University Press for their kindness and patience.

STEVEN RUNCIMAN

LONDON 1952

BOOK I

THE ESTABLISHMENT OF
THE KINGDOM

CHAPTER I

OUTREMER AND ITS NEIGHBOURS

*'Thou land devourest up men, and hast bereaved thy
nations.'* EZEKIEL XXXVI, 13

When the Frankish armies entered Jerusalem, the First Crusade
attained its goal. But if the Holy City were to remain in Christian
hands and if the way thither were to be made easy for pilgrims,
a stable government must be set up there, with reliable defences
and sure communications with Europe. The Crusaders that
planned to settle in the East were well aware of their needs. The
brief reign of Duke Godfrey saw the beginnings of a Christian
kingdom. But Godfrey, for all his estimable qualities, was a weak,
foolish man. Out of jealousy he quarrelled with his colleagues;
out of genuine piety he yielded far too much power into the hands
of the Church. His death and his replacement by his brother
Baldwin saved the young kingdom. For Baldwin possessed the
wisdom, the foresight and the toughness of a statesman. But the
task that lay before him was formidable; and he had few helpers
on whom he could rely. The great warriors of the First Crusade
had all gone northward or returned to their homes. Of the leading
actors of the movement only the most ineffectual remained in
Palestine, Peter the Hermit, of whose obscure life there we know
nothing, and who himself went back to Europe in 1101.[1] The
princes had taken their armies with them. Baldwin himself,
a landless younger son, had not brought to the East any vassals of
his own, but had borrowed men from his brothers. He was now

[1] Hagenmeyer, *Pierre l'Hermite*, pp. 330–44. Peter died at an advanced age
in 1115 (*ibid.* p. 347).

3

dependent upon a handful of devout warriors who had vowed before they left Europe to remain in the Holy Land, and of adventurers, many of them younger sons like himself, who hoped to find estates there and to enrich themselves.

At the time of Baldwin's accession the Franks maintained a precarious hold over the greater part of Palestine. It was most secure along the mountainous backbone of the province, from Bethlehem northward to the plain of Jezreel. Many of the villages there had always been Christian; and most of the Moslems of the district had abandoned their homes on the appearance of the Frankish armies, even deserting their favourite city of Nablus, which they called the Little Damascus. This was an easy district to defend. On the east it was protected by the valley of the Jordan. Between Jericho and Beisan there was no ford across the river and only one track led up from the valley into the mountains. It was almost equally hard of access from the west. Farther north was the principality of Galilee, which Tancred had conquered for Christendom. This included the plain of Esdraelon and the hills from Nazareth to Lake Huleh. Its borders were more vulnerable; it was easily entered from the Mediterranean coast by Acre and from the east along roads to the north and to the south of the Sea of Galilee. But, from there too, much of the Moslem population had emigrated, and only Christians remained, apart from small Jewish colonies in the towns, especially in Safed, long the chief home of the Talmudic tradition. But most of the Jews, after the massacre of their co-religionists at Jerusalem and at Tiberias and their opposition to the Christians at Haifa, preferred to follow the Moslems into exile.[1] The central ridge and Galilee were the core of the kingdom; but tentacles were stretching out into the more Moslem districts around. The principality of Galilee had recently been given an outlet to the sea at Haifa. In the south the Negeb was dominated by the Frankish garrison at Hebron. But the Castle of Saint Abraham, as it was called by the Franks, was little more than an island in a Moslem ocean.[2] The Franks had no control over the

[1] For the Jews, see below, p. 295.   [2] See above, vol. 1, pp. 304, 316.

4

tracks that led from Arabia, round the southern end of the Dead Sea, along the course of the old Spice Road of the Byzantines; by which the Bedouin could infiltrate into the Negeb and link up with the Egyptian garrisons at Gaza and Ascalon on the coast. Jerusalem itself had access to the sea down a corridor running through Ramleh and Lydda to Jaffa; but the road was unsafe except for military convoys. Raiding parties from the Egyptian cities, Moslem refugees from the uplands and Bedouins from the desert wandered over the country and lay in wait for unwary travellers. The Norse pilgrim, Saewulf, who went up to Jerusalem in 1102, after Baldwin had strengthened the defences of the kingdom, was horrified by the dangers of the journey.[1] Between Jaffa and Haifa were the Moslem cities of Arsuf and Caesarea, whose emirs had announced themselves the vassals of Godfrey but kept all the while in touch by sea with Egypt. North of Haifa the whole coast was in Moslem hands for some two hundred miles, up to the outskirts of Lattakieh, where the Countess of Toulouse was living with her husband's household, under the protection of the Byzantine governor.[2]

Palestine was a poor country. Its prosperity in Roman times had not outlasted the Persian invasions; and constant wars since the coming of the Turks had interrupted its partial recovery under the Caliphs. The land was better wooded than in modern times. Despite the devastations of the Persians and the slow destruction by peasants and by goats, there were still great forests in Galilee and along the ridge of Carmel and round Samaria, and a pine-forest by the coast, south of Caesarea. They brought moisture to a countryside naturally short of water. Cornfields flourished in the plain of Esdraelon. The tropical valley of the Jordan produced bananas and other exotic fruits. But for the recent wars, the coastal plain, with its crops and its gardens where vegetables and the bitter orange were grown, would have been prosperous; and many of the mountain villages were surrounded with olive-groves

---

[1] *Pilgrimage of Saewulf* (in *P.P.T.S.* vol. IV), pp. 8–9.
[2] See above, vol. I, pp. 318–19.

and fruit orchards. But in the main the country was arid and the soil shallow and poor, especially round Jerusalem. There was no big industry in any of its towns. Even when the kingdom was at its zenith, its kings never were as rich as the Counts of Tripoli or the Princes of Antioch.[1] The main source of wealth came from tolls; for the fertile lands across the Jordan, Moab and the Jaulan, found their natural outlet in the ports of the Palestine coast. Merchandise travelling from Syria to Egypt passed along Palestinian roads; and caravans laden with spices from southern Arabia had, down the ages, travelled through the Negeb to the Mediterranean Sea. But to ensure this source it was necessary to block all other outlets. The whole frontier from the Gulf of Akaba to Mount Hermon, and even from the Lebanon to the Euphrates, must be controlled by the Franks.

Palestine was, moreover, an insalubrious country. Jerusalem, with its mountain air and its Roman sanitation, was healthy enough, except when the *khamsin* blew, sultry and dust-laden from the south. But the warmer plains, whose fertility attracted the invaders, were the homes of disease, with their stagnant waters, their mosquitoes and their flies. Malaria, typhoid and dysentery flourished there. Epidemics such as cholera and the plague spread rapidly through the crowded insanitary villages. Lepers abounded. The western knights and soldiers, with their unsuitable clothes, their heavy appetites and their ignorance of personal hygiene, easily succumbed to these diseases. The rate of mortality was even higher among the children that they bred there, especially amongst their sons. The cruel prank of nature that makes baby girls tougher than their brothers was in future generations to present a constant political problem to the Frankish kingdom. Later, as the colonists learned to follow native customs, their chances of a long life improved; but the death-rate remained formidable among their infants. It was soon obvious that if the Frankish population of Palestine was to be kept at a sufficient strength to dominate the

[1] A good brief account of Palestine is given in Munro, *The Kingdom of the Crusaders*, pp. 3–9.

country, there must be continuous and ample immigration from Europe.

King Baldwin's first task must be to secure the defence of his kingdom. This would involve offensive action. Arsuf and Caesarea must be taken and their territories absorbed. Ascalon, lost to the Christians in 1099 owing to Godfrey's jealousy of Count Raymond,[1] must be annexed and the Egyptian frontier pushed to the south if the access from Jerusalem to the coast were to be made safe. Advance posts must be established in Transjordan and to the south of the Dead Sea. He must try to link up his kingdom with the Christian states to the north, to open the road for pilgrims and more immigrants; he must advance as far as possible himself along the coast and must encourage the formation of other Christian states in Syria. He must also secure for his kingdom a better seaport than either Jaffa or Haifa. For Jaffa was an open roadstead, too shallow for larger ships to come close inshore. Landings were made in small ferry-boats, and were full of danger if any wind were blowing. If the wind were strong, the ships themselves were in danger. The day after Saewulf landed there in 1102, he witnessed the wrecking of more than twenty ships of the flotilla with which he had voyaged, and the drowning of over a thousand pilgrims.[2] The roadstead at Haifa was deeper and was protected from the south and west winds by the rampart of Mount Carmel, but was dangerously exposed to the north wind. The only port on the Palestinian coast that was safe in all weathers was Acre. For commercial as well as strategical reasons the conquest of Acre must be achieved.

For his internal government Baldwin's chief need was for men and money. He could not hope to build up his kingdom if he were not rich and powerful enough to control his vassals. Manpower could only be obtained by welcoming immigration and by inducing the native Christians to co-operate with him. Money could be obtained by encouraging commerce with the neighbouring countries and by taking full advantage of the pious

[1] See above, vol. I, p. 297. [2] *Pilgrimage of Saewulf*, pp. 6–8.

7

desires of the faithful in Europe to subsidize and endow establishments in the Holy Land. But such endowments would be made in
favour of the Church. To ensure that they would be used to the
advantage of the whole kingdom he must be master of the Church.

The Franks' greatest asset was the disunity of the Moslem world.
It was owing to the jealousies of the Moslem leaders and their
refusal to work together that the First Crusade had achieved its
object. The Shia Moslems, headed by the Fatimid Caliph of Egypt,
loathed the Sunni Turks and the Caliph of Baghdad quite as much
as they loathed the Christians. Amongst the Turks there was
perpetual rivalry between the Seldjuks and the Danishmends,
between the Ortoqids and the house of Tutush, and between the
two sons of Tutush themselves. Individual atabegs, such as
Kerbogha, added to the confusion by their personal ambitions,
while minor Arab dynasties, such as the Banū Ammar of Tripoli
and the Munqidhites of Shaizar profited by the disorder to
maintain a precarious independence. The success of the Crusade
only added to this ineffectual chaos. Despondency and mutual
recrimination made it still harder for the Moslem princes to
co-operate.[1]

The Christians had taken advantage of the discomfiture of
Islam. In the north Byzantium, directed by the supple genius of
the Emperor Alexius, had utilized the Crusade to recover control
of western Asia Minor; and the Byzantine fleet had recently
brought the whole coast-line of the peninsula back into the
Emperor's power. Even the Syrian port of Lattakieh was, owing
to the help of Raymond of Toulouse, once more an imperial
possession.[2] The Armenian principalities of the Taurus and Anti-
Taurus mountains, which had been threatened with extinction by
the Turks, could now feel hopeful of survival. And the Crusade
had given birth to two Frankish principalities, which drove a
wedge into the Moslem world.

[1] An excellent brief account of the Moslem world at this time is given in the
introduction to Gibb's *The Damascus Chronicle* (Ibn al-Qalanisi).
[2] See above, p. vol. I, pp. 318–19.

8

The Principality of Antioch

Of these the wealthier and more secure was the principality of Antioch, founded by the Norman Bohemond, in spite of the opposition of his leading Crusader colleague, Raymond of Toulouse, and of his own sworn obligations to the Emperor Alexius. It did not cover a large area; it consisted of the lower Orontes valley, the plain of Antioch and the Amanus range, with the two seaports of Alexandretta and Saint Symeon. But Antioch itself, despite its recent vicissitudes, was a very rich city. Its factories produced silk cloths and carpets, glass and pottery and soap. Caravans from Aleppo and Mesopotamia ignored the wars between Moslem and Christian to pass through its gates on their way to the sea. The population of the principality was almost entirely Christian, Greeks and Orthodox Syrians, Syrian Jacobites and a few Nestorians, and Armenians, all of them so jealous of each other that it was easy for the Normans to control them.[1] The chief external danger came less from the Moslems than from Byzantium. The Emperor considered that he had been cheated over the possession of Antioch; and now, with the Cilician ports and Lattakieh under his control and his navy based on Cyprus, he awaited an opportunity to reassert his rights. The Orthodox within the principality were eager to see Byzantine rule restored; but the Normans could play off against them the Armenians and the Jacobites. Antioch had suffered a severe blow in the summer of 1100, when Bohemond led his expedition to the upper Euphrates, and his army was destroyed by the Danishmend emir and he himself taken into captivity. But apart from the loss of man-power, the disaster had not done lasting harm to the principality. The prompt action of King Baldwin, who was then still Count of Edessa, had prevented the Turks from following up their victory; and a few months later Tancred came up from Palestine to take over the regency during his uncle's imprisonment. In Tancred the Normans found a leader as energetic and unscrupulous as Bohemond.[2]

[1] For Antioch, see Cahen, *La Syrie du Nord*, pp. 127 ff.
[2] See above, vol. I, pp. 320–1; and below, chapter III.

9

The second Frankish state, the county of Edessa, served as a buffer to protect Antioch from the Moslems. The county, now ruled by Baldwin's cousin and namesake, Baldwin of Le Bourg, was larger than the principality. It sprawled on either side of the Euphrates, from Ravendel and Aintab to a vague frontier in the Jezireh, to the east of the city of Edessa. It lacked natural boundaries and a homogeneous population; for though it was mainly occupied by Christians, Syrian Jacobites and Armenians, it included Moslem towns such as Saruj. The Franks could not hope to set up a centralized government. Instead, they ruled by garrisoning a few strong fortresses from which they could levy taxes and tribute on the surrounding villages and could embark on profitable raids across the border. The whole district had always been border-country, subject to unending warfare, but it contained fertile land and many prosperous towns. From his taxes and his raids the Count of Edessa could raise an adequate revenue. Baldwin I was comparatively far wealthier as Count of Edessa than as King of Jerusalem.[1]

The chief need of the two states was man-power; and even here their need was less than that of Jerusalem. In Palestine the Christian population had been forbidden to bear arms since first the Moslems had invaded the land. There were no native soldiers on whom the new rulers could rely. But Antioch and Edessa lay within the old frontiers of Byzantium. There were Christians there with a long tradition of military prowess, notably the Armenians. If the Armenians would work in with the Frankish prince, he would have an army ready-made. Both Bohemond and Tancred at Antioch and Baldwin I and Baldwin II at Edessa, tried at first to conciliate the Armenians. But they proved themselves to be unreliable and treacherous. They could not be given places of trust. The rulers of Antioch and of Edessa needed western-born knights to lead their regiments and to command their castles, and western-born clerics to administer their government. But while Antioch offered to immigrants the prospect of a fairly secure existence,

[1] Cahen, *op. cit.* pp. 110 ff.

Edessa could only attract adventurers ready to lead the life of a brigand-chief.

Jerusalem was divided from these two northern Frankish states by a long stretch of territory ruled by a number of jealous Moslem potentates. The coast immediately to the north of the kingdom was held by four rich seaports, Acre, Tyre, Sidon and Beirut, each owing an allegiance to Egypt that waxed and waned according to the proximity of the Egyptian fleet.[1] North of Beirut was the emirate of the Banū Ammar, with their capital at Tripoli. The emir of Tripoli had recently profited by the departure of the Crusaders to the south to extend his dominion as far as Tortosa.[2] Jabala, between Tortosa and Lattakieh, was in the hands of a local magnate, the Qadi ibn Sulaiha, who in the summer of 1101 handed it over to Toghtekin, the atabeg of Duqaq of Damascus, from whom it passed to the Banū Ammar.[3] In the Nosairi mountains, behind Tortosa and Jabala, were the small emirates of the Banū Muhris of Marqab and Qadmus and the Banū Amrun of Kahf.[4] The upper Orontes valley was divided between the adventurer Khalaf ibn Mula'ib of Apamea, a Shiite who therefore acknowledged Fatimid suzerainty, the Munqidhites of Shaizar, the most important of these petty dynasties, and Janah ad-Daulah of Homs, a former atabeg of Ridwan of Aleppo, who had quarrelled with his master and enjoyed virtual independence.[5] Aleppo was still in the hands of Ridwan, who as a member of the Seldjuk ruling family bore the title of *Malik*, or King. The Jezireh, to the east, was mainly occupied by members of the Ortoqid dynasty, who had retired there on the Fatimid reconquest of Jerusalem in 1097, and who were considered to be the vassals of Duqaq of Damascus. Duqaq, a *Malik* like his brother Ridwan, ruled in Damascus.[6]

[1] Gibb, *op. cit.* pp. 15–18; Le Strange, *Palestine under the Moslems*, pp. 342–52.
[2] For the Banū Ammar, see Sobernheim's article 'Ibn Ammar', in the *Encyclopaedia of Islam*. [3] Ibn al-Qalanisi (*The Damascus Chronicle*), pp. 51–2.
[4] Cahen, *op. cit.* p. 180.
[5] See Honigman, article 'Shaizar', and Sobernheim, article 'Homs', in *Encyclopaedia of Islam*; also introduction to Hitti, *An Arab-Syrian Gentleman*, pp. 5–6.
[6] See Gibb, *op. cit.* pp. 22–4.

These political divisions were made more unstable by the divergent elements in the population of Syria. The Turks formed a sparse feudal aristocracy; but the smaller emirs were almost all Arabs. In northern Syria and in Damascene territory the urban population was largely Christian, Syrians of the Jacobite church, with Nestorians in the eastern districts and Armenians infiltrating from the north. The territory of the Banū Ammar was largely peopled by the Monothelete sect of the Maronites. In the Nosairi mountains there was the tribe of the Nosairi, a Shiite sect from whom Khalaf ibn Mula'ib drew his strength. On the slopes of the southern Lebanon there were the Druzes, Shiites who accepted the divinity of the Caliph Hakim, and who hated all their Moslem neighbours but who hated the Christians more. The situation was further complicated by the steady immigration into the cultivated lands of Arabs from the desert and of Kurds from the northern mountains, and by the presence of Turcoman companies, ready to hire themselves out to any warring chieftain that would pay them.[1]

Of Syria's Moslem neighbours the most powerful were the Fatimid rulers of Egypt. The Nile valley and the Delta formed the most thickly populated area in the medieval world. Cairo and Alexandria were great industrial cities whose factories produced glass, pottery and metalwork, as well as linens and brocades. The cultivated districts grew vast quantities of corn; and there were huge sugar-plantations in the Delta. Egypt controlled the trade of the Sudan, with its gold and its gum-arabic, its ostrich feathers and ivory. The Far Eastern trade was now carried by ships using the Red Sea route and therefore reached the Mediterranean through Egyptian ports. The Egyptian government could put enormous armies into the field; and, though the Egyptians themselves enjoyed a poor reputation as soldiers, it could afford to hire as many mercenaries as it pleased. Moreover, alone of the Moslem powers, it possessed a considerable navy. The Fatimid Caliph himself as a Shia was the natural protector of the Shia of Syria. But he was

[1] See Gibb, *op. cit.* pp. 27–9.

12

traditionally tolerant; and many of the Sunni Arabs who feared Turkish domination were ready to acknowledge his suzerainty. The Turkish invasions had curtailed the empire of the Fatimids in Syria; and the Frankish capture of Jerusalem and victory over the Egyptian relieving force at Ascalon had damaged their prestige. But Egypt could afford to lose an army. It was clear that Vizier al-Afdal, who ruled Egypt in the name of the young Caliph al-Amir and was himself an Armenian born at Acre, would seek as soon as possible to avenge the defeat and recover Palestine. In the meantime the Egyptian fleet kept in touch with the Moslem cities of the coast.[1]

The rival Caliph, the Abbasid al-Mustazhir, was a shadowy youth, who reigned at Baghdad by the grace of the Seldjuk Sultan. But the Sultan himself, Barkiyarok, the eldest son of the great Malik Shah, lacked his father's power and ability. His brothers continually revolted against him. He had been obliged to enfeoff the youngest, Sanjar, with Khorassan, and from 1099 onwards he was at war with another brother, Mohammed, who eventually secured the province of Iraq. These preoccupations made him a useless ally in the struggle against the Christians.

The head of the youngest branch of the Seldjuk dynasty, the Anatolian *Malik* Kilij Arslan, self-styled Sultan, was at the moment little better placed than his cousin. The First Crusade had deprived him of his capital, Nicaea, and of most of his treasure, lost on the battlefield of Dorylaeum. Much of the land that he had controlled had passed back into Byzantine hands. He was on bad terms with the Seldjuks of the East, whose supremacy he refused to admit. But Turcoman immigrants into Anatolia gave him the means for rebuilding his army and a population that would crowd out the Christians.[2] More effective was the Danishmend emirate, firmly established at Sivas and dominating the north-east of the peninsula. The emir, Gümüshtekin, had recently won renown by his capture of Bohemond. He was the first Moslem leader to win a victory

---

[1] See Wiet, *L'Egypte Musulman*, pp. 260 ff.
[2] See articles, 'Seldjuks' and 'Kilij Arslan', in *Encyclopaedia of Islam*.

over an army of Frankish knights. He too was being continually strengthened by Turcoman immigration.[1]

Between the Turks of Anatolia and the Frankish states of northern Syria was a group of Armenian principalities. There was Oshin, who controlled the central Taurus mountains, and to the east of him the princes of the house of Roupen. There was Kogh Vasil in the Anti-Taurus, Thatoul at Marash and Gabriel at Melitene. Thatoul and Gabriel belonged to the Orthodox Church and were therefore inclined to co-operate with Byzantium. They and Oshin based their juridical position on titles conferred on them by the Emperor. But the Roupenians, who alone of these Armenians succeeded in founding an enduring state, were traditionally hostile both to Byzantium and the Orthodox Church.[2]

The external Christian power most concerned with Syrian affairs was Byzantium. There the Emperor Alexius had been on the throne for nearly twenty years. He had found the Empire at its nadir; but by his diplomacy and his thrift, his judicious handling of his subjects and his rivals, both at home and abroad, he had re-established it on solid foundations. He had used the Crusading movement to recover western Asia Minor from the Turks; and his reorganized fleet gave him control of the coasts. Even at its lowest ebb, Byzantium enjoyed great traditional prestige throughout the East. It was the Roman Empire, with a thousand years of history behind it; and its Emperor was the acknowledged head of Christendom, however much his fellow-Christians might dislike his policy or even his greed. Constantinople, with its innumerable, busy inhabitants, its vast wealth and its formidable fortifications, was the most impressive city in the world. The armed forces of the Empire were the best equipped of their time. The imperial coinage had long been the only sure currency. International exchange was

[1] For the Danishmends, see Mukrimin Halil, article 'Danişmend', in *Islam Ansiklopedisi*.
[2] For the Armenian background, see Tournebize, *Histoire Politique et Religieuse d'Arménie*, pp. 168–70; also above, vol. i, pp. 195 ff.

calculated in terms of the hyperpyron, often called the besant, the gold solidus whose value had been fixed by Constantine the Great. Byzantium was to play a dominant role in Oriental politics for almost a century to come; but in fact its successes were due more to the brilliance of its statesmen and the prestige of its Roman name than to its real strength. The Turkish invasions had destroyed the social and economic organization of Anatolia, from whence of old the Empire had derived the greater part of its soldiers and its food; and though territory might be recovered, it was almost impossible to restore the former organization. The army was now almost entirely mercenary, and therefore both expensive and unreliable. Turkish mercenaries such as the Petchenegs might be safely employed against the Franks or the Slavs, but they could not be trusted against the Turks in Asia. Frankish mercenaries would not willingly fight against fellow-Franks. Early in his reign Alexius had been obliged to buy Venetian help by giving commercial concessions to the Venetians, to the detriment of his own subjects; and these were followed by concessions to the other maritime cities, Genoa and Pisa. The trade of the Empire thus began to pass into alien hands. A little later, in his need for ready-money, Alexius tampered with the coinage, issuing gold pieces that lacked their proper gold content. Confidence in the besant began to diminish; and soon the clients of the Empire insisted on being paid in 'Michaels', the currency minted under the Emperor Michael VII, the last that was known to be trustworthy.

The Emperor's chief concern was the welfare of his Empire. He had welcomed the First Crusade and had been ready to co-operate with its leaders; but Bohemond's ambition and perfidy at Antioch had shocked and angered him. His first desire was to recapture Antioch and to control the roads that led there across Asia Minor. When the Crusaders moved southwards into Palestine his active co-operation ended. The traditional Byzantine policy had been for the past century an alliance with the Fatimids of Egypt against the Sunni Abbasids and the Turks. Except under the mad Caliph Hakim the Fatimids had treated the eastern

Christians with kindly forbearance; and Alexius had no reason to suppose that Frankish rule would be more agreeable to them. He had therefore dissociated himself from the Frankish march on Jerusalem. But at the same time, as patron of the Orthodox, he could not be indifferent to the fate of Jerusalem. If the Frankish kingdom seemed likely to endure, he would have to take steps to see that his rights were recognized. He was ready to show the Franks in Palestine signs of good-will; but his active help would be restricted to co-operation in opening up the routes across Asia Minor. For the Normans at Antioch he felt nothing but hostility and was to prove a dangerous enemy. He seems to have entertained no ambition for the recovery of Edessa. Probably he recognized the value of the Frankish county there as an outpost against the Moslem world.[1]

A new factor had recently been introduced into Oriental politics by the intervention of the Italian merchant-cities. They had at first been diffident of joining in the Crusade till they saw that it promised to be successful. Then Pisa, Venice and Genoa all sent fleets to the East, promising help in return for establishments in any city in whose conquest they shared. The Crusaders welcomed them; for they offered the sea-power without which it would be impossible to reduce the Moslem coastal cities; and their ships provided a swifter and safer route of communication with western Europe than the long journey overland. But the concessions that they demanded and obtained meant that the Frankish governments in the East lost much of their potential revenue.[2]

The complexities of the international situation around him did not give King Baldwin much cause for optimism. His allies were either half-hearted or rapacious, and concerned with their selfish interests. The disunity of his enemies was helpful; but

[1] For the position of Byzantium and the policy of Alexius, see above, vol. I *passim*.
[2] The best summary of the part played by the Italians is in Heyd, *Histoire du Commerce du Levant*, vol. I, pp. 131 ff.

were the Moslem world to find a leader who could bind it together, there was little chance that the Frankish states in the East would survive. In the meantime he was placed with far too few supporters in a land with a deadly climate, that had been down the centuries the battlefield of nations. It was with pleasant expectation that he learnt of new Crusading expeditions setting out from the West.

CHAPTER II

THE CRUSADES OF 1101

'But they said, We will not hearken.'   JEREMIAH VI, 17

The news that the Christians had recovered Jerusalem reached western Europe during the late summer of 1099. It was received with enthusiasm and rejoicing. Everywhere chroniclers interrupted their story of local happenings to record the great instance of God's mercy. Pope Urban himself had died before he could learn of it; but his friends and helpers throughout the Church praised God for the success of his policy. During the winter that followed, many of the Crusading leaders returned home with their men. As is the wont of returning soldiers, the Crusaders no doubt exaggerated both the hardships of their journey and the splendours of the land to which they had penetrated; and they made much of the miracles with which they had been encouraged by Heaven. But they all declared that warriors and colonists were needed in the East, to carry on God's work, and that wealth and great estates lay there to be occupied by the adventurous. They urged a new Crusade to which the preachers of the Church gave their blessing.[1]

It was not until the early autumn of 1100 that the next expedition could start out. The winter months were unsuitable for travel; and then the harvest had to be gathered. But in September 1100 a Crusade of Lombards left Italy for the East. At its head was the greatest personage in Lombardy, the Archbishop of Milan, Anselm of Buis. With him were Albert, Count of Biandrate,

[1] E.g. Pope Paschal's letter in Migne, *Patrologia Latina*, vol. CLXIII, cols. 42 ff. It was thought in the East that if reinforcements did not arrive, the conquered lands might have to be evacuated (*De Translatione S. Nicolai* in *R.H C.Occ.* vol. v, p. 271).

18

Count Guibert of Parma and Hugh of Montebello. The Lombards had played an undistinguished part in the First Crusade. Many of them had journeyed east during its early months and had joined up with Peter the Hermit, and, by intriguing with his German followers against the French, had helped to wreck his expedition. The survivors had then taken service under Bohemond. In consequence, of the Crusading leaders it was Bohemond who enjoyed the highest prestige in Lombardy. The present expedition was little better organized. It included very few trained soldiers and was mainly composed of a rabble drawn from the slums of the Lombard cities, men whose lives had been disorganized by the growing industrialism of the province. With them were large numbers of clerics and women and children. It was a large company; though Albert of Aix's estimate of two hundred thousand souls should be divided by at least ten. Neither the Archbishop nor the Count of Biandrate, who was regarded as the military leader, was able to keep it in control.[1]

During the autumn of 1100 the Lombards made their leisurely way across Carniola and down the valley of the Save, through the territory of the King of Hungary, and entered the Byzantine Empire at Belgrade. Alexius was ready to deal with them. His troops escorted them across the Balkans. Then, as they were too numerous to be provisioned and policed in one camp, they were divided into three companies. One was to spend the winter in a camp outside Philippopolis, the second outside Adrianople and the third outside Rodosto. But even so they were too disorderly to be kept under control. Each company began to raid the district outside its camp, pillaging the villages, breaking into the grain-stores and even robbing the churches. At last, in March, the Emperor brought them all to a camp outside the walls of Constantinople, intending to transport them as soon as possible across into Asia. But they had heard by now that other Crusaders had set out to join them. They refused to cross the Bosphorus until

[1] Albert of Aix, VIII, 1, p. 559; Anna Comnena, XI, viii, 1, vol. III, p. 36, calling them Normans under the command of two brothers called Φλάντρας.

these reinforcements arrived. To oblige them to move, the imperial authorities cut off their supplies; whereupon they at once attacked the city walls and forced their way through into the courtyard of the imperial palace of Blachernae. There they killed one of the Emperor's pet lions, and tried to open the palace gates. The Archbishop of Milan and the Count of Biandrate, who had been well received by the Emperor, were horrified. They rushed out into the midst of the rioting crowds and succeeded at last in persuading them to return to the camp. They then had to face the task of pacifying the Emperor.[1]

Peace was made by Count Raymond of Toulouse. Raymond had been spending the winter as the guest of Alexius, whose complete confidence he now enjoyed. As the senior of all the Crusading princes, the friend of Pope Urban and of Bishop Adhemar, he still had a great reputation. The Lombards listened to him; and on his advice they agreed to move across into Asia. By the end of April they were established in a camp close to Nicomedia, where they awaited newcomers from the West.[2]

Stephen, Count of Blois, had never been allowed to forget his flight from Antioch. He had not fulfilled his Crusading vows and he had shown cowardice in the face of the enemy. His wife, the Countess Adela, daughter of William the Conqueror, was deeply ashamed of him. Even in the private intimacy of their bedchamber she would nag at him to go and redeem his reputation. He could not claim that he was needed at home; for his wife had always been the real ruler of the county. So, wearily and with foreboding, he set out again for the Holy Land in the spring of 1101.[3]

On the news of his expedition many other French knights prepared to join him, under the leadership of Stephen, Count of Burgundy, Hugh of Broyes, Baldwin of Grandpré and the Bishop

---

[1] Albert of Aix, VIII, 2–5, pp. 559–62; Orderic Vitalis, x, 19, vol. IV, p. 120, who muddles the story and says that the Emperor used lions against the Crusaders. [2] Albert of Aix, VIII, 7, p. 563; Anna Comnena, XI, viii, 2, vol. III, pp. 36–7. It was said that Raymond had the so-called Holy Lance with him. See Runciman, 'The Holy Lance found at Antioch', in *Analecta Bollandiana*, vol. LXVIII, pp. 205–6. [3] Orderic Vitalis, x, 19, vol. IV, p. 119.

of Soissons, Hugh of Pierrefonds. They travelled down through Italy and across the Adriatic, and reached Constantinople about the beginning of May. At some point on their journey they were overtaken by a small German contingent, under Conrad, Constable to the Emperor Henry IV.[1]

The French Crusaders were delighted to find Raymond at Constantinople, and were well satisfied by their reception by the Emperor. Probably on the suggestion of Alexius, they decided that Raymond should command the whole expedition; and the Lombards acquiesced. During the last days of May the whole army, Frenchmen, Germans, Lombards, some Byzantines under the General Tsitas, with whom were five hundred Turkish mercenaries, probably Petcheneg, marched out from Nicomedia on the road to Dorylaeum.

The object of the Crusade was to reach the Holy Land and on the way to reopen the route across Asia Minor, a secondary aim that had the Emperor's full support. Stephen of Blois therefore recommended that the army should follow the road taken by the First Crusade, through Dorylaeum and Konya. Raymond, in conformity with the instructions given him by Alexius, agreed with him. But the Lombards, who formed the vast majority of the army, held other views. Bohemond was their hero, the one warrior that they trusted to carry them to victory. And Bohemond lay captive in the Danishmend Emir's castle of Niksar, far away to the north-east of Anatolia. They insisted that their first task must be to rescue Bohemond. Raymond and Stephen protested in vain. Raymond's jealousy of Bohemond was too well known and, for all his qualities, he had never shown himself to be a forceful leader; whilst Stephen's influence was damaged by memories of his past cowardice. The Count of Biandrate and the Archbishop of Milan supported the Lombards, who had their way.[2] On

[1] Albert of Aix, vIII, 6, pp. 562–3; Orderic Vitalis, *loc. cit.*
[2] Albert of Aix, vIII, 7, pp. 563–4, saying that the decision to march east was the Lombards'; Anna, *loc. cit.* She says that the Emperor hoped that Raymond and Tsitas would alter this decision.

leaving Nicomedia the army turned east and took the road to Ankara. The country was largely held by the Byzantines; and the Crusaders were able to find food as they went. Ankara itself now belonged to the Seldjuk Sultan, Kilij Arslan; but when they arrived there on 23 June they found it poorly defended and took it by assault. Very correctly they handed it over to representatives of the Emperor.

On leaving Ankara the Crusaders took a track that led northeastward to Gangra, in southern Paphlagonia, to join the main road to Amasea and to Niksar. On the way to Gangra their troubles began. Kilij Arslan retreated before them, devastating the country as he went, so that they could find little to eat. Meanwhile Malik Ghazi the Danishmend had been thoroughly alarmed. He hastened to renew his alliance with Kilij Arslan and induced Ridwan of Aleppo to send reinforcements up from the south. Early in July the Crusaders reached Gangra; but the Seldjuks were there in force. The fortress proved to be impregnable. After ravaging the countryside and taking what food they could find, the Crusaders were forced to move on. They were weary and hungry; and on the Anatolian tableland the July heat was hard to bear. In their disappointment they listened to Count Raymond, who advised that they should march northward to Kastamuni and from there to some Byzantine city on the Black Sea coast. Such a course would save the army from certain destruction; and no doubt Raymond thought that the Emperor would forgive him his disobedience if he returned having recaptured for the Empire two great fortresses, Ankara and Kastamuni, the latter the *Castra Comnenon* that had been the home of the imperial dynasty.

The journey to Kastamuni was slow and painful. Water was short, and the Turks had destroyed the crops. The Turks themselves moved quickly along parallel tracks, harassing the Crusaders sometimes in the van and sometimes in the rear. They had not gone far before the advance-guard, composed of seven hundred Lombards, was suddenly attacked. The Lombard knights fled in panic, leaving the infantry to be massacred. It was with difficulty that Stephen of Burgundy was able to rally the van and drive off the enemy. During the next days Raymond, in command of the rear, was engaged in continual combat with the Turks. Soon the army was obliged to move in a compact mass, from which it was impossible to send out foraging parties or scouts. By the time that it reached the neighbourhood of Kastamuni it was clear to the leaders that the only chance of safety lay in breaking through as directly as possible to the coast. But once again the Lombards refused to listen to reason. Perhaps they blamed Raymond's choice of the road to Kastamuni for their present troubles; perhaps they thought that when they passed out of Seldjuk territory into Danishmend territory everything would be easier. In their obstinate folly they insisted on turning once more to the east. The princes had to accept this decision; for their small contingents could hardly hope to survive if they left the main army. The Crusade moved on across the river Halys, into the land of the Danish-mend emir. After wantonly sacking a Christian village on the way they reached the town of Mersivan, halfway between the river and Amasea. There the Constable Conrad was lured into an ambush and lost several hundred of his German troops. It was clear now that the Danishmends and their allies were massing for a serious attack; and Raymond drew up the Christian army ready for battle.[1]

When the battle began the Turks employed their favourite tactics. Their archers swooped down and discharged their arrows, then swiftly retreated again, and others would appear from a different direction. The Crusaders were never given the chance of a hand-to-hand combat, in which their greater physical strength

[1] Albert of Aix, VIII, 8–14, pp. 564–7. He says that Raymond was bribed by the Turks to lead the army to Kastamuni. This is unconvincing. Anna, *loc. cit.*, mentions the sacking of the Christian village. Grousset, *Histoire des Croisades*, vol. II, p. 326 n. 2, is clearly right to reject Tomaschak's identification of Albert's 'Maresch' with Amasea (*Topographie von Kleinasien*, p. 88) and to revert to Michaud's identification as Merzifun or Mersivan. Mersivan could easily be changed by an ignorant Frenchman into Maresiam or Marescam, a French form of Marash, but it is difficult to see how an 'r' could intrude into Amasya, the Turkish name for Amasea, or Masa, the Arabic.

and better arms would have been of advantage. Before long the Lombards' nerves gave out. With their leader the Count of Biandrate at their head, they fled in panic, leaving their women and their priests behind them. Soon the Petcheneg mercenaries followed, seeing no reason to await certain death. Raymond, who was fighting with them, found himself deserted. He managed to retreat with his bodyguard to a small rocky hill, where he held out till Stephen of Blois and Stephen of Burgundy could rescue him. Throughout the afternoon the French knights and Conrad the German fought bravely, falling back upon the camp; but by nightfall Raymond had had enough. Under cover of the darkness he fled with his Provençal bodyguard and his Byzantine escort towards the coast. When they learnt that he had fled, his colleagues gave up the fight. Before morning dawned the remnants of the army were in full flight, leaving the camp and the non-combatants in the hands of the Turks.

The Turks paused to butcher the men and old women in the camp, then followed in full cry after the fugitives. Only the knights on horseback were able to escape. The infantry was overtaken and slaughtered almost to a man. The Lombards, whose obstinacy had caused the disaster, were annihilated except for their leaders. The losses were estimated at four-fifths of the whole army. A vast amount of treasure and of arms fell into Turkish hands; and the harems and slave-markets of the East were filled by the younger women and children captured on that day.[1]

Raymond and his escort managed to reach the little Byzantine port of Bafra, at the mouth of the river Halys. There they found a ship to take them to Constantinople. The other knights fought their way back across the river and arrived at the coast at Sinope. From there they travelled slowly by the coast road, through Byzantine territory, to the Bosphorus. They reassembled at Constantinople early in the autumn.[2]

[1] Albert of Aix, VIII, 14–23, pp. 567–73, whose account is consistent with the briefer account of Anna (XI, viii, 3, vol. III, pp. 37–8).
[2] Albert of Aix, VIII, 24, p. 274.

Public opinion amongst the Crusaders, seeking to find a scapegoat, laid the blame for the disaster upon the Byzantines. Count
Raymond, it was said, was obeying the Emperor's instructions
when he led the army out of its course to perish in a prearranged
Turkish ambush. But in fact Alexius was furious with Raymond
and his colleagues. He received them politely but icily and made
no secret of his displeasure.[1] Had the Crusade won for him
Kastamuni and the Paphlagonian interior, he might have forgiven
it; but he was far more anxious to secure the direct road to Syria,
to safeguard his reconquests in the south-west of Asia Minor, and
to enable him to intervene in Syrian affairs. Moreover, he had not
wished to embroil himself in war with the Danishmend emir, with
whom he had opened negotiations to buy the person of Bohemond.
The folly of the Lombards ruined his scheme. But the disaster had
more serious effects. The Christian victories during the First
Crusade had damaged both the reputation and the self-confidence
of the Turks. Now both were gloriously recovered. The Seldjuk
Sultan was able to restore his domination over central Anatolia,
and soon he was to establish his capital at Konya, right on the main
road from Constantinople to Syria; while Malik Ghazi the
Danishmend continued his conquest of the Euphrates valley, to
the borders of the County of Edessa.[2] The land-route from Europe
into Syria was blocked again both for the Crusaders and for the
Byzantines. Moreover, relations between the Crusaders and
Byzantium had worsened. The Crusaders insisted upon considering
the Emperor as the author of their woes, while the Byzantines
were shocked and angered by the stupidity, the ingratitude and the
dishonesty of the Crusaders.

It was not long before the results of the disaster were apparent.
A few days after the Lombards had set out from Nicomedia, a
French army arrived at Constantinople, led by William II, Count
of Nevers. He had left his home in February and, travelling

[1] *Ibid., loc. cit.* He says that Raymond soothed the Emperor's indignation.
[2] Michael the Syrian, III, pp. 189–91. See Cahen, *La Syrie du Nord*,
p. 232.

through Italy, he had crossed the Adriatic from Brindisi to Avlona. His army gave an excellent impression as it marched through Macedonia owing to the strictness of its discipline. The Count was cordially received by Alexius; but he decided not to linger at Constantinople. He had probably expected to join forces there with the Duke of Burgundy, whose neighbour he was at home, so hurried on as quickly as possible in the hope of overtaking him. When he reached Nicomedia he learnt that the Crusade had gone on to Ankara, where he arrived towards the end of July. But at Ankara no one knew the whereabouts of the Franco-Lombard army. William therefore turned back, to take the road to Konya. In spite of the difficulties of the journey through country that had not recovered from devastations at the time of the First Crusade, his army advanced in perfect order. Konya was now held by a strong Seldjuk garrison; and William's attempt to take the city by assault was a failure. He realized that it would be unwise to delay there and moved on. But meanwhile Kilij Arslan and Malik Ghazi learnt of the appearance of this new enemy. Hot from their triumph over the Lombards they hurried southward, probably through Caesarea-Mazacha and Nigde, and reached Heraclea before him. The Nivernais troops marched slowly eastward from Konya. Food was short; the wells by the road had been blocked by the Turks. As they approached Heraclea, weary and weakened, they were ambushed and surrounded by the whole Turkish army, which outnumbered them by far. After a short battle their resistance was broken. The entire French force fell on the field, with the exception of Count William himself and a few mounted knights, who broke through the Turkish lines and after several days of wandering in the Taurus mountains arrived at the Byzantine fortress of Germanicopolis, north-west of Isaurian Seleucia. There the Byzantine governor seems to have offered them an escort of twelve Petcheneg mercenaries to convey them to the Syrian border. A few weeks later Count William and his companions entered Antioch, half-naked and unarmed. They said that the Petchenegs had despoiled them and abandoned them in the desert through which they were passing; but what really happened is unknown.[1]

The Count of Nevers had hardly crossed the Bosphorus before another larger army, composed of Frenchmen and of Germans, arrived at Constantinople. The French contingent was led by William IX, Duke of Aquitaine, who was the most famous troubadour of his time and who was politically the bitter rival of Raymond of Toulouse; for his wife, the Duchess Philippa, was the daughter of Raymond's elder brother and should have inherited his County. With him came Hugh of Vermandois, who had left the First Crusade after the capture of Antioch and was anxious to fulfil his vow to go to Jerusalem. The Aquitanian army set out from France in March and travelled overland, through southern Germany and Hungary. On its way it was joined by Duke Welf of Bavaria, who after a long and illustrious career in Germany planned to spend his declining years fighting for the Cross in Palestine. He brought with him a well-equipped army of German knights and infantry; and he was accompanied by Thiemo, Archbishop of Salzburg, and by the Dowager Margravine Ida of Austria, one of the great beauties of her day, who, now that her youth was over, sought the pious excitement of a Crusade. Their united armies marched together down the Danube to Belgrade and on by the high road across the Balkans. They were an unruly crowd; and by the time that they reached Adrianople their behaviour was so bad that the Byzantine authorities sent Petcheneg and Polovtsian troops to block their further progress. A regular battle began; and it was only when Duke William and Welf intervened in person and guaranteed the future good conduct of their troops that they were allowed to proceed. A strong escort accompanied them to Constantinople. There William and Welf and the Margravine were cordially received by Alexius, who

---

[1] Albert of Aix, VIII, 25–33, pp. 576–8. He is the sole source for this expedition. Hagenmeyer, *Chronologie du Royaume de Jérusalem*, pp. 438–9, 449, 459–60, dates the arrival of the Nivernais at Constantinople in mid-June, their departure from Ankara on about 25 July and from Konya in mid-August.

provided men to transport their men as soon as possible across the Bosphorus. Some of the civilian pilgrims, including the historian Ekkehard of Aura, took ship direct for Palestine, where they arrived after a six weeks' voyage.

It should have been possible for the two Dukes to have caught up with the Count of Nevers and have strengthened their army by the inclusion of his forces. But the Count of Nevers wished to unite with the Count of Burgundy, and Duke William could not be expected to combine with an army led by his old enemy, the Count of Toulouse, while Welf of Bavaria, an old enemy of the Emperor Henry IV, probably had little liking for Henry's Constable, Conrad. The Count of Nevers hastened ahead to Ankara, while the Aquitano-Bavarian army waited for five weeks by the Bosphorus, then moved slowly along the main road to Dorylaeum and Konya. By the time that it reached Dorylaeum the Nivernais army had already passed through the town on its return journey and was well on the way to Konya. The passage of another army along the road a few days previously did not make things easier for the Aquitanians and the Bavarians. The small available supplies of food had already been taken; for which, characteristically, the Crusaders blamed the Byzantines. Like the Nivernais, they found the wells dry or blocked. Philomelium was deserted, and they pillaged it. The Turkish garrison at Konya, which had withstood the Nivernais, abandoned the city before this larger army; but before they left they collected and took with them all the foodstuffs there and stripped bare the orchards and gardens in the suburbs. The Crusaders found little to refresh them. It was about this moment that a hundred miles ahead Kilij Arslan and Malik Ghazi were massacring the men of Nevers.

The Crusaders struggled on from Konya, hungry and thirsty, through the desert towards Heraclea. Turkish horsemen now appeared on their flank, firing arrows into their midst and cutting off foraging parties and stragglers. Early in September they entered Heraclea, which they found deserted as Konya had been. Just beyond the town flowed the river, one of the few Anatolian streams to flow abundantly throughout the summer. The Christian warriors, half-mad from thirst, broke their ranks to rush to the welcoming water. But the Turkish army lay concealed in the thickets on the river banks. As the Crusaders surged on in disorder, the Turks sprang out on them and surrounded them. There was no time to reform ranks. Panic spread through the Christian army. Horsemen and infantry were mixed in a dreadful stampede; and as they stumbled in their attempt to flee they were slaughtered by the enemy. The Duke of Aquitaine, followed by one of his grooms, cut his way out and rode into the mountains. After many days of wandering through the passes he found his way to Tarsus. Hugh of Vermandois was badly wounded in the battle; but some of his men rescued him and he too reached Tarsus. But he was a dying man. His death took place on 18 October and they buried him there in the Cathedral of St Paul. He never fulfilled his vow to go to Jerusalem. Welf of Bavaria only escaped by throwing away all his armour. After several weeks he arrived with two or three attendants at Antioch. The Archbishop Thiemo was taken prisoner and martyred for his faith. The fate of the Margravine of Austria is unknown. Later legends said that she ended her days a captive in a far-off harem, where she gave birth to the Moslem hero Zengi. More probably she was thrown from her litter in the panic and trampled to death.[1]

The three Crusades of the year 1101 had come each of them to a disastrous finish; and their disasters affected the whole story of the Crusading movement. The Turks had avenged their defeat at Dorylaeum. They were not, after all, to be ejected from Anatolia.

---

[1] Albert of Aix, VIII, 34–40, pp. 579–82 (the only full source); Ekkehard, XXIV–XXVI, pp. 30–2. He went by sea from Constantinople, and muddles the land expeditions, as does Fulcher of Chartres, VII, xvi, 1–3, pp. 428–33. There are three *Passiones S. Thiemonis*, describing the Archbishop's martyrdom but giving no details of the expedition. Ida's conjectural fate is told in *Historia Welforum Weingartensis*, in *M.G.H.Ss.*, vol. XXI, p. 462. Ekkehard merely says that she was killed. Several western chroniclers refer in passing to this expedition. Hagenmeyer (*op. cit.* p. 457) dates the pillage of Philomelium on about 10 August and the battle on about 5 September.

The road across the peninsula remained unsafe for Christian armies, Frankish or Byzantine. When the Byzantines wished later to intervene in Syria, they had to operate at the end of communication lines that were long and very vulnerable; while Frankish immigrants from the west were afraid to travel overland through Constantinople, except in vast armies. They could only come by sea; and few of them could afford the fare. And instead of the thousands of useful colonists that the year should have brought to Syria and Palestine, only a small number of quarrelsome leaders who had lost their armies and their reputations on the way penetrated through to the Frankish states, where there was already a sufficiency of quarrelsome leaders.

Not all the Christians, however, had cause to regret the disasters of the year 1101. To the Italian maritime cities the failure to secure the land-route across Asia Minor meant an increase in influence and wealth. For they possessed the ships that provided an alternative means of communication with the Frankish states of the East. Their co-operation was all the more necessary; and they insisted on payment in commercial concessions. The Armenians in the Taurus mountains, particularly the Roupenian princes, welcomed circumstances that made it difficult for Byzantium to re-establish its Empire over the districts where they lived; though the Armenians farther to the east had less cause for rejoicing. Their chief foe was the Danishmend emir, whose triumph soon encouraged him to attack them. And the Normans at Antioch, who, like the Roupenians, feared the Byzantines more than the Turks, were given a useful respite. Bohemond still languished in captivity; but his regent, Tancred, took full advantage of the situation to consolidate the principality at the Emperor's expense. Fate soon placed a trump-card in his hand.

The Duke of Aquitaine, the Count of Bavaria and the Count of Nevers had already arrived with their few surviving comrades at Antioch by the autumn of 1101; but the leaders of the Franco-Lombard Crusade were still at Constantinople. Alexius found it hard to forgive them their follies. Even Raymond, on whom he had built great hopes, had disappointed him. At the end of the year the western princes decided to continue their pilgrimage, and Raymond asked leave to rejoin his wife and his army at Lattakieh. The Emperor willingly let them go and provided ships to convey them to Syria. About the new year Stephen of Blois, Stephen of Burgundy, the Constable Conrad and Albert of Biandrate disembarked at Saint Symeon and hastened up to Antioch, where Tancred gave them a warm welcome. But Count Raymond's ship was separated from the others and put into the port of Tarsus. As he stepped ashore, a knight called Bernard the Stranger came up and arrested him for having betrayed Christendom by his flight from the field of Mersivan. Raymond's small bodyguard was powerless to rescue him. He was taken away under escort and was handed over to Tancred.[1]

[1] Albert of Aix, VIII, 42, pp. 582–3. Bernard the Stranger was in command at Tarsus in September 1101 (see below, p. 33). It is probable that as Radulph of Caen (cxlv, p. 708), followed by Cahen (*La Syrie du Nord*, p. 232, n. 10), suggests, Raymond landed at Longiniada, the port of Tarsus, and not at Saint Symeon with the other Crusaders as Albert implies. Matthew of Edessa, clxxii, p. 242, says that Raymond was imprisoned at 'Sarouantavi', i.e. Sarventikar, in the Taurus. This seems improbable.

CHAPTER III

THE NORMAN PRINCES OF ANTIOCH

'These all do contrary to the decrees of Caesar.' ACTS XVII, 7

Bohemond's defeat and capture by Malik Ghazi the Danishmend, alarming though it had seemed at the time, had not been without its compensations for the Frankish princes. Antioch was in need of a regent; and Tancred was the obvious candidate to take his uncle's place. King Baldwin was thus enabled to rid himself of his most dangerous vassal in Palestine; while Tancred was glad to extricate himself from a position that was embarrassing and insecure and to move to a sphere that offered greater scope and independence. Tancred left Palestine in March 1101, only stipulating that if his uncle returned from captivity within three years and Antioch needed him no more, his fief of Galilee should be restored to him. It was therefore to Baldwin's interest as well as to Tancred's that Bohemond should not be released from his prison too soon. No attempt was made to negotiate with his captor.[1]

Tancred was a correct regent. He did not assume the title of Prince of Antioch. Though he struck coins, the legend, written in bad Greek, merely entitled him 'the servant of God'; and at times he called himself the 'Grand Emir'. It is probable that public opinion in Antioch would have restrained him had his ambitions carried him farther. The Normans still regarded Bohemond as their leader; and Bohemond had a loyal friend in the Patriarch whom he had appointed just before his captivity, the Latin

---

[1] Fulcher of Chartres, I, vii, 1, pp. 390–3; Albert of Aix, VII, 44–5, pp. 537–8.

32

Bernard of Valence, in whose favour he had ejected the Greek, John the Oxite. Tancred's policy was the same as Bohemond's, internally to consolidate the administration of the principality and to Latinize the Church, and externally to enrich himself at the expense of the Byzantines and of the neighbouring Moslem princes. But his ambitions were more local and less world-wide than his uncle's.[1]

His first preoccupation was to guard himself against any attack from Byzantium. The disastrous Crusades of 1101 greatly helped him; for the resurgence of the Anatolian Turks meant that the Emperor could not venture for some time to send an army right across the peninsula to the far south-east. Tancred believed that attack was the best defence. So, in the summer of 1101, probably as soon as the news of the battle at Mersivan reached him, he sent troops into Cilicia to recapture Mamistra, Adana and Tarsus, which the Byzantines had reoccupied three years before. The local Byzantine forces were not strong enough to oppose him. When William of Aquitaine and Hugh of Vermandois arrived as fugitives at Tarsus at the end of September they found Tancred's lieutenant, Bernard the Stranger, in command of the city.[2]

Next, Tancred turned his attention to Lattakieh, the Byzantine port that the Normans had long coveted. It was more formidable; for its Byzantine garrison was reinforced by Raymond's Provençal troops and was protected by a squadron of the Byzantine navy. Before he dared attack, Tancred negotiated to secure the aid of Genoese ships.[3] Meanwhile he occupied the hinterland, and attempted to capture Jabala, to the south. Bohemond had sent a

[1] Schlumberger, *Les Principautés franques du Levant*, pp. 14–15, discusses Tancred's coins, which show him in imperial robes but wearing a *kefieh* on his head. The legend says in Greek, 'Tancred, Servant of God', with a cross and IC XP NIKA (as on Byzantine coins) on the reverse. According to *Historia Belli Sacri*, p. 228, he was not admitted as ruler until he had taken an oath of fidelity to Bohemond. He was vested with the regency by the papal legate, Maurice of Porto.

[2] Radulph of Caen, cxliii, p. 706; Albert of Aix, VIII, 40, p. 582; Orderic Vitalis, XXIII, p. 140.

[3] Caffaro, *Liberatio*, p. 59; Ughelli, *Italia Sacra*, IV, pp. 847–8.

small unsuccessful expedition against Jabala in the summer of 1100, in the course of which his Constable had been taken prisoner. Tancred's expedition in the summer of 1101 was equally ineffective. But it induced Ibn Sulaiha, the qadi of Jabala, to hand the city over to the atabeg of Damascus; and he himself retired to Damascus to enjoy a quiet old age. The atabeg, Toghtekin, sent his son Buri as Governor. But Buri was an unpopular ruler; and the citizens of Jabala after a few months ejected him and put themselves under the protection of the Banū Ammar of Tripoli. Tancred then withdrew his troops from the district.[1]

His capture of Raymond's person enabled Tancred to resume his scheme against Lattakieh. He had incarcerated Raymond at Antioch; but the Patriarch Bernard and Raymond's Crusading colleagues were shocked by his behaviour. At their request he set him free; but Raymond had first to swear an oath that he would never again interfere in northern Syrian affairs.[2] On his release Raymond marched southward, to attack Tortosa. In conformity with his oath, as he passed by Lattakieh he gave orders to his troops and to his Countess to evacuate the town and join him. The Byzantine garrison was left without Provençal support. Then, in the early spring of 1102 Tancred advanced on Lattakieh. But its walls were strong and the garrison fought well, while units of the imperial navy ensured their supplies. The siege lasted for nearly a year; but during the first weeks of 1103 Tancred, who had by now hired ships from the Genoese with which to interrupt communications between Lattakieh and Cyprus, lured the men of the garrison by a stratagem outside the city walls and there fell on them and made them prisoners. The city then capitulated to him.[3]

[1] Ibn al-Qalanisi, *Damascus Chronicle*, pp. 51–2.
[2] Albert of Aix (VIII, 42, pp. 582–3) says that Raymond swore to attempt no conquest in Syria north of Acre, but as no objection was made to his attack on Tortosa, his oath was probably limited to the country from Lattakieh northward.
[3] Radulph of Caen, cxliv, cxlvi, pp. 708–9; Anna Comnena, IX, vii, 7, vol. III, p. 36.

Such actions did not please the Emperor Alexius. He had already been angered by the exile of the Greek Patriarch of Antioch, John the Oxite, and by the news that all the higher Greek clergy were now being dismissed and replaced by Latins. Early in 1102 he received a letter from King Baldwin, who had heard the rumour that Byzantine non-co-operation had helped to wreck the Crusades of 1101, and who wrote to beg the Emperor to give his full support to any subsequent Crusade. The letter was conveyed by a Bishop called Manasses, who had gone to Palestine with Ekkehard in 1101 and was returning from Jerusalem. It seems to have been courteously worded and was accompanied by gifts; and Alexius therefore thought that he could talk frankly to the Bishop and tell him all his grievances. But herein he misjudged his man. The Bishop was a better Latin than Christian, and had no sympathy with the Greeks. At the Emperor's request he went on to Italy and reported to the Pope everything that had been said to him; but he did so in such terms that the Pope's fury was roused against Byzantium. Had Pope Urban II still been alive, no harm would have been done; for Urban had large views and no wish to quarrel with eastern Christendom. But his successor, Paschal II, was a smaller man, short-sighted and easily influenced. He readily fell in with the vulgar Frankish view that the Emperor was an enemy. Alexius obtained no redress.[1]

Tancred next attempted to interfere in the affairs of the kingdom of Jerusalem. King Baldwin banished the Patriarch Daimbert in 1101. Tancred at once welcomed him to Antioch, where he put

---

[1] Albert of Aix, VIII, 41, 47–8, pp. 582, 584–5. Albert calls Manasses Bishop of 'Barzenona' or 'Barcinona', which is usually taken to mean Barcelona (Chalandon, *Règne d'Alexis Ier Comnène*, p. 237; Leib, *Rome, Kiev et Byzance*, pp. 273–4; Norden, *Das Papsttum und Byzanz*, p. 70). But the Bishop of Barcelona at this time was Berengar II, an aged man who never left his diocese (Baudrillart, *Dictionnaire d'Histoire et de Géographie Ecclésiastique*, article 'Barcelone'). It is more probable that the Bishop was an Italian, but it is impossible to identify his see. His complaint was probably made at the Synod which Paschal II is known at have held at Benevento in 1102 (*Annales Beneventani*, ad ann. 1102, in *M.G.H. Ss.*, vol. III, p. 183). Albert of Aix says that he met the Pope at Benevento.

the Church of St George at his disposal. When, a few months later, Baldwin was defeated by the Saracens at Ramleh and asked for help from the princes in the north, Tancred refused to come unless Daimbert were reinstated at Jerusalem. Baldwin agreed; and Tancred's reputation was thereby enhanced. But it fell when Daimbert was condemned by a council and exiled once more. Tancred again offered him hospitality but did not continue to press his cause.[1]

Tancred's activities were not altogether to the liking of his neighbour at Edessa, Baldwin of Le Bourg. Baldwin's father, Count Hugh I of Rethel, was related to the house of Boulogne; and Baldwin, who was a younger son, came out to the East with his cousins, Godfrey of Lorraine and King Baldwin. When Baldwin I established himself at Edessa he had stayed behind with Bohemond and served as intermediary between the two princes. On Bohemond's imprisonment he had taken over the government of Antioch, until Baldwin of Edessa was summoned to Jerusalem. Baldwin of Le Bourg was then enfeoffed with Edessa by his cousin, to rule there autonomously, but under the suzerainty of Jerusalem. It was not an easy position that he inherited. His lands had no natural frontiers and were constantly liable to invasion. He could only rule by garrisoning the principal towns and castles; and for that he needed servants and comrades whom he could trust. Being ill-provided with men of his own race he made it his business to be on excellent terms with the native Christians. Almost his first action as Count of Edessa was to marry a local princess, Morphia, the young daughter of the ancient Gabriel, lord of Melitene, an Armenian by race but an adherent of the Orthodox Church. At the same time he wooed and won the support of the Armenians of the separated Gregorian Church, whose great historian, Matthew of Edessa, was full of praise for his amiable nature and the purity of his private life, though he regretted his ambition and avarice. Baldwin particularly favoured the Armenians, because they could be used as soldiers; but he was kindly also towards his Syrian

[1] See below, pp. 81–3.

Jacobite subjects and even succeeded in healing a schism within their Church. The only complaint against him was his rapacity. He was perpetually in need of money and raised it wherever he could. But his methods were less arbitrary and more gentle than Baldwin I's. His knights were particularly delighted when he managed to extort 30,000 besants from his father-in-law by declaring that he owed that sum to his men and had sworn to them that if he could not pay them he would shave off his beard. The Armenians, like the Greeks, considered a beard necessary to manly dignity and were shocked at the shaven faces of so many Crusaders. Gabriel thought that a beardless son-in-law would be damaging to his prestige; and when Baldwin's men, entering into the comedy, corroborated that their master had indeed sworn such an oath, Gabriel hastened to hand over the necessary cash to prevent so dreadful an humiliation, and made Baldwin swear a fresh oath that never would he pledge his beard again.[1]

Early in his reign Baldwin II had to face an attack from the Ortoqids of Mardin. The emir Soqman led an army against Saruj, a Moslem town which Baldwin I had captured and placed under Fulcher of Chartres. Baldwin II hastened to help Fulcher; but in the ensuing battle he was defeated and Fulcher slain. The town was taken by the Moslems; but the citadel held out under Benedict, Latin Archbishop of Edessa, while Baldwin hastened to Antioch to hire troops to replenish his army. On his return he was more fortunate. Soqman was driven out of the town with heavy losses. The inhabitants that had had dealings with the Ortoqids were massacred; and many prisoners were made, whose ransom enriched Baldwin's exchequer.[2]

Soon afterwards Baldwin acquired a useful lieutenant in the person of his cousin, Joscelin of Courtenay. Joscelin, whose

[1] William of Tyre, x, 24, pp. 437–8, xi, 11, pp. 469–72, tells the story of Baldwin's marriage and his beard. Matthew of Edessa, ccxxv, p. 296, speaks with respect but without affection for him.
[2] Matthew of Edessa, clxviii, pp. 232–3; Ibn al-Qalanisi, pp. 50–1; Al-Azimi, p. 494.

mother was Baldwin's aunt, was the younger and penniless son of the lord of Courtenay and had probably come to the East with his close neighbour, the Count of Nevers. On his arrival Baldwin enfeoffed him with all the land of the county that lay to the west of the Euphrates, with his headquarters at Turbessel. He proved to be a valiant friend; but his loyalty was later to be questioned.[1]

As time went on, Baldwin seems to have grown suspicious of Tancred's ambitions, and desired Bohemond's restoration to Antioch. Together with the Patriarch Bernard he began negotiations with the Danishmend emir to secure his release. Tancred took no part in the transaction. The emir had already been offered the large sum of 260,000 besants from the Emperor Alexius in return for Bohemond's person, and would have accepted, had not the Seldjuk Sultan, Kilij Arslan, come to hear of it. Kilij Arslan, as official overlord of the Anatolian Turks, demanded half of any ransom that the Danishmend might receive. The resultant quarrel between the two Turkish princes prevented the immediate acceptance of the Emperor's offer, but it served the useful purpose of breaking their alliance. Bohemond, in his captivity, was aware of these negotiations. He was still a handsome and glamorous man; and the ladies of the emir's household took an interest in him. Perhaps with their assistance, he was able to persuade his captor that a private arrangement with the Franks of Syria and the promise of their alliance was preferable to a deal with the Emperor, in which the Seldjuks intended to interfere. The emir agreed to release Bohemond for the sum of 100,000 besants.[2]

While the negotiations were continuing, the Danishmend army

[1] William of Tyre, x, 24, pp. 437.
[2] Albert of Aix, ix, 33–6, pp. 610–12; Orderic Vitalis, x, 23, vol. IV, p. 144, tells of Bohemond's love affair with a daughter of the Danishmends, while the *Miracula S. Leonardi* (*Aa. Ss.*, Nov., vol. III, pp. 160–8, 179–82) makes his lady friend a Christian wife of the emir. Matthew of Edessa (clxxviii, p. 252) says that Richard of the Principate was ransomed by Alexius; but Richard was already in Syria before Bohemond's release (*Miracula S. Leonardi*, p. 157). Radulph of Caen says that Baldwin acted from dislike of Tancred (cxlvii, p. 709). The quarrel between the Seldjuk and Danishmend rulers is reported by Ibn al-Qalanisi, p. 59.

attacked Melitene. Its ruler, Gabriel, must have appealed to his son-in-law, Baldwin, for help; but Baldwin did nothing, probably because he was unwilling at this juncture to offend the emir. Gabriel's subjects disliked him for his Orthodox faith. The Syrians, in particular, had never forgiven him for having once put one of their bishops to death for treason. He and his capital were captured; but one of his castles held out. Gabriel was told by his captors to order it to capitulate. When the garrison disobeyed him, he was executed before its walls.[1]

It was at Melitene, a few months later, in the spring of 1103, that Bohemond was handed over to the Franks. His ransom money had been raised by Baldwin and by the Patriarch Bernard, with the help of the Armenian princeling, Kogh Vasil, and of Bohemond's relatives in Italy. Tancred did not contribute to it. Bohemond at once went to Antioch, where he was reinstated in his authority. He publicly thanked Tancred for having administered the principality during his absence, but privately there was some friction between the uncle and the nephew, as Tancred did not see why he should hand over to Bohemond the conquests that he himself had made as regent. Public opinion forced him to give way; and he was rewarded by a small fief within the principality. He could legally have demanded the return of Galilee from Baldwin I, but he did not think it worth his while.[2]

The Franks celebrated Bohemond's return by a general offensive against their neighbours. In the summer of 1103 Bohemond, with Joscelin of Courtenay, raided the territory of Aleppo. They captured the town of Muslimiye, to the north of Aleppo itself, and extracted a large tribute from the Moslems of the district, which was used to repay the Franks who had lent money to Baldwin and the Patriarch for Bohemond's ransom.[3] Next, they turned against

---

[1] Michael the Syrian, III, pp. 185–9.

[2] See above, p. 32. Fulcher (II, xxiii, 1, p. 460) says that Tancred was 'competently' rewarded, but Radulph says that he was only given two small towns (*loc. cit.*).

[3] Kemal ad-Din, p. 591; Ibn al-Athir (*Kamil at-Tawarikh*, p. 212) adds that Bohemond extorted money from Qinnasrin.

the Byzantines. Alexius, after writing to Bohemond to require him to give back the Cilician cities, sent his general Butumites to recover them. But Butumites's force was unreliable. He entered Cilicia in the autumn of 1103 but soon decided that the task was beyond him; and he learnt that the Franks were planning to expand northward against Marash, which the Armenian Thatoul held for the Emperor. He hastened there himself, and, probably, by so doing, he saved Thatoul for the moment. But he was recalled to Constantinople. Early next spring Bohemond and Joscelin marched on Marash. Thatoul was powerless. The Byzantine army was far away. The Danishmend Turks were now on good terms with the Franks. He surrendered his city to Joscelin, who allowed him to retire to Constantinople; while Bohemond took the town of Albistan, to the north of Marash.[1]

The Franks now felt secure from attacks from Anatolia. They could turn against the Moslems of the east. In March 1104 Bohemond reinvaded the lands of Ridwan of Aleppo and took the town of Basarfut, on the road from Antioch to Aleppo; but his attempt against Kafarlata, to the south, failed owing to the resistance of the local tribe of the Banū Ulaim. Joscelin meanwhile cut the communications between Aleppo and the Euphrates.[2] But, if the Moslems of Syria were to be effectively cut off from the Moslems of Iraq and Persia, the great fortress of Harran, situated between Edessa and the Euphrates, in the northern Jezireh, would have to be occupied by the Christians. If they held Harran, the Franks could even contemplate an expedition against Mosul and into Mesopotamia. In the spring of 1104 conditions seemed to be favourable. During 1103 the whole eastern Moslem world had been torn by a civil war between the Seldjuk Sultan Barkiyarok and his brother Mohammed. Peace was made between them in January 1104 by which the Sultan retained Baghdad

---

[1] Anna Comnena, XI, ix, 1–4, vol. III, pp. 40–1; Matthew of Edessa, clxxxvi, p. 257 wrongly placing the capture of Marash after the battle of Harran, Radulph of Caen, cxlviii–cl, pp. 710–2.

[2] Kemal ad-Din, pp. 591–2; *Zettersteen Chronicle*, p. 239.

and the western Iranian plateau. His third brother, Sanjar, already had obtained Khorassan and eastern Iran; and Mohammed obtained northern Iraq and the Jezireh and the suzerainty rights over Diarbekir and over all Syria. It was an uneasy arrangement. Each of the brothers hoped soon to upset it and in the meantime intrigued for allies amongst all the Turkish and Arab princes. In the Jezireh itself the death in 1102 of the atabeg of Mosul, Kerbogha, whom the Franks had defeated at Antioch, had provoked a civil war. The Ortoqid prince of Mardin, Soqman, had failed to secure the succession for his candidate and was at war with the new atabeg, Jekermish, appointed by the Seldjuk Mohammed. Harran itself had belonged to a Turkish general, Qaraja, who had been a mameluke in Malik Shah's service; but his brutal behaviour had caused the inhabitants to rise against him and to hand over the government to a certain Mohammed of Isfahan. Mohammed in his turn was murdered by a former page of Qaraja's, called Jawali, with whom he had rashly become intimate. But Jawali's authority was very insecure; while Harran itself began to suffer severely from raids by the Franks of Edessa, who devastated its fields and interrupted its trade. It was clear that they intended soon to go farther.[1]

Both Soqman at Mardin and Jekermish at Mosul were alarmed. Their common danger induced them to forget their quarrel and to unite in an expedition against Edessa, to attack before they were attacked. Early in May 1104 they marched together on Edessa; Soqman with a considerable force of Turcoman light cavalry and Jekermish with a slightly smaller force composed of Seldjuk Turks, Kurds and Arabs. Baldwin II heard that they were massing at Ras al-Ain, some seventy miles from his capital. He sent for help to Joscelin and to Bohemond, and suggested that they should turn the attack by themselves making an attempt on Harran.

[1] For the background to the Harran campaign, see Cahen, *La Syrie du Nord*, pp. 236–7, with references. Nicholson, in his thesis on Tancred, pp. 138–42, emphasizes that the campaign was not part of a general policy of expansion, but the response to a threat by the Moslems. But Harran was certainly an ultimate objective of the Franks.

Leaving a small garrison at Edessa he made his way to Harran with a small company of knights and of Armenian infantry levies. The Archbishop of Edessa, Benedict, accompanied him. Close to Harran he was joined by Joscelin, with the troops of his lands, and by the Antiochene army under Bohemond, Tancred, the Patriarch Bernard, and Daimbert, ex-Patriarch of Jerusalem. The whole Frankish army numbered nearly three thousand knights and perhaps three times that number of infantry. It represented the full fighting force of the Franks of northern Syria, apart from the garrisons of the fortresses.

The army assembled before Harran while the Moslem princes were still at some distance to the north-east, marching on Edessa. Had the Franks attempted to take the fortress by assault, Harran would have been theirs; but they were unwilling to damage the fortifications, which they hoped to use later themselves. They thought that the garrison could be frightened into surrender. It was a reasonable hope. The Moslems within the town were weak; almost at once they entered into negotiations. But thereupon Baldwin and Bohemond quarrelled over the question, whose standard should first be raised over the walls. The delay caused their downfall. Before they had settled the quarrel the Turkish army had swung southward and was upon them.

The battle took place on the banks of the river Balikh, close to the ancient field of Carrhae, where, centuries before, Crassus and the Roman legions had been annihilated by the Parthians. The Frankish strategy was for the army of Edessa, on the left, to engage the main enemy force, while the Antiochene army lay hidden behind a low hill about a mile to the right, ready to intervene at the decisive moment. But the Moslems made similar plans. A portion of their army attacked the Frankish left, then turned and fled. The Edessenes thought that they had won an easy victory and hurried in pursuit, losing contact with their comrades on the right. They crossed the river and fell straight into an ambush laid by the main Moslem army. Many of them were slaughtered on the spot; the remainder turned and fled. When Bohemond, who had driven off the small detachment opposed to him, prepared to join in the battle, he only found a stream of fugitives pouring from the distance and scrambling back across the river, where fresh bands of Turks fell upon them. He saw that all was lost and moved quickly away, rescuing only a few of the Edessenes. As the combatants passed beneath the walls of Harran, the garrison fell on them and in the confusion enthusiastically killed as many of the Moslem pursuers as of the Franks. The army of Antioch escaped without heavy losses; but the troops of Edessa were almost entirely captured or slain. The Patriarch Bernard was so frightened that as he fled he cut off his horse's tail lest some Turk should catch him by it, though by then none of the enemy was in sight.

Amongst the first to be taken prisoner was the Archbishop Benedict. But, owing either to the compliance of his jailer, a renegade Christian, or to an Antiochene counter-attack, he was soon rescued. Baldwin and Joscelin fled together on horseback but were overtaken in the river-bed. They were brought as prisoners to Soqman's tent.[1]

Rightly fearing that the Turks would next attack Edessa, Bohemond and Tancred hastened there to organize its defence. Once again the misfortune of a colleague turned to Tancred's advantage. The knights remaining in Edessa, with the Archbishop at their head, begged him to take over the regency till Baldwin should be released from captivity. Tancred gladly accepted the offer; and Bohemond, like Baldwin I four years previously, was relieved to see him go. Tancred stayed on in Edessa with the remnants of the Edessene army and with such troops as Bohemond could spare, while Bohemond himself moved back to Antioch, whose neighbours were preparing to take advantage of the Frankish disaster.[2]

[1] Albert of Aix, IX, 38–42, pp. 614–16; Radulph of Caen, cxlviii, pp. 710–11; Fulcher of Chartres, II, xxvii, 1–13, pp. 468–77; Ibn al-Qalanisi, pp. 60–1; Ibn al-Athir, pp. 221–3, Sibt ibn al-Djauzi, p. 537; Matthew of Edessa, clxxxii, pp. 254–5. Michael the Syrian, III, p. 195; *Chron. Anon. Syr.* pp. 78–80. The accounts of the actual battle are somewhat conflicting.
[2] Radulph of Caen, cxlviii, p. 712; Albert of Aix, *loc. cit.*; Matthew of Edessa, clxxxii, p. 256.

The battle of Harran was the complement to the Crusades of 1101. Together, they destroyed the legend of Frankish invincibility. The defeats of 1101 had meant that northern Syria was deprived of the reinforcements from the West that were needed if Frankish domination was to be firmly established there; and Harran meant in the long run that the county of Edessa was doomed and that Aleppo would never pass into Frankish hands. The wedge that the Franks had intended to maintain between the three Moslem centres of Anatolia, Iraq and Syria was insecurely driven in. And not only the Moslems would benefit. The Emperor was watching angrily in Byzantium and was not sorry to hear of the Frankish discomfiture.

The immediate consequences were not as fatal as might have been feared. The alliance between Soqman and Jekermish did not long survive their victory. The former's Turcoman troops had obtained most of the prisoners and the booty; and the latter was jealous. His Seldjuk regiment attacked Soqman's tent and carried off Baldwin. The Turcomans were furious; but Soqman showed sufficient self-control to restrain them from counter-attacking. He reconciled himself to the loss of his valuable prisoner; but, after reducing a few small Christian frontier-forts by the simple ruse of dressing up his soldiers in their Frankish victims' clothes, he retired to Mardin and took no further part in the war.[1] Jekermish fought on. First, to secure himself against Soqman, he overwhelmed the Frankish castles in the Shahbaqtan, to the east of Edessa, then marched on the capital. Frankish delay had saved Harran for Islam. Now the Moslems' delay saved Edessa for Christendom. Tancred had time to repair the city's defences and was able to resist Jekermish's first attack, thanks largely to the loyalty and valour of the local Armenians. But he was so hard pressed that he sent urgently to Bohemond for help. Bohemond had his own problems; but the threat to Edessa must be given precedence. He marched at once to his nephew's assistance; but the poor condition

[1] Ibn al-Athir, *loc. cit.* Soqman is reported to have said: 'I would rather lose my spoil than let the Christians taunt us with folly.'

of the roads delayed him. Tancred, in despair, ordered a sortie of his garrison to take place before dawn. In the darkness his men fell upon the sleeping and confident Turks; and their victory was completed by Bohemond's arrival. Jekermish fled in panic, abandoning the treasures of his camp. Harran was avenged, and Edessa was preserved.[1]

Amongst the prisoners that fell into Tancred's hands was a high-born Seldjuk princess from the Emir's household. So highly did Jekermish value this lady that he at once offered either to pay 15,000 besants to ransom her or else to exchange Count Baldwin himself for her. News of the offer reached Jerusalem; and King Baldwin hastened to write to Bohemond to beg him not to lose this opportunity for obtaining the Count's release. But Bohemond and Tancred needed money, while Baldwin's return would have thrown Tancred out of his present post back on his uncle's hands. They answered that it would be undiplomatic to appear too eager to accept the offer; Jekermish might raise his price if they hesitated. But meanwhile they arranged with the emir to have the money payment; and Baldwin remained in captivity.[2]

Having thus enriched themselves by sacrificing their comrade, Bohemond and Tancred turned to meet the enemies that were pressing round them. Jekermish did not again attempt to attack Edessa; and Tancred was able to repair the city's defences. But Bohemond had at once to face an invasion by Ridwan of Aleppo into the eastern districts of his principality. In June the Armenian inhabitants of Artah handed over their town to the Moslems, delighted to escape from Antiochene tyranny. The towns of Maarrat, Misrin and Sarman on the frontier followed suit; and the small Frankish garrisons of Maarat an-Numan, Albara and Kafartab, who were thus isolated, withdrew back to Antioch. Meanwhile Ridwan ravaged the principality as far as the Iron Bridge. In the far north Bohemond's garrison at Albistan only

[1] Albert of Aix, IX, 43, pp. 617–18; Ibn al-Athir, p. 223; Ibn al-Qalanisi, pp. 69–70.
[2] Albert of Aix, IX, 46, pp. 619–20.

maintained itself by imprisoning the leading local Armenians, who were plotting with the Turks. The whole of Bohemond's state might have been endangered had not Duqaq of Damascus died towards the end of June 1104 whereupon Ridwan's attention was taken up by the struggle for the succession between Duqaq's two sons, Buri and Iltash.[1]

Bohemond's failure to meet Ridwan's attack was due to his preoccupation with Byzantine affairs. The Emperor Alexius was now on good terms with the Frankish states farther to the south. Raymond of Toulouse was still his close friend; and he had won the good-will of King Baldwin by himself paying for the ransom of many distinguished Franks who were held captive in Egypt. His generosity had been wisely calculated. It was in striking contrast to Bohemond and Tancred's behaviour over Baldwin of Edessa; and it reminded the Franks that he had influence and prestige that the Fatimids respected. When therefore he took action against Antioch, its prince received no help from his colleagues. Alexius had already fortified Corycos and Seleucia on the Cilician coast, to prevent Antiochene aggression into western Cilicia. In the summer of 1104 a Byzantine army, under the general Monastras, reoccupied without difficulty the east Cilician cities, Tarsus, Adana and Mamistra; while a naval squadron under the Emperor's admiral, Cantacuzenus, which had come to Cyprian waters in pursuit of a Genoese raiding fleet, took advantage of Bohemond's situation to sail on to Lattakieh, where his men captured the harbour and the lower city. Bohemond hastened with the Frankish troops that he could muster to reinforce the garrison in the citadel and to replace its commander, whom he distrusted. But, lacking sea-power, he did not try to expel the Byzantines from their position.[2]

By the autumn Bohemond felt desperate. In September he held a council of his vassals at Antioch, to which he summoned Tancred.

[1] Radulph of Caen, *loc. cit.*; Kemal ad-Din, pp. 592–3; Sibt ibn al-Djauzi, p. 529; Ibn al-Qalanisi, pp. 62–5.
[2] Anna Comnena, xı, x, 9–xi, 7, vol. ııı, pp. 45–9.

There he told them frankly of the dangers that surrounded the principality. The only solution was, he said, to secure reinforcements from Europe. He would go himself to France and use his personal prestige to recruit the needed men. Tancred dutifully offered to take on this task; but his uncle replied that he did not command sufficient authority in the West. He must remain behind as Regent of Antioch. Arrangements were soon made for Bohemond's departure. Late in the autumn he set sail from Saint Symeon, taking with him all the gold and silver, jewels and precious stuffs that were available, and copies of the *Gesta Francorum*, the anonymous history of the First Crusade told from the Norman point of view. In these copies Bohemond inserted a passage suggesting that the Emperor had promised him the lordship of Antioch.[1]

Tancred then took over the government of Antioch, at the same time taking an oath that he would restore Edessa to Baldwin immediately on his release from captivity. Meanwhile, as Tancred could not rule Edessa satisfactorily from Antioch, he appointed his cousin and brother-in-law, Richard of Salerno, as his deputy across the Euphrates.[2]

Bohemond reached his own lands in Apulia early in the new year. He remained there till the following September, seeing to his personal affairs, which needed his supervision after his nine years' absence, and organizing parties of Normans to join their fellows in the East. Then he went to Rome, where he saw Pope

[1] Anna Comnena, XI, xii, 1–3, vol. III, pp. 50–1, who says that he pretended to be dead so as to embark unnoticed; Albert of Aix, IX, 47, p. 620; Fulcher of Chartres, II, xxix, 1, pp. 482–3; Radulph of Caen, clii, cliii, pp. 712–14; Ibn al-Qalanisi, *op. cit.* p. 66; Matthew of Edessa, clxxxii, pp. 255–6. For the interpolation in the *Gesta*, see Krey, 'A neglected passage in the *Gesta*', in *The Crusades and other Historical Essays*, presented to D. C. Munro. Bohemond's arrival in Italy is recorded in the *Annales Barenses*, p. 155.
[2] Matthew of Edessa, clxxxix, p. 260; Michael the Syrian, III, p. 195; Ibn al-Athir, pp. 262–3. Tancred in his charters henceforward calls himself 'Tancredus Dux et Princeps Antiochenus' (Röhricht, *Regesta*, p. 11). In charters during his first regency he is called 'Princeps' without a territorial designation (*ibid.* p. 5). He was still titular Prince of Galilee.

Paschal. To him Bohemond emphasized that the great enemy of the Latins in the East was the Emperor Alexius. Paschal had already been prejudiced against Alexius by Bishop Manasses and fell in readily with his views. When Bohemond went on into France he was accompanied by the papal legate, Bruno, who was instructed to preach a Holy War against Byzantium. It was a turning-point in the history of the Crusades. The Norman policy, which aimed to break the power of the eastern Empire, became the official Crusading policy. The interests of Christendom as a whole were to be sacrificed to the interests of Frankish adventurers. The Pope was later to regret his indiscretion; but the harm was done. The resentment of the western knights and populace against the haughtiness of the Emperor, their jealousy of his wealth and their suspicions of Christians who used a ritual that they could not understand were all given official sanction by the western Church. Henceforward, though the Pope might modify his views, they felt justified in every hostile action against Byzantium. And the Byzantines, on their side, found their worst suspicions realized. The Crusade, with the Pope at its head, was not a movement for the succour of Christendom, but a tool of unscrupulous western imperialism. This unhappy agreement between Bohemond and Pope Paschal did far more than all the controversy between Cardinal Humbert and Michael Cerularius to ensure the separation between the eastern and western Churches.

Bohemond was well received in France. He spent some time at the Court of King Philip, who gave him permission to recruit men throughout the kingdom; and he enjoyed the active support of that eager Crusader-by-proxy, Adela, Countess of Blois. Adela not only introduced him to her brother, Henry I of England, whom he saw in Normandy at Easter 1106, and who promised to encourage his work, but she also arranged for him to make an impressive marriage-alliance with King Philip's daughter, Constance, the divorced Countess of Champagne. The wedding took place in the late spring of 1106; and at the same time King Philip agreed to offer the hand of his younger daughter, Cecilia, child of his adulterous union with Bertrada of Montfort, to Tancred. Constance never went to the East. Her married life and widowhood were spent in Italy. But Cecilia sailed for Antioch about the end of the year. These royal connections added to the prestige of the Norman princes.[1]

Bohemond remained in France till late in 1106, when he returned to Apulia. There he planned his new Crusade, which was to begin uncompromisingly with an attack on the Byzantine Empire. Cheered by the news that under Tancred's rule Antioch was in no immediate peril, he did not hurry. On 9 October 1107 his army landed on the Epirote coast of the Empire at Avlona; and four days later he appeared before the great fortress of Dyrrhachium, the key to the Balkan peninsula, which the Normans had long coveted and had held for a while a quarter of a century before. But Alexius, too, had had time to make his preparations. To save Dyrrhachium he was ready to sacrifice his south-eastern frontier; and he made peace with the Seldjuk Sultan, Kilij Arslan, from whom he hired mercenaries. Finding the fortress too strong and too vigorously defended by its garrison to be taken by assault, Bohemond settled down to besiege it. But, as in his earlier wars against Byzantium, lack of sea-power was his ruin. Almost at once the Byzantine navy cut off his communications with Italy and blockaded the coast. Then, early next spring, the main Byzantine army closed in round him. As the summer came on, dysentery, malaria and famine weakened the Normans; while Alexius broke their morale by spreading rumours and sending forged letters to

---

[1] Orderic Vitalis, XI, vol. IV, pp. 210–13; Suger, *Vita Ludovici*, pp. 29–30; *Chronicon S. Maxentii*, p. 423; *Chronicon Vindocinense*, pp. 161–2; William of Tyre, XI, 1, p. 450; Anna Comnena, XII, i, 1, vol. III, p. 53. The marriage between Constance and Bohemond took place according to Luchaire, *Louis VI le Gros*, p. 22, in April or May 1106. It was probably after that date that Cecilia set out for the East. Her marriage therefore probably took place later in 1106. Matthew of Edessa (*loc. cit.*) believed that Bohemond was obliged to marry a rich lady, whom he calls the wife of Stephen Pol (apparently muddling Hugh of Champagne with the Crusader Hugh of Saint Pol who was a friend of Bohemond). She imprisoned him till he consented. He would have preferred to return to the East.

their leaders, devices that his daughter Anna described with loving admiration. By September Bohemond knew that he was beaten, and he surrendered to the Emperor. It was a tremendous triumph for Byzantium; for Bohemond was by now the most renowned warrior in Christendom. The sight of this formidable hero, towering personally over the Emperor yet suppliant before him and obedient to his dictation, bore witness which no one could forget to the invincible majesty of the Empire.

Alexius received Bohemond at his camp, at the entrance to the ravines of the river Devol. He was courteous but cold to him, and wasted no time in setting before him the peace treaty that he was to sign. Bohemond hesitated at first; but Nicephorus Bryennius, Anna Comnena's husband, who was in attendance on his father-in-law, persuaded him that he had no option.

The text of the treaty is preserved in full in the pages of Anna Comnena. In it Bohemond first was made to express contrition for the breach of his former oath to the Emperor. Then he swore with the utmost solemnity to become the vassal and liege-man of the Emperor and of the Emperor's heir, the Porphyrogennete John; and he would oblige all his men to do likewise. That there might be no mistake the Latin term for liege was employed, and the duties of a vassal were enumerated. He was to remain Prince of Antioch, which he would govern under the Emperor's suzerainty. His territory would include Antioch itself and its port of Saint Symeon, and the districts to the north-east, as far as Marash, together with the lands that he might conquer from the Moslem princes of Aleppo and other inland Syrian states; but the Cilician cities and the coast round Lattakieh were to be restored to the Emperor's direct rule, and the territory of the Roupenian princes was not to be touched. An appendix was added to the treaty carefully listing the towns that were to constitute Bohemond's dominion. Within his dominion Bohemond was to exercise the civil authority, but the Latin Patriarch was to be deposed and replaced by a Greek. There were special provisions that if Tancred, or any other of Bohemond's men, refused to comply with the demands of the treaty, Bohemond was to force them into obedience.[1]

The Treaty of Devol is of interest because it reveals the solution that Alexius now contemplated for the Crusader question. He was prepared to allow frontier districts and even Antioch itself to pass into the autonomous control of a Latin prince, so long as the prince was bound to him by ties of vassalage according to the Latin custom, and so long as Byzantium kept indirect control through the Church. Alexius, moreover, felt himself to be responsible for the welfare of the eastern Christians, and even wished to safeguard the rights of his unsatisfactory Armenian vassals, the Roupenians. The treaty remained a paper agreement. But it broke Bohemond; who never dared show himself again in the East. He retired humble and discredited to his lands in Apulia, and died there in 1111, an obscure Italian princeling, leaving two infant sons by his French marriage to inherit his rights to Antioch. He had been a gallant soldier, a bold and wily general and a hero to his followers; and his personality had outshone all his colleagues' on the First Crusade. But the vastness of his unscrupulous ambition was his downfall. The time had not yet come for the Crusaders to destroy the bulwark of eastern Christendom.[2]

As Alexius well realized, the Treaty of Devol required the co-operation of Tancred; and Tancred, who was not sorry to see his uncle eliminated from eastern affairs, had no intention of becoming the Emperor's vassal. His ambition was less extensive than Bohemond's, but it was for the creation of a strong independent principality. His prospects were unhopeful. Bohemond had left him with few men and quite without ready money. Nevertheless he decided to take the offensive. A forced loan from the wealthy merchants of Antioch replenished his funds and enabled him to

[1] Anna Comnena, XII, iv, 1–3, viii, 1–ix, 7, XIII, ii, 1–xii, 28, vol. III, pp. 64–5, 77–85, 91–139. See Chalandon, *op. cit.* pp. 237–50.

[2] The date of Bohemond's death is given differently in different chronicles. But Rey (*Histoire des Princes d'Antioche*, p. 334) and Hagenmeyer (*op. cit.* p. 298) both discuss it and give 1111 (6 March, according to the *Nécrologie de l'Abbaye de Molesme*, quoted by Rey).

hire local mercenaries; and he summoned all the knights and cavalrymen that could be spared from Edessa and Turbessel as well as from Antiochene territory. In the spring of 1105 he marched out to recover Artah. Ridwan of Aleppo had been preparing to go to the assistance of the Banū Ammar in their struggle against the Franks farther to the south; but on the news of Tancred's advance he turned to defend Artah. The two armies met on 20 April, at the village of Tizin near Artah, on a desolate plain strewn with boulders. Alarmed by the size of the Turkish host, Tancred suggested a parley with Ridwan, who would have agreed, had not his cavalry commander, Sabawa, persuaded him to attack without delay. The terrain prevented the Turks from using their usual tactics. When their first cavalry onrush was driven back by the Franks they retired to lure the enemy on; but they were unable to re-form their ranks for a second charge, and meanwhile their infantry was cut down by the Frankish knights. At the failure of their plans they panicked. Ridwan and his bodyguard rode off in flight to Aleppo, and most of his cavalry followed. The remainder and the foot-soldiers were butchered on the battle-field.

The victory enabled Tancred to reoccupy all the territory lost in the previous year. The Seldjuk garrison abandoned Artah to him, while his troops pursued the fugitives to the walls of Aleppo and plundered many of the civilian population as they fled in terror from the city. Ridwan sued for peace. He agreed to give up all his territory in the Orontes valley and to pay a regular tribute to Tancred. By the end of 1105 Tancred's dominion stretched once more as far south as Albara and Maarat an-Numan.[1]

In February 1106 the emir of Apamea, Khalaf ibn Mula'ib, who had been not unfriendly to the Franks, was assassinated by fanatics from Aleppo. The murderers then quarrelled with their chief ally within the town, Abu'l Fath, who had assumed its government, and now asked for help from Ridwan. Tancred, invited by the local

[1] Radulph of Caen, cliv, pp. 714–15; Albert of Aix, ix, 47, pp. 620–1; Kemal ad-Din, p. 593; Ibn al-Qalanisi, pp. 69–70; Ibn al-Athir, pp. 227–8.

Armenians, judged it opportune to intervene. He marched south and began to besiege the town. But Abu'l Fath restored order; and the emirs of Shaizar and Hama promised help. Tancred was obliged to retire after three weeks, giving as his excuse that he must succour the garrison at Lattakieh, which, after an eighteen months' blockade by the Byzantines, was faced with famine. He revictualled it and returned to Antioch. A few months later one of Khalaf's sons, Musbih ibn Mula'ib, who had escaped his father's fate, appeared at Antioch with a hundred followers and persuaded Tancred to attack Apamea once again. With Musbih's help he reinvested the town, digging a ditch all round to prevent ingress or egress. None of the neighbouring emirs came to Abu'l Fath's assistance; and after a few weeks, on 14 September 1106, the Moslems capitulated on the condition that their lives should be spared. Tancred agreed to their terms and entered the town; whereupon, to please Musbih, he put Abu'l Fath and three of his companions to death. The other Apamean notables were taken to Antioch, where they remained till Ridwan arranged for their ransom. A Frankish governor was installed at Apamea; while Musbih was enfeoffed with an estate near by.[1] Soon afterwards the Franks reoccupied Kafartab. It was put into the charge of a knight called Theophilus, who soon made himself the terror of the Moslems of Shaizar.[2]

With his eastern and southern frontiers thus secured, Tancred could turn against the foe that he hated the most, Byzantium. In the summer of 1107, when Bohemond's attack on the European provinces was imminent, Alexius was obliged to remove troops from the Syrian frontier in order to face what was a more serious menace. Cantacuzenus was recalled with many of his men from Lattakieh, and Monastras from Cilicia, which was put under the control of the Armenian prince of Lampron, the Sbarabied Oshin.

[1] Ibn al-Qalanisi, *loc. cit.*; *Zettersteen Chronicle*, p. 240; Kemal ad-Din, p. 694; Ibn al-Athir, p. 233; Albert of Aix, x, 17–23, pp. 639–42. Albert says that Abu'l Fath, whom he calls 'Botherus', committed the murder of the emir.

[2] Usama, ed. Hitti, p. 157; Ibn al-Qalanisi, p. 73; Kemal ad-Din, pp. 594–5.

The Norman Princes of Antioch

In the winter of 1108, or early in 1109, soon after Bohemond's humiliation in Epirus, Tancred invaded Cilicia. The Emperor's judgment of men had failed him. Oshin came of high lineage and had been famed in his youth for his courage; but now he had become luxurious and lazy. The key to Cilicia was the fortress of Mamistra, on the river Jihan. When Tancred's forces advanced by land over the Amanus range and by water up the river to besiege the town, Oshin did nothing to stop them. Mamistra fell after a short siege; and it seems that during the next months Tancred re-established his rule over Adana and Tarsus, though western Cilicia remained in imperial hands. Oshin himself retired to his lands in the Taurus.[1]

Lattakieh had already been reconquered. Hitherto the Normans had been hampered by lack of sea-power. But the Byzantine navy was now concentrated far away in the Adriatic; and Tancred was able to purchase the aid of a Pisan squadron. The price that Pisa demanded was a street in Antioch, and a quarter in Lattakieh, with a church and a godown. Petzeas, who had succeeded Cantacuzenus as Byzantine commander there, was powerless to offer resistance. Lattakieh was finally incorporated into the Antiochene principality in the spring of 1108. Next year Tancred extended his dominion farther to the south, taking Jabala, Buluniyas and the castle of Marqab from the dissolving dominions of the Banū Ammar.[2]

Thus, when Bohemond surrendered to the Emperor and signed away his independence, Tancred was reaching the height of his power and was in no way disposed to obey the imperial decree. From the Taurus to the Jezireh and central Syria his was the chief authority. He was ruler of Antioch and Edessa, only their regent, it is true; but Prince Bohemond now lived discredited in Italy and

[1] Anna Comnena, XII, ii, 1–7, vol. III, pp. 56–9; William of Tyre, X, 23, pp. 635–6. (See also Röhricht, *Regesta*, p. 11, and Muratori, *Antiquitates Italicae*, II, pp. 905–6, for Tancred's treaty with the Pisans.)
[2] Dal Borgo, *Diplomata Pisana*, pp. 85–94. See Heyd, *Histoire du Commerce du Levant*, vol. I, pp. 145–6.

would never return to the East, and Count Baldwin languished in Turkish captivity, from which Tancred would make no effort to rescue him. The Prince of Aleppo was his virtual vassal and none of the neighbouring emirs would venture to attack him. And he had triumphantly defied the heir of the Caesars at Constantinople. When the Emperor's ambassadors came to Antioch to remind him of his uncle's engagements, he dismissed them with arrogance. He was, as he said, Ninus the great Assyrian, a giant whom no man could resist.[1]

But arrogance has its limitations. For all his brilliance, Tancred was distrusted and disliked. It was by his own Crusading colleagues that his power was challenged and checked.

[1] Anna Comnena, XIV, ii, 3–5, vol. III, pp. 147–8.

CHAPTER IV

TOULOUSE AND TRIPOLI

'The glory of Lebanon shall come unto thee.' ISAIAH LX, 13

Of all the princes that set out in 1096 for the First Crusade, Raymond, Count of Toulouse, had been the wealthiest and the most distinguished, the man whom many expected to be named as leader of the movement. Five years later he was among the least considered of the Crusaders. His troubles were of his own making. Though he was no greedier and no more ambitious than most of his colleagues, his vanity made his faults too clearly visible. His policy of loyalty to the Emperor Alexius was genuinely based on a sense of honour and a far-sighted statesmanship, but to his fellow-Franks it seemed a treacherous ruse, and it won him small advantage; for the Emperor soon discovered him to be an incompetent friend. His followers respected his piety; but he had no authority over them. They had forced his hand over the march to Jerusalem during the First Crusade; and the disasters of 1101 showed how little fitted he was to direct an expedition. His lowest humiliation had come when he was taken prisoner by his young colleague Tancred. Though Tancred's action, breaking the rules of hospitality and honour, outraged public opinion, Raymond only obtained release on signing away any claims to northern Syria and incidentally destroying the basis of his agreement with the Emperor.[1] But he had the virtue of tenacity. He had vowed to remain in the East. He would keep his vow and would still carve for himself a principality.

There was one area that must be conquered by the Christians if their establishments in the East were to survive. A band of Moslem

[1] See above, p. 34.

emirates separated the Franks of Antioch and Edessa from their brothers in Jerusalem. Of these emirates the most considerable was that of the Banū Ammar of Tripoli. The head of the family, the *qadi* Fakhr al-Mulk Abu Ali, was a man of peace. Though his army was small he ruled a wealthy district, and by a skilful if inconsistent attitude of appeasement towards all his neighbours he maintained a precarious independence, relying in the last resort upon the strength of his fortress-capital, on the peninsula of al-Mina. He had shown considerable friendliness towards the Franks whenever they approached his dominions. He had re-victualled the First Crusade, and he did not oppose its leaders when they besieged his city of Arqa. He had given Baldwin of Boulogne useful help during his perilous journey to assume the crown of Jerusalem. But when the Crusaders receded into the distance he had quietly taken over the cities of Tortosa and Maraclea which they had occupied. He thus controlled the whole coast-road from Lattakieh and Jabala to the Fatimid dependency of Beirut.[1]

The alternative route from northern Syria to Palestine ran up the valley of the Orontes, past the Munqidhite city of Shaizar, past Hama, which owed allegiance to Ridwan, and Homs, where Ridwan's stepfather, Janah ad-Daulah, reigned. There it divided. One branch, followed by Raymond on the First Crusade, forked through the Buqaia to Tripoli and the coast; the other went straight on, past the Damascene dependency of Baalbek, to the head-waters of the Jordan.

Raymond, whose ambitions were never modest, contemplated the establishment of a principality that would command both the coast-road and the Orontes, with its capital at Homs, the city that the Franks called La Chamelle. But his first objective, determined probably by the presence of Genoese ships that might help him, would be the cities of the coast. On his release by Tancred, in the last days of 1101, he set out from Antioch together with the

---

[1] See above, p. 11, also Sobernheim, article 'Ibn Ammar', in *Encyclopaedia of Islam*. Duqaq's son, Buri, had been given Jabala by the local sheikh but had been suspended by Fakhr al-Mulk.

surviving princes of the Crusades of 1101, Stephen of Blois, William of Aquitaine, Welf of Bavaria and their comrades, who were anxious to complete their pilgrimage to Jerusalem. At Lattakieh he was reunited with his wife and with his troops, and with them he marched on to Tortosa. The Genoese flotilla on whose help he counted anchored off the coast as he reached the city walls. Before this double menace, the governor made little resistance. About the middle of February Raymond entered Tortosa, together with his fellow-travellers, who agreed without discussion that it should be his. They supposed that he would then accompany them on to Jerusalem. On his refusal they were angry and, according to Fulcher of Chartres, spoke blasphemous words against him. But Raymond had decided that Tortosa should be the nucleus of his dominion. So they took their leave of him and journeyed on to the south.[1]

Raymond had made no secret of his plans; and the Moslem world was alarmed. Fakhr al-Mulk sent to warn the emirs of Homs and Duqaq of Damascus. But when Raymond appeared before the walls of Tripoli, it was seen that his army numbered little more than three hundred men. The Moslems thought that now was the moment to destroy him. Duqaq hastily provided two thousand horsemen, and Janah ad-Daulah as many more; and the whole army of the Banū Ammar was collected. In all the Moslem host outnumbered Raymond's by twenty to one as it converged on him on the plain outside the city.

Raymond's deeds were poorly reported by the Crusader historians. It is from the Arab Ibn al-Athir that we learn of the extraordinary battle that ensued. Raymond placed a hundred of his men to oppose the Damascenes, a hundred to oppose the Banū Ammar, fifty to oppose the men of Homs, and the remaining fifty to be his own bodyguard. The Homs soldiers began the attack; but when it failed they suddenly panicked; and the panic spread among the troops of Damascus. The Tripolitans were

[1] Fulcher of Chartres, II, xvii, 1-2, pp. 433-5; Albert of Aix, VIII, 43, p. 583; Caffaro, *Liberatio*, p. 69, says that a Genoese fleet helped.

enjoying greater success, when Raymond, finding his other foes in flight, swung his whole army against them. The sudden shock was too much for them; and they too turned and fled. The Frankish cavalry then swept over the battlefield, slaughtering all the Moslems that could not escape. The Arab historian estimated that seven thousand of his co-religionists perished.

The victory not only re-established Raymond's reputation; it also ensured the survival of his Lebanese dominion. The Moslems never again dared to take the offensive against him. But his forces were too small for him to capture Tripoli itself, with its great fortifications on the peninsula of al-Mina. After exacting a heavy tribute in money and horses, he returned to Tortosa, to plan his next campaign.[1]

After spending the following months in establishing himself in the neighbourhood of Tortosa, he set out in the spring of 1103 to conquer the Buqaia, a necessary move if he wished to isolate Tripoli and himself expand towards the Orontes. His attempt to surprise the fortress of Tuban, at the north-eastern entrance to the valley, failed; but undaunted, he settled down to besiege Qalat al-Hosn, the tremendous castle that dominated the whole plain, which his troops had occupied for a week in 1099. These castles belonged to Janah ad-Daulah of Homs, who could not afford to lose them. He prepared an army for their rescue. But, as he came out of the great mosque of Homs, after praying for victory, he was murdered by three Assassins. His death caused disorder in his city. Raymond at once raised the siege of Qalat al-Hosn and marched eastward to profit by it. Public opinion attributed the murder to agents of Ridwan, who had never forgiven Janah for having attacked him three years before, when he was engaged against the Franks of Antioch. But Janah's widow, who was Ridwan's mother, terrified by Raymond's approach, sent to Aleppo to offer Ridwan the city. Janah's counsellors did not support her,

[1] Ibn al-Athir, pp. 211–12; Sibt ibn al-Djauzi (p. 525) placing the battle outside Tortosa, as does Caffaro, *Liberatio, loc. cit.* Radulph of Caen, cxlv, p. 707.

but instead summoned Duqaq of Damascus to their rescue. Duqaq hastened up in person from the south with his atabeg Toghtekin and took over the government, which he entrusted to Toghtekin. Raymond was not in a position to fight against him, and withdrew to the coast.[1]

When he returned to Tortosa he learnt that a Genoese squadron of forty vessels had put into Lattakieh. He at once hired its help for an attack on Tripoli. The attack failed; so the allies moved southward and captured the port of Jebail, or Gibelet, the Byblos of the ancients. The Genoese were rewarded with one-third of the town.[2] But Raymond was determined to conquer Tripoli itself. During the last months of 1103 he set up a camp in the suburbs of the city and began to construct a huge castle on a ridge, some three miles inland. Shortly before, to please the Byzantines, he had tried to divert Tancred from Lattakieh. In return they provided him from Cyprus with materials and with skilled masons. By the spring of 1104 it was completed and Raymond was in residence. He called it Mount Pilgrim; but to the Arabs it was known as Qalat Sanjil, the castle of Saint-Gilles.[3]

Tripoli was now in a state of permanent siege, but it remained inviolate. Raymond controlled the land approaches, but he lacked permanent sea-power. With their great hoards of wealth the Banū Ammar could still maintain a large merchant-fleet and bring in provisions to the city from the Egyptian ports to the south. But Raymond's castle menaced their freedom. In the late summer they made a sortie and burnt the suburbs up to its walls; and Raymond himself was injured by a burning roof which fell on him. Early next spring Fakhr al-Mulk was induced to arrange a truce with the Christians, by which he abandoned the suburbs to them. The negotiations were hardly concluded, when Raymond, who had

---

[1] Ibn al-Athir, p. 213. His dating is obscure. Kemal ad-Din, pp. 590-1.
[2] Albert of Aix, IX, 26, pp. 605-6; Caffaro, *Liberatio*, p. 71.
[3] Anna Comnena, XI, viii, 5, vol. III, p. 389; Albert of Aix, IX, 32, p. 510; Caffaro, *Liberatio*, p. 70; Radulph of Caen, *loc. cit.*; William of Tyre, X, 17, p. 441; Ibn al-Athir, pp. 217-18; Abu'l Mehasin, p. 275.

never fully recovered from his burns six months before, fell mortally ill. He died at Mount Pilgrim on 28 February 1105. The gallant adventures of his later years had quite restored his fame. He was mourned as a great Christian knight who had preferred the hardships of the Holy War to all the pleasures of his native land.[1]

This tribute was deserved. For Raymond, unlike his fellow-Crusaders now settled in the East, who were of small account in their home-countries, had possessed a rich heritage in Europe. Though he had sworn never to return to it, yet he had kept some control over its government. His death created a problem of succession in Toulouse as well as in the Lebanon. He had left Toulouse under the rule of his eldest son, Bertrand. But Bertrand's right to inherit the county was questioned, probably because he was a bastard. Of Raymond's children by the Countess Elvira all had died save one small boy, Alfonso-Jordan, born a few months ago in the castle of Mount Pilgrim. It was clear that an infant could not take over the government of a precarious military state in the Lebanon; while his very existence was probably not yet known at Toulouse. Bertrand continued to govern his father's European lands; and in the East Raymond's soldiers chose as Raymond's successor, probably in conformity with Raymond's own last wishes, his cousin, William-Jordan, Count of Cerdagne. William-Jordan, whose maternal grandmother had been Raymond's maternal aunt, had only recently arrived in the East. He regarded himself as regent for his baby cousin and refrained from taking any title from his eastern territory. But, so long as Alfonso-Jordan lived, neither William-Jordan nor Bertrand could be secure in his government.[2]

[1] Albert of Aix, *loc. cit.*; Caffaro, *Liberatio*, p. 72; Bartolf of Nangis, LXVIII, p. 539. William of Tyre, XI, 2, p. 452; Ibn al-Athir (*Kamil at-Tawarikh*, p. 230, making him die ten days after his accident); William of Tyre speaks of him as 'Bonae memoriae' and 'vir religiosus et timens Deum, vir per omnia commendabilis'.

[2] Albert of Aix, IX, 50, pp. 123–4. According to Vaissette, *Histoire de Languedoc*, ed. Molinier, vol. IV, 1, pp. 195–9, Bertrand was the son of Raymond

William-Jordan continued his predecessor's policy, pressing on the blockade and preserving the alliance with Byzantium. At the Emperor's request, the governor of Cyprus, Eumathius Philocales, sent him an ambassador to receive his homage and in return to make him valuable presents. As a result of William-Jordan's compliance, regular supplies were sent from Cyprus to the Franks before Tripoli, and Byzantine troops occasionally helped in the blockade of the city. While provender flowed into the Frankish camp, Tripoli itself was now threatened with starvation. No food could reach it by land. There were ships from the Fatimid ports and even from Tancred's territory that ran the blockade; but they could not bring enough for its large population. Prices for foodstuffs rose fantastically; a pound of dates cost a gold piece. Everyone that could escape from the city emigrated. Within the walls there was misery and disease, which Fakhr al-Mulk tried to alleviate by distributing food, paid for by special taxes, among the soldiers and the sick. Certain city notables fled to the Frankish camp; and two of them revealed to the besiegers the paths by which goods were still smuggled into the city. Fakhr al-Mulk offered William-Jordan vast sums of money for the persons of these traitors. When the Count refused to give them up, they were found murdered in the Christian camp.[1]

Fakhr al-Mulk did not know where to turn for help. If he applied to the Fatimids, they would insist on the annexation of his state. He was, for some reason, on bad terms with Toghtekin of

by his first wife, the daughter of the Marquis of Provence. This marriage was later annulled on grounds of consanguinity. Such an annulment did not always bastardize the children. But it is clear that though Raymond regarded Bertrand as his heir in Toulouse when he went off to the East accompanied by his children by Elvira (whose sexes are unknown), Bertrand's claims were considered to be inferior to those of the indubitably legitimate Alfonso-Jordan in Toulouse; and, later, Alfonso-Jordan's claim to Tripoli alarmed Bertrand's grandson, Raymond II (see below, p. 280). William of Malmesbury, who is not always very accurate, calls Bertrand Raymond's son by a concubine (II, 9. 456). Caffaro (*Liberatio*, p. 72), writing as a contemporary, calls him a bastard.

[1] Anna Comnena, *loc. cit.*; Ibn al-Athir, p. 236, who says that the town received good supplies from the Greeks of Lattakieh.

Homs, his most natural ally, who had taken over the government of Damascus on Duqaq's death in 1104, and who himself kept up constant warfare with William-Jordan. Distant allies seemed the safest; so in 1105 he sent an urgent appeal to Mardin, to Soqman the Ortoqid. Soqman, who was not unwilling to re-enter the arena of the Syrian coast, set out with a large army across the desert. But when he reached Palmyra he suddenly died, and his generals hurried back to the Jezireh to dispute about the succession.[1] Thanks to his wealth and his diplomacy Fakhr maintained himself in Tripoli, amid increasing misery, throughout 1106 and 1107. His relations with Toghtekin improved; and Toghtekin's diversions against the Franks, as when he recaptured Rafaniya from them in 1105, were of assistance to him.[2] But the Franks were now firmly established on the Lebanese coast; and no neighbouring Moslem power seemed prepared or able to eject them. In the spring of 1108 Fakhr al-Mulk, in his despair, decided personally to beg for help from the head of his religion, the Caliph of Baghdad, and from its greatest potentate, the Seldjuk Sultan Mohammed.

Leaving the government of Tripoli in the hands of his cousin, Abu'l Manaqib ibn Ammar, and giving all his soldiers six months' pay in advance, Fakhr set out from Tripoli in March. He had already informed Toghtekin of his intentions, and it seems that he obtained permission from William-Jordan to pass through Frankish-held territory. He took a bodyguard of five hundred men, and numerous costly gifts for the Sultan. When he arrived at Damascus, Toghtekin received him with every mark of respect, and the leading Damascene emirs showered gifts on him though, as a precaution, he lodged outside the city walls. When he continued his journey, Toghtekin's own son, Taj al-Mulk Buri, joined his escort. As he approached Baghdad he was honoured with every flattering attention. The Sultan sent his own barge to transport him across the Euphrates, and he lay on the cushion usually honoured by the Sultan's body. Though he had never

[1] Ibn al-Athir, pp. 226–7.
[2] Ibn al-Qalanisi, *op. cit.* p. 60; Ibn al-Athir, p. 230.

assumed a title higher than that of *qadi*, he entered Baghdad with the ceremony accorded to a sovereign prince. Both the Caliph and the Sultan showed him brotherly affection and praised him for his services to the Faith. But when it came to the discussion of business, the emptiness of these compliments was revealed. The Sultan promised him that a great Seldjuk army would come to relieve Tripoli; but first there were a few little tasks to be completed nearer Baghdad. For instance, the emir of Mosul, Jawali, must be reduced to a more obedient state of mind. Fakhr understood that in fact Mohammed had no desire to intervene. After spending four luxurious and fruitless months at the Sultan's Court, he began his homeward journey, only to find that now he had no home.[1]

Abu'l Manaqib and the notables of Tripoli were realists. They saw that only one Moslem power was in a position to help them, the Fatimids who still had some command of the seas. They invited the Egyptian vizier, al-Afdal, to send a governor to take over the city. In response, al-Afdal appointed Sharaf ad-Daulah, who arrived in Tripoli in the summer of 1108, laden with supplies of corn for the populace. He had no difficulty in assuming control. All the partisans of Fakhr al-Mulk were arrested and shipped off to Egypt. Fakhr had reached Damascus before he heard of the revolution. He still possessed Jabala, to the north of Tortosa, and he made his way thither. But his rule in Jabala was of short duration. In May 1109 Tancred of Antioch appeared in full force before the city. Fakhr at once capitulated on the understanding that he should hold the town as a fief from Tancred. But Tancred broke his word. Fakhr was forced to leave, and made his way without molestation into retirement in Damascus. He spent the rest of his life as Toghtekin's pensioner.[2]

Though Fakhr al-Mulk lost Tripoli, the Egyptians could not hold it; nor did William-Jordan win it. On Raymond's death, the barons of Toulouse had accepted Bertrand's succession, because he

[1] Ibn al-Qalanisi, *op. cit.* pp. 83–6; Ibn al-Athir, pp. 255–7.
[2] Ibn al-Qalanisi, pp. 86–90; Ibn al-Athir, p. 274; Sibt ibn al-Djauzi, p. 536.

had already governed them for nearly ten years and because they were not aware that Raymond had left a legitimate son. But when they learnt of the existence of the young Alfonso-Jordan, they sent out to the East to ask him to take over his rightful inheritance. The Countess Elvira cannot be blamed for preferring for her son the rich lands of southern France to a precarious lordship in the East. She arrived with him at Toulouse in the course of 1108.[1]

Their coming obliged Bertrand to consider his future. It is probable that a family compact was arranged by which Bertrand gave up any claims that he might have to his father's lands in Europe, and in return Alfonso-Jordan, in order to be well rid of him from Toulouse, abandoned in his favour his inheritance in the Lebanon. Bertrand set out for the East in the summer of 1108. He was determined to round off his future principality by the conquest of Tripoli; and he probably anticipated that he might have some difficulty with William-Jordan. To achieve his aims he brought with him an army of four thousand cavalry and infantry and a flotilla of forty galleys, provided by the ports of Provence. His young son, Pons, travelled with him. His first visit was to Genoa, from whom he hoped to obtain the naval help needed for the reduction of Tripoli. William-Jordan had also tried to arrange an alliance with the Genoese; but his embassy found Bertrand already accepted as the Republic's ally. Genoa had promised to aid Bertrand to take over his father's conquests in the East and to crown them with the capture of Tripoli, in which they would be given the favoured commercial position. When Bertrand sailed on eastward in the autumn, a Genoese squadron sailed with him.[2]

Next, Bertrand planned to visit Constantinople, to secure the support of his father's friend, the Emperor. Storms obliged his fleet to put into the Gulf of Volo, to the harbour of Almyro, where his men made an excellent impression by abstaining from

[1] See above, p. 61.
[2] Albert of Aix, XI, 3, p. 664, says that Bertrand visited Pisa when he means Genoa; Caffaro, *Liberatio*, p. 72.

the usual Western habit of pillaging the countryside. Consequently, when he arrived at Constantinople, Alexius was prejudiced in his favour and received him as a son. Bertrand was given many valuable presents and the promise of imperial favours to come. In return he swore allegiance to the Emperor.[1]

From Constantinople Bertrand and his allies sailed to Saint Symeon, the port of Antioch, and sent an envoy to Tancred to ask for an interview. Tancred at once came down to see him. But their conversation did not go smoothly. Bertrand arrogantly demanded that Tancred should hand over to him the portions of the city of Antioch that his father once had held. Tancred replied that he would consider this if Bertrand would assist him in the campaign on which he was about to embark against Mamistra and the Byzantine cities of Cilicia. To Bertrand, who had just sworn an oath of allegiance to Alexius and who counted on Byzantine subsidies, the proposition was unacceptable; but he offered instead to conquer for Tancred the town of Jabala, in which Fakhr al-Mulk had taken refuge. Tancred insisted on co-operation in the Cilician expedition; and when Bertrand categorically refused because of his oath to the Emperor, Tancred ordered him to leave his principality and forbade his subjects to sell him supplies. Bertrand was obliged to move on down the coast, and sailed into Tortosa harbour.[2]

Tortosa was held by one of William-Jordan's lieutenants; who at once admitted Bertrand into the town and gave him all the provisions that he required. Next day Bertrand sent a messenger to William-Jordan's headquarters at Mount Pilgrim, requiring the surrender of all his father's inheritance in the lands of La Chamelle, that is to say the principality of Homs that Raymond had hoped to found. But William-Jordan had recently won a signal success. When the Egyptians took over Tripoli, the town of

---

[1] Anna Comnena, xiv, ii, 6, vol. iii, p. 149, says that Bertrand (Πελκτράνος) swore allegiance to Alexius when he was already in Tripoli. But Albert of Aix, *loc. cit.*, mentions his visit via Halmyrus to Constantinople.

[2] Albert of Aix, xi, 5–7, pp. 665–7.

Arqa, under the leadership of one of Fakhr's favourite pages, had placed itself under the protection of Toghtekin of Damascus. Toghtekin set out in person to inspect his new dependency; but the winter rains delayed his progress through the Buqaia. While waiting for the weather to improve, he attacked certain forts that the Christians had built near the frontier. William-Jordan, with three hundred horsemen and two hundred native infantrymen, crept over the shoulder of the Lebanon and fell on him unexpectedly, near the village of Akun. The Damascene army, with Toghtekin at its head, fled in panic to Homs, pursued by the Franks, who could not venture to attack the city, but then turned northward to raid the territory of Shaizar. The Munqidhite brothers, Murshid and Sultan, emirs of Shaizar, hearing that the Frankish army was small, came out in the confident expectation that it could easily be captured. But the Franks attacked at once so fiercely that the men of Shaizar broke and fled. William-Jordan then returned to Arqa, which capitulated to him after a siege of only three weeks.[1]

Encouraged by these victories, William-Jordan was in no mood to abdicate in Bertrand's favour. He replied that he held Raymond's lands by the right of inheritance and that moreover he had defended them and added to them. But the size of Bertrand's armada alarmed him. He sent to Antioch to ask Tancred to intervene in his favour. In return he promised to become Tancred's vassal. His move obliged Bertrand to take corresponding action. He sent a messenger to Jerusalem, to put his case before King Baldwin, to whom he appealed as supreme arbiter of the Franks in the East and whom he thereby recognized as his suzerain.[2]

Baldwin, whose statesmanship saw that the Franks in the East must work together and whose ambition pictured himself as their leader, at once answered the appeal. He was already angry with Tancred over his treatment of Baldwin of Edessa and Joscelin of

---

[1] Usama, ed. Hitti, p. 78; Ibn al-Athir, pp. 226–7.
[2] Fulcher of Chartres, II, xi, 1, pp. 526–30; Albert of Aix, XI, 1–2, 8, pp. 663–4, 666.

Courtenay. Bertrand had moved southward to Tripoli, where his army was conducting the double task of continuing the blockade of the Moslem city and besieging William-Jordan's supporters on Mount Pilgrim. William-Jordan had meanwhile left Mount Pilgrim and had reoccupied Tortosa, where he awaited Tancred. No sooner had Tancred joined him than they were visited by the envoys of the King, Eustace Garnier and Pagan of Haifa, who ordered them both to appear at the Royal Court before Tripoli, to settle the question of Raymond's inheritance as well as the restitution of Edessa and Turbessel to their rightful owners. William-Jordan wished to refuse the summons; but Tancred realized that defiance was impracticable.

In June 1109 all the princes of the Frankish East assembled outside the walls of Tripoli. Bertrand was there with his army. King Baldwin came up from the south with five hundred knights and as many infantrymen. Tancred brought seven hundred of his best knights; and Baldwin of Edessa and Joscelin arrived with their bodyguards. At a solemn session in the castle of Mount Pilgrim Tancred was formally reconciled with Baldwin of Edessa and with Joscelin, while the Toulousain inheritance was divided. William-Jordan was to keep Tortosa and his own conquest, Arqa; and Bertrand was to have Jebail and Tripoli as soon as it was captured. The former swore allegiance to Tancred, and the latter to King Baldwin; and it was agreed that on the death of either candidate the other should inherit his lands.[1]

With peace made between its leaders, the Frankish army set seriously about the capture of Tripoli. The Egyptian governor, Sharaf ad-Daulah, had been desperately demanding help from the authorities in Egypt, who equipped a huge fleet, with transports for an army and boats laden with supplies. But intrigues and quarrels amongst the Egyptian commanders had delayed its departure from the ports of the Delta. Months passed by, while the vizier half-heartedly tried to compose the quarrels; and now at last orders were given for it to sail. But the north wind blew

[1] Fulcher of Chartres, II, xli, 1, p. 531; Albert of Aix, XI, 9-12, pp. 666-8.

68

steadily and the ships could not leave harbour. When at last they set out reduced in number, it was too late.[1]

The garrison of Tripoli, cut off from help by sea by the fleets of Genoa and Provence, and with their land-wall battered by all the machines that the Frankish army could muster, soon abandoned all thought of resistance. Sharaf ad-Daulah sent to King Baldwin offering to surrender on terms. He asked that the citizens wishing to emigrate from the city should be allowed to go in safety with their movable goods, and that those wishing to remain should become Frankish subjects and should keep all their possessions, merely paying a special yearly tax; he himself would be permitted to depart with his troops to Damascus. Baldwin agreed; and on 12 July 1109 the Christians entered Tripoli.

Baldwin himself kept to his agreement. In the districts that he took over there was no pillage or destruction. But the Genoese marines, finding the city undefended, forced their own way in. They began to sack and to burn houses and to slay every Moslem that they met; and it was some time before the authorities could restrain them. In the tumult the great library of the Banū Ammar, the finest in the Moslem world, was burnt to the ground, and all its contents perished.[2]

When the city was fully occupied and order was restored, Bertrand was installed as its ruler. He took the title of Count of Tripoli and reaffirmed his vassaldom to the Kingdom of Jerusalem. His obligations to the Emperor Alexius were ignored. The Genoese were rewarded by a quarter in Tripoli, by a castle, known as the Castle of the Constable, ten miles south of Tripoli, and the remaining two-thirds of the town of Jebail. Jebail was given by them to the Admiral Hugh Embriaco, whose descendants formed it into a hereditary fief.[3]

[1] Ibn al-Athir, p. 274; Ibn al-Qalanisi, p. 89.
[2] Fulcher of Chartres, II, xli, 2–4, pp. 531–3; Albert of Aix, XI, 13, p. 668; Ibn al-Qalanisi, pp. 89–90; Ibn al-Athir, *loc. cit.*; Abu'l Mahâsin, p. 489; Ibn Hamdun, p. 455; Sibt ibn al-Djauzi, p. 536.
[3] Caffaro, *Liberatio*, pp. 72–3. See Rey, 'Les Seigneurs de Gibelet', in *Revue de l'Orient Latin*, vol. III, pp. 399–403.

Toulouse and Tripoli

Bertrand did not have long to wait before he secured the whole of his father's eastern inheritance. While the Frankish army was still at Tripoli William-Jordan was shot by an arrow. The circumstances remained a mystery. It seemed that he rashly intervened in a scuffle that had broken out between two grooms, and as he tried to separate the men, someone fired on him. Suspicion inevitably fell on Bertrand; but nothing could be proved. Bertrand at once took over all William-Jordan's lands; which thus passed under the allegiance of King Baldwin. Tancred had backed the wrong horse.[1]

So it was that Raymond's son fulfilled his father's ambition of founding a state in the East. It was a lesser principality than Raymond had envisaged. The lands of La Chamelle were never to form part of it; and instead of acknowledging the distant suzerainty of the Emperor at Constantinople, it had an overlord close at hand at Jerusalem. But it was a rich and prosperous heritage. By its wealth and by its position, linking the Franks of northern Syria with the Franks of Palestine, it was to play a vital part in the history of the Crusades.

[1] Fulcher of Chartres, *loc. cit.*; Albert of Aix, XI, 15, pp. 669–70.

CHAPTER V

KING BALDWIN I

*'His heart is as firm as a stone; yea, as hard as a piece of the
nether millstone.'*   JOB XLI, 24

King Baldwin's intervention at Tripoli in 1109 revealed him as the
chief potentate of the Frankish East. He had won his position by
patient and arduous industry and by boldness of enterprise. When
he arrived in Jerusalem, against the allied opposition of the
Patriarch Daimbert and the Prince of Antioch, it was to inherit an
empty treasury and a scattered dominion, made up of the central
mountain-ridge of Palestine, the plain of Esdraelon and a few
outlying fortresses set in a hostile countryside, and a tiny army of
lawless, arrogant knights and untrustworthy native mercenaries.
The only organized body in the kingdom was the Church; and
within the Church there were two parties, Daimbert's and
Arnulf's. Godfrey's central administration had been conducted by
his household, which was small and ill-suited to govern a country.
The barons to whom border castles had been entrusted were left
to rule their territories as they pleased.

Baldwin saw that the most pressing danger was of a Moslem
attack before his state could be set in order. Believing that the
best defence is to take the offensive, he started out, before he had
even settled the urgent question of his relations with Daimbert or
had himself assumed the crown, on a campaign to awe the infidel.
His exploits at Edessa and his victory at the Dog River had given
him a terrible reputation, from which he sought to profit. Barely a
week after his arrival at Jerusalem he marched down to Ascalon and
made a demonstration in front of its walls. But the fortress was too
strong for his little army to attack; so he moved eastward to Hebron
and thence down into the Negeb to Segor, in the salt land at the

71

southern tip of the Dead Sea, burning villages as he went, and on through the wilderness of Edom to Mount Hor, and its ancient monastery of St Aaron, by Petra. Though he made no permanent settlements in the region, his progress cowed the Arabs. For the next few years they refrained from infiltrating into his territory.[1]

He returned to Jerusalem a few days before Christmas. The Patriarch Daimbert had had time to reflect on his situation. He bowed to the inevitable; and on Christmas Day, 1100, he crowned Baldwin King of Jerusalem. In return, he was confirmed in the Patriarchate.[2]

In the early spring of 1101 Baldwin heard that a rich Arab tribe was passing through Transjordan. At once he led a detachment across the river and fell by night on its encampment. Only a few of the Arabs escaped. The majority of men were slain in their tents, and the women and children were carried off into captivity, together with a great hoard of money and precious stuffs. Amongst the captives was the wife of one of the sheikhs of the tribe. She was on the point of bearing a child; and when Baldwin learnt of her condition, he gave orders that she should be released with her maid-servant, two female camels and a good supply of food and drink. She gave birth successfully by the wayside, where her husband soon found her. Deeply moved by Baldwin's courtesy he hurried after him to thank him and to promise that some day he would repay him for his kindness.[3]

News of the raid added to Baldwin's fame. In March embassies came to Jerusalem from the coastal cities, Arsuf, Caesarea, Acre and Tyre, bearing valuable gifts; while Duqaq of Damascus sent to offer the sum of fifty thousand gold besants for the ransom of the captives that Baldwin had made at the battle of the Dog River. Baldwin's most pressing financial problem was thereby solved.[4]

[1] Fulcher of Chartres, II, iv, i–5, ii, pp. 370–83 (Fulcher accompanied the expedition); Albert of Aix, VII, 28–42, pp. 533–6. There was a Greek monastery on the present Jebel Harun (Mount Hor) and a settlement of monks round the great Nabatean tomb known now as the Deir, or Monastery.
[2] See above, vol. I, p. 326.   [3] William of Tyre, X, 11, p. 415.
[4] Albert of Aix, VII, 52, pp. 541–2.

Their tribute did not long benefit Arsuf or Caesarea. In March a Genoese squadron was sighted off Haifa, and on 15 April it put in at Jaffa. Amongst the passengers was Maurice, Cardinal-Bishop of Porto, sent out as Legate by Pope Paschal. Hitherto Baldwin had been dependent for sea-power on the small Pisan fleet that had accompanied the Pisan archbishop, his enemy Daimbert, to the East. An alliance with the Genoese, chief rivals of the Pisans, suited him better. He hurried down to Haifa to greet them and to receive the Legate, and took their leaders with them to spend Easter at Jerusalem. There they made an agreement to serve him for a season. Their payment was to be one-third of all the booty that might be captured, of goods as well as of money, and a street in the bazaar quarter of every conquered town. As soon as the pact was signed, the allies moved against Arsuf, Baldwin by land and the Genoese by sea. Resistance soon broke down. The authorities of the town offered to capitulate on condition that the inhabitants might emigrate safely with their families and their possessions to Moslem territory. Baldwin accepted their terms. They were escorted by his troops to Ascalon. Baldwin then garrisoned the town, after assigning their share to the Genoese.[1]

From Arsuf the allies went to Caesarea, whose siege began on 2 May. The garrison, relying on its old Byzantine walls, refused to surrender; but on 17 May it was taken by assault. The victorious soldiers were given permission to pillage the city as they pleased; and the horrors of the sack shocked even their own leaders. The cruellest massacre took place in the Great Mosque, which once had been the synagogue of Herod Agrippa. Many of the citizens had taken refuge there and begged for mercy. But they were butchered, men and women alike, till the floor was a lake of blood. In all the city only a few girls and young infants were spared, and the chief magistrate and the commander of the garrison, whom Baldwin himself saved in order to obtain good ransom-money. The ferocity was deliberate. Baldwin wished to show that he

---

[1] Fulcher of Chartres, II, viii, 1-7, pp. 393-400; Albert of Aix, VII, 54, pp. 452-3.

would keep his word to all that came to terms with him. Otherwise he would be pitiless.[1]

Baldwin had only time to divide the booty according to his pact and to instal a Frankish garrison before the news came to him that an Egyptian army had entered Palestine.

The Fatimid vizier, al-Afdal, was eager to avenge the disaster at Ascalon, two years before, and had fitted out an expedition under the command of the Mameluk, Sa'ad ed-Daulah al-Qawasi. It reached Ascalon in mid-May and advanced as far as Ramleh, hoping, perhaps, to penetrate to Jerusalem while Baldwin was still occupied at Caesarea. Baldwin hastened with his forces to Ramleh; whereupon Sa'ad fell back on Ascalon to await reinforcements. After fortifying Ramleh, Baldwin set up his headquarters at Jaffa, so as to be able to watch the Egyptians' movements and at the same time keep in touch with his maritime communications. Apart from a short visit to Jerusalem for administrative purposes in July, he remained at Jaffa all through the summer. At the end of August an intercepted letter told him that new detachments had reached the Egyptians and that they were preparing to march on Jerusalem.

On 4 September Sa'ad moved his forces slowly up to the outskirts of Ramleh. Two days later Baldwin held a council of war and decided to attack at dawn, without waiting to be attacked. He had only two hundred and sixty horsemen and nine hundred infantrymen; but they were well armed and experienced; while the huge army of the Egyptians, which he estimated at eleven thousand horsemen and twenty-one thousand infantry, was lightly armed and untrained. He divided his troops into five corps, one under a knight called Bervold, the second under Geldemar Carpenel, lord of Haifa, the third under Hugh of Saint-Omer, who had succeeded Tancred as Prince of Galilee, and the fourth

[1] Fulcher of Chartres, IX, 1–9, pp. 400–4; Albert of Aix, VII, 55–6, pp. 453–4. William of Tyre, X, 16, p. 423, reports that the Genoese took as part of their booty a green cup that they believed to be made of a solid emerald. It is still in the treasury of the cathedral of San Lorenzo at Genoa, and was later considered to be the Holy Grail. See Heyd, *Histoire du Commerce du Levant*, I, p. 137.

and fifth under himself. Inspired by the presence of the True Cross, by a stirring sermon delivered by Arnulf of Rohes, and by a special absolution given by the Cardinal-Legate, the Franks marched out to Ramleh and at sunrise fell on the Egyptians, near Ibelin, south-west of the town.

Bervold led the attack; but his troops were mown down by the Egyptians and he himself slain. Geldemar Carpenel hurried to his rescue, only to perish also with all his men. The Galilean corps followed; but they made no effect on the Egyptian masses. After heavy losses Hugh of Saint-Omer extricated his men and fled towards Jaffa, pursued by the Egyptian left. It seemed that all was lost. But King Baldwin, after publicly confessing his sins before the True Cross and then haranguing his company, mounted on his brave Arab charger, Gazelle, galloped at the head of his knights into the heart of the enemy. The Egyptians, confident of victory, were taken by surprise. After a brief struggle their centre turned and fled; and the panic spread to their right. Baldwin, forbidding his men to stop to pillage corpses or to sack the enemy camp, chased them to the walls of Ascalon. Then he rallied his men and retired to divide the spoils won on the battlefield.[1]

Meanwhile Hugh of Saint-Omer had arrived at Jaffa, to report that the battle was lost. The Queen and her court were waiting there. Hearing of the disaster and believing that the King was dead, they sent a messenger at once to the only man that they thought could help them now, to Tancred at Antioch. Next morning an army came into sight. They thought that it was the Egyptians; and great was their rejoicing when they discerned the Frankish banners and recognized the King. A second messenger was dispatched to Antioch, with the news that all was well; and Tancred, who had been prepared, with some relish, to set out for the south, was told that he could stay at home.[2]

For the moment the danger was averted. The Egyptians had suffered heavy losses and were not disposed to renew the campaign

---

[1] Fulcher of Chartres, II, xi, 1–xiii, 5, pp. 407–20; Albert of Aix, VII, 66–70, pp. 550–3.   [2] Fulcher of Chartres, II, xiv, 1–8, pp. 420–4.

that season. But the resources of Egypt were enormous. Al-Afdal had no difficulty in equipping a second army that should continue the struggle next year. In the meantime Baldwin received the visit of the princes that had survived the Anatolian Crusades of 1101. Led by William of Aquitaine, Stephen of Blois and Stephen of Burgundy and the Constable Conrad, and accompanied by various barons from the Low Countries and by Ekkehard of Aura and Bishop Manasses, most of whom had come by sea to Antioch, they reached the neighbourhood of Beirut in the early spring of 1102. To ensure their safe passage through enemy country Baldwin sent an escort to meet them there and to convey them to Jerusalem. After celebrating Easter at the Holy Places the leaders prepared to return home. William of Aquitaine safely embarked for Saint Symeon at the end of April; but the ship in which Stephen of Blois and Stephen of Burgundy, with several others, had taken their passage was driven ashore by a storm off Jaffa. Before another ship could be found to accommodate them, there was news that a fresh Moslem host was marching up from Egypt. Owing to this fateful mishap they remained to assist in the coming struggle.[1]

In mid-May 1102 the Egyptian army, consisting of some twenty thousand Arabs and Sudanese, under the command of the Vizier's own son, Sharaf al-Ma'ali, assembled at Ascalon and moved up towards Ramleh. Baldwin had made his preparations. An army of several thousand Christians waited at Jaffa; and the Galilean garrisons were ready to send detachments when required. But Baldwin's scouts misled him. Believing the Egyptians to be a small body of raiders he decided to destroy them himself without calling upon his reserves. He had with him at Jerusalem his friends from the West, Stephen of Blois, Stephen of Burgundy, the Constable Conrad, Hugh, Count of Lusignan and various Belgian knights. He proposed to them to set out with his cavalry to finish off the job. Stephen of Blois ventured to suggest that it was a rash undertaking; a better reconnaissance would be desirable. But

[1] Fulcher of Chartres, II, xv, 1-6, pp. 424-8.

76

nobody even listened to Stephen, remembering his cowardice at Antioch. He joined his comrades without further complaint.

On 17 May King Baldwin set out with some five hundred horsemen from Jerusalem. They rode gaily, with little order. When they came out into the plain and suddenly saw before them the vast Egyptian army, Baldwin realized his mistake. But there could be no turning back. They were already seen, and the Egyptian light cavalry was riding up to cut off their retreat. Their only chance was to charge headlong into the enemy. The Egyptians, believing at first that this must be the vanguard of a greater army, nearly gave up before the impact; but when they saw that no other force followed, they rallied and closed in on the Franks. Baldwin's ranks broke. A few knights, led by Roger of Rozoy and Baldwin's cousin, Hugh of Le Bourg, cut their way through the Egyptian host and reached the safety of Jaffa. Many, such as Gerard of Avesnes and Godfrey's former chamberlain, Stabelon, were killed on the field. But King Baldwin himself and his chief comrades made their way into the little fortress of Ramleh, where they were surrounded by the Egyptian army.

Nightfall saved them from immediate attack. But the defences of Ramleh were pitiable. Only one tower, built by Baldwin the previous year, might possibly be held; and into that they crowded. In the middle of the night an Arab came to the gate and asked to see the King. He was admitted and revealed himself as the husband of the lady to whom Baldwin had shown courtesy during his raid on Transjordan. In gratitude he warned the King that the Egyptian assault would begin at dawn and that he must escape at once. Baldwin took his advice. However much he may have regretted the desertion of his comrades—and he was not a man with a highly developed sense of honour—he saw that on his own preservation depended the preservation of the kingdom. With a groom and three other companions he slipped out on horseback, through the enemy lines, trusting his Gazelle to take him to safety. During the same night, Lithard of Cambrai, Viscount of Jaffa, and Gothman of Brussels separately made their escape.

Gothman, though severely wounded, managed to reach Jerusalem, where he brought tidings of the disaster but counselled resistance; for he believed that Baldwin was still alive.

Early next morning the Egyptians stormed over the walls of Ramleh, and piled faggots round the tower in which the knights had taken refuge. Rather than perish in the flames, the Frankish chivalry charged out at the enemy, with the Constable Conrad at their head. But there was no escape. They were all hewn down on the spot or captured. Conrad's bravery so impressed the Egyptians that they spared his life. He and more than a hundred of his companions were sent in captivity to Egypt. Of the other leaders Stephen of Burgundy, Hugh of Lusignan and Geoffrey of Vendôme were killed in the battle, and with them died Stephen of Blois, who thus by his glorious death redeemed his reputation. The Countess Adela could sleep content.[1]

The Queen and the Court were once more at Jaffa. There Roger of Rozoy and his fellow-fugitives told them of terrible defeat. They feared that the King had fallen with all his knights, and they made plans to flee by sea while there was still time. But on 20 May the Egyptian army came up to the city walls and the Egyptian fleet approached over the southern horizon. Their worst fears seemed realized when an Egyptian soldier brandished before them a head that was recognized as the King's, but which was, in fact, that of Gerbod of Winthinc, who greatly resembled him. At that moment, as though by a miracle, a little ship was seen sailing down from the north with the King's own standard at the mast-head.

On his escape from Ramleh, Baldwin had made for the coast,

<hr>

[1] Fulcher of Chartres, II, xviii, 1–xix, 5, pp. 436–44; Ekkehard of Aura, *Hierosolymita*, pp. 33–5; Albert of Aix, IX, 2–6, pp. 591–4; Bartolf of Nangis, pp. 533–5; William of Tyre, x, 20–1, pp. 429–32, who tells of the intervention of the Sheikh; Ibn al-Athir, pp. 213–16 (a garbled account based on two different versions). I accept Hagenmeyer's dating (*op. cit.* pp. 162–6), though the *Chronicon S. Maxentii*, p. 421, says 27 May, and Albert of Aix 'about Pentecost', i.e. about 25 May; of Stephen of Blois's death, according to Guibert of Nogent, p. 245, nothing definite was known; *Cartulaire de Notre Dame de Chartres*, III, p. 115, dates it 19 May.

in an attempt to reach the army at Jaffa. But Egyptian troops were scouring the countryside. For two nights and two days he wandered through the foothills north of Ramleh, then hastened across the plain of Sharon to Arsuf. He arrived there on the evening of the 19th, to the astonished delight of its governor, Roger of Haifa. That same evening the troops of Galilee, eighty picked knights, under Hugh of Saint-Omer, who had hurried south on the news of the Egyptian advance, joined him at Arsuf. Next morning Hugh marched south with his men, to try to break his way into Jaffa, while Baldwin persuaded an English adventurer called Goderic to take him on his ship through the Egyptian blockade. To cheer his court, Baldwin hoisted his standard. The Egyptians noticed it, and at once sent ships to intercept him. But a strong north wind was blowing, against which the Egyptians could not get under weigh, while it carried Baldwin swiftly into harbour.

At once he set about reorganizing his forces. Before the Egyptians had entirely closed in round the city he broke his way out to meet Hugh of Galilee's company and to take them within the walls. Next, he sent up to Jerusalem to summon all the men that could be spared from there and from Hebron. A local monk was found who was ready to take the message through the enemy lines. He left Jaffa under darkness, but it took him three days to reach Jerusalem. When he confirmed that the King was alive, there was great rejoicing. A troop of some ninety knights and rather more mounted sergeants was collected and was fortified by a piece of the True Cross. It hastened down to Jaffa. The knights, better mounted and better armed, forced their way into the town; but the sergeants were driven into the sea. They abandoned their horses there and swam round into the harbour. Meanwhile, Baldwin wrote to Tancred and to Baldwin of Edessa, to report his heavy losses and to ask for reinforcements.

Before the northern princes could set out, unexpected help arrived. In the last days of May a fleet of two hundred ships, mostly English, and filled with soldiers and pilgrims from England, France and Germany, sailed in Jaffa roads, with the help of the wind, through the Egyptian blockade. They provided Baldwin with the additional men that he needed. On 27 May he led his army out against the enemy. The details of the battle are unknown. It seems that the Egyptians vainly tried to lure him on and then encircle him, and that eventually a charge of the heavy Frankish cavalry broke their ranks and sent them fleeing in panic. After a few hours the whole Egyptian force was in headlong flight to Ascalon, and their camp, with all its booty, was in Christian hands.[1]

Baldwin and his kingdom had been saved by a series of accidents, in which the Christians, not unnaturally, saw the hand of God. Not least of these accidents was the incompetent strategy of the Egyptians. A small detachment of their troops could have captured Jerusalem immediately after the battle of Ramleh without seriously weakening the encirclement of Jaffa. But the vizier al-Afdal was losing his grip. His son Sharaf was weak and ill-obeyed. Rivalry between his various lieutenants paralysed his movements. Next summer his father sent out a new expedition, by sea and land. But while the fleet sailed up to Jaffa, the land forces refused to advance beyond Ascalon, as its commander, the mameluk Taj al-Ajam, was jealous of the admiral, the *qadi* Ibn Qadus. Taj al-Ajam was subsequently imprisoned for his disloyalty; but the harm was done. The best opportunity for the reconquest of Palestine was missed.[2]

Tancred and Baldwin of Le Bourg, when they heard of the plight of Jerusalem, made their arrangements to set out as soon as possible for the south. With them came William of Aquitaine, who had been at Antioch when King Baldwin's letter arrived. They travelled all together up the Orontes valley, past Homs, and down the upper Jordan, in such force that the local Moslem authorities made no attempt to stop their passage. They reached Judaea towards the end of September. Baldwin by now was no longer in urgent need of their help; but their presence enabled him

[1] Fulcher of Chartres, II, xx, 1–xxi, 18, pp. 444–55; Ekkehard of Aura, *loc. cit.*; Albert of Aix, IX, 7–12, pp. 595–7; Ibn al-Athir, *loc. cit.*
[2] Ibn al-Athir, *loc. cit.*

to attack the Egyptian army at Ascalon. The skirmishes were favourable for the Christians; but they did not venture to assault the fortress.[1]

The meeting of the Frankish potentates was of use to Baldwin for other reasons. Tancred had intended to give his help on his own terms; but in fact he enabled Baldwin to solve his most difficult internal problem. The Patriarch Daimbert had crowned Baldwin on Christmas Day, 1100; but he had done so unwillingly, and Baldwin knew it. It was necessary for Baldwin to control the Church, for the Church was well organized, and it was to the Church, not to the lay authorities, that pious sympathizers from the West gave donations and legacies. Daimbert's elevation to the Patriarchate had been doubtfully legal, and complaints had been laid at Rome. At last Pope Paschal sent out a legate, Maurice, Cardinal-Bishop of Porto, to inquire into the situation. He arrived in time for Easter, 1101; and at once Baldwin accused Daimbert of treachery before him, showing him the letter that Daimbert had written to Bohemond on Godfrey's death, calling on Bohemond to oppose Baldwin's succession by force if need be. He moreover declared that Daimbert had tried to assassinate him on his journey southward. However false that latter charge might be, the letter was incontrovertible. Maurice forbade Daimbert to take part in the Easter ceremonies, which he performed alone. Daimbert, fearful for his future, sought out Baldwin and knelt in tears before him begging for forgiveness. But Baldwin was adamant, till Daimbert murmured that he had three hundred besants to spare. Baldwin always needed ready-money. He secretly accepted the gift, then went to the legate to announce magnanimously that he would forgive Daimbert. Maurice, a man of peace, was delighted to effect a reconciliation.[2]

[1] Albert of Aix, IX, 15, p. 599; Ibn Moyessar, p. 464; Ibn al-Athir, p. 213 who says that the northern princes insisted on retreat.

[2] Albert of Aix, VII, 46–51, pp. 538–41, an account that is hostile to Daimbert. William of Tyre (X, 26–7, pp. 438–40), who was throughout a defender of Daimbert's cause in the interests of the independence of the Church, disingenuously omits to report the investigations of Maurice. Riant, *Inventaire*, pp. 218–19.

After some months Baldwin again needed money, and applied to Daimbert; who gave him two hundred marks, saying that that was all that the Patriarchal coffers contained. But clerics belonging to Arnulf's party told the King that in fact Daimbert was concealing vast hoards. It happened that a few days later the Patriarch gave a sumptuous banquet in honour of the Legate, whose support he was assiduously cultivating. Baldwin burst in upon them and harangued them on their luxurious living when the forces of Christendom were starving. Daimbert angrily answered that the Church could use its money as it pleased and that the King had no authority over it, while Maurice anxiously tried to appease them both. But Baldwin could not be silenced. His early training as a priest enabled him to quote canon law; and his eloquence was such that Maurice was impressed. He induced Daimbert to promise to pay for a regiment of horsemen. The sums, however, were never paid, despite Baldwin's incessant demands. In the autumn of 1101 an envoy came from Prince Roger of Apulia with a gift of a thousand besants for the Patriarch. A third was to be devoted to the Holy Sepulchre, a third to the Hospital and a third to the King for his army. Daimbert rashly kept the whole for himself. But the terms of the gift were known. When the King made complaint, the legate could no longer support Daimbert, who was declared deprived of the Patriarchate. He retired to Jaffa, where he spent the winter, and in March he went on to Antioch. His old friend Tancred received him gladly and gave him the charge of one of the richest churches in the city, that of St George. Baldwin meanwhile kept the Patriarchate vacant, on the plea that Rome must be informed; and his officials raided the Patriarchal treasury, where they found that Daimbert had concealed twenty thousand besants. Maurice acted as locum tenens; but his health had been shattered by these scandals. He died in the spring of 1102.[1]

When Tancred came south in the autumn to rescue Baldwin, he announced that his terms were the restitution of Daimbert; and

[1] Albert of Aix, vII, 58–64, pp. 545–9.

Daimbert accompanied him. Baldwin was most accommodating. But at that moment a new papal legate arrived, Robert, Cardinal of Paris. The King therefore insisted that matters must be regularized by the session of a Synod, under Robert's presidency. Tancred and Daimbert could not refuse. A council temporarily reinstated the latter till a full investigation could be heard. Tancred therefore joined his troops to the King's for the campaign against Ascalon. Soon afterwards the Synod was held in the Church of the Holy Sepulchre. The legate presided, assisted by the visiting Bishops of Laon and Piacenza; and all the Palestinian bishops and abbots attended, as well as the Bishop of Mamistra, from Tancred's territory. The accusations against Daimbert were made by the prelates of Caesarea, Bethlehem and Ramleh, inspired by Arnulf of Rohes. They declared that on his journey to Palestine in 1099 at the head of his Pisans, he had attacked fellow-Christians in the Ionian Islands, that he had sought to provoke a civil war between King Baldwin and Prince Bohemond, and that he had kept for himself money given him for the welfare of pilgrims at the Hospital and for the soldiers of Christ. The charges were undeniably true. The Cardinal-Legate had no option but to declare Daimbert unworthy of his see and to depose him. Tancred could not object to so canonical a procedure. He had to admit defeat. Daimbert accompanied him back to Antioch and was re-established in the Church of St George till he could find an opportunity to go to Rome. He had shown himself a corrupt and miserly old man; and his departure was unregretted in Palestine. His appointment as Legate had been the one great error committed by Pope Urban II.[1]

Arnulf of Rohes, who had been Baldwin's willing adjutant in the whole affair, was too wily to attempt to take Daimbert's place. Instead, when the legate asked for a candidate for the Patriarchate, the Palestinian bishops suggested an aged priest from Therouannes, called Evremar. Evremar, who had come East with the First Crusade, was known for his piety and his charity. Though he was a compatriot of Arnulf's he had taken no part in his intrigues but

---

[1] Albert of Aix, IX, 14, 16–17, pp. 598–600; William of Tyre, *loc. cit.*

was universally respected. The legate was delighted to consecrate so blameless a cleric; and Baldwin was satisfied, knowing Evremar to be a harmless old man who would never venture to take part in politics. Meanwhile Arnulf could continue to make his own plans without hindrance.

Daimbert did not despair. When his protector Bohemond went to Italy in 1105 he accompanied him and proceeded to Rome to lay his grievance before the Pope. Paschal was cautious at first; but after some delay he decided, probably under Bohemond's fatal influence, to support him. Baldwin was required to send to Rome to answer Daimbert's charges. But the King, probably because he knew that Bohemond had the Pope's ear, took no notice. Paschal therefore cancelled Daimbert's deposition, which, he said, was due to the interference of the civil power. Fortunately, the Pope's folly was amended by the hand of God. Daimbert, as he prepared to set out in triumph to resume his patriarchal throne, fell seriously ill. He died at Messina on 15 June 1107.[1]

The troubles of the patriarchate were not over. Baldwin grew dissatisfied with Evremar. Probably he realized that the Church was too important an organization to be allowed to remain in the hands of a nonentity. He needed an efficient ally at its head. When Evremar had heard of Daimbert's official reinstatement, he set out himself for Rome. He arrived there to find his rival dead, with his own complaints against the civil power. But when the news of Daimbert's death reached Palestine, Arnulf hurried to Rome to act for the King there. Paschal now inclined towards Evremar; but he understood that the case was more complicated than he had thought. He entrusted it to the Archbishop of Arles, Gibelin of Sabran, an ecclesiastic of immense age and vast experience. In the spring of 1108, Gibelin arrived in Palestine, whither both Evremar and Arnulf had preceded him. He saw that Evremar was unfitted for the position and that no one wished for his restitution. He therefore declared the see vacant and held a synod to appoint a successor. To his embarrassed delight, Baldwin proposed that he

[1] William of Tyre, XI, 1, pp. 450-1.

should be the candidate. He accepted; and Evremar was consoled with the Archbishopric of Caesarea, which had fortunately fallen vacant.

Gossip said that Arnulf had persuaded the King to choose Gibelin because of his age. The Patriarchate would soon be vacant again. And, indeed, Gibelin only lived for four more years: and on his death Arnulf was, at last, elected without opposition to his throne.[1]

Arnulf was, from Baldwin's point of view, an ideal Patriarch. In spite of trouble later on over the King's remarriage, and in spite of the hatred of many of his subordinates, he maintained his position. He was undoubtedly corrupt. When his niece Emma made a satisfactory marriage with Eustace Garnier, he endowed her with a valuable estate at Jericho which belonged to the Holy Sepulchre. But he was active and efficient, and devoted to the King. Thanks to him, the unworkable scheme envisaged by most of the participants in the First Crusade, by which Jerusalem should be a theocracy, with a monarch merely as a minister for defence, was finally and utterly abandoned. He saw to it that the whole Church in Palestine shared his views, even deposing the canons of the Holy Sepulchre whom Godfrey of Lorraine had appointed, because he did not trust their loyalty. When the kingdom was expanded by conquest, he fought hard to see that the civil and ecclesiastical jurisdiction coincided, against the opposition of Pope Paschal, who, with his disastrous predilection for the Norman princes of Antioch, defended the historical but impracticable rights of the Antiochene see. Arnulf was not an estimable person, but he was a valuable servant of the kingdom of Jerusalem. Its great historian, William of Tyre, execrated his memory and besmirched his name, unfairly, for he did much to consolidate the work of the First Crusade.[2]

---

[1] Albert of Aix, x, 589, pp. 650–9, xii, 24, p. 704; William of Tyre, *loc. cit.* and xi, 4, pp. 455–6.

[2] William of Tyre, xi, 15, p. 479. William disapproved of Arnulf as a time-server. See below, p. 104.

To Arnulf also, and to his master King Baldwin, must be given the credit of the good relations that were established between the Latin hierarchy and the native Christians. During his first tenure of the Patriarchate in 1099, Arnulf had ejected the eastern sects from the Church of the Holy Sepulchre and had despoiled them. But Daimbert was a worse enemy. His policy was to banish all the native Christians not only from the Church itself but from their monasteries and establishments in Jerusalem, whether they were Orthodox, like the Greeks and the Georgians, or heretics, like the Armenians, the Jacobites and the Nestorians. He also offended local propriety by introducing women to serve in the Holy Places. Because of these enormities all the lamps in the Church of the Holy Sepulchre went out on the eve of Easter, 1101, and the Sacred Fire would not descend from heaven to light them again till the five dispossessed communities prayed together that the Franks might be forgiven. Baldwin took heed of the lesson. He insisted that the wrongs of the natives should be righted. The keys of the Sepulchre itself were restored to the Greeks. Thenceforward he seems to have enjoyed the support of all the Christians of Palestine. The higher clergy were all Franks, though there were Greek canons at the Holy Sepulchre. The Orthodox natives accepted this; for their own higher clergy had left the country in the troubled yeasr just before the Crusade. The Latin hierarchs were never liked; but local Orthodox monasteries carried on without hindrance, and Orthodox pilgrims that visited Palestine during the days of the Frankish kingdom found no cause for complaint against the lay powers either on their own behalf or on behalf of their native brothers. The heretic Churches seem to have been equally content. It was very different from the position in the Frankish states of northern Syria, where both Orthodox and heretic alike resented the Franks as oppressors.[1]

---

[1] See below, pp. 320–3. There is a long account of the ceremony given in one MS. of Fulcher of Chartres, which is printed in the edition in the *Recueil des Historiens des Croisades*. Hagenmeyer, in his edition of Fulcher, notes that it only appears in one MS. (L) and rejects it all except the introductory words

The Egyptian defeat at Jaffa in 1102, and the fiasco of the expedition in the spring of 1103 did not entirely exhaust al-Afdal's efforts. But it took him longer to raise another army. Baldwin used the respite to strengthen his hold on the Palestinian sea-coast. Though he possessed the towns on the coast from Jaffa up to Haifa, Moslem marauders haunted the roads between them, in particular round the slopes of Mount Carmel. Even the road from Jaffa to Jerusalem was unsafe, as the pilgrim Saewulf noted.[1] From the Egyptian-held ports of Tyre and Acre pirates would slip out to intercept Christian merchantmen. In the late autumn of 1102 the ships that were transporting home the pilgrims whose coming had saved Baldwin at Jaffa in May were driven ashore by storms at various parts of the coast, some near Ascalon and some between Tyre and Sidon. The passengers were either all slain or sold in the slave-markets of Egypt.[2] In the spring of 1103 Baldwin, who still had some of the English ships to assist him, undertook the siege of Acre. The garrison was about to surrender to him when twelve Fatimid galleys and a large transport from Tyre and Sidon sailed into the port, laden with men and with engines for firing Greek fire. Baldwin had to raise the siege.[3] Later in the summer Baldwin attempted to clear Mount Carmel of its robbers. He was only partly successful; for in a skirmish he was severely wounded in the kidneys; and for a while they despaired of his life. While he lay sick in Jerusalem there was news of the double expedition of Taj al-Ajam and Ibn Qadus. But Taj al-Ajam's refusal to advance

'conturbati sunt omnes propter ignem quem die sabbati non habuimus ad Sepulcrum Domini' (II, viii, 2, p. 396). See his note 5, pp. 395–6, for a full discussion. He prints the interpolated text, with those found in Bartolf of Nangis and Guibert of Nogent, in an appendix (*ibid.* pp. 831–7). As Fulcher was Baldwin's chaplain he must himself have been present at the ceremony. Daniel the Higumene (ed. de Khitrowo, pp. 75–83) gives an account of the ceremony in 1107. It is clear from this narrative that the Greeks had charge of the Sepulchre itself.

[1] *Pilgrimage of Saewulf* (*P.P.T.S.* vol. IV), pp. 8–9.
[2] Albert of Aix, IX, 18, pp. 600–1.
[3] Albert of Aix, IX, 15, p. 599; Ibn al-Athir, p. 213, giving the wrong year (495 A.H., instead of 496).

beyond Ascalon obliged Ibn Qadus to attempt the siege of Jaffa alone. His efforts were half-hearted. As soon as Baldwin had recovered sufficiently to lead an army down to the coast, the Egyptian fleet sailed away.[1]

Next May the Genoese armada of seventy galleys which had helped Raymond of Toulouse to capture Jebail sailed into Haifa. Baldwin met its leaders there and secured their alliance for the reduction of Acre, promising the usual fee of one-third of the booty and commercial privileges and a quarter in the bazaar. The allies began the siege on 6 May. The Fatimid commander, the mameluk Bena Zahr ad-Daulah al-Juyushi, put up a stubborn resistance; but he received no aid from Egypt. After twenty days he offered to capitulate, on terms similar to those granted at Arsuf. Such citizens as wished could leave safely with their movable belongings; the others would become subjects of the Frankish king. Baldwin for his part accepted and kept to these terms, even allowing a mosque to be reserved for his Moslem subjects. But the Italian sailors could not bear to see so much wealth escape them. They fell on the emigrants, slaying many and robbing them all. Baldwin was furious. He would have attacked the Genoese to punish them had not the Patriarch Evremar arrived and patched up a reconciliation.[2]

The possession of Acre gave Baldwin what he sorely needed, a harbour that was safe in all weathers. Though it was more than a hundred miles from the capital, it at once became the chief port of the kingdom, replacing Jaffa with its open roadstead. It was moreover the chief port through which merchandize from Damascus was shipped to the West; and its conquest by the Franks did not interrupt this traffic, to which the Moslems still resident in Acre gave encouragement.[3]

---

[1] Fulcher of Chartres, II, xxiv, 1, pp. 460–1; Albert of Aix, IX, 22–3, pp. 103–4.
[2] Fulcher of Chartres, II, xxv, 1–3, pp. 462–4; Albert of Aix, IX, 27–9, pp. 606–8; Caffaro, *Liberatio*, pp. 71–2; Charter of Baldwin in *Liber Jurium Reipublicae Genuensis*, vol. I, pp. 16–17.
[3] See below, p. 318. The trade was still continuing in Ibn Jubayr's time (1183).

1105: Third Battle of Ramleh

In the summer of 1105 the vizier al-Afdal made a final attempt to reconquer Palestine. A well-equipped army of five thousand Arab horsemen and Sudanese infantry, under his son Sena al-Mulk Husein, assembled at Ascalon at the beginning of August. Profiting by the lessons of their previous failures, the Egyptians decided to ask for the co-operation of the Turkish rulers of Damascus. In 1102 or 1103 Damascene help would have been invaluable. But Duqaq of Damascus had died in June 1104 and his family disputed the inheritance with his atabeg Toghtekin, while Ridwan of Aleppo came south to seek a share of it. Toghtekin first placed Duqaq's one-year-old son Tutush on the throne, then replaced him by Duqaq's twelve-year-old brother, Irtash. Irtash soon suspected his guardian's intentions, and fled to the Hauran, whose leading emir, Aytekin of Bosra, gave him asylum. From Bosra he appealed to King Baldwin, who invited him to Jerusalem. Under these circumstances Toghtekin was glad to help the Egyptians but could not venture to send a large force to join them. He sent his general Sabawa south with thirteen hundred mounted archers.[1] In August the Egyptian army moved up into Palestine, where the Damascene troops joined it, after having come down through Transjordan and across the Negeb. Baldwin was waiting at Jaffa. When the Egyptian fleet hove into sight he took up a position on the inevitable battlefield of Ramleh. Jaffa was kept under the command of Lithard of Cambrai, with three hundred men. With Baldwin was the young Damascene pretender, Irtash, and the whole of the rest of the Frankish troops in Palestine, the garrisons of Galilee, Haifa and Hebron as well as the central army, five hundred horsemen and two thousand infantry. At Baldwin's request the Patriarch Evremar came down from Jerusalem with one hundred and fifty men that he had recruited there and with the True Cross.

The battle took place on Sunday, 27 August. At dawn the Patriarch rode up and down in front of the Frankish lines, in his full robes, the Cross in his hand, giving his blessing and absolution.

[1] Ibn al-Qalanisi, p. 71; Ibn al-Athir, p. 229.

Then the Franks attacked. A counter-attack by the Damascene
Turks nearly broke their ranks; but Baldwin, taking his standard
into his own hands, led a charge that scattered them. The Egyptians
fought more bravely than usual; but their left wing had gone off
in a vain attempt to surprise Haifa, and returned too late. By
evening the Moslems were beaten. Sabawa and his Turks fled
back to their own land, and the Egyptians retreated on Ascalon,
whence their commander, Sena al-Mulk, hurried back to Cairo.
Their losses had been heavy. The governor of Ascalon was slain,
and the ex-commanders of Acre and Arsuf captured and later
ransomed at a high price. Fulcher of Chartres could not help
regretting that Sena al-Mulk had escaped, because of the rich
ransom that he would have commanded. But the Frankish losses
also were heavy. After pillaging their camp Baldwin did not
further pursue the Egyptians. Nor did he continue his support of
the young Prince Irtash, who retired disconsolate to ar-Rahba on
the Euphrates. The Egyptian fleet sailed back to Egypt, having
achieved nothing except the loss of some ships in a storm.[1]

This third battle of Ramleh ended the last large-scale attempt of
the Fatimids to reconquer Palestine. But they still were dangerous
to the Franks; and a smaller raid in the autumn of 1106 nearly
succeeded where their greater armies had failed. That October,
when Baldwin was engaged on the Galilean frontier, some
thousand Egyptian horsemen suddenly attacked a pilgrim camp
between Jaffa and Arsuf and massacred its inhabitants. They then
rode on Ramleh, which was defended only by eight knights, who
were easily overwhelmed. The governor of Jaffa, Roger of Rozoy,
went out against them but fell into an ambush and only extricated
himself by flying headlong back to Jaffa. So hotly was he pursued
that forty of his foot-soldiers were caught outside the gates and
slain. Next, the Egyptians rode up towards Jerusalem, and
attacked a small castle, Chastel Arnaud, that Baldwin had not
quite completed to guard the road. The workmen surrendered,

[1] Albert of Aix, IX, 48–50, pp. 621–4; Fulcher of Chartres, II, XXXI, I–xxxiii,
3, pp. 489–503; Ibn al-Athir, pp. 228–9; Ibn Moyessar, p. 466.

but were killed, with the exception of their commander, Geoffrey, Castellan of the Tower of David, who was taken off to be ransomed. But by now Baldwin had heard of the raid and marched south in force. The Egyptians retired to Ascalon.[1]

The following year an Egyptian expedition nearly captured Hebron, but was driven off by Baldwin in person; and in 1110 the Egyptians penetrated to the walls of Jerusalem, only to retire at once.[2] Similar raids on a lesser scale took place from time to time during the next ten years, rendering life unsafe for Christian settlers and pilgrims in the coastal plain and in the Negeb; but they became little more than reprisals for Baldwin's own raids into Moslem territory.

Baldwin therefore felt free to continue his attempt to expand the kingdom. His chief objectives were the coastal cities, Ascalon in the south and Tyre, Sidon and Beirut in the north. Both Ascalon and Tyre were strong fortresses with a large permanent garrison; their reduction would need careful preparation. In the spring of 1106 the presence in the Holy Land of a large convoy of English, Flemish and Danish pilgrims induced Baldwin to plan an expedition against Sidon. The governor of Sidon, learning of this, hastened to send the King an enormous sum of money. Baldwin, always in need of money, accepted the gift; and for two years Sidon was left in peace.[3]

In August 1108 Baldwin marched out again against Sidon, with the support of a squadron of sailor-adventurers from various Italian cities. The governor at once hired the support of the Turks of Damascus for thirty thousand besants, while a powerful Egyptian squadron sailed up from Egypt and defeated the Italians in a sea-battle outside the harbour. Baldwin was obliged to raise the siege. Thereupon the Sidonians refused to admit the Turks into the city, fearing, with some reason, that Toghtekin had designs on it. The governor even refused to pay the promised besants. The Turks threatened to summon back Baldwin; but when he showed

[1] Albert of Aix, x, 10–14, pp. 635–8.
[2] *Ibid.* x, 33, pp. 646–7; xi, 28, p. 676.   [3] *Ibid.* x, 4–7, pp. 632–4

signs of returning they agreed to retire, with nine thousand besants as compensation.[1]

Next summer Baldwin assisted Bertrand of Toulouse to capture Tripoli; and in return, early in 1110, Bertrand sent men to help Baldwin attack Beirut. Genoese and Pisan ships were at hand to blockade the town; and Tripoli provided them with a convenient base. Fatimid ships from Tyre and Sidon tried in vain to break the blockade. The siege lasted from February till mid-May, when the governor, despairing of further help, fled by night through the Italian fleet to Cyprus, where he gave himself up to the Byzantine governor. The city that he had abandoned was taken by assault on 13 May. The Italians conducted a general massacre of the inhabitants before Baldwin could restore order.[2]

During that summer further naval reinforcements reached Baldwin from the West. In 1107 a fleet set out from Bergen in Norway under Sigurd, who shared the Norwegian throne with his two brothers, and, sailing across the North Sea and round by Gibraltar, calling on the way in England, Castile, Portugal, the Balearic Islands and Sicily, arrived at Acre just as Baldwin was returning from the capture of Beirut. Sigurd was the first crowned head to visit the kingdom; and Baldwin received him with great honour, conducting him personally to Jerusalem. Sigurd agreed to help the Franks to besiege Sidon. The allies began the siege in October. Sidon was vigorously defended. The Norwegian ships were nearly dispersed by a powerful Fatimid flotilla from Tyre, but were saved by the arrival of a Venetian squadron, under the command of the Doge himself, Ordelafo Falieri. Meanwhile, the governor of Sidon devised a plan for Baldwin's assassination. A renegade Moslem in Baldwin's personal service agreed for a large sum to undertake the murder. But the native Christians in Sidon heard of the plot and shot an arrow with a message fixed on

[1] *Ibid.* x, 48–51, pp. 653–5; Ibn al-Qalanisi, p. 87.
[2] Fulcher of Chartres, ii, xlii, 1–3, p. 536, giving the date as 13 May in an astronomical poem; Albert of Aix, p. 671, gives the date as 27 May; Ibn al-Qalanisi, pp. 99–101 (13 May).

it into the Frankish camp to warn the King. Sidon eventually capitulated on 4 December, on the same terms that had been granted to Acre. The notables of the town left with all their belongings for Damascus; but the poorer folk remained and became subjects of the Frankish king; who promptly levied from them a tax of twenty thousand gold besants. The Venetians were rewarded by the gift of a church and some property at Acre. Sidon was entrusted as a barony to Eustace Garnier, who was already governor of Caesarea, and who soon after consolidated his position by his politic marriage to the Patriarch Arnulf's niece Emma.[1]

The Franks now controlled the whole of the Syrian coast, with the exception of the two fortresses of Ascalon at the southern end and Tyre in the centre. The governor of Tyre was nervous. In the autumn of 1111 he sent to Toghtekin at Damascus to hire from him for the sum of twenty thousand besants a corps of five hundred archers, and at the same time he asked permission for himself and his notables to send their more valuable possessions to Damascus for their preservation. Toghtekin agreed; and a rich caravan containing the money and the goods set out from the coast. As it had to pass through the country held by the Franks, the Tyrian governor, Izz al-Mulk, bribed a Frankish knight called Rainfred to guide it and to guarantee its safety. Rainfred accepted the terms and promptly informed Baldwin; who fell upon the unsuspecting Tyrians and robbed them of all their wealth. Encouraged by this windfall Baldwin brought up his whole army at the end of November to attack the walls of Tyre. But he had no fleet to help him, apart from twelve Byzantine vessels under the Byzantine ambassador Butumites; and the Byzantines were not prepared to take hostile action against the Fatimids, with

[1] Fulcher of Chartres, II, xliv, 1-7, pp. 543-8; Albert of Aix, XI, 26, 30-4, pp. 675, 677; William of Tyre, XI, 14, pp. 476-9, who tells of the native Christians; *Sigurdar Saga* in *Agrip af Noregs Konungasögum, passim*; *Sigurdar Saga Jórsalafara ok Broedra Hans*, pp. 75 ff.; Ibn al-Qalanisi, pp. 106-8; Ibn al-Athir, p. 275; Dandolo in Muratori, *Ss. R.I.* vol. XII, p. 264; Tafel and Thomas, I, 86, 91, 145; Riant, *Les Scandinaves en Terre Sainte*, chap. IV, *passim*.

whom their relations were good, unless they were given serious compensation. They demanded that Baldwin should in return help them to recover the cities that they had lost to the princes of Antioch. As Baldwin hesitated to commit himself, the Byzantines did no more than supply the Frankish army with provisions. The siege of Tyre lasted till the following April. The Tyrians fought well, burning down the huge wooden siege-towers that Baldwin had constructed; but at least they were reduced to seeking aid from Toghtekin. Before taking this step Izz al-Mulk wrote to the Egyptian court to justify his action. Toghtekin's first attempt to establish contact failed, as a carrier-pigeon was intercepted by an Arab in Frankish service. His Frankish comrade wished to let the bird go, but he took it to Baldwin. Men were sent in disguise to meet the Damascene ambassadors, who were captured and put to death. But nevertheless Toghtekin advanced on Tyre, surprising a Frankish foraging party and besieging the Franks in their camp while he raided the countryside. Baldwin was obliged to lift the siege and to fight his way back to Acre.[1]

He was equally unsuccessful at Ascalon. He had marched against the fortress immediately after his capture of Sidon. The governor, Shams al-Khilafa, being commercially minded, was weary of all this fighting. He bought an armistice for a sum which he then tried to levy from the people of Tyre, which was under his jurisdiction. His actions were reported to Egypt; and al-Afdal sent loyal troops there with orders to depose him. Shams al-Khilafa, suspecting their purpose, refused to admit them, and even dismissed those of his troops that he suspected of Fatimid sympathies, recruiting Armenian mercenaries in their place. He then went himself to Jerusalem to put himself and his city under Baldwin's protection. He returned with three hundred Frankish soldiers whom he installed in the citadel. But this treason shocked the Ascalonites. In July 1111, with help from Egypt, they staged a *coup d'état*, murdering Shams and massacring the Franks. Bald-

[1] Albert of Aix, xii, 3–7, pp. 690–3; Ibn al-Athir, p. 257; Ibn Moyessar, p. 467.

win hurried down to rescue his men but arrived too late. Ascalon was to remain a thorn in the Franks' flesh for another forty years.[1]

A similar attempt to establish a protectorate over Baalbek with the help of the governor, the eunuch al-Taj Gümüshtekin, had failed in the spring of 1110. Toghtekin heard of the plot and replaced Gumushtekin by his own son Taj al-Mulk Buri.[2]

Baldwin's main preoccupation had been to secure for his kingdom an adequate coast-line. But he was also concerned to give it suitable land frontiers and at the same time to take full advantage of its proximity to the great Arab trade-routes from Iraq and Arabia to the Mediterranean and to Egypt. When Tancred had left Palestine for Antioch, Baldwin entrusted the principality of Galilee, which retained the grandiloquent name that Tancred had given it, to his former neighbour in France, Hugh of Saint-Omer; and Hugh had been encouraged in an aggressive policy against the Moslems. His first action was to construct in the mountains, over the road between Tyre and Banyas and Damascus, a castle called Toron, the Tibnin of to-day. Then, in order the better to conduct raids in the rich lands east of the Sea of Galilee, he built another castle on the hills south-west of the lake, called by the Arabs al-Al. These two fortresses were completed by the autumn of 1105; but the second had a short life in Christian hands. Toghtekin of Damascus could not allow such a threat to his territory. At the end of the year, when Hugh was returning to al-Al, heavily laden after a successful raid, the Damascene army fell on him. He was mortally wounded in the battle and his men scattered. Toghtekin was then able without difficulty to take over the castle. Hugh's brother, Gerard of Saint-Omer, who was seriously ill at the time, did not long survive Hugh. Baldwin therefore gave the fief of Galilee to a French knight, Gervase of Basoches.[3]

---

[1] Albert of Aix, XI, 36-7, pp. 680-1; Ibn al-Qalanisi, pp. 108-10.
[2] Ibn al-Qalanisi, *op. cit.* p. 106; Sibt ibn al-Djauzi, p. 537.
[3] William of Tyre, XI, 5, pp. 459-60; Ibn al-Qalanisi, pp. 72, 75; Ibn al-Athir, pp. 229-30; Albert of Aix, X, 8, pp. 635-6.

Guerrilla warfare continued. In 1106 the Tyrians made a raid against Toron, to coincide with a Damascene raid against Tiberias. Neither raid was successful; and on Baldwin's approach, the Damascenes sent to his camp to arrange for a short armistice. His gracious and munificent reception of their envoys did much to enhance his reputation among the Moslems. But the truce was brief.[1] In the spring of 1108 Toghtekin again raided Galilee and in a battle outside Tiberias managed to capture Gervase of Basoches, together with most of his staff. He then sent to Baldwin to say that the price for their liberation was the three cities of Tiberias, Acre and Haifa. When Baldwin refused the offer, Gervase was put to death, and his scalp, with its white locks waving, was carried on a pole before the victorious Moslem army.[2] Baldwin then gave back the title of Prince of Galilee to Tancred, but probably administered the principality from Jerusalem. In 1113, after Tancred's death, when Baldwin of Edessa banished Joscelin of Courtenay from his county, the exile was compensated by the King with Galilee.[3]

At the end of 1108 Baldwin and Toghtekin, both of whose main interests lay elsewhere, made a ten years' truce, dividing the revenues of the districts of Sawad and Ajlun, that is to say, northern Transjordan, between them. A third was to go to Baldwin, a third to Toghtekin and a third was to remain with the local authorities.[4] The reasons for the truce were probably commercial. Raids were ruining the carrying trade that went through the country; and all parties would benefit by its resumption. The truce was purely local. It did not keep Toghtekin from coming to the help of the Moslem coastal cities, nor did it restrain Baldwin from his attempt to turn Baalbek into a vassal-city. But Arab historians remarked with gratitude that owing to it Baldwin did

[1] Albert of Aix, X, 25–6, pp. 642–3; Ibn al-Qalanisi, p. 75.
[2] Albert of Aix, X, 57, p. 658; Ibn al-Qalanisi, pp. 86–7; Ibn al-Athir, pp. 268–9. He calls Gervase the son of Baldwin's sister.
[3] Albert of Aix, XI, 12, p. 668; William of Tyre, XI, 22, p. 492.
[4] Ibn al-Qalanisi, p. 92; Ibn al-Athir, p. 269.

not invade Damascene land when Toghetin's defeat by William-Jordan at Arqa would have offered a useful opportunity.[1] The desire for a truce may have arisen on Baldwin's side as a result of Gervase's defeat and the consequent danger of raids from Transjordan into Galilee, and on the Moslems' after two recent raids, one conducted by a newly arrived pilgrim to Palestine, Robert of Normandy's son, William Cliton, on a wealthy Arab princess who was journeying with all her belongings from Arabia to Damascus, and the other on a merchant caravan bound from Damascus to Egypt. On the first occasion the Franks obtained four thousand camels, and on the second all the merchandise of the caravan, whose survivors were slaughtered later by the Bedouin.[2] The treaty was broken in 1113, when Baldwin invaded Damascene territory.[3]

From 1111, after his failure before Tyre, Baldwin was for a time occupied by affairs in northern Syria. He had already made it clear, at Tripoli in 1109, that he intended to be master of all the Frankish East; and events at Antioch and Edessa enabled him to reassert his claim.[4] He could also once more turn his attention to the aggrandizement of his personal domain. He had always been aware that Palestine was open to invasion and infiltration from the south-east, through the Negeb, and that the command of the country between the Dead Sea and the Gulf of Akaba was necessary in order to cut off Egypt from the eastern Moslem world. In 1107 Toghtekin had sent a Damascene army into Edom, at the invitation of the local Bedouin, to establish a base from which Judaea could be raided. The Idumaean wilderness contained several Greek monasteries; and one of the monks, a certain Theodore, urged Baldwin to intervene. Baldwin marched down close to the Turkish encampment in the Wadi Musa, near Petra; but he wished to avoid a battle. Theodore therefore offered to go as though a fugitive to Toghtekin's general, to warn him that a huge Frankish army was at hand. The Turks were alarmed and retreated

[1] Ibn al-Athir, pp. 269–70.
[2] Albert of Aix, x, 45, p. 653; Ibn al-Athir, p. 272.
[3] See below, p. 126.   [4] See above, pp. 67–8 and pp. 115–16.

at full speed back to Damascus. Baldwin then punished the Bedouin by smoking them out of the caverns in which they lived and carrying off their flocks. When he returned northward, he took with him many of the native Christians, who feared reprisals from the Bedouin.[1]

Baldwin returned to the Idumaean country in 1115. He decided that it must be permanently occupied. Coming down from Hebron round the base of the Dead Sea and across the Wadi al-Araba, the stark valley that runs from the Dead Sea towards the Gulf of Akaba, he arrived at one of the few fertile spots in that bleak region, Shobak, on a wooded range between the depression and the Arabian desert. There, almost a hundred miles from the nearest Frankish settlement, he constructed a great castle, in which he left a garrison, well stocked with arms, and to which he gave the name of The Royal Mountain, Le Krak de Montreal. Next year, at the head of his army and with a long train of mules bearing provisions, he plunged farther into unknown Arabia. He revisited Montreal and marched on southward, till at last his weary men reached the shores of the Red Sea, at Akaba. There they bathed their horses in the sea and caught the fishes for which those waters are renowned. The local inhabitants, terrified, took to their boats and fled. Baldwin occupied the town, called by the Franks Aila or Elyn, and fortified it with a citadel. He then sailed across to the little island, the Jesirat Far'un, called by the Franks Graye, where he built a second castle. Garrisons were left in both strongholds. Thanks to them, the Franks now dominated the roads between Damascus and Arabia and Egypt. They could raid the caravans at their ease, and made it difficult for any Moslem army to reach Egypt from the East.[2]

On his return from the shores of the Red Sea, Baldwin marched again against Tyre, but contented himself with setting up a strict

[1] Albert of Aix, x, 28–9, pp. 644–5; Ibn al-Qalanisi, pp. 81–2. For the Greek monasteries in the district see above, p. 72, n. 1.
[2] Albert of Aix, xII, 21–2, pp. 702–3; William of Tyre, xI, 29, p. 505. For Aila, see Musil, article 'Aila', in *Encyclopaedia of Islam*.

blockade of the city from the land. To that end he built a castle at Scandelion, where the coast road begins to climb up the side of the cliff to the pass known as the Ladder of Tyre.[1] Sidon already controlled the approach to Tyre from the north and the castle of Toron from the east. Scandelion completed its encirclement.

Encouraged by his achievements, Baldwin embarked in 1118 on a bolder expedition. Fatimid armies from Ascalon had twice lately conducted successful raids into his territory. In 1113, when he was engaged against the Turks in the north, they had advanced as far as the walls of Jerusalem, pillaging as they came; and in 1115 they almost succeeded in surprising Jaffa. Baldwin's answer now was to invade Egypt itself. Early in March, after careful negotiations with the sheikhs of the desert tribes, he led a small army of two hundred and sixteen horsemen and four hundred foot-soldiers, well supplied with provisions, from Hebron across the Sinai peninsula, to the Mediterranean coast at Farama, well within the Egyptian frontier, close to the mouth of the Pelusian branch of the Nile. He prepared to take the city by assault, but the garrison had fled in panic. He marched on to the Nile itself; and his men were agape to see the famous river. But there a mortal illness struck him down. He retired back dying towards Palestine.[2]

By his unwearying campaigns and his use of every opportunity King Baldwin had raised his inheritance to be a consolidated state comprising the whole historic province of Palestine. With only Tyre and Ascalon still out of his grasp, he controlled the country from Beirut in the north to Beersheba in the south, with the Jordan as his eastern frontier and with outposts in the far south-east to command the approaches from Arabia. His fellow-Christians in the Frankish East acknowledged his hegemony; and he had won the respect of his Moslem neighbours. His work had ensured that the kingdom of Jerusalem would not easily be destroyed.

Of the internal administration of his kingdom we have very little evidence. Broadly speaking, it was feudal. But Baldwin

[1] Fulcher of Chartres, II, lxii, 1, pp. 605–6; William of Tyre, XI, 30, p. 507.
[2] Albert of Aix, XII, 25, p. 705; Ibn al-Athir, p. 314.

kept most of the country in his own hands, appointing viscounts as his deputies. Even the greatest of the fiefs, the principality of Galilee, was for some years without its lord. The fiefs were not yet considered to be hereditary. When Hugh of Saint-Omer was killed, it was thought that his brother Gerard would have succeeded to his principality had his health permitted, but his right was not absolute. Baldwin himself evolved a rough constitution for the kingdom. He himself governed through a household that was increasing in size; and his feudatories had their own. To Baldwin were due the arrangements with the Italians in the seaports, who were not obliged to assist on military campaigns, but had to take part in the naval defence of their localities.[1]

Baldwin had made it clear that he intended to control the Church. Once he was sure of its support he treated it generously, freely endowing it with lands conquered from the infidel. His generosity was to some degree mistaken; for the Church was free of the obligation to provide soldiers. On the other hand he expected it to provide him with money.

Frequent incidents showed that Baldwin was popular with the native Christians. Ever since the episode at Easter, 1101, he had been careful to have regard for their susceptibilities. At his courts they were allowed to use their own languages and to follow their own customs; and the Church was not allowed to interfere with their religious practices. In the last years of his reign he encouraged the immigration of Christians, heretic as well as Orthodox, from the neighbouring countries under Moslem rule. He needed an industrious peasant population to occupy the lands left empty in Judaea by the departure of the Moslems. He favoured marriage between the Franks and the natives, for which he himself had set an example. Very few of the barons took local brides; but the practice became common among the poorer Frankish soldiers and settlers. Their cross-bred children were to provide the kingdom later with most of its soldiers.[2]

[1] See La Monte, *Feudal Monarchy*, pp. 228–30; see below, p. 292.
[2] See below, p. 294.

Baldwin and the Eastern Peoples

Baldwin showed similar affability towards the Moslems and Jews that consented to become his subjects. A few mosques and synagogues were permitted. In the law courts Moslems might swear on the Koran and Jews on the Torah; and infidel litigants could rely on obtaining justice.[1] Intermarriage with Moslems was allowed. In 1114 the Patriarch Arnulf was severely scolded by Pope Paschal for having performed a marriage ceremony between a Christian and a Moslem lady.[2]

Therein Pope Paschal showed once again his misunderstanding of the East. For if the Franks were to survive there, they must not remain an alien minority but must become part of the local world. Baldwin's chaplain, Fulcher of Chartres, in a lyrical chapter in his History, remarked on the miraculous work of God in turning Occidentals into Orientals. That eastern and western races should blend seemed to him admirable; he saw it as a step towards the union of nations. Throughout the existence of the Crusading states we find the same story. Wise Frankish statesmen in the East followed Baldwin's tradition, adopting local customs and forming local friendships and alliances, while newcomers from the West brought with them chauvinistic ideas that were disastrous for the country.

The King had already offended the Pope, when his conquests along the Syrian coasts had brought into his power towns, notably Sidon and Beirut, whose churches historically belonged to the Patriarch of Antioch. The proper administration of the kingdom demanded that they should be transferred to the jurisdiction of the Patriarch of Jerusalem; and Baldwin thereupon transferred them. The Patriarch of Antioch, Bernard, protested to the Pope against such an uncanonical act. Paschal had in 1110 informed Jerusalem that in view of changed circumstances the historic position could be ignored. In 1112, with his habitual weakness, he veered round and supported the claims of Antioch. Baldwin blandly ignored the Pope's new decision. In spite of a petulant

[1] See below, p. 304.
[2] Röhricht, Regesta, no. 83, p. 19.

101

reproof from Paschal, the bishoprics remained under the Patriarchate of Jerusalem.[1]

Baldwin himself made one serious lapse with regard to his marriage. He had never much cared for his Armenian bride since the day that her father, terrified of his ruthless son-in-law, had decamped with her promised dowry. Baldwin was fond of amorous adventures; but he was discreet and the presence of a queen at the court prevented him from indulging in his tastes. The Queen also had a reputation for gaiety and had even, it was said, bestowed her favours upon Moslem pirates when she was voyaging down from Antioch to take over her throne. There were no children to bind them together. After a few years, when there was no longer the smallest political advantage to the marriage, Baldwin dismissed her from the Court on the grounds of adultery and obliged her to enter into the convent of St Anne in Jerusalem, which, to salve his conscience, he richly endowed. But the Queen had no vocation for the monastic life. She soon demanded and received permission to retire to Constantinople, where her parents had been living since their ejection from Marash by the Franks. There she abandoned her monastic robe and settled down to taste all the pleasures that the great city provided.[2] Meanwhile Baldwin rejoiced to find himself able to lead a bachelor life once more. But he still needed money; and in the winter of 1112 he learnt that the most eligible widow in Europe was seeking a husband. Adelaide of Salona, Countess-Dowager of Sicily, had just retired from the regency of her county on the coming-of-age of her young son, Roger II. She was immensely rich; and a royal title attracted her. To Baldwin she was desirable not only for her dowry but also for her influence over the Normans of Sicily; whose alliance would help to supply him with sea-power and would act as a counter-weight against the Normans of Antioch. He sent to ask for her hand. The Countess accepted on

[1] William of Tyre, XI, 28, pp. 502–5.
[2] Guibert of Nogent, p. 259, telling of her loose life; William of Tyre, XI, 1, pp. 451–2, suggesting that she took to evil ways after her divorce.

her own terms. Baldwin was childless. The children of his first wife had died in Anatolia during the First Crusade; and his Armenian Queen had borne him none. Adelaide insisted that if no baby was born of her marriage to Baldwin—and the ages of the bride and bridegroom gave little promise of a baby—the crown of Jerusalem was to pass to her son, Count Roger.

The contract was made; and in the summer of 1113 the Countess set out from Sicily in such splendour as had not been seen on the Mediterranean since Cleopatra sailed for the Cydnus to meet Mark Antony. She lay on a carpet of golden thread in her galley, whose prow was plated with silver and with gold. Two other triremes accompanied her, their prows equally ornate, bearing her military escort, prominent amongst whom were the Arab soldiers of her son's own bodyguard, their dark faces shining against the spotless white of their robes. Seven other ships followed in her wake, their holds laden with all her personal treasure. She landed at Acre in August. There King Baldwin met her, with all the pomp that his kingdom could provide. He and all his Court were clad in costly silks; and their horses and mules were hung with purple and gold. Rich carpets were laid in the streets, and from the windows and balconies fluttered purple banners. The towns and villages along the road to Jerusalem bore like finery. All the country rejoiced, but not so much at the coming of its new, ageing mistress as at the wealth that she brought in her train.[1]

Despite its gorgeous beginning, the marriage was not a success. Baldwin at once took over the Queen's dowry, which he used to pay off the overdue wages of his soldiers and to spend on works of fortification; and the money coming into circulation enriched the commerce of the country. But the effect soon wore off; and the disadvantages of the marriage became apparent. Pious folk

[1] Albert of Aix, XII, 13–14, pp. 696–8; William of Tyre, XI, 21, pp. 487–9; Fulcher of Chartres, II, li, pp. 575–7. Adelaide was the daughter of a Marquis Manfred and niece of Boniface of Salona, and had married Roger I of Sicily as his third wife in 1089. For her genealogy, see Chalandon, *Histoire de la Domination Normande en Italie*, II, p. 391 n. 5.

remembered that Baldwin's previous wife had never been legally divorced. They were shocked that the Patriarch Arnulf had so willingly performed what was in fact a bigamous marriage ceremony; and Arnulf's many enemies were quick to make use of this irregularity. Their attack might have been less effective had not all Baldwin's subjects been angered when they discovered that he proposed to dispose of the succession to the kingdom without consulting his council. Complaints against Arnulf poured into Rome. A year after the royal marriage a papal legate, Berengar, Bishop of Orange, arrived at Jerusalem. When he found that added to the charges of simony against Arnulf there was the certainty that he had condoned and blessed an adulterous connection, he summoned the bishops and abbots of the Patriarchate to a synod and declared Arnulf deposed. But Arnulf could not be disposed of so easily. He saw to it that no successor was appointed and himself went off in the winter of 1115 to Rome. There he used all his persuasive charm on the Pope and the Cardinals, whose sympathies were strengthened by the well-chosen gifts that he made to them. Paschal fell under his influence and repudiated his legate's decision. Arnulf made one concession; he promised to order the King to dismiss his Sicilian Queen. On those terms the Pope not only declared that Arnulf's deposition was void but himself presented him with the pallium, thus placing his position beyond all question. In the summer of 1116 Arnulf returned triumphant to Jerusalem.[1]

The concession was willingly made; for Arnulf knew that Baldwin, now that Adelaide's dowry was spent, was half-regretful of his marriage. Nor did Adelaide, used to the luxuries of the palace at Palermo, find the discomforts of Solomon's Temple at Jerusalem much to her liking. But Baldwin hesitated; he was unwilling to lose the advantages of the Sicilian alliance. He resisted Arnulf's demands; till in March 1117 he fell seriously ill. Face to face with death he listened to his confessors, who told

[1] Letter of Paschal II of 15 July 1116, *M.P.L.*, vol. CLXIII, cols. 408–9; Albert of Aix, XII, 24, p. 704; William of Tyre, XI, 24, pp. 499–500.

him that he was dying in a state of sin. He must dismiss Adelaide and call his former wife to his side. He could not carry out all their wishes; for the ex-Queen was not prepared to leave Constantinople, whose gallant pleasures she so richly enjoyed. But when he recovered, he announced the annulment of his marriage to Adelaide. Adelaide herself, shorn of her wealth and almost unescorted, sailed angrily back to Sicily. It was an insult that the Sicilian Court never forgave. It was long before the kingdom of Jerusalem was to receive any aid or sympathy from Sicily.[1]

On 16 June 1117 there was an eclipse of the moon and another on 11 December, and five nights later the rare phenomenon of the aurora borealis flickered through the Palestinian sky. It was a terrible portent, foretelling the death of princes.[2] Nor did it lie. On 21 January 1118 Pope Paschal died at Rome.[3] On 16 April the ex-Queen Adelaide ended her humiliated existence in Sicily.[4] Her false friend the Patriarch Arnulf survived her for only twelve days.[5] 5 April saw the death of the Sultan Mohammed in Iran.[6] On 6 August the Caliph Mustazhir died at Baghdad.[7] On 15 August, after a long and painful illness, the greatest of the eastern potentates, the Emperor Alexius, died at Constantinople.[8] In the early spring King Baldwin returned fever-stricken from Egypt. His worn, overstrained body had no resistance left in it. His soldiers carried him back, a dying man, to the little frontier-fort of el-Arish. There, just beyond the borders of the kingdom

---

[1] Albert of Aix, *loc. cit.*; William of Tyre, *loc. cit.*; Fulcher of Chartres, ii, lix, 3, p. 601.

[2] Fulcher of Chartres, ii, lxi, 1–3, lxiii, 1–4, pp. 604–5, 607–8. Hagenmeyer's notes discuss the dating. Fulcher mentions the death of Paschal, Baldwin, Adelaide, Arnulf and Alexius.

[3] *Annales Romani, M.G.H. Ss.*, vol. v, p. 477; William of Tyre, xii, 5, p. 518.

[4] *Necrologia Panormitana*, in *Forschungen zur deutschen Geschichte*, vol. xviii, pp. 472, 474; William of Tyre, xii, 5, p. 518.

[5] See below, p. 144.

[6] Ibn al-Qalanisi, p. 156; Ibn al-Athir, p. 303, dates it 18 April.

[7] Ibn al-Athir, pp. 310–11; Matthew of Edessa, ccxxvi, p. 297.

[8] Zonaras, p. 759; William of Tyre, xii, 5, p. 517; Ibn al-Qalanisi, p. 157, and Matthew of Edessa, ccxxviii, pp. 300–1, also record his death.

which owed to him its existence, he died on 2 April, in the arms of the Bishop of Ramleh. His corpse was brought to Jerusalem, and on Palm Sunday, 7 April, it was laid to rest in the Church of the Holy Sepulchre, by the side of his brother Godfrey.[1]

Lamentations accompanied the funeral procession, from Franks and native Christians alike; and even the visiting Saracens were moved. He had been a great King, harsh and unscrupulous, not loved but deeply respected for his energy, his foresight and the order and justice of his rule. He had inherited a tenuous, uncertain realm, but by his martial vigour, his diplomatic subtlety and his wise tolerance he had given it a solid place amongst the kingdoms of the East.

[1] Fulcher of Chartres, II, xiv, 1-5, pp. 609-13; Albert of Aix, XII, 26-9, pp. 706-9; William of Tyre, XI, 31, pp. 508-9; Ibn al-Qalanisi, *loc. cit.*

CHAPTER VI

EQUILIBRIUM IN THE NORTH

'They shall fight every one against his brother, and every one against his neighbour.' ISAIAH XIX, 2

Some years before he died, King Baldwin I had established himself as the unquestioned leader of the Franks in the East. It had not been an easy achievement; and Baldwin succeeded in it by his subtle use of circumstances.

The capture of Baldwin of Le Bourg and Joscelin of Courtenay at Harran and the departure of Bohemond to the West had left Tancred without a rival among the Franks of northern Syria; and dissensions amongst the Moslems had enabled him to take full advantage of his opportunities. The Seldjuk empire was crumbling to pieces, less from pressure from outside than from the quarrels of its princes. The victory at Harran had brought Jekermish, the atabeg of Mosul, to the fore amongst the Turkish magnates in northern Syria and the Jezireh. The disastrous failure of his attempt to pursue the offensive against the Franks had not weakened his position among his fellow-Moslems. His former ally and rival, Soqman the Ortoqid of Mardin, had died early in 1105, on his way to help beleaguered Tripoli; and Soqman's brother Ilghazi and son Ibrahim disputed the inheritance.[1] Ridwan of Aleppo had hoped that the victory of Ilghazi, who had formerly served under him, would give him influence in the Jezireh; but Ilghazi forgot past loyalties; and Ridwan himself was too deeply involved against the Franks of Antioch to assert his old over-

[1] Ibn al-Fourat, quoted by Cahen, *La Syrie du Nord*, p. 248, n. 26; Ibn al-Athir, pp. 226-7. Ilghazi took Mardin from Ibrahim in 1107. For the complicated history of the Moslem emirs, see Cahen, *op. cit.* pp. 246-9.

lordship.[1] The great Danishmend emir, Malik Ghazi Gümüshte-kin, died in 1106, leaving his dominions divided. Sivas and his Anatolian lands went to Ghazi, his elder son, and Melitene and his Syrian lands to the younger, Sangur. Sangur's youth and in-experience tempted Kilij Arslan, who had recently made peace with Byzantium, to turn eastward and to attack Melitene, which he captured in the autumn of 1106.[2] He then attempted to have his self-assumed title of Sultan recognized throughout the Turkish world and was ready to make friends with anyone that would humour him in this.[3]

Jekermish did not enjoy his pre-eminence for long. He was inevitably involved in the quarrels of the Seldjuk Sultanate of the East. When the Sultan Barkiyarok in 1104 was obliged to share his dominion with his brother Mohammed, Mosul was allotted to the latter's sphere. Jekermish tried to achieve independence by declaring that his allegiance was to Barkiyarok alone, and defied Mohammed's troops; but in January 1105, Barkiyarok died and his inheritance passed in its entirety to Mohammed. Jekermish was deprived of his excuse and hastened to submit to Mohammed; who for the moment professed friendship and retired eastward without venturing to make a triumphant entry into Mosul.[4] Probably at Mohammed's request, Jekermish then set about the organization of a new campaign against the Franks. He formed a coalition with Ridwan of Aleppo and Ridwan's lieutenant, the *aspahbad* Sabawa, Ilghazi the Ortoqid, and his own son-in-law, Albu ibn Arslantash of Sinjar. The allies suggested to Ridwan and Albu that it would be more politic and profitable to please the Sultan by an attack on Jekermish. They marched together on his second city, Nisibin; but there his agents succeeded in embroiling Ridwan with Ilghazi, whom Ridwan kidnapped at a banquet before the walls of Nisibin and loaded with chains. The Ortoqid

---

[1] Ibn al-Athir, *loc. cit.*   [2] Michael the Syrian, III, p. 192.
[3] See article, 'Kilij Arslan', in *Encyclopaedia of Islam*. Ibn al-Qalanisi, Ibn al-Athir, and the other Arab chroniclers carefully only call him Malik. Matthew of Edessa calls him Sultan, as does Michael the Syrian.   [4] Ibn al-Athir, pp. 224-5.

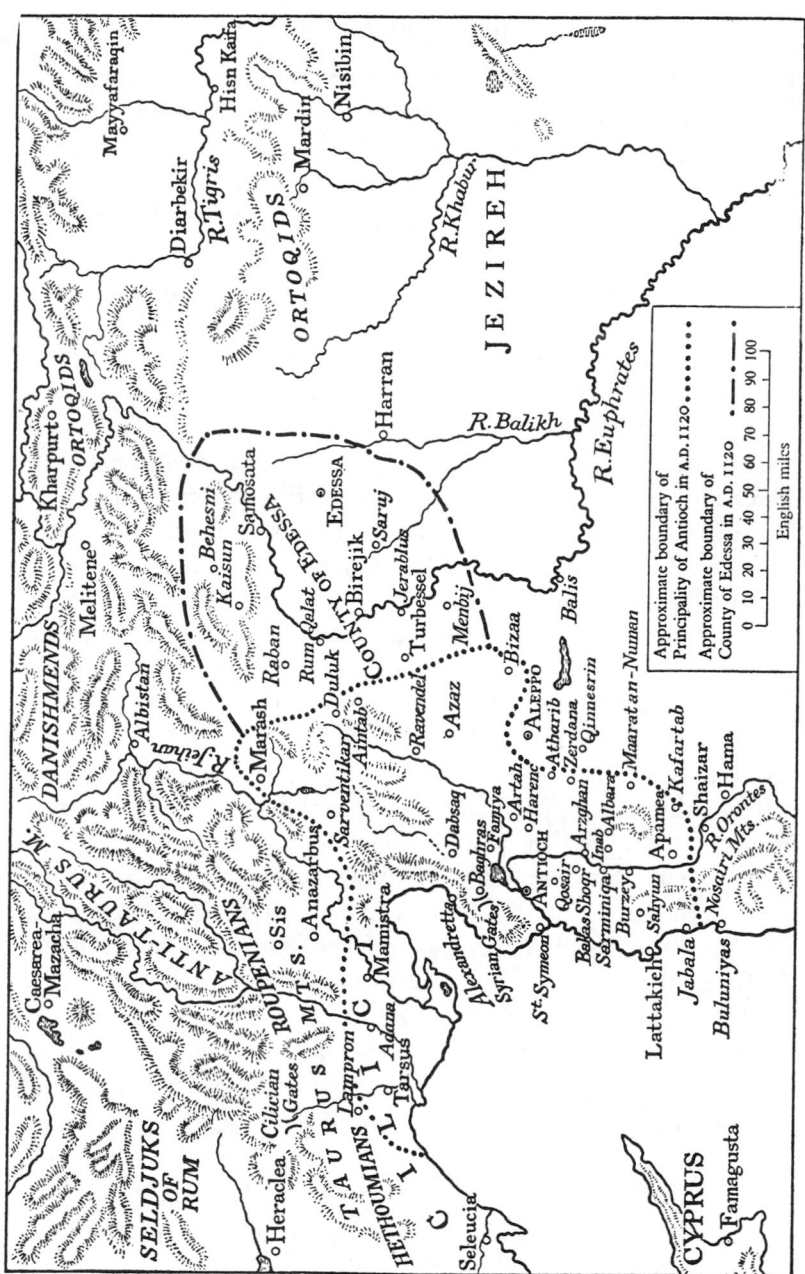

Map 1. Northern Syria in the twelfth century.

troops then attacked Ridwan and forced him to retire to Aleppo.[1]
Jekermish was thus saved, and then himself attacked Edessa; but
after successfully defeating a sortie of Richard of the Principate's
troops, he returned home, to face fresh trouble.[2]

Meanwhile Kilij Arslan, who had just taken over Melitene, in
his turn made an attempt against Edessa; but, finding it too
strongly defended, he moved on to Harran, which was surrendered to him by Jekermish's garrison. It was clear that the
Seldjuks of Rum sought to expand their power in the Moslem
world at the expense of their Persian cousins.[3]

The Sultan Mohammed had never forgiven Jekermish for his
independent airs, and he suspected some collusion between him
and Kilij Arslan. In the winter of 1106 he officially deprived him of
Mosul and gave it, with the lordship of the Jezireh and Diarbekr,
to a Turkish adventurer called Jawali Saqawa. Jawali led an army
against Jekermish, who advanced to meet him but was defeated
just outside the city and was himself captured. The inhabitants of
Mosul, where Jekermish had been a popular ruler, at once proclaimed his young son Zenki as atabeg; while friends outside the
city summoned the help of Kilij Arslan. Jawali thought it prudent
to retire, especially as Jekermish, whom he had hoped to use as
a bargaining counter, suddenly died on his hands. Mosul opened
its gates to Kilij Arslan, who promised to respect its liberties.[4]

Jawali established himself in the Euphrates valley and from there
he entered into negotiations with Ridwan of Aleppo. They agreed
first to displace Kilij Arslan and then together to attack Antioch.
In June 1107 they led four thousand men against Mosul. Kilij
Arslan, operating far from his home, had an even smaller army, but
he came out to meet the allies on the banks of the river Khabar.
Despite his personal bravery, he was utterly defeated, and himself
perished when fleeing across the river.[5]

[1] Ibn al-Athir, pp. 225–6.   [2] Matthew of Edessa, clxxxix, pp. 260–1.
[3] Ibn al-Athir, p. 239.   [4] *Ibid.* pp. 260–4.
[5] *Ibid.* pp. 246–7; Matthew of Edessa, cxcvi, p. 264. He considered Kilij
Arslan's death a disaster for the whole Christian world, i.e. the Armenians.

1107: Release of Joscelin

The elimination of Kilij Arslan affected the whole Oriental world. It removed a potential danger from Byzantium at the crucial moment when Bohemond was about to attack the Balkans; it enabled the Seldjuk Sultanate of Persia to endure for nearly a century; and it was the first serious stage in the severance of the Anatolian Turks from their brothers farther east. At the moment it deprived Moslem Syria of the one force capable of bringing it unity.

Jawali was now able to enter Mosul, where he soon made himself odious by the savagery of his rule. Nor did he show more deference to his overlord the Sultan Mohammed than Jekermish had shown. After a year Mohammed planned to replace him, and sent against him an army led by the Mameluk Mawdud, who for the next few years became the chief protagonist of Islam.[1]

During all this commotion Baldwin of Le Bourg had been living as a prisoner at Mosul, while his cousin, Joscelin of Courtenay, had passed at Soqman's death into the hands of Ilghazi, who was planning to turn his nephew Ibrahim out of Mardin. Ilghazi needed money and allies. He therefore agreed to release Joscelin for the sum of twenty thousand dinars and the promise of military aid. Joscelin's subjects at Turbessel willingly promised the ransom-money; and Joscelin was released in the course of 1107.[2] Thanks to the arrangement, Ilghazi was able to capture Mardin. Joscelin then sought to secure the release of Baldwin, who, with all Jekermish's belongings, was in Jawali's power. The moment was well chosen; for Jawali needed help against the coming attack of Mawdud. He demanded sixty thousand dinars, the release of the Moslem captives held at Edessa, and a military alliance. While the negotiations were in progress, Jawali was driven from Mosul,

[1] Ibn al-Athir, pp. 259–61; Bar-Hebraeus, trans. Budge, I, p. 241.
[2] Michael the Syrian, III, pp. 195–6, who says that the citizens of Turbessel gave themselves as hostages till the money should be raised, then escaped, so that in fact none was paid. But Joscelin returned into captivity as hostage for Baldwin, and made an excellent impression on the Sultan of Mosul who specially asked to see him. Ibn al-Athir, p. 261, assumes that the money was duly paid.

III

where he had found no support from the citizens, who opened their gates to Mawdud. He established himself in the Jezireh, taking Baldwin with him.[1]

Joscelin succeeded in finding thirty thousand dinars without great difficulty. He came himself with the money to the castle of Qalat Jabar, on the Euphrates, where Jawali now lived, and he offered himself as hostage if Baldwin might be released to raise the remainder of the ransom. Jawali was moved by the gesture and impressed by the gallantry of the Frankish prince. He accepted Joscelin in Baldwin's place, then, a few months later, partly from chivalry and partly from self-interest—for he greatly desired this Frankish alliance—he set Joscelin free, relying on his word that the money would be paid. His trust was justified.[2]

Tancred had now been for four years the master of Edessa, where his cousin, Richard of the Principate, governed in his name. He had no wish to give it up to Baldwin. When Baldwin appeared at Edessa, he agreed to raise the required thirty thousand dinars, but he refused to hand back the town unless Baldwin swore allegiance to him. Baldwin, as vassal to the King of Jerusalem, could not agree, and went angrily to Turbessel, where Joscelin joined him; and they sent to Jawali for help. Tancred marched on Turbessel, where there was a slight skirmish, after which the combatants sat down to an embarrassed banquet together, to discuss the question once more. No settlement was reached; and Baldwin, after sending as a present to Jawali a hundred and sixty Moslem captives whom he freed and re-equipped, moved north to find other allies. Richard's government of Edessa was harsh and extortionate and was particularly resented by the Armenians. Baldwin therefore went to visit the leading Armenian prince of the neighbourhood, Kogh Vasil of Kaisun, who had recently enhanced his prestige by inducing the Armenian Catholicus to live under his protection. Kogh Vasil received Baldwin at Raban and promised him aid;

---

[1] Ibn al-Athir, p. 260; Bar-Hebraeus, *loc. cit.*
[2] Michael the Syrian, *loc. cit.*; *Chron. Anon. Syr.* pp. 81–2; Bar-Hebraeus, trans. Budge, I, p. 243; Ibn al-Athir, p. 261.

while the Armenian Oshin, governor of Cilicia under the Byzantines, glad to take any action against Tancred, sent three hundred Petcheneg mercenaries to Baldwin. With these confederates Baldwin returned to Turbessel. Tancred was not prepared to offend the whole Armenian world; and the Patriarch of Antioch, Bernard, brought his influence to bear on Baldwin's behalf. With a bad grace Tancred withdrew Richard of the Principate from Edessa, where Baldwin was received with rejoicing.[1]

It was only a temporary truce. Baldwin was faithful to his friendship with Jawali. He sent him back many Moslem captives; he allowed the mosques to be rebuilt in the town of Saruj, whose population was mainly Moslem; and he disgraced and executed the chief magistrate of Saruj, who was particularly unpopular as a renegade from Islam. This alliance alarmed Ridwan of Aleppo. Jawali threatened his possessions on the Euphrates. He countered by raiding a convoy of merchandise, including some of Baldwin's ransom-money, sent from Turbessel to Jawali's court. In September 1108 Jawali attacked and captured the town of Balis, on the Euphrates, only fifty miles from Aleppo, and crucified Ridwan's chief supporters in the town. Ridwan at once sought help from Tancred. Early in October Baldwin and Joscelin brought their knights, a few hundred in number, to join Jawali's army at Menbij, between Aleppo and the Euphrates. Jawali had with him some five hundred Turks and rather more Bedouins, who were under the son of the emir Sadaqa of the Banū Mazyad. The united army numbered about two thousand men. Ridwan had about six hundred men to oppose to them; but Tancred came up with a force of fifteen hundred. The battle, Christian and Moslem against Christian and Moslem, was hard contested. Jawali's troops were gradually pushing the Franks of Antioch back with heavy losses, when the Bedouin noticed the horses that

[1] Fulcher of Chartres, II, xxviii, 1-5, pp. 477-81; Albert of Aix, x, 37, p. 648; Matthew of Edessa, cxcix, p. 266; Ibn al-Athir, pp. 262-3 (calling the Patriarch Bernard 'the equivalent to the Christians of an *imam* to the Moslems').

Baldwin's knights kept in reserve and could not resist the temptation that they offered. They deserted the field in order to steal and ride off with them. Seeing them go, Jawali's Turks turned and fled; and Baldwin and Joscelin were left almost alone. They, too, were obliged to fly with the remnant of their troops, each of them barely escaping capture. The Christian losses on the battlefield were said to have numbered nearly two thousand.[1]

Joscelin retired to Turbessel and Baldwin to Dulak, north of Ravendel, where Tancred made a half-hearted attempt to besiege him, but desisted on the rumour of Jawali's approach. Eventually Baldwin and Joscelin regained Edessa. They found the city in a panic. The citizens, fearing that Baldwin was dead and that they might again be subjected to the hated rule of Richard of the Principate, had held an assembly in the Church of St John, where the Latin bishop was invited by the Armenians of the city to join in the establishment of an interim government, till the situation should be clearer. When Baldwin arrived two days later he suspected treason; he believed that the Armenians had been planning to regain their independence. He struck swiftly and severely. Many Armenians were arrested and some were blinded. The Armenian bishop only saved his eyes by paying a heavy fine subscribed by his flock. There was a forced exodus of Armenians from the city. What had really happened is unknown; but it is clear that Baldwin must have been thoroughly alarmed so drastically to reverse his Armenian policy.[2]

In spite of his own victory and in spite of Jawali's decision a few months later to reconcile himself with his overlord the Sultan, who gave him a command far away in Persia, Tancred did not attempt any further move to evict Baldwin from Edessa. Instead, in the autumn of 1108, he led an expedition against Shaizar, where after miraculously slaying a small company of the enemy whom he caught in a cave, he allowed himself to be bought off by the gift

[1] Matthew of Edessa, cxcix, pp. 266–7; Ibn al-Athir, pp. 265–7; Kemal ad-Din, p. 595; Ibn al-Fourat, quoted in Cahen, *op. cit.* p. 250 n. 34.
[2] Matthew of Edessa, cxciv, pp. 267–8.

of a superb horse.[1] Next spring he became involved in the quarrel between William-Jordan and Bertrand of Toulouse for the possession of the Frankish lands in the Lebanon. His acceptance of William-Jordan as his vassal was countered by King Baldwin's speedy intervention as overlord of all the Franks in the East. When the King summoned Tancred with the other Frankish leaders to accept his arbitration in the camp before Tripoli, he did not dare to disobey. Before the assembled princes the King not only divided the Toulousain inheritance, but he obliged Tancred and Baldwin of Edessa and Joscelin to be reconciled and to work together against the infidel. Tancred, in admitting the King's right to arbitrate, acknowledged his suzerainty. In return, he was allowed to retain William-Jordan as his vassal, and he was given back the title of Prince of Galilee, and the ownership of the Temple at Jerusalem, with the promise that he could resume the government of the fief were Bohemond to return to Antioch. These advantages were lessened when William-Jordan was murdered and his lands passed to Bertrand, who recognized King Baldwin alone as his overlord. Tancred was, however, encouraged to attack Jabala, the last possession of the Banū Ammar, which he captured in July 1109, thus bringing his frontier down to march with Bertrand's.[2]

A reconciliation of the Frankish princes under King Baldwin's leadership was needed; for early in 1110 the atabeg Mawdud of Mosul, in obedience to the instructions of his master the Sultan, organized an expedition against the Franks. With the help of Ilghazi the Ortoqid and his Turcoman troops and of the emir of Mayyafaraqin, Soqman el-Qutbi, who was popularly known as the Shah of Armenia, he marched on Edessa in April. On the news that the Moslem troops were mustering Baldwin of Le Bourg sent Joscelin to Jerusalem to beg urgent help from King Baldwin and to voice his suspicion that Tancred was encouraging the

---

[1] Usama, ed. Hitti, pp. 99–100.
[2] See above, pp. 66–8, and Albert of Aix, XI, 3–13, pp. 664–8, 685–6; Ibn al-Athir, p. 274.

enemy. Tancred's friends, for their part, made a similar, but less convincing, charge against Baldwin. The King was engaged in the siege of Beirut, and would not move till he had captured it. Then he hurried north, avoiding Antioch, partly to save time and partly because he did not trust Tancred, and arrived before Edessa at the end of June. As he approached the city he was joined by Armenian forces sent by Kogh Vasil and by the lord of Birejik, Abu'lgharib, chief of the Pahlavouni. Mawdud had been besieging Edessa for two months, but had not been able to penetrate its fortifications. When the knights of Jerusalem came into sight, their banners waving and their armour gleaming in the sun, he retired to Harran, hoping to lure them to make a rash offensive.[1]

Baldwin of Le Bourg emerged gladly from his fortress to meet his cousin and overlord, and at once complained of Tancred. The King therefore sent to Antioch to demand that Tancred should come in force to join the Christian coalition and to answer these accusations. Tancred himself hesitated; but his Great Council insisted that he should obey the summons. On his arrival he promptly made a counter-claim against Baldwin of Le Bourg. The province of Osrhoene, in which Edessa was situated, had always, he said, depended upon Antioch throughout history, and he was its rightful overlord. King Baldwin answered sternly that as the chosen king he was leader of eastern Christendom, in whose name he demanded that Tancred be reconciled with Baldwin of Le Bourg. If Tancred refused and preferred to continue his intrigues with the Turks, he would no longer be considered as a Christian prince but would be combatted mercilessly as an enemy. The assembled knights approved the royal words; and Tancred was obliged to make his peace.[2]

The united Frankish army then marched in pursuit of Mawdud, who retreated farther to draw it on into hostile territory, intending

[1] Albert of Aix, XI, 16–18, pp. 670–2; Matthew of Edessa, cciv, pp. 270–3; Ibn al-Qalanisi, p. 103.
[2] Albert of Aix, XI, 20–4, pp. 672–4; Fulcher of Chartres, II, xliii, 1–6, pp. 532–41; Ibn al-Qalanisi, p. 102.

to outflank it by a sudden swerve to the north. King Baldwin was warned in time and stopped to besiege the castle of Shinav, to the north-west of Harran. But there the coalition dispersed. Tancred heard rumours that Ridwan of Aleppo was preparing to attack Antioch. Messengers came from Palestine to tell the King of a threatened Egyptian move against Jerusalem. The campaign in the Jezireh was abandoned. Tancred retired to Samosata; and Baldwin of Le Bourg, on the King's advice, took the decision that it was useless to try and protect the country east of the Euphrates. He had wept to see how it was ravaged by Mawdud while he was besieged at Edessa. He planned to keep garrisons only in the two great fortresses of Edessa and Saruj and in a few smaller castles, but to make no attempt to guard the frontiers. The Christian population was advised to leave the land for the safer territory on the right bank of the great river. The advice was taken. The Christians of the countryside, mostly Armenians, collected their belongings and moved slowly westward. But spies had informed Mawdud of what was being planned. He came up quickly on their tracks. When he reached the Euphrates he found the Frankish leaders already across the river; but their two great ferry boats had been overladen with soldiers and had sunk before the civilians had crossed. He fell on them, unarmed as they were; and scarcely a man, woman or child survived. The fierce elimination of these Armenian peasants, politically unreliable but prosperous and hardworking, who had been settled in Osrhoene since before the opening of the Christian era, dealt the province a blow from which it never fully recovered. Though Frankish Counts might rule on in Edessa itself for a few more years, it had been proved that the Frankish dominion beyond the Euphrates was doomed to inevitable failure; and the failure brought ruin to the miserable native Christians who had submitted to its government.[1]

In his fury Baldwin of Le Bourg led back a contingent across the river, to take vengeance upon Mawdud. But his men were

[1] Albert of Aix, *loc. cit.*; William of Tyre, XI, 7, p. 464; Matthew of Edessa, cclv, p. 273; Ibn al-Qalanisi, pp. 103–4.

Equilibrium in the North

hopelessly outnumbered and would have been annihilated had not King Baldwin hastened up, together with a rather unwilling Tancred, to rescue him.[1]

King Baldwin returned to the south; and Tancred turned to punish Ridwan whose attack on his territory he considered as treachery. He took by assault the castle of Naqira, just over the frontier, then marched on Athareb, only some twenty miles from Aleppo. Ridwan obtained no help from his fellow-Moslems. He attempted to buy off Tancred, whose terms were too high; and the negotiations were dropped when Ridwan's own treasurer fled with part of his master's treasure to Tancred's camp. At last, when Tancred's engines had pounded the walls of Athareb to pieces, the town surrendered in December 1110. Ridwan purchased peace at the price of the loss of Athareb and Zerdana, a little to the south, the sum of twenty thousand dinars, and ten of his best Arab horses.[2] Next, Tancred moved on against Shaizar and Hama. The Munqidhite emir of Shaizar bought a few months' respite at the cost of four thousand dinars and another horse; but when the truce was ended, in the spring of 1111, Tancred advanced again and built on a neighbouring hill a strong castle at Ibn Mashar, from which he could watch every movement to and from the city. Soon afterwards he occupied the fort of Bisikra'il, on the road from Shaizar to Lattakieh. The emir of Homs paid two thousand dinars and was left in peace.[3]

Tancred's successes were helped by two factors. First, the Byzantines were not ready to counter-attack. The death of Kilij Arslan in 1107 had left the situation in Anatolia fluid. His eldest son, Malik Shah, had been captured in the battle of the Khabar and was now in the power of the Sultan Mohammed. His widow seized Melitene and the eastern provinces for her youngest son,

[1] Albert of Aix, XI, 25, p. 675.
[2] Matthew of Edessa, cciv, p. 274; Bar-Hebraeus, trans. Budge, p. 243; Ibn al-Qalanisi, pp. 105–6; Kemal ad-Din, pp. 596–8; Ibn al-Athir, p. 278.
[3] Albert of Aix, XI, 43–6, pp. 684–6; Usama, ed. Hitti, pp. 95–6; Kemal ad-Din, p. 599; Ibn al-Qalanisi, p. 114.

118

Toghrul. Another son, Mas'ud, was living at the Danishmend court; while a fourth, Arab, seems to have held Konya. The Sultan Mohammed, fearing that either Mas'ud or Toghrul would take over the whole inheritance, added to the confusion by releasing Malik Shah, who established himself in Konya and ungratefully assumed the title of Sultan.[1] The breakdown of the central Seldjuk government in Anatolia was not entirely beneficial to the Byzantines, as it led the Seldjuks to make numerous irresponsible raids into Byzantine territory; but it enabled the Emperor Alexius to occupy various fortresses on the frontier. He was not, however, willing to risk a campaign in Cilicia or Syria.[2] His enforced inaction benefited not only Tancred but also the Armenian Kogh Vasil; who, probably with imperial approval, succeeded in strengthening his principality in the Anti-Taurus and in warding off Turkish attacks. The Roupenian princes in the Taurus, more exposed to Seldjuk aggression and prevented by Tancred's troops from expansion into Cilicia, were unable to increase their power; and Kogh Vasil was thus without a rival in the Armenian world.[3]

More helpful to Tancred, and more disastrous for any Moslem counter-Crusade, was the appearance of a new and disruptive sect in the Islamic world. During the last decades of the eleventh century the Persian Hasan as-Sabah founded and organized the religious body known later as the Hashishiyun or the Assassins. Hasan had been converted to the Ismaili doctrine, of which the Fatimid Caliphs were the patrons, and had become an adept in the *batanya*, its esoteric lore. Wherein exactly his teaching improved on the mystical and allegorical theology of the Ismaili is obscure. His outstanding achievement was more practical. It was to build up an Order, united in strict obedience to himself as Grand Master, which he used for political purposes, directed against the Abbasid Caliphs of Baghdad, whose legitimacy he challenged, and more

[1] Michael the Syrian, III, pp. 194–5; Ibn al-Qalanisi, p. 81 (a vague story). See Cahen, *op. cit.* pp. 253–4.

[2] Anna Comnena, XIV, i, v–vi, pp. 141–6, 166–72. See Chalandon, *op. cit.* pp. 254–6.

[3] For Kogh Vasil, see Matthew of Edessa, clxxxvii, pp. 258–9; ccx, pp. 281–2.

especially against their Seldjuk masters, whose power enabled the Caliphate to endure. His chief political weapon was one for which his followers were to provide the name, assassination. Murder in the interest of religious belief had often been practised by heterodox sects in Islam, but in Hasan's hands it reached a high efficiency; for the unquestioned devotion of his disciples and their readiness to travel far and to risk their own lives at his orders enabled him to strike at any adversary throughout the Moslem world. In 1090 Hasan set up his headquarters in Khorassan, in the impregnable citadel of Alamut, the Eagle's Nest. In 1092 the first of his assassinations took place, that of the great vizier Nizam al-Mulk, whose ability had been the main prop of the Seldjuk dynasty in Iran. Later legend enhanced the horror of the deed by declaring that Nizam and Hasan, together with the poet Omar Khayyam, had been pupils together of the learned Muwaffaq of Nishapur, and each had sworn to aid the others throughout life. The Seldjuk Sultans were well aware of the danger that the Assassins created; but all their attempts to reduce Alamut were unavailing. Soon after the turn of the century lodges of the Assassins were set up in Syria. Ridwan of Aleppo, permanently on bad terms with his Seldjuk cousins, and perhaps genuinely impressed by Assassin doctrines, gave them his patronage. A Persian goldsmith, Abu Tahir, who had great influence over Ridwan, was their chief. To the Assassins, the Christians were no more odious than the Sunni Moslems; and Ridwan's readiness to co-operate with Tancred may have been largely due to his sympathy with their doctrine. Their first achievement in Syria was the murder of the emir of Homs, Janah ad-Daulah, in 1103. Three years later they slew the emir of Apamea, Khalaf ibn Mula'ib; but it was only the Franks of Antioch who profited by his death. Though as yet the Assassins only revealed their policy by isolated murders, they were an element in Islamic politics that even the Christians would have to respect.[1]

[1] For the Assassins, see von Hammer, *Histoire de l'Ordre des Assassins*; also articles 'Assassins' and 'Ismaili', in *Encyclopaedia of Islam*; Browne, *Literary History of Persia*, vol. II, pp. 193 ff.

In 1111 Mawdud of Mosul once again prepared to lead an army against the Franks, at the demand of his master the Sultan. Early that year a deputation from the citizens of Aleppo, angered by the heterodoxy of their ruler and his subservience to Tancred, arrived at the Caliph's court at Baghdad to urge a holy war to free them from the Frankish menace. When they were put off with empty promises they stirred up the people of Baghdad to riot before the mosque of the palace. At the same time the Caliph received an embassy from the Emperor at Constantinople. There was nothing unusual in this; Constantinople and Baghdad had a common interest in their hostility to the Seldjuk dynasty of Rum; but it seems that Alexius instructed his envoys to discuss with the Moslem authorities the possibility of joint action against Tancred.[1] These negotiations enabled the rioters to denounce the Caliph as being a worse Moslem than the Christian Emperor. Al-Mustazhir was alarmed by all this enthusiasm, especially as the disorders had prevented him from receiving his wife in proper state when she returned from a visit to her father, the Sultan Mohammed, at Ispahan.[2] He sent to his father-in-law; who at once instructed Mawdud to form a new coalition, whose nominal leader was to be his own young son Mas'ud. Mawdud enlisted the help of Soqman of Mayyafaraqin, of Ilghazi's son Ayaz, of the Kurdish princes Ahmed-Il of Maragha and Abu'l Haija of Arbil, and of some Persian lords headed by Bursuq ibn Bursuq of Hamadan. In July the allies were ready and marched swiftly across the Jezireh to besiege Joscelin's fortress of Turbessel. On the news the emir Sultan of Shaizar sent to beg them to hurry to his rescue; and Ridwan thought it politic to tell them to hasten as he could not

---

[1] Ibn al-Qalanisi, *op. cit.* pp. 112–13, saying that the Emperor (he uses the term 'usurper', *mutamelik*) sent to warn the Moslems of the designs of the Franks and implies that the embassy visited Damascus. Alexius in fact probably only suggested action against Tancred. He could find no support amongst the Frankish leaders in his attempt to make Tancred carry out the Treaty of Devol (see above, p. 51). Ibn al-Athir, pp. 279–80, reports the embassy to Baghdad, quoting Ibn Hamdun.
[2] Ibn al-Athir, *loc. cit.*

hold out long against Tancred. Mawdud was impressed by Ridwan's change of heart; and on the suggestion of Ahmed-Il, with whom Joscelin had established secret relations, he raised the siege of Turbessel and led the army off to Aleppo. But Ridwan's message had not been sincere. On the approach of the Moslem allies, he closed the gates against them and took the precaution of imprisoning many of the leading citizens as hostages to prevent riots. Mawdud was thwarted; so, after ravaging the country round Aleppo, he moved south to Shaizar. There he was joined by Toghtekin of Damascus, who came to seek his help for the reconquest of Tripoli.[1]

Tancred, who had been encamped before Shaizar, retired to Apamea and sent to King Baldwin for help. The King responded and summoned all the chivalry of the Frankish East to join him. With him came the Patriarch Gibelin and the chief vassals of the kingdom, Eustace Garnier of Sidon and Walter of Hebron. Bertrand of Tripoli joined him on his way. From the north came Baldwin of Edessa with his two great vassals, Joscelin of Turbessel and Pagan of Saruj. Tancred brought his vassals from the perimeter of the Antiochene principality, Guy, surnamed the Goat, from Tarsus and Mamistra, Richard of Marash, Guy, surnamed the Beech, of Harenc, Robert of Suadieh, Pons of Tel-Mannas, Martin of Lattakieh, Bonaplus of Sarmeda, Roger of Hab and Enguerrand of Apamea. Kogh Vasil and the Roupenians sent an Armenian detachment; and even Oshin of Lampron provided a few men, whose role was probably to spy on behalf of the Emperor. The north was denuded of troops, to the advantage of Toghrul Arslan of Melitene, who at once captured Albistan and the neighbourhood from its small Frankish garrison and carried out a raid into Cilicia.[2]

Before the Frankish concentration, which numbered some six-

---

[1] Ibn al-Qalanisi, pp. 114–15; Kemal ad-Din, pp. 600–1; Ibn al-Athir, p. 282; Albert of Aix, XI, 38, p. 681.
[2] Albert of Aix, XI, 39–40, pp. 682–3, for the list of allies; Matthew of Edessa, ccvi, p. 275; Michael the Syrian, III, p. 205, reports the loss of Albistan.

teen thousand men, Mawdud cautiously retired behind the walls of Shaizar and refused to be drawn out to fight a pitched battle. Things were not going well in his army. Toghtekin would not provide help unless Mawdud undertook to campaign farther south, a move that was strategically far too risky. The Kurd Bursuq was ill and wished to return to his home. Soqman suddenly died; and his troops retired north with his corpse. Ahmed-Il promptly deserted, to try to snatch some of the inheritance. Ayaz the Ortoqid remained; but his father, Ilghazi, attacked the cortege carrying Soqman's bier, hoping, in vain, to secure his treasure. With his forces daily diminishing, Mawdud could not take the offensive; and he was unwilling to winter so far from his base. In the autumn he retreated back to Mosul.[1]

His failure showed that the Moslems were in no condition to counter-attack the Franks so long as the Franks were united; and King Baldwin had achieved the task of forcing union upon them. For the moment the Frankish establishments were saved. Mawdud carried out a profitable but inconclusive raid into Edessene territory next summer; while Toghtekin patched up an alliance with Ridwan, somewhat generously, for Ridwan had tried to persuade his Assassin friends to murder him.[2] But for the moment the Moslem menace was lessened. Inevitably the Christians began to quarrel once more. First, the Franks decided to attack Kogh Vasil, of whose growing power both Baldwin of Edessa and Tancred were jealous. Tancred invaded his lands and captured Raban and was preparing to besiege Kaisun before peace was made.[3] Next, Baldwin of Edessa suddenly turned against his cousin Joscelin. When Mawdud had attacked Edessa in the summer of

---

[1] Fulcher of Chartres, II, xlv, 1–9, pp. 549–57; Albert of Aix, XI, 41–3, pp. 683–4; Ibn al-Qalanisi, pp. 116–19; Usama, ed. Hitti, pp. 97–8; Kemal ad-Din, p. 600; Ibn al-Athir, p. 83, muddles the story, which he derives from Ibn al-Qalanisi and Ibn Hamdun. See Cahen, *op. cit.* p. 363 n. 33.

[2] Kemal ad-Din, pp. 601–2; Albert of Aix (XI, 43, p. 684) reports the capture of Azaz about now, but Azaz was still in Moslem hands in 1118. (See below p. 134.)

[3] Matthew of Edessa, ccix, pp. 280–1.

1112 Joscelin discovered an Armenian plot to hand the city over to the Moslems and had saved Baldwin by warning him and joining him in prompt action against the traitors. But during the following winter Baldwin heard rumours that Joscelin talked of supplanting him. The fief of Turbessel was rich, whereas the land of Edessa had suffered terribly from raids and forced emigration. The Armenians liked Joscelin, whereas they now hated Baldwin. There was nothing in Joscelin's own conduct to account for Baldwin's suspicions, which were, perhaps, based on jealousy. At the end of the year Joscelin was summoned to Edessa; Baldwin said that he was ill and must discuss the succession. On his arrival, all unsuspecting, he was accused of having failed to supply Edessa with sufficient food from his territory and was thrown into prison. It was only when he promised to give up his fief that he was released. He retired southward, about the new year, to Jerusalem, where King Baldwin enfeoffed him with the principality of Galilee.[1]

The year 1112 saw many other changes in northern Syria. Kogh Vasil died on 12 October. His widow hastily sent presents to Tancred, including her own diadem for the Princess Cecilia, to secure his help for the succession of her adopted son, Vasil Dgha; but Tancred himself coveted the inheritance.[2] Among the Franks, Richard of the Principate had died some time in the spring[3] and Bertrand of Tripoli in January or February. Bertrand's young son and successor, Pons, did not share his father's liking for the Byzantines nor his hatred for Tancred; and his council probably thought that Tancred's good-will was necessary if the youthful count was to hold his position. There was a reconciliation between

---

[1] William of Tyre, XI, 22, pp. 489–92; Matthew of Edessa, ccviii, p. 280, hints of a plot against the Franks during Mawdud's siege; *Chron. Anon. Syr.* p. 86; Ibn al-Qalanisi, *op. cit.* p. 133.

[2] Matthew of Edessa, ccx, pp. 281–2. The exact date of Richard's death is unknown. He was already dead by the time of Tancred's death, but alive the previous winter.

[3] Ibn al-Qalanisi, p. 127, says that the news of Bertrand's death reached Damascus on 3 February.

the Courts of Tripoli and Antioch, which added to Tancred's influence.[1] With Joscelin in disgrace, the Count of Tripoli his friend, and the great prince of the Armenians dead, Tancred's supremacy seemed sure. He was planning an expedition to conquer Kogh Vasil's land when suddenly he fell ill. There were inevitable whispers of poison; but the illness was probably typhoid. When it was certain that he would not recover he named his nephew Roger of Salerno, son of Richard of the Principate, as his heir, but he forced Roger to swear to hand over his power to Bohemond's young son, should the boy come to the East. At the same time he requested Pons to marry his girl-widow, Cecilia of France. He died on 12 December 1112, aged only thirty-six.[2]

Tancred's personality does not shine clearly through the mists of history. He was immensely active and able, a subtle diplomat and a brilliant soldier; and he grew wiser as he grew older. But he never acquired the glamour that surrounded his uncle, Bohemond; nor does he seem to have been popular with his men, apart from his sycophantic biographer, Radulph of Caen. He was hard, self-seeking and unscrupulous, correct and yet disloyal towards Bohemond and a faithless colleague to Baldwin of Edessa. But for the intervention of King Baldwin, his equal in relentlessness and his superior in width of vision, his particularism might have gone far to wreck the Frankish East. His aim was the firm establishment and the aggrandizement of the Antiochene principality; and therein he was superbly successful. Without his work Bohemond's foundation would have crumbled. The long history of the princes of Antioch was the fruit of his energy. Of all the princes of the First Crusade, only King Baldwin, a penniless adventurer like himself, enjoyed a more impressive career. Yet, when he was being taken to his burial in the porch of the Cathedral

---

[1] Pons seems to have been attached at some time to Tancred's household and to have received knighthood from him.
[2] Fulcher of Chartres, II, xlvii, 1, pp. 562–3 (12 December); Albert of Aix, XII, 8, p. 693 (about Advent); Ibn al-Qalanisi, pp. 131–2 (11 December); Michael the Syrian, III, p. 203 (5 December).

of St Peter the chroniclers could find few scenes of grief to report. Only the Armenian Matthew of Edessa wrote warmly of him and lamented his death.[1]

The accession of Roger as Prince of Antioch—for, notwithstanding his acknowledgement of the claims of Bohemond's son, he took the princely title—brought harmony to the Franks. He was married to Baldwin of Edessa's sister, Cecilia;[2] and, though he was a notoriously unfaithful husband, he was always on affectionate terms with his brother-in-law. His sister Maria became the second wife of Joscelin of Courtenay.[3] Pons of Tripoli, who, following Tancred's wishes, at once married Tancred's widow, Cecilia of France, remained his constant friend.[4] And all three princes united in regarding King Baldwin as their overlord. This rare solidarity, combined with fresh quarrels among the Moslems, brought the Frankish dominion in northern Syria to its apogee.

In 1113 King Baldwin began a campaign against Toghtekin of Damascus, who succeeded at last in securing the aid of Mawdud and of Ayaz the Ortoqid. The Moslem allies lured the King into Damascene territory, to Sennabra on the upper Jordan, where, forgetting for once his usual caution, he was attacked and suffered a severe defeat.[5] He had summoned Pons and Roger to his aid; and their arrival with all their chivalry enabled him to extricate himself. The enemy advanced as far as the neighbourhood of

---

[1] Matthew of Edessa, *loc. cit.* 'The greatest of all the Faithful'.

[2] William of Tyre, XI, 9, p. 523, calls Roger Baldwin's brother-in-law, as does Walter the Chancellor, II, 16, p. 131. Cecilia's name is given in a Charter of 1126 (Röhricht, *Regesta, Additamenta,* p. 9). Orderic Vitalis, X, 23, IV, p. 158, gives Roger a Turkish wife called Melaz, the Danishmend emir's daughter who according to him secured Bohemond's release. See above, p. 38.

[3] Maria is known only for a quarrel arising later because of her dowry. See below, pp. 161, 181. *Chron. Anon. Syr.* says that Joscelin married her in 1121 (p. 89), but it is clear that the marriage was arranged in Roger's lifetime. Their daughter Stephanie was considered an old woman in 1161—see below, p. 362, n. 1.

[4] According to Albert of Aix (XII, 19, p. 701) the marriage did not take place till 1115. But Pons's son Raymond II seems to have been twenty-two in 1136.

[5] Ibn al-Qalanisi, pp. 132–6.

Tiberias, but would not venture to face the whole Frankish army. After a few weeks of hesitation, Mawdud retired with Toghtekin to Damascus. There on the last Friday in September, as he was entering the Great Mosque with his host, he was stabbed to death by an Assassin. Toghtekin promptly put the murderer to death, to dissociate himself from the crime. Public opinion held him guilty, but gave him the excuse that Mawdud had designs on Damascus.[1]

Mawdud's death freed the Franks of a formidable adversary. It was followed two months later, on 10 December 1113, by the death of Ridwan of Aleppo.[2] His chilly relations with his fellow-Moslems had done much to help the establishment of the Franks in Syria; but his elimination did not greatly benefit Islam. He was succeeded by his son, Alp Arslan, a weak, vicious and cruel boy of sixteen, completely in the hands of his favourite eunuch, Lulu. The Assassins, whom Ridwan had protected, found themselves cold-shouldered by the new administration, at the express orders of the Sultan Mohammed. His envoy, the Persian Ibn Badi, forced Alp Arslan to issue a warrant for the execution of Abu Tahir and the other leaders of the sect; and the populace of Aleppo, who had long loathed the Assassins, set about massacring all that they could catch. In self-defence the Order had tried unsuccessfully to capture the citadel while Ridwan lay dying.[3] Soon afterwards sectarians tried to surprise the citadel at Shaizar, when the emir's family were out watching the Christian Easter festival; but the townsfolk joined with the emir against them. Their one success was to take the fortress of Qolaia, near Balis, where the road from Aleppo to Baghdad approaches the Euphrates. Elsewhere they went underground, or fled to the protection of the Franks; but they were still powerful and began to turn their attention to the Lebanon.[4] Alp Arslan's reign was short. He paid

---

[1] *Ibid.* pp. 137–42.   [2] *Ibid.* p. 144; Kemal ad-Din, p. 602.
[3] Ibn al-Qalanisi, pp. 145–6; Kemal ad-Din, pp. 603–4. See Cahen, *op. cit.* pp. 267–8.
[4] Ibn al-Qalanisi, pp. 146–8; Usama, ed. Hitti, pp. 146, 153 (without giving a date for the *coup* at Shaizar).

a friendly visit to Damascus, where Toghtekin received him with royal honours; but in September 1114 his wanton behaviour induced the eunuch Lulu, terrified for his life, to have him murdered in his bed and to place on the throne his six-year-old brother, Sultanshah. For the next few years Lulu and his general Shams as-Shawas, ex-emir of Rafaniya, held the citadel and controlled the army of Aleppo; but the real power was in the hands of the notables of the city, whose wishes Lulu did not dare to disregard. Its lack of a strong prince and the small size of its army left Aleppo powerless to do more than defend its own walls; while, though the Assassins had been banished, the new authorities were considered by their neighbours to have dangerously Shian tendencies, due to the influence of Persians in the city. In consequence Lulu was ready to carry on Ridwan's policy of subservient friendship with the Franks of Antioch.[1]

On Mawdud's death the Sultan gave Mosul to his representative at the Caliph's court, Aqsonqor il-Bursuqi, a Turkish soldier of fortune like his predecessor. It became his duty to direct operations against the Franks. In May 1114 he led an army of fifteen thousand men against Edessa. With him were the Sultan's son, Mas'ud, Temirek, emir of Sinjar, and a young Turk called Imad ed-Din Zengi, son of an earlier Aqsonqor who had been governor of Aleppo and Hama in the years before the Crusade. Ilghazi of Mardin had been summoned to join the expedition but refused. Its first step therefore was to march on Mardin; whereupon Ilghazi agreed to send his son Ayaz with a detachment of Turcoman troops. For two months the Moslems sat before Edessa; but the city was well garrisoned and well provisioned, whereas the ravaged countryside could not feed the besieging forces. Il-Bursuqi was obliged to lift the siege and contented himself with ravaging the countryside, till the Armenians offered him new scope for action.[2]

[1] Ibn al-Qalanisi, pp. 148–9; Kemal ad-Din, pp. 605–6.
[2] Matthew of Edessa, ccxii, pp. 282–3; ccxvi, p. 287; *Chron. Anon. Syr.* p. 86; Ibn al-Athir, pp. 292–3.

The Armenian plot to hand over Edessa to Mawdud in 1112 had been followed by a similar plot next year, when Mawdud was about to invade Frankish territory and Baldwin was at Turbessel, taking over Joscelin's fief. It was discovered in time; and Baldwin firmly transferred the whole Armenian population of his capital to Samosata. Having taught the Armenians a lesson, he allowed them to return early in 1114; but some had gone on into the territory of Vasil Dgha, Kogh Vasil's heir, who was anyhow alarmed by Frankish attempts on his inheritance. He and his adopted mother now invited Il-Bursuqi to deliver them from the Franks. Il-Bursuqi sent one of his generals, Sonqor the Long, to negotiate with Vasil Dgha at Kaisun. The Franks heard of it, and vainly attacked Sonqor and the Armenians. But before the Moslems could take advantage of the new alliance Il-Bursuqi quarrelled with Ayaz the Ortoqid and imprisoned him. Ayaz's father, Ilghazi, therefore summoned his clan and his Turcomans and marched against Il-Bursuqi, whom he severely defeated and forced to retreat back to Mosul. Once again the Moslem counter-Crusade ended in a fiasco.[1]

The Armenians paid for it. The Franks advanced to punish Vasil Dgha. They were unable to take his fortress capital at Raban; but he thought it wise to seek the alliance of the Roupenian prince Thoros. Thoros, after inviting him to come to discuss a marriage alliance, imprisoned him and sold him to Baldwin of Edessa. Vasil was only released on a promise to cede all his lands to Baldwin. He then was allowed to retire to Constantinople. Having thus annexed Raban and Kaisun in 1116, Baldwin decided to suppress the remaining Armenian principalities in the Euphrates valley. In 1117 he first displaced Abu'lgharib, lord of Birejik, who had been established there with the help of Baldwin during the First Crusade. He gave Birejik to his cousin, Waleran of Le Puiset, who married Abu'lgharib's daughter. Next he attacked Baldwin I's old friend and later enemy, Bagrat, Kogh Vasil's brother, who

[1] Matthew of Edessa, ccxii, pp. 282–4; Michael the Syrian, III, pp. 216–17; Ibn al-Athir, pp. 292–3.

129

now possessed a small lordship at Khoros, west of the Euphrates. Finally, he overran the territory of another of Baldwin's allies, Prince Constantine of Gargar, whom he captured and imprisoned at Samosata, where the unfortunate victim soon perished in an earthquake. The Roupenian prince soon found himself, to his satisfaction, the only independent Armenian potentate that remained. But, apart from the Roupenians, the Armenian people lost confidence in the Franks.[1]

Baldwin of Edessa's Armenian conquests were helped by a diminution of danger from the East. The previous years had been full of anxiety. A tremendous earthquake in November 1114 had devastated Frankish territory, from Antioch and Mamistra to Marash and Edessa. Roger of Antioch hastily toured his chief fortresses to repair their walls; for there was a rumour that the Sultan Mohammed was preparing a new expedition.[2]

Mohammed was the last of the great Seldjuk Sultans. He had taken over a decadent state from his brother Barkiyarok, and he had restored order in Iraq and Iran, suppressing the rebel Arabs of the eastern desert in ⸱108 and keeping the Assassins in check. The Caliph al-Mustazhir, indolently writing love-poems in his palace at Baghdad, obeyed his authority. But his attempts to organize a campaign to drive the Franks from Syria had failed one after the other; and he realized that to succeed he must establish his authority over the Moslem princes there, whose jealousies and insubordination had regularly ruined his cause. In February 1115, after securing the loyalty of Mosul by sending his son Mas'ud to take charge of its government, he dispatched a large army westward, under the governor of Hamadan, Bursuq ibn Bursuq, with Juyush-beg, former governor of Mosul, and Temirek, emir of Sinjar, to aid him.

[1] Matthew of Edessa, ccxiii–ccxiv, pp. 293–5. *Chron. Anon. Syr.* p. 86. Waleran was probably the brother of Hugh of Le Puiset, whose mother Alice was Baldwin II's aunt and Tancred's first cousin. See below, p. 190.

[2] Fulcher of Chartres, II, lii, 1–5, pp. 578–80; Walter the Chancellor, I, pp. 83–4; Matthew of Edessa, ccxvii, pp. 287–9; Ibn al-Qalanisi, p. 149; Kemal ad-Din, p. 607.

1115: Expedition of Bursuq ibn Bursuq

The Moslem princes of Syria were as alarmed as the Franks. The Sultan's only reliable vassals there were the Munqidhites of Shaizar and Ibn Qaraja, emir of Homs. On the rumour of the expedition the Ortoqid Ilghazi hastened to Damascus to confirm his alliance with Toghtekin, but on his return he was waylaid and captured by the emir of Homs; who, however, threatened by Toghtekin, let him go on condition that he sent his son Ayaz in his place. Ilghazi was able to return to Mardin and collect his troops. Then he retired westward again to join up with Toghtekin. The eunuch Lulu, regent in Aleppo, after promising support to both sides, decided that the Sultan's victory would not suit him and ranged himself with Toghtekin and Ilghazi. Meanwhile Roger of Antioch had collected his forces and took up a position by the Iron Bridge across the Orontes. There, on whose initiative we cannot tell, he made a pact with Toghtekin and his allies and invited their army to join his own before the walls of Apamea, a good vantage-point for watching Bursuq's movements when he should cross the Euphrates and advance towards his friends at Shaizar. The Franks provided some two thousand knights and infantrymen and their Moslem allies about five thousand.

Bursuq met with no opposition as he led his great army through the Jezireh. He had hoped to make his headquarters at Aleppo, but, hearing that Lulu had joined his enemies and that Toghtekin was at their head, he turned southward against the latter. With the help of the emir of Homs he made a surprise attack on Hama, which belonged to Toghtekin and contained much of his baggage. The town was captured and pillaged, to the fury of the local Moslems; and he then marched on the Frankish fort of Kafartab. Roger would have liked to make a diversion, but Toghtekin persuaded him that it would be too risky. Instead, the allies appealed for help to Baldwin of Jerusalem and Pons of Tripoli, who hastened northward, the former with five hundred knights and a thousand infantrymen, the latter with two hundred knights and two thousand infantrymen. They entered the camp at Apamea to the fanfare of trumpets. Bursuq, who was now based on Shaizar, thought it prudent to retreat towards the Jezireh. His ruse was effective. Baldwin and Pons considered the danger to be ended and returned home; and the allied army broke up. Bursuq then suddenly swept back again to Kafartab. After a short struggle he took the castle and handed it over to the Munqidhites. Lulu of Aleppo, whether from treachery or cowardice, at once wrote to him apologizing for past sins and asking him to send a detachment to occupy Aleppo; and Bursuq weakened his forces by dispatching Juyush-beg and his corps. Roger had not disbanded his army. He could not wait for help to arrive from King Baldwin nor from Pons, nor even from Toghtekin. After summoning Baldwin of Edessa to his rescue and asking the Patriarch Bernard to bless the troops and to send with them a fragment of the True Cross, he left Antioch on 12 September and marched southward up the Orontes to Chastel Rouge, while Bursuq marched northward along a parallel line further inland. Neither army knew the other's position, till a knight named Theodore Berneville came galloping to the camp at Chastel Rouge from a scouting expedition to say that he had seen the Sultan's army moving through the forest towards the hill of Tel-Danith, near to the town of Sirmin. On the morning of the 14th the Frankish army crept over the intervening ridge and fell upon Bursuq as his troops were carelessly marching on. The baggage animals were in the van; and already detachments had stopped to erect tents for the noonday halt. Some of the emirs had taken parties to forage in the neighbouring farms; others had gone off to occupy Biza'a. When the battle began Bursuq was without his best lieutenants.

The Franks' attack was quite unexpected. They sprang out suddenly from the trees and quickly stormed the half-prepared camp. Soon the whole Moslem army was in disorder. Bursuq could not rally his men. He himself barely avoided capture and retired with a few hundred horsemen to a spur of the hill of Tel-Danith. There he beat off the enemy for a while and sought to be killed in the fighting rather than face the disgrace of such a defeat. At last his bodyguard persuaded him that nothing more could be done; and he rode off in flight to the east. The emir of Sinjar, Temirek, had at first been more successful and had driven back the Frankish right. But Guy Fresnel, lord of Harenc, brought up fresh troops; and soon the men of Sinjar were surrounded, and only the swiftest horsemen escaped alive. By evening the remnants of the Moslem army were hastening in disorder towards the Jezireh.[1]

The Frankish victory at Tel-Danith ended the last attempt of the Seldjuk Sultans of Iran to recover Syria. Bursuq died a few months later, humiliated and ashamed; and the Sultan Mohammed was not prepared to risk a further expedition. The only danger to the Franks from the East came now from the semi-independent emirs, who for the moment were disunited and discouraged. The prestige of Roger, Prince of Antioch, was at its height. His men quickly reoccupied Kafartab, which had been given to the Munqidhites by Bursuq.[2] The rulers of Aleppo and Damascus were seriously alarmed. The latter, Toghtekin, hastened to make his peace with the Sultan Mohammed, who forgave him but provided him with no material aid.[3] At Aleppo the eunuch Lulu watched helpless while the Franks consolidated their positions around him. He sought to make a closer alliance with Toghtekin. But he was generally discredited; and in May 1117 he was murdered by Turks of his garrison. His successor was a fellow-eunuch, the Armenian renegade Yaruqtash, who at once sought Frankish support by yielding to Roger the fortress of al-Qubba, on the road from Aleppo to Damascus used by the pilgrims to Mecca, and the right to levy tolls on the pilgrims.[4] The concession did Yaruqtash no good. Lulu's murderers had acted in the name of Ridwan's youngest son, Sultanshah, who would not recognize

---

[1] Fulcher of Chartres, II, liv, 1–6, pp. 586–90; Albert of Aix, XII, 19, p. 701; Walter the Chancellor, I, 6–7, pp. 92–6 (the fullest account); al-Azimi, p. 509; Ibn Hamdun in Ibn al-Athir, pp. 295–8; Usama, ed. Hitti, pp. 102–6; Michael the Syrian, III, p. 217; *Chron. Anon. Syr.* p. 86.

[2] Usama, ed. Hitti, p. 106.

[3] Ibn al-Qalanisi, pp. 151–2, implying that the overtures came from the Sultan's side. Ibn Hamdun, *loc. cit.*

[4] Ibn al-Qalanisi, pp. 155–6.

him. Yaruqtash appealed for help to Ilghazi the Ortoqid; but when Ilghazi's troops arrived at Aleppo they found Yaruqtash fallen and the government directed by Sultanshah's minister, the Damascene Ibn al-Milhi. Ilghazi therefore retired, leaving his son Kizil as his representative in Aleppo and taking over the fortress of Balis on the Euphrates, which was granted him as the price of his help should il-Bursuqi, who was now established at ar-Rahba and claimed to have been allotted Aleppo by the Sultan, try to make good his claim. Ibn al-Milhi then decided that Ilghazi was too uncertain an ally and handed over Aleppo and Kizil to Khirkan, emir of Homs, and prepared with Frankish help to recover Balis. But Ilghazi's alliance with Toghtekin held good. While the latter marched on Homs and obliged Khirkan to retire, Ilghazi relieved Balis and entered Aleppo in the summer of 1118. Ibn al-Milhi had already been displaced by a black eunuch, Qaraja, who, together with Ibn al-Milhi and the prince Sultanshah, were imprisoned by the Ortoqid.[1] During all these movements and intrigues Frankish intervention had been sought by all parties in turn; and though Roger was never master of Aleppo itself, he was able to occupy the territory to the north of the city, occupying Azaz in 1118 and early in 1119 Biza'a, thus cutting off Aleppo from the Euphrates and the East.[2]

About the same time Roger improved his southern frontier by capturing the castle of Marqab, on its high hill overlooking the sea behind Buluniyas.[3]

Thus, by the end of 1118, there was an equilibrium in northern Syria. The Franks had become an accepted part of the pattern of the country. They were still far from numerous, but they were well-armed and were building fortresses, and were learning to

[1] Ibn al-Qalanisi, *loc. cit.* Kemal ad-Din, pp. 610-15; Ibn al-Athir, pp. 308-9.
[2] Matthew of Edessa, ccxxvii, pp. 297-8; Kemal ad-Din, pp. 614-15.
[3] For the Arabic sources, see the discussion in Cahen, *op. cit.* p. 279 n. 16. Pons of Tripoli seems to have helped Roger, after a slight quarrel over the dower of Pons's wife, Tancred's widow, Cecilia, who claimed Jabala but was eventually satisfied with Chastel Rouge and Arzghan (William of Tyre, xiv, 5, p. 612).

adapt themselves to local life. Moreover, for the moment they were united. Roger of Antioch was by far the greatest of the northern Christian princes; but his hegemony was not resented by Baldwin of Edessa nor by Pons of Tripoli; for he made no attempt to be their overlord but like them acknowledged the suzerainty of the King of Jerusalem. The Moslem princes were numerically stronger, but they were disunited and jealous. Only the alliance between Toghtekin of Damascus and the Ortoqids kept them from chaos. The balance thus was slightly tilted in favour of the Franks. No external power was in a position to upset this balance. King Baldwin of Jerusalem, with the Fatimid menace in his rear, could not often intervene in the north. The Seldjuk Sultan of Iran, after the disaster at Tel-Danith, abstained from further practical attempts to assert authority in Syria. The two chief powers of Anatolia, Byzantium and the Seldjuks of Rum, for the moment were balanced against each other.

Even the native Christians maintained a balance. The Armenian subjects of Edessa and Antioch were disillusioned and disloyal; but the only free Armenian state that remained, the Roupenian principality on the Taurus, was ready to work in with the Franks. Its prince, Leo, had brought a contingent to help Roger of Antioch at the siege of Azaz.[1] A schism divided the Jacobite Church. In about 1118, its head, the Patriarch Athanasius, who resided at Antioch, quarrelled with his metropolitan at Edessa, Bar-Sabuni, over the possession of some sacred books, and placed him under an interdict. Bar-Sabuni, to make trouble, appealed for help to the Latin Patriarch of Antioch, Bernard; who summoned Athanasius to discuss the matter at a synod held in the Latin cathedral. Athanasius came protesting. The incompetence of an interpreter led Bernard to believe that the dispute was over a private debt between the two prelates, and he pronounced that it was simoniacal of Athanasius not to forgive the debtor. Athanasius was infuriated by a decision whose validity he did not recognize and whose sense

---

[1] Matthew of Edessa, *loc. cit.* For the history of the Roupenians, see Tournebize, *op. cit.* pp. 168 ff.

he did not understand. He protested rudely; whereupon Bernard ordered him to be scourged. On the advice of an Orthodox friend, the philosopher Abd' al-Massih, Athanasius appealed to Roger, who had been away at the time. Roger angrily reproved Bernard for interfering in a matter that did not concern him, and permitted Athanasius to leave Antioch for his former home, the monastery of Mar Barsauma. There Athanasius was in the territory of the Ortoqids, who gave him their protection. He excommunicated Bar Sabuni and placed the Jacobite Church of Edessa under an interdict. Many of the Edessene Jacobites, thus deprived of the services of their Church, went over to the Latin rite. Others obeyed the Patriarch. Peace was not restored for many years, till after the death of Athanasius.[1]

The Orthodox congregations in Antioch and Edessa disliked Latin rule, but, unlike the Armenians and Jacobites, they were never tempted to intrigue with the Moslems. They only sighed for the return of Byzantium. But the loathing which Armenians and Jacobites united in bearing to them limited their power.

Nevertheless, though the Franks in Edessa might rightly fear that some new danger would arise in the East, to the Franks of Antioch Byzantium remained the chief enemy. The Emperor Alexius had never forgotten his claim to Antioch. He was prepared to recognize a Latin kingdom at Jerusalem; and he had shown his good-will by his generous ransom of the Frankish prisoners taken by the Fatimids at Ramleh in 1102 and by the presence of his ships at the ineffectual siege of Acre in 1111. King Baldwin on his side always acted courteously and correctly towards the Emperor, but refused to put any pressure on Tancred to carry out the terms of the Treaty of Devol.[2] Ever since the Crusade of 1101 Franco-Byzantine relations had been darkened by suspicion; while Pope Paschal's intervention on Bohemond's behalf in 1106 had never been forgiven by Constantinople. Alexius was too supple a statesman to allow resentment to colour his policy. During the years

[1] Michael the Syrian, III, pp. 193–4, 207–10.
[2] Anna Comnena, XIV, ii, 12–13, pp. 152–3.

1111 and 1112 he carried on a series of negotiations with the Pope, using the Abbot of Monte Cassino as an intermediary. With the promise to settle the outstanding differences between the Roman and Greek Churches he induced the Roman authorities to offer the imperial crown of the West to him or to his son, and he suggested that he would visit Rome himself. Paschal, who was at that moment in great difficulties with the Emperor Henry V, was willing to pay a high price for Byzantine support; but Turkish wars and his own ill-health prevented Alexius from carrying out his project.[1] The negotiations came to nothing. The Archbishop of Milan, Peter Chrysolan, visited Constantinople in 1113 to discuss Church affairs; but his theological argument with Eustratius, Bishop of Nicaea, did not restore better feeling between the Churches.[2] It is probable that Alexius himself never took his ambitious Italian scheme very seriously. Papal friendship was of value to him mainly as a means of putting a break on Norman ambitions and of enhancing his authority over the Latins in the East.

In the meantime there was little that the Byzantines could do to recover Antioch. The Emperor's treaty with Bohemond remained a dead letter. Tancred had not only disregarded it but had increased his territory at Byzantine expense. Roger had continued Tancred's policy. Alexius had hoped that the Counts of Tripoli would be his agents in Syria, and he had provided money to be kept at Tripoli for joint Byzantine and Tripolitan enterprises. But on Bertrand's death his son Pons worked in co-operation with the Antiochenes. The Byzantine Ambassador-at-large to the Latin states, Butumites, therefore demanded the return of the money; and it was only when he threatened to cut off the provisions that Tripoli obtained from Cyprus that it was handed over to him. He then judged it prudent to give back to Pons the gold and precious

---

[1] See Chalandon, *op. cit.* pp. 260–3, with full references.
[2] Landolph, in Muratori, *Ss. R.I.* vol. v, p. 487; Chrysolan's speeches in *M.P.L.* vol. cxxvii, col. 911–19; Eustratius's speeches in Demetracopoulos, *Bibliotheca Ecclesiastica,* vol. i, p. 15.

stuffs that had been promised personally to Bertrand. In return
Pons took an oath of allegiance to the Emperor, probably the oath
of non-injury that his grandfather Raymond had taken. The money
recovered by Butumites was used to buy for the Byzantine army
horses from Damascus, Edessa and Arabia.[1]

It was clear that Pons could not be inveigled to act against
Antioch; while Turkish action prevented the Emperor from
making a direct intervention in Syria. Since the death of the
Danishmend Malik Ghazi Gümüshtekin in 1106 and that of the
Seldjuk Kilij Arslan in 1107, there had been no great Turkish
potentate in Anatolia; and Alexius was able, as far as he was not
distracted by the Normans, slowly to restore his authority in its
western districts and along the south coast. The leading Moslem
emir was now the Cappadocian Hasan, who in 1110 attempted to
raid Byzantine territory, even advancing towards Philadelphia,
with Smyrna as his goal. Eustathius Philocales had recently been
given a land-command in south-west Anatolia, with orders to clear
the province of the Turks. He managed, with the small forces that
he controlled, to catch Hasan's army when it was divided up into
various raiding-parties, which he defeated one by one. Hasan
speedily retired; and the Aegean coasts were spared further raids.
But that same year Kilij Arslan's eldest son, Malik Shah, was
released from his Persian captivity. He made Konya his capital
and soon held the bulk of his due inheritance, defeating Hasan and
annexing his lands. Warned by his father's fate he avoided entanglement in the East, but as soon as he felt strong enough, he set
out to recover the territory lost by Kilij Arslan at the time of the
First Crusade. During the early months of 1112 he began incursions into the Empire, marching on Philadelphia, where he was
checked by the Byzantine general, Gabras. He sued for a truce,
but in 1113 he attacked again, sending a hurried expedition
through Bithynia to the very walls of Nicaea, while his lieutenant
Mohammed penetrated to Poemamenum, farther to the west,
where he defeated and captured a Byzantine general, and another

[1] Anna Comnena, XIV, ii, 14, pp. 153-4.

138

lieutenant, Manalugh, raided Abydos on the Hellespont, with its rich custom-houses. Malik Shah himself attacked and captured Pergamum. The Emperor set out to meet the invaders, but waited to catch them on their return, heavily laden with booty. Coming south through Dorylaeum he fell on them near Coty-aeum. He won a complete victory and recovered all the loot and prisoners that they had taken. In 1115 there was news that Malik Shah was preparing to renew the attack; and Alexius spent much of the year in patrolling the Bithynian hills. Next year, though he was already very ill, he decided himself to take the offensive. He marched southward towards Konya and met the Turkish army near Philomelium. Once again he was victorious; and Malik Shah was forced to sign a peace in which he promised to respect the frontiers of the Empire, which now controlled all the coast from Trebizond to Cilician Seleucia and the interior west of Ankara, the Salt Desert and Philomelium. Malik Shah's attempts at reconquest had failed; and a few months later he was dethroned and killed by his brother Mas'ud, in alliance with the Danishmend. But the Turks remained firmly entrenched in the centre of Anatolia, and Byzantium was still unable to take effective action in Syria. The chief beneficiaries of these wars were the Armenians in the Taurus and the Frankish Prince of Antioch.[1]

[1] Anna Comnena, xiv, v–vi, xv, i–ii, iv–vi, pp. 164–72, 187–72, 187–94, 199–213. See Chalandon, *op. cit.* pp. 265–71.

BOOK II

THE ZENITH

CHAPTER I

KING BALDWIN II

'There shall not fail thee a man upon the throne of Israel.' I KINGS IX, 5

Baldwin I had neglected his final duty as King; he made no arrangement for the succession to the throne. The council of the kingdom hastily met. To some of the nobles it seemed unthinkable that the crown should pass from the house of Boulogne. Baldwin I had succeeded his brother Godfrey; and there was still a third brother, the eldest, Eustace, Count of Boulogne. Messengers were hastily dispatched over the sea to inform the Count of his brother's death and to beg him to take up the heritage. Eustace had no wish to leave his pleasant country for the hazards of the East; but they told him that it was his duty. He set out towards Jerusalem. But when he reached Apulia he met other messengers, with the news that it was too late. The succession had passed elsewhere. He refused the suggestion that he should continue on his way and fight for his rights. Not unwillingly, he retraced his steps to Boulogne.[1]

Indeed, few of the council had favoured his succession. He was far away; it would mean an interregnum of many months. The most influential member of the council was the Prince of Galilee, Joscelin of Courtenay; and he demanded that the throne be given to Baldwin of Le Bourg, Count of Edessa. He himself had no cause to love Baldwin, as he carefully reminded the council; for Baldwin had falsely accused him of treachery and had exiled him from his lands in the north. But Baldwin was a man of proved ability and courage; he was the late King's cousin; and he was the

---

[1] William of Tyre, XII, 3, pp. 513–16. It is uncertain what arrangements he made for Boulogne. His wife, Mary of Scotland, died in 1116.

sole survivor of the great knights of the First Crusade. Moreover, Joscelin calculated that if Baldwin left Edessa for Jerusalem the least that he could do to reward the cousin who had requited his unkindness so generously was to entrust him with Edessa. The Patriarch Arnulf supported Joscelin and together they persuaded the council. As if to clinch their argument, on the very day of the King's funeral, Baldwin of Le Bourg appeared unexpectedly in Jerusalem. He had heard, maybe, of the King's illness of the previous year and thought it therefore opportune to pay an Easter pilgrimage to the Holy Places. He was received with gladness and unanimously elected king by the Council. On Easter Sunday, 14 April 1118, the Patriarch Arnulf placed the crown on his head.[1]

Baldwin II differed greatly as a man from his predecessor. Though handsome enough, with a long fair beard, he lacked the tremendous presence of Baldwin I. He was more approachable, genial and fond of a simple joke, but at the same time subtle and cunning, less open, less rash, more self-controlled. He was capable of large gestures but in general somewhat mean and ungenerous. Despite a high-handed attitude to ecclesiastical affairs, he was genuinely pious; his knees were callous from constant prayer. Unlike Baldwin I's, his private life was irreproachable. With his wife, the Armenian Morphia, he presented a spectacle, rare in the Frankish East, of perfect conjugal bliss.[2]

Joscelin was duly rewarded with the county of Edessa, to hold it as vassal to King Baldwin, just as Baldwin himself had held it under Baldwin I. The new King was also recognized as overlord by Roger of Antioch, his brother-in-law, and by Pons of Tripoli. The Frankish East was to remain united under the crown of Jerusalem.[3] A fortnight after Baldwin's coronation the Patriarch Arnulf died. He had been a loyal and efficient servant of the state;

[1] Fulcher of Chartres, III, i, 1, pp. 615–16; Albert of Aix, XII, 30, pp. 707–10; William of Tyre, XII, 4, p. 517.
[2] William of Tyre, XII, 2, pp. 512–13. See above, p. 36.
[3] Immediately on his accession Baldwin summoned Roger and Pons to fight under him against the Egyptians. (See below, p. 146.)

CYPRUS

Lattakieh
Jabala   Shaiza
                  Hama
          Safita   Montferrand
Tortosa Krak des Réfanye
         Chevaliers Homs
         The Bukaia
TRIPOLI
Botrun
Jebeil
Beirut   Baalbek
Sidon
Beaufort   DAMASCUS
Tyre   Banyas
    Toron
Acre   Jacob's Ford
Haifa Tiberias Hauran
    Nazareth
    Beisan
Caesarea   Bosra
Arsuf   Nablus
Jaffa
    Ramleh Jericho
    Ibelin
Ascalon JERUSALEM
        Bethlehem
    Hebron
Gaza
Daron   Kerak

                Montreal

         Petra
         Le Vaux Moise

Ile de Graye Aila
              (Akaba)

Approximate frontiers of the
Christian states about A.D. 1165 · — · — · — ·

0   50   100

English miles

Map 2. Southern Syria in the twelfth century.

145

but, in spite of his prowess as a preacher, he had been involved in too many scandals to be respected as an ecclesiastic. It is doubtful if Baldwin much regretted his death. In his place he secured the election of a Picard priest, Gormond of Picquigny, of whose previous history nothing is known. It was a happy choice; for Gormond combined Arnulf's practical qualities with a saintly nature and was universally revered. This appointment, following on the recent death of Pope Paschal, restored good relations between Jerusalem and Rome.[1]

King Baldwin had barely established himself on the throne before he heard the ominous news of an alliance between Egypt and Damascus. The Fatimid vizier, al-Afdal, was anxious to punish Baldwin I's insolent invasion of Egypt; while Toghtekin of Damascus was alarmed by the growing power of the Franks. Baldwin hastily sent him an embassy; but confident of Egyptian help Toghtekin demanded the cession of all Frankish lands beyond Jordan. In the course of the summer a great Egyptian army assembled on the frontier and took up its position outside Ashdod; and Toghtekin was invited to take command of it. Baldwin summoned the militia of Antioch and Tripoli to reinforce the troops of Jerusalem, and marched down to meet them. For three months the armies faced each other, neither side daring to move; for everyone, in Fulcher of Chartres's words, liked better to live than to die. At last the soldiers on either side dispersed to their homes.[2]

Meanwhile, Joscelin's departure for Edessa was delayed. He was more urgently needed in Galilee than in the northern county, where, it seems, Queen Morphia remained, and where Waleran, Lord of Birejik, carried on the government.[3] As Prince of Galilee it was for Joscelin to defend the land against attacks from Damascus. In the autumn Baldwin joined him in a raid on Deraa

---

[1] Albert of Aix, *loc. cit.*; William of Tyre, xii, 6, p. 519.
[2] Fulcher of Chartres, iii, ii, 1-3, pp. 617-19; William of Tyre, xii, 6, pp. 518-19; Ibn al-Athir, pp. 314-15.
[3] *Chron. Anon. Syr.* p. 86.

in the Hauran, the granary of Damascus. Toghtekin's son Buri went out to meet them and owing to his rashness was severely defeated. After this check Toghtekin turned his attention again to the north.[1]

In the spring of 1119 Joscelin heard that a rich Bedouin tribe was pasturing its flocks in Transjordan, by the Yarmuk. He set out with two leading Galilean barons, the brothers Godfrey and William of Bures, and about a hundred and twenty horsemen, to plunder it. The party divided to encircle the tribesmen. But things went wrong. The Bedouin chief was warned and Joscelin lost his way in the hills. Godfrey and William, riding up to attack the camp, were ambushed. Godfrey was killed, and most of his followers taken prisoner. Joscelin returned unhappily to Tiberias and sent to tell King Baldwin; who came up in force and frightened the Bedouin into returning the prisoners and paying an indemnity. They were then allowed to spend the summer in peace.[2]

When Baldwin was pausing at Tiberias on his return from this short campaign, messengers came to him from Antioch, begging him to hasten with his army northward, as fast as he could travel.

Ever since Roger of Antioch's victory at Tel-Danith, the unfortunate city of Aleppo had been powerless to prevent Frankish aggression. It had reluctantly placed itself beneath the protection of Ilghazi the Ortoqid; but Roger's capture of Biza'a in 1119 left it surrounded on three sides. The loss of Biza'a was more than Ilghazi could endure. Hitherto neither he nor his constant ally, Toghtekin of Damascus, had been prepared to risk their whole strength in a combat against the Franks; for they feared and disliked still more the Seldjuk Sultans of the East. But the Sultan Mohammed had died in April 1118; and his death had let loose the ambition of every governor and princeling throughout his empire. His youthful son and successor, Mahmud, tried pathetically to assert his authority, but eventually, in August 1119, he was obliged to hand over the supreme power to his uncle Sanjar, the King of Khorassan, and spent the rest of his short life in the

[1] Ibn al-Athir, pp. 315–16.   [2] *Ibid.* pp. 325–6.

pleasures of the chase. Sanjar, the last of his house to rule over the whole eastern Seldjuk dominion, was vigorous enough; but his interests were in the East. He never concerned himself with Syria. Nor were his cousins of the Sultanate of Rum, distracted with quarrels amongst themselves and with the Danishmends and by wars with Byzantium, better able to intervene in Syrian affairs.[1] Ilghazi, the most tenacious of the local princes, at last had his opportunity. His wish was not so much to destroy the Frankish states as to secure Aleppo for himself, but the latter aim now involved the former.

During the spring of 1119 Ilghazi journeyed round his dominions collecting his Turcoman troops and arranging for contingents to come from the Kurds to the north and from the Arab tribes of the Syrian desert. As a matter of form he applied for assistance from the Sultan Mahmud, but received no answer. His ally, Toghtekin, agreed to come up from Damascus; and the Munqidhites of Shaizar promised to make a diversion to the south of Roger's territory.[2] At the end of May, the Ortoqid army, said to be forty thousand strong, was on the march. Roger received the news calmly; but the Patriarch Bernard urged him to appeal for help to King Baldwin and to Pons of Tripoli. From Tiberias Baldwin sent to say that he would come as quickly as possible and would bring the troops of Tripoli with him. In the meantime Roger should wait on the defensive. Baldwin then collected the army of Jerusalem, and fortified it with a portion of the True Cross, in the care of Evremar, Archbishop of Caesarea.[3]

While the Munqidhites made a raid on Apamea, Ilghazi sent Turcoman detachments south-west, to effect a junction with them and with the army coming up from Damascus. He himself with his main army raided the territory of Edessa but made no attempt against its fortress-capital. In mid-June he crossed the Euphrates

[1] Ibn al-Athir, pp. 318–23. See articles 'Sandjur' and 'Seldjuks', in *Encyclopaedia of Islam*.
[2] Ibn al-Qalanisi, pp. 157–7; Kemal ad-Din, pp. 615–16.
[3] Walter the Chancellor, II, 1, pp. 100–1.

at Balis and moved on to encamp himself at Qinnasrin, some fifteen miles south of Aleppo, to await Toghtekin. Roger was less patient. In spite of King Baldwin's message, in spite of the solemn warning of the Patriarch Bernard and in spite of all the previous experience of the Frankish princes, he decided to meet the enemy at once. On 20 June he led the whole army of Antioch, seven hundred horsemen and four thousand infantrymen, across the Iron Bridge, and encamped himself in front of the little fort of Tel-Aqibrin, at the eastern edge of the plain of Sarmeda, where the broken country afforded a good natural defence. Though his forces were far inferior to the enemy's, he hoped that he could wait here till Baldwin arrived.

Ilghazi, at Qinnasrin, was perfectly informed of Roger's movements. Spies disguised as merchants had inspected the Frankish camp and reported the numerical weakness of the Frankish army. Though Ilghazi wished to wait for Toghtekin's arrival, his Turcoman emirs urged him to take action. On 27 June part of his army moved to attack the Frankish castle of Athareb. Roger had time to rush some of his men there, under Robert of Vieux-Ponts; then, disquieted to find the enemy so close, when darkness fell he sent away all the treasure of the army to the castle of Artah on the road to Antioch.

Throughout the night Roger waited anxiously for news of the Moslems' movements, while his soldiers' rest was broken by a somnambulist who ran through the camp crying that disaster was upon them. At dawn on Saturday, 28 June, scouts brought word to the Prince that the camp was surrounded. A dry enervating *khamsin* was blowing up from the south. In the camp itself there was little food and water. Roger saw that he must break through the enemy ranks or perish. The Archbishop of Apamea was with the army, Peter, formerly of Albara, the first Frankish bishop in the East. He summoned the soldiers together and preached to them and confessed them all. He confessed Roger in his tent and gave him absolution for his many sins of the flesh. Roger then boldly announced that he would go hunting. But first he sent out another scouting-party which was ambushed. The few survivors hurried back to say that there was no way through the encircle-ment. Roger drew up the army in four divisions and one in reserve. Thereupon the Archbishop blessed them once more; and they charged in perfect order into the enemy.

It was hopeless from the outset. There was no escape through the hordes of Turcoman horsemen and archers. The locally recruited infantrymen, Syrians and Armenians, were the first to panic; but there was no place to which they could flee. They crowded in amongst the cavalry, hindering the horses. The wind suddenly turned to the north and rose, driving a cloud of dust into the Franks' faces. Early in the battle less than a hundred horsemen broke through and joined up with Robert of Vieux-Ponts, who had arrived back from Athareb too late to take part. They fled on to Antioch. A little later Reynald Mazoir and a few knights escaped and reached the little town of Sarmeda, in the plain. No one else in the army of Antioch survived. Roger himself fell fighting at the foot of his great jewelled cross. Round him fell his knights except for a few, less fortunate, who were made prisoners. By midday it was all over. To the Franks the battle was known as the *Ager Sanguinis*, the Field of Blood.[1]

At Aleppo, fifteen miles away, the faithful waited eagerly for news. About noon a rumour came that a great victory was in store for Islam; and at the hour of the afternoon prayer the first exultant soldiers were seen to approach. Ilghazi had only paused on the battlefield to allot the booty to his men, then marched to Sarmeda, where Reynald Mazoir surrendered to him. Reynald's proud bearing impressed Ilghazi, who spared his life. His com-rades were slain. The Frankish prisoners were dragged in chains

[1] Walter the Chancellor, II, 2–6, pp. 101–11 (the fullest account); William of Tyre, XII, 9–10, pp. 523–6; Fulcher of Chartres, III, iii, 2–4, pp. 621–3 (a short account in which he attributed the disaster to God's displeasure at Roger's adulterous habits); Matthew of Edessa, ccxxvi, pp. 276–7; Michael the Syrian, III, p. 204; Ibn al-Qalanisi, pp. 159–61; Kemal ad-Din, pp. 616–18; Usama, ed. Hitti, pp. 148–9; Ibn al-Athir, pp. 324–5. Fulcher gives the Frankish losses as seven thousand and the Turkish as twenty.

across the plain behind their victors. While Ilghazi parleyed with Reynald, they were tortured and massacred amongst the vineyards by the Turcomans, till Ilghazi put a stop to it, not wishing the populace of Aleppo to miss all the sport. The remainder were taken on to Aleppo, where Ilghazi made his triumphant entry at sundown; and there they were tortured to death in the streets.[1]

While Ilghazi feasted at Aleppo in celebration of his victory, the terrible news of the battle reached Antioch. All expected that the Turcomans would come up at once to attack the city; and there were no soldiers to defend it. In the crisis the Patriarch Bernard took command. His first fear was of treason from the native Christians, whom his own actions had done so much to alienate. He at once sent round to disarm them and impose a curfew on them. Then he distributed the arms that he could collect among the Frankish clergy and merchants and set them to watch the walls. Day and night they kept vigil, while a messenger was sent to urge King Baldwin to hurry faster.[2]

But Ilghazi did not follow up his victory. He wrote round to the monarchs of the Moslem world to tell them of his triumph; and the Caliph in return sent him a robe of honour and the title of Star of Religion.[3] Meanwhile he marched on Artah. The Bishop who was in command of one of the towers surrendered it in return for a safe-conduct to Antioch; but a certain Joseph, probably an Armenian, who was in charge of the citadel, where Roger's treasure was housed, persuaded Ilghazi that he himself sympathized with the Moslems, but his son was a hostage at Antioch. Ilghazi was impressed by the story, and left Artah in Joseph's hands, merely sending one of his emirs to reside as his representative in the town.[4] From Artesia he returned to Aleppo, where he settled down to so pleasant a series of festivities that his health began to suffer. Turcoman troops were sent to raid the suburbs of Antioch and sack the port of Saint Symeon, but

---

[1] Kemal ad-Din, *loc. cit.*; Walter the Chancellor, II, 7, pp. 111–13.
[2] Walter the Chancellor, II, 8, pp. 114–15. [3] Ibn al-Athir, p. 332.
[4] Walter the Chancellor, II, 8, p. 114.

reported that the city itself was well garrisoned. The fruits of the Field of Blood were thus thrown away by the Moslems.[1]

Nevertheless the position was serious for the Franks. Baldwin had reached Lattakieh, with Pons close behind him, before he heard the news. He hurried on, not stopping even to attack an undefended Turcoman encampment near to the road, and arrived without incident at Antioch in the first days of August. Ilghazi sent some of his troops to intercept the relieving army; and Pons, following a day's march behind, had to ward off their attack but was not much delayed. The King was received with joy by his sister, the widowed Princess Cecilia, by the Patriarch and by all the people; and a service giving thanks to God was held in St Peter's Cathedral. He first cleared the suburbs of marauders, then met the notables of the city to discuss its future government. The lawful prince, Bohemond II, whose ultimate rights Roger had always acknowledged, was a boy of ten, living with his mother in Italy. There was no representative of the Norman house left in the East; and the Norman knights had all perished on the Field of Blood. It was decided that Baldwin, as overlord of the Frankish East, should himself take over the government of Antioch till Bohemond came of age, and that Bohemond should then be married to one of the King's daughters. Next, Baldwin redistributed the fiefs of the principality, left empty by the disaster. Wherever it was possible, the widows of the fallen lords were married off at once to suitable knights in Baldwin's army or to newcomers from the West. We find the two Dowager Princesses, Tancred's widow, now Countess of Tripoli, and Roger's widow, installing new vassals on their dower-lands. At the same time Baldwin probably rearranged the fiefs of the county of Edessa; and Joscelin, who followed the King up from Palestine, was formally established as its Count. Having assured the administration of the land, and having headed a barefoot procession to the cathedral, Baldwin led his army of about seven

---

[1] Usama, ed. Hitti, pp. 148–9; Ibn al-Athir, pp. 332–3. According to Usama, if Ilghazi drank wine he felt drunk for twenty days.

hundred horsemen and some thousand infantrymen out against the Moslems.[1]

Ilghazi had now been joined by Toghtekin; and the two Moslem chieftains set out on 11 August to capture the Frankish fortresses east of the Orontes, beginning with Athareb, whose small garrison at once surrendered in return for a safe-conduct to Antioch. The emirs next day went on to Zerdana, whose lord, Robert the Leper, had gone to Antioch. Here again the garrison surrendered in return for their lives; but they were massacred by the Turcomans as soon as they emerged from the gates. Baldwin had hoped to save Athareb; but he had hardly crossed the Iron Bridge before he met its former garrison. He went on south, and heard of the siege of Zerdana. Suspecting that the Moslems intended to move southward to mop up the castles round Maarat an-Numan and Apamea, he hurried ahead and encamped on the 13th at Tel-Danith, the scene of Roger's victory in 1115. Early next morning he learnt that Zerdana had fallen and judged it prudent to retire a little towards Antioch. Meanwhile Ilghazi had come up, hoping to surprise the Franks as they slept by the village of Hab. But Baldwin was ready. He had already confessed himself; the Archbishop of Caesarea had harangued the troops and held up the True Cross to bless them; and the army was ready for action.

The battle that followed was confused. Both sides claimed a victory; but in fact the Franks came off the best. Toghtekin drove back Pons of Tripoli, on the Frankish right wing; but the Tripolitans kept their ranks. Next to him Robert the Leper charged through the regiment from Homs and eagerly planned to recapture Zerdana, only to fall into an ambush and be taken captive. But the Frankish centre and left held their ground, and at the crucial moment Baldwin was able to charge the enemy with

[1] Walter the Chancellor, II, 9–10, pp. 115–18; Fulcher of Chartres, III, vii, 1–3, pp. 633–5; Orderic Vitalis (XI, 25, vol. IV, p. 245) tells of Cecilia, Countess of Tripoli, enfeoffing knights. Roger's widow enfeoffed knights in 1126 (Röhricht, *Regesta, Additamenta*, p. 9). It was probably at this time that Marash was transferred from the suzerainty of Antioch to that of Edessa.

troops that were still fresh. Numbers of the Turcomans turned and fled; but the bulk of Ilghazi's army left the battlefield in good order. Ilghazi and Toghtekin retired towards Aleppo with a large train of prisoners, and were able to tell the Moslem world that theirs was the victory. Once again the citizens of Aleppo were gratified by the sight of a wholesale massacre of Christians, till Ilghazi, after interrupting the killing to try out a new horse, grew disquieted at the loss of so much potential ransom-money. Robert the Leper was asked his price and replied that it was ten thousand pieces of gold. Ilghazi hoped to raise the price by sending Robert to Toghtekin. But Toghtekin had not yet satisfied his blood-lust. Though Robert was an old friend of his from the days of 1115, he himself struck off his head, to the dismay of Ilghazi, who needed money for his soldiers' pay.[1]

At Antioch soldiers fleeing from Pons's army had brought news of a defeat; but soon a messenger arrived for the Princess Cecilia bearing the King's ring as token of his success. Baldwin himself did not attempt to pursue the Moslem army but moved on south to Maarat an-Numan and to Rusa, which the Munqidhites of Shaizar had occupied. He drove them out but then made a treaty with them, releasing them from the obligation to pay yearly dues that Roger had demanded. The remaining forts that the Moslems had captured, with the exception of Birejik, Athareb and Zerdana, were also recovered. Then Baldwin returned to Antioch in triumph, and sent the Holy Cross southward to arrive at Jerusalem in time for the Feast of the Exaltation, on 14 September. He himself spent the autumn in Antioch, completing the arrangements that he had begun before the recent battle. In December he journeyed back to Jerusalem, leaving the Patriarch Bernard to administer Antioch in his name, and installing Joscelin in Edessa.[2] He brought south with him from Edessa his wife and their little

---

[1] Walter the Chancellor, II, 10–15, pp. 118–28; William of Tyre, XII, 11–12, pp. 527–30; Kemal ad-Din, pp. 620–2; Usama, ed. Hitti, pp. 149–50.
[2] Walter the Chancellor, II, 16, pp. 129–31; William of Tyre, XII, 12, p. 530.

daughters; and at the Christmas ceremony at Bethlehem Morphia was crowned queen.[1]

Ilghazi had not ventured to attack the Franks again. His army was melting away. The Turcoman troops had come mainly for the sake of plunder. After the battle of Tel-Danith they were left idle and bored and their pay was in arrears. They began to go home, and with them the Arab chieftains of the Jezireh. Ilghazi could not prevent them; for he himself had fallen ill once more and for a fortnight he hung between life and death. When he recovered it was too late to reassemble his army. He returned from Aleppo to his eastern capital at Mardin, and Toghtekin returned to Damascus.[2]

Thus the great Ortoqid campaign fizzled out. It had achieved nothing material for the Moslems, except for a few frontier-forts and the easing of Frankish pressure on Aleppo. But it had been a great moral triumph for Islam. The check at Tel-Danith had not counterbalanced the tremendous victory of the Field of Blood. Had Ilghazi been abler and more alert, Antioch might have been his. As it was, the slaughter of the Norman chivalry, their Prince at their head, encouraged the emirs of the Jezireh and northern Mesopotamia to renew the attack, now that they were free from the tutelage of their nominal Seldjuk overlord in Persia. And soon a greater man than Ilghazi was to arise. For the Franks the worst result of the campaign had been the appalling loss of man-power. The knights and, still more, the infantrymen fallen on the Field of Blood could not easily be replaced. But the lesson had now been thoroughly learnt that the Franks of the East must always co-operate and work as a unit. King Baldwin's prompt intervention had saved Antioch; and the needs of the time were recognized by the readiness of all the Franks to accept him as an active overlord. The disaster welded together the Frankish establishments in Syria.

[1] Fulcher of Chartres, III, vii, 4, p. 635; William of Tyre, XII, 12, p. 531.
[2] Walter the Chancellor, *loc. cit.*; Ibn al-Qalanisi, p. 161; Kemal ad-Din, pp. 624-5.

King Baldwin II

On his return to Jerusalem Baldwin busied himself over the administration of his own kingdom. The succession to the princi-pality of Galilee was given to William of Bures, in whose family it remained. In January 1120 the King summoned the ecclesiastics and tenants-in-chief of the kingdom to a council at Nablus to discuss the moral welfare of his subjects, probably in an attempt to curb the tendency of the Latin colonists in the East to adopt the easy and indolent habits that they found there. At the same time he was concerned with their material welfare. Under Baldwin I an increasing number of Latins had been encouraged to settle in Jerusalem, and a Latin bourgeois class was growing up there by the side of the warriors and clerics of the kingdom. These Latin bourgeois were now given complete freedom of trade to and from the city, while, to ensure a full supply of food, the native Christians and even Arab merchants were allowed to bring vegetables and corn to the city free of customs-dues.[1]

The most important internal event of these years was the founda-tion of the Military Orders. In the year 1070 some pious citizens of Amalfi had founded a hostel at Jerusalem for the use of poor pilgrims. The Egyptian governor then in possession of the city had allowed the Amalfitan consul to choose a suitable site; and the establishment was dedicated to Saint John the Almsgiver, the charitable seventh-century Patriarch of Alexandria. The hostel was staffed mainly by Amalfitans, who took the usual monastic vows and were under the direction of a Master, who in his turn was under the Benedictine authorities established in Palestine. At the time of the Crusaders' capture of Jerusalem the Master was a certain Gerard, probably an Amalfitan. With his co-religionists he had been banished from Jerusalem by the Moslem governor before the siege began; and his knowledge of local conditions had been of value to the Crusaders. He persuaded the new Frankish government to make endowments to the Hospital. Many of the pilgrims joined his staff, which was soon released from its obedience

[1] Röhricht, *Regesta*, p. 20; Mansi, *Concilia*, vol. xxi, pp. 262–6; William of Tyre, xii, xiii, p. 531.

156

to the Benedictines and raised to be an Order of its own, under the name of the Hospitallers, owing direct obedience to the Pope. More lands were conferred on it and most of the great ecclesiastics of the realm offered it a tithe from their revenues. Gerard died in about 1118. His successor, the Frenchman Raymond of Le Puy, had larger ideas. He decided that it was not enough for his Order to guide and entertain pilgrims; it must be ready to fight to keep the pilgrim-routes open. The Order still contained brothers whose duties were purely pacific; but its main function was now to keep up an establishment of knights bound by the religious vows of personal poverty, chastity and obedience, and dedicated to fight against the heathen. About the same time, as though to mark the greater status of the Hospital, John the Almsgiver was imperceptibly replaced as its patron saint by John the Evangelist. The distinctive badge of the Knights Hospitaller was the white cross that they wore on their tunics over their armour.

This transformation was helped by the simultaneous establishment of the Knights Templar. Indeed, the idea of an Order that should be both religious and military probably sprang from the brain of a knight from Champagne, Hugh of Payens, who in 1118 persuaded King Baldwin I to allow him to instal himself and a few companions in a wing of the royal palace, the former mosque al-Aqsa, in the Temple area. Like the Hospitallers the Templars first followed the Benedictine rule but were almost at once established as an independent Order, with three classes, the knights, all of noble birth, the sergeants, drawn from the bourgeoisie, who were the grooms and stewards of the community, and the clerics, who were chaplains and in charge of non-military tasks. Their badge was the red cross, worn on a white tunic by the knights and on a black by the sergeants. The first avowed duty of the Order was to keep the road from the coast to Jerusalem free from bandits, but soon they took part in any campaign in which the kingdom was involved. Hugh himself spent much of his time in western Europe, gaining recruits for his Order.

King Baldwin gave the military Orders his full support. They were independent of his authority, owing allegiance only to the Pope. Even the great estates with which he and his vassals began to endow them involved no obligation to fight in the King's army; but a generation passed before they were rich enough to challenge the royal authority. In the meantime they provided the kingdom with what it most needed, a regular army of trained soldiers, whose permanent presence was assured. In the lay fiefs the sudden death of the lord and the passing of the inheritance to a woman or a child might interrupt the organization of his troops and perpetually involve the suzerain in anxious and tiresome business. Nor could he count on replacing the lords that he lost by newcomers from the West whenever he needed them. But the Military Orders, with their efficient organization and with their glamour and prestige spreading through western Christendom, could ensure a regular supply of devoted fighting-men who would not be distracted by thoughts of personal ambition and gain.[1]

In 1120 Baldwin returned to Antioch. Ilghazi's governor of Athareb, Bulaq, had begun to raid Antiochene territory, while Ilghazi himself had marched on Edessa. Both raids were checked; but Ilghazi passed on to the neighbourhood of Antioch. The Patriarch Bernard sent nervously to Jerusalem, to the King; and in June Baldwin started northward, bearing with him once more the True Cross, to the distress of the Church of Jerusalem, which disliked to see its precious relic exposed to the risk of war. The Patriarch Gormond himself accompanied the army, to take charge of the relic. When Baldwin arrived in the north he found that Ilghazi, weakened by desertions from his Turcoman troops, had already retired; and so alarmed were the Moslems that Toghtekin was summoned to Aleppo. During the campaign that followed each side marched to and fro, till at last the Moslems were

---

[1] For the Military Orders, see William of Tyre, xii, 7, pp. 520–1 (the Templars); xviii, 4, pp. 822–3 (the Hospitallers). For good modern accounts see Delaville Le Roulx, *Les Hospitaliers en Terre Sainte*; Curzon, *La Règle du Temple*; Melville, *La Vie des Templiers*. A full account of the Templars (called the 'Frankish Phrer') is given by Michael the Syrian, iii, pp. 201–3. See also La Monte, *Feudal Monarchy*, pp. 217–25.

wearied. Toghtekin retired to Damascus; and Ilghazi made a truce with Baldwin. A definite frontier-line was drawn between their zones of influence, in one place cutting a mill and in another a castle in half so that by mutual consent the buildings were destroyed. Zerdana, which remained a Moslem enclave, was dismantled.[1] Early next spring Baldwin returned home, having won a bloodless moral victory. He was needed in the south, as Toghtekin, believing him fully occupied in the north, had carried out an extensive raid into Galilee. In July 1121 Baldwin, in reprisal, crossed the Jordan and ravaged the Jaulan, occupying and destroying a fort that Toghtekin had built at Jerash.[2] Meanwhile Joscelin made a profitable razzia in Ilghazi's lands in the Jezireh.[3]

During the summer of 1121 a new factor made itself felt in eastern politics. Away to the north, in the Caucasian foothills, the Bagratid Kings of Georgia had established their hegemony over the Christian peoples there that still remained independent of Moslem domination; and King David II had extended his rule to the south of the Araxes valley, where he came into conflict with the Seldjuk prince, Toghrul, governor of Arran. After a defeat by David's forces Toghrul invited Ilghazi to join him in a Holy War against the impudent Christian. The campaign that followed was disastrous for the Moslems. In August 1121 the united army of Toghrul and Ilghazi was almost annihilated by the Georgians; and Ilghazi barely escaped with his life as he fled back to Mardin. King David was able to establish himself in the old Georgian capital of Tiflis, and by 1124 he had acquired northern Armenia and the metropolis of Ani, the ancient home of his house. Henceforward the whole Turkish world was desperately conscious of the danger that Georgia, with its superb strategic position, presented to them; nor

---

[1] Fulcher of Chartres, III, ix, 1–7, pp. 638–42; Walter the Chancellor, II, 16, p. 131; Matthew of Edessa, ccxxx, pp. 302–3; Michael the Syrian, III, pp. 205–6; Kemal ad-Din, p. 627; Ibn al-Qalanisi, p. 162; Grousset, *op. cit.* I, p. 574, following Michael the Syrian, confuses Bulaq with Ilghazi's nephew Balak, who was now campaigning farther north (Ibn al-Qalanisi, *loc. cit.*).

[2] Fulcher of Chartres, III, x, 1–6, pp. 643–5.

[3] Ibn al-Qalanisi, *op. cit.* p. 163; Kemal ad-Din, pp. 623–6.

was the danger lessened by David II's death in 1125.[1] His successors inherited his vigour. Their prowess, by keeping the Moslems perpetually nervous of their northern flank, was of great value to the Franks, though there seems to have been no direct contact between the two Christian powers. The Georgians, bound by links of religion and tradition to Byzantium, had no liking for the Franks; and the chilly treatment accorded to their religious establishments at Jerusalem was not such as would please a proud people.[2]

Nevertheless, Ilghazi's fate at their hands gave Baldwin an opportunity that he did not miss. Ilghazi's son, Suleiman, recently appointed governor of Aleppo by his father, rashly profited by his father's defeat to declare his independence, and, finding himself unable to meet the attack that Baldwin at once launched against him, he made peace with the Franks, ceding to them Zerdana and Athareb, the fruits of Ilghazi's victory. Ilghazi hastened to punish his disloyal son, but judged it prudent to confirm the treaty with Baldwin; who returned to Jerusalem, well pleased with the year's achievements.[3]

Early in 1122 Pons, Count of Tripoli, suddenly refused to pay allegiance to the King. The reason for his insubordination is unknown. It is difficult to see what support he hoped to find that would enable him to maintain it. Baldwin was furious and at once summoned his vassals to come and punish the rebel. The royal army marched up from Acre; and on its approach Pons submitted and was forgiven.[4] His submission was timely; for

---

[1] *Georgian Chronicle* (in Georgian), pp. 209–10, 215; Matthew of Edessa, ccxxxi–ii, ccxxxix, ccxliii, pp. 303–5, 310–11, 313–14; Ibn al-Qalanisi, p. 164; Ibn al-Athir, pp. 330–2; Kemal ad-Din, pp. 628–9; Walter the Chancellor, ii, 16, p. 130 (who gives the credit of the Georgian victory to Frankish mercenaries); Michael the Syrian, iii, p. 206.

[2] For the Georgian establishments in Jerusalem, see *Georgian Chronicle*, pp. 222–3 and Brosset, *Additions et Eclaircissements*, x, pp. 197–205. A brief notice is given in Rey, *Les Colonies Franques*, pp. 93–4. It is possible that the Georgians, by continually threatening the Ortoqids and the Seldjuks of Persarmenia, indirectly helped the growth of Zengi's power.

[3] Kemal ad-Din, p. 629; Ibn al-Athir, pp. 349–50.

[4] Fulcher of Chartres, iii, xi, pp. 647–8; William of Tyre, xii, 17, pp. 536–7.

Ilghazi, urged on by his nephew Balak, formerly prince of Saruj and now lord of Khanzit, was on the warpath once more. Baldwin, when the news was brought to him, refused to believe it. He had made a treaty with Ilghazi, and he believed that a gentleman—the Arab chronicler uses the word 'sheikh'—kept his word. But Ilghazi was no gentleman; and he had the promise of Toghtekin's help. He laid siege to Zerdana, which the Franks had rebuilt, and had captured part of the fortifications when Baldwin approached. There followed another campaign without a battle, as Baldwin refused to be lured by the habitual Turkish stratagem of a feigned flight. Once again the Moslems were the first to weary of the marching to and fro and returned to their homes. Baldwin contentedly sent the Cross back to Jerusalem and himself went to Antioch.[1]

Before the Cross had reached its destination, bad news came from Edessa. On 13 September 1122, Count Joscelin and Waleran of Birejik were riding with a small force of horsemen near Saruj when they suddenly came across Balak's army. They charged the enemy; but a heavy shower of rain turned the plain into mud. The horses slid and stumbled; and the light-armed Turcomans had no difficulty in surrounding the Franks. Joscelin, Waleran and sixty of their comrades were captured. Balak at once offered them their liberty in return for the cession of Edessa. On Joscelin's refusal to listen to such terms, the prisoners were taken by Balak to his castle of Kharpurt.[2]

Joscelin's capture did not much affect the man-power of the Crusading states. We find the knights of Edessa successfully raiding Moslem territory during the following month. But it was a blow to Frankish prestige; and it forced Baldwin to add to his

[1] Fulcher of Chartres, III, xi, 3–7, pp. 648–51; Kemal ad-Din, pp. 632–3; Ibn al-Qalanisi, p. 166.

[2] Fulcher of Chartres, III, xii, 1, pp. 651–2; Matthew of Edessa, ccxxxiv, pp. 306–7; Kemal ad-Din, p. 634; *Anon. Chron. Syr.* p. 90, says that Joscelin was bringing home his new wife, Roger's sister. But there is no mention of her capture and, as Roger endowed his sister, the marriage must have taken place before Roger's death.

labours by taking over once more the administration of Edessa. Fortunately, in November, Ilghazi died at Mayyafaraqin, and his sons and nephews divided up the Ortoqid inheritance. His elder son Suleiman took Mayyafaraqin and the younger, Timurtash, Mardin. Aleppo went to a nephew, Badr ad-Daulah Suleiman; and Balak increased his possessions in the north and took Harran to the south.[1]

The Moslems had recently reoccupied Athareb; and in April next year Baldwin took advantage of the present confusion to force the feeble new ruler of Aleppo to give it back once and for all. After recapturing Birejik, the King then proceeded to Edessa to make arrangements for its government. He placed Geoffrey the Monk, lord of Marash, at the head of its administration, and went on with a small force north-eastward, to reconnoitre the scene of Joscelin's captivity. He encamped on 18 April not far from Gargar on the Euphrates. As he prepared to enjoy a morning's sport with his falcon, Balak, of whose proximity he knew nothing, fell upon the camp. Most of the army was massacred, and the King himself was taken prisoner. He was treated with respect and sent under escort to join Joscelin in the fortress of Kharpurt.[2]

Once again Baldwin and Joscelin found themselves together in captivity. But it was more serious than in 1104, for Baldwin now was king, the centrepiece of the whole Frankish fabric. It was a testimony to his administrative ability that the structure remained standing. Geoffrey the Monk continued to govern in Edessa. At Antioch when the news came there the Patriarch Bernard once more made himself the responsible authority. At Jerusalem it was first rumoured that the King was killed. The Patriarch Gormond summoned the council of the kingdom to

[1] Ibn al-Qalanisi, p. 166; Ibn Hamdun, p. 516; Kemal ad-Din, pp. 632–4; Matthew of Edessa, *loc. cit.* (an ignorant account of the Ortoqid succession).
[2] Fulcher of Chartres, III, xvi, 1, pp. 658–9; William of Tyre, XII, 11, p. 537; Orderic Vitalis, XI, 26, vol. IV, p. 247; Matthew of Edessa, CCXXV, pp. 307–8; Ibn al-Qalanisi, p. 167; Ibn al-Athir, p. 352.

meet at Acre. By the time that it assembled the truth about his captivity was known. The council elected Eustace Garnier, lord of Caesarea and Sidon, to act as constable and bailiff of the kingdom till the King should be delivered. In all three territories administrative life went on undisturbed.[1]

The emir Balak had acquired a vast prestige; but he used it, not to deliver a death-blow against the Franks, but to establish himself in Aleppo. It was a harder task than he expected, for he was unpopular there. By June he was its master; and he then attacked the Frankish possession farther south, capturing Albara in August, only to be summoned north again by extraordinary news from Kharpurt.[2]

Joscelin had always been well-liked by the Armenians. Soon after his arrival in the East he had, like Baldwin I and Baldwin II, married an Armenian wife, the sister of the Roupenian Thoros, and she, unlike the two Queens of Jerusalem, was not born Orthodox but of the Separated Armenian Church and therefore in greater sympathy with most of her compatriots. She was dead now, and Joscelin had remarried; but his intimacy with the Armenians had continued and he had never shown against them the severity shown by his predecessor Baldwin II. The castle of Kharpurt lay in Armenian country; and a local peasant agreed to take a message to Joscelin's Armenian friends. Fifty of them came in various disguises to Kharpurt and were allowed entry as being monks and merchants of the district with a grievance that they asked to lay before the governor. Once inside the fortress they produced arms from beneath their garments and overpowered the garrison. Baldwin and Joscelin suddenly found themselves the masters of their prison. After a brief conference it was decided that Joscelin should leave the fortress before the Ortoqid army came up and should seek help, while Baldwin should try to hold

---

[1] Fulcher of Chartres, III, xvi, 1–3, pp. 659–61; William of Tyre, XII, 17, p. 538.

[2] Kemal ad-Din, pp. 636–7; Ibn al-Qalanisi, pp. 167–8. For various accounts of Balak's capture of Aleppo, see Cahen, *op. cit.* p. 296 n. 35.

the fortress. Joscelin slipped out with three Armenian comrades. When he had managed to pass between the gathering Turkish forces, he sent one of his men back to reassure the King. He himself went on through the dangerous enemy country, hiding by day and tramping wearily by night. At last the fugitives reached the Euphrates. Joscelin could not swim; but he had two wine-skins in which he had carried water. Blowing them up with his breath he used them as floats; and his two companions, both strong swimmers, were able to push him across through the darkness. Next day they were found by a peasant, who recognized the Count and welcomed him with joy; for Joscelin had given him alms in the past. With the help of the peasant and his family Joscelin travelled on cautiously to Turbessel, where he revealed himself to his wife and the court. He would not stay there but hurried to Antioch to raise troops to rescue the King. But the army of Antioch was small and the Patriarch Bernard was nervous. At his suggestion Joscelin rode at full speed to Jerusalem. His first act was to offer his chains at the altar of Calvary. Then he summoned the council of the kingdom and told his story. With the eager help of the Patriarch Gormond and of the Constable Eustace, troops were collected and, with the True Cross at their head, set out under his leadership by forced marches to Turbessel. But when they arrived there they heard that it was too late.

When the news of the revolution at Kharpurt reached Balak he at once brought his army up from the south at a speed that astounded contemporaries. On his arrival he offered Baldwin a safe-conduct to his home if he would surrender the castle. Baldwin refused, either distrusting the emir or not wishing to abandon his comrades. But the castle was less impregnable than he had thought. Balak's engineers soon undermined a wall, and the Ortoqid army broke in. Balak now showed no mercy. His harem had been in the castle and its sanctity had been violated. Every defender of the castle, Frank or Armenian, and every woman who had aided them—there were, probably, Armenian slaves in the harem—was hurled over the battlements to death.

Only the King, a nephew of his and Waleran were spared. They were moved for greater safety to the castle of Harran.[1]

Joscelin could not risk the hazards of a campaign against Harran. After utilizing his army for a successful raid in the neighbourhood of Aleppo he dismissed it and returned to Tur-bessel. But Balak was equally unable to profit by the situation. His lieutenant in Aleppo could only answer the Franks by converting the churches of Aleppo into mosques, thereby outraging the local Christians and in no way harming the Latins. Balak himself came to Aleppo to organize a fresh campaign. But, early in 1124, the governor of Menbij revolted against his authority. He was arrested by the Ortoqid Timurtash, whom Balak asked to crush the rebellion; but the rebel's brother Isa held the citadel and appealed to Joscelin for help. Balak met Joscelin's army and defeated it, slaying Geoffrey the Monk. He went on to Menbij, eager to restore order there as he had just received an urgent summons from the south, from Tyre. But a stray arrow from the citadel ended his life, on 6 May. He died murmuring that his death was a mortal blow for Islam. He was right; for of all the Turkish leaders that the Crusaders had encountered he had shown the greatest energy and wisdom. The power of the Ortoqids did not long survive him.[2]

In the kingdom of Jerusalem itself Baldwin's absence in captivity

[1] Fulcher of Chartres, III, xxiii–xxvi, 6, pp. 676–93; Orderic Vitalis, XI, 26, vol. IV, pp. 248–10. He says that the Armenian-born Queen Morphia helped to recruit compatriots for the King's rescue. He adds that captives were sent to Persia but later released. William of Tyre, XII, 18–20, pp. 538–41; Matthew of Edessa, ccxxxvi, pp. 308–10; Ibn al-Qalanisi, p. 169 (unfortunately with a lacuna in the text); Kemal ad-Din, p. 637; Michael the Syrian, III, p. 211. Baldwin's nephew was probably a brother of Manasses of Hierges, son of his sister Hodierna (see below, p. 233). We are told by Michael, who calls him Bar Noul (Arnulf?), that he was the son of a sister. Baldwin's other sister Mahalda, Lady of Vitry, seems to have had only one son, who married an heiress-cousin and succeeded to Rethel. William of Tyre, XII, 1, pp. 511–12.

[2] Fulcher of Chartres, III, xxxi, 1–10, pp. 721–7; Orderic Vitalis, XI, 26, vol. IV, p. 260; William of Tyre, XIII, 11, pp. 570–1; Matthew of Edessa, ccxl, pp. 311–12; Kemal ad-Din, pp. 641–2; Usama, ed. Hitti, pp. 63, 76, 130; Ibn al-Qalanisi, pp. 168–9 (but does not mention Balak's death).

had had no harmful effect. It had tempted the Egyptians once more to invade the country. In May 1123 a large Egyptian army moved out from Ascalon towards Jaffa. Eustace Garnier at once led the army of Jerusalem to oppose it. With him went the True Cross; while the Christian civilians of Jerusalem made barefoot processions to the churches. These pious precautions were barely needed; for when the Franks came up with the Egyptians at Ibelin, on 29 May, the enemy, despite his vast numerical superiority, turned and fled, leaving his camp to be plundered by the Christians.[1] It was Eustace's last achievement. On 15 May he died. Following the custom of the kingdom, his widow, the Patriarch Arnulf's rich niece Emma, promptly took a new husband, Hugh of Le Puiset, Count of Jaffa, in order that her lands should not lack an effective tenant. The office of Constable of the Kingdom was given by the council to William of Bures, Prince of Galilee.[2]

In 1119, just after the Field of Blood, King Baldwin had written to the Republic of Venice to plead for its help. The Egyptians might not be formidable on land, but their fleet still dominated Palestinian waters. In return he offered Venice commercial advantages. The Pope supported his appeal; and the Doge, Domenico Michiel, decided to answer it. Nearly three years passed before the Venetian expedition was ready. On 8 August 1122, a fleet of well over a hundred great men-of-war set sail from Venice, carrying a number of men and horses and siege-material. But it did not sail direct for Palestine. Venice had recently quarrelled with Byzantium, over an attempt of the Emperor John Comnenus to reduce its trading privileges. So the Venetians paused to attack the Byzantine island of Corfu. For some six months, throughout the winter of 1122-3, the Doge laid

---

[1] Fulcher of Chartres, III, xvi, 3-xix, 1, pp. 661-8; William of Tyre, XII, 1, pp. 543-5.
[2] Fulcher of Chartres, III, xxii, pp. 674-5; William of Tyre, *loc. cit.* For Hugh of Le Puiset, see below, p. 191. He had married Emma before April 1124 (Röhricht, *Regesta*, p. 25).

siege, ineffectively, to the city of Corfu. At the end of April a ship sailing swiftly from Palestine told the Venetians of the disaster to the King. Reluctantly the Doge lifted the siege and took his armada eastward, merely stopping to attack whatever Byzantine ships he met. He arrived at Acre at the end of May and heard that the Egyptian fleet was cruising off Ascalon. He sailed down to meet it and, to lure it to battle, sent his lighter-armed ships ahead. The Egyptians fell into the trap. Thinking to have an easy victory they sailed out only to find themselves caught between two Venetian squadrons and outnumbered. Scarcely an Egyptian ship escaped from disaster. Some were sunk, others captured; and the Venetians added to their triumph when, sailing back to Acre, they met and captured a merchant-fleet of ten richly laden vessels.[1]

The presence of the Venetians was too valuable to be wasted. There was a debate whether their fleet should be used to capture Ascalon or Tyre, the two remaining Moslem strongholds on the coast. The nobles of Judea favoured the attack on Ascalon, those of Galilee that on Tyre. The Venetians finally decided upon Tyre. Its harbour was the best along the coast and it was now the port of the rich lands of Damascus; it was a far more important trading-centre than Ascalon, with its open roadstead and its poor hinterland. But they insisted on their price. Negotiations about the terms dragged on throughout the autumn. At Christmas 1123, the Venetian commanders were sumptuously entertained at Jerusalem and attended the services at Bethlehem. Early in the new year a treaty was signed at Acre between the representatives of the Republic on the one hand and the Patriarch Gormond, the Constable William and the Chancellor Pagan on the other, in the name of the captive King. The Venetians were to receive a street, with a church, baths and a bakery, free of all customary obligations, in every town of the kingdom. They were to be free to use their own weights and measures in all their transactions, not only amongst themselves. They were to be excused all tolls and

---

[1] Fulcher of Chartres, III, xx, 1–8, pp. 669–72; William of Tyre, XII, 23, pp. 546–7; *Historia Ducum Veneticorum, M.G.H. Ss.* vol. XIV, p. 73.

customs-duties throughout the kingdom. They were to receive additional houses in Acre and a third of the cities of Tyre and Ascalon, if they helped in their capture. In addition they were to be paid an annual sum of three hundred Saracen besants, chargeable on royal revenues at Acre. They agreed in return to continue the customary payment of a third of the fare charged for pilgrims to the royal treasury. The Venetians further demanded that the kingdom should not reduce the customs-dues charged on other nationals without Venetian consent. The Patriarch Gormond swore on the Gospel that King Baldwin would confirm the treaty when he was released. This was in fact done two years later, though Baldwin refused to accept the last clause, which would entirely have subordinated the commerce of the kingdom to Venetian interests.[1] When the treaty was signed the Frankish army moved up the coast to Tyre and the Venetian fleet sailed parallel to it. The siege of Tyre was begun on 15 February 1124.[2]

Tyre still belonged to the Fatimid Caliphate. In 1112 its citizens, shocked by the little support that they had received from Egypt during the siege of the city in 1111, had allowed Toghtekin to install a governor. He sent one of his ablest captains, the emir Mas'ud, to take over the city. At the same time the suzerainty of Egypt was recognized and prayers in the mosques were made for the Fatimid Caliph, who was periodically asked to send naval help to the city.[3] The dyarchy worked smoothly for ten years, largely because the vizier al-Afdal was anxious to keep on good terms with Toghtekin, whose friendship was needed against the Franks. But in December 1121 al-Afdal was murdered by an Assassin in the streets of Cairo. The Caliph al-Amir, who then at last became his own master, wished to recover control of Tyre. He sent a fleet to Tyre in 1122, as though to strengthen its defences. The admiral invited Mas'ud to inspect the ships and, when he came,

---

[1] Tafel and Thomas, I, pp. 84–9; Röhricht, *Regesta*, pp. 23–5; William of Tyre, XII, 4–5, pp. 547–53; Fulcher of Chartres, III, xxvii, 1–3, pp. 693–5.
[2] Fulcher of Chartres, III, xviii, 1, pp. 695–6.
[3] Ibn al-Qalanisi, pp. 128–30, 142.

kidnapped him and brought him to Cairo. He was well received there and sent with every mark of honour to Toghtekin, who agreed not to dispute the Fatimid restoration. But when the Franks approached the city, al-Amir, declaring that with his fleet destroyed he could do nothing to save it, formally handed over its defences to Toghtekin; who rushed up seven hundred Turkish troops and provisions against the siege.[1]

The city of Tyre was joined to the mainland only by the narrow isthmus that Alexander the Great had constructed; and its fortifications were in good order. But it had one weakness; the drinking water came through an aqueduct from the mainland, for there was no well on the peninsula. The day after their arrival the Franks cut this aqueduct. But winter rains had filled the city cisterns; it was some time before the shortage of water made itself felt. The Franks settled down in a camp in the gardens and orchards where the isthmus joined the mainland. The Venetians beached their vessels alongside of them, but always kept at least one galley at sea to intercept any vessel that might attempt to sail through to the harbour. The supreme commander of the army was the Patriarch Gormond, who was felt to possess greater authority than the Constable. When the Count of Tripoli came up with his army to join the besieging forces, he showed himself willing to obey the Patriarch in everything, a concession that he would not probably have made to William of Bures.[2]

The siege lasted on throughout the spring and early summer. The Franks kept up a steady bombardment of the walls across the isthmus from engines whose material had been brought up by the Venetians. The defenders on their side were well equipped with machines for hurling stones and Greek fire on their assailants. They fought magnificently; but they were not sufficiently numerous to attempt sorties. Fearing lest hunger and thirst and shortage of man-power might force them to capitulate, their

[1] *Ibid.* pp. 165–6, 170–1; Ibn al-Athir, pp. 356–8.
[2] Fulcher of Chartres, III, xxviii, 1–xxx, 13, pp. 695–720 (including a long digression on the history of Tyre); William of Tyre, XIII, 7, p. 565.

messengers slipped out of the city to urge Toghtekin and the Egyptians to hurry to their rescue. An Egyptian army attempted a diversion against Jerusalem itself and reached the outskirts of the Holy City. But its civilians, merchants, clerks and priests, hastened to man its tremendous walls; and the Egyptian commander did not venture to attack them. Soon afterwards a second Egyptain army sacked the little town of Belin, or La Mahomerie, a few miles to the north, and massacred its inhabitants. But such isolated raids would not save Tyre. Toghtekin was even less enterprising. When the siege began he moved with his army to Banyas, by the source of the Jordan, waiting for news of an Egyptian fleet with which he could concert his attack on the Frankish camp. But no Egyptian fleet sailed up the coast; the Caliph could not muster one. The Franks had feared this combination. The Venetian fleet lay for some weeks off the Ladder of Tyre to intercept the Egyptians; and the Patriarch detached Pons of Tripoli and William of Bures with a considerable army to go to meet Toghtekin. When they approached towards Banyas, Toghtekin decided not to risk a battle and retired to Damascus. The only hope of the besieged city now lay in Balak the Ortoqid, the renowned captor of the King. Balak planned to come to their aid; but in May he was killed at Menbij.

By the end of June the situation inside Tyre was desperate. Food and water were alike running out, and many of the garrison had fallen. Toghtekin was warned that it must surrender. He sent to the Frankish camp offering its capitulation on the usual terms; that those of the inhabitants that wished to leave the city should do so in peace with all their movable belongings and those that wished to remain should keep their rights as citizens. The Frankish and Venetian leaders accepted the offer, though the common soldiers and sailors were furious to hear that there would be no looting and threatened mutiny. On 7 July 1124 the gates were opened and the Christian army took over the city. The King's standard was hoisted over the main gate, and the Count of Tripoli's and the Doge's over towers on either side. The leaders kept their word. There was no looting; and a long procession of Moslems passed safely through the Crusader camp. The last Moslem town on the coast north of Ascalon thus passed to the Christians. Their army returned rejoicing to Jerusalem; and the Venetians sailed back to Venice, having extracted their pound of flesh.[1]

The good news reached King Baldwin at Shaizar. On Balak's death his custody had passed to Ilghazi's son Timurtash, who disliked the responsibility of it and preferred the idea of a rich ransom. He asked the emir of Shaizar to open negotiations with the Franks. Queen Morphia had journeyed to the north to be as near as possible to her husband; and she and Count Joscelin arranged terms with the emir. The price demanded was high. The King was to pay Timurtash eighty thousand dinars and was to cede to Aleppo, where Timurtash had succeeded to Balak's power, the towns of Athareb, Zerdana, Azaz, Kafartab and the Jasr; he must also help Timurtash in suppressing the Bedouin leader Dubais ibn Sadaqa, who had settled in the Jezireh. Twenty thousand dinars were to be paid in advance; and hostages were to be deposited at Shaizar for the payment of the remainder. As soon as they were handed over to the Moslems, Baldwin would be freed. For hostages Timurtash demanded the King's youngest child, the four-year old Princess Joveta, and the son and heir of Joscelin, a boy of eleven, and ten scions of the nobility. The emir Sultan of Shaizar, to show his good faith, sent various members of his family to Aleppo. At the end of June 1124 Baldwin left Harran, on his own charger, which had been restored to him by Timurtash, together with many costly gifts. He went to Shaizar, where the emir, who remembered him kindly for his remission of the money due from Shaizar to Antioch five years before, offered

---

[1] Fulcher of Chartres, III, xxxii, 1–xxxiv, 13, pp. 728–39, fixing the date of the capture (he unfairly blames the Antiochenes for not co-operating); William of Tyre, XIII, 13–14, pp. 573–6; Ibn al-Qalanisi, pp. 170–2, giving the date; Ibn al-Athir, pp. 358–9 (dating it 9 July); Abu'l Feda, pp. 15–16 (dating it 5 July); Matthew of Edessa, ccxliv, p. 314.

him lavish entertainment. He met there his daughter and her fellow-hostages. On their arrival he was allowed to proceed to Antioch, which he reached in the last days of August.[1]

Now that he was free Baldwin did not honour the terms that he had accepted. The Patriarch Bernard pointed out to him that he was only the overlord and regent of Antioch; he had no right to give away its territory, which belonged to the youthful Bohemond II. Baldwin was willingly convinced by the argument and sent to tell Timurtash very apologetically that most unfortunately he could not disobey the Patriarch. Timurtash, who was more concerned to receive money than territory, forgave the offence for fear of losing the remainder of the ransom. Discovering Timurtash to be so compliant, Baldwin next dishonoured the clause by which he had promised to aid him against the Bedouin emir Dubais. Instead, he received an embassy from Dubais to plan common action against Aleppo. An alliance was made; and in October the armies of Antioch and Edessa joined Dubais's Arabs before the walls of Aleppo. Their coalition was soon strengthened by the arrival in their camp of the Seldjuk claimant to the throne of Aleppo, Sultanshah, who had recently escaped from an Ortoqid prison, together with his cousin Toghrul Arslan, brother of the Sultan of Rum, who had recently been evicted from Melitene by the Danishmends and was searching for allies.

Timurtash made no attempt to defend Aleppo. His brother Suleiman of Mayyafaraqin was dying; and he wanted to make sure of the inheritance. He remained at Mardin, leaving the notables of the city to hold out as best they could. For three months they resisted, while their emissaries, ill-received by Timurtash, who had no wish to be further bothered about them, went on to Mosul and aroused the interest of its atabeg, Aqsonqor il-Bursuqi, who

[1] Usama, ed. Hitti, pp. 133, 150; Kemal ad-Din, pp. 643-4; Matthew of Edessa, ccxli, pp. 312-13 (mentioning that Joscelin and the Queen arranged the ransom and adding that Waleran and the King's nephew were put to death by Timurtash—this was possibly because the King broke the terms of his ransom). Michael the Syrian, III, pp. 212, 225. Joveta is variously called in charters, Yvette, Ivetta or Juditta.

had led the Sultan's armies against the Franks in 1114. Il-Bursuqi, who hated the Ortoqids, sent officers to take over the citadel of Aleppo, and himself, though ill, set out with an army and with the Sultan's blessing. When he approached Aleppo he ordered the emir of Homs, Khirkan, and Toghtekin of Damascus to join him; and both sent contingents. Before this display of force the Franco-Bedouin alliance broke up. Dubais moved with his tribe eastward, while Baldwin retired to the fortress of Athareb. At the end of January il-Bursuqi entered Aleppo, but made no attempt to pursue the Franks. Seeing this, the King returned to Antioch and went on to Jerusalem, where he arrived in April 1125, after two years' absence.[1]

He did not remain there for long; for il-Bursuqi was more formidable than the Ortoqids. Master of Mosul and Aleppo, and backed by the Sultan's authority, he was able to coalesce the Moslems of northern Syria under his rule. Toghtekin and the emir of Homs submitted to his hegemony. In March he visited Shaizar, whose emir Sultan, always anxious to be the friend of everyone of importance, handed over to him the Frankish hostages, the Princess Joveta and young Joscelin and their comrades. In May, at the head of a new Moslem alliance, he attacked and captured the Frankish fort of Kafartab and laid siege to Zerdana. Baldwin hastened northward and led the armies of Antioch, Tripoli and Edessa, eleven hundred horsemen and two thousand foot-soldiers, to save Zerdana. The Moslems moved on to Azaz; and there, at the end of May, took place one of the most bloodthirsty battles in the history of the Crusades. The Moslems, relying on their superior numbers, attempted a hand-to-hand contest; but the superior armour and physique of the Franks was too much for them, and they were decisively beaten. From the rich booty that he acquired, Baldwin was able to amass the eighty thousand dinars owing for the ransom of the hostages, each Frankish knight

[1] Fulcher of Chartres, III, xxxviii–xxxix, 9, 2, pp. 751–6; William of Tyre, XIII, 15, pp. 576–7; Ibn al-Qalanisi, pp. 172–3; Kemal ad-Din, pp. 643–50 Usama, ed. Hitti, p. 133; Matthew of Edessa, ccxlv, pp. 314–15.

giving up a portion of his share to rescue the King's daughter. Though the money was really due to Timurtash, il-Bursuqi accepted it and returned the hostages. Another sum, sent to Shaizar, redeemed prisoners and hostages that were still detained there. On their release, they were attacked by the emir of Homs; but the Munqidhites hurried to their rescue and sent them on their way.

After the battle a truce was made. The Moslems kept Kafartab, which was given to the emir of Homs, but no other territorial changes were made. After leaving a garrison in Aleppo, il-Bursuqi returned to Mosul. For eighteen months the north was left in peace.[1]

Baldwin went back to Palestine, where in the autumn of 1125, he conducted a raid on Damascene lands and a demonstration against Ascalon. In January 1126 he decided to lead a serious expedition against Damascus and invaded the Hauran. Toghtekin came out to meet him. The armies clashed at Tel es-Saqhab, some twenty miles south-west of Damascus. At first the Moslems had the better of the fight, and Toghtekin's Turcoman regiment penetrated to the royal camp; but in the end Baldwin won the victory. He pursued the enemy half-way to Damascus, but in view of his heavy losses he judged it prudent to abandon the campaign and retired, laden with booty, to Jerusalem.[2]

In March 1126 Pons of Tripoli attacked the Moslem fortress of Rafaniya, which dominated the entry to the Buqaia from the Orontes valley. It had long been a Christian objective since its recapture by Toghtekin in 1105. While its governor appealed for help to Toghtekin and to il-Bursuqi, Pons applied for King Baldwin's aid. The two Christian princes marched quickly on the fortress, long before the Moslems were ready to come to its

[1] Fulcher of Chartres, III, xlii, 1–xliv, 4, pp. 761–71; William of Tyre, XIII, 11, pp. 578–80; Sigebert of Gembloux, *M.G.H.Ss.* vol. VI, p. 380; Kemal ad-Din, p. 651; *Bustan*, p. 519; Usama, *loc. cit.*; Matthew of Edessa, ccxlvii, pp. 315–18; Michael the Syrian, III, p. 221.
[2] Fulcher of Chartres, III, xlvi, 1–7, l, 1–15, pp. 772–4, 784–93; William of Tyre, XIII, 17–18, pp. 581–5; Ibn al-Qalanisi, pp. 574–7.

rescue; and it surrendered to them after a siege of eighteen days. Its capture was valuable to the Franks; for it safeguarded not only the county of Tripoli itself but communications between Jerusalem and Antioch.[1]

Meanwhile the Egyptians had rebuilt their fleet. In the autumn of 1126 it set sail from Alexandria to ravage the Christian coast. Hearing of this il-Bursuqi planned a simultaneous attack in the north and laid siege to Athareb. Baldwin rightly decided that the latter was the greater danger and hurried to Antioch. In fact the Egyptians, after attempting a costly raid on the suburbs of Beirut, found the coastal cities so well garrisoned that they soon returned to the Nile.[2] In the north Baldwin, who was joined by Joscelin, obliged the Moslems to retire from Athareb. Neither side would risk a battle; and the truce was soon re-made. Il-Bursuqi, after installing his son Izz ed-Din Mas'ud as governor of Aleppo, went home to Mosul. On the very day of his arrival, 26 November, he was stabbed to death by an Assassin.[3]

Il-Bursuqi's death brought chaos to the Moslems, which worsened when his son Mas'ud, with whom Toghtekin had already quarrelled, died, probably of poison, a few months later. Aleppo passed to and fro between Mas'ud's nominee Tuman, a Mameluk sent by the Sultan called Kutluh, the Ortoqid Badr ad-Daulah Suleiman, and a son of Ridwan's, Ibrahim the Seldjuk.[4]

About the same time Baldwin gladly found himself relieved of the regency of Antioch. The young Bohemond II was now aged eighteen and came to take over his inheritance. Abandoning his lands in Italy to his cousin, Roger II of Sicily, he sailed from

[1] Fulcher of Chartres, III, li, 4, lii, 1, pp. 795–7, 798–9; William of Tyre, XIII, 19, pp. 585–6; Ibn al-Qalanisi, p. 180; Kemal ad-Din, p. 652.
[2] Fulcher of Chartres, III, lvi, 1–5, pp. 803–5; William of Tyre, XIII, 20, pp. 587–8.
[3] Fulcher of Chartres, III, lv, 5, pp. 802–3; Ibn al-Qalanisi, pp. 177–8; Kemal ad-Din, pp. 653–4.
[4] Ibn al-Qalanisi, pp. 181–2; Kemal ad-Din, p. 654; Michael the Syrian, III, p. 225.

Otranto in September 1126 with a squadron of twenty-four ships, carrying a number of troops and horses. He landed at Saint Symeon early in October, and came straight up to Antioch, where King Baldwin welcomed him with every mark of honour. He made an excellent impression. He had his father's magnificent appearance, being tall, fair-haired and handsome, and he showed an air of high breeding that came from his mother Constance, daughter of King Philip I of France. King Baldwin at once handed over the principality, with all its possessions, into his hands, with the utmost scrupulousness. The ambassador from Shaizar was deeply impressed to see that the King henceforward paid cash to the Prince for the corn consumed by the horses of the army of Jerusalem. With him the King had his second daughter, the Princess Alice; and, in conformity with the plan that had been made, the young couple were married. Bohemond began his reign brilliantly, with an attack on Kafartab, which he recovered from the emir of Homs; and soon afterwards we hear of his gallantry in skirmishes against the army of Shaizar.[1]

King Baldwin could at last return to the south feeling that the death of il-Bursuqi and the coming of Bohemond would leave him free to see to his own kingdom. He spent the year 1127 so peacefully that we know nothing of his movements, except for a short campaign east of the Dead Sea in August.[2] Early in 1128 his faithful friend, the Patriarch Gormond, died. His successor was another French priest, Stephen of La Ferté, abbot of Saint-Jean-en-Vallée at Chartres, a man of noble birth, related to King Baldwin. If Baldwin had hoped that the ties of cousinhood would make for cordial co-operation, he was soon disillusioned. The new

[1] Fulcher of Chartres, III, lvii, 1-4, lxi, 1-5, pp. 805-9, 819-22. (The intervening chapters tell of the perils of the Mediterranean Sea and the species of serpents to be found on its shores. After a further chapter on a plague of mice in 1127 Fulcher's narrative ends.) William of Tyre, XIII, 21, pp. 588-9; Orderic Vitalis, XI, 9, vol. IV, p. 266; Matthew of Edessa, ccl, p. 319 (saying that Baldwin promised Bohemond the succession to Jerusalem); Michael the Syrian, III, p. 224; Usama, ed. Hitti, p. 150.
[2] Ibn al-Qalanisi, p. 182.

Patriarch at once revived the question of the agreement that Godfrey had made with the Patriarch Daimbert. He claimed Jaffa as the autonomous possession of the Patriarchate; and he reminded the King that as soon as Ascalon should be conquered Jerusalem itself must be yielded up to him. Baldwin refused to listen to these demands but did not know how to deal with them. Relations between the royal Court and the Patriarchate worsened throughout 1129; but an open breach was avoided by Stephen's death after a short illness, early in 1130. His friends suspected poison. When the King came to visit the dying Patriarch, to ask how he was, the latter bitterly remarked: 'Sire, I am faring as you desire.' Indeed, his death was desirable. As his successor Baldwin secured the election of the Prior of the Holy Sepulchre, William of Messines, a man of great piety and goodness, though a little simple and ill-educated. He had no political ambitions and was glad to do whatever the King wished. In consequence he became universally beloved.[1]

Baldwin's next important task was to arrange for the succession to the throne. Queen Morphia had borne him no sons; but there were four daughters, Melisende, Alice, Hodierna and Joveta. Alice was now Princess of Antioch, Hodierna and Joveta still were children. Melisende was to be his successor in conjunction with a suitable husband. In 1128, after consulting his council, he sent William of Bures, together with the lord of Beirut, Guy Brisebarre, to France, to ask the King of France, Louis VI, to select from the French nobility a man suitable for this high position. Louis recommended the Count of Anjou, Fulk V. Fulk was aged about forty, the son of Fulk IV, Rechin, and of Bertrada of Montfort, notorious for her adultery with King Philip I of France. He was the head of a great house that during the last two centuries had built up one of the richest and most formidable appanages in France; and he himself, by war, marriage and intrigue, had considerably added to its extent. That very year he had achieved

---

[1] William of Tyre, XIII, 25–6, pp. 594–5, 598; William is sometimes called 'of Malines'. Messines is in western Flanders.

a family triumph in marrying his young son and heir, Geoffrey, to the Empress Matilda, the only surviving legitimate child of Henry I of England and heiress of England and Normandy. A widower now himself, he had decided to abandon the family lands to his son and to dedicate himself to the service of the Cross. He had already been to Jerusalem on a pilgrimage in 1120 and was therefore personally known to Baldwin. So notable a candidate, backed by the King of France and endorsed by the Pope, Honorius II, was readily accepted by King Baldwin, who had been anxious that his arrangements for the succession should be to the liking of the barons of his kingdom. It would be impossible for any of them to dispute the claims of a warrior-prince of such eminence, married to their King's eldest daughter.

Fulk left France in the early spring of 1129, accompanied by William of Bures and Guy Brisebarre. They landed at Acre in May and went on to Jerusalem. There, at the end of the month, Fulk and Melisende were married amid great festivities and rejoicing. The arrangement had the approval of the whole country, with perhaps one exception. The Princess Melisende herself was unmoved by the short, wiry, red-haired, middle-aged man whom political advantages had forced upon her.[1]

With Fulk to aid him Baldwin embarked in 1129 on the great project of his reign, the conquest of Damascus. Toghtekin of Damascus died on 12 February 1128. He had been for many years the complete master of the city and the most respected Moslem figure in western Syria.[2] Some years previously a leader of the

---

[1] William of Tyre, XIII, 24, p. 593, XIV, 2, p. 608; Halphen et Poupardin, *Chroniques des Comtes d'Anjou, Gesta Ambaziencium Dominorum*, p. 115 and *Gesta Consulum Andegavorum*, pp. 69–70. Fulk had married Arenburga or Guiberga, heiress of Maine in about 1109, and had continued wars with Henry I of England over her inheritance. The marriage of his son Geoffrey (17 June 1128) to the Empress Matilda had solved the quarrel. His daughter Sibylla had already married Thierry of Alsace, Count of Flanders. He had already paid a pilgrimage to Jerusalem in 1120 (William of Tyre, p. 608). Pope Honorius II's letter of commendation to Baldwin is given in Rozière, *Cartulaire du Saint Sépulcre*, pp. 17–18.

[2] Ibn al-Qalanisi, pp. 183–6; Ibn al-Athir, pp. 317–18.

178

Assassins, Bahram of Asterabad, had fled from Persia to Aleppo and established himself as leader of the underground Ismaili movement in northern Syria. But, though he enjoyed the support of Ilghazi, the people of Aleppo loathed the sect; and Bahram was obliged to move on. Armed with a recommendation from Ilghazi, he came to Damascus, where Toghtekin received him graciously. He settled there, gradually gathering adherents round him, and he won the sympathy of Toghtekin's vizier, al-Mazdaghani. The sect grew in power, to the disapproval of the Sunni population of Damascus. Bahram therefore asked al-Mazdaghani for protection; and at the vizier's request Toghtekin handed over to the sect, in November 1126, the frontier-fortress of Banyas, which was menaced by the Franks, hoping thus to make good use of its energies. Bahram re-fortified the castle and gathered all his followers round him. Soon they began to terrorize the neighbourhood; and Toghtekin, though he still officially protected them, began to plan their elimination, but he died before he found any suitable opportunity. A few months afterwards Bahram was killed in a skirmish with an Arab tribe near Baalbek, whose sheikh he had murdered. His position was taken over by another Persian, called Ismail.[1]

Toghtekin's successor as atabeg of Damascus was his son Taj al-Mulk Buri. Buri determined to rid himself of the Assassins. His first step, in September 1129, was suddenly to have their protector, the vizier al-Mazdaghani, murdered as he sat in council in the Rose Pavilion at Damascus. At once riots, prepared by Buri, broke out in Damascus; and every Assassin found there was slaughtered. Ismail, at Banyas, was alarmed. To save his sectaries he opened negotiations with the Franks.

This was the occasion for which King Baldwin had been waiting. On hearing of Toghtekin's death he sent Hugh of Payens, Grand Master of the Templars, to Europe, to recruit soldiers there, stating that Damascus was his objective. When Ismail's emissaries arrived, Frankish troops set out to take over Banyas from the

[1] Ibn al-Qalanisi, pp. 179–80, 187–91; Ibn al-Athir, pp. 382–4.

Assassins and to settle Ismail and his sect within Frankish territory. There Ismail fell ill of dysentery, dying a few months later; and his followers dispersed.[1] Baldwin himself came to Banyas early in November, with the whole army of Jerusalem, swelled by newly arrived men from the West. He marched on without serious opposition and encamped at the Wooden Bridge, some six miles south-west of Damascus. Buri drew up his army opposite to them, with the city at its rear. For some days neither army moved. Baldwin meanwhile sent detachments, mainly composed of the new-comers, under William of Bures, to collect food and material before he should venture to close in round the city. But William was unable to control his men, who were more interested in securing booty for themselves than in systematically gathering supplies. Buri learnt of this. Early one morning in late November his Turcoman cavalry fell on William twenty miles south of the Frankish camp. The Franks fought well but were overwhelmed. Only William himself and forty-five comrades survived to tell the news to the King.[2]

Baldwin decided to march at once against the enemy while they were celebrating their victory, and gave the order to advance. But at that moment rain began to fall in torrents. The plain became a sea of mud, with deep rivers cutting across the roads. In such conditions an attack was impossible. Bitterly disappointed, the King abandoned all idea of continuing the siege. The Frankish army retreated slowly in perfect order back to Banyas and into Palestine, where it dispersed.[3]

Events in the north made the disappointment particularly cruel. Baldwin had hoped that Bohemond II and Joscelin would profit by the chaos in Aleppo to take possession at last of the great Moslem city. But, though each in turn successfully raided its territory during the autumn of 1127, they would not co-operate. Each was jealous of the other. Joscelin had obtained by a truce

---

[1] Ibn al-Qalanisi, pp. 191–5; Ibn al-Athir, pp. 384–6.
[2] Ibn al-Qalanisi, pp. 195–8.
[3] William of Tyre, xiii, 26, pp. 595–7; Ibn al-Qalanisi, pp. 198–200.

with il-Bursuqi districts that had been held for a while by Antioch. Worse still, Joscelin's second wife, Roger of Antioch's sister Maria, had been promised as her dowry the town of Azaz. Bohemond considered that Roger had only been a regent in his name and had no right to give away Antiochene territory. He denounced the agreement. Joscelin thereupon led his troops, aided by Turkish mercenaries, to raid Antiochene villages near his borders. An interdict hurled by the Patriarch Bernard against the whole county of Edessa did not deter him. News of the quarrel was brought to King Baldwin, who was furious. He hurried north, early in 1128, and forced the two princes to make peace with each other. Fortunately, Joscelin, who was the more truculent, fell suddenly ill and saw his illness as a punishment from heaven. He agreed to restore to Bohemond the booty that he had taken, and apparently abandoned his claim to Azaz. But it was too late. As at Damascus the following year, a golden opportunity was missed and would never recur. For Islam had found a new and greater champion.[1]

During the last months of 1126 the Abbasid Caliph al-Mustarshid, who succeeded the amiable poet al-Mustazhir in 1118, thought to utilize the family quarrels of the Seldjuk Sultans to free himself of their control. The Sultan, Mahmud, in whose dominions Baghdad lay, was obliged to interrupt his hunting to send an army there; and he placed it under his captain, Imad ad-Din Zengi. Zengi, whose father Aqsonqor had been governor of Aleppo before the period of the Crusades, had already made a name in wars against the Franks. After a brief campaign he routed the Caliph's forces at Wasit and reduced the Caliph to obedience. His tactful behaviour after the victory pleased al-Mustarshid; and when on il-Bursuqi's death it was necessary to appoint a new atabeg for Mosul, Mahmud, who had first thought of naming the Bedouin leader Dubais, agreed with the Caliph that Zengi was a better candidate. The Sultan's youthful son Alp

[1] William of Tyre, xiii, 22, p. 590; Michael the Syrian, iii, p. 224; Kemal ad-Din, p. 665.

Arslan was installed as governor of Mosul with Zengi as his atabeg. Zengi spent the winter of 1127 at Mosul organizing his government there. In the spring of 1128 he marched on to Aleppo, claiming it as part of il-Bursuqi's dominions. The citizens of Aleppo, tired of the anarchy through which they had passed, received him gladly. He made his solemn entry there on 28 June.[1]

Zengi saw himself as the champion of Islam against the Franks. But he was unwilling to strike until he was ready. He made a truce with Joscelin, to last for two years, while he consolidated his power in Syria. The emirs of Shaizar and Homs hastened to acknowledge his suzerainty. He had no fears of the former. The latter was induced to assist him on a campaign against the Damascene possession of Hama, with the promise of its reversion. But as soon as Hama was conquered, Zengi seized it for himself and imprisoned Khirkan of Homs, though he was unable to secure Homs itself. Buri of Damascus, who had promised to join him in a Holy War against the Christians, was too fully occupied by his war against Jerusalem to make any active protest. By the end of 1130 Zengi was unquestioned master of Syria as far south as Homs.[2]

That same year the Franks suffered a great disaster. It was the ambition of Bohemond II to restore to his principality all the lands that it had ever contained. In Cilicia Antiochene power had declined. Tarsus and Adana were still in Frankish hands; they formed, it seems, the dower of Roger's widow Cecilia, King Baldwin's sister; and a Frankish garrison remained at Mamistra. But farther inland Anazarbus had fallen into the possession of the Armenian prince, Thoros the Roupenian, who had established his capital at Sis, close by. Thoros died in 1129 and his son Constantine a few months later, in the course of a palace intrigue. The next prince was the brother of Thoros, Leo I.[3] Bohemond thought that the moment had come to recover Anazarbus. In February 1130

[1] For Zengi's history till 1128, see Cahen, *op. cit.* pp. 306–7, and nn. 12 and 13 (with references).
[2] Ibn al-Qalanisi, pp. 200–2; Kemal ad-Din, p. 658; Matthew of Edessa, cclii, p. 320.   [3] Vahram, *Armenian Rhymed Chronicle*, p. 500.

he marched with a small force up the river Jihan towards his objective. Leo was alarmed and appealed for help to the Danish-mend emir, Ghazi, whose lands now reached the Taurus mountains. Bohemond knew nothing of this alliance. As he progressed carelessly up the river, meeting only light resistance from the Armenians, the Danishmend Turks fell on him and massacred the whole of his army. It was said that had they recognized the Prince himself, they would have saved him for the ransom that he would bring. As it was, his head was brought to the Danishmend emir, who had it embalmed and sent it as a gift to the Caliph.[1]

It was due to Byzantine intervention that the Turks did not follow up their victory; and Anazarbus remained in Armenian hands.[2] But Bohemond's death was a disaster for Antioch. Bohemond had succeeded to Antioch by hereditary right. Sentiment demanded that his rights should pass to his heir. But his marriage with Alice had produced only one child, a daughter two years old, called Constance. Without waiting for her father the King to appoint a regent, according to his right as overlord, Alice at once assumed the regency. But she was ambitious. It was soon rumoured in Antioch that she wished to rule not as a regent but as a reigning sovereign. Constance was to be immured in a convent or, as soon as might be, married off to some ignoble husband. The unnatural mother lost popularity in the principality, where already many men felt that in such times a warrior was needed as regent. When she heard that the King was already on his way from Jerusalem, Alice saw power slipping from her grasp, and took a desperate step. A messenger leading a splendid horse splendidly caparisoned was sent to Aleppo, to the atabeg Zengi, to whom she announced that she was ready to pay homage if he would guarantee her possession of Antioch.

---

[1] William of Tyre, XIII, 27, pp. 598–9; Orderic Vitalis, XI, 10, vol. IV, pp. 267–8; Romuald, *M.G.H.Ss.* vol. XIV, p. 420; Michael the Syrian, III, p. 227; *Chron. Anon. Syr.* pp. 98–9; Ibn al-Athir, p. 468.

[2] Michael the Syrian (III, p. 230) says that John Comnenus at once started an offensive against the Turks. See below, p. 210.

On the news of Bohemond's death King Baldwin hastened northward with his son-in-law Fulk, to take over the custody of its heiress and to nominate the regent. As he approached the city, his troops captured Alice's envoy to Zengi. The King at once had him hanged. When he appeared before Antioch he found that his daughter had shut the gates in his face. He summoned Joscelin to his aid and encamped before the city. Within, Alice had won temporary support by a lavish distribution of money from the princely treasury to the soldiers and people. It is possible that with her Armenian blood she was popular amongst the native Christians. But the Frankish nobility would not support a woman against their sovereign. After a few days a Norman knight, William of Aversa, and a monk, Peter the Latin, opened the Gate of the Duke to Joscelin and the Gate of Saint Paul to Fulk. Next day the King entered. Alice barricaded herself in a tower, and only emerged when the notables of the city guaranteed her life. There was a painful interview between Baldwin and his daughter, who knelt in terrified shame before him. The King wished to avoid a scandal; and doubtless his father's heart was touched. He forgave her; but he removed her from the regency and banished her to Lattakieh and Jabala, the lands that had been settled on her by Bohemond II as her dower. He himself assumed the regency and made all the lords of Antioch take an oath to him and to his granddaughter jointly. Then, after charging Joscelin with the guardianship of Antioch and its child-princess, he returned to Jerusalem in the summer of 1130.[1]

It was his last journey. A long life of endless activity only interrupted by two miserable periods of captivity had worn him out. In 1131 his health began to fail. When August came he was clearly dying. At his wish he was moved from the Palace at Jerusalem to the Patriarch's residence, attached to the buildings of the Holy Sepulchre, that he might die as near as possible to Calvary. As the end approached he summoned the nobles of the

[1] William of Tyre, XIII, 27, pp. 599–601; Michael the Syrian, III, p. 230; Kemal ad-Din, pp. 660–1.

realm to his room, and with them his daughter Melisende and her husband Fulk and their little one-year-old son, called Baldwin after him. He gave Fulk and Melisende his blessing and bade all present to accept them as their sovereigns. Then he himself assumed the robe of a monk and was admitted a canon of the Holy Sepulchre. The ceremony was barely done before he died, on Friday, 21 August 1131. He was buried in the Church of the Holy Sepulchre, amid mourning worthy of a great king.[1]

His cousin and old comrade, Joscelin of Edessa, did not long survive him. About the time of Baldwin's death he went to besiege a small castle north-east of Aleppo; and while he was inspecting his lines a mine that his men had laid collapsed beneath him. He was horribly wounded, and there was no hope of his recovery. As he lay dying, news came that the Danishmend emir, Ghazi, had marched against the town of Kaisun, the great fortress where Joscelin had recently installed the Jacobite Patriarch of Antioch. Kaisun was hard pressed by the Turks; and Joscelin ordered his son to go to its rescue. But the younger Joscelin replied that the army of Edessa was too small to be of use. Thereupon the aged Count hoisted himself from his bed and was carried in a litter at the head of his army to fight the Turks. The news of his coming startled Ghazi, who had thought him already dead. Disquieted, he raised the siege of Kaisun. A messenger rode hurriedly to tell Joscelin; who had his litter laid on the ground that he might thank God. The effort and the emotion were too much for him; and he died there by the roadside.[2]

With Baldwin and with Joscelin dead, the old generation of pioneer Crusaders was ended. In the years to come we find a new pattern of conflict between the Crusaders of the second generation, men and women like Joscelin II, like the Princess Alice, or like the

---

[1] William of Tyre, XIII, 28, pp. 601-2; Orderic Vitalis, XII, 23, vol. IV, p. 500; Ibn al-Qalanisi, pp. 207-8, dating it Thursday, 25 Ramadan, but giving the wrong year (A.H. 526).

[2] William of Tyre, XIV, 3, pp. 609-11; Michael the Syrian, III, 232; *Chron. Anon. Syr.* pp. 99-100.

house of Tripoli, ready to fit themselves into the eastern way of life and seeking only to hold what they possessed, and the new-comers from the West, aggressive, unadapted and uncompre-hending, like Fulk, like Raymond of Poitiers, or like the fatal Reynald of Châtillon.[1]

[1] Ibn al-Athir, pp. 389–90, realizes the changed circumstances, with the disappearance of the pioneer Crusaders on the one hand and the beginning of Moslem unity under Zengi on the other.

CHAPTER II

THE SECOND GENERATION

'They have begotten strange children.' HOSEA V, 7

On 14 September 1131, three weeks after King Baldwin II had been laid to rest in the Church of the Holy Sepulchre, the same church witnessed the coronation of King Fulk and Queen Melisende. The succession of the new sovereign was celebrated with joyful festivities.[1]

But while the barons of the Kingdom of Jerusalem accepted King Fulk without demur, the Frankish princes of the north were less ready to admit him as overlord. Baldwin I and Baldwin II had acted as suzerains of all the Frankish states because they had had the power and personality to do so. But the juridical position was by no means clear. In the case of Edessa Joscelin I had, like Baldwin II before him, paid homage to his predecessor when his predecessor became King of Jerusalem and personally bequeathed him the fief. Did the arrangement make Joscelin's heirs the vassals of Baldwin II's? At Tripoli Count Bertrand had submitted to Baldwin I's suzerainty in order to protect himself against Tancred's aggression; but his son Pons had already tried to repudiate Baldwin II's rights and had only recognized them because he was not strong enough to defy the King's forces. At Antioch Bohemond I had considered himself a sovereign prince; and Tancred, though he had only been regent, not prince, refused to regard himself as the King's vassal except for his principality of Galilee. Though Roger and Bohemond II had recognized Baldwin II as overlord, it could be argued that they had been wrong to do so. The position was complicated by the rights that

[1] William of Tyre, XIV, 2, pp. 608–9.

187

the Byzantine Emperor legitimately claimed over Antioch and Edessa, through the treaty made between the Princes and the Emperor at Constantinople during the First Crusade, and over Tripoli because of the homage paid by Count Bertrand to the Emperor.

Fulk's accession raised the whole question. The opposition to his overlordship was led by Alice, his sister-in-law. She had submitted to her father, King Baldwin, with a very bad grace. She now reasserted her claim to be her daughter's regent. It was not ill-founded, if it could be maintained that the King of Jerusalem was not overlord of Antioch; for it was usual, both in Byzantium and in the West, for the mother of a child-prince to be given the regency. Joscelin I's death, barely a month after Baldwin's, gave her an opportunity; for Joscelin had been guardian of the young Princess Constance, and the barons at Antioch would not install Joscelin II in his father's place. Disappointed, the new Count of Edessa listened to Alice's blandishments. He, too, was doubtless unwilling to accept Fulk as his suzerain. Pons of Tripoli also offered her support. His wife, Cecilia, had received from her first husband, Tancred, the dower-lands of Chastel Rouge and Arzghan: and through her he was thus one of the great barons of the Antiochene principality. He realized that the emancipation of Antioch from Jerusalem would enable Tripoli to follow suit. Alice had already won over the most formidable barons in the south of the principality, the brothers, William and Garenton of Zerdana, Lords of Sahyun, the great castle built by the Byzantines in the hills behind Lattakieh; and she had her partisans in Antioch itself. But the majority of the Antiochene lords feared a woman's rule. When they heard rumours of Alice's plot, they sent a messenger to Jerusalem to summon King Fulk.

Fulk set out at once with an army from Jerusalem. It was a challenge that he could not ignore. When he reached the confines of Tripoli, Pons refused him passage. The Countess Cecilia was Fulk's half-sister; but Fulk's appeal to the duties of kinship was made in vain. The army of Jerusalem had to proceed by sea, from

Beirut

Sidon

DAMASCUS

Beaufort

Tyre
Hunin
Scandelion
Banyas
Toron
Jacob's Ford
Safed
Acre
GALILEE
Haifa
Sephoria
Alal
Nazareth
Sennabra
Tiberias
La Fève
M.t Tabor
Habis Jaldak
Belvoir
Caesarea
Beisan
Bosra

R. Jordan

R. Litani

Jerash

Arsuf
Sebastea
Nablus
Jaffa
Lydda
La Grande
Ramleh
Mahomerie
Amman
Ibelin
Jericho
JERUSALEM
Ascalon
Bethlehem
Blanchegarde
St Sabas
Beth Gibelin
Gaza
Hebron
Daron
OULTREJOURDAIN
Kerak

0   10   20   30   40   50
English miles

Map 3. The Kingdom of Jerusalem in the twelfth century.

Beirut to Saint Symeon. As soon as he landed in Antiochene territory the King marched southward and defeated the rebel allies at Chastel Rouge. But he was not strong enough to punish his enemies. Pons apologized to him and was reconciled. Alice remained unharmed at Lattakieh, in her dower-lands. The brothers William and Garenton of Sahyun were forgiven, as was Joscelin of Edessa; who had not been present in the battle. It is doubtful whether Fulk obtained an oath of allegiance from either Pons or Joscelin; nor did he succeed in breaking up Alice's party. William of Sahyun was killed a few months later, in the course of a small Moslem raid against Zerdana; and Joscelin promptly married his widow Beatrice, who probably brought him Zerdana as her dower. But for the meantime peace was restored. Fulk himself retained the regency of Antioch but entrusted its administration to the Constable of the principality, Reynald Mazoir, lord of Marqab. He himself returned to Jerusalem, to take part in a terrible drama at the Court.[1]

There was amongst his nobles a handsome youth, Hugh of Le Puiset, lord of Jaffa. His father, Hugh I of Le Puiset in the Orleannais, a first cousin of Baldwin II, had been the leader of the baronial opposition to King Louis VI of France; who in 1118 destroyed the castle of Le Puiset and deprived him of his fief. Hugh's brothers Gildoin, abbot of Saint Mary Josaphat, and Waleran of Birejik had already gone to the East and, as Baldwin had recently become King of Jerusalem, Hugh decided to follow them with his wife Mabilla.[2] They set out with their

---

[1] William of Tyre, xiv, 4-5, pp. 611-14; Michael the Syrian, iii, p. 233; Kemal ad-Din, p. 664, who says that William of Zerdana was killed in the civil war. But Ibn al-Qalanisi (p. 125) says that William was killed early in 1133. Alice's revolt is probably to be dated early in 1132.

[2] Hugh I of Le Puiset's mother, Alice of Montlhéry, was sister of Baldwin II's mother Melisende. Cuissard, *Les Seigneurs du Puiset*, p. 89. Abbot Gildoin of St Mary Josaphat and Waleran of Birejik were apparently his brothers. Mabilla was the daughter of Hugh, Count of Roucy, and Robert Guiscard's daughter Sibylla. See below, Appendix III, for genealogical trees, I, 1 and 2. William of Tyre (see reference below, p. 193 n. 1) wrongly assumes that Hugh II was born in Apulia, in which case he married at the age of six.

young son Hugh. As they passed through Apulia the boy fell ill; so they left him there at the Court of Bohemond II, who was Mabilla's first cousin. On their arrival in Palestine they were given by Baldwin the lordship of Jaffa. Hugh I died soon afterwards, whereupon Mabilla and the fief passed to a Walloon knight, Albert of Namur. Both Mabilla and Albert soon followed him into the grave; and Hugh II, now aged about sixteen, sailed from Apulia to claim his heritage. Baldwin received him well and handed his parents' fief over to him; and he was brought to live at the royal Court, where his chief companion was his cousin, the young Princess Melisende. About 1121 he married Emma, niece of the Patriarch Arnulf and widow of Eustace Garnier, a lady of mature age but of vast possessions. She delighted in her tall, handsome husband; but her twin sons, Eustace II, heir of Sidon, and Walter, heir of Caesarea, hated their stepfather who was little older than themselves.[1] Meanwhile Melisende was married to Fulk, for whom she never cared, despite his great love for her. After her accession she continued her intimacy with Hugh. There was gossip at the Court; and Fulk grew jealous. Hugh had many enemies, headed by his stepsons. They fanned the King's suspicions, till at last Hugh in self-defence gathered round him a party of his own, of which the leading member was Roman of Le Puy, lord of the lands of Oultrejourdain. Soon all the nobility of the kingdom was divided between the King and the Count, who was known to have the sympathy of the Queen. Tension grew throughout the summer months of 1132. Then one day in the late summer, when the palace was full of the magnates of the

---

[1] The names of the sons of Eustace Garnier are uncertain. Walter appears as Lord of Caesarea and Sidon in a diploma of 21 September, 1131 (Röhricht, *Regesta*, p. 35); Eustace II was Lord of Sidon in 1126 (Röhricht, *Regesta*, *Additamenta*, p. 8), and Eustace and Walter appear as the sons of Eustace I in a diploma of the same year (Röhricht, *Regesta*, p. 28). But the *Lignages* calls the two sons Gerard and Walter, and Gerard is also called Guy in *Assises*. See La Monte, 'The Lords of Sidon', in *Byzantion*, vol. XVII, pp. 188–90, who makes Gerard the son of Eustace II, and places the latter's death before 1131 when Walter became regent for Gerard.

realm, Walter Garnier stood up and roundly accused his stepfather of plotting against the life of the King, and challenged him to justify himself in single combat. Hugh denied the charge and accepted the challenge. The date for the duel was fixed by the High Court; and Hugh retired to Jaffa and Walter to Caesarea, each to prepare himself.

When the day arrived, Walter was ready at the lists, but Hugh stayed away. Perhaps the Queen, alarmed that things had gone too far, begged him to absent himself, or perhaps it was the Countess Emma, appalled at the prospect of losing either husband or son; or perhaps Hugh himself, knowing his guilt, was afraid of God's vengeance. Whatever its cause might be, his cowardice was read as the proof of his treason. His friends could support him no longer. The King's council declared him guilty by default. Hugh then panicked and fled to Ascalon to ask for protection from the Egyptian garrison. An Egyptian detachment brought him back to Jaffa and from there began to ravage the plain of Sharon. Hugh's treason was now overt. His chief vassal, Balián, lord of Ibelin and Constable of Jaffa, turned against him; and when a royal army came hastily down from Jerusalem, Jaffa itself surrendered without a blow. Even the Egyptians abandoned Hugh as a profitless ally. He was obliged to make his submission to the King.

His punishment was not severe. The Queen was his friend, and the Patriarch, William of Messines, counselled mercy. The King himself was anxious to smooth things over; for already the dangers of civil war had been made clear. On 11 December, when the royal army had been summoned to march against Jaffa, the atabeg of Damascus had surprised the fortress of Banyas and recovered it for Islam. It was decided that Hugh should go for three years into exile; then he might return with impunity to his lands.

While awaiting a boat for Italy, Hugh came up to Jerusalem early in the new year to say good-bye to his friends. As he was playing dice one evening at the door of a shop in the Street of the Furriers, a Breton knight crept up behind him and stabbed him through his head and through his body. Hugh was carried off bleeding to death. Suspicion at once fell upon the King; but Fulk acted promptly and prudently. The knight was handed over for trial by the High Court. He confessed that he had acted on his own initiative, hoping thus to win the favour of the King, and was sentenced to death by having his limbs cut off one by one. The execution took place in public. After the victim's arms and legs had been struck off but while his head remained to him he was made to repeat his confession. The King's reputation was saved. But the Queen was not satisfied. So angry was she with Hugh's enemies that for many months they feared assassination; and their leader, Raourt of Nablus, dared not walk in the streets without an escort. Even King Fulk was said to be afraid for his life. But his one desire was to win his wife's favour. He gave way to her in everything; and she, thwarted in love, soon found consolation in the exercise of power.[1]

Hugh survived his attempted murder, but not for long. He retired to the Court of his cousin, King Roger II of Sicily, who enfeoffed him with the lordship of Gargano, where he died soon afterwards.[2]

It was no doubt with relief that Fulk turned his attention once more to the north. The situation there was more ominous for the Franks than in Baldwin II's days. There was no effective prince ruling in Antioch. Joscelin II of Edessa lacked his father's energy and political sense. He was an unattractive figure. He was short and thick-set, dark-haired and dark-skinned; his face was pock-marked, with a huge nose and prominent eyes. He was capable of generous gestures, but was lazy, luxurious and lascivious, and quite unfitted to command the chief outpost of Frankish Christendom.[3]

The dearth of leadership among the Franks was the more serious

---

[1] The story is given at length by William of Tyre, xiv, 15–17, pp. 627–33. Ibn al-Qalanisi, p. 215, tells briefly of dissensions amongst the Franks—'not usual with them'.

[2] William of Tyre, xiv, 17, p. 633.

[3] William of Tyre, xiv, 3, p. 610. Joscelin II was born in 1113 (*Chron. Anon. Syr.* p. 35).

because the Moslems now had in Zengi a man capable of assembling the forces of Islam. As yet Zengi was biding his time. He was too heavily entangled in events in Iraq to take advantage of the situation among the Franks. The Sultan Mahmud ibn Mohammed died in 1131, leaving his possessions in Iraq and southern Persia to his son Dawud. But the dominant member of the Seldjuk family, Sanjar, decided that the inheritance should pass to Mahmud's brother Tughril, lord of Kazwin. The other two brothers of Mahmud, Mas'ud of Fars and Seldjuk-Shah of Azerbaijan, then put in claims. Dawud soon retired, supported neither by Mustarshid nor by his subjects. For a while Tughril, armed by Senjar's influence, was accepted at Baghdad; and Mas'ud was forced by Sanjar to retire. But Sanjar soon lost interest; whereupon Seldjuk-Shah came to Baghdad and won the Caliph's support. Mas'ud appealed to Zengi to help him. Zengi marched on Baghdad, only to be severely defeated by the Caliph and Seldjuk-Shah near Tekrit. Had not the Kurdish governor of Tekrit, Najm ed-Din Ayub, conveyed him across the river Tigris, he would have been captured or slain. Zengi's defeat encouraged the Caliph, who now dreamed to resurrect the past power of his house. Even Sanjar was alarmed; and Zengi as his representative once again attacked Baghdad in June 1132, this time in alliance with the volatile Bedouin chieftain, Dubais. In the battle that followed Zengi was at first victorious; but the Caliph intervened in person, routed Dubais and turned triumphantly on Zengi, who was forced to retire to Mosul. Mustarshid arrived there next spring at the head of a great army. It seemed that the Abbasids were to recover their old glory; for the Seldjuk Sultan of Iraq was now little more than a client of the Caliph. But Zengi escaped from Mosul and began relentlessly to harass the Caliph's camp and to cut off his supplies. After three months Mustarshid retired.[1] The Abbasid revival was cut short. During the next year the Seldjuk prince Mas'ud gradually displaced the other claimants to the

[1] Ibn al-Athir, pp. 398–9 (and *Atabegs of Mosul*, pp. 78–85); see articles 'Mas'ud ibn Mohammed', 'Tughril I', and 'Sandjar' in *Encyclopaedia of Islam*.

Sultanate of Iraq. Mustarshid vainly tried to check him. At a battle at Daimarg in June 1135 the Caliph's army was routed by Mas'ud and he himself captured. He was sent into exile to Azerbaijan and there was murdered by Assassins, probably with Mas'ud's connivance. His son and successor in the Caliphate, Rashid, appealed to the Seldjuk claimant Dawud and to Zengi, but in vain. Mas'ud secured Rashid's deposition by the cadis at Baghdad. His successor, Moqtafi, managed by lavish promises to seduce Zengi away from Rashid and Dawud. Fortified by fresh titles of honour from Moqtafi and from Mas'ud, Zengi was able, from 1135 onwards, to turn his attention to the West.[1]

While Zengi was engaged in Iraq, his interests in Syria were cared for by a soldier from Damascus, Sawar, whom he made governor of Aleppo. He could not afford to send him many troops; but at his instigation various bodies of freebooting Turcomans entered Sawar's services, and with them Sawar prepared in the spring of 1133 to attack Antioch. King Fulk was summoned by the frightened Antiochenes to their rescue. As he journeyed north with his army he was met at Sidon by the Countess of Tripoli, who told him that her husband had been ambushed by a band of Turcomans in the Nosairi mountains and had fled to the castle of Montferrand, on the edge of the Orontes valley. At her request Fulk marched straight to Montferrand; and on his approach the Turcomans retired. The episode restored cordial relations between Fulk and Pons. Soon afterwards Pons's son and heir Raymond was married to the Queen's sister, Hodierna of Jerusalem; while his daughter Agnes married the son of Fulk's constable at Antioch, Reynald Mazoir of Marqab.[2]

Having rescued the Count of Tripoli, Fulk moved on to Antioch. There he learnt that Sawar had already successfully raided the Edessene city of Turbessel and had assembled an army to use

---

[1] Abu'l Feda, pp. 21–3; Ibn al-Athir, *Atabegs of Mosul*, pp. 88–91; Ibn at-Tiqtaqa, *Al Fakhiri*, pp. 297–8.

[2] William of Tyre, XIV, 6, pp. 614–15; Ibn al-Qalanisi, pp. 221–2; Ibn al-Athir, pp. 399–400.

against Antioch. After a cautious delay of several days Fulk advanced towards the Moslem camp at Qinnasrin and made a surprise attack on it by night. He forced Sawar to retire and to abandon his tents; but the victory was far from complete. In subsequent skirmishes the Moslems annihilated several detachments of Franks. But Fulk made a triumphant entry into Antioch before he returned to Palestine in the summer of 1133. As soon as he was gone, Sawar's raids on Christian territory recommenced.[1]

Apart from such frontier raids the year 1134 passed peaceably enough. Next year the Moslem world was weakened by revolutions. In Egypt the Fatimid Caliph al-Hafiz had attempted to curb the power of the vizierate by appointing his own son Hasan as vizier. But the young man showed himself to be almost insanely ferocious. After forty emirs had been beheaded on a trumpery charge, there was a revolt. The Caliph only saved himself by poisoning his son and handing over the corpse to the rebels. He then appointed as vizier an Armenian, Vahram, who was more interested in enriching his friends and fellow-Christians than in aggressive action against the Franks.[2] Damascus was equally rendered impotent. Toghtekin's son Buri died in 1132 and was succeeded as atabeg by his son Ismail. Ismail's rule began brilliantly with the recapture of Banyas from the Franks and Baalbek and Hama from his rivals; but soon he began to combine a tyrannous cruelty with oppressive taxation. His behaviour provoked an attempt to murder him, which he punished with wholesale executions, even walling up alive his own brother, Sawinj, on the faintest of suspicions. Next, he planned the elimination of his father's trusted counsellor, Yusuf ibn Firuz. His mother, the dowager Princess Zumurrud, had borne the death of her son Sawinj with equanimity; but Yusuf was her lover. She plotted to save him. Ismail became aware that he was unsafe even in his own palace. In alarm he wrote to his father's old enemy Zengi, offering

---

[1] William of Tyre, xiv, 7, pp. 615–16; Ibn al-Qalanisi, pp. 222–3; Kemal ad-Din, p. 665.
[2] Ibn al-Athir, pp. 405–8.

to become his vassal if Zengi would maintain him in power. If he would not help him, then Ismail would hand over Damascus to the Franks. It was inconvenient for Zengi to leave Mosul with the Abbasid Caliph Mustarshid still unbeaten. But he could not ignore the appeal. He received it too late. He crossed the Euphrates on 7 February; but six days previously Zumurrud had achieved the assassination of Ismail and the succession of her younger son, Shihab ed-Din Mahmud. The new atabeg, with the support of his people, gave a polite refusal to the envoys that Zengi sent to him asking for his submission. When Zengi advanced on Damascus, receiving the surrender of Hama as he came, he found the city in a state of defence. His attempt to storm the walls failed. Soon supplies ran short at his camp; and some of his troops deserted him. At that moment an embassy reached him from the Caliph Mustarshid, courteously requesting him to respect Damascene independence. Zengi gratefully accepted an excuse that enabled him to retire without dishonour. Peace was made between Zengi and Mahmud; and Zengi paid a state visit to Damascus. But Mahmud did not trust Zengi sufficiently to pay a return visit; he sent his brother in his stead.[1]

The episode, coinciding with the weakness of Egypt, offered a rare opportunity for recovering Banyas and taking aggressive action. But Fulk let the chance go by. Zengi, having extricated himself from Damascus, employed his forces in an attack on Antiochene territory. While his lieutenant Sawar threatened Turbessel, Aintab and Azaz, preventing a junction between the armies of Antioch and Edessa, Zengi swept up past the fortresses of the eastern frontier, Kafartab, Maarrat, Zerdana and Athareb, capturing them one by one. Fortunately for the Franks, he was then obliged to return to Mosul; but the frontier defences were lost.[2]

---

[1] Ibn al-Qalanisi, pp. 211–36, a very full account, but ascribing praiseworthy motives to the dowager's murder of her son. He says that Ismail's chief minister was a Christian Kurd, Bertrand the Infidel; *Bustan*, p. 329; Kemal ad-Din, pp. 667–70; Ibn al-Athir, pp. 403–5.

[2] Kemal ad-Din, p. 670.

These disasters brought Fulk again to the north. He was still nominal regent of Antioch, but authority there was represented by the venerable Patriarch Bernard. Bernard died in the early summer. He had been an able statesman, energetic, firm and courageous, but strict towards the Frankish nobility and intolerant towards the native Christians. On his death the populace acclaimed as his successor the Latin Bishop of Mamistra, Radulph of Domfront, who assumed the Patriarchal throne without waiting for a canonical election. Radulph was a very different man, handsome, despite a slight squint, a lover of pomp, open-handed and affable, not well educated but an eloquent persuasive speaker, and, behind a gracious façade, worldly, ambitious and sly. He had no wish to be dominated by the King and the King's men; so he opened negotiations with the dowager Princess Alice, who was still living on her lands at Lattakieh. Alice saw her opportunity and appealed to her sister Queen Melisende. Fulk arrived at Antioch in August for a short visit. He did not feel strong enough to protest against Radulph's irregular election, and he could now refuse his wife nothing. Alice was allowed to return to Antioch. Fulk remained regent, but the power was shared in an uneasy alliance between the dowager and the Patriarch.[1]

Radulph soon quarrelled with his clergy; and Alice was left mistress of the city. But her position was precarious. Her main support came from the native Christian population. As her intrigues with Zengi had shown, she had little regard for Frankish sentiment. She thought now of a better scheme. At the end of 1135 she sent an envoy to Constantinople to offer the hand of her daughter the Princess Constance to the Emperor's younger son Manuel. Her action may have been, as the horrified Crusaders declared, due to the caprice of her ambition; but in fact it offered the best solution for the preservation of northern Syria. The Greek element was strong in Antioch. The Moslem menace was growing under Zengi; and the Empire was the only power strong

[1] William of Tyre, XIV, 9, 20, pp. 619–20, 636. Fulk was in Antioch in August 1135 (Röhricht, *Regesta*, p. 39).

enough to check it. A vassal-state ruled under imperial suzerainty first by the half-Armenian Alice and then jointly by a Byzantine prince and a Frankish princess, might well have served to weld Greek and Frank together for the defence of Christendom. But the Frankish nobles were aghast; and the Patriarch Radulph saw himself displaced in favour of a hated Greek. It seems that during his visit to Antioch King Fulk had been consulted by the barons about a suitable husband for Constance. Now a messenger went secretly to him to say that one must urgently be found. After reviewing all the French princes of his acquaintance, Fulk decided upon the younger son of Duke William IX of Aquitaine, Raymond of Poitiers, at present in England at the Court of King Henry I, whose daughter had recently married Fulk's son Geoffrey. A knight of the Hospital, Gerard Jebarre, was sent to England to fetch him out. The greatest secrecy was observed. Alice must know nothing; nor would it be safe even to inform the Queen. Another danger lay in the hostility of King Roger of Sicily, who had never forgiven the Kingdom of Jerusalem for the insult done to his mother Adelaide and whose Mediterranean ambitions would never let him offer free passage to a claimant for the hand of the greatest heiress in the East. Gerard reached the English court, and Raymond accepted the proposal. But King Roger learnt of the secret; for the Normans of England and of Sicily were always in close touch with each other. He determined to arrest Raymond, who could not find a ship for Syria except from a south Italian port. Raymond was obliged to divide up his company and to disguise himself sometimes as a pilgrim, sometimes as a merchant's servant. He managed to slip through the blockade, and in April 1136 he arrived at Antioch.

His arrival could not be kept hidden from Alice. He therefore at once went to see the Patriarch. Radulph offered him help on terms. Raymond must pay him homage and defer to him in everything. On Raymond's agreement Radulph demanded an audience with Alice to tell her that the glamorous stranger had arrived as a candidate for her hand. The story was convincing, for

Raymond was aged thirty-seven, Alice was under thirty, and Constance barely nine. Then, while Alice waited in her palace to receive her future betrothed, Constance was kidnapped and taken to the cathedral, where the Patriarch hastily wedded her to Raymond. Alice was defeated. Against the lawful husband of the heiress a dowager had no rights. She retired once more to Lattakieh, to remain there disconsolate for the remainder of her short existence.[1]

Raymond was in the prime of life. He was handsome and of immense physical strength, not well educated, fond of gambling and impetuous and at the same time indolent, but with a high reputation for gallantry and for purity of conduct.[2] His popularity soon awed the Patriarch, whose troubles with his own clergy continued, and who found himself treated with deference but in fact shorn of power. The nobles solidly supported Raymond; for indeed the situation was too serious for them to do otherwise. The principality was losing ground. Not only were the eastern defences gone. In the south, in the Nosairi mountains, a Turco-man adventurer captured the castle of Bisikra'il from its owner, Reynald Mazoir, in 1131, and early in 1136 he was with difficulty prevented from taking Balatonos. Bisikra'il was recovered soon afterwards. Farther to the south, where the Franks had acquired the castle of Qadmus in 1129, in 1131 it passed back to the Moslem emir of Kahf, Saif ed-Din ibn Amrun, who next year sold it to the Assassin leader Abu'l Fath. In 1135 the Assassins bought Kahf itself from Saif ed-Din's sons; and in the winter of 1136 they captured Khariba from the Franks.[3] Cilicia had already been lost. In 1131, soon after Bohemond II's death, the Roupenian Prince Leo, protected in his rear by an alliance with the Danishmend emir, descended into the plain and seized the three cities of Mamistra,

---

[1] William of Tyre, XIV, 20, pp. 635–6; Cinnamus, pp. 16–17; Robert of Torigny (I, p. 184) believed that Raymond married Bohemond II's widow.

[2] William of Tyre, XIV, 21, pp. 637–8; Kemal ad-Din, ed. Blochet, p. 522, describes how he could bend an iron bar. Cinnamus (p. 125) compares him to Hercules.

[3] Ibn al-Qalanisi, p. 241; Usama, ed. Hitti, p. 157; Kemal ad-Din, p. 680.

Tarsus and Adana. His brother and predecessor Thoros had already a few years before ejected the small Byzantine garrisons from Sis and Anazarbus, farther inland. In 1135 Leo captured Sarventikar, on the slopes of the Amanus, from Baldwin, Lord of Marash. But the Armenian hold over Cilicia was weak. Bandits found refuge there, and pirates hung about its coasts.[1]

The county of Edessa was no better off. Timurtash the Ortoqid had recently annexed some of its territory in the east. To the north the Armenian Prince of Gargar, Michael, unable to maintain himself against the Turks, ceded his lands to Count Joscelin, who rashly handed them over to Michael's personal enemy Basil, brother of the Armenian Catholicus. A civil war between the two Armenians broke out. Joscelin was obliged to garrison Gargar himself, but could not prevent the countryside from being ravaged by Armenians and Turks in turn. Sawar raided the district of Turbessel in 1135, and in April 1136, about the time of Raymond of Poitiers's arrival in the East, his general, Afshin, not only broke his way through Antiochene territory to Lattakieh in the south, burning and pillaging the villages as he passed, but afterwards turned northward past Marash to Kaisun. The chief vassal of the Count of Edessa, Baldwin, lord of Marash and Kaisun, was powerless to defend his lands.[2]

Raymond decided that his first action must be to recover Cilicia. His rear must be protected before he could venture to oppose Zengi. With King Fulk's approval he marched with Baldwin of Marash against the Roupenians. But the alliance was incomplete. Joscelin of Edessa, though he was Fulk's vassal and Baldwin's suzerain, was also Leo's nephew; and his sympathies were with his uncle. The King of Jerusalem's authority was no longer sufficient to reunite the Frankish princes. With Joscelin's help, Leo drove back the Antiochene army. Triumphant, he

[1] Gregory the Priest, p. 152; Michael the Syrian, III, pp. 230–3; *Armenian Rhymed Chronicle*, p. 499; Sembat the Constable, p. 615.
[2] Michael the Syrian, III, p. 244; Ibn al-Qalanisi, pp. 239–40; Kemal ad-Din, p. 672.

agreed to have a personal interview with Baldwin, who treacherously made him prisoner and sent him off to captivity in Antioch. In Leo's absence his three sons quarrelled. The eldest, Constantine, was eventually captured and blinded by his brothers. But meanwhile the Franks derived no profit. The Danishmend emir, Mohammed II ibn Ghazi, invaded Cilicia, destroyed the harvests, then moved on into Baldwin's lands, which he ravaged as far as Kaisun. Shaken by these disasters, Leo bought his freedom by offering to give up the Cilician cities to Raymond; but on his return home he forgot his promise. A desultory war broke out again, till, early in 1137, Joscelin patched up a truce between the combatants, who were terrified by news from the north, news that showed Princess Alice not to have been so foolish after all.[1]

King Fulk had not been able to give any practical aid to his friend Raymond. He had to face dangers nearer home. The government of the young atabeg Mahmud of Damascus had been dominated by the peaceful influence of his mother's lover, Yusuf; but one spring evening, in 1136, as the atabeg was walking on the maidan with Yusuf and a mameluk commander, Bazawash, the latter suddenly stabbed Yusuf to death and fled to his regiment at Baalbek. From there he threatened to march on Damascus and depose the atabeg, unless he was made chief minister. Mahmud yielded to his wishes. At once the Damascenes took up an aggressive attitude against the Franks. Early next year they invaded the County of Tripoli. The local Christians, who felt no loyalty towards the Franks, guided them secretly through the passes of the Lebanon into the coastal plain. Count Pons was taken by surprise. He came out with his small army to meet them and was disastrously defeated. Pons himself, who fled into the mountains, was betrayed to the Moslems by a Christian peasant, and was instantly put to death. The Bishop of Tripoli, Gerard, who was captured in the battle, was fortunately not recognized and was soon exchanged as

[1] Gregory the Priest, *loc. cit.* (and note by Dulaurier); Sembat the Constable, p. 616; Matthew of Edessa, ccliii, pp. 320–1.

a man of no importance. Bazawash captured one or two frontier castles, but did not venture to attack Tripoli itself. He soon retired to Damascus laden with booty.[1]

Pons had ruled over Tripoli for twenty-five years. He seems to have been a competent administrator but a feckless politician, always anxious to throw off the suzerainty of the King of Jerusalem but too weak to achieve independence. His son and successor, Raymond II, was of a more passionate temperament. He was now aged twenty-two, and had recently married Queen Melisende's sister, Hodierna of Jerusalem, to whom he was jealously devoted. His first act was to avenge his father's death, not on the mamelukes of Damascus, who were too powerful for him, but on the disloyal Christians of the Lebanon. Marching on the villages suspected of helping the enemy, he massacred all their men-folk and took the women and children to be sold as slaves in Tripoli. His ruthlessness cowed the Lebanese, but it made them no fonder of the Franks.[2]

Bazawash's activity was not to the liking of Zengi. He was unwilling to attack the Franks with an independent and aggressive Moslem state on his flank. At the end of June he marched on Homs, which was held for the atabeg of Damascus by an elderly mameluke, Unur. For about a fortnight Zengi lay before the city, when news came that a Frankish army from Tripoli was approaching. Whatever Count Raymond's intention may have been, his move caused Zengi to raise the siege of Homs and turn on the Franks. As Raymond retired before him, he advanced to besiege the great castle of Montferrand, on the eastern slopes of the Nosairi hills, guarding the entrance to the Buqaia. Meanwhile Raymond sent to Jerusalem to ask for help from King Fulk.

Fulk had just received an urgent appeal from Antioch; but a Moslem threat to Tripoli could not be ignored. He hurried up with all the men that he could collect to join Raymond, and together they made a forced march round the Nosairi foothills to

[1] William of Tyre, xiv, 23, p. 640; Ibn al-Qalanisi, pp. 240–1; Ibn al-Athir, pp. 419–20.
[2] William of Tyre, *loc. cit.*

Montferrand. It was a difficult journey; and their army soon was in a pitiable state. Zengi had moved away on their approach, but, hearing of their condition, he returned and closed in round them as they came out of the hills near to the castle. The weary Franks were taken by surprise. They fought bravely, but the battle was soon over. Most of the Christians lay dead on the field. Others, including the Count of Tripoli, were taken prisoner, while Fulk with a small bodyguard escaped into the fortress.[1]

Before Zengi could move up to invest Montferrand, the King sent messengers to the Patriarch of Jerusalem, to the Count of Edessa and to the Prince of Antioch, begging for immediate help. All three, ignoring other risks, answered his appeal; for the capture of the King and all his chivalry might well mean the end of the kingdom. The Patriarch William gathered together the rest of the militia left in Palestine, and led it, with the Holy Cross at its head, up to Tripoli. Joscelin of Edessa, forgetting his local worries, came down from the north, and on his way was joined by Raymond of Antioch, who could ill afford at that moment to leave his capital. Fortunately for Palestine, bared as it was of every fighting man, its neighbours were not in the mood to be aggressive. Egypt was paralysed by a palace revolution, which had replaced the Armenian vizier Vahram by a violent anti-Christian, Ridwan ibn al-Walakshi, who was fully occupied in slaying his predecessor's friends and in quarrelling with the Caliph. The garrison of Ascalon carried out a raid on Lydda, but no more.[2] The mameluke Bazawash of Damascus was more dangerous; and as soon as the Patriarch had left the country, he permitted himself to ravage it as far south as the open city of Nablus, whose inhabitants he put to the sword. But he was too fearful of the consequences to Damascus should Zengi enjoy too complete a victory to wish to press the Franks very far.[3]

---

[1] William of Tyre, xiv, 25, pp. 643–5; Ibn al-Qalanisi, pp. 242–3 (tactfully omitting to mention the Franco-Damascene alliance); Kemal ad-Din, pp. 672–3; Ibn al-Athir, p. 420.
[2] William of Tyre, xiv, 26, pp. 645–7. [3] *Idem*, xiv, 27, p. 647.

At the end of July the relieving force assembled in the Buqaia. Meanwhile in Montferrand the King was growing desperate. He was cut off from news of the outside world. His supplies were running out; and day and night Zengi's ten great mangonels pounded at the walls of the castle. At last he sent a herald to Zengi to ask for his terms. To his incredulous joy, Zengi demanded only the cession of Montferrand. The King might go free with all his men. Moreover, the leading knights captured in the battle, including the Count of Tripoli, should be set at liberty. No ransom would be charged. Fulk accepted at once. Zengi kept to his engagement. Fulk and his bodyguard were brought before Zengi, who treated them with every mark of honour and presented the King with a sumptuous robe. Their comrades were restored to them; and they were sent peaceably on their way. In the Buqaia they met the relieving army, much nearer than they had thought. Some of them were vexed to find that had they held out longer they might have been rescued; but the wiser were glad to have escaped so lightly.[1]

Indeed, Zengi's forbearance has never ceased to astonish historians. But Zengi knew what he was doing. Montferrand was no mean prize. Its possession would prevent the Franks from penetrating into the upper Orontes valley. It was also admirably situated to control Hama and the Damascene city of Homs. To obtain it without further fighting was well worth while; for he had no wish to risk a battle with the Frankish relieving force so near to the frontiers of Damascus, whose rulers would at once take advantage of any check that he might suffer. Moreover, like his Frankish enemies, he was disquieted by news from the north.

[1] William of Tyre, xiv, 28–9, pp. 545–51; Ibn al-Qalanisi, *loc. cit.*; Kemal ad-Din, *loc. cit.*; Ibn al-Athir, pp. 421–3.

CHAPTER III

THE CLAIMS OF THE EMPEROR

'Let not him that is deceived trust in vanity: for vanity shall be his recompence.'　　　　　　　　　　　　JOB XV, 31

The news that had patched up a peace between the Franks and the Armenians, that had made Prince Raymond loth to leave Antioch, and that now induced Zengi to show mercy to his enemies was of a great army marching into Cilicia, led in person by the Emperor John Comnenus. Ever since the Emperor Alexius had failed to come to Antioch during the First Crusade the politicians of the Frankish East had blandly ignored Byzantium. Even though Bohemond's attempt to invade the Empire from the west had utterly failed, Alexius had been quite unable to secure that the terms of his treaty with Bohemond were implemented. As the Franks in Antioch well knew, he was distracted by cares nearer home.[1]

Theses cares endured for nearly thirty years. There were intermittent wars on all the frontiers of the Empire. There were Polovtsian invasions across the lower Danube, as in 1114 and 1121. There was continual tension with the Hungarians on the middle Danube, which flared into open war in 1128; the Hungarians invaded the Balkan peninsula as far as Sofia, but were driven back and defeated in their own territory by the Emperor. The Italian merchant cities periodically raided the Empire in order to extract commercial privileges. Pisa obtained a favourable treaty in 1111; and Venice, after four years of war, following on the Emperor John's refusal to renew his father's concessions, recovered all its rights in 1126. The Normans of southern Italy, cowed since

---

[1] See above, pp. 108–9, 137.

Bohemond's defeat at Dyrrhachium, became a menace once more in 1127, when Roger II of Sicily annexed Apulia. Roger II, who assumed the title of King in 1130, possessed to the full his family's hatred of Byzantium, though he loved to copy its methods and to patronize its arts. But his ambitions were so vast that it was usually possible to find allies against him. Not only did he seek to dominate Italy, but he claimed Antioch as the only surviving representative in the male line of the House of Hauteville, and Jerusalem itself in virtue of the treaty made by his mother Adelaide with Baldwin I.[1]

In Asia Minor there was no peace. During and after the First Crusade Alexius had consolidated his hold over the western third of the peninsula and over the northern and southern coasts; and had he had only to deal with the Turkish princes he could have kept his possessions intact. But groups of Turcomans were still seeping into the interior, where they and their flocks multiplied; and inevitably they overflowed into the coastal valleys, to seek a gentler climate and richer pastures. Their coming inevitably destroyed the settled agricultural life of the Christians. Indeed, the weaker the princes became, the more unruly and dangerous to the Empire were their nomad subjects.[2]

At the time of the Emperor Alexius's death in 1118, Turkish Anatolia was divided between the Seldjuk Sultan Mas'ud, who reigned from Konya over the southern centre of the peninsula, from the Sangarius to the Taurus, and the Danishmend emir Ghazi II, whose lands stretched from the Halys to the Euphrates. Between them they had absorbed and eliminated the smaller emirates, except for Melitene in the east, where Mas'ud's youngest brother Toghrul reigned under the regency of his mother and her

[1] For Roger II, see Chalandon, *Domination Normande en Italie*, II, pp. 1-51. The Polovtsian invasion of 1121 was graphically described by the Jacobite Basil of Edessa for the benefit of Michael the Syrian (III, p. 207).
[2] A good summary of the course and effect of the Turcoman invasions is given in Ramsay, 'War of Moslem and Christian for the Possession of Asia Minor', in *Studies in the History and Art of the Eastern Provinces of the Roman Empire*, pp. 295-8.

second husband, the Ortoqid Balak. In spite of the Byzantine victory at Philomelion in 1115 and the subsequent attempted delineation of the frontier, the Turks had during the following years recaptured Phrygian Laodicea and penetrated into the Meander valley, and had cut off the road to Attalia. At the same time the Danishmends were pressing westward into Paphlagonia. The Emperor Alexius was planning a campaign to restore the Anatolian frontiers when his last illness supervened.[1]

The accession of the Emperor John brought new vigour to Byzantium. John, whom his subjects called Kaloioannes, John the Good, was one of those rare characters of whom no contemporary writer, with one exception, had anything derogatory to say. The exception was his own sister. Anna Comnena was the eldest of Alexius's children. As a child she had been betrothed to the young co-Emperor Constantine Ducas, to whom Alexius had promised the eventual succession. His early death, which followed closely on her brother's birth, was a cruel blow to her ambitions; and she sought ever afterwards to redress the injustice of Providence by persuading her father, with her mother's approval, to leave his throne to her husband, the Caesar Nicephorus Bryennius. Even when the Emperor lay dying, devotedly nursed by his wife and daughter, the two ladies punctuated their ministrations with demands for John's disinheritance. But Alexius had decided that his son must succeed him. When John was admitted to bid him farewell, the dying man quietly passed him his ring with the imperial seal, and John hurried from the death-bed, to secure the gates of the palace. His promptness was rewarded. The army and the senate acclaimed him at once as reigning Emperor; and the Patriarch hastily endorsed their acclamation at a coronation ceremony in Saint Sophia. Anna and the Empress-Mother were outwitted. But John feared lest their partisans should make an attempt on his life. He even refused to attend his father's funeral, having good reason to believe that his murder was planned for

[1] Anna Comnena, xv, i, 6–vi, 10, pp. 187–213; Chalandon, *Règne d'Alexius I Comnène*, pp. 268–71.

the occasion. A few days later Anna organized a plot to eliminate him, while he was staying at the quiet suburban palace of Philopatium. But the plot had one grave weakness. It was to place on the throne Nicephorus Bryennius; and he had no desire for the throne. It was possibly he that warned the Emperor. John punished the conspirators very lightly. The Empress-Mother Irene probably was not privy to the plot, but retired nevertheless to a convent. Anna's leading supporters had their possessions confiscated, but many of them later received them back. Anna herself was deprived of her possessions for awhile, and henceforward lived in complete seclusion. Nicephorus went unpunished. Both he and his wife consoled themselves for the loss of a crown by adopting the less exigent calling of historian.[1]

John was now secure. He was in his thirtieth year, a small, thin man, dark-haired, dark-eyed and remarkably dark of complexion. His tastes were austere; he did not share in the delight taken by most of his family in literature and theological discussion. He was above all a soldier, happier on campaigns than in the palace. But he was an able and just administrator, and, despite his severity towards himself, generous to his friends and to the poor and ready to appear himself in ceremonial splendour should it be required. He was affectionate and forbearing to his family and faithful to his wife, the Hungarian Princess Piriska, rechristened Irene; but she, though she shared in his austerities and his charities, had little influence over him. His only intimate friend was his Grand Domestic, a Turk called Axuch, who had been taken prisoner as a boy at the capture of Nicaea in 1097 and had been brought up in the palace. John's conception of his imperial role was high. His father had left him a strong fleet, an army that was made up from a medley of races but was well organized and well equipped and a treasury that was full enough to permit an active policy. He wished not only to conserve the Empire's frontiers but to restore

[1] Anna Comnena, XV, xi, 1–23, pp. 229–42; Zonaras, III, p. 759 (a less subjective account); see Chalandon, *op. cit.* pp. 273–6, and *Les Comnènes*, pp. 1–8.

The Claims of the Emperor

it to its ancient boundaries, and to realize the imperial claims in northern Syria.[1]

John began his first campaign against the Turks in the spring of 1119. He marched down through Phrygia and recaptured Laodicea. Urgent business then recalled him to Constantinople; but he returned a month later to take Sozopolis and reopen the road to Attalia. While he himself attacked the Seldjuks in the west, he had arranged for an attack on the Danishmends in the east. Constantine Gabras, Duke of Trebizond, took advantage of a quarrel between the emir Ghazi and his son-in-law, Ibn Mangu, a Turkish princeling established at Taranaghi in Armenia, to take up arms in support of the latter. But Ghazi, with Toghrul of Melitene as his ally, defeated and captured Gabras; who had to pay thirty thousand dinars to ransom himself. A timely dispute between Ghazi and Toghrul prevented the Turks from following up their victory.[2]

For the next few years John was unable to intervene in Anatolia. These years saw an alarming growth in the power of the Danishmends. In 1124, when Toghrul of Melitene's stepfather, Balak the Ortoqid, was killed fighting in the Jezireh, the emir Ghazi invaded Melitene and annexed it, to the delight of the native Christians there, who found his rule mild and just. Next, he turned westward and took Ankara, Gangra and Kastamuni from the Byzantines and extended his power down to the Black Sea coast. Constantine Gabras, thus cut off by land from Constantinople, took advantage of his isolation to declare himself independent ruler of Trebizond. In 1129, on the death of the Roupenian Prince Thoros, Ghazi turned his attention to the south; and next year, in alliance with the Armenians, he slew Prince Bohemond II of Antioch on the banks of the Jihan. Whatever views John might hold about Antioch, he had no wish for it to pass into the possession of a powerful Moslem prince. His prompt invasion of Paphlagonia kept Ghazi from following up his victory. Fortunately during these years the Anatolian Seldjuks were incapacitated by family

[1] Chalandon, op. cit. pp. 8–11, 19.   [2] Ibid. pp. 35–48.

210

disputes. In 1125 the Sultan Mas'ud was displaced by his brother, Arab. Mas'ud fled to Constantinople, where the Emperor received him with every honour. He then went on to his father-in-law, the Danishmend Ghazi, whose help enabled him, after a struggle of four years, to recover his throne. Arab in his turn sought refuge at Constantinople, where he died.[1]

Yearly from 1130 to 1135 John campaigned against the Danishmends. Twice his work was interrupted by the intrigues of his brother, the Sebastocrator Isaac, who fled from the Court in 1130 and spent the next nine years plotting with various Moslem and Armenian princes; and in 1134 the sudden death of the Empress recalled him from the wars. By September 1134, when the death of the emir Ghazi eased the situation, he had reconquered all the lost territory except for the town of Gangra, which he recaptured next spring. Ghazi's son and successor, Mohammed, harassed by family squabbles, could not afford to be aggressive; and Mas'ud, deprived of Danishmend help, came to terms with the Emperor.[2]

With the Anatolian Turks cowed, John was ready to intervene in Syria. But first he had to protect his rear. In 1135 a Byzantine embassy arrived in Germany at the Court of the western Emperor Lothair. On John's behalf it offered Lothair large financial subsidies if he would attack Roger of Sicily. The negotiations lasted some months. Eventually Lothair agreed to attack Roger in the spring of 1137.[3] The Hungarians had been defeated in 1128 and the Serbians reduced to submission by a campaign in 1129. The defences on the lower Danube were secure.[4] The Pisans had been detached from their Norman alliance by the treaty of 1126; and the Empire was now on good terms with both Venice and Genoa.[5]

In the spring of 1137 the imperial army, with the Emperor and

[1] Chalandon, pp. 77-91; Nicetas Choniates, p. 45; Michael the Syrian, III, pp. 223-4, 227, 237.
[2] Cinnamus, pp. 14-15; Nicetas Choniates, pp. 27-9; Michael the Syrian, III, pp. 237-49.
[3] Peter Diaconus, in *M.G.H. Ss.* vol. VII, p. 833.
[4] Chalandon, *op. cit.* pp. 59-63, 70-1. [5] *Ibid.* pp. 158-61.

his sons at its head, assembled at Attalia and advanced eastward into Cilicia. The imperial fleet guarded its flank. The Armenians and the Franks were equally taken by surprise at the news of its approach. Leo the Roupenian, master now of the east Cilician plain, moved up in an attempt to check its progress by taking the Byzantine frontier fortress of Seleucia, but was forced to retire. The Emperor swept on, past Mersin, Tarsus, Adana and Mamistra, which all yielded to him at once. The Armenian prince relied on the great fortifications of Anazarbus to hold him up. Its garrison resisted for thirty-seven days; but the siege-engines of the Byzantines battered down its walls, and the city was forced to surrender. Leo retreated into the high Taurus, where the Emperor did not trouble now to follow him. After mopping up several Armenian castles in the neighbourhood, he led his forces southward past Issus and Alexandretta, and over the Syrian Gates into the plain of Antioch. On 29 August he appeared before the walls of the city and encamped on the north bank of the Orontes.[1]

Antioch was without its prince. Raymond of Poitiers had gone to rescue King Fulk from Montferrand; and Joscelin of Edessa was with him. They reached the Buqaia to find the King released. Fulk had intended himself to go to Antioch to meet the Byzantines, but after his recent experiences he preferred now to return to Jerusalem. Raymond hastened back to Antioch to find that the Emperor's siege had begun, but the investiture of the city was not yet complete. He was able to slip in with his bodyguard through the Iron Gate close under the citadel.

For several days the Byzantine machines pounded at the fortifications. Raymond could hope for no help from outside; and he was uncertain of the temper of the population within the walls. There were many even of his barons who began to see the

[1] Cinnamus, pp. 16–18; Nicetas Choniates, pp. 29–35; William of Tyre, XIV, 24, pp. 341–2; Matthew of Edessa, ccliv, p. 323; Sembat the Constable, pp. 616–17; Gregory the Priest, pp. 152–3; Michael the Syrian, III, p. 45; Ibn al-Athir, p. 424; Ibn al-Qalanisi, pp. 240–1 (the editor, p. 240 n. 2, wishes to alter the reading Kiyālyāni, i.e. Kaloioannes, for Imānyāl, Emmanuel. But it is of John that the chronicler is speaking).

wisdom of Alice's thwarted policy. It was not long before
Raymond sent a message to the Emperor offering to recognize
him as suzerain if he might keep the principality as Imperial Vicar.
John in answer demanded unconditional surrender. Raymond
then said that he must consult King Fulk; and letters were sent
post-haste to Jerusalem. But Fulk's reply was unhelpful. 'We all
know', said the King, 'and our elders have long taught us that
Antioch was part of the Empire of Constantinople till it was taken
from the Emperor by the Turks, who held it for fourteen years,
and that the Emperor's claims about the treaties made by our
ancestors are correct. Ought we then to deny the truth and oppose
what is right?' When the King whom he regarded as his overlord
offered such advice, Raymond could not resist longer. His envoys
found the Emperor ready to make concessions. Raymond was to
come to his camp and swear a full oath of allegiance to him,
becoming his man and giving him free access into the city and
citadel. Moreover, if the Byzantines with Frankish help conquered
Aleppo and the neighbouring towns, Raymond would hand back
Antioch to the Empire and receive instead a principality consisting
of Aleppo, Shaizar, Hama and Homs. Raymond acquiesced. He
came and knelt before the Emperor and paid him homage. John
did not insist then on entering Antioch; but the imperial standard
was hoisted over the citadel.[1]

The negotiations showed the uneasiness of the Frankish attitude
towards the Emperor. Fulk's reply may have been dictated by
the immediate needs of the moment. He knew too well that
Zengi was the great enemy of the Frankish kingdom and he would
not offend the only Christian power capable of checking the
Moslems; and it may be that Queen Melisende's influence was
exerted in favour of a policy that would justify her sister Alice and
would humiliate the man that had tricked her. But his verdict was
probably the considered view of his lawyers. Despite all the
propaganda of Bohemond I, the more scrupulous Crusaders held

---

[1] William of Tyre, xiv, 30, pp. 651–3; Orderic Vitalis, xiii, 34, pp. 99–101;
Cinnamus, pp. 18–19; Nicetas Choniates, pp. 36–7.

that the treaty made between Alexius and their fathers at Constantinople still was valid. Antioch should have been returned to the Empire; and Bohemond and Tancred, by violating the oaths that they had sworn, had forfeited any claims that they might have made. This was a more extreme imperialist view than the Emperor himself held. The imperial government was always realistic. It saw that it would be impracticable and unwise to try to eject the Franks from Antioch without offering compensation. Moreover, it liked to line the frontier with vassal-states whose general policy would be controlled by the Emperor but who meanwhile would bear the brunt of enemy attacks. The Emperor therefore based his claims not on the treaty made at Constantinople but on the treaty made with Bohemond at Devol. He demanded the unconditional surrender of Antioch as from a rebellious vassal; but he was prepared to let Antioch continue as a vassal-state. His immediate need was that it should co-operate in his campaigns against the Moslems.[1]

It was now too late in the year for a campaign; so John, having asserted his authority, returned to Cilicia to finish off its conquest. The Roupenian princes fled before him into the high Taurus. Three of Leo's sons, Mleh, Stephen and the blind Constantine, took refuge with their cousin, Joscelin of Edessa. The family castle of Vahka held out for some weeks under its valiant commander Constantine, whose personal combat with an officer of the Macedonian regiment, Eustratius, impressed the whole imperial army. Soon after its fall Leo and his elder sons, Roupen and Thoros, were captured. They were sent to prison in Constantinople, where Roupen was soon put to death; but Leo and Thoros gained the favour of the Emperor and were allowed to live under surveillance at the Court. Leo died there four years later. Thoros eventually escaped and returned to Cilicia. When the conquest of the province was completed, John went into winter quarters in the Cilician plain, where Baldwin of Marash came to pay him homage and to ask for protection against the Turks. At the same

[1] See Chalandon, *op. cit.* pp. 122–7, 130–3, and below, p. 215.

time an imperial embassy was sent to Zengi, in order to give him the impression that the Byzantines were unwilling to start upon an aggressive adventure.

Next February, by orders from the Emperor, the authorities in Antioch suddenly arrested all the merchants and travellers from Aleppo and the neighbouring Moslem towns, lest they might report to their homes of the military preparations that they had seen. Towards the end of March the imperial army moved up to Antioch and was joined there by the troops of the Prince of Antioch and the Count of Edessa, together with a contingent of Templars. On 1 April the allies crossed into enemy territory and occupied Balat. On the 3rd they appeared before Biza'a, which held out under its commander's wife for five days. Another week was spent in rounding up the Moslem soldiers in the district, most of whom took refuge in the grottoes of el-Baba, from whence they were smoked out by the Byzantines. Zengi was with his army before Hama from which he was trying to expel the Damascene garrison when scouts told him of the Christian invasions. He hastily sent troops under Sawar to reinforce the garrison of Aleppo. John had hoped to surprise Aleppo; but when he arrived before the walls on 20 April and launched an attack he found it strongly defended. He decided not to undertake the ardours of a siege, but turned southward. On the 22nd he occupied Athareb, on the 25th Maarat an-Numan and on the 27th Kafartab. On 28 April his army was at the gates of Shaizar.

Shaizar belonged to the Munqidhite emir, Abu'l Asakir Sultan, who had managed to preserve his independence from Zengi. Perhaps John hoped that Zengi would not therefore concern himself with the city's fate. But its possession would give the Christians control of the middle Orontes and would hinder Zengi's farther advance into Syria. The Byzantines began the siege with great vigour. Part of the lower town was soon occupied; and the Emperor brought up his great mangonels to bombard the upper town on its precipitous hill over the Orontes. Latin and Moslem sources alike tell of the Emperor's personal courage and energy and of the efficiency of his bombardment. He seemed to be everywhere at once, in his golden helmet, inspecting the machines, encouraging the assailants and consoling the wounded. The emir's nephew Usama saw the terrible damage done by the Greek catapults. Whole houses were destroyed by a single ball, while the iron staff on which the emir's flag was fixed came crashing down piercing and killing a man in the street below. But while the Emperor and his engineers were indefatigable, the Franks held back. Raymond feared that if Shaizar were captured he might be obliged to live there in the front line of Christendom and to abandon the comforts of Antioch; while Joscelin, who privately hated Raymond, had no wish to see him installed in Shaizar and perhaps later in Aleppo. His whispering encouraged Raymond's natural indolence and his mistrust of the Byzantines. Instead of joining in the combat, the two Latin princes spent their days in their tents playing at dice. The Emperor's reproaches could only goad them into perfunctory and short-lived activity. Meanwhile Zengi gave up the siege of Hama and moved towards Shaizar. His envoys hurried to Baghdad, where at first the Sultan would not offer help, till a popular riot, crying for a Holy War, forced him to send an expedition. The Ortoqid prince Dawud promised an army of fifty thousand Turcomans from the Jezireh. Letters were also sent to the Danishmend emir, requesting him to make a diversion in Anatolia. Zengi was also well aware of the dissensions between the Byzantines and the Franks. His agents in the Christian army fanned the Latin princes' resentment against the Emperor.

Despite all John's vigour the great cliffs of Shaizar, the courage of its defenders and the apathy of the Franks defeated him. Some of his allies suggested that he should go out to meet Zengi, whose army was smaller than the Christian. But he could not afford to leave his siege-machinery unguarded nor could he now trust the Franks. The risk was too great. He managed to take the whole of the lower city; then, on about 20 May, the emir of Shaizar sent to him offering to pay him a large indemnity and to present him with his best horses and silken robes and his two most precious treasures, a table studded with jewels and a cross set with rubies that had been taken from the Emperor Romanus Diogenes at Manzikert, sixty-seven years before. He agreed further to recognize the Emperor as his overlord and to pay him a yearly tribute. John, disgusted by his Latin allies, accepted the terms, and on 21 May he raised the siege. As the great imperial army moved back towards Antioch, Zengi came up towards Shaizar; but, apart from a few light skirmishes, he did not venture to interfere with the retreat.[1]

When the army reached Antioch, John insisted on making a ceremonial entry into the city. He rode on horseback, with the Prince of Antioch and the Count of Edessa walking as his grooms on either side. The Patriarch and all the clergy met him at the gate and led him through streets hung with bunting to the Cathedral for a solemn mass, and on to the palace where he took up his residence. There he summoned Raymond and, hinting that the Prince had recently failed in his duties as vassal, he demanded that his army should be allowed to enter the city and that the citadel should be handed over to him. The future campaigns against the Moslems must, he said, be planned at Antioch, and he needed the citadel to store his treasure and his war-material. The Franks were horrified. While Raymond asked for time to consider the request, Joscelin slipped out of the palace. Once outside he told his soldiers to spread a rumour round the Latin population of the city that the Emperor was demanding their immediate expulsion, and to incite them to attack the Greek population. Once the rioting was started, he rushed back to the palace and cried to John that he had come at the risk of his life to warn him of the danger that he ran. There was certainly tumult in the streets, and unwary Greeks were

[1] William of Tyre, xv, 1–2, pp. 655–8; Cinnamus, pp. 19–20; Nicetas Choniates, pp. 37–41; Michael the Syrian, *loc. cit.*; Usama, ed. Hitti, pp. 26, 124, 143–4; Ibn al-Qalanisi, pp. 248–52; Kemal ad-Din, pp. 674–8; Ibn al-Athir, pp. 426–8. The congratulatory poem addressed by Prodomus to the Emperor suggests that Shaizar was saved by the weather. (*M.P.G.* vol. cxxxiii, cols. 1344–9.)

being massacred. In the East there is no telling where a riot may end. John wished neither that the Greeks in the city should suffer nor that he himself should be cut off in the palace with only his bodyguard, and his main army on the far banks of the Orontes. Moreover he had learnt that, thanks to Zengi's diplomacy, the Anatolian Seldjuks had invaded Cilicia and raided Adana. He saw through Joscelin's trickery; but before he could risk an open breach with the Latins he must be absolutely sure of his communications. He sent for Raymond and Joscelin and said that for the moment he would ask for no more than a renewal of their oath of vassaldom and that he must return now to Constantinople. He left the palace to rejoin the army; and at once the princes stilled the riot. But they were still nervous and very anxious to recapture the Emperor's goodwill. Raymond even offered to admit imperial functionaries into the city, guessing rightly that John would not accept so insincere an offer. Shortly afterwards John said good-bye to Raymond and Joscelin with an outward show of friendship and complete mutual mistrust. He then led his army back into Cilicia.[1]

It is remarkable that during all John's negotiations over Antioch nothing was said about the Church. By the treaty of Devol the Patriarchate was to be given back to the Greek line; and it is clear that the Latin church authorities feared that the Emperor might insist on that clause; for, in March 1138 almost certainly in answer to an appeal from Antioch, Pope Innocent II issued an order forbidding any member of his Church to remain with the Byzantine army should it take any action against the Latin authorities in Antioch. John must have been unwilling to stir up any religious trouble till he was politically and strategically on surer ground. Had he succeeded in providing Raymond with a principality in lieu of Antioch, then he would have reintroduced a Greek Patriarch into the city. But in the meantime he publicly condoned the presence of a Latin when on his solemn entry Radulph

[1] William of Tyre, xv, 3-5, pp. 658-65; al-Azimi (p. 352) is the only other chronicler to mention the plot.

of Domfront came to greet him and conducted him to mass at the cathedral.[1]

John journeyed slowly back to Constantinople, after sending part of his army to punish the Seldjuk Mas'ud for his raid into Cilicia. Mas'ud asked for peace and paid an indemnity. During 1139 and into 1140 the Emperor was occupied with the Danishmend emir, who was a far more dangerous enemy than the Seldjuk. In 1139 Mohammed not only invaded upper Cilicia and took the castle of Vahka, but he also led an expedition westward as far as the Sangarius river. His alliance with Constantine Gabras, the rebel Duke of Trebizond, guarded his northern flank. During the summer of 1139 John drove the Danishmends out of Bithynia and Paphlagonia, and in the autumn he marched eastwards along the Black Sea coast. Constantine Gabras made his submission; and the imperial army turned inland to besiege the Danishmend fortress of Niksar. It was a difficult undertaking. The fortress was naturally strong and well defended; and in that wild mountainous country it was difficult to keep communications open. John was depressed by the heavy losses suffered by his troops and by the desertion to the enemy of his nephew John, his brother Isaac's son, who became a Moslem and married Mas'ud's daughter. The Ottoman Sultans claimed to be descended from him. In the autumn of 1140 John abandoned the campaign and brought his army back to Constantinople, intending to recommence next year. But next year the emir Mohammed died, and the Danishmend power was temporarily put out of action by civil war between his heirs. John could revert to his larger schemes and turn his attention again to Syria.[2]

There the benefits of his campaign against the Moslems in 1137 had been quickly lost. Zengi had recovered Kafartab from the

---

[1] William of Tyre, xv, 3, p. 659. But Ibn al-Qalanisi (p. 245) says that John demanded a Greek Patriarch for Antioch. Possibly he confused John's demands with those later made by Manuel. Innocent's letter, dated 25 March 1138, is given in *Cartulaire du Saint Sépulcre*, ed. Rozière, p. 86.

[2] Nicetas Choniates, pp. 44–9; Michael the Syrian, III, p. 248.

Franks in May 1137 and Maarat an-Numan, Bizaa and Athareb in the autumn. During the next four years, when Zengi was fully occupied in his attempt to conquer Damascus, the indolent Franks of the north failed to take advantage of his difficulties. Every year Raymond and Sawar of Aleppo exchanged raids into each other's territories; but no major engagement took place.[1] The county of Edessa enjoyed a comparative peace, owing to the internecine quarrels of the Moslem princes round the frontiers, intensified by the death of the Danishmend Mohammed. To the Emperor John, carefully watching events from Constantinople, it seemed clear that the Franks of northern Syria were valueless as soldiers of Christendom.

Raymond's apparent nonchalance was partly due to shortage of man-power and partly to his quarrel with the Patriarch Radulph. He had never intended to keep to his oath to obey the Patriarch in all things; and Radulph's arrogance enraged him. He found allies in the cathedral chapter, led by the Archdeacon Lambert and a canon, Arnulf of Calabria. Encouraged by Raymond they left for Rome towards the end of 1137 to complain of Radulph's uncanonical election. As they passed through King Roger II's dominions, Arnulf, who was born his subject, incited him against Radulph by pointing out that Radulph had secured the throne of Antioch, which Roger coveted, for Raymond. Radulph was obliged to follow them to Rome to justify himself. When he in his turn arrived in southern Italy, Roger arrested him; but such was his charm of manner and so persuasive his tongue that he soon won over the King to his side. He proceeded to Rome, where once again his charm triumphed. He voluntarily laid down his pallium on the altar of St Peter's and received it back from the Pope. When he journeyed back through southern Italy to resume his patriarchal throne, King Roger treated him as an honoured guest. But when he arrived at Antioch his clergy, backed by Raymond, refused to pay him the customary compliment of meeting him at the city gates. Radulph, playing the part of a meek,

[1] Kemal ad-Din, pp. 681–5.

injured man, retired discreetly to a monastery near St Symeon; where he remained till Joscelin of Edessa, always eager to embarrass Raymond, invited him to pay a ceremonious visit to his capital, where the Archbishop was received as spiritual overlord. Raymond soon decided that it was safer to have him back in Antioch. When he returned he was greeted with all the honours that he could desire.

But thanks to Raymond's agitations, the inquiry into his position was reopened at Rome. In the spring of 1139 Peter, Archbishop of Lyons, was sent out to hear the case on the spot. Peter, who was very old, went first to visit the Holy Places; and on his journey north he died at Acre. His death discountenanced Radulph's enemies; and even Arnulf of Calabria offered his submission. But Radulph in his arrogance refused to accept it; whereupon Arnulf, enraged, returned to Rome and persuaded the Pope to send out another legate, Alberic, Bishop of Ostia. The new legate arrived in November 1139 and at once summoned a synod which was attended by all the Latin prelates of the East, including the Patriarch of Jerusalem. It was clear that the sympathy of the synod was with the Prince and the dissident clergy. Radulph therefore refused to attend its sessions in the Cathedral of St Peter, while his only supporter, Serlon, Archbishop of Apamea, when he attempted to defend the Patriarch, was ejected from the assembly. After disobeying three summonses to appear to answer the charges against him, Radulph was declared deposed. In his place the synod elected Aimery of Limoges, the head of the chapter, a gross, energetic and almost illiterate man who had owed his first advancement to Radulph but had wisely made friends with Raymond. On his deposition the ex-Patriarch was thrown into prison by Raymond. Later he escaped and made his way to Rome, where once again he won the favour of the Pope and the Cardinals. But before he could use their help to restore himself he died, it was thought from poison, some time in 1142. The episode ensured for Raymond the loyal co-operation of the Church of Antioch; but the high-handed treatment of the

Patriarch left behind an ugly impression, even amongst the ecclesiastics who had most disliked him.[1]

In the spring of 1142 John was ready to return to Syria. As in 1136 he protected his rear by an alliance with the German monarch against Roger of Sicily. His ambassadors visited the Court of Conrad III, Lothair's successor, to make the necessary arrangements and to seal the friendship with a marriage. They returned in 1142, bringing with them Conrad's sister-in-law, Bertha of Sulzbach, who under the name of Irene was to be the wife of John's youngest son, Manuel. The good-will of the Italian maritime cities was also assured.[2] In the spring of 1142 John and his sons led his army across Anatolia to Attalia, driving back the Seldjuks and their Turcoman subjects who once again were trying to break through into Phrygia, and strengthening the frontier defences. While he waited at Attalia the Emperor suffered a heavy loss. His eldest son, Alexius, his appointed heir, fell ill and died there. His second and third sons, Andronicus and Isaac, were detailed to convey the body by sea to Constantinople; and during the voyage Andronicus also died.[3] Despite his grief, John pushed on to the east, giving out that he was bound for upper Cilicia, to reconquer the fortresses that the Danishmends had taken; for he did not wish to rouse the suspicions of the Franks.[4] The army passed by forced marches through Cilicia and across the upper Amanus range, the Giaour Dagh, and in mid-September it appeared unexpectedly at Turbessel, the second capital of Joscelin of Edessa. Joscelin, taken by surprise, hurried over to pay homage to the Emperor and to offer him as hostage his daughter Isabella.

[1] William of Tyre, xiv, 10, pp. 619–20, xv, 11–16, pp. 674–85. He is our only source.
[2] Chalandon, *op. cit.* pp. 161–2, 171–2.
[3] Cinnamus, p. 24; Nicetas Choniates, pp. 23–4. Cinnamus (p. 23) says that John had intended that Alexius should inherit the Empire but that Manuel, his youngest son, should have a principality consisting of Antioch, Attalia and Cyprus.
[4] William of Tyre, xv, 19, p. 688, indicates that Raymond had invited John's intervention out of fear of Zengi, but Nicetas Choniates (p. 52) talks of him disguising his plans and his actual arrival in Syria was a surprise (William of Tyre, *ibid.* p. 689).

John then turned towards Antioch, and on 25 September he arrived at Baghras, the great Templar castle that commanded the road from Cilicia to Antioch. Thence he sent to Raymond to demand that the whole city be handed over to him, and he repeated his offer to provide the Prince with a principality out of his future conquests.

Raymond was frightened. It was certain that the Emperor was now determined to follow up his demands with force; and it seems that the native Christians were ready to help the Byzantines. The Franks tried to gain time. Entirely changing the juridical position on which he had based himself in 1131, Raymond answered that he must consult his vassals. A council was held at Antioch at which the vassals, probably prompted by the new Patriarch, declared that Raymond only ruled Antioch as the husband of its heiress and therefore had no right to dispose of her territory, and that even the Prince and Princess together could not alienate nor exchange the principality without the consent of their vassals; who would dethrone them should they attempt to do so. The Bishop of Jabala, who brought the council's answer to John, backed up the rejection of the imperial demand by citing the authority of the Pope; but he offered John a solemn entry into Antioch. This answer, completely counter to all Raymond's previous undertakings, left John with no alternative but war. But the season was too far advanced for immediate action. After pillaging the property of the Franks in the neighbourhood of the city, he retired into Cilicia, to recover the castles taken by the Danishmends, and to spend the winter.[1]

From Cilicia John sent an embassy to Jerusalem to King Fulk, to announce his desire of paying a visit to the Holy Places, and of discussing with the King joint action against the infidel. Fulk was embarrassed. He had no wish for the great imperial army to descend into Palestine; the price of the Emperor's aid would inevitably be the recognition of his suzerainty. The Bishop of Bethlehem, Anselm, accompanied by Roard, castellan of Jeru-

---

[1] William of Tyre, xv, 19–20, pp. 688–91; Nicetas Choniates, pp. 52–3; Gregory the Priest, p. 156; Matthew of Edessa, cclv, p. 325.

salem, and by Geoffrey, abbot of the Temple, who was a good Greek scholar, was sent to John to explain that Palestine was a poor country which could not supply provender for the maintenance of so large an army as the Emperor's, but if he would care to come with a smaller escort the King would be delighted to welcome him. John decided not to press his request further for the moment.[1]

In March 1143, when the Emperor's preparations for the reduction of Antioch were made, he took a brief holiday to go hunting the wild boar in the Taurus mountains. In the course of a hunt he was accidentally wounded by an arrow. He paid little attention to the wound; but it became septic and soon he was dying of blood-poisoning. John faced his end with composure. To the last he was at work arranging for the succession and the smooth continuance of the government. His two elder sons were dead. The third, Isaac, who was at Constantinople, was a youth of uncertain temper. John decided that the youngest and most brilliant, Manuel, should be his heir, and he persuaded his great friend, the Grand Domestic Axuch, to support Manuel's claim. With his own feeble hands he placed the crown on Manuel's head and summoned in his generals to acclaim the new Emperor. After making his last confession to a holy monk from Pamphylia he died on 8 April.[2]

John's death saved Frankish Antioch. While Axuch hurried to Constantinople ahead of the news, to secure the palace and the government from any attempt by John's son Isaac to claim the throne, Manuel led the army back across Anatolia. Till he was sure of his capital there could be no further adventures in the East. The imperial project was laid aside, but not for long.[3]

[1] William of Tyre, xv, 21, pp. 691–3. John had prepared offerings for the Holy Sepulchre (Cinnamus, p. 25).

[2] William of Tyre, xv, 22–3, pp. 693–5; Cinnamus, pp. 26–9; Nicetas Choniates, pp. 56–64; Matthew of Edessa, cclv, p. 325; Gregory the Priest, p. 156; Michael the Syrian, III, p. 254; Ibn al-Qalanisi, p. 264; *Bustan*, p. 537.

[3] Cinnamus, pp. 29–32, telling of an insolent Antiochene embassy to Manuel who replied that he would return to assert his rights. Nicetas Choniates, pp. 65–9; William of Tyre, xv, 23, p. 696.

CHAPTER IV

THE FALL OF EDESSA

'An inheritance may be gotten hastily at the beginning; but the end thereof shall not be blessed.' PROVERBS XX, 21

It was with relief that the Franks of the East learnt of the Emperor's death; and in their contentment they did not notice how much more greatly relieved was their arch-enemy, the atabeg Zengi.[1] From 1141 for two years Zengi had been embarrassed by a desire of the Sultan Mas'ud to reassert his authority over him. It was only by a timely show of submission, accompanied by a gift of money and the dispatch of his son as a hostage that Zengi averted an invasion into the territory of Mosul by the Sultan's army.[2] A Byzantine conquest of Syria at that moment would have put an end to his western schemes. They were further endangered by an alliance, formed by common fear of him, between the King of Jerusalem and the atabeg of Damascus.

After the breakdown of the Franco-Byzantine alliance in 1138, Zengi returned to the task of conquering Damascus. His siege of Homs had twice been interrupted, first by the Frankish advance to Montferrand, and secondly by the Byzantine siege of Shaizar. He now returned in full force to Homs, and sent to Damascus to demand in marriage the hand of the atabeg's mother, the Princess Zumurrud, with Homs as her dowry. The Damascenes were in no position to refuse. In June 1138 the dowager was married to Zengi; and his troops entered Homs. As a gesture of good-will he enfeoffed the governor of Homs, the aged mameluke Unur,

---

[1] The Moslem attitude towards the Byzantines is exemplified by Ibn al-Qalanisi (p. 252) who when he talks of the Emperor's retreat in 1138 says 'all hearts were set at rest after their distress and fear'.

[2] Ibn al-Athir, pp. 241–2.

with the newly conquered fortress of Montferrand and some neighbouring castles.[1]

Fortunately for the Burid dynasty of Damascus, Unur did not take up his residence at Montferrand but came to Damascus. There, on the night on 22 June 1139, the young atabeg, Shihab ed-Din Mahmud, was murdered in his bed by three of his favourite pages. If Zengi, whose complicity was suspected, had hoped thereby to take over the government, he was disappointed. Unur at once assumed control. The murderers were crucified; and the atabeg's half-brother, Jemal ed-Din Mohammed, governor of Baalbek, was summoned to take over Mahmud's throne. In return Mohammed gave his mother and Baalbek to Unur. But Unur stayed on at Damascus, in charge of the government. This did not suit Zengi, who was urged on by his wife Zumurrud, and by a brother of Mohammed's, Bahram Shah, a personal enemy of Unur. In the late summer of 1139 he laid siege to Baalbek, with a large army and fourteen siege-engines. The town capitulated on 10 October; on the 21st the garrison of the citadel, formed out of the ruins of the great temple of Baal, also surrendered, after Zengi had sworn on the Koran to spare the lives of its members. But Zengi broke his oath. They were all brutally massacred and their women sold into captivity. The massacre was intended to terrify the Damascenes, but it only hardened their resistance and led them to regard Zengi as a foe outside the pale of the Faith.[2]

During the last days of the year Zengi encamped close to Damascus. He offered the atabeg Mohammed Baalbek or Homs, in exchange for Damascus; and the young prince would have accepted had Unur permitted him. On his refusal Zengi moved in to besiege the city. At this crisis, on 29 March 1140, Mohammed died. But Damascus was loyal to the Burids; and Unur without difficulty elevated Mohammed's youthful son Mujir ed-Din Abaq to the throne. At the same time he decided that he would be justified, religiously as well as politically, to call in the help of the

[1] Ibn al-Qalanisi, p. 252; Kemal ad-Din, pp. 678–9.
[2] Ibn al-Qalanisi, pp. 253–6; Ibn al-Athir, p. 431.

Christians against his perfidious enemy. An embassy led by the Munqidhite prince Usama left Damascus for Jerusalem.[1]

King Fulk had been attempting to take advantage of the embarrassments of the Damascenes to strengthen his hold of Transjordan. During the summer of 1139 he had received a visit from Thierry of Alsace, Count of Flanders, whose wife Sibylla was his daughter by his first marriage; and with Thierry's help he invaded Gilead and with some difficulty captured a small fortress near Ajlun, massacring its defenders.[2] The effort had brought him little profit; and when Unur offered him twenty thousand besants a month and the return of the fortress of Banyas if he would drive Zengi from Damascus, he was easily persuaded to change his policy. The idea of such an alliance was not new. Already early in 1138 Usama had journeyed to Jerusalem on Unur's behalf to discuss its feasibility. But though the Frankish Court had given him an honourable reception, his suggestions were rejected. Now the menace afforded by Zengi's growing power was better understood. When Fulk summoned his council to consider the offer there was a general feeling that it should be accepted.[3]

After hostages had been received from Damascus, the Frankish army set out in April for Galilee. Fulk moved cautiously and halted near Tiberias while his scouts went ahead. Zengi came down the opposite coast of the Sea of Galilee to watch his movements, but, finding him stationary, returned to the siege of Damascus. Thereupon Fulk advanced northward. Zengi would not risk being caught between the Franks and the Damascenes. He drew away from Damascus; and when Fulk met Unur's forces a little to the east of Lake Huleh, early in June, they learnt that Zengi had retired to Baalbek. Some of Zengi's troops returned later in the month to raid right up to the walls of Damascus, but he and his main army retreated on unscathed to Aleppo.[4] The

---

[1] Ibn al-Qalanisi, pp. 256–9.   [2] William of Tyre, xv, 6, pp. 665–8.
[3] *Ibid.* xv, 7, pp. 668–9; Ibn al-Qalanisi, pp. 259–60.
[4] William of Tyre, xv, 8, pp. 669–70; Ibn al-Qalanisi, p. 260; Kemal ad-Din, p. 682.

alliance had saved Damascene independence without a battle.
Unur remained true to his bargain. For some months past his
troops had been conducting a desultory siege of Banyas. Zengi's
lieutenant, Ibrahim ibn Turgut took advantage of a lull in the
siege to raid the coast near Tyre. There he was surprised by an
army led by Raymond of Antioch, who had come south to help
Fulk in the Damascene campaign. Ibrahim was defeated and killed.
When Unur himself appeared before Banyas, and was joined by
Fulk and Raymond, who were further encouraged by the visiting
papal legate, Alberic of Beauvais, the defenders soon decided to
capitulate. Unur arranged that they should be compensated with
lands near Damascus. He then handed the city over to the Franks,
who installed its former governor, Rainier of Brus, while Adam,
Archdeacon of Acre, was appointed its bishop.[1]

The alliance between Fulk and Unur was sealed by a visit that
Unur paid soon afterwards, accompanied by Usama, to the King's
Court at Acre. They were given a cordial and flattering reception,
and went on to Haifa and Jerusalem, returning through Nablus
and Tiberias. The tour was conducted in an atmosphere of the
greatest good-will, though Usama by no means approved of
everything that he saw.[2] Fulk further showed his honest desire
for friendship with the Damascenes, when they complained to
him of the raids against their flocks committed by Rainier of Brus
from Banyas. Rainier was sternly ordered to end his forays and
to pay compensation to his victims.[3]

By about the year 1140 King Fulk had reason to be satisfied with
his government. The position in northern Syria had deteriorated
since his predecessor's days; nor did he enjoy such prestige or
authority there. It is doubtful whether Joscelin of Edessa even
recognized him as overlord. But in his own domain he was secure.
He had learnt the lesson that for the Franks to survive there, they
must be less intransigent towards the Moslems, but must be ready
to make friends with the less dangerous of them; and he had

[1] William of Tyre, xv, 9–11, pp. 770–6; Ibn al-Qalanisi, pp. 260–1.
[2] Usama, ed. Hitti, pp. 166–7, 168–9, 226.　　[3] *Ibid.* pp. 93–4.

carried his nobles with him in this policy. At the same time he had worked hard for the country's defences. On the southern frontier three great castles had been built to guard against raids from the Egyptians at Ascalon. At Ibelin, some ten miles south-west of Lydda, at a well-watered spot that commanded the junction of the roads from Ascalon to Jaffa and to Ramleh, he used the ruins of the old Roman town of Jamnia to erect a splendid fortress that was entrusted to Balian, surnamed 'the Old', brother of the Viscount of Chartres. Balian had owned the land under the lords of Jaffa, and had won Fulk's favour by supporting the King against Hugh of Le Puiset. As chatelain of Ibelin he was raised to the rank of a tenant-in-chief; and he married Helvis, heiress of Ramleh. His descendants were to form the best-known noble family in the Frankish East.[1]

South of Ibelin the direct road from Ascalon to Jerusalem was guarded by the castle of Blanchegarde, on the hill called by the Arabs Tel as-Safiya, the shining mound. Its custodian, Arnulf, became one of the richest and most powerful barons of the realm.[2] The third castle was built at Bethgibelin at the village that the Crusaders wrongly identified with Beersheba. It commanded the road from Ascalon to Hebron; and its maintenance was entrusted to the Hospitallers.[3] These fortifications were not complete enough to prevent all raids from Ascalon. In 1141 the Egyptians broke through and defeated a small Crusader force on the plain of Sharon.[4] But they could hold up any serious attack from the south on Jerusalem, and were centres for local administration.

At the same time Fulk took steps to bring the country east and south of the Dead Sea under stricter control. The seigneurie of Montreal, with its castle in an oasis in the Idumaean hills, had given to the Franks a loose command of the caravan-routes leading

---

[1] William of Tyre, xv, 24, pp. 696-7. For Balian's origin, see Ducange, *Familles d'Outre Mer*, ed. Rey, pp. 360-1.

[2] William of Tyre, xv, 25, pp. 697-9.

[3] *Ibid.* xiv, 22, pp. 638-9. Martin, 'Les premiers princes croisés et les Syriens jacobites de Jérusalem. ii', *Journal Asiatique*, 8me série, vol. xiii, pp. 34-5, gives Syrian evidence suggesting that the castle was being built in 1135.

[4] Ibn al-Qalanisi, p. 263.

The Fall of Edessa

from Egypt to Arabia and to Syria; but Moslem caravans still
passed unscathed along the roads, and raiders from the desert were
still able to break through into Judaea. At the time of Fulk's
accession the lord of Montreal and Oultrejourdain had been
Roman of Le Puy, whom Baldwin I had enfeoffed about the year
1115. But Roman had supported Hugh of Le Puiset against the
King, who therefore, in about 1132, dispossessed and disinherited
his son, and gave the fief to Pagan the Butler, one of the high
officials of his Court. Pagan was a vigorous administrator who
tried to establish a tighter control over the large area that he
governed. He seems to have succeeded in policing the country to
the south of the Dead Sea; but in 1139, when Fulk was engaged in
Gilead, a band of Moslems managed to cross the Jordan close to its
junction with the Dead Sea and to raid Judaea, where they lured
to its destruction by the tactics of a feigned retreat a company of
Templar knights sent against them. It was probably to control
the north as well as the south end of the Dead Sea that Pagan
moved his headquarters from Montreal in Idumaea to Moab. There,
in 1142, on a hill called by the chroniclers Petra Deserti, the Stone
of the Desert, he built with the King's approval a great fortress
known as Kerak of Moab. It was superbly situated for dominating
the only practicable roads from Egypt and western Arabia into
Syria, and it was not too far from the fords of the lower Jordan.
Baldwin I had already established a look-out post down on the
shore of the Gulf of Akaba, at Elyn or Aila. Pagan installed a
stronger garrison there and at the Fort of the Valley of Moses, by
the ancient Petra. These castles, with Montreal and Kerak, gave
the lord of Oultrejourdain the mastery of the lands of Idumaea and
Moab, and their rich cornfields and the saltpans by the Dead Sea,
though there was no serious Frankish colonization there and the
Bedouin tribes continued their old nomad life in the barren
districts, merely paying occasional tribute to the Franks.[1]

[1] William of Tyre, xv, 21, pp. 692-3. For the products of the district, see
Abel, *Géographie de la Palestine*, I, p. 505. For the effect on Moslem trade, see
Wiet, *op. cit.* pp. 320-1. See Rey, 'Les Seigneurs de Montréal et de la Terre

The internal security of the realm improved during Fulk's reign. At the time of his accession the road between Jaffa and Jerusalem was still unsafe because of the bandits who not only molested pilgrims but also interrupted the food-supply to the capital. In 1133, while the King was absent in the north, the Patriarch William organized a campaign against the bandits and constructed a castle called Chastel Ernaut, near Beit Nuba, where the road from Lydda climbs into the hills. Its erection made it easier for the authorities to police the road; and after the fortification of the Egyptian frontier travellers seldom met with trouble on their journey from the coast.[1]

Of the government of the kingdom during Fulk's later years we hear little. Once Hugh of Le Puiset's revolt had been crushed and the Queen's desire for vengeance had been allayed, the barons supported the Crown with perfect loyalty. With the Church of Jerusalem Fulk's relations were consistently good. The Patriarch William of Messines, who had crowned him and who was to survive him, remained a faithful and deferential friend. As she grew older, Queen Melisende took to pious works, though her chief foundation was intended for the greater glory of her family. She was devoted to her sisters. Alice became Princess of Antioch; Hodierna was now Countess of Tripoli; but for the youngest, Joveta, who had spent a year of her childhood as a hostage with the Moslems, there was no suitable husband to be found. She had entered religion and became a nun at the Convent of St Anne in Jerusalem. The Queen in 1143 bought from the Holy Sepulchre, in exchange for estates near Hebron, the village of Bethany; and there she built a convent in honour of Saint Lazarus and his sisters Martha and Mary, endowing it with Jericho and all its orchards and surrounding farms, and fortifying it with a tower.

d'Oultre Jourdain', in *Revue de l'Orient Latin*, vol. IV, pp. 19 ff. The castle at the Valley of Moses is on the precipitous hill now known as Wueira on the outskirts of Petra, where extensive Crusader ruins look across to Wadi Musa. There are also ruins of a small medieval fort on the hill of al-Habis in the centre of Petra.

[1] William of Tyre, XIV, 8, p. 617.

Lest her motive should be too clearly apparent she appointed as its first abbess an excellent but elderly and moribund nun, who tactfully died a few months later. The convent then dutifully elected the twenty-four-year-old Joveta as Abbess. Joveta in her dual role as princess of the blood royal and abbess of Palestine's richest convent occupied a distinguished and venerable position for the rest of her long life.[1]

This was the most lavish of Melisende's charitable endowments; but she persuaded her husband to make several grants of land to the Holy Sepulchre, and she continued to found religious houses on a generous scale throughout her widowhood.[2] She was also responsible for improving relations with the Jacobite and Armenian Churches. Before the Crusaders' capture of Jerusalem the Jacobites had fled in a body to Egypt. When they returned they found that the estates of their church in Palestine had been given to a Frankish knight, Gauffier. In 1103 Gauffier was captured by the Egyptians, and the Jacobites recovered their lands. But in 1137 Gauffier, whom everyone thought dead, returned from his captivity and claimed his property. Owing to the direct intervention of the Queen, the Jacobites were allowed to remain in possession, after paying Gauffier three hundred besants as a compensation. In 1140 we find the Armenian Catholicus attending a synod of the Latin Church there. Melisande also gave endowments to the Orthodox Abbey of St Sabas.[3]

Fulk's commercial policy was a continuation of his predecessors'. He honoured his obligations to the Italian cities, who now controlled the export trade of the country. But he refused to give any one the monopoly; and in 1136 he made a treaty with the merchants of Marseilles, promising to give four hundred besants a year,

---

[1] William of Tyre, xv, 26, pp. 699–700. Joveta was responsible for the education of her grand-niece the future Queen Sibylla (see below, p. 407). She died some time before 1178, when the Abbess Eva of Bethany refers to her as her predecessor (*Cartulaire de Ste Marie Josaphat*, ed. Kohler, p. 122).

[2] E.g. Röhricht, *Regesta*, pp. 43, 44, 45.

[3] Nau, 'Le croisé lorrain, Godefroy de Ascha', in *Journal Asiatique*, 9me série, vol. xiv, pp. 421–31; Röhricht, *Regesta*, pp. 106–7. See below, pp. 321–3.

drawn from the revenues of Jaffa, for the maintenance of their establishment there.[1]

In the autumn of 1143 the Court was at Acre, enjoying the lull that Zengi's retreat from Damascus had afforded. On 7 November the Queen desired to go for a picnic. As the royal party rode out into the country a hare was flushed, and the King galloped off in pursuit of it. Suddenly his horse stumbled and Fulk was thrown off; and his heavy saddle struck him on the head. They carried him back unconscious and with ghastly head-wounds to Acre. There, three days later, he died. He had been a good king for the realm of Jerusalem, but not a great king nor a leader of the Franks in the East.[2]

Queen Melisende's vocal grief, much as it moved all the Court, did not distract her from taking over the kingdom. Of the children that she had born to Fulk two sons survived, Baldwin, who was aged thirteen, and Amalric, aged seven. Fulk had possessed the throne as her husband; and her rights as heiress were fully recognized. But the idea of a sole Queen-regnant was unthought of by the barons. She therefore appointed her son Baldwin as her colleague and herself assumed the government. Her action was regarded as perfectly constitutional and was endorsed by the council of the realm when she and Baldwin were crowned together by the Patriarch William on Christmas Day.[3] Melisende was a capable woman who in happier times might have reigned with success. She took as her adviser her first cousin, the Constable Manasses of Hierges, son of a Walloon lord who had married Baldwin II's sister, Hodierna of Rethel. Manasses had come out as a young man to his uncle's court, where his abilities

---

[1] Röhricht, *Regesta*, p. 40. See La Monte, *Feudal Monarchy*, p. 272. Sixteen years later Baldwin III gave them a quarter in Jerusalem. Röhricht, *Regesta*, p. 70.

[2] William of Tyre, xv, pp. 700-2; Matthew of Edessa, cclvi, p. 325; Ibn al-Qalanisi, p. 265. St Bernard wrote a letter of condolence to Queen Melisende (no. 354, *M.P.L.* vol. clxxxii, cols. 556-7).

[3] William of Tyre, xvi, 3, p. 707. For Melisende's constitutional position, see La Monte, *Feudal Monarchy*, pp. 14-18.

and his royal connections secured him steady advancement. When Balian the Old of Ibelin died, soon after King Fulk's death, Manasses married his widow Helvis, heiress of Ramleh, who in her own right and her sons' controlled the whole Philistian plain. The barons were in time to resent Manasses's power, for the Queen and he inclined towards autocracy; but for the moment there was no opposition to the Queen.[1]

Her accession brought one serious disadvantage. Under Fulk the King of Jerusalem's position as overlord of the Crusading states had been growing theoretical rather than practical; and it was unlikely that the princes of the north would pay greater attention to the suzerainty of a woman and a child. When quarrels broke out between the Prince of Antioch and the Count of Edessa, a strong king of Jerusalem, such as Baldwin II, would have marched north and forcibly composed the differences. Neither a queen nor a boy-king could do so; and no one else had the overriding authority.

Since the Emperor John's death and Zengi's check before Damascus, Raymond of Antioch's self-confidence had revived. He sent at once to the new Emperor, Manuel, to demand the return of Cilicia to his principality, and when Manuel refused he invaded the province. Manuel himself was obliged during the first months of his reign to remain at Constantinople; but he sent a land and sea expedition under the Contostephanus brothers and the converted Turk Bursuk and the admiral Demetrius Branas, which not only drove Raymond out of Cilicia but followed his troops to the walls of Antioch.[2] A few months previously Raymond had added Aleppan territory as far as Biza'a while Joscelin of Edessa advanced to the Euphrates to meet him. But Joscelin suddenly made a truce with Sawar, governor of Aleppo, which ruined Raymond's schemes. Relations between Raymond

[1] William of Tyre, xvi, 3, p. 707, for a eulogy of the Queen. For Manasses, see below, p. 334. His marriage is recorded by William, xvii, 18, p. 780, and Helvis's name often appears in charters, e.g. Röhricht, *Regesta*, pp. 22, 76.
[2] Cinnamus, pp. 33-4.

234

and Joscelin were worsening. It seems that since about 1140 Joscelin had been obliged to accept Raymond as his overlord; but there was never any cordiality between them. Joscelin had irritated Raymond by his intervention in favour of the Patriarch Radulph; and this truce brought them almost to an open rupture.[1]

Zengi was watching these quarrels. The death of the Emperor had freed him of his most dangerous potential enemy. The Damascenes would take no action against him without Frankish help; and the Kingdom of Jerusalem was unlikely now to embark on adventures. The opportunity must not be missed. In the autumn of 1144 Zengi attacked Kara Arslan, the Ortoqid prince of Diarbekir, who had recently made an alliance with Joscelin. In support of the alliance Joscelin marched out of Edessa with the bulk of his army down to the Euphrates, apparently to cut off Zengi's communications with Aleppo. Zengi was informed by Moslem observers at Harran of Joscelin's movements. He sent at once a detachment under Yaghi-Siyani of Hama to surprise the city. But Yaghi-Siyani lost his way in the darkness of the rainy November night, and reached Edessa no sooner than Zengi with the main army, on 28 November. By now the Edessenes had been warned and the defences had been manned.

The siege of Edessa lasted for four weeks. Joscelin had taken with him all his leading soldiers. The defence was therefore entrusted to the Latin archbishop, Hugh II. The Armenian bishop John and the Jacobite bishop Basil loyally supported him. Any hope that Zengi may have had of seducing the native Christians from their Frankish allegiance was disappointed. Basil the Jacobite suggested asking for a truce, but public opinion was against him. But the defenders, well though they fought, were few in numbers. Joscelin himself retired to Turbessel. The historian William of Tyre cruelly criticizes him for sloth and cowardice in refusing to go to his capital's rescue. But his army was not strong enough to

[1] Azimi, p. 537; Ibn al-Qalanisi, p. 266. Joscelin dates a diploma of 1141 'Raimundo Antiochiae principe regnante' (Röhricht, *Regesta*, p. 51), and William of Tyre (XVI, 4, p. 710) makes him allude to Raymond as his lord in 1144.

risk a battle with Zengi's. He had confidence that the great fortifications of Edessa could hold out for some time. At Turbessel he could interrupt any reinforcements that Zengi might summon from Aleppo; and he counted on help from his Frankish neighbours. He had sent at once to Antioch and to Jerusalem. At Jerusalem Queen Melisende held a Council and was authorized to gather an army, which she dispatched under Manasses the Constable, Philip of Nablus and Elinand of Bures, prince of Galilee. But at Antioch Raymond would do nothing. All Joscelin's appeals to him as his overlord were in vain. Without his help Joscelin dared not attack Zengi. He waited at Turbessel for the arrival of the Queen's army.

It came too late. Zengi's army was swelled by Kurds and Turcomans from the upper Tigris; and he had good siege-engines. The clerics and merchants who formed the bulk of the garrison were inexpert in warfare. Their counter-attacks and counterminings were unsuccessful. Archbishop Hugh was thought to be holding back the treasure that he had amassed, badly though it was needed for the defence. On Christmas Eve a wall collapsed near the Gate of the Hours; and the Moslems poured in through the breach. The inhabitants fled in panic to the citadel, to find the gates closed against them by order of the Archbishop, who himself stayed outside in a vain attempt to restore order. Thousands were trampled to death in the confusion; and Zengi's troops, hard on their heels, slew thousands more, including the bishop. At last Zengi himself rode up and ordered the massacre to cease. The native Christians were spared; but all the Franks were rounded up and done to death, and their women sold into slavery. Two days later a Jacobite priest, Barsauma, who had taken over command of the citadel, surrendered to Zengi.[1]

Zengi treated the conquered city kindly once the Franks were

---

[1] William of Tyre, xvi, 4–5, pp. 708–12: Matthew of Edessa, cclvii, pp. 326–8; Michael the Syrian, iii, pp. 259–63; *Chron. Anon. Syr*, pp. 281–6 (the fullest account, with details not found elsewhere). Nerses Shnorhal, *Elegy on the fall of Edessa*, pp. 2 ff.; Bar-Hebraeus, trans. Budge, pp. 268–70; Kemal

removed. He appointed as governor Kutchuk Ali of Arbil; but the native Christians, Armenians, Jacobites and even Greeks, were allowed a certain measure of autonomy. Though the Latin churches were destroyed, theirs were untouched, and they were encouraged to bring their co-religionists in to re-people the city. In particular the Syrian bishop Basil enjoyed the favour of the conquerors, because of his proud reply, when they questioned if he was trustworthy, that his loyalty to the Franks showed how capable he was of loyalty. The Armenians, amongst whom the dynasty of Courtenay had always been popular, took less willingly to the new régime.[1]

From Edessa Zengi moved on to Saruj, the second great Frankish fortress east of the Euphrates, which fell to him in January. He then advance to Birejik, the town that commanded the chief ford across the river. But the Frankish garrison put up a stiff resistance. Joscelin was near at hand; and the Queen's army was approaching. At that moment Zengi had rumours of trouble in Mosul. He raised the siege of Birejik and hurried eastward. He was still in name merely the atabeg of Mosul for the young Seldjuk prince Alp Arslan, son of Mas'ud. He returned to Mosul to find that Alp Arslan, in an attempt to assert his authority, had murdered the atabeg's lieutenant Shaqar. It was an ill-chosen moment, for Zengi, as the conqueror of a Christian capital, was at the height of his prestige in the Moslem world. Alp Arslan was dethroned and his advisers were put to death; while the Caliph sent Zengi an embassy laden with gifts, to confer on him the honour of King and conqueror.[2]

The news of the fall of Edessa reverberated throughout the

ad-Din, pp. 685–6; Ibn al-Qalanisi, pp. 266–8; Ibn al-Athir, pp. 443–6. Many European chronicles make some mention of the fall of Edessa. St Bernard's letter no. 256, *M.P.L.* vol. CLXXXII, col. 463, refers to it. Ibn al-Athir tells us of a Moslem at King Roger of Sicily's court who had a telepathic vision of the capture.

[1] Michael the Syrian, *loc. cit.*; *Chron. Anon. Syr. loc. cit.*
[2] *Chron. Anon. Syr.* pp. 286–8; Ibn al-Qalanisi, pp. 268–9; Ibn al-Athir, pp. 445–8; Ibn al-Furat, quoted by Cahen, *La Syrie du Nord*, p. 371 n. 11.

world. To the Moslems it brought new hope. A Christian state that had intruded into their midst had been destroyed, and the Franks restricted to the lands by the Mediterranean. The roads from Mosul to Aleppo now were cleared of the enemy, and there was no longer a Christian wedge driven between the Turks of Iran and the Turks of Anatolia. Zengi had well earned his royal title. To the Franks it brought despondency and alarm; and to the Christians of western Europe it came as a terrible shock. For the first time they realized that things were not well in the East. A movement was set on foot to preach a new Crusade.

Indeed, a Crusade was needed; for the Frankish princes of the East, despite their peril, still could not bring themselves to cooperate. Joscelin attempted to rebuild his principality in the lands that he held west of the Euphrates, with Turbessel as his capital.[1] But, though it was clear that Zengi would soon attack him, he could not forgive Raymond for having refused him help. He openly broke with him and rejected his suzerainty. Raymond was equally averse to a reconciliation. But he was alive to the danger of isolation. In 1145, after defeating a Turcoman raid, he decided to travel to Constantinople, to ask for help from the Emperor. When he arrived, Manuel would not receive him. It was only after he had knelt in humble contrition at the tomb of the Emperor John that he was allowed an audience. Manuel then treated him graciously, loading him with gifts and promising him a money subsidy. But he would not promise him immediate military aid, for the Byzantines had a Turkish war on their hands. There was talk of an expedition in the future; and the visit, humiliating though it was to Raymond's pride and unpopular amongst his barons, had one useful result. It was not unremarked by Zengi; who therefore decided to postpone a further attack on the northern Franks and to turn his attention once more to Damascus.[2]

In May 1146 Zengi moved to Aleppo to prepare for his Syrian

[1] Joscelin still owned the territory from Samosata, through Marash (held by his vassal Baldwin) south to Birejik, Aintab, Ravendal and Turbessel.
[2] Cinnamus, p. 35; Michael the Syrian, III, p. 267.

expedition. As he passed through Edessa he learnt of an attempt by the Armenians there to shake off his rule and restore Joscelin. Kutchuk Ali easily crushed it; and Zengi ordered the ringleaders to be executed and a part of the Armenian population to be banished. Its place was taken by three hundred Jewish families, introduced by Zengi because the Jews were notoriously ready to support the Moslems against the Christians.[1] In the summer Zengi led his army southward to Qalat Jabar, on the direct route from the Euphrates to Damascus, where a petty Arab prince refused to recognize him as overlord. While he was besieging the town, on the night of 14 September 1146, he quarrelled with a eunuch of Frankish origin whom he caught drinking wine from his own glass. The eunuch, furious at the rebuke, waited till he slept, then murdered him.[2]

Zengi's sudden disappearance was welcome news to all his enemies, who hoped that the dynastic disputes that usually followed the death of Moslem princes would disrupt his realm. While his corpse lay unburied and deserted, the eldest of his sons, Saif ed-Din Ghazi, accompanied by the vizier Jamal ed-Din of Isfahan, hurried to Mosul to take over the government there, and the second, Nur ed-Din, seizing the ring of office from the corpse's finger, went to be proclaimed at Aleppo by the Kurd Shirkuh, whose brother Ayub had saved Zengi's life when the Caliph defeated him in 1132. The division of the realm was the signal for its foes to invade. In the south Unur's troops from Damascus reoccupied Baalbek and reduced the governor of Homs and Yaghi-Siyani, governor of Hama, to vassalage. In the east the Seldjuk Alp Arslan made another bid for power, but in vain, while the Ortoqids of Diarbekir recovered towns that they had lost.[3] In the centre Raymond of Antioch led a raid up to the very

[1] Michael the Syrian, III, pp. 267–8; *Chron. Anon. Syr.* p. 289; Ibn al-Qalanisi, p. 270; Ibn al-Furat, *loc. cit.*
[2] William of Tyre, XVI, 7, p. 714; Michael the Syrian, III, p. 268; *Chron. Anon. Syr.* p. 291; Ibn al-Qalanisi, pp. 270–1; Kemal ad-Din, p. 688.
[3] Ibn al-Qalanisi, pp. 272–4; Ibn al-Athir, pp. 455–6; see Cahen, 'Le Diyarbekr' in *Journal Asiatique*, 1935, p. 352.

The Fall of Edessa

walls of Aleppo, while Joscelin planned to reoccupy Edessa. His agents made contact with the Armenians in the city and won over the Jacobites. Joscelin then set out himself with a small army, which was joined by Baldwin of Marash and Kaisun. Raymond once more refused his help, this time with good reason, for the expedition was ill-planned. Joscelin had hoped to surprise Edessa; but the Moslems were warned. When he arrived before its walls, on 27 October, he was able, thanks to native help, to break his way into the city itself, but the garrison of the citadel was ready for him. His troops were too few to enable him to storm its fortifications. He lingered in the city uncertain what to do. Meanwhile messengers had reached Nur ed-Din at Aleppo. His army was now counter-attacking Raymond in Antiochene territory; but he at once summoned it back and demanded help from the neighbouring Moslem governors. On 2 November he appeared before Edessa. Joscelin was caught between him and the citadel. He saw that his only chance lay in an immediate evacuation. During the night he managed to slip out with his men and with large numbers of the native Christians, and made his way towards the Euphrates. Nur ed-Din followed on his heels. Next day a battle was fought. The Franks held their ground well till Joscelin rashly ordered a counter-attack. It was driven back; and the Frankish army broke up in panic. Baldwin of Marash was killed on the field. Joscelin, wounded in the neck, escaped with his bodyguard and took refuge in Samosata, where he was joined by the Jacobite bishop Basil. The Armenian bishop John was captured and taken to Aleppo. The native Christians, deserted by the Franks, were massacred to a man, and their wives and children enslaved. At Edessa itself the whole Christian population was driven into exile. The great city, which claimed to be the oldest Christian commonwealth in the world, was left empty and desolate, and has never recovered to this day.[1]

[1] William of Tyre, xvi, 14–16, pp. 728–32; Matthew of Edessa, cclviii, pp. 328–9 (giving the wrong date 1147–8); Michael the Syrian, III, pp. 270–2. Basil the Doctor, *Elegy on Baldwin*, p. 205; *Anon. Chron. Syr.* pp. 292–7; Ibn al-Qalanisi, pp. 274–5; Ibn al-Athir, pp. 455–8 (and *Atabegs*, p. 156); *Bustan*, p. 541.

The episode showed Zengi's enemies that they had gained little by his death. Moreover his sons, though they had small affection for each other, were wise enough not to quarrel. Saif ed-Din Ghazi, whose hands were fully occupied with the Ortoqids, took the initiative in arranging an interview with his brother, at which the division of the inheritance was peaceably confirmed. Saif ed-Din took the lands in Iraq and Nur ed-Din those in Syria. About the same time Nur ed-Din's position was strengthened by an unexpected act of folly committed by the Franks in Jerusalem. Early in 1147 one of Unur's lieutenants, Altuntash, governor of Bosra and Salkhad in the Hauran, an Armenian converted to Islam, declared his independence of Damascus and came to Jerusalem for support. He offered to hand Bosra and Salkhad to the Franks if they would set him up in a lordship in the Hauran. Queen Melisende very correctly summoned her Council to discuss the suggestion. It was an important decision to make, for to support Altuntash would mean the rupture of the alliance with Damascus. But it was a tempting offer. The population in the Hauran was largely Christian, Melkite, of the Orthodox rite. With this Christian help it should be easy to colonize the Hauran; and its control would put Damascus at the mercy of the Franks. The barons hesitated. They ordered the army to be assembled at Tiberias; but they sent an embassy to Unur to say that they proposed to reinstate Altuntash. Unur was angry, but for fear of Nur ed-Din he wished to avoid a rupture. He answered reminding the Queen that, according to her feudal law, a ruler could not support the rebellious vassal of a friendly power against his master; but he offered to repay her for any expenses that her proposed expedition had involved. The Queen then sent a knight called Bernard Vacher to Damascus to say that unfortunately she was committed to the support of Altuntash whom her army would convey back to Bosra, but she undertook in no way to cause damage to Damascene territory. Bernard soon returned, convinced by Unur that the proposal was unwise and wrong. He brought the young king Baldwin round to his views; and, when the matter was discussed again before the Council it was decided to abandon the expedition. But by now the soldiers' enthusiasm had been aroused. Demagogues in the army, furious at the cancellation of a profitable raid against the infidel, denounced Bernard as a traitor and insisted on war. The King and the barons were frightened and gave way.

In May 1147 the Frankish army, with the King at its head, crossed the Jordan and marched into the Jaulan. But it was not the triumphal progress that the soldiers had anticipated. Unur had had full warning. His light Turcoman troops combined with the Arabs of the district to harrass them as they toiled up the Yarmuk valley towards Deraa. Unur himself had already sent an embassy to Aleppo to ask for help from Nur ed-Din. It was an appeal that Nur ed-Din was delighted to receive. An alliance was made. Nur ed-Din received Unur's daughter's hand in marriage and promised to come at once to his rescue; he was to be given back Hama but was to respect Damascene independence. At the end of May the Franks reached Deraa, just over halfway between the frontier and Bosra. Meanwhile, Unur had hurried to Salkhad, which lay farther to the east. Altuntash's garrison there asked for a truce; and Unur moved on westward to join with Nur ed-Din, who had come down at full speed from Aleppo. Together they marched on Bosra, which was surrendered to them by Altuntash's wife. News of the surrender reached the Franks on the evening when, weary and short of water, they arrived within sight of Bosra. They were in no state to attack the Moslems. There was nothing to be done but retreat. The return journey was more arduous than the advance. Food ran short; many of the wells had been destroyed. The enemy hung on their rear and killed the stragglers. The boy King showed great heroism, refusing a suggestion that he should leave the main army and hurry on to safety with a picked bodyguard. Thanks to his example, discipline remained high. The barons at last decided to make their peace with Unur, and dispatched an Arabic-speaking messenger, probably Bernard Vacher, to beg for a truce; but the messenger was killed on his way. However, when the army reached ar-Rahub, on the edge of the Jebel Ajlun, a messenger came from Unur, to offer to revictual the Franks. With Nur ed-Din at hand, he had no wish for the Frankish army to be completely wiped out. The King haughtily rejected the offer; but it was remarked that a mysterious stranger on a white horse with a scarlet banner appeared to lead the army safely to Gadara. After a last skirmish there it crossed the Jordan back into Palestine. The expedition had been costly and pointless. It showed the Franks to be good fighters but foolish in their politics and their strategy.[1]

One man alone had profited from it, Nur ed-Din. Unur had indeed recovered the Hauran. When Altuntash came to Damascus hoping to be pardoned, he was blinded and imprisoned, and his friends were disgraced. But Unur was desperately conscious of Nur ed-Din's strength. He was alarmed for the future and longed to restore his Frankish alliance. Nur ed-Din, however, abode by his treaty with Unur. He returned northward to continue the task of stripping the principality of Antioch of all its lands east of the Orontes. By the end of 1147 Artah, Kafarlata, Basarfut and Balat were in his hands.[2]

Nur ed-Din thus emerged as the principal enemy of the Christians. He was now aged twenty-nine; but he was wise for his years. Even his opponents admired his sense of justice, his charity and his sincere piety. He was perhaps a less brilliant soldier than his father Zengi, but he was less cruel and less perfidious and a far better judge of men. His ministers and generals were able and loyal. His material sources were less than his father's; for Zengi had been able to call on the riches of Upper Iraq, which now had passed to Saif ed-Din. But Saif ed-Din had therefore inherited Zengi's difficulties with the Ortoqids and with the Caliph and the Seldjuk sultanate, leaving Nur ed-Din free to give his full attention to the West. Moreover, the sons of Zengi

---

[1] William of Tyre, XVI, 8–13, pp. 715–28; Ibn al-Qalanisi, pp. 276–9; Abu Shama, pp. 50–3.
[2] Kemal ad-Din, ed. Blochet, pp. 515–16; Ibn al-Athir, pp. 461–2.

remained true to their family pact. Saif ed-Din would send help if need be to Nur ed-Din, without any desire to annex his share of the family lands. A third brother, Nasr ed-Din, was established as Nur ed-Din's vassal at Harran, while the youngest of the family, Qutb ed-Din, was growing up at his eldest brother's court at Mosul. Secure from danger from his fellow-Moslems by his family connections and his alliance with Unur, Nur ed-Din was well fitted to lead the counter-attack of Islam. If the Christians in the East were to survive, it was against him that they must concentrate their efforts.[1]

[1] Ibn al-Athir, p. 456, and *Atabegs*, pp. 152–8.

BOOK III

THE SECOND CRUSADE

CHAPTER I

THE GATHERING OF THE KINGS

'Arise therefore, and be doing, and the Lord be with
thee.'   I CHRONICLES XXII, 16

As soon as it was known in Jerusalem that Edessa had fallen,
Queen Melisende sent to Antioch to consult with the government
there about the dispatch of an embassy to Rome, to break the news
to the Pope and to ask for a new Crusade. It was decided that the
ambassador should be Hugh, Bishop of Jabala, whose opposition
to the demands of the Emperor John had given him renown
amongst the Latin Christians. Despite the urgency of his message
the bishop did not arrive until the autumn of 1145 at the Papal
Curia. Pope Eugenius III was at Viterbo, as Rome was in the
hands of a commune resentful of papal rule. With him was the
German chronicler, Otto of Freisingen, who recorded the Pope's
reception of the dreadful news, though he himself was more
interested by information brought by the bishop of a Christian
potentate who lived to the east of Persia and was conducting a
successful war against the infidel. His name was John, and he was
a Nestorian. Already he had conquered the Persian capital of
Ecbatana, but he had gone northward to a region of ice and snow,
where he had lost so many men that he had returned to his home.
This was the first entry of the legendary Prester John into the
pages of history.[1]

Pope Eugenius did not share the chronicler's hope that Prester
John would rescue Christendom. He was seriously disquieted.
About the same time a delegation reached him of Armenian
bishops from Cilicia, eager for support against Byzantium.[2] The

---

[1] Otto of Freisingen, *Chronica*, pp. 363–7. See Gleber. *Papst Eugen III*, p. 36.
[2] See Tournebize, *Histoire Politique et Religieuse de l'Arménie*, pp. 235–9.

Pope could not neglect his Oriental duties. While Bishop Hugh went on to inform the courts of France and Germany, Eugenius decided to preach the Crusade.[1] But the Papacy was not in the position to direct the movement as Pope Urban had tried to do. Since his accession in February, Eugenius had not been able to enter Rome. He could not yet afford to travel beyond the Alps. Fortunately he was on good terms with the two chief potentates of western Europe. Conrad of Hohenstaufen, King of Germany, had owed his throne to ecclesiastical support, and had been crowned by the papal legate. With Louis VII, the pious King of France, papal relations were even more cordial. After some early misdemeanours, due to the influence of his wife, Eleanor of Aquitaine, he had repented and allowed himself to be guided in all things by ecclesiastical advisers, notably by the great Abbot of Clairvaux, Saint Bernard. It was to King Louis that the Pope decided to apply for help for the East. He needed Conrad's help in Italy, for the subjection of the Romans and the curbing of the ambitions of Roger II of Sicily. He did not wish Conrad to assume other obligations. But Louis was king of the land from which most of the Frankish princes and lords in the East had come; he was the obvious leader for the expedition that was to relieve them. On 1 December 1145, Eugenius addressed a bull to King Louis and all the princes and the faithful of the kingdom of France, urging them to go to the rescue of eastern Christendom and promising them security for their worldly possessions and remission for their sins.[2]

The news of the fall of Edessa horrified the West. The interest and enthusiasm aroused by the First Crusade had quietened down. The capture of Jerusalem had fired men's imagination; and immediately afterwards large reinforcements had willingly set out

---

[1] *Chronicon Mauriniacense, R.H.F.* vol. XII, p. 88; Otto of Freisingen, *Gesta Friderici*, pp. 54–7.

[2] Jaffé-Wattenbach, *Regesta*, no. 8796, vol. II, p. 26. Caspar 'Die Kreuzzugsbullen Eugens III', in *Neues Archiv*, vol. XLV, pp. 285–306, proves that the Bull must definitely be dated 1 December 1145, which destroys the French theory that Louis VII instigated the Crusade.

in answer to appeals from the East, as the Crusades of 1101 had shown. But the Crusades of 1101 had ended in disaster; and, in spite of that, the Frankish states in the East had held and consolidated their position. Reinforcements still came, but in driblets. There was a steady stream of pilgrims, many of whom would stay long enough to fight in a summer campaign. Among these were potentates like Sigurd of Norway; or there might be a great company of humbler folk, such as the Englishmen, Flemings and Danes who came in 1106. The Italian maritime cities would from time to time send a fleet to help in the capture of some seaport; but their motive was frankly commercial interest, which also brought in a growing number of individual Italian merchants. But since Baldwin I's reign there had been few of these armed pilgrim companies. Of recent years the only one of note had been that led by King Fulk's son-in-law, Thierry, Count of Flanders. Immigrants had continued to arrive, younger sons, like Balian of Chartres, founder of the house of Ibelin, or barons like Hugh of Le Puiset or Manasses of Hierges, who hoped to take advantage of kinship with the royal house. A more constant and valuable element was provided by the knights that came out to join the great Military Orders, the Hospitallers and the Templars. The Orders were gradually assuming the role of the standing army of the kingdom; and the many grants of lands made to them by the Crown and its vassals showed how highly they were appreciated. But ever since the dispersal of the armies of the First Crusade there had not been in the East a Frankish force strong enough to undertake a grand offensive against the infidel.[1]

It needed the shock of the disaster at Edessa to rouse the West again. For meanwhile in the perspective of western Europe the Crusader states of Syria had seemed merely to form the left-flank of the Mediterranean-wide campaign against Islam. The right flank was in Spain, where there were still tasks for a Christian knight to perform. The progress of the Cross in Spain had been held up during the second and third decades of the century, owing

[1] See above, pp. 91–2, 227.

to the quarrels between Queen Urraca of Castile and her husband King Alfonso I of Aragon. But the Queen's son and heir by her first, Burgundian, marriage, Alfonso VII brought about a renaissance in Castile. In 1132, six years after his accession, he began a series of campaigns against the Moslems, which brought him by 1147 to the gates of Cordova, where he was recognized as suzerain. Already in 1134 he had taken the title of Emperor, to show that he was overlord of the peninsula and vassal to no man. Meanwhile Alfonso I, freed by Urraca's death of Castilian complications, spent his last years taking the offensive, with varying success, in Murcia; and along the coast Raymond-Berenger III, Count of Barcelona, pushed his power southward. Alfonso I died in 1134. His brother, the ex-monk Ramiro, reigned disastrously for three years; but in 1137 Ramiro's two-year old daughter, Queen Petronilla, was married to Raymond-Berenger IV of Barcelona, and Catalonia and Aragon were united to form a power whose naval strength enabled it to complete the reconquest of north-eastern Spain.[1] Thus by 1145 things were going well in the Spanish theatre; but a storm was brewing. The Almoravids, who had dominated Moslem Spain for the last half-century, had fallen into a hopeless decay. Their place in Africa had already been taken by the Almohads, a sect of ascetic reformers, almost Gnostic in its theology and its insistence on a class of adepts, founded by the Berber prophet Ibn Tumart, and carried on even more aggressively by his successor Abd al-Mumin. Abd al-Mumin defeated and slew the Almoravid monarch, Tashfin ibn Ali, near Tlemcen in 1145. In 1146 he completed the conquest of Morocco and was ready to move into Spain.[2] With such preoccupations the Christian knights in Spain were insensible to an appeal from the East. On the other hand, now that the Spanish kingdoms were securely founded, they no longer offered the same scope as in the previous century to the knights and princes of France.

[1] See Bellasteros, *Historia de España*, II, pp. 247–62.
[2] For the Almohads, see Codera, *Decadencia y Desaparición de los Almoravides en España*, and Bel, article 'Almohads', in *Encyclopaedia of Islam*.

Roger II of Sicily

The centre of the battlefield against Islam was occupied by King
Roger II of Sicily. Roger had united all the Norman dominions
in Italy and assumed the royal title in 1130. He was well aware of
the strategic importance of his kingdom, which was ideally placed
to control the Mediterranean. But, to make that control complete,
it was necessary for him to have a footing on the African coast
opposite to Sicily. The quarrels and rivalries of the Moslem
dynasties in northern Africa, intensified by the declining power of
the Almoravids in Morocco and the ineffectual suzerainty of the
Fatimids in Tunisia, together with the dependence of the African
cities upon the import of grain from Sicily, gave Roger his chance.
But his first campaigns, from 1123 to 1128, brought him no profit
beyond the acquisition of the island of Malta. In 1134 by judi-
ciously timed assistance he induced El-Hasan, lord of Mahdia, to
accept him as overlord; and next year he occupied the island of
Jerba in the Gulf of Gabes. Successful raids on Moslem shipping
whetted his appetite, and he began to attack the coastal towns.
In June 1143 his troops entered Tripoli, but were forced to retire.
Exactly three years later he recaptured the city, just as an internal
revolution was installing an Almoravid prince as its governor.
This time he could not be dislodged; and Tripoli became the
nucleus for a Norman colony in Africa.[1]

King Roger was thus admirably fitted to take part in the new
Crusade. But he was suspect. His behaviour to the Papacy had
never been dutiful and seldom deferential. His presumption in
crowning himself king had been resented by the other potentates
of Europe; and Saint Bernard had commented to Lothair of
Germany that 'whoever makes himself King of Sicily attacks the
Emperor'.[2] Saint Bernard's disapproval meant the disapproval of
French public opinion. Roger was still more unpopular among
the princes in the East; for he had made it clear that he had never
forgiven the kingdom of Jerusalem for its treatment of his mother
Adelaide and his own failure to secure the succession promised in

[1] Chalandon, *Domination Normande en Italie*, pp. 158–65.
[2] Saint Bernard, letter no. 139, in *M.P.L.* vol. CLXXXII, col. 294.

her marriage-contract, while he claimed Antioch as sole heir in the male line of his cousin Bohemond. His presence on the Crusade was not desired; but it was hoped that he would carry on the war against Islam in his own particular sector.[1]

The Pope's choice of King Louis of France to organize the new Crusade was easy to understand; and the King responded eagerly to the call. When the papal Bull arrived, following close on the news brought by the Bishop of Jabala, Louis had just issued a summons to his tenants-in-chief to meet him at Christmas at Bourges. When they were assembled he told them that he had decided to take the Cross and he begged them to do likewise. He was sadly disappointed in their answer. The lay nobility showed no enthusiasm. The chief elder statesman of the realm, Suger, Abbot of Saint-Denis, voiced his disapproval of the King's projected absence. Only the Bishop of Langres spoke up in support of his sovereign.[2]

Chilled by his vassals' indifference, Louis decided to postpone his appeal for three months, and summoned another assembly to meet him at Easter at Vézélay. In the meantime he wrote to the Pope to tell him of his own desire to lead a Crusade; and he sent for the one man in France whose authority was greater than his own, Bernard, Abbot of Clairvaux. Saint Bernard was now at the height of his reputation. It is difficult now to look back across the centuries and appreciate the tremendous impact of his personality on all who knew him. The fire of his eloquence has been quenched in the written words that survive. As a theologian and a controversialist he now appears rigid and a little crude and unkind. But from the day in 1115 when, at the age of twenty-five, he was appointed Abbot of Clairvaux, till his death nearly forty years later he was the dominant influence in the religious and political life of western Europe. It was he who gave the Cistercian Order its impetus; it was he who, almost single-handed, had rescued the Papacy from the slough of the schism of Anacletus. The fervour

[1] Odo of Deuil, pp. 22-3.
[2] *Vita Sugerii Abbatis*, pp. 393 ff.; Odo of Deuil, p. 121.

and sincerity of his preaching combined with his courage, his vigour and the blamelessness of his life to bring victory to any cause that he supported, save only against the embittered Cathar heretics of Languedoc. He had long been interested in the fate of eastern Christendom and had himself in 1128 helped in drawing up the rule for the Order of the Temple. When the Pope and the King begged for his help in preaching the Crusade, he eagerly complied.[1]

The assembly met at Vézélay on 31 March 1146. The news that Saint Bernard was going to preach brought visitors from all over France. As at Clermont, half a century before, the crowd was too great to be fitted into the Cathedral. Saint Bernard spoke from a platform erected in a field outside the little town. His words have not been handed down. We only know that he read out the papal Bull asking for a holy expedition and promising absolution to all that took part in it, and that he then made use of his incomparable rhetoric to show the urgency of the papal demand. Very soon his audience was under his spell. Men began to cry for Crosses—'Crosses, give us Crosses!'—It was not long before all the stuff that had been prepared to sew into Crosses was exhausted; and Saint Bernard flung off his own outer garments to be cut up. At sunset he and his helpers were still stitching as more and more of the faithful pledged themselves to go on the Crusade.[2]

King Louis was the first to take the Cross; and his vassals forgot their earlier coolness in their eagerness to follow him. Amongst them were his brother Robert, Count of Dreux, Alfonso-Jordan, Count of Toulouse, who had himself been born in the East, William, Count of Nevers, whose father had led one of the unfortunate expeditions of 1101, Henry, heir to the County of Champagne, Thierry of Flanders, who had already fought in the East and whose wife was Queen Melisende's stepdaughter, the

---

[1] Odo of Deuil, p. 21. According to Otto of Freisingen the barons wished to consult St Bernard before they committed themselves (*Gesta Friderici*, p. 58). For St Bernard and the Templars, see Vacandard, *Vie de Saint Bernard*, II, pp. 227–49.

[2] Odo of Deuil, p. 22; *Chronicon Mauriniacense, loc. cit.*; Suger, *Gesta Ludovici*, ed. Molinier, pp. 158–60.

The Gathering of the Kings

King's uncle, Amadeus of Savoy, Archimbald, Lord of Bourbon, the Bishops of Langres, Arras and Lisieux and many nobles of the second rank. An even greater response came from humbler people.[1] Saint Bernard was able to write a few days later to the Pope, saying: 'You ordered; I obeyed; and the authority of him who gave the order has made my obedience fruitful. I opened my mouth; I spoke; and at once the Crusaders have multiplied to infinity. Villages and towns are now deserted. You will scarcely find one man for every seven women. Everywhere you see widows whose husbands are still alive.'[2]

Encouraged by his success Saint Bernard undertook a tour of Burgundy, Lorraine and Flanders, preaching the Crusade as he went. When he was in Flanders he received a message from the Archbishop of Cologne, begging him to come at once to the Rhineland. As in the days of the First Crusade, the enthusiasm aroused by the news of the movement had been turned against the Jews. In France the Abbot of Cluny, Peter the Venerable, eloquently complained that they were not paying a financial contribution towards the rescue of Christendom. In Germany the resentment took a fiercer form. A fanatical Cistercian monk called Rudolf was inspiring Jewish massacres throughout the Rhineland, in Cologne, Mainz, Worms, Spier and Strasburg. The Archbishops of Cologne and Mainz did what they could to save the victims, and the latter summoned Bernard to deal with the Cistercian. Bernard hastened from Flanders and ordered

[1] The Bishop of Langres was Godfrey de la Roche Faillée, a monk of Clairvaux and a relative of St Bernard. Of Alvisus, Bishop of Arras, formerly Abbot of Anchin, little is known. Later legends made him Suger's brother, without any foundation. Arnulf of Séez, Bishop of Lisieux, was a classical scholar of distinctively secular tastes. The bishops of Langres and Lisieux considered themselves to have been given the position of Papal Legates, though in fact the Legates were the German Theodwin, Cardinal of Porto, and the Florentine Cardinal Guido. John of Salisbury (*Historia Pontificalis*, pp. 54–5) considered that the quarrels between the two bishops and their joint resentment of the Cardinals contributed largely to the failure of the Crusade. He thought Godfrey of Langres more reasonable than Arnulf of Lisieux.
[2] St Bernard, letter no. 247, in *op. cit.* col. 447.

Rudolf back into his monastery. When calm was re-established, Bernard stayed on in Germany; for it seemed to him that the Germans too should join in the Crusade.[1]

The Germans hitherto had played an undistinguished part in the Crusading movement. Their Christian zeal had, rather, been directed towards the forcible evangelization of the heathen Slavs on their eastern frontiers. Since the beginning of the century missionary work and German colonization had been going on in the Slav districts in Pomerania and Brandenburg; and the German lords regarded this expansion of Christendom as a more important task than a war against Islam, whose menace was to them remote and theoretical. They were therefore disinclined to respond to Saint Bernard's preaching. Nor was their King, Conrad of Hohenstaufen, greatly though he admired the Saint, much more eager to listen to him. He had Mediterranean interests; but they were restricted to Italy, where he had promised the Pope help against the recalcitrant Romans and against Roger of Sicily, in return for his much desired imperial coronation. And his position was still insecure in Germany itself. Despite his victory at Weinsburg in 1140 he still was faced with the enmity of the supporters of the house of Welf; while the antics of his Babenberger half-brothers and sisters raised trouble for him along all his eastern flank. When Saint Bernard, after writing round to secure the co-operation of the German bishops, met the King at Frankfort-on-the-Main in the autumn of 1146, Conrad prevaricated; and Bernard would have gone back to Clairvaux, had the bishops not begged him to continue his preaching. He therefore turned southward to preach the Crusade at Freiburg, at Basle, at Schaffhausen and Constance. The tour was immediately successful, even though the sermons had to be translated by a German interpreter. The humbler people flocked

[1] St Bernard, letters nos. 363, 365, in *op. cit.* cols. 564–8, 570–1; Otto of Freisingen, *Gesta Friderici*, pp. 58–9; Joseph ben Joshua ben Meir, *Chronicle*, trans. Biellablotzky, I, pp. 116–29. The rumours of their murder of a Christian child at Norwich helped to rouse feeling against the Jews. See Vacandard, *op. cit.* II, pp. 274–81.

to take the Cross. The crops in Germany had failed that year, and there was famine in the land. Starvation breeds a mystic exaltation; and it is probable that many in Bernard's audiences thought, like the pilgrims of the First Crusade, that the journey eastward would bring them to the riches of the New Jerusalem.[1]

King Conrad agreed to meet Saint Bernard again at Christmas 1146, when he would be holding a Diet at Spier. Saint Bernard's sermon on Christmas Day, once more asking him to take the Cross, failed to move the King. But two days later Bernard preached again before the Court. Speaking as though he were Christ Himself he rounded on the King, reminding him of the benefits that Heaven had showered on him. 'Man,' he cried, 'what ought I to have done for you that I have not done?' Conrad was deeply moved and promised to follow the Saint's bidding.[2]

Saint Bernard left Germany well pleased with his work. He travelled through eastern France, supervising the arrangements for the Crusade and writing to the Cistercian houses all over Europe to bid them encourage the movement. He was back in Germany in March to assist at a council at Frankfort, when it was decided to send a Crusade against the heathen Slavs east of Oldenburg. His presence was intended to show that while he advocated an Oriental Crusade, he did not desire the Germans to neglect their nearer duties. This German Crusade, though the Pope allowed the participants to wear the Cross, was in its outcome a fiasco that did much to retard the conversion of the Slavs. From

[1] Bernhardi, *Konrad III*, pp. 563–78, a full summary of the Crusades against the Slavs. St Bernard's letter no. 457 (*op. cit.* cols. 651–2) orders the Christians of Germany to crusade in the East and no. 458, cols. 652–4, gives the same order to the King and people of Bohemia. Chroniclers such as William of Tyre, Odo of Deuil, and most modern historians refer to Conrad as Emperor; but in fact he never received an imperial coronation.

[2] Otto of Freisingen, *Gesta Friderici*, pp. 60–3; *Vita S. Bernardi*, cols. 381–3. It is possible that Conrad was influenced by hearing that his rival Welf VI of Bavaria had decided to take the Cross. (See Cosack, 'Konrad III's Entschluss zum Kreuzzug', in *Mitteilungen des Instituts für österreichische Geschichtsforschung*, vol. xxxv; but Welf's decision was made so shortly before Conrad's that the latter can hardly have heard of it. See Gleber, *op. cit.* pp. 53–4.)

Frankfort Bernard hurried to his abbey at Clairvaux, to receive a visit from the Pope.[1]

Pope Eugenius had spent Christmas 1145 in Rome; but difficulties with the Romans forced him soon to withdraw again to Viterbo, while Rome itself passed under the influence of the anti-clerical agitator, Arnold of Brescia. Eugenius realized that without the help of King Conrad he could not hope to re-establish himself in the Holy City. In the meantime he decided to cross the Alps into France, to see King Louis and to superintend the Crusade. He left Viterbo in January 1147 and reached Lyon on 22 March. As he journeyed he received news of Saint Bernard's activities. He was not altogether pleased. His practical sense had made him envisage a purely French Crusade, under the lay leadership of the King of France, without the divided command that had so nearly wrecked the First Crusade. Saint Bernard had turned the movement into an international enterprise; and the splendour of his conception might well be outweighed in practice by the rivalry of the kings. Besides, the Pope could not spare King Conrad, on whose aid he was counting in Italy. He gave the news of German participation a very chilly reception. But he could not countermand it.[2]

Proceeding into France, the Pope met King Louis at Dijon in the first days of April and arrived at Clairvaux on 6 April. Conrad sent him an embassy there to ask for an interview at Strassburg on the 18th; but Eugenius had promised to spend Easter, on 20 April, at Saint-Denis and would not alter his plans. Conrad prepared to depart for the East without the personal blessing of the Pontiff. Eugenius meanwhile had many interviews with the abbot Suger, who was to govern France while Louis was away. He held a council at Paris to deal with the heresy of Gilbert de la Porée, and he saw Louis again, at Saint-Denis, on 11 June. Then, while Louis completed his last preparations, he moved slowly southward to return to Italy.[3]

[1] See St Bernard, letter no. 457, *loc. cit.*; Vacandard, *op. cit.* II, pp. 297-8.
[2] See Gleber, *op. cit.* pp. 22-7, 48-61.   [3] Odo of Deuil, pp. 24-5.

While the Kings of France and Germany were preparing for the Crusade, planning a long overland journey, a humbler expedition composed of Englishmen, together with some Flemings and Frisians, was inspired by the preaching of Saint Bernard's agents to set out by sea for Palestine. The ships left England in the late spring of 1147; and early in June bad weather forced them to take refuge at the mouth of the river Douro, on the Portuguese coast. There they were met by emissaries from Alfonso-Henry, Count of Portugal. He had recently established his country's independence and was negotiating with the Papacy for the title of King, giving as its justification his successful campaigns against the Moslems. Taking advantage of the difficulties of the Almoravids, he had won a great victory at Ourique in 1139, and in March of 1147 he had reached the banks of the Tagus and had captured Santarem. He now wished to attack the local Moslem capital, Lisbon, and needed naval help for it. The Crusaders' arrival was timely. His chief envoy, the Bishop of Oporto, pointed out to them that there was no need to make the long voyage to Palestine if they wished to fight for the Cross. There were infidels close at hand, and not only spiritual merit but rich estates could be won here and now. The Flemings and Frisians agreed at once; but the English contingent hesitated. They had vowed to go to Jerusalem; and it needed all the influence of their leader, Henry Glanville, Constable of Suffolk, whom the Bishop had won over, to persuade them to remain. Once the terms were arranged, the flotilla sailed down to the Tagus, to join the Portuguese army; and the siege of Lisbon was begun. The Moslems defended their city valiantly. It was only in October, after four months of fighting, that the garrison surrendered, on the guarantee that their lives and property would be preserved. The Crusaders promptly broke the terms and indulged in a glorious massacre of the infidel, in which the English, congratulating themselves on their virtue, only played a minor part. After the campaign was over, some of the Crusaders continued their journey to the East, but many more remained as settlers under the Portuguese crown. The episode, though it heralded the long alliance between England and Portugal and though it laid the foundations for the spread of Christianity beyond the oceans, did little to help Christians in the East, where sea-power would have been invaluable to the cause.[1]

While the northerners delayed in Portugal, the Kings of France and Germany set out by land to the East. King Roger of Sicily had sent to each of them to offer to transport them and their armies by sea. To Conrad, who had long been Roger's enemy, the offer was obviously inacceptable, and Louis also declined it. The Pope did not wish for Roger's co-operation; and it is doubtful whether in fact the Sicilian marine was large enough to carry all the soldiers bound for the Crusade. Louis had no desire to entrust himself, separated from half his army, to a man whose record for duplicity was notorious and who was bitterly hostile to the French Queen's uncle. It was safer and cheaper to travel by land.[2]

King Conrad intended to leave Germany at Easter, 1147. In December he had received a Byzantine embassy at Spier, which he told of his immediate departure to the East. In fact it was not till the end of May that he started his journey. He left Ratisbon towards the last days of the month and passed into Hungary. His army was of formidable proportions. Awed chroniclers spoke of a million soldiers; and it is probable that the whole company, armed men and pilgrims, numbered nearly twenty thousand. With Conrad came two vassal-kings, Vladislav of Bohemia and Boleslav IV of Poland. The German nobility was headed by Conrad's nephew and heir, Frederick, Duke of Swabia. There was a contingent from Lorraine, led by Stephen, Bishop of Metz, and Henry, Bishop of Toul. It was a turbulent army. The German magnates were jealous of each other; and there was constant

[1] The chief original source for the Portuguese Crusade is Osborn, *De expugnatione Lyxbonensi*, printed in Stubbs, *Memorials of the Reign of Richard I*, vol. I, pp. cxliv–clxxxii. See also Erdmann, 'Die Kreuzzugegedanke in Portugal', in *Historische Zeitschrift*, vol. CXLI, pp. 23–53.

[2] King Louis had announced the Crusade to Roger (Odo of Deuil, p. 22), but when Roger suggested active participation he rejected his help to the retrospective grief of Odo (*ibid.* p. 24).

friction between the Germans, the Slavs and the French-speaking Lorrainers. Conrad was not the man to keep it under control. He was now well over fifty years of age, of indifferent health and a weak, uncertain temperament. He had begun to delegate much of his authority into the vigorous but inexperienced hands of his nephew Frederick.[1]

During June the German army moved through Hungary. The young King Geza was well disposed; and there was no unpleasant incident. A Byzantine embassy, led by Demetrius Macrembolites and the Italian Alexander of Gravina, met Conrad in Hungary and asked him on the Emperor's behalf whether he came as a friend or foe and to beg him to take an oath to do nothing against the welfare and interests of the Emperor. This oath of non-injury was well chosen; for in certain parts of the West it was the usual oath for a vassal to take to his overlord; it was the oath that Raymond of Toulouse had taken to Alexius during the First Crusade; yet it was so framed that Conrad could hardly refuse to take it without labelling himself as the Emperor's enemy. He took it; and the Byzantine ambassadors then promised him every assistance while he should be in imperial territory.[2]

About 20 July Conrad crossed into the Empire at Branitchevo. Byzantine ships helped to convey his men across the Danube. At Nish the governor of the Bulgarian province, Michael Branas, met him and provided the army with food that had been stored up against its arrival. At Sofia, which it reached a few days later, the governor of Thessalonica, the Emperor's cousin, Michael Palaeologus, gave Conrad an official welcome from the Emperor. So far all had gone well. Conrad wrote to friends in Germany that he was satisfied with everything. But after leaving Sofia his men began to pillage the countryside and to refuse to pay the villagers for what they took, even slaughtering those who protested. When complaints were made to Conrad, he confessed that he could not discipline the rabble. At Philippopolis there were

[1] Odo of Freisingen, *Chronica*, p. 354 and *Gesta Friderici*, pp. 63–5.
[2] Cinnamus, pp. 67–9.

worse disorders. More food was stolen, and a riot occurred when a local juggler, who had hoped to gain some money from the soldiers by showing off his tricks, was accused by the Germans of sorcery. The suburbs were burnt down; but the city walls were too strong for the Germans to attack. The Archbishop, Michael Italicus, protested so vigorously to Conrad that he was shamed into punishing the ringleaders. Manuel then sent troops to accompany the Crusaders and to keep them to the road. This only produced worse disorders, as the Byzantines and Germans frequently came to blows. The climax came near Adrianople, when some Byzantine bandits robbed and killed a German magnate who had lingered behind sick; whereupon Frederick of Swabia burnt down the monastery near which the crime had been committed and slew its inhabitants. Drunken stragglers, who were abundant amongst the Germans, were slain in retaliation whenever they fell into Byzantine hands. When the Byzantine commander Prosuch had restored peace and the army resumed its march, an embassy came from Manuel, who was now seriously alarmed, to urge Conrad to take the road to Sestos on the Hellespont and cross from there into Asia. It would be regarded as an unfriendly act were the Germans to march on to Constantinople. Conrad would not agree. Manuel then seems to have decided to oppose the Crusaders by force, but at the last moment countermanded his orders to Prosuch. The Germans were soon visited by divine punishment. As they lay encamped at Cheravas on the Thracian plain a sudden inundation swept through their tents, drowning many of the soldiers and destroying much property. Only Frederick's detachment, encamped on higher ground, were unharmed. There was, however, no further serious incident till the army reached Constantinople, on about 10 September.[1]

King Louis and the French army followed about a month behind. The King himself set out from Saint-Denis on 8 June and

---

[1] Cinnamus, pp. 69–74; Nicetas Choniates, pp. 82–7; Odo of Deuil, p. 38. The juggler is mentioned by him earlier, p. 36. Odo of Freisingen, *Gesta Friderici*, pp. 65–7.

summoned his vassals to meet him at Metz a few days later. His expedition was probably a little smaller than Conrad's. All the nobles who had taken the Cross with him at Vézélay came to fulfil their vows; and with the King was his wife, Eleanor of Aquitaine, the greatest heiress in France and niece to the Prince of Antioch. The Countesses of Flanders and Toulouse and many other great ladies travelled with their husbands. The Grand Master of the Temple, Everard of Barre, joined the army with a regiment of recruits for his Order.[1] The King himself was aged twenty-six. He was famed for piety rather than for a strong personality. His wife and his brother both wielded influence over him. As a commander he was untried and indecisive.[2] On the whole his troops were better disciplined and less wanton than the Germans, though there were disorders at Worms at the crossing of the Rhine.[3]

When all the French contingents had joined the King the army set out through Bavaria. At Ratisbon, where it arrived on 29 June, ambassadors from the Emperor Manuel were waiting. These were Demetrius Macrembolites, who had already interviewed Conrad in Hungary, and a certain Maurus. They asked for guarantees that Louis would behave as a friend while in imperial territory and that he would promise to restore to the Empire any of its former possessions that he should conquer. Apparently they did not require him to swear the oath of non-injury, whose significance he might have realized too well. Louis declared formally that he was coming as a friend, but he gave no promise about his future conquests, finding the request dangerously vague.[4] From

---

[1] A list of Crusaders is given in Suger, *Gesta Ludovici*, ed. Molinier, pp. 158–60. The legend that Queen Eleanor came at the head of a company of Amazons is based on a remark of Nicetas (p. 80) that the German army contained a number of fully armed women.

[2] The portrait of him given in Suger's *Gesta* and in his own letters is not of a decisive man.

[3] Odo of Deuil, p. 27.

[4] Cinnamus, p. 82. He calls the Germans ''Αλεμανοί' and the French 'Γερμανοί'; Odo of Deuil, pp. 28–30. He says that Louis made representatives swear on his behalf.

Ratisbon the French journeyed peaceably for fifteen days through Hungary and reached the Byzantine frontier at the end of August.[1] They crossed the Danube at Branitchevo and followed the main road through the Balkans. They found some difficulty in procuring sufficient food; for the Germans had consumed all that was available, and the excesses committed by the Germans made the local inhabitants suspicious and unwilling to help. Moreover, the local merchants were far too ready to give short measure after insisting on pre-payment. But the Byzantine officials were friendly, and the French commanders kept their men in order. There was no serious trouble till the army drew near to Constantinople, though the French began to feel resentment against both the Byzantines and the Germans. At Adrianople the Byzantine authorities tried, as with Conrad, to persuade Louis to by-pass the capital and cross the Hellespont into Asia, but with equal unsuccess. Meanwhile, some of the French, impatient with the leisurely progress of their army, hurried ahead to join with the Germans. But the Germans were unfriendly, refusing to spare them rations. The contingents from Lorraine, already on bad terms with their German comrades, joined with these Frenchmen and inflamed French public opinion against the Germans.[2] Thus, before ever the French King arrived at Constantinople, relations between the two Crusading armies were suspicious and embittered, and Germans and French alike were ill-disposed towards Byzantium. It did not augur well for the success of the Crusade.

[1] Odo of Deuil, pp. 30–4. [2] *Ibid.* pp. 35–44.

CHAPTER II

CHRISTIAN DISCORD

'Debates, envyings, wraths, strifes, backbitings, whisperings, swellings, tumults.' II CORINTHIANS XII, 20

When the news of the coming of the Crusade first reached Constantinople, the Emperor Manuel was engrossed in Anatolian affairs. Despite his father's and his grandfather's campaigns, the situation in the Asiatic provinces of the Empire was still worrying. Only the coastal districts were free from Turkish invasions. Farther inland almost yearly a Turkish raiding force would sweep over the territory, avoiding the great fortresses and eluding the imperial armies. The inhabitants of the frontier-lands had abandoned their villages and fled to the cities or to the coast. It was Manuel's policy to establish a definite frontier-line, guarded by a closely knit line of forts. His diplomacy and his campaigns were aimed at securing such a line.

The Danishmend emir Mohammed ibn Ghazi died in December 1141. He had been the chief Moslem power in Asia Minor; but his death was followed by civil wars between his sons and his brothers. Before the end of 1142 the emirate was split into three. His son Dhu'l Nun held Caesarea-Mazacha, his brothers Yakub Arslan ibn Ghazi and Ain ed-Daulat ibn Ghazi Sivas and Melitene respectively. The Seldjuk Sultan of Konya, Mas'ud, saw in the division his chance of establishing a hegemony over the Anatolian Turks. He invaded Danishmend territory and established his control over districts as far east as the Euphrates. Frightened by his aggression the brothers Yakub Arslan and Ain ed-Daulat sought the alliance of Byzantium, and by a treaty, probably concluded in 1143, they became to some degree his vassals. Manuel then turned his attention towards Mas'ud, whose raiders had penetrated to Malagina, on the road from Nicaea to Dorylaeum. He drove them back, but returned soon to Constantinople owing to his own ill-health and the fatal illness of his beloved sister Maria, whose loyalty to him had been proved when her husband, the Norman-born Caesar John Roger, had plotted for the throne at the time of his accession. In 1145 Mas'ud invaded the Empire again and captured the little fortress of Pracana in Isauria, thereby threatening Byzantine communications with Syria, and soon afterwards raided the valley of the Meander, almost as far as the sea. Manuel decided that the time had come to strike boldly at Mas'ud and to march on Konya. He had recently been married, and it was said that he wished to show to his German wife the splendours of Byzantine chivalry. In the summer of 1146 he sent the Sultan a formal declaration of war and set out in gallant style along the road past Dorylaeum down to Philomelium. There Turkish detachments attempted to check him but were repulsed. Mas'ud retired towards his capital but, though he strengthened its garrison, he kept himself to the open country and sent urgently for reinforcements from the East. The Byzantine army encamped for several months before Konya, which was defended by the Sultana. Manuel's attitude towards his enemies was courteous. When it was rumoured that the Sultan was killed, he sent to inform the Sultana that the story was untrue; and he attempted, vainly, to make his soldiers respect the Moslem tombs outside the city. Suddenly he gave the order to retire. It was said later that he had heard rumours of the coming Crusade; but he could hardly have been notified yet of the decision made at Vézelay that spring. He was definitely suspicious of Sicilian intentions, and he may already have realized that something was afoot. He learnt, too, that Mas'ud had received a considerable addition to his army, and he was afraid of being caught with long and risky lines of communication. He retreated slowly in perfect order back to his own territory.[1]

[1] See Chalandon, *Les Comnènes*, pp. 248–58. Michael the Syrian (III, p. 275), says that Manuel made peace with the Turks for fear of the Crusaders and that he managed to hold them up for two years.

Before there could be another campaign against Konya, Manuel was faced with the actual prospect of the Crusade. He was disquieted, with reason; for the Byzantines' experience of Crusaders was not reassuring. When, therefore, Mas'ud sent to him in the spring of 1147 to suggest a truce and to offer to give back Pracana and his other recent conquests, Manuel agreed. For this treaty he has been called a traitor to Christendom. But Conrad's hostility, demonstrated before news of the treaty could have reached the Germans, shows that his precautions were wise. He had no obligations towards a fellow-Christian who openly thought of attacking Constantinople. Nor could Manuel be pleased by an expedition which would undoubtedly encourage the Prince of Antioch to forget his recent homage and subservience. If he were engaged in a serious war against the Turks it might help the Crusaders in their passage across Anatolia, but it would permit them to do infinite harm to the Empire that was the bulwark of Christendom. He preferred to have no entanglement that might weaken him at so delicate a time, especially as a war with Sicily was imminent.[1]

With Conrad, Manuel's relations had hitherto been good. A common fear of Roger of Sicily had brought them together; and Manuel had recently married Conrad's sister-in-law.[2] But the behaviour of the German army in the Balkans and Conrad's refusal to take the route across the Hellespont alarmed him. When Conrad arrived before Constantinople he was allotted as his residence the suburban palace of Philopatium, near the land-walls; and his army encamped around him. But within a few days the Germans so pillaged the palace that it was no longer habitable; and Conrad moved across the head of the Golden Horn to the palace of Picridium, opposite to the Phanar quarter. Meanwhile his soldiers committed violence against the local population, and

[1] Chalandon, *op. cit.* pp. 266–7. The war with Sicily broke out in fact in the summer of 1147 (*op. cit.* p. 318 n. 1). Odo of Deuil refers to it (p. 53).
[2] See above, p. 222. The marriage took place in January 1146 (Chalandon, *op. cit.* p. 262 n. 3).

Byzantine soldiers were sent out to repress them. A series of skirmishes ensued. When Manuel asked for redress Conrad at first said that the outrages were unimportant; then he angrily threatened to come back next year and take over the capital. It seems that the Empress, Conrad's sister-in-law, was able to pacify the two monarchs. Manuel, who had been urging the Germans to cross quickly over the Bosphorus, as he feared the consequences of the junction with the French, suddenly found the Germans amenable, as the Germans were already beginning to quarrel with the first French arrivals. An outward concord was restored; and Conrad and his army passed over to Chalcedon, enriched by costly presents. Conrad himself received some handsome horses. But he refused the suggestion that he should leave some of his men to take service with the Emperor and should in return be allotted some of the Byzantine troops in Cilicia, an arrangement that Manuel would have found convenient for his war against Roger of Sicily.[1]

When he arrived in Chalcedon, Conrad asked Manuel to provide him with guides to take him across Anatolia; and Manuel entrusted the task to the head of the Varangian Guard, Stephen. At the same time he advised the Germans to avoid the road straight across the peninsula but to go by the coast-road round to Attalia, thus keeping within imperial-controlled land. He also suggested that it would be wise to send home all the non-combatant pilgrims whose presence would only embarrass the army. Conrad took no notice of this advice, but set out to Nicaea. When his army arrived there, he thought again and decided to divide the expedition. Otto of Freisingen was to take a party, including most of the non-combatants, by a road through Laodicea-on-the-Lycus

[1] Cinnamus, pp. 74–80; Nicetas Choniates, p. 87; letter of Conrad to Wibald, *Wibaldi Epistolae* in Jaffé, *Bibliotheca*, I, p. 166 (saying that he was well received by the Emperor); *Annales Herbipolenses*, pp. 4–5; Romuald of Salerno, p. 424; Odo of Deuil, pp. 39–40. He says that according to the Greeks' computation 900,566 German soldiers and pilgrims crossed the Bosphorus. Possibly 9566 is the correct figure. He also says that Conrad did not have a personal interview with Manuel.

Christian Discord

to Attalia, while he himself and the main fighting force would follow the route of the First Crusade through the interior.[1]

Conrad's army left Nicaea on 15 October, with Stephen the Varangian as chief guide. For the next eight days, whilst they were in the Emperor's territory, they were well fed, though they later complained that his agents mixed chalk with the flour that was provided and also gave them coins of a debased value. But they made no provisions for their march into Turkish territory. In particular they lacked water. On 25 October, as they reached the little river Bathys, near to Dorylaeum, close to the site of the great Crusader victory half a century before, the whole Seldjuk army fell upon them. The German infantry were weary and thirsty. Many of the knights had just dismounted, to rest their exhausted horses. The sudden, swift and repeated attacks of the light Turkish horsemen caught them unawares. It was a massacre rather than a battle. Conrad vainly tried to rally his men; but by evening he was in full flight with the few survivors on the road back to Nicaea. He had lost nine-tenths of his soldiers and all the contents of his camp. The booty was sold by the victors in the bazaars throughout the Moslem East, as far as Persia.[2]

Meanwhile King Louis and the French army had passed through Constantinople. They arrived there on 4 October, to find their advance-guard and the army of Lorraine disgusted on the one hand by the savagery of the Germans and on the other by the news of Manuel's truce with the Turks. Despite the pleading of Louis's envoy, Everard of Barre, Grand Master of the Temple, the Byzantine authorities made difficulties about the junction of the Lorrainers with the French.[3] The Bishop of Langres, with the un-Christian intolerance of a monk of Clairvaux, suggested to the King that he should change his policy and make an alliance with

[1] Cinnamus, pp. 80-1.
[2] Cinnamus, pp. 81-2; Nicetas Choniates, p. 89; letter of Conrad to Wibald, *Wibaldi Epistolae*, p. 152; *Annales Palidenses*, p. 82; *Annales Herbipolenses, loc. cit.*; Odo of Deuil, pp. 53, 56-8; William of Tyre, XVI, 21-2, pp. 740-4; Michael the Syrian, III, p. 276.
[3] Odo of Deuil, pp. 40-1.

Roger of Sicily against the perfidious Greeks. But Louis was too scrupulous to listen, to the disappointment of his barons. He was satisfied by his reception at the Byzantine Court and preferred the suave advice of the humanist Bishop of Lisieux. He was lodged at Philopatium, which had been cleaned after the German occupation, and he was welcomed to banquets at the imperial palace at Blachernae and conducted by the Emperor round the sights of the great city. Many of his nobility were equally charmed by the attentions paid to them.[1] But Manuel saw to it that the French army passed soon over the Bosphorus; and when it was established at Chalcedon he used the pretext of a riot caused by a Flemish pilgrim who thought he had been cheated to cut off supplies from the French. Though Louis promptly had the culprit hanged, Manuel would not revictual the camp until Louis at last swore to restore to the Empire its lost possessions that he might help to recover, and agreed that his barons should pay homage in advance for any that they might occupy. The French nobility demurred; but Louis considered the demand reasonable, considering his urgent need for Byzantine assistance, particularly as rumours came through of the German disaster.[2]

At the beginning of November the French army reached Nicaea. There they learnt definitely of Conrad's defeat. Frederick of Swabia rode into the French camp to tell the story, and asked Louis to come at once to see Conrad. Louis hastened to the German headquarters; and the two Kings consulted together. They decided both to take the coast route southward, keeping within Byzantine territory. For the moment there was amity between the two armies. When the Germans could find no food in the area where they were encamped, as the French had taken all that was available, and they therefore began to raid the neighbouring villages, Byzantine police-troops at once attacked them. They were rescued by a French detachment under the

---

[1] Cinnamus, pp. 82–3; Louis VII, letter to Suger, *R.H.F.* vol. xv, p. 488 Odo of Deuil, pp. 45–6, 47–8.
[2] Odo of Deuil, pp. 48–51.

Christian Discord

Count of Soissons, who hurried up at Conrad's request. Conrad was meantime able to restore some sort of order among his troops. Most of the pilgrims who survived left him to struggle back to Constantinople. Their further history is unknown.[1]

The armies moved on together. On 11 November they encamped at Esseron, near the modern Balikesri. There they made a further change of plan. It is probable that reports had come to them of the journey made by Otto of Freisingen along the direct route to Philadelphia and Laodicea. We know little of that journey save that his expedition arrived at last at Attalia weary and reduced in numbers, leaving by the wayside the many dead whom their own privations or Turkish raiders had slain. The Kings decided to keep closer to the coast, through more fertile country, and to remain in touch with the Byzantine fleet. They marched on down through Adramyttium, Pergamum and Smyrna and came to Ephesus. Louis's army was in the van, and the Germans struggled on about a day behind, taunted by their allies for their slowness. The Byzantine historian Cinnamus records the cry of 'Pousse Allemand' which was hurled at them by the contemptuous French.[2]

When they arrived at Ephesus Conrad's health was so bad that he remained there. Hearing this the Emperor Manuel sent him costly presents and persuaded him to return to Constantinople where he received him kindly and took him to lodge in the palace. Manuel was passionately interested in medicine and insisted on being his guest's own doctor. Conrad recovered, and was deeply touched by the attentions shown him by the Emperor and the Empress. It was during this visit that a marriage was arranged between his brother, Henry, Duke of Austria, and the Emperor's niece, Theodora, daughter of his brother Andronicus. The German

---

[1] Odo of Deuil, pp. 58–60; William of Tyre, xvi, 23, pp. 744–5.
[2] Odo of Deuil, pp. 61–3. Cinnamus (p. 84) discusses the difference between the two armies. The French were better on horseback and with the lance, the Germans on foot and with swords. He transliterates 'Pousse Allemand' as Πούτζη Ἀλεμανέ.

King and his household remained in Constantinople till the beginning of March 1148, when a Byzantine squadron conveyed them to Palestine.[1]

During the four days that he spent at Ephesus King Louis received a letter from Manuel informing him that the Turks were on the war-path and advising him to avoid any conflict with them but to keep as far as possible within the range of shelter afforded by the Byzantine fortresses. Manuel clearly feared that the French would suffer at the hands of the Turks and he would be blamed; at the same time he had no wish, with the Sicilian war on his hands, that anything should occur to break his peace with the Sultan. Louis returned no answer, nor did he reply when Manuel wrote to warn him that the Byzantine authorities could not prevent their people from taking vengeance for the damage caused to them by the Crusaders. The discipline of the French army was breaking down, and complaints were reaching the capital of its lawlessness.[2]

The French army wound its way up the valley of the Meander. At Decervium, where Christmas was spent, the Turks made their appearance and began to harass the Crusaders till they reached the bridge across the river, at Pisidian Antioch. There was a pitched battle there; but the Frenchmen forced their way over the bridge, and the Turks retired behind the walls of Antioch. Under what circumstances the Turks were able to take refuge within this Byzantine fortress is unknown. The French not unnaturally saw it as treason to Christendom; but whether the local garrison had yielded to superior force or had made some private arrangement with the infidel, it is unlikely that the Emperor himself had sanctioned the plan.[3]

The battle before the bridge at Antioch took place about 1 January 1148. Three days later the Crusaders arrived at Laodicea,

---

[1] Cinnamus, pp. 85–6; letter of Conrad to Wibald, *Wibaldi Epistolae*, p. 153; *Annales Herbipolenses*, p. 6; Odo of Deuil, pp. 63–4; William of Tyre, XVI, 23, pp. 745–6.

[2] Cinnamus, *loc. cit.*; Odo of Deuil, pp. 63–5.

[3] Odo of Deuil, pp. 65–6; William of Tyre, XVI, 24, pp. 746–7.

to find it deserted; for their reputation had driven the inhabitants to the hills, with all their provisions. It was difficult for the army to collect any food for the arduous stage that lay ahead.[1] The road to Attalia wound over high desolate mountains. It was a hard journey at the best of times. For a hungry army, struggling through the January storms, with the Turks relentlessly hanging on its flanks and picking off the stragglers and the sick, it was a nightmare. All along the road the soldiers saw the corpses of the German pilgrims who had perished on their march a few months before. There was no longer any attempt at discipline, except with the company of the Knights Templar. The Queen and her ladies shivered in their litters, vowing never again to face such an ordeal. One afternoon, as the army began to descend toward the sea, the advance-guard, under Geoffrey of Rancon, disobeyed the King's orders to camp on the summit of the pass and moved down the hill, losing touch with the main army, which the Turks at once attacked. The Crusaders held their ground; but it was only the falling of darkness that saved the King's life, and the losses among the Frenchmen were heavy.[2]

Thenceforward the way was easier. The Turks did not venture down into the plain. At the beginning of February the Crusade arrived at Attalia. The Byzantine governor there was an Italian called Landolph. On the Emperor's orders he did what he could to succour the Westerners. But Attalia was not a large town with great resources of food. It was set in a poor countryside ravaged recently by the Turks. Winter stocks were low by now; and the German pilgrims had taken what there had been to spare. It was no wonder that few provisions were available and that prices had soared high. But to the angry disappointed Frenchmen

[1] Odo of Deuil, *loc. cit.*

[2] *Ibid.* pp. 67-7, 71-2; William of Tyre, xvi, 25, pp. 747-9. For the baseless story that Queen Eleanor was responsible for the disaster, see Walker, 'Eleanor of Aquitaine and the disaster at Cadmos Mountain', in *American Historical Review*, vol. lv, pp. 857-61. Odo of Deuil was responsible for much good work in victualling the army. He is too modest himself to mention it. (William the Monk, *Dialogus Apologeticus*, p. 106.)

all this was just another proof of Byzantine treachery. King Louis now decided that the journey must be pursued by sea, and negotiated with Landolph for ships. It was not easy at that time of year to assemble a flotilla at a port on the wild Caramanian coast. While the transports were being collected, the Turks came down and made a sudden attack on the Crusader camp. Once again the French blamed the Byzantines; who indeed probably made no effort to defend the unwanted guests to whose presence they owed these Turkish raids. When the ships arrived they were too few to take all the company. Louis therefore filled them with his own household and as many cavalrymen as could be taken, and sailed off to Saint Symeon, where he arrived on 19 March. To salve his conscience for his desertion of his army, the King gave Landolph the sum of five hundred marks, asking him to care for the sick and wounded and to send on the remainder, if possible, by sea. The Counts of Flanders and Bourbon were left in charge. The day after the King's departure the Turks swept down into the plain and attacked the camp. Without sufficient cavalry it was impossible to drive them off effectively; so the Crusaders obtained permission to take refuge within the walls. There they were well treated and their sick given treatment; and Landolph hastily tried to collect more ships. Again he could not find sufficient for all the expedition. So Thierry of Flanders and Archimbald of Bourbon followed their King's example and themselves embarked with their friends and the remaining horsemen, telling the foot-soldiers and the pilgrims to make their way by land as best they could.[1] Deserted by their leaders the unhappy remnant refused to stay in the camp prepared for them by Landolph, who wished to move them out of the town. They thought that they would be too badly exposed there to attacks from Turkish archers. Instead, they set out at once along the eastern road. Ignorant, undisciplined and distrustful of their guides, continually harassed by the Turks, with whom they were convinced the Byzantines were in league, the

[1] Odo of Deuil, pp. 73–6. He tries awkwardly to gloss over the King's desertion of the army. William of Tyre, XVI, 26, pp. 749–51.

miserable Frenchmen, with what remained of Conrad's German infantry dragging on behind, made their painful way to Cilicia. Less than half of them arrived in the late spring at Antioch.[1]

In one of his many letters home to the abbot Suger, letters whose unvaried theme is a request for more money, King Louis ascribed the disasters in Anatolia to 'the treachery of the Emperor and also our own fault'. The charge against Manuel is repeated more constantly and more passionately by the official French chronicler of the Crusade, Odo of Deuil, and it has been echoed by western historians, with few exceptions, to this day.[2] The misfortunes of the Crusades did so much to embitter relations between western and eastern Christendom that the accusation must be examined more closely. Odo complains that the Byzantines provided insufficient food-supplies for which they charged exorbitant prices, in-adequate transport and inefficient guides and, worst of all, that they allied themselves with the Turks against their fellow-Christians. The first charges are absurd. No medieval state, even one so well organized as the Byzantine, possessed sufficient stocks of food to be able to supply two exceptionally large armies which had arrived uninvited at short notice; and when food is scarce, its prices inevitably rise. That many local merchants and some government officials tried to cheat the invaders is certain. Such behaviour has never been a rare phenomenon in commerce, particularly in the Middle Ages and in the East. It was unreasonable to expect Landolph to supply a sufficient number of ships for a whole army at the little port of Attalia in mid-winter; nor could the guides, whose advice was seldom taken, be blamed if they did not know of the latest destruction of bridges or wells by the Turks, or if they fled before the threats and hostility of the men that they were conducting. The question of the Turkish alliance is more serious, but it must be regarded from Manuel's viewpoint. Manuel neither invited nor wished for the Crusade. He had good reasons

[1] Odo of Deuil, pp. 76–80.
[2] Louis VII, letter to Suger, *R.H.F.* vol. xv, pp. 495–6; Odo of Deuil is throughout hysterically anti-Greek.

for deploring it. Byzantine diplomacy had learnt well by now how to play off the various Moslem princes against each other and thus to isolate each of them in turn. A well advertised expedition like the Crusade would inevitably again bring together a united front against Christendom. Moreover, for Byzantine strategy against Islam it was essential to control Antioch. Byzantium had at last won this control, when Prince Raymond made his abject submission at Constantinople. The coming of a Crusade with his niece and her husband at its head would inevitably tempt him to throw off his vassalage. The behaviour of the Crusaders when they were guests in his territory was not such as to increase the Emperor's liking for them. They pillaged; they attacked his police; they ignored his requests about the routes that they should take; and many of their prominent men talked openly of attacking Constantinople. Seen in such a light his treatment of them seems generous and forbearing; and some of the Crusaders so recognized it. But the westerners could not comprehend nor forgive his treaty with the Turks. The broad needs of Byzantine policy were beyond their grasp; and they chose to ignore, though they certainly were aware of the fact, that while they demanded help from the Emperor against the infidel his own lands were being subjected to a venomous attack from another Christian power. In the autumn of 1147 King Roger of Sicily captured the island of Corfu and from there sent an army to raid the Greek peninsula. Thebes was sacked, and thousands of its workers kidnapped to help the nascent silk-industry of Palermo; and Corinth itself, the chief fortress of the peninsula, was taken and bared of all its treasures. Laden with spoil the Sicilian Normans fell back to Corfu, which they planned to hold as a permanent threat to the Empire and a stranglehold on the Adriatic Sea. It was the imminence of the Norman attack that had decided Manuel to retire from Konya in 1146 and to accept the Sultan's overtures for peace next year. If Manuel was to rank as a traitor to Christendom, King Roger certainly took precedence over him.

The Byzantine army was large but not ubiquitous. The best

troops were needed for the war against Roger. Then there were rumours of unrest in the Russian Steppes, which was to result in the summer of 1148 in a Polovtsian invasion of the Balkans. With the Crusade at hand, Manuel could not denude his Cilician frontier of men; and the passage of the Crusaders through the Empire meant that a large increase must be made in the military police. With these preoccupations, the Emperor could not provide full frontier forces to cover his long Anatolian borderlands. He preferred a truce that would enable his Anatolian subjects to live their lives free from the menace of Turkish raids. The Crusaders endangered this truce. Conrad's march on Dorylaeum was a direct provocation to the Turks; and Louis, though he kept within Byzantine territory, publicly announced himself as the enemy of all Moslems and refused the Emperor's request to remain within the radius guarded by Byzantine garrisons. It is quite possible that Manuel, faced by this problem, made an arrangement with the Turks by which he condoned their incursions into his territory so long as they only attacked the Crusaders, and that they kept to the bargain, thus giving the clear impression that they were in league with the local inhabitants; to whom indeed it was indifferent whether their flocks and foodstocks were stolen by Crusaders or by Turks, and who under these circumstances would naturally prefer the latter.[1] But it is impossible to believe with Odo of Deuil that they definitely attacked the Crusaders at the Turks' side. He makes this accusation against the inhabitants of Attalia immediately after saying that they were later punished by the Emperor for having shown kindness to the Crusaders.[2]

The main responsibility for the disasters that befell the Crusaders in Anatolia must be placed on their own follies. The Emperor could indeed have done more to help them, but only at a grave

[1] For Manuel's preoccupations at this time, see Chalandon. Michael the Syrian repeats many of the Frankish accusations against the Greeks (III, p. 276). But Moslem sources, e.g. Abu Shama, p. 54, say that Manuel made common cause with the Franks.
[2] Odo of Deuil, p. 79.

PLATE II

JERUSALEM FROM THE MOUNT OF OLIVES

The Dome of the Rock (Solomon's Temple) and the Mosque al-Aqsa are in the left foreground of the city. The Tower of David shows on the horizon behind them. The Holy Sepulchre is behind the right corner of the Dome of the Rock.

PLATE III

TRIPOLI

Raymond's castle of Mount Pilgrim is in the foreground. The walls facing the ravine are mainly Raymond's original construction. The Saracen town, al-Mina, is in the background on the left.

PLATE IV

THE EMPEROR JOHN COMNENUS

PLATE V

DAMASCUS

Seen from the north-west. The orchards through which the Second Crusade
attacked are on the far side of the city.

PLATE VI

SEALS OF BALDWIN III, KING OF JERUSALEM; BOHEMOND III,
PRINCE OF ANTIOCH; PONS, COUNT OF TRIPOLI;
WILLIAM OF BURES, PRINCE OF GALILEE

PLATE VII

THE EMPEROR MANUEL COMNENUS AND HIS
WIFE, MARIA OF ANTIOCH

PLATE VIII

ALEPPO

risk to his Empire. But the real issue lay deeper. Was it to the better interest of Christendom that there should be occasional gallant expeditions to the East, led by a mixture of unwise idealists and crude adventurers, to succour an intrusive state there whose existence depended on Moslem disunity? Or that Byzantium, who had been for so long the guardian of the eastern frontier, should continue to play her part unembarrassed from the West? The story of the Second Crusade showed even more clearly than that of the First that the two policies were incompatible. When Constantinople itself had fallen and the Turks were thundering at the gates of Vienna, it would be possible to see which policy was right.

CHAPTER III

FIASCO

'Take counsel together, and it shall come to nought.' ISAIAH VIII 10

When news arrived on 19 March 1148 that King Louis had landed at Saint Symeon, Prince Raymond and all his household rode down from Antioch to welcome him and escort him up to the city. The next days were spent in feasting and merriment. The gallant nobles of Antioch did their best to please the Queen of France and the great ladies in her train; and in the cheerful weather of the Syrian spring amid the luxuries of the Antiochene Court the visitors forgot the hardships through which they had passed. As soon as they had recovered Raymond began to discuss with the French leaders plans for a campaign against the infidel. Raymond hoped for great results from the coming of the Crusade. His position was precarious. Nur ed-Din was established now along the Christian frontier from Edessa to Hama and had spent the autumn of 1147 picking off one by one the Frankish fortresses east of the Orontes. Count Joscelin was fully occupied in holding his own at Turbessel. If the Moslems were to attack Antioch in force the only power that could help Raymond was Byzantium; and the Byzantine troops might well arrive too late and would anyhow insist on a tighter subservience. The French army, though the accidents of the journey had reduced its infantry strength, provided such formidable cavalry reinforcements that the Franks of Antioch would be able to take the offensive. Raymond urged upon the King that they should strike together at the heart of Nur ed-Din's power, the city of Aleppo; and he induced many of the French knights to join him in a preliminary reconnaissance up to its walls, to the consternation of its inhabitants.[1]

[1] William of Tyre, XVI, 27, pp. 751–3; William of Nangis, I, p. 44.

But when it came to the point, King Louis hesitated. He said that his Crusader vow obliged him first to go to Jerusalem before he started on any campaign; but the excuse was made to veil his indecision. All the princes of the Frankish East were demanding his help. Count Joscelin hoped to use him for the recovery of Edessa; for had not its fall set the whole Crusade in motion? Raymond of Tripoli, claiming a cousin's right—for his mother had been a French princess—sought his help for the recovery of Montferrand. Then in April there arrived at Antioch the Patriarch of Jerusalem himself, sent by the High Court of the Kingdom to beg him to hasten south and to tell him that King Conrad was already in the Holy Land.[1] In the end a purely personal motive made up the King's mind for him. Queen Eleanor was far more intelligent than her husband. She saw at once the wisdom of Raymond's scheme; but her passionate and outspoken support of her uncle only roused Louis's jealousy. Tongues began to wag. The Queen and the Prince were seen too often together. It was whispered that Raymond's affection was more than avuncular. Louis, alarmed for his honour, announced his immediate departure; whereat the Queen declared that she at least would remain in Antioch, and would seek a divorce from her husband. In reply Louis dragged his wife by force from her uncle's palace and set out with all his troops for Jerusalem.[2]

King Conrad had landed at Acre with his chief princes in the middle of April and had been given a cordial and honourable reception at Jerusalem by Queen Melisende and her son.[3] Similar honours were paid to King Louis on his entry into the Holy Land a month later. Never had Jerusalem seen so brilliant an assembly of knights and ladies.[4] But there were many notable absentees.

---

[1] The Patriarch was Fulcher of Angoulême, former Archbishop of Tyre, appointed by Melisende on the death of William of Messines in 1147.

[2] William of Tyre, *loc. cit.* He calls Eleanor a 'fatuous' woman but does not suggest that she was unfaithful. The King's suspicions are reported by John of Salisbury (*Historia Pontificalis*, p. 53).

[3] William of Tyre, XVI, 28, pp. 753–4; Otto of Freisingen, *Gesta Friderici*, pp. 88–9.   [4] William of Tyre, XVI, 29, pp. 754–6.

Raymond of Antioch, furious at Louis's behaviour, washed his hands of the whole Crusade. He could not in any case afford to leave his hard-pressed principality for some adventure in the south. Nor could Count Joscelin leave Turbessel. The Count of Tripoli's absence was due to a sinister family tragedy. Amongst the Crusaders to take the vow with King Louis at Vézélay had been Alfonso-Jordan, Count of Toulouse. With his wife and his children he had travelled by sea from Constantinople and landed at Acre a few days after Conrad. His arrival with a strong contingent had heartened the Franks in the East to whom he was a romantic figure. For he was the son of the old Crusader Raymond of Toulouse and he had been born in the East, at Mount Pilgrim, while his father was besieging Tripoli. But his coming was an embarrassment to the reigning Count of Tripoli, the grandson of old Count Raymond's bastard son Bertrand. If Alfonso-Jordan put in a claim to Tripoli, it would be hard to deny it; and it seems that he liked to mention his rights. On his way up to Jerusalem from Acre he paused at Caesarea, and there quite suddenly he died in agony. It may have been some acute illness such as appendicitis that caused his death; but everyone at once suspected poison, and the dead man's son Bertrand openly accused his cousin Raymond of Tripoli of instigating the murder. Others believed that the culprit was Queen Melisende, acting at the behest of her beloved sister, the Countess Hodierna, Raymond's wife. Nothing was proven; but Raymond in his indignation at the charge abstained from any dealing with the Crusade.[1]

When all the Crusaders had arrived in Palestine Queen Melisende and King Baldwin invited them to attend a great assembly to be held at Acre on 24 June 1148. It was an impressive gathering. The hosts were King Baldwin and the Patriarch Fulcher, with the Archbishops of Caesarea and Nazareth, the Grand Masters of the Temple and the Hospital, and the leading prelates and barons of the kingdom. With Conrad were his half-brothers, Henry

[1] William of Tyre, XVI, 28, p. 754; William of Nangis, I, p. 43, suggests that Melisende was implicated in the murder.

Jasomirgott of Austria, and Otto of Freisingen, his nephew, Frederick of Swabia, Welf of Bavaria and many lesser princes. Lorraine was represented by the Bishops of Metz and Toul. With King Louis were his brother Robert of Dreux, his future son-in-law Henry of Champagne, Thierry, Count of Flanders, as well as the young Bertrand, Alfonso-Jordan's bastard. We do not know what was the course of the debate nor who made the final proposal. After some opposition the assembly decided to concentrate all its strength on an attack against Damascus.[1]

It was a decision of utter folly. Damascus would indeed be a rich prize, and its possession by the Franks would entirely cut off the Moslems of Egypt and Africa from their co-religionists in northern Syria and the East. But of all the Moslem states the Burid kingdom of Damascus alone was eager to remain in friendship with the Franks; for, like the farther-sighted among the Franks, it recognized its chief foe to be Nur ed-Din. Frankish interests lay in retaining Damascene friendship till Nur ed-Din should be crushed, and to keep open the breach between Damascus and Aleppo. To attack the former was, as the events of the previous year had shown, the surest way to throw its rulers into Nur ed-Din's hands. But the barons of Jerusalem coveted the fertile lands that owed allegiance to Damascus, and they smarted under the recollection of their recent humiliation, for which their high-spirited young King must have longed for revenge. To the visiting Crusaders Aleppo meant nothing, but Damascus was a city hallowed in Holy Writ, whose rescue from the infidel would resound to the glory of God. It is idle to try to apportion blame for the decision; but a greater responsibility must lie with the local barons, who knew the situation, than with the new-comers to whom all Moslems were the same.[2]

The Christian army, the greatest that the Franks had ever put into the field, set out from Galilee through Banyas in the middle

---

[1] William of Tyre, XVII, 1, pp. 758–9; he gives a list of the ecclesiastical and secular magnates present; Otto of Freisingen, *Gesta Friderici*, p. 89; Suger, *Gesta Ludovici*, pp. 403–4.　　　　[2] William of Tyre, *loc. cit.*

of July. On Saturday, 24 July, it encamped on the edge of the gardens and orchards that surrounded Damascus. The emir Unur had not at first taken the news of the Crusade very seriously. He had heard of its heavy losses in Anatolia, and in any case he had not expected it to make Damascus its objective. When he discovered the truth he hastily ordered his provincial governors to send him all the men that they could spare; and a messenger hurried off to Aleppo, to ask for help from Nur ed-Din. The Franks first halted at Manakil al-Asakir some four miles to the south of the city, whose white walls and towers gleamed through the thick foliage of the orchards; but they moved quickly up to the better watered village of al-Mizza. The Damascene army attempted to hold them there but was forced to retire behind the walls. On their victory the Crusader leaders sent the army of Jerusalem into the orchards to clear them of guerrilla fighters. By afternoon the orchards to the south of the city were in the possession of the Franks, who were building palisades out of the trees that they cut down. Next, thanks chiefly to Conrad's personal bravery, they forced their way to Rabwa, on the river Barada, right under the walls of the city. The citizens of Damascus thought now that all was lost and began to barricade the streets ready for the last desperate struggle. But next day the tide turned. The reinforcements summoned by Unur began to pour in through the north gates of the city and with their help he launched a counter-attack which drove the Christians back from the walls. He repeated the attacks during the next two days, while guerrilla fighters penetrated once more into the gardens and orchards. So dangerous were their actions to the camp that Conrad, Louis and Baldwin met together and decided to evacuate the orchards south of the city and to move eastward, to encamp in a spot where the enemy could find no such cover. On 27 July the whole army moved to the plain outside the east wall. It was a disastrous decision, for the new site lacked water and faced the strongest section of the wall; and Damascene sally parties could now move more freely about the orchards. Indeed, many of the Frankish soldiers believed that the Palestinian barons who advised the Kings must have been bribed by Unur to suggest it. For with the move the last chance of their taking Damascus vanished. Unur, whose troops were increasing in number and who knew that Nur ed-Din was on his way southward, renewed his attacks on the Frankish camp. It was the Crusading army, not the beleaguered city, that was now on the defensive.[1]

While discouragement and murmurs of treachery passed through the Christian army, its leaders openly quarrelled over the future of Damascus when they should capture it. The barons of the kingdom of Jerusalem expected Damascus to be incorporated as a fief of the Kingdom, and had agreed that its lord should be Guy Brisebarre, the lord of Beirut, whose candidature was, it seems, confirmed by Queen Melisende and the Constable Manasses. But Thierry of Flanders coveted Damascus, which he wished to hold as a semi-independent fief, of the same type as Tripoli. He won the support of Conrad and Louis, and of King Baldwin, whose half-sister was his wife. The anger of the local baronage when they learnt that the Kings favoured Thierry inclined them to slacken their efforts. Those amongst them that had always opposed the attack on Damascus won more converts. Perhaps they were in secret touch with Unur. There were whispers of vast sums, paid, it is true, in money that was found to be counterfeit, passing between Damascus and the Court of Jerusalem and Elinand, Prince of Galilee. Perhaps Unur told them that if they retreated at once he would abandon his alliance with Nur ed-Din. This argument, whether or no Unur made specific use of it, undoubtedly swayed the nobles of the Kingdom. Nur ed-Din was already at Homs, negotiating the terms of his aid to Unur. His troops must, he demanded, be allowed entry into Damascus; and Unur was playing for time. The Frankish army was in a difficult position before Damascus. It could expect no reinforcements,

[1] William of Tyre, XVII, 2–5, pp. 760–7; Ibn al-Qalanisi, pp. 282–6; Abu Shama, pp. 55–9; Usama, ed. Hitti, p. 124.

whereas in a few days Nur ed-Din's men could be in the field. If they arrived, not only might the whole Crusading force be annihilated, but Damascus would surely pass into Nur ed-Din's power.[1]

The Palestinian barons were all now, too late, convinced of the folly of continuing the war against Damascus; and they pressed their views on King Conrad and King Louis. The westerners were shocked. They could not follow the subtle political arguments, but they knew that without the help of the local Franks there was little to be done. The Kings complained publicly of the disloyalty that they had found amongst them and of their lack of fervour for the cause. But they ordered the retreat.[2]

At dawn on Wednesday, 28 July, the fifth day after their arrival before Damascus, the Crusaders packed up their camp and began to move back towards Galilee. Though Unur's money may have bought their retreat, he did not let them depart in peace. All day long, and during the next few days, Turcoman light horsemen hung on their flanks, pouring arrows into their masses. The road was littered with corpses, of men and of horses, whose stench polluted the plain for many months to come. Early in August the great expedition returned to Palestine and the local troops went home. All that it had accomplished was to lose many of its men and much of its material and to suffer a terrible humiliation. That so splendid an army should have abandoned its objective after only four days of fighting was a bitter blow to Christian prestige. The legend of invincible knights from the West, built up during

[1] William of Tyre, XVII, 6, pp. 767–8. Rey, 'Les Seigneurs de Barut', in *Revue de l'Orient Latin*, vol. IV, pp. 14–15, identifies the baronial candidate as Guy of Beirut, from *Assisses*, II, p. 458. Michael the Syrian (III, p. 276) reports the rumour of the money paid to King Baldwin and Elinand, which they accepted for fear of Conrad's ambitions. Bar Hebraeus (trans. Budge, p. 274), says that he does not find the story in any Arab writer. Ibn al-Qalanisi (p. 268) says that the Franks were alarmed by the approach of Moslem armies. Ibn al-Athir (pp. 469–70) says that Unur definitely warned the local Franks of it and sowed dissension between them and the King of Germany.

[2] William of Tyre, XVII, 7, pp. 768–70. The French translation inserts an attack on the Pulani. Conrad casts the blame on the local baronage. See letter in *Wibaldi Epistolae*, pp. 225–6.

the great adventure of the First Crusade, was utterly shattered. The spirits of the Moslem world revived.[1]

King Conrad did not linger in Palestine after the return from Damascus. Together with his household he embarked from Acre on 8 September on a ship bound for Thessalonica. When he landed there he received a pressing invitation from Manuel to spend Christmas at the imperial Court. There was now perfect concord between the two monarchs. Though his young nephew Frederick might continue to bear rancour against the Byzantines, blaming them for the German losses in Anatolia, Conrad only thought of the value of Manuel's alliance against Roger of Sicily and he was captivated by Manuel's personal charm and his delightful hospitality. During his visit the marriage of his brother, Henry of Austria, to Manuel's niece Theodora was celebrated with the greatest pomp. Shocked Byzantines wept to see the lovely young princess sacrificed to so barbarous a fate—'immolated to the beast of the West', as a court poet wrote sympathetically to her mother—but the wedding marked the complete reconciliation of the German and Byzantine Courts. When Conrad left Constantinople in February 1149 to return to Germany an alliance had been made between them against Roger of Sicily, whose lands on the Italian peninsula it was proposed to divide.[2]

While Conrad enjoyed the comforts of Constantinople, King Louis lingered on in Palestine. The abbot Suger wrote to him again and again to beg him to come back to France; but he could not make up his mind. Doubtless he wished to spend an Easter at Jerusalem. His return would, he knew, be followed by a divorce and all its political consequences. He sought to postpone the evil day. In the meantime, while Conrad renewed his friendship with

---

[1] William of Tyre, *loc. cit.*; Ibn al-Qalanisi, pp. 286–7.

[2] William of Tyre, xvii, 8, pp. 770–1; Cinnamus, pp. 87–8; *Annales Palidenses*, p. 83; Otto of Saint Blaise, p. 305; Otto of Freisingen, *Gesta Friderici*, p. 96. A poem by Prodromus in honour of Theodora's marriage is given in *R.H.C.G.* ii, p. 772; but he refers to her being sacrificed 'to the beast of the West' in a poem to her mother, *ibid.* p. 768.

Byzantium, Louis's resentment against the Emperor increased the more he thought of it. He changed his policy, and sought the alliance of Roger of Sicily. His quarrel with Raymond of Antioch had removed the chief obstacle to this alliance, which would enable him to gratify his hatred of Byzantium. At last in the early summer of 1149 Louis left Palestine in a Sicilian ship, which soon joined the Sicilian squadron cruising in eastern Mediterranean waters. The Sicilian war against Byzantium was still in progress; and as the fleet rounded the Peloponnese it was attacked by ships of the Byzantine navy. King Louis hastily gave orders for the French flag to be flown on his vessel and was therefore allowed to sail on. But a ship containing many of his followers and his possessions was captured and taken as a war-prize to Constantinople. Many months passed before the Emperor would agree to send back the men and the goods to France.[1]

Louis landed at Calabria at the end of July and was received by King Roger at Potenza. The Sicilian at once suggested the launching of a new Crusade whose first object should be to take vengeance on Byzantium. Louis and his advisers readily agreed and went on to France telling everyone as they went of the perfidy of the Byzantines and the need to punish them. Pope Eugenius, whom King Louis met at Tivoli, was lukewarm; but there were many of his Curia who welcomed the scheme. Cardinal Theodwin set about finding preachers to promote it. Peter the Venerable lent his support. When Louis arrived in France he persuaded Suger to agree; and, most important of all, Saint Bernard, puzzled by the ways of Providence that had permitted his great Crusade to come to so lamentable an end, greedily accepted Byzantium as the source of all its disasters, and flung his whole energy into the task of abetting divine vengeance on the guilty Empire. But, if the movement were to succeed, it must have the help of Conrad of Germany; and Conrad would not co-operate. He saw too clearly the hand

---

[1] Cinnamus, p. 87; letter of Suger (*Sugeri Opera*, ed. de la Marche, pp. 258–60); William of Nangis, I, p. 46. The ship containing Queen Eleanor was detained for a while by the Byzantines (John of Salisbury, *Historia Pontificalis*, p. 61).

of his enemy Roger and saw no reason to break his alliance with Manuel in order to add to Roger's power. Vain appeals were made to him by Cardinal Theodwin and by Peter the Venerable; and Saint Bernard himself besought him and thundered at him in vain. The last time that Conrad had taken the Saint's advice had been over the Second Crusade. He was not to fall into the trap again. With Conrad's refusal to help, the scheme had to be dropped. The great betrayal of Christendom, urged by Saint Bernard, was postponed for another half-century.[1]

Only one of the princes of the Second Crusade remained on in the East; and his sojourn was involuntary. The young Bertrand of Toulouse, Count Alfonso's bastard son, could not endure to see the rich inheritance of Tripoli remain in the hands of a cousin whom he suspected as his father's murderer. He stayed on in Palestine till King Louis left, then marched his men of Languedoc northward, as though he intended to embark from some north Syrian port. After passing across the plain where the Buqaia opens out towards the sea, he suddenly turned inward and seized the castle of Araima. There he defied the troops that Count Raymond sent from Tripoli to dislodge him. It was a well-placed eyrie, for it dominated the roads from Tripoli to Tortosa and from Tripoli inland up the Buqaia. Count Raymond found no sympathy amongst his fellow-Christian princes, so he sent to Damascus for help from Unur. Unur responded gladly and invited Nur ed-Din to join him. He could thus show his willingness to co-operate with Nur ed-Din against the Christians without damaging his attempt to restore good relations with the Kingdom of Jerusalem. Indeed, he would gratify Queen Melisende by helping her brother-in-law. The two Moslem princes descended on Araima, which was unable to hold out long against so great a host. The Moslem victors razed the castle to the ground, after sacking it completely. They then

---

[1] For a summary of these negotiations, see Bernhardi, *op. cit.* p. 810, and Vacandard, *op. cit.* II, pp. 425–8. The letters of St Bernard and Theodwin advocating an anti-Greek Crusade are lost but their sense is to be found in a letter of Wibald (no. 252, *Wibaldi Epistolae*, p. 377).

left it for Count Raymond to reoccupy and retired with a long string of captives. Bertrand and his sister fell to Nur ed-Din's share. He took them to Aleppo where they were to spend twelve years in captivity.[1]

It was a fitting end to the Second Crusade that its last Crusader should be held captive by the Moslem allies of the fellow-Christian prince whom he had tried to despoil. No medieval enterprise started with more splendid hopes. Planned by the Pope, preached and inspired by the golden eloquence of Saint Bernard, and led by the two chief potentates of western Europe, it had promised so much for the glory and salvation of Christendom. But when it reached its ignominious end in the weary retreat from Damascus, all that it had achieved had been to embitter the relations between the western Christians and the Byzantines almost to breaking-point, to sow suspicions between the newly-come Crusaders and the Franks resident in the East, to separate the western Frankish princes from each other, to draw the Moslems closer together, and to do deadly damage to the reputation of the Franks for military prowess. The Frenchmen might seek to throw the blame for the fiasco on others, on the perfidious Emperor Manuel or on the lukewarm Palestinian barons, and Saint Bernard might thunder against the wicked men who interfered with God's purpose; but in fact the Crusade was brought to nothing by its leaders, with their truculence, their ignorance and their ineffectual folly.

[1] Ibn al-Qalanisi, pp. 287–8; Ibn al-Athir, pp. 470–1, and *Atabegs*, p. 162; Kemal ad-Din, ed. Blochet, p. 517. According to Frankish legend Bertrand's sister married Nur ed-Din and was the mother of his heir as-Salih (Robert of Torigny, II, p. 53).

BOOK IV

THE TURN OF THE TIDE

CHAPTER I

LIFE IN OUTREMER

'Ye...have done after the manners of the heathen that are round about you.' EZEKIEL XI, 12

The failure of the Second Crusade marked a turning-point in the story of Outremer. The fall of Edessa completed the first stage in the renascence of Islam; and the gains of Islam were confirmed by the pitiful collapse of the great expedition that was to have restored Frankish supremacy.

Amongst the chief reasons for this failure had been the difference in habits and outlook between the Franks resident in the East and their cousins from the West. It was a shock for the Crusaders to discover in Palestine a society whose members had in the course of a generation altered their way of life. They spoke a French dialect; they were faithful adherents of the Latin Church, and their government followed the customs that we call feudal. But these superficial likenesses only made the divergences more puzzling to the newcomers.

Had the colonists been more numerous they might have been able to keep up their occidental ways. But they were a tiny minority in a land whose climate and mode of life was strange to them. Actual numbers can only be conjectural; but it seems that at no time were there as many as a thousand barons and knights permanently resident in the Kingdom of Jerusalem. Their non-combatant relatives, women and old men, cannot have numbered much more than another thousand. Many children were born, but few survived. That is to say, apart from the clergy, who numbered a few hundreds, and the knights of the Military Orders, there can only have been from two to three thousand adult members of the Frankish upper classes.[1] The combined population of the knightly classes in the Principality of Antioch and the counties of Tripoli and Edessa was probably about the same.[2] These classes remained on the whole racially pure. In Edessa and Antioch there was some intermarriage with the local Greek and Armenian aristocracy; both Baldwin I and Baldwin II had, when Counts of Edessa, married Armenian wives of the Orthodox persuasion, and we are told that some of their nobles followed their example. Joscelin I's wife and the wife of Waleran of Birejik were Armenians of the separated Church. But farther south there was no local Christian aristocracy; the only eastern element was the Armenian blood in the royal family and the house of Courtenay and, later, the descendants, royal and Ibelin, of the Byzantine Queen, Maria Comnena.[3]

The class of the 'sergeants' was more numerous. The sergeants were in origin the fully armed infantry of Frankish stock, who settled on the lords' fiefs. As they had no pride of birth to maintain, they married with the native Christians; and by 1150 they were beginning to form a class of *poulains* already merging with the native Christians. By 1180 the number of sergeants was estimated at little more than 5000; but we cannot tell what proportion remained of pure Frankish blood. The 'sodeers' or mercenary soldiers probably also claimed some Frankish descent. The 'Turcopoles', raised locally and armed and trained after

[1] The great army that was defeated at Hattin probably had 1200 knights, of which 300 were Templars, and probably nearly as many Hospitallers. The lay barons and knights cannot have been more than 700, yet every available knight was present. Only two remained at Jerusalem. This army included a few knights from Tripoli or Antioch. A certain number of knights had recently left the kingdom with Baldwin of Ibelin. See below, pp. 454, 464. John of Ibelin estimates that in Baldwin IV's time the kingdom could raise 577 knights apart from the Orders and 5025 sergeants (Ibelin, pp. 422–7).

[2] Figures for Antioch and Tripoli can only be conjectured. Edessa probably never contained more than 100 noble and knightly Frankish families. The County of Tripoli contained perhaps 200 and Antioch considerably more. In 1111 Turbessel is said by Albert of Aix (XI, 40–1, pp. 182–3) to have provided 100 knights and Edessa 200, but many of these must have been Armenians.

[3] See below, genealogical trees.

the model of the Byzantine light cavalry, whose name they took, consisted partly of native Christians and converts and partly of half-castes. There was perhaps a difference between the

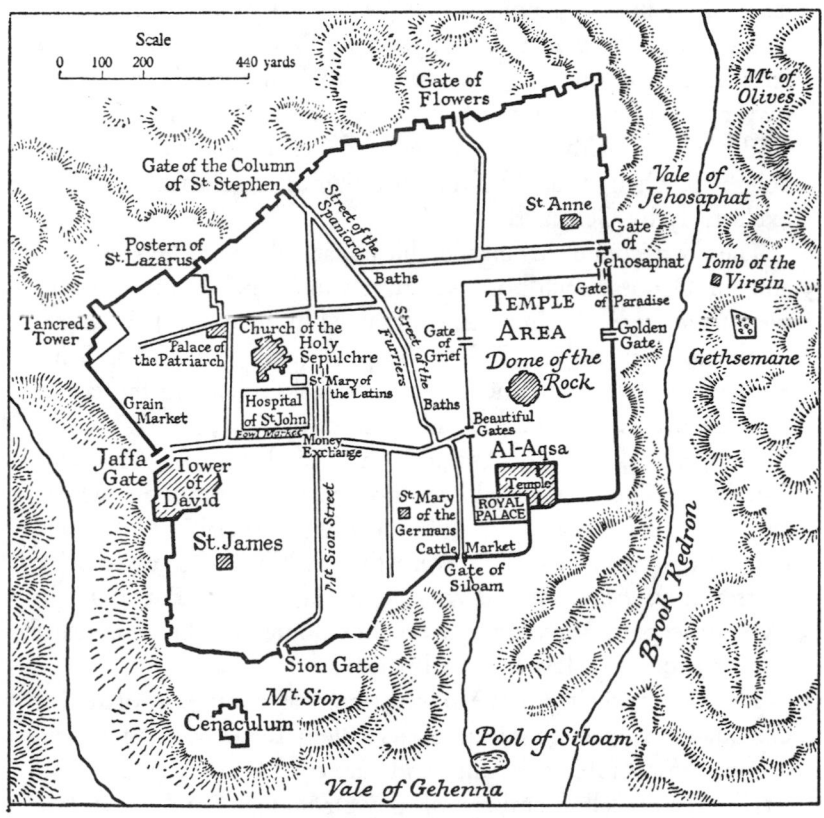

Map 4. Jerusalem under the Latin Kings.

half-castes who spoke their fathers' tongue and those that spoke their mothers'. The Turcopoles were probably drawn from the latter.[1]

[1] See La Monte, *Feudal Monarchy*, pp. 160–2; Munro, *The Kingdom of the Crusaders*, pp. 106–7, 120–1.

Except in the larger towns, the settlers were almost all of French origin; and the language spoken in the kingdom of Jerusalem and the principality of Antioch was the *langue d'œil*, familiar to the northern French and the Normans. In the County of Tripoli, with its Toulousain background, the *langue d'oc* was probably employed at first. The German pilgrim, John of Wurzburg, who visited Jerusalem in about 1175, was vexed to find that the Germans played no part in Frankish society, although, as he claimed, Godfrey and Baldwin I had been of German origin. He was delighted when at last he found a religious establishment staffed exclusively by Germans.[1]

The towns contained considerable Italian colonies. The Venetians and the Genoese each possessed streets in Jerusalem itself. There were Genoese establishments, guaranteed by treaty, in Jaffa, Acre, Caesarea, Arsuf, Tyre, Beirut, Tripoli, Jebail, Lattakieh, Saint Symeon and Antioch, and Venetian establishments in the larger of these towns. The Pisans had colonies in Tyre, Acre, Tripoli, Botrun, Lattakieh and Antioch, the Amalfitans in Acre and Lattakieh. These were all self-governing communes, whose citizens spoke Italian and did not mingle socially with their neighbours. Akin to them were the establishments owned by Marseilles in Acre, Jaffa, Tyre and Jebail, and by Barcelona in Tyre. Except in Acre, these merchant colonies numbered none of them more than a few hundred persons.[2]

The vast majority of the population was composed of native Christians. In the kingdom of Jerusalem these were of mixed origin, most Arabic-speaking, and carelessly known as Christian Arabs, almost all members of the Orthodox Church. In the County of Tripoli some of the inhabitants were members of the Monothelete sect called the Maronites. Farther north the in-

[1] John of Wurzburg (*P.P.T.S.* vol. v), *passim*.
[2] Cahen, 'Notes sur l'histoire des Croisades et de l'Orient latin. III. L'Orient latin et commerce du Levant', in *Bulletin de la Faculté des Lettres de Strasbourg*, 29me année, no. 7, points out that the trade activities of the Italians during the twelfth century were mainly concentrated on Egypt and Constantinople. The Syrian coastal ports were far less important to them.

digenous inhabitants were mostly Monophysites of the Jacobite Church, but there were very large colonies of Armenians, almost all of the Separated Armenian Church, and, in Antioch, Lattakieh and Cilicia, considerable groups of Greek-speaking Orthodox. In addition there were in the Holy Land religious colonies of every Christian denomination. The monasteries were mainly Orthodox and Greek-speaking; but there were also Orthodox Georgian establishments, and, especially in Jerusalem itself, colonies of Monophysites, both Egyptian and Ethiopian Copts and Syrian Jacobites, and a few Latin groups who had settled there before the Crusades.[1] Many Moslem communities had emigrated when the Christian kingdom was set up. But there were still Moslem villages round Nablus;[2] and the population of many districts that were conquered later by the Franks remained Moslem. In northern Galilee, along the road from Banyas to Acre, the peasants were almost exclusively Moslem. Farther north, in the Buqaia, the Nosairi mountains and the Orontes valley there were heretical Moslem sects acknowledging Frankish rule.[3] Along the southern frontier and in Oultrejourdain there were nomad Bedouin tribes. Massacres and the fear of massacre had greatly reduced the number of Jews in Palestine and Christian Syria. Benjamin of Tudela was distressed to see how small their colonies were when he visited the country in about 1170.[4] In Damascus alone they were more numerous than in all the Christian states.[5] But at some time during the twelfth century they purchased the monopoly of dye-making from the Crown; and glass manu-

[1] There is little direct evidence about the native Christians in Palestine during the twelfth century. See below, pp. 319–23, and Rey, *Les Colonies Franques*, pp. 75–94. See Gerulli, *Etiopi in Palestina*, pp. 8 ff., for Copts and Abyssinians.

[2] The Moslems round Nablus caused alarm to the Franks after Hattin (Abu Shama, p. 302); Ibn Jubayr, ed. Wright, pp. 304–7, for the Moslems in and round Acre.

[3] See Cahen, *La Syrie du Nord*, pp. 170 ff. Burchard of Mt Sion refers to the various Moslem sects in northern Syria (*P.P.T.S.* vol. XII, p. 18).

[4] Benjamin of Tudela, ed. Adler, Hebrew text, pp. 26–47.

[5] *Ibid.* pp. 47–8.

facture was largely in their hands.¹ A small Samaritan community
lived on at Nablus.²

These various communities formed the basis of the Frankish
states; and their new masters did little to disturb them. Where
natives could prove their title to lands they were allowed to keep
them; but in Palestine and Tripoli, with the exception of estates
owned by the native churches, the landowners had almost all been
Moslems who had emigrated as a result of the Frankish conquest,
leaving large territories in which the new rulers could install their
compatriot vassals. It seems that there were no free villages left,
such as had existed in earlier Byzantine times. Each village community was tied to the land and paid a portion of its produce to
the lord. But there was no uniformity about this proportion.
Over the greater part of the country where the villagers followed
a simple mixed agriculture the lord probably expected enough
produce to feed his household and his *poulains* and Turcopoles who
lived grouped round the castle; for the native peasant was not
fitted to be a soldier himself. In the rich plains agriculture was run
on a more commercial basis. Orchards, vineyards and above all
sugar-cane plantations were exploited by the lord, and the peasant
probably worked for little more than his keep. Except in the
lord's household there was no slave labour, though Moslem
prisoners might temporarily be used on the King's or the great
lords' estates. The villagers' dealings with their lord were conducted through their headman, called sometimes by the Arabic
name of *rais*, sometimes by a latinized form *regulus*. On his side
the lord employed a compatriot as his factor or *drogmannus*
(dragoman), an Arabic-speaking secretary who could keep the
records.³

¹ Benjamin of Tudela, ed. Adler, Hebrew text, p. 35 (dye-monopoly at
Jerusalem). Jews made glass at Antioch and Tyre. *Ibid.* pp. 26–47.
² *Ibid.* pp. 33–4, 1000 families according to Benjamin, who found others at
Caesarea and Ascalon (pp. 32, 44).
³ See Cahen, 'Notes sur l'histoire des Croisades et de l'Orient latin. II. Le
régime rural syrien au temps de la domination franque', in *Bulletin de la
Faculté des Lettres de Strasbourg*, 29me année, no. 7, an invaluable study of this
very obscure question.

Though there was little change in the lives of the peasants, the kingdom of Jerusalem was superficially reorganized according to the pattern of fiefs that we call 'feudal'. The royal domain consisted of the three cities of Jerusalem, Acre and Nablus and, later, the frontier town of Daron, and the territory around them. It had occupied a larger proportion of the kingdom, but the first kings and especially Queen Melisende were lavish in the gifts of land that they made to friends and to the Church and the religious Orders. Further portions might be temporarily alienated as dowers for widowed queens. The four chief fiefs of the kingdom were the County of Jaffa, usually reserved for a cadet of the royal house; the principality of Galilee, which owed its grandiose title to Tancred's ambition; the Seigneurie of Sidon; and the Seigneurie of Oultrejourdain. The holders of these fiefs seem to have had their own high officers in imitation of the King's. So also did the Lord of Caesarea, whose fief was almost as important, though it ranked with the twelve secondary fiefs. After Baldwin II's reign tenure was based on hereditary right, females succeeding in default of the direct male line. A tenant could only be evicted by a decision of the High Court after some gross misdemeanour. But he owed the King, or his superior lord, a fixed number of soldiers whenever it was required of him; and it seems that there was no time-limit to their service. The Count of Jaffa, the Lord of Sidon and the Prince of Galilee owed a hundred fully armed knights, and the Lord of Oultrejourdain sixty.[1]

The size of the fiefs was variable. The secular fiefs had been set up by conquest and formed solid blocks of land. But the estates of the Church and the Military Orders, which had grown chiefly through charitable gifts and bequests or, in the case of the Orders, from strategical convenience, were scattered throughout the Frankish territories. The unit in which estates were measured was the village, or *casal*, or, very rarely, a half or a third of a village; but villages also varied in size. Round Safed, in northern Galilee, they seem to have averaged only forty male inhabitants, but we

[1] La Monte, *Feudal Monarchy*, pp. 138–65; Rey, *op. cit.* pp. 1–56, 109–64.

hear of larger villages round Nazareth and smaller villages round Tyre, where, however, the general population was thicker.[1]

Many of the lay-lords also owned money-fiefs. That is to say, they were granted a fixed money revenue from certain towns and villages and in return had to provide soldiers in proportionate numbers. These grants were heritable and almost impossible for the King to annul.[2] As with the landed fiefs he could only hope that the possessor would die without heirs, or at least with only a daughter, for whom he had the right to choose a husband or to insist on the choice of a husband out of the three candidates that he proposed.[3]

The royal cities were obliged to produce soldiers, according to their wealth. Jerusalem was scheduled for sixty-one, Nablus for seventy-five and Acre for eighty. But they were provided not by the bourgeoisie but by the nobility resident in the city, or owners of house-property there. The leading ecclesiastics also owed soldiers in respect of their landed estates or house-property. The bourgeoisie paid its contribution to the government in money taxes. Regular taxes were levied on ports and exports, on sales and purchases, on anchorage, on pilgrims, on the use of weights and measures. There was also the terraticum, a tax on bourgeois property, of which little is known. In addition there might be a special levy to pay for some campaign. In 1166 non-combatants had to pay ten per cent on the value of their movables; and in 1183 there was a capital levy of one per cent on property and debts from the whole population, combined with two per cent on income from the ecclesiastical foundations and the baronage. Beside the produce that their villages had to provide, every peasant owed a personal capitation-tax to his lord; and Moslem

[1] Cahen, *op. cit.* pp. 291-8.
[2] La Monte, *op. cit.* pp. 144-51.
[3] The assize allowing the heiress to choose one of three husbands suggested by the King is dated after 1177 by Grandclaude, 'Liste d'Assises de Jérusalem', in *Mélanges Paul Fournier*, p. 340. But Baldwin III offered Constance of Antioch the choice of three suitors in 1150. He could not, however, force her to accept any of them (see below, p. 331).

subjects were liable to a tithe or *dime* which went to the Church. The Latin hierarchs continually tried to extend the *dime* to apply to Christians belonging to the heretic churches. They did not succeed, though they forced King Amalric to refuse an offer made by the Armenian prince Thoros II to send colonists to the depopulated districts of Palestine by their insistence that they should pay the *dime*.[1] But even with the *dime* the Moslems found the general level of taxation lower under the Franks than under neighbouring Moslem lords. Nor were Moslems excluded from minor governmental posts. They, as well as Christians, could be employed as customs-officers and tax-collectors.[2]

It is impossible to give a precise account of the constitution of the Frankish states because at no moment was there a fixed constitution. Customs developed or were modified by particular pronouncements. When later lawyers produced such compilations as the *Livre au Roi* or the *Assises de Jerusalem*, they were attempting to find out where definite decisions had altered accepted custom rather than to lay down an established governmental code. There were local variants. The Prince of Antioch and the Counts of Edessa and Tripoli normally had little trouble from their vassals. The King of Jerusalem was in a weaker position. He was the Lord's Anointed, the accepted head of the Franks in the East, with no rival after Baldwin I had demolished the pretensions of the Patriarchate. But, while the lords of Antioch and Tripoli could hand on their power by the accepted rules of hereditary succession, the kingship was elective. Public feeling might support a hereditary claim. In 1174 Baldwin IV was accepted without question to succeed his father, though he was only thirteen years old and a leper. But the confirmation by election was needed. Sometimes the electors made their terms, as when Amalric I was obliged to divorce his wife Agnes before they would allow him the crown. When the natural heir was a woman there were further complications. Her husband might be elected as King; but it seems that he

---

[1] Cahen, *op. cit.* pp. 299–302. The offer of Thoros is reported by Ernoul, pp. 27–30.   [2] Ibn Jubayr, ed. Wright, p. 305.

was regarded as deriving his rights through her. In the case of
Queen Melisende and her son Baldwin III no one quite knew what
was the juridical position; and the whole constitutional problem
was disastrously illustrated after Baldwin V's death in 1186.[1]

The King was at the apex of the social pyramid, but it was a low
apex. As the Lord's Anointed he commanded some prestige. It
was high treason to do him an injury. He presided at the High
Court, and he was commander-in-chief of the forces of the realm.
He was responsible for the central administration and he appointed
its officials. As his vassals' suzerain he could prevent them from
alienating their lands, and he could choose husbands for their
heiresses. Having no superior lord to consider, he could make
grants as he pleased from his own domain, though, like his nobles
when they alienated lands, he usually associated his wife and
children in the grant, lest there should be some later complaint over
the widow's dower or the son's inheritance. But there the royal
power ended. The royal revenues were restricted and were
reduced by over-generous gifts. The King was always short of
money. He was at the head of the kingdom but he was under the
law of the kingdom; and the law was represented by the High
Court. The High Court consisted of the tenants-in-chief of the
realm, the lords who owed allegiance direct to the Crown.
Leading ecclesiastics attended in virtue of their landed holdings,
and foreign communities who possessed land in the kingdom,
such as the Venetians or Genoese, sent representatives. Distinguished visitors might be invited to be present, though they
did not form part of the Court and had no vote in it.[2]

The High Court was fundamentally a court of law. As such it
had two main functions. First, it had to elucidate what was the
law on particular points. This meant that it passed legislation; for
each *assise* was in theory merely a statement of the law, but in fact
was also the definition of a new law. Secondly, it tried those of

[1] La Monte, *op. cit.* pp. 87–137, *passim.* See above, p. 233, and below,
pp. 334, 443.
[2] *Ibid.* pp. 87–104.

300

its members who were guilty of crime and heard cases that they might bring against each other. Trial by peers was an essential feature of Frankish custom; and the King ranked with his tenant-in-chief as *primus inter pares,* their president but not their master. The theory behind it was that the kingdom had not been conquered by a king but by a company of peers who then elected their king. This theory justified the Court in electing subsequent kings and, in the case of a minority or the King's captivity, a regent or *bailli.* The High Court was also consulted on major matters of policy; this was an inevitable development, for without the co-operation of his vassals the King would seldom have been able to carry out his policy. In 1166 the High Court was enlarged to include *arrière*-vassals, as part of Amalric I's scheme to find support for the Crown against the chief vassals. In 1162 he had obliged the Court to pass an *assise* allowing *arrière*-vassals to appeal against their lords to the High Court, and if the lord refused to answer the summons his tenants could put themselves under the Crown. Though this law provided the King with a useful weapon against the nobility, in the long run it merely added to the power of the High Court and could be used against the King. The Court seems to have heard cases carefully and conscientiously, though the result of trial by battle was accepted as proof. It had no fixed seat but could be summoned by the King wherever was convenient. During the First Kingdom this was usually at Jerusalem or at Acre. The nobles, in their desire to attend, began to neglect their fiefs and to establish residences in either city.[1] But their power as a collective body was weakened by their perpetual quarrels and family feuds, which were intensified and complicated as time went on and almost all the noble houses were connected by intermarriage.

In accordance with the principle of trial by peers, non-noble Frankish settlers had their own *cours des bourgeois.* These Bourgeois Courts were to be found in every large city. Their president was always the Viscount of the city. There were twelve jurors to each

[1] *Ibid.* pp. 106–13. Usama gives instances of trial by single combat and by water (ed. Hitti, pp. 167–9).

Court, chosen by the lord from his free-born Latin subjects. They acted as judges, though a litigant could engage one of them as counsel. In this case the counsel-juror took no part in the verdict. Jurors were also required to witness any deed or charter made in court. Unlike the practice in the High Court, careful records were kept of all proceedings. The Bourgeois Courts met regularly on Mondays, Wednesdays and Fridays, except on feast-days. A case between a noble and a bourgeois was held before the Bourgeois Court. The Bourgeois Court admitted the ordeal by battle and the ordeal by water.[1]

The native communities had at first their own courts for petty cases, under the presidency of the local headman, appointed by the Viscount, where their customary law applied. But during King Amalric I's reign a *Cour de la Fonde* was instituted in each of the thirty-three chief market towns. This dealt with commercial questions and took over all cases, even criminal, that involved the native population. It was under a *bailli* appointed by the local lord and six jurors, two Franks and four natives. Native litigants took the oath each on his own holy book. Moslems could use the Koran; and Moslem visitors admired the fairness of the proceedings. The *Cour de la Fonde* also registered sales and gifts of all property other than real and was an office for the collection of purchase taxes. There was a right of appeal to the Bourgeois Court whose general procedure it copied. Amalric also set up a *Cour de la Chaine* in all maritime cities, to cover cases to do with shipping and to be a registry of customs and anchorage dues. Its jurors were drawn from merchants and sailors. In addition, the Italian and Provençal commercial communities had their own consular courts for their internal affairs. The chief feudatories had their own courts 'baron' to deal with disputes between their knightly vassals. There were twenty-two of them, as well as four for the King's domain. Each of these many courts had its clearly defined sphere; but where a case involved litigants of different rank, it was heard in the Court appropriate to the inferior.[2]

[1] La Monte, *op. cit.* pp. 105-8. [2] *Ibid.* pp. 108-9.

Owing to the medieval concept of law which demanded specific laws only when the need arose to define a particular point, the legislative activity of the government seems arbitrary and fitful. Of the laws given in the thirteenth-century *Assises de Jérusalem* it is probable that six date from Duke Godfrey's time and another nineteen, of which eleven can be roughly dated, from the period up to 1187.[1]

The administration was in the hands of the chief officers of the household, who were chosen from the tenants-in-chief of the kingdom. First in precedence came the Seneschal. He was master of ceremonies, and as such he carried the sceptre before the King at the coronation; and he was head of the civil service. In particular he was in charge of the treasury, the *Secrète*, the office into which moneys due to the Crown were paid and from which salaries were taken, and which kept a register of all financial dealings in which the government was involved. The *Secrète* was a loosely organized bureau, which the Franks took over from the Arabs who in their turn had taken it from the Byzantines. Next after the Seneschal came the Constable, who was greater in actual power. He was head of the Army, under the King, and was responsible for all its organization and administration. At the coronation he carried the King's banner and held the King's horse, which became his perquisite. He was responsible for military supplies and military justice. Mercenaries, whether hired by the King or by a lord, were under his special jurisdiction and he saw to it that they were paid properly. If the King or his *bailli* were absent from a campaign, he had complete control of the expedition. He was assisted by the Marshal, who was his lieutenant in everything. The Chamberlain was in charge of the King's personal household and finances. On ceremonial occasions he acted as chief Lord-in-Waiting. His was

[1] Grandclaude, *op. cit.* pp. 322 ff., gives a list of the assizes that can be assigned to the period 1099–1187. He assigns six to Godfrey's rule and eleven to the Kings from Baldwin I to Baldwin IV (though one ordering the sale of fiefs without heirs to pay for the King's ransom is believed by him to postdate Guy's capture at Hattin. It might, however, refer to Baldwin II's captivity). There are also eight to which no precise date can be given.

a profitable office, as vassals paying homage were expected to make a gift to him. Certain lands were assigned to the office; but in 1179 the Chamberlain John of Bellesme sold them without apparently causing offence to the King. The functions of the Butler are unknown. His duties were probably purely ceremonial. The Chancellor, as in the West, was always an ecclesiastic, though he was not, as often in the West, the royal chaplain. As head of the chancery, it was his business to draw up and register all charters and to fix the royal seal on them. The chancery remained a records office. As there was no royal justice nor common law, it was never required to issue writs nor set up its own court. Its records seem to have been well kept, though few have survived. The language of the chancery in the twelfth century was Latin. The dating was by the <i>anno Domini</i> and the Roman Indiction, with sometimes the regnal year or the year from the capture of Jerusalem added. The year began at Christmas. The Kings numbered themselves from Baldwin I, regardless of their names. Their title did not at first follow a fixed formula but was eventually standardized as 'per Dei gratiam in sancta civitate Jerusalem Latinorum Rex'.[1]

The chief local official was the Viscount, who represented the King in the royal cities and the lord in the baronial cities. He collected local taxes and transmitted them to the treasury after taking out what he needed for the expenses of local government. He was responsible for the local law-courts and for keeping order generally in his city. He was chosen from a noble family, but his post was not hereditary. His second in command was known by the Arabic title of <i>mathesep</i>, or sometimes the Master-Sergeant, who had originally been the official responsible for marketing regulations.[2]

The King of Jerusalem claimed suzerainty over all the Frankish states in the East and considered that he was entitled to demand their rulers to send troops to join him on his expeditions. In fact the suzerainty existed only when the King was strong enough to

[1] La Monte, <i>op. cit.</i> pp. 114–37, the best summary of the functions of the Officers of State.　　[2] <i>Ibid.</i> pp. 135–6, 167–8.

304

enforce it, and even in theory neither Antioch nor Tripoli was considered to be part of the kingdom. The earlier kings achieved a personal suzerainty over Tripoli. Count Bertrand paid homage to Baldwin I for his lands in 1109. Count Pons endeavoured to renounce his allegiance to Baldwin II in 1122 but was forced to submit by his own High Court. In 1131 he refused to allow King Fulk to pass through his lands but was punished by the King and forced again into submission. From 1164 to 1171 King Amalric was regent of Tripoli for the child Count Raymond III, but this was probably as the boy's nearest male relative rather than as his overlord. Raymond III, when he grew up, never admitted the suzerainty, though he was the King's vassal in respect of his wife's principality of Galilee. During the campaign of 1187 in which he took part as Prince of Galilee his County of Tripoli declared itself neutral. With the County of Edessa the Kings had a personal bond. Baldwin I, when he appointed Baldwin II to succeed him there, took from him an oath of vassaldom, and Baldwin II followed his example with Joscelin of Courtenay. But Joscelin in his later days acknowledged the Prince of Antioch also as his overlord. Antioch was in a different position, Bohemond I admitted no one as his suzerain; nor did the regents Tancred and Roger, both of them appointed by the High Court of the Principality. Baldwin II acted as regent for the young prince Bohemond II from 1119 to 1126, but, it seems, not by legal right but by invitation of the High Court. He was invited again in 1131, with the additional reason that he was grandfather to the young Princess Constance, whose interests appeared to the Court to be endangered by her mother Alice. After his death, when Alice once again tried to seize power, the High Court invited King Fulk to take over the regency in his place. But here again the King was the young Princess's nearest male relative, as the husband of her aunt. Had there been in the East a male member of the house of Hauteville he would have been selected. Similarly when the King chose a husband for the Princess he was acting at the request of the High Court and not as suzerain. Baldwin II had asked the King of France to select a husband for his heiress Melisende, without any suggestion that he accepted French suzerainty. When the time came for Constance to take a second husband she made her own choice as a sovereign princess. If she asked permission from King Baldwin III it was because her chosen husband Reynald was his vassal. In 1160 the Antiochenes invited Baldwin II to take over the regency; but here again the King was their young Prince's nearest male relative. The legal position was never clearly defined. Probably the Prince of Antioch regarded the King of Jerusalem as his senior but not as his superior.[1]

Antioch was also distinct from Tripoli and Edessa in its governmental system. Of the Edessene we know little. Such charters as the Count may have issued are lost. Presumably he had a court of his vassals like any great feudal lord; but the position of the county on the very outpost of Christendom prevented any constitutional development. He lived more like one of the Turkish emirs who surrounded him. The Frankish colonists were few, and there were few great fiefs. The Count depended largely on Armenian officials trained in Byzantine methods. Almost perpetual warfare compelled him to act more autocratically than would have been allowed in a more tranquil land. The constitution of the County of Tripoli seems to have resembled that of Jerusalem. The Count had his High Court by whose rulings he was bound. But his title was hereditary not elective, and his personal domains were far larger than those of any of his vassals. Except on one or two grave matters of policy, as when Pons defied the King of Jerusalem, the Count had little trouble from his barons, who, with the exception of the Genoese lords of Jebail, were descended from his ancestors' Toulousain vassals. The chief officials of the Court had the same titles and functions as those of Jerusalem. The towns were similarly administered by viscounts.[2]

---

[1] La Monte, *op. cit.* pp. 187–202. See also Cahen, *La Syrie du Nord*, pp. 436–7. Bohemond II was, however, Amalric I's vassal because of a money-fief that he held at Acre.

[2] La Monte, *op. cit., loc. cit.*; Richard, *Le Comté de Tripoli*, pp. 30–43.

The Principality of Antioch

In the principality of Antioch the institutions superficially resembled those of the kingdom of Jerusalem. There was a High Court and a Bourgeois Court and the same high officials. Antioch had its own *Assises*, but their general tenour conformed with that of the *Assises* of Jerusalem. Under the surface there were, however, many differences. The princely title was hereditary, and the High Court only intervened to appoint a regent if need be. The Prince from the outset kept in his own hands the chief towns of the principality and much of its lands and was chary of making grants of territory except in frontier districts. The money-fief suited him better. It seems that jurors appointed by the Prince sat in the High Court and his personal representatives controlled the Bourgeois Courts. For the administration of the towns and the princely domain, the Prince took over the Byzantine system with its competent bureaucracy and its careful means for raising taxes. Antioch, Lattakieh and Jabala had each its Duke, who was in complete charge of the municipality. He was appointed by the Prince and could be dismissed at his pleasure; but during his period of office he seems to have sat in the High Court. The Dukes of Lattakieh and Jabala were often drawn from the native population. The Duke of Antioch was of noble Frankish birth but was aided by a viscount who might be a native. Like their cousins in Sicily, the Princes of Antioch strengthened themselves against the nobility by making use of native-born officials who were entirely dependent upon the princely favour. They had found in Antioch an educated local society, Greek, Syrian and Armenian in origin, surviving from Byzantine times. A further control of the High Court was secured by appointing jurors, as in the Bourgeois Courts, to sit in it to decide on purely legal questions. The Princes inherited the Byzantine system of assessing and collecting taxes; their *Secrète* had its own bureaucracy and was not dependent for revenue on local courts as in Jerusalem. They directed policy with little regard to the High Court. They made their own treaties with foreign powers. The whole organization of the principality was closer knit and more effective than that of

Life in Outremer

the other Frankish states. Had it not been for constant wars, for minor or captive princes and the substitution of a French for a Norman dynasty, Antioch might have developed a government as efficient as that of Sicily.[1]

The peculiar position of Antioch was further enhanced by its special relationship with the Byzantine Emperor. According to Byzantine theory the Emperor was the head of the Christian commonwealth. Though he never made any attempt to establish suzerainty over the monarchs of the West, he considered eastern Christendom to be his own sphere. Orthodox Christians under the Caliphate had been under his protection, and his obligations to them were recognized by the Moslems. He had no intention of abdicating his duties because of the Frankish conquest. But there was a difference between Antioch and Edessa on the one hand and Jerusalem and Tripoli on the other. The latter two countries had not been part of the Empire since the seventh century, but the former had been imperial provinces within the lifetime of Alexius I. Alexius, when he induced the leaders of the First Crusade to pay him homage, distinguished between former imperial lands, like Antioch, which were to be restored to him, and further conquests, over which he only claimed an undefined suzerainty. The Crusaders failed to keep their oaths; and Alexius was unable to enforce them. Byzantine policy was always realist. After his victory over Bohemond Alexius modified his demands. By the Treaty of Devol he allowed the Norman dynasty to rule at Antioch but strictly as a vassal; and he demanded certain safeguards, such as the installation of a Greek as Patriarch. This treaty formed the basis of Byzantine claims; but the Franks ignored it. Frankish public opinion seems to have been that Bohemond had indeed behaved badly towards the Emperor, but the Emperor had ruined his case by failing to appear in person. When, however, an Emperor did appear in person, his rights were recognized. That is to say, to judge from King Fulk's advice in 1137, his claim to

[1] Cahen, op. cit. pp. 435 ff., a full account of the Antiochene constitution and its development.

suzerainty was accepted as being juridically sound when he was in a position to enforce it. If he did not choose to do so, it could be disregarded. There were a few other occasions when the Emperor was treated as overlord, as when the Princess Constance applied to Manuel to choose her a husband. But as his choice was displeasing to her she ignored it. Imperial suzerainty was thus fitful and lightly borne, but the Princes of Antioch and their lawyers were uneasy about it; and it remained a potential limitation to the Prince's sovereign independence.

The Count of Edessa admitted imperial overlordship in 1137; but Edessa was further from the imperial frontier, and the question was less urgent. Frankish opinion approved of the Countess of Edessa selling the remaining Edessene lands to the Emperor in 1150; but that was because they were obviously untenable against the Moslems. Raymond of Toulouse had been willing to admit the Emperor as suzerain; and his son Bertrand did homage to Alexius for his future county in 1109. Raymond II repeated this homage to the Emperor John in 1137. Raymond III, though he attacked Byzantium in 1151, received help from the Byzantines in 1163, which may have been a gesture by Manuel to show his overlordship. But it may be that this homage was limited to Tortosa and its neighbourhood which traditionally belonged to the territory of Antioch as part of the *theme* of Lattakieh.

With the kingdom of Jerusalem Byzantine juridical relations were still less precise. Baldwin III paid homage to the Emperor Manuel at Antioch in 1158; and Amalric visited Constantinople as a vassal, though as a highly honoured vassal, in 1171. Both Baldwin and Amalric regarded Byzantine friendship as being essential to their policy and were therefore ready to make concessions. But it seems that their lawyers never regarded this vassaldom as more than a temporary expedient.[1]

[1] Cahen, *op. cit.* pp. 437–8, for the relations of Antioch with Byzantium. Richard, *op. cit.* pp. 26–30, for those of Tripoli with Byzantium. For the whole question of Byzantine pretensions over the Crusader states, see La Monte, 'To what extent was the Byzantine Empire the Suzerain of the Crusading States?' in *Byzantion*, vol. VII. See also below, p. 391.

If the King of Jerusalem had any overlord it was the Pope. The First Crusade anticipated a theocratic state in Palestine; and, had Adhemar of Le Puy lived on, some such organization might have been evolved. It was probably this idea that kept Godfrey from accepting a royal crown. Adhemar's successor Daimbert envisaged a state controlled by the Patriarch of Jerusalem. Baldwin I countered by assuming the crown and by making use of Daimbert's enemies within the Church. It was clear that the Papacy would not approve of an over-powerful Patriarchate in Jerusalem, which might from its special position and its increasing wealth have set itself up, as Daimbert hoped, to be an Oriental equal of Rome. It was thus easy for the King to play off Pope against Patriarch. He was traditionally obliged to pay homage to the Patriarch at his coronation, but he sought confirmation of his title from the Papacy. The vassaldom was little more than nominal and no stricter than that claimed by the Popes over the Spanish kingdoms; but it was useful to the kingdom, for the Popes felt themselves responsible for keeping up supplies of men and money for the Holy Land and for giving diplomatic help whenever it was needed. The Papacy could also be used to put a check on the Patriarchate and to exercise some control on the Military Orders. But on the other hand the Pope might support the Military Orders against the King; and he often intervened when the King attempted to put some curb on the Italian merchant-cities.[1]

The Church in the kingdom was under the Patriarch of Jerusalem. After the initial trouble caused by Daimbert's ambition, he was in effect a servant of the Crown. He was elected by the Chapter of the Holy Sepulchre, who nominated two candidates of which the King selected one. Under the Patriarch were the four archbishops of Tyre, Caesarea, Nazareth and Rabboth-Moab, and nine bishops, nine mitred abbots and five priors; but certain other abbeys depended directly on the Papacy, as did the Military Orders. The Palestinian Church was immensely wealthy in lands and in money-fiefs. The leading ecclesiastics usually owed

[1] La Monte, *Feudal Monarchy*, pp. 203-16.

sergeant-service rather than knights-service. The Patriarch and the
Chapter of the Holy Sepulchre each owed five hundred sergeants,
the Bishop of Bethlehem two hundred, the Archbishop of Tyre
a hundred and fifty, as did the abbots of Saint Mary Josaphat and
Mount Sion. The Convent of Bethany, founded by Queen
Melisende for her sister, possessed the whole town of Jericho. In
addition the Patriarchate and many of the more celebrated abbeys
had been given vast estates all over western Europe, from which
the revenues were sent to Palestine. The Church had its own
courts, to deal with cases concerning heresy and religious discipline, marriage, including divorce and adultery, and testaments.
They followed the usual rules and procedure of the Canon Law
Courts in the West.[1]

The territories of Antioch, Tripoli and Edessa, were ecclesias-
tically under the Patriarch of Antioch. The delineation of the
Patriarch's spheres had given rise to difficulties; for traditionally
Tyre was included in the Patriarchate of Antioch, though it
formed by conquest part of the kingdom of Jerusalem. Paschal II
ruled that Tyre, with its dependent bishoprics of Acre, Sidon and
Beirut, should be transferred to Jerusalem. This was done, as it
corresponded to political realities. But the attempts of the
Patriarchs of Jerusalem to obtain jurisdiction over the three
Tripolitan bishoprics of Tripoli, Tortosa and Jabala failed, in spite
of fitful support from the Papacy. Raymond of Toulouse seems to
have hoped for an autonomous Church in his future county; but
his successors admitted the ecclesiastical suzerainty of Antioch. It
weighed lightly on them; for they appointed their bishops without interference.

Like his brother of Jerusalem the Patriarch of Antioch was
elected by the Chapter but in fact appointed by the secular ruler,
who could also secure his deposition. We know that certain
Princes paid homage to the Patriarch at their coronation; but it
was probably only under exceptional circumstances. Under the
Patriarch were the Archbishops of Albara, Tarsus and Mamistra,

[1] La Monte, *op. cit.* pp. 215-16; Rey, *op. cit.* pp. 268-9.

311

as well as Edessa. The archbishopric of Turbessel was set up later, with the official title of Hierapolis (Menbij). The number of bishoprics varied according to political circumstances. There were nine Latin abbeys and two priories. The chief monastic establishments were those of Saint Paul and Saint George, where the Benedictines seem to have displaced Greek monks, and Saint Symeon, where the two rites existed side by side. The Antiochene Church was not quite so wealthy as that of Jerusalem; indeed, many Palestinian establishments owned estates in the principality.[1]

Long before the end of the twelfth century the secular Church in the Frankish states was completely overshadowed by the Military Orders. Since their establishment they had grown steadily in numbers and in wealth, and by 1187 they were the chief landowners in Outremer. Gifts and purchase continually increased their estates. Many Palestinian nobles joined their ranks; and recruits came in steadily from the West. They answered an emotional need of the time, when there were many men anxious to take up the religious life but wishful still to be active and to do battle for the Faith. And they answered a political need. There was a perpetual shortage of soldiers in Outremer. The feudal organization depended too much on the accidents of family life in the noble houses to provide a replacement for the men that died in battle or of sickness. Visiting Crusaders would fight well for a season or two, but then they returned home. The Military Orders produced a constant supply of devoted professional soldiers who cost the King nothing and who were rich enough besides to build and maintain castles on a scale that few secular lords could undertake. Without their assistance the Crusader-states would have perished far sooner. Of their actual numbers we have only incidental evidence. The Hospitallers sent five hundred knights with a proportionate number of other ranks on the Egyptian campaign of 1158; and the Templar knights taking part in the campaign of 1187 numbered about three hundred. In each case these probably represented knights from the kingdom of Jerusalem

[1] Cahen, *op. cit.* pp. 501–10.

alone; and a certain number would have been kept back for garrison duties. Of the two Orders the Hospitallers were probably the larger and the richer; but they were still busily concerned with charitable activities. Their hostel in Jerusalem could house a thousand pilgrims; and they maintained a hospital for the needy sick there that survived the Saracen reconquest. They distributed alms daily amongst the poor with a generosity that astounded visitors. Both they and the Templars policed the pilgrim-routes, taking particular care of the sacred bathing-places in the Jordan. The Templars also distributed alms, but less lavishly than the Hospitallers. Their attention was given more exclusively to military affairs. They were famed for their courage in attack and regarded themselves as being dedicated to offensive warfare. They devoted themselves also to banking and soon made themselves the financial agents for visiting Crusaders; and they were later to win unpopularity by the suspicion of strange esoteric rites; but as yet they were universally esteemed for their bravery and chivalry.[1]

The advantages brought by the Military Orders were balanced by grave disadvantages. The King had no control over them, for their only suzerain was the Pope. Lands that were given to them were held in mortmain; no services were due from them. They refused to let their tenants pay the *dime* due to the Church. The knights fought with the King's armies merely as voluntary allies. Occasionally the King or a lord might put a castle under their temporary control, and they were sometimes asked to act as trustees for a minor. In such cases they were liable for the proper services. The Grand Masters or their deputies sat in the High Court of the kingdom; and their representatives on the High Courts of the Prince of Antioch and the Count of Tripoli. But the advice that they gave there was apt to be irresponsible. If they disliked the official policy they might refuse to co-operate, as when the Templars boycotted the expedition to Egypt in 1158. The perpetual rivalry between the two Orders was a constant danger. It was seldom that they could be induced to campaign

[1] For references about the Orders, see above, p. 158 n. 1.

together. Each Order followed its own line in diplomacy, regardless of the official policy of the kingdom. We find both Orders
making their treaties with Moslem rulers; and the story of the
negotiations with the Assassins in 1172 shows the Templars'
readiness to upset an obviously desirable arrangement in the
interest of their financial advantages and their frank disdain of the
authority of the royal courts. The Hospitallers were throughout
more temperate and unselfish; but even with them the Order took
precedence over the kingdom.

A similar balance of advantage and disadvantage was shown
in the relations between the Frankish states and the Italian and
Provençal merchant-cities.[1] The Frankish colonists were soldiers,
not sailors. Tripoli and Antioch each later developed a small fleet,
and the Orders built flotillas, but the kingdom itself, with its few
good harbours and general shortage of timber, never had an
adequate naval establishment. For any expedition that involved
sea-power such as the conquest of the coastal towns or the
campaigns against Egypt, it was necessary to invoke the help
of some maritime power. The two great sea-powers of the East
were Byzantium and Egypt. But Egypt was always a potential
and often a real enemy, and Byzantium was always suspect. The
Sicilian fleet could have been useful; but Sicilian policy was
untrustworthy. The Italians and southern French were better
allies; and their help was further needed to keep open the sea-
routes to the West and to transport pilgrims, soldiers and colonists
to Outremer. But the merchant-cities had to be paid. They
demanded trading facilities and rights, their own quarters in the
larger towns, and the complete or partial freedom from customs-
dues; and their colonies had to be given extra-territorial privileges.
These concessions were not on the whole resented by the Frankish
authorities. Any loss in revenue was balanced by the trade that
they stimulated; and the royal courts had no wish to have to
administer Genoese or Venetian law, especially as cases involving
a citizen of the kingdom, or of serious crime, such as murder, were

[1] See below, chapters II and III, *passim*.

reserved to them. Occasionally there were disputes. The Venetians were at perpetual enmity with the Archbishop of Tyre; and the Genoese had a long quarrel with King Amalric I. In both cases the Papacy supported the Italians, who probably had legal right on their side. But the merchant-cities were out not for the welfare of Christendom but for their own commercial gain. Usually the two interests coincided; but if they clashed the immediate commercial interest prevailed. The Italians and Provençals were therefore unsteady friends for the King. Moreover, the jealousy between the two great Orders was pale beside that between the various merchant-cities. Venice would far sooner help the Moslems than help Genoa or Pisa or Marseilles; and her rivals held similar views. Thus, while the help given by them all was essential in maintaining the existence of Outremer, intrigues and riots between their colonists and their bland readiness to betray the common cause for momentary profit cancelled out much of its value.[1]

To pilgrims in particular they seemed shamefully greedy and un-Christian. The conquest greatly stimulated the pilgrim-traffic; the huge hostel of the Hospitallers was usually full. Despite the original purpose of the Crusade the route across Anatolia was still unsafe. Only a well-armed company could brave its dangers. The average pilgrim preferred to travel by sea. He had to obtain a berth in an Italian ship; and the fares were very high. A number of pilgrims might band together to charter a whole ship, but even so a captain and crew were costly to hire. It was cheaper for a pilgrim from northern France or England to travel in one of the small convoys that sailed yearly from the Channel ports to the East. But that was a long, perilous journey. Atlantic storms had to be faced; there were Moslem corsairs lying in wait in the Straits of Gibraltar and along the African coast. From Oporto or Lisbon to Sicily there were no ports at which water or provisions could be safely obtained, and it was difficult to carry sufficient supplies for the men and horses on board. It was far simpler to go overland to Provence or Italy and there embark in vessels well

[1] Heyd, *op. cit.* pp. 129–63, a full summary.

used to the voyage. For a single pilgrim a berth was found more easily and cheaply in ports in the King of Sicily's domain; but large parties were dependent on the fleets of the great merchant-cities.[1]

When he landed at Acre or Tyre or St Symeon, the traveller found himself at once in a strange atmosphere. Beneath the feudal superstructure Outremer was an eastern land. The luxury of its life impressed and shocked Occidentals. In western Europe life was still simple and austere. Clothes were made of wool and seldom laundered. Washing facilities were few, except in some old towns where the tradition of Roman baths lingered on. Even in the greatest castle furniture was rough and utilitarian and carpets were almost unknown. Food was coarse and lacked variety, especially during the long winter months. There was little comfort and little privacy anywhere. The Frankish East made a startling contrast. There were not, perhaps, many houses as large and splendid as the palace built early next century by the Ibelins at Beirut, with its mosaic floors, its marble walls and its painted ceilings, and great windows looking, some westward over the sea, and others eastward over gardens and orchards to the mountains. The Royal Palace at Jerusalem, lodged in part of al-Aqsa Mosque, was certainly humbler, though the palace at Acre was a sumptuous edifice. But every noble and rich bourgeois filled his town-house with similar splendour. There were carpets and damask hangings, elegantly carved and inlaid tables and coffers, spotless bed-linen and table-linen, dinner-services in gold and silver, cutlery, fine faience and even a few dishes of porcelain from the Farther East. In Antioch water was brought by aqueducts and pipes to all the great houses from the springs at Daphne. Many houses along the Lebanese coast had their private supplies. In Palestine, where water was less abundant, the cities had well-organized storage tanks; and in Jerusalem the sewerage system installed by the Romans was still in perfect order. The great

[1] See Cahen, 'Notes sur l'histoire des Croisades et de l'Orient latin. III. L'Orient latin et commerce du Levant', in *Bulletin de la Faculté des Lettres de Strasbourg*, 1951, p. 333.

frontier-fortresses were almost as comfortably appointed as the town-houses, grim and fierce though life might be outside the walls. They had baths, elegant chambers for the ladies of the household and sumptuous reception halls. Castles belonging to the Military Orders were slightly more austere; but in the great family seats, such as Kerak in Moab or Tiberias, the chatelain lived more splendidly than any king in western Europe.[1]

The clothes of the settlers soon became as Oriental and luxurious as their furnishings. When a knight was not in armour he wore a silk burnous and usually a turban. On campaigns he wore a linen surcoat over his armour, to protect the metal from the heat of the sun, and a *kefieh* in the Arab style over his helmet. The ladies adopted the traditional eastern fashion of a long under-robe and a short tunic or coat, heavily embroidered with gold thread and maybe with jewels. In winter they wore furs, as did their husbands. Out of doors they were veiled like the Moslem women, but less from modesty than to protect their complexions, which were generously covered with paint; and they affected a mincing gait. But, for all their airs of delicacy and langour, they were as courageous as their husbands and brothers. Many a noblewoman was called upon to lead the defence of her castle in the absence of her lord. The wives of merchants copied the ladies of the aristocracy and often outshone them in the richness of their apparel. The successful courtesans—a class unknown hitherto in western society—were equally gorgeous. Of Paschia de Riveri, the shopkeeper's wife from Nablus whose charms ensnared the Patriarch Heraclius, the chronicler says that you would have thought her a countess or a baroness from her silks and jewels.[2]

Strange though this luxury seemed to the western pilgrim, it

[1] Rey, *op. cit.* pp. 3–10. Cahen, *La Syrie du Nord*, pp. 129–32, giving an account of Antioch and its amenities.

[2] Tancred's coins show him in a turban (see above, p. 33). In 1192 Henry of Champagne, thanking Saladin for the gift of a turban, announces that such things are liked by his compatriots and he will often wear it (see Rey, *op. cit.* pp. 11–12). Ibn Jubayr (ed. Wright, p. 309) describes the clothes at a Christian wedding at Acre in 1184. For Paschia, see below, p. 425.

was natural to a visitor from the Moslem East or from Byzantium. The Frankish colonists had inevitably to try to fit into their new environment, and they could not escape contact with their subjects and their neighbours. There was the climate to consider. Winters in Palestine and Syria can be almost as bleak and cold as in western Europe, but they are short. The long, sweltering summers soon taught the colonists that they must wear different clothes, eat different foods and keep different hours. The vigorous habits of the north were out of place. Instead, they must learn native ways. They must employ native servants. Native nurses looked after their children, and native grooms their horses. There were strange diseases about, for which their own doctors were useless; they soon had to rely on native medicine.[1] Inevitably they learnt to understand the natives and to work in with them. In the Kingdom of Jerusalem and the County of Tripoli the absence of a native aristocracy to challenge their rule, once the Moslems had fled, made this easy. Farther north, the Greek and Armenian aristocracy were jealous of them and politics interfered with their mutual understanding; though the Armenians in the end met them half-way and adopted many Frankish habits.[2]

Between the Franks and their Moslem neighbours there could never be lasting peace, but there was increasing contact. The revenues of the Frankish states came largely from tolls levied on the trade between the Moslem interior and the coast. Moslem merchants must be allowed to come down freely to the seaports and must be treated fairly. Out of their commercial connections friendship grew. The Order of the Temple, with its great banking activities, was ready to extend its operations to oblige infidel

[1] The Tripolitan doctor who was supposed to have poisoned Baldwin III was a native (see below, p. 361). Native doctors proved themselves wiser than the Frankish over Amalric I's death-bed (see below, p. 399). Amalric employed a certain Suleiman ibn Daoud and his elder son as Court doctors, while Suleiman's second son was Court riding master. See Cahen, 'Indigènes et Croisés', *Syria*, 1934. Usama was unimpressed by Frankish medicine (see below, p. 320).
[2] See Cahen, *La Syrie du Nord*, pp. 561–8.

clients and kept officials who could specialize in Moslem affairs. At the same time the wiser statesmen amongst the Franks saw that their kingdom could only last if the Moslem world were kept disunited; and for this purpose diplomatic missions passed to and fro. Frankish and Moslem lords were often received with honour at courts of the rival faith. Captives or hostages often spent years in the enemies' castles or palaces. Though few Moslems troubled to learn French, many Franks, nobles as well as merchants, spoke Arabic. A few, like Reynald of Sidon, even took an interest in the Arabic literature. In times of war each side appreciated gestures of gallantry and chivalry. In times of peace lords from either side of the frontier would join together in hunting expeditions.[1]

Nor was there complete religious intolerance. The two great Faiths shared a common background. The Moslem chroniclers were as interested as the Christian when relics believed to be of Abraham, Isaac and Jacob were discovered at Hebron.[2] Even in times of hostility Frankish pilgrims could penetrate to the shrine of Our Lady of Sardenay in the hills behind Damascus;[3] and the protection given by the Bedouins to the great monastery of St Catherine in the Sinai desert was usually extended to its visitors.[4] Reynald of Châtillon's brutal treatment of Moslem pilgrims shocked his fellow-believers almost as much as it infuriated Saladin. William of Tyre was ready to pay tribute to Nur ed-Din's piety, though he disagreed with his creed. Moslem writers often showed admiration of Frankish chivalry.[5]

[1] For Reynald of Sidon, see below, p. 469. The Moslems insisted on financial guarantees by Knights Templar when negotiating with Christian rulers, e.g. Abu Shama, p. 32. Raymond III of Tripoli spoke Arabic, William of Tyre almost certainly read Arabic, or employed secretaries who knew Oriental languages. See below, p. 476.

[2] Ibn al-Qalanisi, p. 161, refers to the discovery. See also Kohler, 'Un nouveau récit de l'invention des Patriarches Abraham, Isaac et Jacob à Hébron', in *Revue de l'Orient Latin*, vol. IV, pp. 477 ff.

[3] For Our Lady of Sardenay, see Rey, *op. cit.* pp. 291–6.

[4] For Saint Catherine and its pilgrims, see Rey, *op. cit.* pp. 287–91.

[5] E.g. William of Tyre (xx, 31, p. 1000) calls Nur ed-Din 'princeps justus, vafer et providus, et secundum gentis suae traditiones religiosus'.

The atmosphere of the time is best illustrated in the memoirs of the Munqidhite prince Usama of Shaizar. The Munqidhites were a petty dynasty in constant fear of absorption by more powerful co-religionists. They were therefore ready to come to terms with the Franks; and Usama himself spent many years at the courts of Damascus and Cairo when both were in close diplomatic connection with Jerusalem. As an envoy, a tourist and a sportsman Usama often visited Frankish lands, and, though when writing he consigns them all piously to perdition, he had many Frankish friends whose conversation he enjoyed. He was shocked by the crudity of their medicine, though he learnt from them a sure cure for scrofula, and he was astounded by the latitude allowed to their women; and he was embarrassed when a Frankish acquaintance offered to send his son to be educated in western Europe. He thought them a little barbarous, and would laugh about them with his native Christian friends. But they were people with whom he could reach an understanding. The one bar to friendship was provided by newcomers from the West. Once when he was staying with the Templars at Jerusalem and was praying with their permission in the corner of the old Mosque al-Aqsa, a knight roughly insulted him; whereupon another Templar hurried up to explain that the rude man had only just arrived from Europe and did not as yet know any better.[1]

It was indeed the immigrants, come to fight for the Cross and determined to brook no delay, whose crudity continually ruined the policy of Outremer. They were particularly strong in the Church. Not one of the Latin Patriarchs of Jerusalem in the twelfth century was born in Palestine, and of the great ecclesiastics only William, Archbishop of Tyre, to whom the Patriarchate was refused. The influence of the Church was seldom in favour of an understanding with the infidel; and it was even more disastrous in its relations with the native Christians. The native Christians had great influence at the Moslem courts. Many of the best-known

[1] Usama, ed. Hitti, *passim*, esp. pp. 161–70.

Arabic writers and philosophers and almost all the physicians were Christian. They could have formed a bridge between the eastern and western worlds.

The Orthodox communities in Palestine had accepted the Latin hierarchy because at the time of the conquest its own upper clergy were all in exile. The Patriarch Daimbert had attempted to deprive their clergy of their positions at the Holy Sepulchre, but strange events at the ceremony of the Holy Fire in 1101 and the influence of the King had restored Greek canons to the church and had allowed the celebration of the Orthodox rite there. The Crown throughout was friendly to the Orthodox. Morphia, Baldwin II's queen and Melisende's mother was an Orthodox princess as were the queens of Melisende's two sons. The Abbot of St Sabas, the leading Orthodox hierarch left in Palestine, was treated with honour by Baldwin I; and Melisende gave lands to the abbey, which probably owed service to the Crown. The Emperor Manuel was able to maintain a protective interest in the Orthodox, illustrated by the repairs for which he was responsible in the two great Churches of the Holy Sepulchre and the Nativity. The monastery of St Euthymius in the Judaean wilderness was rebuilt and redecorated about the same time, perhaps with his help. But there was no increase in cordiality between the Latin and Greek clergy. The Russian pilgrim, Daniel, in 1104 was hospitably received in Latin establishments; but the Greek pilgrim, Phocas, in 1184, though he visited Latin establishments, had no liking for Latins, except for a Spanish hermit who had at one time lived in Anatolia; and he relates with glee a miracle that discomfited the Latin ecclesiastic whom he calls the 'intruder' Bishop of Lydda. It is probable that the attempt of the Latin hierarchy to make the Orthodox pay the *dime*, together with resentment that their rite was seldom permitted in the great churches of their Faith, lessened the liking of the Orthodox for Frankish rule, and made them ready, once Manuel's protection had ended, to accept and even to welcome Saladin's reconquest. In Antioch the presence of a powerful Greek community and political developments had caused an open hostility between Greeks and Latins which seriously weakened the principality.[1]

In the kingdom itself the heretic sects were of little importance outside of Jerusalem, where almost all of them kept establishments at the Holy Sepulchre. Daimbert had tried to eject them too, without success. The Crown protected their rights. Indeed, Queen Melisende gave her personal support to the Jacobite Syrians when they had a lawsuit against a Frankish knight.[2] In the County of Tripoli the chief heretic Church was that of the Maronites, the surviving adherents of Monothelete doctrine. With them the western Church acted with rare tact and forbearance; and about 1180 they agreed to admit the supremacy of the Roman See, provided that they might keep their Syriac liturgy and customs; nor did they renounce their heretical doctrine of Christ's single will. The negotiations, of which too little is known, were ably managed by the Patriarch Aimery of Antioch. The admission of this first Uniate Church showed that the Papacy was ready to permit divergent usages and even doubtful theology, provided that its ultimate authority was recognized.[3]

[1] See Daniel the Higumene, *passim*, and John Phocas, *A Brief Description*, *passim*. See also Rey, *op. cit.* pp. 75–93, and Cahen, *loc. cit.* The Russian pilgrim Euphrosyne of Polotsk, when dying in Palestine, applied to the Abbot of Saint Sabas as the chief Orthodox ecclesiastic to find her a suitable burying place. See de Khitrowo, 'Pèlerinage en Palestine de l'Abbesse Euphrosyne', in *Revue de l'Orient Latin*, vol. III, pp. 32–5. Later Orthodox writers such as the seventeenth-century Dositheus, disliking to admit that the Orthodox had accepted the Latin Patriarchs from 1099 to 1187, have evolved a list of six or seven Patriarchs between Symeon's death in 1099 and 1187 (Dositheus, II, p. 1243; Le Quien, *Oriens Christianus*, III, pp. 498–503). There is a John, Patriarch of Jerusalem, who subscribed to the condemnation of Soterichus in 1157, and a John of Jerusalem, presumably the same, wrote a treatise against the Latins about this time (Krumbacher, *Gesch. der Byz. Literatur*, p. 91). It is possible that Manuel had the recapture of the Jerusalem Patriarchate in mind and kept a Patriarch in storage against that day. But it is clear that the Orthodox in Palestine submitted to the Latin Patriarch. The presence of Greek canons at the Holy Sepulchre is attested in the *Cartulaire du Saint Sépulcre*, ed. Rozière, p. 177.
[2] See above, p. 232.
[3] See Dib, article 'Maronites', in Vacant et Mangenot, *Dictionnaire de Théologie Catholique*, vol. x, 1.

In the principality of Antioch the separated Armenian Church was powerful and was encouraged by the Princes, who found it a useful counter against the Orthodox; and in Edessa the Armenians, though they were distrusted by Baldwin I and Baldwin II, enjoyed the friendship of the house of Courtenay. Many Armenian bishops came to recognize papal supremacy, and some attended Synods of the Latin Church, forgiving in the Latin doctrines what they thought unpardonable in the Greek. The Jacobite Syrians were at first frankly hostile to the Crusaders and preferred Moslem rule. But, after the fall of Edessa, they became reconciled to the Prince of Antioch, nominally because of a miracle at the tomb of St Barsauma, but actually from a common fear and hatred of Byzantium. The Jacobite Patriarch Michael, one of the great historians of the time, was a friend of the Patriarch Aimery and paid a cordial visit to Jerusalem. None of the other heretic churches was of importance in the Frankish states.[1]

The Franks' Moslem subjects accepted their masters calmly and admitted the justice of their administration; but they would obviously be unreliable if things went badly for the Christians. The Jews, with good reason, preferred the rule of the Arabs, who always treated them honestly and kindly, if with a certain contempt.[2]

To the contemporary western pilgrim Outremer was shocking because of its luxury and licence. To the modern historian it is rather the intolerance and dishonourable barbarity of the Crusaders that is to be regretted. Yet both aspects can be explained by the atmosphere that reigned there. Life amongst the Frankish colonists was uneasy and precarious. They were in a land where intrigue and murder flourished and enemies lay in wait across the near-by frontiers. No one knew when he might not receive a knife-thrust from a devotee of the Assassins or poison from one of his servants. Mysterious diseases of which they knew little were rife. Even

---

[1] See below, p. 371, also the preface to Nau's edition of Michael the Syrian.
[2] Ibn Jubayr, ed. Wright, pp. 304-5. Benjamin of Tudela's statistics show the greater prosperity of the Jews under the Moslems.

with the help of local doctors, no Frank lived for long in the East. Women were more fortunate than men. They avoided the risks of battle and, owing to better medical knowledge, childbirth was less dangerous there than in the West. But infant mortality was high, especially among the boys. Fief after fief fell into the hands of an heiress, whose inheritance might lure gallant adventurers from the West; but too often great estates lacked a lord at the hour of crisis, and every marriage was a matter of dispute and of plotting. Marriages were often sterile. Many of the toughest warriors failed to father a child. Intermarriage between the few noble families increased personal rivalries. Fiefs were joined and divided with little regard to geographical convenience. There were perpetual quarrels between the next-of-kin.

The social structure that the Franks brought from the West demanded a steady hereditary succession and a maintenance of man-power. The physical decline of the human element was full of danger. Fear made them brutal and treacherous, and uncertainty encouraged their love of frivolous gaiety. As their tenure weakened, their feats and tournaments grew more lavish. Visitors and natives alike were horrified by the extravagance and the immorality that they saw all around them, and the worst offender was the Patriarch Heraclius.[1] But a wise visitor would understand that beneath the splendid surface all was not well. The King, for all his silk and gold, often lacked the money to pay his soldiers. The proud Templar, counting his money bags, might at any moment be summoned to battles more cruel than any that the West had known. Revellers like the wedding guests at Kerak in 1183 might rise from the table to hear the mangonels of the infidel pounding against the castle walls. The gay, gallant trappings of life in Outremer hung thinly over anxiety, uncertainty and fear; and an onlooker might well wonder whether even under the best of rulers the adventure could endure for long.

[1] *Estoire d'Eracles*, II, p. 88; Ernoul, pp. 83–7; *Itinerarium Regis Ricardi*, pp. 5–6; Caesarius of Heisterbach, *Dialogus Miraculorum*, I, p. 188, attributing the fall of Jerusalem to the corruption of the Franks of Outremer.

CHAPTER II

THE RISE OF NUR ED-DIN

'He went forth conquering, and to conquer.' REVELATION VI, 2

Raymond of Antioch had been right to urge the leaders of the Second Crusade to march against Aleppo. His failure to persuade them cost him his life. The chief enemy of Christendom was Nur ed-Din; and in 1147 a great army could have crushed him. He was master of Aleppo and Edessa; but Unur of Damascus and the petty independent emirs of the Orontes valley would not have come to his rescue; nor could he have counted on help from his brother Saif ed-Din at Mosul, who had troubles of his own in Iraq. But the folly of the Crusaders drove Unur into alliance with him for as long as the danger lasted; and the chance given him of intervention in the affairs of Tripoli allowed him to strengthen his hold on central Syria.

Raymond was further justified in refusing to join the Crusade. Neither he nor Joscelin of Edessa could afford to leave their lands exposed to Nur ed-Din. Even while the Crusaders were before Damascus troops from Aleppo raided Christian territory. Under a flag of truce Count Joscelin went himself to Nur ed-Din's camp to beg for clemency. All that he obtained was a temporary respite.[1] Meanwhile, the Sultan of Konya, Mas'ud, at peace with Byzantium, took advantage of the discomfiture of the Franks to attack Marash. Raymond prepared to meet him; so Mas'ud sent to ask Nur ed-Din to make a diversion. His request was granted; but Raymond with the alliance of a Kurdish chief of the Assassins, Ali ibn Wafa, who hated Nur ed-Din far more than the Christians, surprised Nur ed-Din in November 1148 as he swept through the

---

[1] Ibn al-Furat, quoted by Cahen, *La Syrie du Nord*, p. 382.

villages in the plain of the Aswad at Famiya, on the road from Antioch to Marash. Nur ed-Din's two chief lieutenants, the Kurd Shirkuh and the Aleppan notable Ibn ed-Daya, had quarrelled. The former refused to take part in the battle; and the whole Moslem army was forced into a hasty and ignominious retreat. Next spring Nur ed-Din invaded the country again and defeated Raymond at Baghras, close to the former battlefield. He then turned south to besiege the fortress of Inab, one of the few strongholds left to the Christians east of the Orontes. Raymond with a small army and a few Assassin allies under Ali ibn Wafa hurried to its rescue; and Nur ed-Din, misinformed of the strength of his force, retreated. In fact the Moslem army of six thousand horse outnumbered the Frankish of four thousand horse and one thousand infantrymen. Against Ali's advice Raymond then decided to reinforce the garrison of Inab. But Nur ed-Din was now aware of Raymond's weakness. On 28 June 1149 the Christian army encamped in a hollow by the Fountain of Murad, in the plain between Inab and the marsh of Ghab. During the night Nur ed-Din's troops crept up and surrounded them. Next morning Raymond realized that his only chance was to charge his way out. But the terrain was against him. A wind rose and blew dust in the eyes of his knights as they pressed their horses up the slope. In a few hours his army was annihilated. Amongst the dead were Reynald of Marash and the Assassin leader Ali. Raymond himself perished by the hand of Shirkuh, who thus regained his master's favour lost at Famiya. The Prince's skull, set in a silver case, was sent by Nur ed-Din as a gift to his spiritual master, the Caliph of Baghdad.[1]

Joscelin of Edessa, enjoying an uneasy truce with the Moslems, had refused to work in with his old rival, Raymond. His turn

---

[1] William of Tyre, XVII, 9, pp. 771–3; letter of Seneschal of Temple to the Grand Master Everard in *R.H.F.* vol. XV, p. 541; Cinnamus, pp. 122–3; Michael the Syrian, III, pp. 288–9; *Chron. Anon Syr.* (Syriac edition), p. 296; Matthew of Edessa, cclix, p. 329; Gregory the Priest, p. 142; Ibn al-Qalanisi, pp. 288–92; Abn Shama, pp. 10–12; Ibn al-Furat, *loc. cit.* identifying the site as Ard al-Hatim.

came next. Nur ed-Din passed on through Antiochene territory completing his hold on the middle Orontes by the capture of Arzghan and Tel-Kashfahan, then overpowering the garrisons of Artah and Harenc farther north and turning west to appear before the walls of Antioch itself and raid as far as Saint Symeon.[1] Joscelin made no attempt to rescue his fellow-Franks but marched on Marash in the hope of taking over the inheritance of Reynald, who was his son-in-law. He entered the city but retired when the Sultan Mas'ud approached. The garrison that he left behind surrendered to the Seldjuks on the promise that Christian lives should be spared; but as they and the clergy were taking the road to Antioch they were massacred one and all. Mas'ud pursued Joscelin to the neighbourhood of Turbessel. But Christian reinforcements were approaching; while Nur ed-Din had no wish to see Joscelin, who was still his client, lose his lands to the Seldjuks. Mas'ud found it politic to retire. Next, the Ortoqids of the Jezireh, limited on the south by Nur ed-Din and his brothers, sought to expand along the Euphrates at the expense of the Armenians of Gargar, who had been tributaries to Reynald. Joscelin dissipated his energies in vainly sending help to Basil of Gargar. The Ortoqid Kara Arslan took over the whole district of Gargar and Kharpurt, to the delight of the Jacobite Christians to whom his rule was infinitely preferable to that of Reynald with his strong pro-Armenian and anti-Jacobite sentiments.[2] In the winter of 1149 Nur ed-Din broke with Joscelin. His first attacks were unsuccessful; but in April 1150, as Joscelin was riding to Antioch to consult with the government there, he was separated from his escort and fell into the hands of some Turcoman freebooters. They were ready to release him for a heavy ransom; but Nur ed-Din heard of his capture and sent a squadron of cavalry to

---

[1] William of Tyre, xvII, 10, pp. 774–5; letter to Everard, *loc. cit.*; *Chron. Anon. Syr.* (Syriac edition), p. 299; Ibn al-Qalanisi, p. 293; Ibn al-Athir, *Atabegs*, p. 180.

[2] Matthew of Edessa, cclix, pp. 330–1; Gregory the Priest, p. 162; Michael the Syrian, III, pp. 209–11, 294–6, and Armenian version, p. 346.

take him from his captors. He was blinded and imprisoned at
Aleppo. There he died, nine years later, in 1159.[1]

Thus, by the summer of 1150, both the Principality of Antioch
and the remains of the County of Edessa had lost their lords. But
Nur ed-Din did not venture to go farther. When news reached
Antioch of the death of Prince Raymond, the Patriarch Aimery
put the city into a state of defence and sent urgently south to
ask King Baldwin to come to its rescue. He then obtained
a short truce from Nur ed-Din by promising to surrender
Antioch if Baldwin did not arrive. The arrangement suited Nur
ed-Din, who was shy of attempting the siege of the city and
who meanwhile was able to capture Apamea, the last Antiochene
fortress in the Orontes valley. King Baldwin hastened north
with a small company, mostly composed of Knights Templar.
His appearance induced Nur ed-Din to accept a more lasting
truce, and it served to help to keep Mas'ud from attacking
Turbessel. But though Antioch was saved, the Principality was
now reduced to the plain of Antioch itself and the coast from
Alexandretta to Lattakieh.[2]

It then remained to settle the government of the two lordless
domains. On Joscelin's capture, Nur ed-Din had attacked
Turbessel; but the Countess Beatrice put up so spirited a defence

[1] William of Tyre, xvii, 11, pp. 776–7; Matthew of Edessa, cclix, pp. 331–2;
Michael the Syrian, iii, p. 295; *Chron. Anon. Syr.*, p. 300; Ibn al-Furat,
quoted by Cahen, *op. cit.* p. 386: Kemal ad-Din, ed. Blochet, pp. 523–4;
Bustan, p. 544; Ibn al-Qalanisi, p. 300; Ibn al-Athir, p. 481; Sibt ibn el-Djauzi,
p. 122. The circumstances vary in each account. William says that he was going
to Antioch to answer an appeal from the Patriarch; Matthew of Edessa and
Ibn al-Furat to seek help there; the Anonymous Chronicle to secure the
regency. William attributes his separation from his company to the demands of
nature, Sibt to an amour with a Turcoman girl; Ibn al-Furat to a fall when his
horse collided with a tree, which, according to Michael, only existed in his
imagination (the Syriac chroniclers saw Joscelin's capture as divine vengeance
for his persecution of the Jacobites); the Syriac chroniclers say that he was
identified by a Jew. The Anonymous Chronicle alone says that he was blinded.
Michael adds that he was not allowed a Latin confessor but was confessed on
his death-bed by the Jacobite Bishop of Edessa.

[2] William of Tyre, xvii, 15, pp. 783–4; Ibn al-Qalanisi, pp. 293–4, 300–1.

that he withdrew. It was clear, nevertheless, that Turbessel could
not be held. It was overcrowded with Frankish and Armenian
refugees from the outlying districts. The Jacobite Christians were
openly disloyal; and the whole area was cut off from Antioch by
Nur ed-Din's conquests. The Countess was preparing to abandon
her lands when a message came through from the Emperor
Manuel. He was aware of the situation, and he offered to purchase
from her all that was left of her county. Beatrice dutifully referred
the offer to King Baldwin, who was at Antioch. The lords of his
kingdom who were with him and the lords of Antioch discussed
the offer. They were loth to hand over territory to a hated Greek;
but they decided that it would at least be the Emperor's fault now
if the places were lost to Christendom. The Byzantine governor
of Cilicia, Thomas, brought bags of gold—how many, we are not
told—to the Countess at Antioch; and in return she handed over
to his soldiers the six fortresses of Turbessel, Ravendel, Samosata,
Aintab, Duluk and Birejik. The King's army accompanied the
Byzantine garrisons on their journey, and escorted back the many
Frankish and Armenian refugees who distrusted Byzantine rule and
preferred the greater safety of Antioch. The Countess reserved
one fortress from the sale, Ranculat or Rum Kalaat, on the
Euphrates near Samosata, which she gave to the Armenian
Catholicus. It remained his residence, under Turkish suzerainty,
for a century and a half. As the royal army and the refugees
travelled back, Nur ed-Din tried to surprise them at Aintab; but
the King's excellent organization preserved them. His chief
barons, Humphrey of Toron and Robert of Sourdeval, vainly
begged him to allow them to take possession of Aintab in his
name; but he abode by the bargain with the Emperor.[1]

[1] William of Tyre, xvii, 16–17, pp. 784–9. The Byzantine historians make
no mention of the transaction. For the dating and Moslem evidence, see Cahen,
op. cit. p. 388 n. 24; Michael the Syrian, iii, p. 297, and Armenian version,
p. 343. Vartan, p. 435, and Vahram, *Rhymed Chronicle*, p. 618, tell of the cession
of Rum Kalaat to the Catholicus. Michael's Syriac version says that the
Countess asked the Catholicus to aid an Armenian lord in Rum Kalaat, but the
Catholicus installed himself there by trickery.

Why the Emperor made the bargain is uncertain. The Franks believed that in his pride he thought that he could hold them. It is unlikely that he was so badly misinformed. Rather, he was looking ahead. He hoped before long to come in force to Syria. If he lost them now he could recover them then; and his claim would be beyond dispute. In fact, he lost them in less than a year, to an alliance between Nur ed-Din and the Seldjuk Mas'ud. The alliance had been made on the morrow of Joscelin's capture, and had been sealed by the marriage of Nur ed-Din to Mas'ud's daughter. Turbessel was to be her dowry. But Mas'ud had not joined his son-in-law in his attack on Beatrice; he contented himself with capturing Kaisun and Behesni, in the north of the county, giving them to his son Kilij Arslan. But in the spring of 1151 he and Nur ed-Din both attacked the Byzantine garrisons; and the Ortoqids hurried to take their share. Aintab and Duluk fell to Mas'ud, Samosata and Birejik to the Ortoqid Timurtash of Mardin, and Ravendel to Nur ed-Din. At Turbessel itself the Byzantines resisted for a while but were starved out and surrendered to Nur ed-Din's lieutenant, Hasan of Menbij, in July 1151.[1] All traces of the County of Edessa were gone. The Countess Beatrice retired to Jerusalem with her children, Joscelin and Agnes; who in time to come were to play disastrous parts in the downfall of the kingdom.[2]

Edessa was gone, but Antioch remained. Raymond's death left the Princess Constance a widow with four young children. The throne was hers by right; but it was felt that in such times a man must govern. Her elder son, Bohemond III, was five years old at his father's death. Till he came of age there must be a male regent. The Patriarch Aimery had taken charge at the moment of crisis; but lay opinion disliked the idea of a clerical regency. It was clear

---

[1] William of Tyre, *loc. cit.*; Bar-Hebraeus, trans. Budge, p. 277; Michael, Armenian version, p. 297; Ibn al-Qalanisi, p. 309; Ibn al-Athir, *Atabegs*, p. 132 (with the wrong date).

[2] Joscelin II's other daughter Isabella (see above, p. 222) was probably dead, though William of Tyre (p. 777) mentions her as alive when her father died.

that the young Princess ought to remarry. In the meantime the proper regent should be her cousin, King Baldwin, acting as her nearest male relative rather than as an overlord. Baldwin had hastened to Antioch on the news of Raymond's death. He dealt with the situation with a wisdom rare in a boy of nineteen, and his authority was universally accepted. He returned in the early summer of 1150, to give his authority to the sale of Countess Beatrice's lands. But he had too many anxieties in the south to wish to remain responsible for Antioch. He urged Constance, who was only twenty-two, to choose another husband and himself suggested three alternative candidates, first, Yves of Nesle, Count of Soissons, a wealthy French noble who had come to Palestine in the wake of the Second Crusade and was ready to make his home there; secondly, Walter of Falconberg, of the family of Saint-Omer, which had held the lordship of Galilee in the past; and thirdly Ralph of Merle, a gallant baron of the County of Tripoli. But Constance would have none of them; and Baldwin had to return to Jerusalem leaving her in possession of her government.[1]

Irritated by her young cousin's importunities, Constance at once changed her policy and sent an embassy to Constantinople to ask the Emperor Manuel as her overlord to choose her a husband.[2] Manuel was eager to comply with her wishes. Byzantine influence had been declining along the south-eastern frontier of the Empire. About the year 1143 the Armenian Prince, Thoros the Roupenian, had escaped from Constantinople and taken refuge at the Court of his cousin, Joscelin II of Edessa. There he gathered a company of compatriots, with which he recaptured the family stronghold of Vahka, in the eastern Taurus mountains. Two of his brothers, Stephen and Mleh joined him, and he made friends with a neighbouring Frankish lord, Simon of Raban, whose daughter he married. In 1151, while the Byzantines were distracted by the

---

[1] William of Tyre, XVII, 18, pp. 789–91. He suggests that the Patriarch Aimery encouraged Constance to refuse the candidates, for fear of his power being reduced.
[2] Cinnamus, p. 178.

Moslem attack on Turbessel, he swept down into the Cilician plain and defeated and slew the Byzantine governor, Thomas, at the gates of Mamistra. Manuel at once sent his cousin Andronicus with an army to recover the territory lost to Thoros; and now there came the timely chance to place his own candidate on the throne of Antioch.

Neither project succeeded. Andronicus Comnenus was the most brilliant and fascinating member of his talented family, but he was rash and careless. As he moved up to besiege Thoros at Mamistra, the Armenians made a sudden sortie and caught him unawares. His army was routed and he fled back in disgrace to Constantinople. In choosing a husband for Constance, Manuel showed greater ingenuity than sense. He sent his brother-in-law, the Caesar John Roger, the widower of his favourite sister Maria. John Roger was a Norman by birth, and though he had once plotted to secure the imperial throne, he was now a proved and trusted friend of the Emperor; who knew that he could count on his loyalty but believed that his Latin birth would make him acceptable to the Frankish nobility. He forgot about Constance herself. John Roger was frankly middle-aged and had lost all his youthful charm. The young Princess, whose first husband had been famed for his beauty, would not consider so unromantic a mate. She bade the Caesar return to the Emperor. It would have been better if Manuel had sent Andronicus to Antioch and John Roger to fight in Cilicia.[1]

King Baldwin would have welcomed almost any husband for his cousin; for he had recently acquired a new responsibility. The married life of Count Raymond II of Tripoli and his wife Hodierna of Jerusalem was not entirely happy. Hodierna, like her sisters Melisende and Alice, was headstrong and gay. Doubts were whispered about the legitimacy of her daughter Melisende. Raymond, passionately jealous of her, attempted to keep her in

[1] Cinnamus, pp. 121–4, 178; Matthew of Edessa, cclxiii, pp. 334–6; Gregory the Priest, p. 166; Sembat the Constable, p. 619; Vahram, *Rhymed Chronicle*, pp. 504–6; Michael the Syrian, III, p. 281.

a state of Oriental seclusion. Early in 1152 their relations were so bad that Queen Melisende felt it her duty to intervene. Together with her son the King, she travelled to Tripoli to patch up a reconciliation. Baldwin used the opportunity to summon Constance to Tripoli, where her two aunts scolded her for her obstinate widowhood. But, perhaps because neither of them had made an outstanding success of married life, their lectures were unavailing. Constance returned to Antioch promising nothing. With Raymond and Hodierna the Queen was more effective. They agreed to compose their quarrel; but it was thought best that Hodierna should enjoy a long holiday at Jerusalem. Baldwin decided to stay on at Tripoli for a while as there were rumours that Nur ed-Din was going to attack the County. The Queen and the Countess set out on the road southward, escorted for a mile or so by the Count. As he rode back through the south gate of his capital a band of Assassins leapt out on him and stabbed him to death. Ralph of Merle and another knight who were with him tried to protect him, only to perish themselves. It was all over so quickly that his guard were unable to catch the murderers. The King was playing at dice in the castle when cries came up from the city below. The garrison rushed to arms and poured into the streets, slaying every Moslem that they saw. But the Assassins escaped; nor was the motive of their act ever known.[1]

Messengers were sent to bring back the Queen and the Countess, and Hodierna assumed the regency in the name of her twelve-year old son, Raymond III. But, as at Antioch, a man was needed as guardian of the government; and Baldwin, as the nearest male relative was obliged to take on the guardianship. Nur ed-Din at once made an incursion as far as Tortosa, which his troops held for a while. They were soon driven out; and Baldwin, with Hodierna's consent, handed over Tortosa to the Knights of the Temple.[2]

Baldwin was glad to be able to return to Jerusalem. Queen Melisende, conscious of her hereditary right, was unwilling to

---

[1] William of Tyre, XVII, 18–19, pp. 789–92.
[2] *Ibid., loc. cit.*; Ibn al-Qalanisi, p. 312.

hand power over to her son. But he was now over twenty-two years of age and public opinion demanded his coronation as an adult ruler. The Queen therefore arranged with the Patriarch Fulcher that she should be crowned again by his side, in order that her joint authority should be explicitly admitted. The coronation was to take place on Easter Sunday, 30 March; but Baldwin postponed it. Then, on the Tuesday, when his mother suspected nothing, he entered the Church of the Holy Sepulchre with an escort of knights and forced the angry Patriarch to crown him alone. It was the signal for an open breach. The Queen had many friends. Manasses of Hierges, her protégé, was still Constable; his family connections included the great Ibelin clan, which controlled the Philistian plain; and many of the nobles of southern Palestine were of his party. It was noticeable that when Baldwin went to Antioch in 1149, few of the nobility would accompany an expedition in which the Queen was not interested. Baldwin's friends came from the north. They were led by Humphrey of Toron and William of Falconberg, whose estates were in Galilee. The King did not venture to have recourse to force. He summoned a great council of the realm, before which he pleaded his claims. Thanks to the influence of the clergy, he was obliged to accept a compromise. He could have Galilee and the north as his realm; but Melisende would retain Jerusalem itself and Nablus, that is to say, Judaea and Samaria; and the coast, where the King's young brother Amalric held the County of Jaffa, was under her sovereignty. It was an impossible solution; and before many months were passed, the King demanded from his mother the cession of Jerusalem. Without Jerusalem, he said, he could not undertake the defence of the kingdom. With Nur ed-Din's power growing daily, the argument was forceful; and even her best supporters began to desert the Queen's cause. But she held firm and fortified Jerusalem and Nablus against her son. Unfortunately, the Constable Manasses was surprised and captured by the King's troops at his castle of Mirabel, on the edge of the coastal plain. His life was spared on his promise to leave the East and never to return.

Nablus thereupon surrendered to the King. Melisende, deserted by the lay nobility but supported still by the Patriarch, tried to hold out in Jerusalem. But the citizens also turned against her and obliged her to give up the struggle. After a few days she yielded the city to her son. He took no strong action against her; for legal opinion seems to have held that right, if not expediency, was on her side. She was allowed to retain Nablus and the neighbourhood as her dower; and, though she retired from lay politics, she retained the patronage over the Church. Baldwin, supreme now in the lay government, replaced Manasses as Constable with his friend Humphrey of Toron.[1]

These dynastic troubles in the ruling Frankish families had been very much to Nur ed-Din's liking. He did not trouble to make any serious attacks against the Christians during these years; for he had a more urgent task to complete, the conquest of Damascus. After the failure of the Second Crusade Unur of Damascus kept up a desultory war against the Christians for a few months; but fear of Nur ed-Din made him glad to accept peace overtures from Jerusalem. In May 1149 a two-years' truce was arranged. Unur died soon afterwards, in August; and the Burid emir, Toghtekin's grandson Mujir ed-Din, in whose name Unur had ruled, took over the government.[2] His weakness gave Nur ed-Din his

---

[1] William of Tyre, XVII, 13-14, pp. 779-83. Nablus was held by Philip of Milly, who had supported the Queen. On 31 July, 1161, a few weeks before the Queen's death, he was given the seigneurie of Oultrejourdain in exchange for Nablus (Röhricht, *Regesta*, p. 96). Queen Melisende was not consulted, probably because she was too ill, though her sister, Hodierna, Dowager Countess of Tripoli, approved the transaction. Presumably Philip held his lands from Melisende, not from Baldwin, and it was only on her death-bed that Baldwin was able to make a change, which would have deprived her of her friend and chief vassal. Philip's wife Isabella or Elizabeth was the niece of Pagan of Oultrejourdain, and eventual heiress to his successor Maurice. On her death he joined the Templars. Her sister Maria's husband Walter Brisebarre III of Beirut seems later to have been lord of Oultrejourdain, for which he exchanged his own fief of Beirut, but on the death of his wife and her infant daughter he presumably lost the fief, which passed to Philip's daughter Stephanie. See Rey, 'Les Seigneurs de Montréal' and 'Les Seigneurs de Barut', *passim*.   [2] Ibn al-Qalanisi, p. 295. Unur died of dysentery, 'jūsantiryā'.

opportunity. He did not act at once; for his own brother Saif ed-Din died in November, and a rearrangement of the family lands ensued. The youngest brother, Qutb ed-Din, inherited Mosul and the territory in Iraq, but he seems to have recognized Nur ed-Din as his superior.[1] In March next year Nur ed-Din advanced on Damascus; but heavy rains slowed his progress and gave Mujir ed-Din time to ask for help from Jerusalem. Nur ed-Din therefore retired on receiving a promise that his name should be mentioned on the coinage and in the public prayers at Damascus after those of the Caliph and the Sultan of Persia. His rights to a vague overlordship were thus admitted.[2]

In May 1151 Nur ed-Din again appeared before Damascus, and again the Franks came to the rescue. After camping for a month close to the city Nur ed-Din retreated to the neighbourhood of Baalbek, which was governed by his lieutenant, Shirkuh's brother Ayub. Meanwhile the Franks under King Baldwin moved up to Damascus. Many of them were allowed to visit the bazaars within the walls, while Mujir ed-Din paid a cordial visit to the King in the Christian camp. But the allies were not strong enough to go in pursuit of Nur ed-Din. Instead, they marched on Bosra, whose emir, Sarkhak, had accepted help from Nur ed-Din in a revolt against Damascus. The expedition was unsuccessful; but soon afterwards Sarkhak, with the usual volatility of the minor Moslem princes, made friends with the Franks; and Mujir ed-Din was obliged to call in Nur ed-Din's help to reduce him to obedience. When Nur ed-Din went north again, Mujir ed-Din followed him on a visit to Aleppo, where a treaty of friendship was signed.[3] But the Damascenes still refused to renounce their alliance with the Franks. In December 1151 a band of Turcomans tried to raid Banyas, probably at Ayub's orders. The garrison countered by a raid on the territory of Baalbek, which Ayub drove off. Mujir ed-Din carefully disclaimed any connection with

---

[1] Ibn al-Athir, *Atabegs*, pp. 171–5; Ibn al-Qalanisi, pp. 295–6. See Cahen, *op. cit.* p. 393 n. 12, for MS. sources.

[2] Ibn al-Qalanisi, pp. 97–300.   [3] *Ibid.* pp. 302–11.

the warfare.[1] He was more embarrassed when suddenly, in the autumn of 1152, the Ortoqid prince Timurtash of Mardin appeared with a Turcoman army that he had taken by forced marches round the edge of the desert and asked for help for a surprise attack on Jerusalem. He had probably heard of the quarrels between Baldwin and Melisende and thought that a bold stroke might succeed. Mujir ed-Din compromised by allowing him to purchase supplies but sought to dissuade him from going farther. Timurtash then dashed across the Jordan, and, while the Frankish nobility was attending a council at Nablus, doubtless to arrange for Melisende's dower, pitched his camp on the Mount of Olives. But the garrison of Jerusalem made a sudden sortie on the Turcomans, who, finding that their surprise had failed, retreated to the Jordan. There, on the river bank, the army of the Kingdom fell on them and won a complete victory.[2]

During the next months the attention of Christians and Moslems alike was turned to Egypt. The Fatimid Caliphate seemed near to complete disruption. Since the murder of the vizier al-Afdal there had been no competent ruler in Egypt. The Caliph al-Amir had reigned on till October 1129 when he, too, was murdered; but the government had been conducted by a series of worthless viziers. Al-Amir's successor, his cousin al-Hafiz, showed more character and tried to free himself from the shackles of the vizierate by appointing his own son Hasan to the post. But Hasan was disloyal and was put to death at his father's orders in 1135. The next vizier, the Armenian-born Vahram, filled the administration with his compatriots, only to provoke a reaction in 1137, when for days the streets of Cairo ran with Christian blood. Nor was al-Hafiz luckier with his later viziers, though he clung precariously to his throne till his death in 1149. The reign of his son, al-Zafir, began with open civil war between his two leading generals. Amir ibn Sallah won and became vizier, only to be murdered himself three years afterwards.[3] This unending

[1] *Ibid.* p. 311–12.   [2] William of Tyre, XVII, 20, pp. 792–4.
[3] Ibn al-Athir, pp. 475, 486–7. See Wiet, *L'Egypte Arabe*, pp. 190–5.

story of intrigue and blood raised the hopes of Egypt's enemies. In 1150 King Baldwin began to repair the fortifications of Gaza. Ascalon was still a Fatimid fortress, and its garrison still made frequent raids into Christian territory. Gaza was to be the base for operations against Ascalon. The vizier Ibn Sallah was alarmed. Amongst the refugees at the Fatimid court was the Munqidhite prince Usama, who had previously been in Zengi's service. He was sent to Nur ed-Din, who was now encamped before Damascus, to ask him to make a diversion into Galilee; the Egyptian fleet would meanwhile raid the Frankish seaports. The mission was unsuccessful; Nur ed-Din had other preoccupations. Usama on his way back stopped at Ascalon for two years to conduct operations against the local Franks; then he returned to Egypt in time to witness the intrigues that followed the murder of Ibn Sallah by the son of his stepson Abbas, with the connivance of the Caliph.[1]

This drama, following soon on his own triumph over his mother, decided King Baldwin to attack Ascalon. He made careful preparations; and on 25 January 1153 the whole army of the Kingdom, with all the siege engines that the King could amass, appeared before its walls. With the King were the Grand Masters of the Hospital and the Temple, with the pick of their men, the great lay lords of the realm, the Patriarch, the Archbishops of Tyre, Caesarea and Nazareth, and the Bishops of Bethlehem and Acre. The relic of the True Cross accompanied the Patriarch. Ascalon was a tremendous fortress, spreading from the sea in a great semicircle, with its fortifications in excellent repair; and the Egyptian government had always kept it well stocked with armaments and provisions. For some months the Frankish army, though it could completely blockade the city, could make no impression on its walls. The pilgrim-ships that arrived about Easter-time added reinforcements to its ranks. But they were countered by the arrival of an Egyptian fleet in June. The Fatimids

[1] Usama, ed. Hitti, pp. 40–3; Ibn al-Qalanisi, p. 314. The Egyptian raid on the Frankish coast in 1151 is reported by Ibn al-Qalanisi, pp. 307–8, who also reports an Egyptian raid from Ascalon in April 1152 (p. 312).

did not venture to attempt to relieve Ascalon by land, but they sent a squadron of seventy ships laden with men and arms and supplies of all sorts. Gerard of Sidon, who commanded the twenty galleys that were all that the Christians could muster, dared not attack them, and the Egyptian ships sailed triumphantly into the harbour. The defenders were heartened; but the ships sailed away again after they had been unloaded; and the siege dragged on. Most formidable of the Frankish siege-machines was a great wooden tower that overtopped the walls, from which stones and flaming faggots could be shot right into the city streets. One night, in late July, some of the garrison crept out and set fire to it. But a wind arose, and the flaming mass was blown against the wall. The intense heat caused the masonry to disintegrate, and by morning a breach was made. The Templars, who manned that sector, determined that they alone should have the credit of the victory. While some of their men stood by to prevent any other Christian approaching, forty of their knights penetrated into the city. The garrison at first thought that all was lost, but then, seeing how few the Templars were, rounded on them and slew them. The breach was hastily repaired, and the Templar corpses were hung out over the city walls.

While a truce was held to enable each side to bury its dead, the King held a Council in his tent, before the relic of the Holy Cross. The lay nobles, discouraged by the reverse, wished to abandon the siege; but the Patriarch and the Grand Master of the Hospitallers, Raymond of Le Puy, persuaded the King to continue with it; and their eloquence moved the barons. The attack was renewed more vigorously than before.

On 19 August, after a fierce bombardment of the city, the garrison decided to surrender, on condition that the citizens should be allowed to depart in safety with their movable belongings. Baldwin accepted the terms and abode by them loyally. As a great stream of Moslems poured out of the city, by road and sea, to retire to Egypt, the Franks entered in state and took over the citadel, with its vast store of treasure and of arms. The lordship of

Ascalon was given to the King's brother, Amalric, Count of Jaffa. The great mosque became the Cathedral of St Paul, and the Patriarch consecrated as bishop one of his canons, Absalom. Later, the Bishop of Bethlehem, Gerard, secured a ruling from Rome that the see depended on his own.[1]

The capture of Ascalon was the last great triumph of the Kings of Jerusalem, and it raised their prestige to a formidable height. To have won at last the city known as the Bride of Syria was a resounding achievement; but in fact it brought no great substantial gain. Though the fortress had been the base for petty raids into Frankish lands, Egypt no longer seriously threatened the Christians; but now, with Ascalon in their hands, the Franks were lured on to dangerous adventures by the Nile. It was perhaps for that reason that Nur ed-Din, with his far-sighted policy, had not attempted to interfere in the campaign, except for a projected expedition against Banyas which he planned with Mujir of Damascus, but which came to nothing owing to mutual quarrels. He could not regret that Egypt was weakened, nor that Frankish attention should be diverted to the south. Mujir of Damascus was more easily impressed. He hastened to assure Baldwin of his devoted friendship, and he agreed to pay him a yearly tribute. While Frankish lords journeyed and raided as they pleased over Damascene territory, Frankish ambassadors came to the city to collect the money for their King.[2]

To Mujir and his counsellors, mindful of their own safety, a Frankish protectorate was preferable to their fate should Nur ed-Din become their master. But to the ordinary citizen of Damascus the insolence of the Christians was unbearable. The Burid dynasty was proving itself traitor to the Faith. Ayub, Emir of Baalbek, took advantage of this sentiment. His agents penetrated the city, spreading resentment against Mujir. There

[1] William of Tyre, XVII, 1–5, 27–30, pp. 794–802, 804–13; Ibn al-Qalanisi, pp. 314–17; Abu Shama, pp. 77–8; Ibn al-Athir, p. 490.
[2] Ibn al-Qalanisi, pp. 315–16 (he is reticent about Frankish influence in Damascus); Ibn al-Athir, p. 496, and *Atabegs*, p. 189.

happened at this time to be a food-shortage in Damascus; so Nur ed-Din held up the convoys that were bringing corn from the north, and Ayub's agents spread the rumour that this was Mujir's fault for refusing to co-operate with his fellow-Moslems. Next, Nur ed-Din persuaded Mujir that many of the Damascene notables were plotting against him; and Mujir in panic took action against them. When Mujir had thus lost the favour of both the rich and the poor, Ayub's brother Shirkuh arrived as Nur ed-Din's ambassador before Damascus, but he came truculently, with an armed force unusual for a friendly mission. Mujir would not admit him to the city nor would he go out to meet him. Nur ed-Din took this as an insult to his ambassador and advanced with a large army to Damascus. Mujir's desperate appeal to the Franks was sent out too late. Nur ed-Din encamped before the walls on 18 April 1154. Exactly a week later, after a brief skirmish outside the eastern wall, a Jewess admitted some of his soldiers into the Jewish quarter, and at once the populace opened the eastern gate to the bulk of his army. Mujir fled to the citadel, but capitulated after only a few hours. He was offered his life and the emirate of Homs. A few weeks later he was suspected of plotting with old friends in Damascus and was ejected from Homs. He refused the offer of the town of Balis on the Euphrates, and retired to Baghdad.

Meanwhile the citizens of Damascus received Nur ed-Din with every sign of joy. He forbade his troops to pillage, and he at once filled the markets with foodstuffs and removed the tax on fruit and vegetables. When Nur ed-Din returned to Aleppo, he left Ayub in charge of Damascus. Baalbek was given to a local noble, Dhahak, who later revolted against Nur ed-Din and had to be suppressed.[1]

Nur ed-Din's capture of Damascus heavily outbalanced Baldwin's capture of Ascalon. His territory now stretched down the whole eastern frontier of the Frankish states, from Edessa to

[1] Ibn al-Qalanisi, pp. 318–21; Ibn al-Athir, pp. 496–7, and *Atabegs*, pp. 190–2; Kemal ad-Din, ed. Blochet, pp. 527–8.

Oultrejourdain. Only a few petty emirates in Moslem Syria retained their independence, such as Shaizar. Though Frankish possessions were larger in area and richer in resources, Nur ed-Din's had the advantage of union under one master who was far less trammelled by arrogant vassals than the rulers of the Franks. His star was in the ascendant. But he was too cautious to follow up his triumph too quickly. He seems to have reaffirmed the alliance between Damascus and Jerusalem and to have renewed the truce for another two years in 1156, when he made a payment of 8000 ducats in continuance of the tribute paid by Mujir ed-Din. His forbearance was chiefly due to his rivalry with the Anatolian Seldjuks, from whom he wished to take their share of the former County of Edessa.[1]

The Sultan Mas'ud died in 1155; and his sons, Kilij Arslan II and Shahinshah, at once quarrelled over the inheritance. The former won the support of the Danishmend princes, Dhu'l Nun of Caesarea and Dhu'l Qarnain of Melitene; the latter that of the eldest Danishmend, Yaghi Siyan of Sivas. Yaghi Siyan asked Nur ed-Din for help; and Nur ed-Din readily responded by attacking and annexing the Seldjuk share of the Edessan towns, Aintab, Dukuk and probably also Samosata. Kilij Arslan defeated his brother; but, though he tried to build up an alliance with the Armenians and Franks against Nur ed-Din, he was obliged to accept the loss of his Euphratesian province.[2]

Secure in the north, Nur ed-Din turned south again. In February 1157 Baldwin broke his truce with Nur ed-Din. Relying on the truce, large numbers of Turcomans had brought their flocks of sheep and their horses to graze on the rich pastures near the frontier at Banyas. King Baldwin, heavily in debt owing to a taste for luxury, could not resist the temptation to attack the unsuspecting shepherds and make off with their animals. This shameless breach of his engagements brought him the most valuable booty that Palestine had seen for many decades, but it

[1] Ibn al-Qalanisi, pp. 322, 327.
[2] *Ibid.* pp. 324–5; Nicetas Choniates, pp. 152–4; Gregory the Priest, p. 176.

roused Nur ed-Din to vengeance. While he paused at Baalbek, to reduce its rebellious emir, his general Shirkuh defeated some Latin raiders from the Buqaia; and his brother Nasr ed-Din routed a company of the Hospitallers near Banyas. In May Nur ed-Din himself set out from Damascus to besiege Banyas. Shirkuh defeated a small relieving force, and joined his master before the walls. The lower town was soon taken, but the citadel, two miles away up a steep mountain, held out under the Constable, Humphrey of Toron. Humphrey was on the point of surrendering when news came of the King's approach. Nur ed-Din set fire to the lower town and retired, letting Baldwin enter Banyas and repair its walls. As the Franks returned south down the Jordan, Nur ed-Din fell on them just north of the Sea of Galilee and won a great victory. The King barely escaped to Safed; and the Moslems were able to return to the siege of Banyas. But after a few days, on news from the north of a projected attack by Kilij Arslan, Nur ed-Din abandoned the attempt and hurried back to Aleppo.[1]

There were other reasons for wishing to avoid an open war at that moment. In the early autumn of 1156 a series of earthquakes was felt throughout Syria. Damascus was not severely damaged, but news of destruction came in from Aleppo and Hama, while a bastion collapsed at Apamea. In November and December there were further shocks, in which the town of Shaizar suffered. Cyprus and the coastal cities north of Tripoli were affected by shocks during the following spring. In August 1157 the Orontes valley underwent even more serious shocks. Many lives were lost at Homs and Aleppo. At Hama the damage was so appalling that the earthquake was called by the chroniclers the Hama earthquake. At Shaizar the family of the Munqidhites were gathered together to celebrate the circumcision of a youthful prince when the great walls of the citadel crashed down on them. Only the Princess of Shaizar, rescued from the ruins, and Usama, away on his diplomatic missions, survived of all the dynasty. Both

[1] William of Tyre, XVIII, 11-15, pp. 834-45; Ibn al-Qalanisi, pp. 325-6, 330-7.

Moslems and Franks were too busy repairing shattered fortresses to think of serious aggressive expeditions for some time to come.[1]

In October 1157, two months after his return from Banyas, Nur ed-Din suddenly fell desperately ill at Sarmin. Thinking that he was dying he insisted upon being carried in a litter to Aleppo. There he made his will. His brother, Nasr ed-Din was to succeed to his states, with Shirkuh ruling Damascus under his suzerainty. But when Nasr ed-Din entered Aleppo to be ready to take over the heritage, he met with opposition from the governor, Ibn ed-Daya. There were disturbances in the streets that were only quelled when the notables of Aleppo were summoned to their prince's bedside and saw that he still lived. Indeed, the crisis was now past, and he began slowly to recover. But he seemed to have lost something of his initiative and energy. He was no longer the invincible warrior. Other forces were appearing in Syria to dominate the scene.[2]

[1] Robert of Torigny, I, p. 309; Michael the Syrian, III, pp. 315–16, Armenian version, p. 356; *Chron. Anon. Syr.* (Syriac edition), p. 302; Ibn al-Qalanisi, pp. 338–41; Ibn al-Athir, p. 503; Kemal ad-Din, ed. Blochet, p. 529. According to Ibn al-Qalanisi Nur ed-Din feared that the Franks would attack his defence-less fortresses and kept his army assembled to prevent any such move. Usama's elegy on the destruction of his family, with which he had quarrelled, is given in Abu Shama, Cairo edition, vol. I, p. 112.

[2] William of Tyre, XVIII, 17, pp. 847–8; Ibn al-Qalanisi, p. 341; Kemal ad-Din, ed. Blochet, pp. 531–1; Abu Shama, p. 110 (in *R.H.C.Or.*).

CHAPTER III

THE RETURN OF THE EMPEROR

'For the king of the north shall return, and shall set forth a multitude
greater than the former, and shall certainly come after certain years with
a great army and with much riches.'　　　　　　DANIEL XI, 13

In 1153, while Nur ed-Din's attention was fixed upon Damascus and
while King Baldwin and his army lay before Ascalon, the Princess
of Antioch decided her own destiny. Amongst the knights that
followed King Louis of France to the Second Crusade was the
younger son of Geoffrey, Count of Gien and lord of Châtillon-
sur-Loing. Reynald of Châtillon had no prospects in his own
country; so he had stayed behind in Palestine when the Crusaders
returned home. There he took service under the young King Baldwin, whom he accompanied to Antioch in 1151. The widowed
Princess soon took notice of him. He seems to have remained in
her principality, no doubt in possession of some small fief; and it
may have been his presence that induced her to refuse the husbands
suggested for her by the King and the Emperor. In the spring of
1153 she decided to marry him. Before she announced her intention
she asked permission of the King; for he was official guardian of her
state and the overlord of her bridegroom. Reynald hastened to
Ascalon, where the King's camp had just been established, and
delivered Constance's message. Baldwin, knowing Reynald to be
a brave soldier, and, above all, thankful to be relieved of the responsibility for Antioch, made no difficulty. As soon as Reynald arrived
back in Antioch the marriage took place and Reynald was installed
as Prince. It was not a popular match. Not only the great families
of Antioch but also the humbler subjects of the Princess thought
that she was degraded by giving herself to this upstart.[1]

[1] William of Tyre, XVII, 26, p. 802, saying that she was secretly married
before obtaining the King's permission. Cinnamus, p. 178, calling him

It would have been courteous and correct of Constance to have asked permission also from the Emperor Manuel. The news of the marriage was ill-received at Constantinople. But Manuel was at the moment involved in a campaign against the Seldjuks. He could not give practical expression to his wrath. Conscious of his rights, he therefore sent to Antioch offering to recognize the new Prince if the Franks of Antioch would fight for him against the Armenian Thoros. He promised a money-subsidy if the work were properly done. Reynald willingly complied. Imperial approval would strengthen him personally; moreover, the Armenians had advanced into the district of Alexandretta, which the Franks claimed as part of the Antiochene principality. After a short battle near Alexandretta he drove the Armenians back into Cilicia; and he presented the reconquered country to the Order of the Temple. The Order took over Alexandretta, and to protect its approaches reconstructed the Castles of Gastun and Baghras, which commanded the Syrian Gates. Reynald had already decided to work in with the Templars and thus started a friendship that was to be fatal for Jerusalem.[1]

Having secured the land that he wanted, Reynald demanded his subsidies from the Emperor, who refused them, pointing out that the main task had yet to be done. Reynald changed his policy. Encouraged by the Templars he made peace with Thoros and his brothers; and while the Armenians attacked the few remaining Byzantine fortresses in Cilicia, he decided to lead an expedition against the rich island of Cyprus. But he lacked money for the enterprise. The Patriarch Aimery of Antioch was very rich; and he had been outspoken in his disapproval of Constance's marriage. Reynald determined to punish him to his own profit. Aimery had

'a certain Reynald'—'Ρεινάλδῳ τινί'; Michael the Syrian, Armenian version, p. 310. Schlumberger (*Renaud de Châtillon*, p. 3) establishes his origin. The marriage took place before May, when Reynald confirmed Venetian privileges in Antioch (Röhricht, *Regesta*, p. 72).

[1] William of Tyre, XVIII, 10, pp. 834–5; Michael the Syrian, III, p. 314 and Armenian version, p. 349, giving a version more favourable to Thoros; Bar-Hebraeus, trans. Budge, p. 283.

earned the respect of the Antiochenes by his courage and energy in the dark days after Prince Raymond's death; but his illiteracy and the looseness of his morals damaged his reputation and made him vulnerable. Reynald demanded money from him and on his refusal lost his temper and cast him into prison. There the prelate was cruelly beaten on the head. His wounds were then smeared with honey, and he was left for a whole summer day chained in blazing sunshine on the roof of the citadel to be a prey for all the insects of the neighbourhood. The treatment achieved its object. The miserable Patriarch hastened to pay rather than face another day of such torment. Meanwhile the story reached Jerusalem. King Baldwin was horrified and sent at once his chancellor, Ralph, and the Bishop of Acre to insist on the Patriarch's immediate release. Reynald, having secured the money, let him go; and Aimery accompanied his rescuers back to Jerusalem, where he was received with the highest honours by the King and Queen Melisende and his brother-Patriarch. He refused meanwhile to return to Antioch.[1]

The Patriarch's experience shocked responsible Frankish circles; but Reynald was unabashed. He could now attack Cyprus; and in the spring of 1156 he and Thoros made a sudden landing on the island. Cyprus had been spared the wars and invasions that had troubled the Asian continent during the last century. It was contented and prosperous under its Byzantine governors. Half a century before, Cypriot food-parcels had done much to help the Franks of the First Crusade when they lay starving at Antioch; and, apart from occasional administrative disputes, relations between the Franks and the island government had been friendly. As soon as he heard of Reynald's plan, King Baldwin sent a hasty message to warn the island. But it was too late; reinforcements could not be rushed there in time. The governor was the Emperor's nephew, John Comnenus; and with him in the island was the distinguished soldier Michael Branas. When news came of the Frankish landing, Branas hurried with the island militia down to

---

[1] William of Tyre, xviii, 1, pp. 816–17; Cinnamus, p. 181.

the coast and won a small initial victory. But the invaders were too numerous. They soon overpowered his troops and captured him himself; and when John Comnenus came to his aid, he too was taken prisoner. The victorious Franks and Armenians then marched up and down the island robbing and pillaging every building that they saw, churches and convents as well as shops and private houses. The crops were burnt; the herds were rounded up, together with all the population, and driven down to the coast. The women were raped; children and folk too old to move had their throats cut. The murder and rapine was on a scale that the Huns or the Mongols might have envied. The nightmare lasted about three weeks. Then, on the rumour of an imperial fleet in the offing, Reynald gave the order for re-embarkation. The ships were loaded up with booty. The herds and flocks for which there was no room were sold back at a high price to their owners. Every Cypriot was forced to ransom himself; and there was no money left in the island for the purpose. So the governor and Branas, together with the leading churchmen, the leading proprietors and the leading merchants, with all their families, were carried off to Antioch to remain in prison till the money should be forthcoming; except for some who were mutilated and sent in derision to Constantinople.[1] The island of Cyprus never fully recovered from the devastation caused by the Frenchmen and their Armenian allies. The earthquakes of 1157, which were severe in Cyprus, completed the misery; and in 1158 the Egyptians, whose fleet had not ventured into Cypriot waters for many decades, made some raids on the defenceless island, possibly without the formal permission of the Caliph's government; for amongst the prisoners captured was the governor's brother, who was received honourably at Cairo and sent back at once to Constantinople.[2]

[1] William of Tyre, XVIII, 10, pp. 834–5; Cinnamus, pp. 78–9; Michael the Syrian, III, p. 315, and Armenian version, p. 350; Bar-Hebraeus, trans. Budge, p. 284; Gregory the Priest, p. 187, who says that Reynald cut off the noses of the Greek priests that he captured.
[2] Ibn Moyessar, p. 473.

In 1157 Thierry, Count of Flanders, returned to Palestine with a company of knights; and in the autumn Baldwin III determined to profit by his arrival and by Nur ed-Din's illness to re-establish the Frankish positions on the middle Orontes. Reynald was persuaded to join the royal army in an attack upon Shaizar. After the disastrous earthquake in August the citadel had fallen to a band of Assassin adventurers. The Christian army arrived there at the end of the year. The lower town fell at once to them; and the ruined citadel seemed likely to surrender, when a quarrel broke out amongst the besiegers. Baldwin promised the town and its territory to Thierry as the nucleus of a principality to be held under the Crown; but Reynald, claiming that the Munqidhites had been tributaries to Antioch, demanded that Thierry should pay him homage for it. To the Count the idea of paying homage to a man of such undistinguished origin was unthinkable. Baldwin could only solve the difficulty by abandoning the disputed territory. The army moved away northwards to occupy the ruins of Apamea, then laid siege to Harenc. This was undeniably Antiochene property; but Baldwin and Thierry were prepared to help Reynald recapture it in view of its strategic importance. After a heavy bombardment by mangonels it capitulated in February 1158, and was given a little later to one of Thierry's knights, Reynald of Saint-Valery, who held it under the Prince of Antioch.[1]

The Prince of Antioch's conduct had not been satisfactory; and the King decided to reorientate his policy. He knew of Reynald's bad relations with the Emperor, who was unlikely to forgive the raid on Cyprus, and he knew that the Byzantine army was still the most formidable in Christendom. In the summer of 1157 he had sent an embassy to Constantinople to ask for a bride from the imperial family. It was led by Achard, Archbishop of Nazareth,

---

[1] William of Tyre, xviii, 17–19, pp. 847–53; Robert of Torigny, i, p. 316; Michael the Syrian, Armenian version, pp. 351–3; Ibn al-Qalanisi, pp. 342, 344; Reynald of Saint-Valery was still a baron of Jerusalem in 1160 (Röhricht, *Regesta,* p. 94) but returned to the West soon afterwards. Robert of Torigny alone tells us that he was given Harenc.

who died on the journey, and Humphrey II of Toron. The Emperor Manuel received them well. After some negotiation he offered his niece Theodora, with a dowry of 100,000 golden hyperperi, and another 10,000 for wedding expenses, and gifts worth 30,000 more. In return she was to be given Acre and its territory as her dower, to keep should her husband die childless. When his embassy came back and Baldwin had confirmed the terms, the young princess set out from Constantinople. She arrived at Acre in September 1158 and travelled in state to Jerusalem. There she was married to the King by the Patriarch Aimery of Antioch, as the Patriarch-elect of Jerusalem had not yet been confirmed by the Pope. She was aged thirteen, but well-grown and very lovely. Baldwin was delighted with her and was a faithful husband, abandoning the easy morals of his bachelor days.[1]

During the negotiations it seems that Manuel promised to join in an alliance against Nur ed-Din, and that Baldwin agreed that Reynald should be humbled. Meanwhile the King campaigned on the Damascene frontier. In March 1158 he and the Count of Flanders made a surprise march on Damascus itself and on 1 April laid siege to the castle of Dareiya in the suburbs. But Nur ed-Din, now convalescent, was already on his way south to put an end to the intrigues that had flourished there during his illness. He arrived in Damascus on 7 April to the great delight of its inhabitants; and Baldwin thought it prudent to retire. Nur ed-Din then made a counter-offensive. While his lieutenant Shirkuh raided the territory of Sidon, he himself attacked the castle of Habis Jaldak, which the Franks had built as an outpost south-east of the Sea of Galilee, by the banks of the river Yarmuk. The garrison was so hard pressed that it soon agreed to capitulate if help did not arrive within ten days. Baldwin therefore set out with Count Thierry to its relief, but instead of going straight to it he took the road north of the lake leading to Damascus. The ruse worked. Nur ed-Din feared for his communications and raised the

[1] William of Tyre, xviii, 16, 22, pp. 846, 857–8; Gregory the Priest, pp. 186–9; Matthew of Edessa, cclxxiii, pp. 352–3.

siege. The two armies met at the village of Butaiha, on the east of the upper Jordan valley. At the first glimpse of the Moslems, the Franks attacked, believing them to be only a scouting party; when the whinny of a mule that the King had given to a sheikh whom they knew to be with Nur ed-Din—it had recognized the smell of its old friends amongst the Frankish horses—showed them that the whole Moslem force had arrived. But the impetus of their attack had been so great that the Moslems wavered. Nur ed-Din, whose health was still frail, was persuaded to leave the battlefield; and on his departure his whole army turned and retired in some disorder. The Frankish victory was sufficient to induce Nur ed-Din to ask for a truce. For the next few years there was no serious warfare on the Syro-Palestinian frontier. Both Baldwin and Nur ed-Din could turn their attention to the north.[1]

In the autumn of 1158 the Emperor set out from Constantinople at the head of a great army. He marched to Cilicia; and while the main force followed slowly along the difficult coast-road eastward, he hurried ahead with a force of only five hundred horsemen. So secret were his preparations and so quick his movements that no one in Cilicia knew of his coming. The Armenian Prince Thoros was at Tarsus, suspecting nothing, when suddenly, one day in late October, a Latin pilgrim whom he had entertained came rushing back to his Court to tell him that he had seen Imperial troops only a day's march away. Thoros collected his family, his intimate friends and his treasure and fled at once to the mountains. Next day Manuel entered the Cilician plain. While his brother-in-law, Theodore Vatatses, occupied Tarsus, he moved on swiftly; and within a fortnight all the Cilician cities as far as Anazarbus were in his power. But Thoros himself still eluded him. While Byzantine detachments scoured the valleys he fled from hill-top to hill-top and at last found refuge on a crag called Dadjig, near the sources of the Cydnus, whose ruins had been uninhabited for

---

[1] William of Tyre, xviii, 21, pp. 855–6; Ibn al-Qalanisi, pp. 346–8; Abu Shama, pp. 97–100 (who says that Baldwin asked for a truce, probably relying on an equivocal sentence in Ibn al-Qalanisi).

generations. Only his two most trusted servants knew where he lay hidden.[1]

The Emperor's arrival terrified Reynald. He knew that he could not resist against this huge Imperial army; and this knowledge saved him. For by making an immediate submission he could obtain far better terms than if he were defeated in battle. Gerard, Bishop of Lattakieh, the most perspicacious of his counsellors, pointed out to him that the Emperor's motive was prestige rather than conquest. So Reynald sent hastily to Manuel offering to surrender the citadel of Antioch to an Imperial garrison. When his envoy was told that that was not enough, he himself put on a penitent's dress and hurried to the Emperor's camp, outside the walls of Mamistra. Envoys from all the neighbouring princes were arriving to greet the Emperor, from Nur ed-Din, from the Danishmends, from the King of Georgia, and even from the Caliph. Manuel kept Reynald waiting a little. It seems that about this moment he received a message from the exiled Patriarch Aimery suggesting that Reynald should be brought before him in chains and be deposed. But it suited the Emperor better to have him a humble client. At a solemn session, with the Emperor seated enthroned in his great tent, his courtiers and the foreign ambassadors grouped around him and the crack regiments of the army lining the approaches, Reynald made his submission. He and his suite had walked barefoot and bareheaded through the town and out to the camp. There he prostrated himself in the dust before the imperial platform, while all his men raised their hands in supplication. Many minutes passed before Manuel deigned to notice him. Then pardon was accorded to him on three conditions. Whenever it was asked of him he must hand his citadel over to an Imperial garrison; he must provide a contingent for the Imperial army; and he must admit a Greek Patriarch of Antioch instead of the Latin. Reynald swore to obey these terms. Then he was dismissed and sent back to Antioch.

[1] Cinnamus, pp. 179–81; Matthew of Edessa, *loc. cit.*; Gregory the Priest, p. 187.

1159: The Emperor in Antioch

The news of Manuel's approach had brought King Baldwin, with his brother Amalric and the Patriarch Aimery, hastening from the south. They arrived at Antioch soon after Reynald's return. Baldwin was a little disappointed to hear of Reynald's pardon and he wrote at once to Manuel to beg for an audience. Manuel hesitated, apparently because he believed that Baldwin desired the principality for himself. This may have been part of Aimery's suggestion. But when Baldwin insisted, Manuel yielded. Baldwin rode out from Antioch escorted by citizens praying him to reconcile them with the Emperor. The interview was an immense success. Manuel was charmed by the young King, whom he kept as his guest for ten days. While they discussed plans for an alliance, Baldwin succeeded in securing a pardon for Thoros, who went through the same procedure as Reynald had done, and who was allowed to keep his territory in the mountains. It was probably due to Baldwin that Manuel did not insist on the immediate installation of the Greek Patriarch. Aimery was re-established on his patriarchal throne and was formally reconciled with Reynald. When Baidwin returned to Antioch, laden with gifts, he left his brother behind with the Emperor.

On Easter Sunday, 12 April 1159, Manuel came to Antioch and made his solemn entry into the city. The Latin authorities tried to keep him away by saying that there was a plot to assassinate him there; but he was not intimidated. He merely insisted that the citizens should give him hostages and that the Latin princes who were to take part in the procession should be unarmed. He himself wore mail beneath his robes. There was no untoward incident. While the imperial banners floated over the citadel, the cortège passed over the fortified bridge into the city. First came the superb Varangians of the Imperial Guard. Then the Emperor himself, on horseback, in a purple mantle, and on his head a diadem dripping with pearls. Reynald, on foot, held his bridle, and other Frankish lords walked beside the horse. Behind him rode Baldwin, uncrowned and unarmed. Then there followed the

353

high functionaries of the Empire. Just inside the gates waited the Patriarch Aimery, in full pontificals, with all his clergy, to lead the procession through streets strewn with carpets and with flowers, first to the Cathedral of St Peter, then on to the palace.

For eight days Manuel remained in Antioch; and festivity followed festivity. He himself, though proud and majestic on solemn occasions, radiated a personal charm and friendliness that captivated the crowds; and the lavishness of his gifts, to the nobles and the populace alike, enhanced the general rejoicing. As a gesture to the Occident he organized a tournament and made his comrades join him in the jousts. He was a fine horseman and acquitted himself with honour; but his commanders, to whom horsemanship was a means, and not an end, were less impressive in comparison with the knights of the West. The intimacy between the Emperor and his nephew-by-marriage, the King, grew closer. When Baldwin broke his arm out hunting, Manuel insisted on treating it himself, just as he had acted as medical adviser to Conrad of Germany.[1]

This splendid week marked the triumph of the Emperor's prestige. But Gerard of Lattakieh was right. It was prestige, not conquest, that he wanted. When all the feasts were ended, he rejoined his army outside the walls and moved eastward to the Moslem frontier. He was met almost at once by ambassadors from Nur ed-Din, with full powers to negotiate a truce. To the fury of the Latins, who had expected him to march on Aleppo, he received the embassy, and discussions began. When Nur ed-Din offered to release all the Christian captives, to the number of six thousand, that were in his prisons and to send an expedition against the Seldjuk Turks, Manuel agreed to call off the campaign.

He had probably never intended to carry on with it; and though

[1] William of Tyre, xviii, 23–5, pp. 859–64; Cinnamus, pp. 181–90; Nicetas Choniates, pp. 141–5; Prodromus, in *R.H.C.G.* ii, pp. 752, 766; Matthew of Edessa, cclxxiv, pp. 354–5; Gregory the Priest, pp. 188–9; Vahram, *Rhymed Chronicle*, p. 505; Ibn al-Qalanisi, pp. 349, 353. See also La Monte, 'To what extent was the Byzantine Empire the suzerain of the Crusading States?' in *Byzantion*, vol. vii.

the Crusaders and their modern apologists might cry treason, it is hard to see what else he could have done. To the Crusaders Syria was all-important, but to Manuel it was only one frontier-zone out of many and not the most vital to his Empire. He could not afford to remain for many months at the end of a long and vulnerable line of communications, nor, magnificent though his army was, could he risk heavy losses to it with impunity. Moreover he had no wish to cause the break-up of Nur ed-Din's power. He knew from bitter experience that the Franks only welcomed him when they were frightened. It would be folly to remove their chief source of fear. And Nur ed-Din's alliance was a valuable asset in the wars against a far more dangerous enemy to the Empire, the Turks of Anatolia. But, as the sequel showed, he would give help to prevent Nur ed-Din's conquest of Egypt; for that would fatally upset the equilibrium. Perhaps, had he been less precipitate, he might have obtained better terms. But he had received worrying news of a plot at Constantinople and troubles on his European frontier. He could not anyhow afford to stay much longer in Syria.[1]

Nevertheless his truce with Nur ed-Din was a psychological mistake. For a moment the Franks had been prepared to accept him as leader; but he had shown himself, as wiser men would have foreseen, more interested in his Empire's fate than in theirs. Nor were they much consoled by the release of the Christian captives. They included some important local warriors, such as the Grand Master of the Temple, Bertrand of Blancfort; but they were for the most part Germans captured during the Second Crusade, and amongst them was the claimant to Tripoli, Bertrand of Toulouse, whose reappearance might have been embarrassing had his health not been broken by captivity.[2]

[1] William of Tyre, XVIII, 25, p. 864 (in no way blaming the Emperor); Otto of Freisingen, *Gesta Friderici*, p. 229; Cinnamus, pp. 188–90; Gregory the Priest, pp. 190–1; Matthew of Edessa, cclxxv, pp. 355–8; Ibn al-Qalanisi, pp. 353–5.

[2] William of Tyre, *loc. cit.*; Cinnamus, p. 188, specially mentioning 'τὸν Σαγγέλη υἱέα' (the son of Saint Gilles) and 'τὸν τέμπλου μαῖστορα'.

When the truce was concluded, the Emperor and his army retreated westward, slowly at first, then faster as more alarming news arrived from his capital. Some of Nur ed-Din's followers tried to harass it, against their master's wishes; and when, to save time, it cut through Seldjuk territory, there were skirmishes with the Sultan's troops. But it arrived intact at Constantinople in the late summer. After some three months, Manuel crossed again into Asia to campaign against the Seldjuks, to try out against them a new and more mobile form of tactics. Meanwhile his envoys were building up the coalition against the Seldjuk Sultan, Kilij Arslan II. Nur ed-Din, deeply relieved by Manuel's departure, advanced into Seldjuk territory from the middle Euphrates. The Danishmend prince Yakub Arslan attacked from the north-east, so successfully that the Sultan was obliged to cede to him the lands round Albistan in the Anti-Taurus. Meanwhile the Byzantine general, John Contostephanus, collected the levies that Reynald and Thoros were bound by treaty to provide, and, with a contingent of Petchenegs, settled by Manuel in Cilicia, moved up through the Taurus passes; and Manuel and the main Imperial army, reinforced by troops provided by the Prince of Serbia and Frankish pilgrims recruited when their ships called in at Rhodes, swept up the valley of the Meander. The Sultan had to divide his forces. When Contostephanus won a complete victory over the Turks sent to oppose him, Kilij Arslan gave up the struggle. He wrote to the Emperor offering in return for peace to give back all the Greek cities occupied in recent years by the Moslems, to see that the frontiers were respected and that raiding ceased, and to provide a regiment to fight in the Imperial army whenever it might be required. Manuel agreed to the terms; but he kept in reserve the Sultan's rebellious brother Shahinshah, who had come to him for protection. So, to confirm the treaty, Kilij Arslan sent his Christian chancellor, Christopher, to Constantinople to suggest an official visit to the imperial Court. Hostilities ended in the summer of 1161; and next spring Kilij Arslan was received at Constantinople. The ceremonies were splendid. The Sultan was

treated with great honour and showered with gifts, but was
treated as a vassal-prince. The news of the visit impressed all the
princes of the East.[1]

It is in this general light that we must judge Manuel's eastern
policy. He had won a very valuable victory of prestige and he had,
temporarily at least, humbled the Seldjuks, who had been the main
threat to his Empire. This success brought certain advantages to
the Franks. Nur ed-Din had not been defeated, but he had been
scared. He would not attempt a direct attack on Christian
territory. At the same time the peace with the Seldjuks reopened
the land route for pilgrims from the West. There was an increase
in their numbers; and that more did not arrive was due to western
politics, to the wars between the Hohenstaufen and the Papalists in
Germany and Italy and between the Capetians and the Plantagenets in France. But, though Byzantium was to remain for the
next twenty years the greatest influence in northern Syria, its
genuine friends among the Franks were very few.

Events in 1160 showed both the nature and the value of the
Imperial suzerainty over Antioch. King Baldwin had returned to
the south and was engaged on a few minor raids in Damascene
territory, taking advantage of Nur ed-Din's preoccupations in the
north, when he heard that Reynald had been taken prisoner by
Nur ed-Din. In November 1160 the seasonal movement of herds
from the mountains of the Anti-Taurus into the Euphratesian plain
tempted the Prince to make a raid up the river valley. As he
returned, slowed down by the droves of cattle and camels and horses
that he had rounded up, he was ambushed by the governor of
Aleppo, Nur ed-Din's foster-brother Majd ed-Din. He fought
bravely; but his men were outnumbered and he himself was
unhorsed and captured. He was sent with his comrades, bound, on
camel-back, to Aleppo, where he was to remain in gaol for sixteen
years. Neither the Emperor nor the King of Jerusalem nor even the

[1] Cinnamus, pp. 191–201, 204–8; Nicetas Choniates, pp. 152–64; Gregory
the Priest, pp. 193–4, 199; Matthew of Edessa, cclxxxii, p. 364; Michael the
Syrian, III, p. 320; *Chron. Anon. Syr.* p. 302; Ibn al-Athir, p. 544.

people of Antioch showed any haste to ransom him. In his prison he found young Joscelin of Courtenay, titular Count of Edessa, who had been captured on a raid a few months previously.[1]

Reynald's elimination raised a constitutional problem in Antioch, where he had reigned as the husband of the Princess Constance. She now claimed that the power reverted to her; but public opinion supported the rights of her son by her first marriage, Bohemond, surnamed the Stammerer, who was however only aged fifteen. It was a situation similar to that of Queen Melisende and Baldwin III in Jerusalem a few years previously. There was no immediate danger, because Nur ed-Din's fear of Manuel kept him from attacking Antioch itself. But some effective government must be provided. Strictly speaking, it was for the Emperor as the accepted suzerain of Antioch to settle the question. But Manuel was far away, and the Antiochenes had not accepted him without reservations. The Norman princes of Antioch had considered themselves as sovereign princes; but the frequent minorities amongst their successors had obliged the Kings of Jerusalem to intervene, more as kinsmen than as suzerains. There had, however, grown up in Antioch a sentiment that regarded the King as suzerain; and there is little doubt that Manuel had only been accepted so easily because Baldwin was present to give his approval to the arrangement. It was to Baldwin, not to Manuel, that the people of Antioch looked now for a solution. On their invitation he came to Antioch, declared Bohemond III to be the rightful prince, and entrusted the government to the Patriarch Aimery till the Prince should be of age. The decision displeased Constance, and its method displeased Manuel. The Princess promptly appealed to the Imperial Court.[2]

[1] William of Tyre, xviii, 28, pp. 868–9; Matthew of Edessa, cclxxxi, pp. 363–4; *Chron. Anon. Syr.* p. 302; Gregory the Priest, p. 308; Kemal ad-Din, ed. Blochet, p. 533; Cahen (*op. cit.* p. 405 n. 1) gives additional sources and discusses the topography.

[2] William of Tyre, xviii, 30, p. 874; Michael the Syrian, iii, p. 324, who says that Constance was removed from the rule of Antioch by Thoros.

1161: Melisende of Tripoli

About the end of the year 1159 the Empress Irene, born Bertha of Sulzbach, had died leaving only a daughter behind her. In 1160 an embassy led by John Contostephanus, accompanied by the chief interpreter of the Court, the Italian Theophylact, arrived at Jerusalem to ask the King to nominate one of the eligible princesses of Outremer as bride for the widowed Emperor. There were two candidates, Maria, daughter of Constance of Antioch, and Melisende, daughter of Raymond II of Tripoli, both of them Baldwin's cousins and both famed for their beauty. Distrusting a close family alliance between the Emperor and Antioch, Baldwin suggested Melisende. The ambassadors went on to Tripoli to report on the Princess, whom the whole Frankish East saluted as the future Empress. Raymond of Tripoli proudly determined to give his sister a worthy dowry and spent vast sums on her trousseau. Presents poured in from her mother Hodierna and her aunt Queen Melisende. Knights from all parts hurried to Tripoli in the hope of being asked to the wedding. But no confirmation came from Constantinople. The ambassadors sent to Manuel glowing and intimate accounts of Melisende's person, but they also recorded a rumour about her birth, based on her mother's known quarrel with her father. There seems to have been in fact no doubt about her legitimacy; but the gossip may have made the Emperor hesitate. Then he heard of Baldwin's intervention at Antioch and received Constance's appeal. In the early summer of 1161 Raymond, having grown impatient, sent one of his knights, Otto of Risberg, to Constantinople to ask what was afoot. About August Otto returned with the news that the Emperor repudiated the engagement.[1]

The shock and humiliation were too much for Melisende. She fell into a decline and soon faded away, as the *Princesse Lointaine*

[1] William of Tyre, XVIII, 30, pp. 874–6; Cinnamus, pp. 208–10, who says that Melisende's health was unsatisfactory, in addition to the rumours about her legitimacy. Melisende is mentioned as 'futurae Imperatricis Constantino-politanae' in the charter of 31 July 1161, when Oultrejourdain was given to Philip of Milly. She and her brother were then with the King at Nazareth (Röhricht, *Regesta*, p. 96).

of medieval French romance. Her brother Raymond was furious. He demanded angrily to be recouped for the sums that he had spent on her trousseau; and when that was refused, he fitted out the twelve galleys that he had ordered to convey her to Constantinople as men-of-war and led them to raid the coasts of Cyprus.[1] King Baldwin, who was staying with his cousins waiting for news, was seriously disquieted, especially when the Byzantine ambassadors received orders to go to Antioch. He hurried after them, to find in Antioch a splendid embassy from the Emperor, headed by Alexius Bryennius Comnenus, son of Anna Comnena, and the Prefect of Constantinople, John Camaterus. They had already negotiated a marriage contract between their master and the Princess Maria of Antioch; and their presence had sufficed to establish Constance as ruler of the principality. Baldwin had to accept the situation. Maria, who was lovelier even than her cousin Melisende, set sail from Saint Symeon in September, proud to be an Empress and happy in her ignorance of her ultimate destiny. She was married to the Emperor in December in the Church of Saint Sophia at Constantinople by the three Patriarchs, Luke of Constantinople, Sophronius of Alexandria and the titular Patriarch of Antioch, Athanasius II.[2]

Baldwin had seen the value of a Byzantine alliance; but Manuel's success had been greater than he wished in the Christian north and less effective against Nur ed-Din, though it kept the Moslems quiet for the next two years. After this diplomatic check over the Emperor's marriage, the King returned towards his kingdom. There his government had gone smoothly ever since his mother's fall from power. She had emerged in 1157 to preside over a council of regency when Baldwin was away at the wars; and she kept ecclesiastical patronage in her hands. When the Patriarch Fulcher died in November 1157 she secured the appointment as his successor of a simple cleric whom she knew, Amalric of Nesle,

[1] William of Tyre, xviii, 31, 33, pp. 876, 878–9.
[2] *Ibid.* xviii, 31, pp. 875–6; Cinnamus, p. 210–11; Nicetas Choniates, p. 151, a great eulogy of the beauty of the new Empress.

well-educated but unworldly and unpractical. Hernes, Archbishop of Caesarea, and Ralph, Bishop of Bethlehem, opposed his elevation; and Amalric was obliged to send Frederick, Bishop of Acre, to Rome to secure papal support. Frederick's tact and, it was hinted, his bribes obtained confirmation from the papal Curia.[1] In her church-patronage, Melisende was seconded by her stepdaughter, Sibylla of Flanders, who refused to return to Europe with her husband Thierry in 1158 but stayed on as a nun in the abbey that Melisende had founded at Bethany. When Melisende died in September 1161, while the King was at Antioch, Sibylla succeeded to her influence in the royal family and in the Church till her own death four years later.[2]

While he was passing through Tripoli, King Baldwin fell ill. The Count of Tripoli sent his own doctor, the Syrian Barac, to tend him; but the King grew worse. He moved on to Beirut, and there, on 10 February 1162, he died. He had been a tall, strongly-built man, whose florid complexion and thick fair beard suggested good health and virility; and all the world believed that Barac's drugs had poisoned him. He was in his thirty-third year. Had he lived longer, he might have been a great king; for he had energy and a far-sighted vision and a personal charm that was irresistible. He was well-lettered, learned both in history and in law. His subjects mourned him bitterly; and even the Moslem peasants came down from the hills to pay respect to his body as the funeral cortège moved slowly to Jerusalem. Some of Nur ed-Din's friends suggested to the Atabeg that now was the time to attack the Christians. But he, just returned from a long-postponed pilgrimage to Mecca, refused to disturb a people bewailing the loss of so great a prince.[3]

[1] William of Tyre, xviii, 20, p. 854. Examples of Melisende's religious charities in 1159 and 1160 are given in Röhricht, *Regesta*, pp. 88, 94.

[2] William of Tyre, *loc. cit.* mentions Sibylla's participation. Ernoul, p. 21, for Sibylla's refusal to leave the Holy Land.

[3] William of Tyre, xvi, 2, pp. 705-6, gives a character sketch of Baldwin III.

CHAPTER IV

THE LURE OF EGYPT

'No; but we will go into the land of Egypt.' JEREMIAH XLII, 14

Baldwin III left no children. His Greek Queen, Theodora, was still only sixteen when she was widowed. The heir to the kingdom was his brother Amalric, Count of Jaffa and Ascalon. Eight days after Baldwin's death he was crowned king by the Patriarch Amalric. There had, however, been some question about his succession. The barons were unwilling to abandon their right of election, even though there was no other possible candidate. They had one legitimate grievance. Some four years before, Amalric had married Agnes of Courtenay, daughter of Joscelin II of Edessa. She was his third cousin, and therefore within the degrees prohibited by the Church; and the Patriarch had refused to confirm the marriage. There were other reasons for disliking Agnes. She was considerably older than Amalric. Her first husband, Reynald of Marash, had been killed in 1149, when Amalric was aged thirteen; and her reputation for chastity was not good. The Patriarch and the barons demanded that the marriage be annulled. Amalric consented at once, but he insisted that the legitimacy and rights of inheritance of his two children, Baldwin and Sibylla, should be recognized.[1]

---

[1] William of Tyre, XIX, 1, 4, pp. 883-4, 888-90. Robert of Torigny, I, p. 309, dates Amalric's marriage 1157. For Agnes's first husband, see above, p. 326. William of Tyre's continuators disliked her intensely for good reasons (see below, p. 407). They may have exaggerated her faults, but it is unlikely that the distant consanguinity alone would have made the barons insist on the divorce. According to William the relationship was pointed out by the Abbess Stephanie, daughter of Joscelin I, and Maria of Salerno: but it must have been well known that Baldwin I and Joscelin I were first cousins, and the Patriarch

Amalric was now twenty-five. He was as tall and handsome as his brother, with the same high colouring and thick blond beard, though critics considered him too plump in the chest. He was less learned, though well informed on legal matters. While his brother loved to talk, he stammered a little and was taciturn, but was

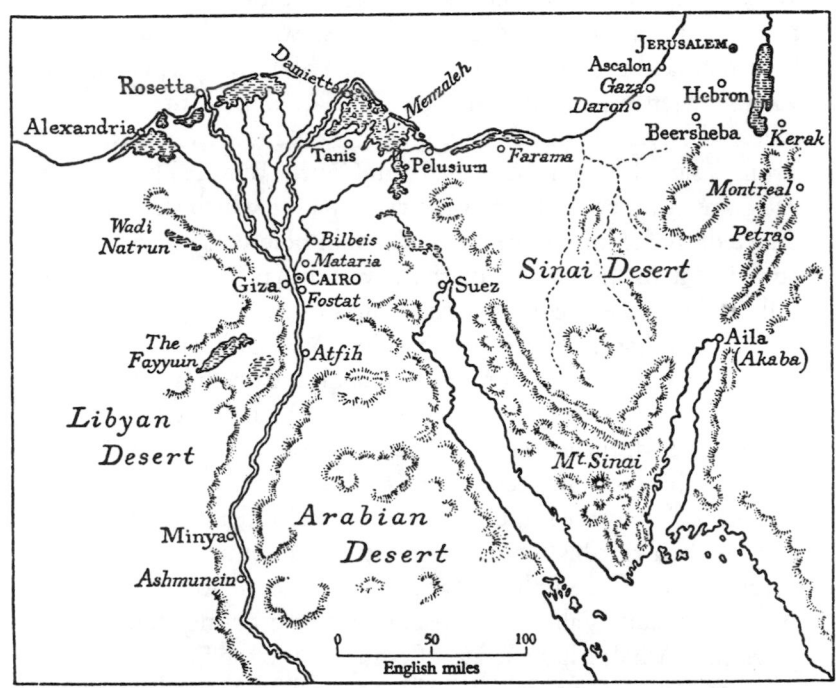

Map 5. Egypt in the twelfth century.

given to frequent paroxysms of loud laughter, which somewhat impaired his dignity. He was never as popular as his brother, lacking his charm and open manner; and his private life was unpraiseworthy.[1] His quality as a statesman was shown within

had already refused to bless the wedding. Agnes was probably born in 1133— her mother Beatrice's first husband died in 1132, and she married Joscelin of Edessa very soon afterwards.

[1] William of Tyre, XIX, 2–3, pp. 884–8.

a few months of his accession, when Gerard, lord of Sidon and Beaufort, dispossessed one of his vassals without due cause, and the vassal appealed to the Crown. Amalric insisted upon the case being heard before the High Court of the realm. He then passed an *assise*, based on other such precedents, which empowered vassals to appeal against their lord to the High Court. If the lord failed to appear before the Court, the case was held to have gone by default and the vassal was reinstated. This law, by bringing the vassals of tenants-in-chief into direct relation with the King, to whom they had to pay liege homage, gave immense power to a strong king who dominated the High Court. But the High Court itself was composed of that very class against which the law was directed. If the king were weak, it could be used against him by applying it to the tenants of the royal domain.[1] This *assise* was followed by others regulating the King's relations with his vassals.

When he had firmly established his royal authority at home, Amalric could attend to foreign affairs. In the north he was ready to sacrifice Antioch to the Byzantines. About the end of 1162 there were disturbances in Cilicia following the murder of Thoros's brother Stephen, who was on his way to attend a banquet given by the Imperial governor Andronicus. Thoros, who had his own reasons for desiring Stephen's elimination, accused Andronicus of complicity and swept down on Mamistra, Anazarbus and Vahka, surprising and murdering the Greek garrisons. Amalric hastened to offer support to the Emperor; who replaced Andronicus with an able general of Hungarian birth, Constantine Coloman. Coloman came with strengthened forces to Cilicia; and Thoros retired with apologies back to the mountains.[2] Bohemond of Antioch was now eighteen and of an age to govern. In her desire to keep her power Constance appealed to

[1] For this important *assise*, see above, p. 301. La Monte, *Feudal Monarchy*, pp. 22–3, 99, 153; also Grandclaude, 'Liste d'Assises de Jérusalem' in *Mélanges Paul Fournier*, pp. 329 ff. He dates this *assise* 1166 and lists the other assizes that can be attributed to Amalric.

[2] Cinnamus, p. 227; Gregory the Priest, p. 200; Sembat the Constable, p. 621; Michael the Syrian, III, p. 319, Armenian version, pp. 349, 356.

364

Coloman for military aid. The rumour of her appeal provoked
a riot in Antioch. Constance was exiled and Bohemond III installed in her place. She died soon afterwards.[1] The Emperor made
no objection to the change of régime, probably because Amalric
gave guarantees that his suzerainty would be respected. But as
a safeguard he invited Constance's second son Baldwin and, later,
her children by Reynald, to Constantinople. Baldwin joined the
imperial army and died in battle.[2] While King Amalric openly
supported the Byzantines, he wrote at the same time to King
Louis VII of France to ask if there was any hope of his sending
help to the Latins of Syria.[3]

Byzantine good-will was necessary to Amalric to carry out his
chief political ambition, which was the control of Egypt. The
existence of the Latin states depended, as he well understood, on
disunion amongst their Moslem neighbours. Moslem Syria was
now united; but so long as Egypt was at enmity with Nur ed-Din,
the situation was not desperate. The Fatimid Caliphate was, however, in such decadence that its end seemed imminent. It was
essential that it should not fall into Nur ed-Din's hands. Since the
loss of Ascalon there had been increasing chaos at the Caliph's
Court. The vizier Abbas survived the disaster for a year. His son
Nasr was the favourite of the young Caliph al-Zafir; and their
intimacy gave rise to scandalous gossip. This infuriated Abbas, not
for moral reasons but because he rightly suspected that al-Zafir
intended to play off the son against the father. Usama, who was
still at the Court, learnt that Nasr had indeed agreed to murder

[1] Michael the Syrian, III, p. 324, confirmed by *Chron. Anon. Syr.* They seem
to coalesce the events of 1160 and 1162–3. Ughelli, *Italia Sacra*, VII, p. 203,
quotes a charter of 1167 where Bohemond III calls himself 'Prince of Antioch,
Lord of Laodicea and Gibel'. As Lattakieh and Jabala were his mother's dower,
she had presumably died.

[2] For Baldwin, see below, p. 413. Constance's daughter by Reynald, Agnes,
was married later to the Hungarian pretender Alexius or Bela III, who became
King of Hungary in 1173 (Nicetas Choniates, p. 221).

[3] Letters of Amalric in Bouquet, *R.H.F.* vol. XVI, pp. 36–7, 39–40. The
second letter speaks of the Byzantine threat to Antioch. Bohemond III wrote
about the same time to King Louis (*ibid.* pp. 27–8).

Abbas. He hastened to reconcile them and soon persuaded Nasr
that it would be better to murder the Caliph instead. Nasr
invited his benefactor to a midnight orgy at his house and there
stabbed him. Abbas affected to believe that the murderers were
the Caliph's own brothers. He put them to death and, while
seizing the Caliph's treasure for himself, placed on the throne
al-Zafir's young son, al-Fa'iz, a boy of five, who had witnessed his
uncles' deaths and thereafter suffered from chronic convulsions.
The princesses of the family suspected the truth and summoned
the governor of upper Egypt, Ibn Ruzzik, an Armenian by birth,
to rescue them. He marched on Cairo and won round the officers
of the garrison. Abbas and Nasr packed up their treasure and on
29 May 1154 fled from the capital, taking with them Usama, who
had begun to intrigue with Ibn Ruzzik. As they emerged from
the deserts of Sinai, Frankish troops from Montreal fell on them.
Usama escaped safely and eventually reached Damascus. But
Abbas was slain, and Nasr and all the treasure was captured. Nasr
was handed over to the Templars and at once announced his wish
to become a Christian. But the Court of Cairo offered the Order
60,000 dinars for his person; so his instruction was interrupted and
he was sent in chains to Cairo. There the late Caliph's four widows
personally mutilated him. He was then hanged, and his body
swung for two years at the Zawila Gate.[1]

Ibn Ruzzik governed till 1161. In 1160 the boy-Caliph died, to
be succeeded by his nine-year old cousin, al-Adid, who next year
was forced to marry Ibn Ruzzik's daughter. But the Caliph's aunt,
al-Zafir's sister, distrusted the vizier's ambition. She induced her
friends to stab him in the hall of the palace. Before he died, in
September 1161, he was able to summon the princess to his
presence and killed her himself. His son, al-Adil, succeeded as
vizier and ruled for fifteen months. Then he in his turn was dis-

[1] Usama, ed. Hitti, pp. 43–54 (whose account does not quite conceal his
volatile disloyalties): Ibn al-Athir, pp. 492–3; William of Tyre, XVIII, 9,
pp. 832–4. For the history of Egypt at this period, see Wiet, *L'Egypte Arabe*,
pp. 191 ff.

placed and killed by the governor of upper Egypt, Shawar, who survived for eight months, till August 1163 when he was ejected by his Arab chamberlain, Dhirgham. Dhirgham, to consolidate his power, put to death everyone whose ambition he feared; which left the Egyptian army almost entirely void of senior officers.[1]

In 1160 Baldwin III had threatened to invade Egypt and had been bought off by the promise of a yearly tribute of 160,000 dinars. It had never been paid; and in September of 1163 Amalric made this the excuse for a sudden descent on Egypt. He crossed the isthmus of Suez without difficulty and laid siege to Pelusium. But the Nile was in flood; and by breaking one or two dykes Dhirgham forced him to retire.[2] His intervention had been remarked by Nur ed-Din, who profited by his absence to attack the weakest of the Crusading states, Tripoli. He invaded the Buqaia in order to lay siege to the Castle of Krak, which dominated the narrow plain. Fortunately for the Franks, Hugh, Count of Lusignan, and Geoffrey Martel, brother of the Count of Angoulême, were passing through Tripoli with their following on their return from a pilgrimage to Jerusalem. They joined Count Raymond; and an urgent appeal to Antioch brought not only Bohemond III but also the Imperial general Constantine Coloman down from the north. The united Christian army marched swiftly through the hills, and surprised the Moslems at their camp below Krak. After a short battle, in which Coloman and his troops particularly distinguished themselves, Nur ed-Din fled in disorder to Homs. There he regrouped his army and received reinforcements. The Christians therefore abandoned the pursuit.[3]

[1] Ibn al-Athir, p. 529; Abu Shama, p. 107.
[2] William of Tyre, XIX, 5, pp. 890–1; letter of Amalric, R.H.F. vol. XVI, pp. 59–60. He assures King Louis that Egypt could be conquered with a little additional aid; Michael the Syrian, III, p. 317.
[3] William of Tyre, XIX, 8, pp. 894–5; Ibn al-Athir, p. 531, and Atabegs, pp. 207–9; Kemal ad-Din, ed. Blochet, p. 534. Michael the Syrian, III, p. 324. Ibn al-Athir mentions the Byzantines as being the most formidable element in the Christian army.

The Lure of Egypt

Soon afterwards the ex-vizier, Shawar, who had escaped from Egypt, appeared at Nur ed-Din's Court and offered, if Nur ed-Din would send an army to re-establish him in Cairo, to pay the expenses of the campaign, to cede districts on the frontier, to recognize Nur ed-Din's suzerainty and to provide a yearly tribute of a third of his country's revenues. Nur ed-Din hesitated. He feared to risk an army along roads dominated by the Franks of Oultrejourdain. It was only in April 1164, after seeking advice by opening the Koran at random, that he ordered his most trusted lieutenant, Shirkuh, to set out with a large detachment and go with Shawar across the desert, while he himself made a diversion by attacking Banyas. With Shirkuh went his nephew Saladin, son of Najm ed-Din Ayub, a young man of twenty-seven, who was not over anxious to join the expedition. Dhirgham in terror sent off to ask help from Amalric; but so quickly did Shirkuh move that he was across the Isthmus of Suez before the Franks were ready to intervene. Dhirgham's brother, with the few troops that he could muster, was defeated near to Pelusium. By the end of May 1164 Shawar was reinstalled in Cairo and Dhirgham was dead.[1]

Restored to power, Shawar repudiated his bargain and told Shirkuh to go back to Syria. Shirkuh refused, and seized Bilbeis. Shawar then appealed to King Amalric, and bade him make haste, offering him a thousand dinars for each of the twenty-seven stages of the journey from Jerusalem to the Nile and promising a further present to the Knights of the Hospital that accompanied him and the expenses for the fodder of their horses. After putting his kingdom into a good state of defence, Amalric marched swiftly early in August to Faqus on the Nile. There Shawar joined him and they moved to besiege Shirkuh in Bilbeis. The fortress held out for three months and was likely to fall when Amalric, who had news from Syria, decided to raise the siege on condition that Shirkuh evacuated Egypt. Shirkuh agreed and the two armies, Frankish and Syrian, marched on parallel routes out across the

[1] William of Tyre, xix, 5, 7, pp. 891-2, 893; Abu Shama, p. 107; Ibn al-Athir, p. 533, and *Atabegs*, pp. 215-6; Beha ed-Din, *P.P.T.S.* pp. 46-8.

Sinai peninsula, leaving Shawar in control of his realm. Shirkuh was the last of his company to leave. When he bade farewell to the Franks, one of them, newly come to the East, asked him, was he not afraid of treachery? He answered proudly that his whole army would avenge him, and the Frank replied gallantly that he now understood why Shirkuh's reputation stood so high with the Crusaders.[1]

The news that had brought Amalric hurrying home came from Antioch. When he knew that Amalric had left for Egypt, Nur ed-Din struck at the northern principality and laid siege to the key-fortress of Harenc. With him was his brother's army from Mosul and troops of the Ortoqid princes of Diarbekir and Mardin and Diert and Kir. While the lord of Harenc, Reynald of Saint-Valery, put up a brave defence, Prince Bohemond called upon Raymond of Tripoli, Thoros of Armenia and Constantine Coloman to come to his rescue. They set out together in mid-August. At the news of their coming, Nur ed-Din raised the siege. He was, we are told, particularly alarmed by the presence of the Byzantine contingent. As he retired, Bohemond, who had some six hundred knights with him, decided to follow in pursuit, against the advice of Reynald of Saint-Valery; for the Moslem army was considerably larger. The armies made contact on 10 August, near Artah. Ignoring a warning from Thoros, Bohemond attacked at once and when the Moslems feigned flight rushed headlong after them, only to fall into an ambush and to find himself and his knights surrounded by the army of Mosul. Thoros and his brother Mleh, who had been more cautious, escaped from the battlefield. The rest of the Christian army was captured or slain. Amongst the prisoners were Bohemond, Raymond of Tripoli, Constantine Coloman and Hugh of Lusignan. They were taken, bound together, to Aleppo.[2]

[1] William of Tyre, XIX, 7, pp. 893–4; Ibn al-Athir, pp. 534–6, and *Atabegs*, pp. 217–9; Abu Shama, p. 125.

[2] William of Tyre, XIX, 9, pp. 895–7, dating it erroneously 1165; Robert of Torigny, I, p. 355; letters of Amalric I and of Gaufred Fulcher to Louis VII,

Nur ed-Din's advisers urged him to march on the defenceless city of Antioch. But he refused. If he moved towards Antioch, he said, the Greeks would hastily send a garrison into the citadel; and though he might take the city, the citadel could hold out until the Emperor arrived. It was better, he thought, to have a petty Frankish state there than to let it become part of a great Empire. So anxious was he not to offend Byzantium that he freed Constantine Coloman almost at once, in return for a hundred and fifty silken robes. Once again Antioch was saved for Christendom by the prestige of the Emperor.

Amalric, as he hurried northwards, was joined by Thierry of Flanders, who had come on his fourth pilgrimage to Palestine. With this reinforcement he paused at Tripoli to establish his right to be regent of the County during the Count's captivity, then moved on to Antioch. There he entered into negotiations with Nur ed-Din, who agreed to release Bohemond and Thoros for a large ransom, but only because they were the vassals of the Emperor; he would not allow Raymond of Tripoli to go, nor his older prisoner, Reynald of Châtillon.[1] Amalric himself was disquieted when an Imperial envoy came to ask him what he was doing at Antioch. He replied by sending to Constantinople the Archbishop of Caesarea and his Butler, Odo of Saint-Amand, to ask the Emperor for the hand of an Imperial princess and to suggest an alliance for the conquest of Egypt.[2] Manuel kept the embassy waiting two years for an answer. Meanwhile Amalric had to return south; for Nur ed-Din, instead of attacking Antioch, had suddenly appeared in October before Banyas, whose lord, Humphrey II of Toron, was with Amalric's army. He had spread

in *R.H.F.* vol. XVI, pp. 60–2; Cinnamus, p. 216 (a very brief reference to Coloman's capture); Michael the Syrian, III, p. 324; *Chron. Anon. Syr.* p. 304; *Bustan*, p. 559; Kemal ad-Din, ed. Blochet, p. 510; Abu Shama, p. 133; Ibn al-Athir, *Atabegs*, pp. 220–3.
[1] William of Tyre, XIX, 10, 11, pp. 898, 900–1; *Bustan*, p. 561; Michael the Syrian, III, p. 326, Armenian version, p. 360, saying that Thoros, who was released first, insisted on Bohemond's release.
[2] Cinnamus, pp. 237–8; William of Tyre, XX, 1, p. 942.

rumours that his objective was Tiberias; and the local Frankish militia was concentrated there. The garrison at Banyas put up a brave resistance at first. It was hoped that Thierry of Flanders, who had just arrived in Palestine, would come to the rescue, when suddenly, owing perhaps to treason, the fortress capitulated. Nur ed-Din occupied the surrounding country and threatened to march on into Galilee, whose barons bought him off by promising a tribute.[1]

Bohemond of Antioch, as soon as he was released, went to Constantinople to visit his sister and to beg his brother-in-law for money with which to pay part of his ransom that he still owed to Nur ed-Din. Manuel gave the required aid. In return Bohemond journeyed back to Antioch with a Greek Patriarch, Athanasius II. The Latin Patriarch Aimery went protesting into exile to the Castle of Qosair.[2] For the next five years the Greeks dominated the Antiochene Church. It does not seem that Latin bishops were ejected; but vacant sees were filled by Greeks. The dependent Latin Church of Tripoli was unaffected. The coming of the Greeks threw the Jacobite Church into the arms of the Latins. They had been on friendly terms since 1152 when a miracle at the tomb of the Syrian Saint Barsauma had cured a lame Frankish child; and in 1156 the Jacobites, to the delight of their Patriarch, Michael the historian, had been allowed to build a new cathedral, at whose dedication the Princess Constance and the Armenian Prince Thoros assisted. Now the Patriarch Michael went to visit Aimery at Qosair to assure him of his sympathy. Michael's dislike of the Greeks went so far that he refused in 1169 a friendly invitation from the Emperor to come to Constantinople for one of the religious debates in which Manuel delighted.[3]

Nur ed-Din spent 1165 and 1166 in making surprise attacks on

[1] William of Tyre, XIX, 10, pp. 898–900; Ibn al-Athir, p. 540–2, and *Atabegs*, p. 234; Kemal ad-Din, ed. Blochet, p. 541.
[2] William of Tyre, XIX, 11, p. 901; Michael the Syrian, III, p. 326. Athanasius II had been appointed Patriarch of Antioch in 1157 when the Patriarch-designate, Panteugenes Soterichus, was accused of heresy.
[3] Michael the Syrian, III, pp. 301–4, 332, 334–6.

The Lure of Egypt

fortresses on the eastern slopes of the Lebanon, while Shirkuh raided Oultrejourdain, destroying a castle that the Templars had built in a grotto south of Amman.[1] At the end of 1166 Shirkuh at last obtained permission from his master to invade Egypt once more. He persuaded the Caliph at Baghdad to represent the project as a holy war against the heretic Caliphate of the Shia Fatimids; and this argument probably affected Nur ed-Din, who had grown deeply religious since his illness. He provided reinforcements from Aleppo for Shirkuh and his army. Shirkuh set out from Damascus in January 1167. Once again he took Saladin with him. He had made no secret of his intentions; and Shawar had time again to call on Amalric's help. The King was at Nablus and summoned his barons to meet him there. After he had pointed out the danger to Palestine should the Sunni Syrians conquer Egypt, the High Court agreed on a full expedition to save Shawar. The whole fighting force of the kingdom was to take part or else to stay on the frontiers to guard against attacks in the King's absence. Anyone who could not come was to pay a tenth of his year's income. Before the army was ready news came that Shirkuh was passing through the Sinai desert. Amalric sent the troops that were at hand to intercept him, but it was too late.[2]

A terrible sand-storm almost overwhelmed Shirkuh's army; but he reached the isthmus about the first days of February. There he heard that the Frankish army had set out on 30 January. He therefore marched south-westward, through the desert, to reach the Nile at Atfih, forty miles above Cairo. There he crossed and came

[1] William of Tyre, XIX, 11, pp. 901-2; Beha ed-Din, P.P.T.S. p. 501, dating the capture of Munietra after the Egyptian campaign of 1167; Ibn al-Athir, pp. 545-6, and Atabegs, pp. 235-6. Nur ed-Din took Munietra, on the road from Jebail to Baalbek, while Shirkuh took Shaqif Titun, or the Cave of Tyron, identified by Rey (Colonies Franques, p. 513) as Qalat an-Ninha, about 15 miles east of Sidon. The location of the Templar fortress near Amman is unknown. Beha ed-Din calls it Akaf. It may be the grotto of Kaf, south-east of Amman, which contains Roman remains but no sign of medieval masonry.
[2] William of Tyre, XIX, 13, 16, pp. 902-4, 907-8; Beha ed-Din, P.P.T.S. p. 48, saying that Nur ed-Din obliged Saladin to accompany Shirkuh; Ibn al-Athir, p. 547, and Atabegs, p. 236.

down the west bank and set up his camp at Giza, opposite the capital. Meanwhile the Frankish army approached Cairo from the north-east. Shawar met it some way from the city and guided it to an encampment on the east bank of the Nile, a mile from the city walls. After he had refused a suggestion from Shirkuh to unite against the Christians, he made a pact with Amalric. The Franks were to be paid 400,000 besants, half at once, half a little later, on condition that Amalric solemnly swore not to leave Egypt until Shirkuh had been driven out. The King sent Hugh, Lord of Caesarea, and a Templar called Geoffrey, who probably spoke Arabic, into Cairo to obtain the Caliph's formal confirmation of the treaty. Their reception at the palace was superb. They were led past colonnades and fountains and gardens where the Court menageries and aviaries were kept, through hall after hall, heavy with hangings of silk and golden thread, studded with jewels, till at last a great golden curtain was raised, to show the boy-Caliph seated veiled on his golden throne. The oaths to keep the treaty were sworn; and Hugh then, as his King's deputy, wished to seal the pact in the western fashion by shaking the Caliph's bare hand. The Egyptian courtiers were horrified; but at last their sovereign, smiling contemptuously, was persuaded to remove his glove. The ambassadors then retired, deeply impressed, as was intended, by the accumulated wealth of the Fatimid Empire.[1]

For a month the armies glared at each other, neither able to cross the river in face of the other's opposition. Then Amalric managed to effect a crossing on to an island at the head of the Delta, a little to the north, and from there on to the left bank; where he surprised one of Shirkuh's corps. Shirkuh, whose army was outnumbered by the Franco-Egyptian, retired southward up the Nile. Amalric and Shawar followed, but as a precaution they left a strong garrison in Cairo under Shawar's son Kamil and Hugh

---

[1] William of Tyre, XIX, 17–19, pp. 908–13; Ernoul, p. 19, comments that only the Emperor's Court at Constantinople was richer than that of Cairo; Abu Shama, p. 130. William continues his narrative with an account of the difference between the Sunni and the Shia sects.

of Ibelin. The entry of Hugh's regiment into Cairo and the free access to the palace allowed to the officers horrified the stricter Moslem circles in the city.

Not far from Minya in middle Egypt Shirkuh prepared to cross the Nile again with the idea of falling back to invade the Syrian frontier. He encamped at Ashmunein, amongst the ruins of the ancient Hermoupolis. There the Franco-Egyptian army caught up with him. It was larger than his, even without the garrison left at Cairo; but Shirkuh's army was chiefly composed of light Turkish horse, whereas the Egyptians were infantrymen, and the Franks had only a few hundred knights with them. Against the advice of his emirs he decided to give battle. Amalric on his side hesitated. But Saint Bernard then made one of his unfortunate interventions into Crusading history. He appeared in a vision to the King and taunted him as being unworthy of the fragment of the True Cross that he wore round his neck. Only when the King vowed to be a better Christian would he bless the relic. Thus encouraged, Amalric next morning, 18 March 1167, led an attack on the Syrians. Shirkuh adopted the usual Turkish tactics. His centre, under Saladin, yielded, and when the King and his knights galloped on in pursuit, he flung his right wing against the Franco-Egyptian left, which crumbled. Amalric found himself surrounded. That he escaped alive was due, it was thought, to his blessed relic; but many of his best knights were slain, and others, including Hugh of Caesarea, taken prisoner. Amalric and Shawar and the remnants of their army retreated precipitately to Cairo, to join the forces of the garrison.[1]

Shirkuh was victorious; but there was still an allied army in the field. Instead of attempting an attack on Cairo he recrossed the river and moved swiftly north-west through the Fayyum. Within a few days he appeared before Alexandria; and the great

[1] William of Tyre, XIX, 22–5, pp. 917–28 (including a description of Egypt and the Nile); Ibn al-Athir, pp. 547–9, dating the battle of Ashmunein 18 March, and *Atabegs*, p. 23, dating the battle 18 April. *Vita S. Bernardi*, *M.P.L.* vol. CLXXXV, cols. 366–7, dating the battle 19 March.

city, where Shawar was hated, opened its gates to him. Meanwhile Amalric and Shawar reformed their army outside Cairo. Despite its losses it still was larger than Shirkuh's. They therefore followed him to Alexandria and blockaded the city. A few reinforcements arrived from Palestine; and Frankish ships sailed in to complete the blockade. After about a month Shirkuh was threatened with starvation. Leaving Saladin with about a thousand men to hold the city, he slipped out one night in May with the greater part of his army, past Amalric's camp, and made for upper Egypt. Amalric was furious and wished to go in pursuit; but Shawar advised that Shirkuh should be allowed if he wished to pillage the upper Egyptian towns. It was more important to recover Alexandria. By the end of June Saladin's position within the city was so desperate, that he had to beg his uncle to return. Shirkuh realized that nothing more could be done. He approached Alexandria and sent one of his Frankish prisoners, Arnulf of Turbessel, after Hugh of Caesarea had refused the task, to Amalric's camp to suggest peace on the basis that both he and the Franks should evacuate Egypt, and that Shawar should promise not to penalize those of his subjects who at Alexandria and elsewhere had supported the invaders. Amalric, who was nervous about affairs in Palestine and Tripoli, accepted his terms. On 4 August, the Frankish army, with the King at its head, entered Alexandria. Saladin and his army were escorted out with full military honours, though the local population would have gladly torn him to pieces, blaming him for their recent misery. But their troubles were not over. No sooner did Shawar's officials enter the city than anyone suspected of collaboration with the Syrians was arrested. Saladin complained to Amalric, who ordered Shawar to let the prisoners go. He himself provided boats to convey Shirkuh's wounded by sea to Acre; where unfortunately those that had recovered were sent to work in the sugar-plantations till the King came in person to release them. During the negotiations Saladin made many friends amongst the Franks; and it was believed afterwards that he had been knighted by the Constable

Humphrey of Toron. Shirkuh and Saladin left Egypt about 10 August and reached Damascus in September. Amalric and his army went to Cairo, to relieve Hugh of Ibelin from his garrison duty; but Shawar was made to sign a pact promising to pay a yearly tribute of 100,000 pieces of gold and to keep a Frankish high commissioner and a small Frankish garrison in Cairo, in control of the gates of the city. The King then returned to Palestine, reaching Ascalon on 20 August.[1]

Some of the Frankish lords thought that a better bargain could have been made. But Amalric was unwilling to risk his forces further in Egypt without safeguarding Frankish Syria against Nur ed-Din's attacks. While he was still in Egypt Nur ed-Din had led a raid into the territory of Tripoli but without capturing any important fortresses. It was necessary to reorganize the defence of the country. The chief problem was always man-power. The resident families were reduced by death or by capture. Visiting Crusaders like Thierry of Flanders could only be used for specific campaigns. Amalric therefore mainly depended on the Military Orders, to whom in 1167 and the succeeding years a large number of fortresses with the surrounding lands were handed over. The gifts were particularly important in Tripoli, whose Count was still a captive and where there were few great noble families. Tortosa and almost the whole of the north of the county passed to the control of the Templars, while the Hospitallers, who probably already held Krak, known after them as 'des Chevaliers', were given charge of the Buqaia. In the kingdom the Templars, already installed at Gaza in the south, were given Safed in the north, while the Hospitallers acquired Belvoir, which commanded the fords of the Jordan to the south of the Sea of Galilee. In Antioch Bohemond III followed Amalric's example. The Templars' holdings round Baghras, on the Syrian Gates, were increased, and

---

[1] William of Tyre, XIX, 26–32, pp. 928–39; Abu Shama, pp. 130–4; Ibn al-Athir, pp. 547–51, and *Atabegs*, pp. 236–46; Beha ed-Din, *P.P.T.S.* pp. 49–51; Imad ed-Din. The story of Saladin's knighthood is given in the *Itinerarium Regis Ricardi*, p. 9.

the Hospitallers were allotted a huge wad of territory at the south of the principality, most of which was actually in Moslem hands. Had the Orders been less irresponsible and jealous, their power might well have preserved the kingdom's defences.[1]

While the Orders were to lead the defence of the realm, Amalric also sought a closer alliance with Byzantium. In August 1167, when he had just come back from Egypt, news reached him that his ambassadors to Constantinople, the Archbishop of Caesarea and the Butler Odo, had landed at Tyre with the Emperor's lovely young grand-niece, Maria Comnena. He hastened to meet her; and their marriage was celebrated pompously in the Cathedral of Tyre by the Patriarch Amalric on 29 August. The Queen was given Nablus and its territory as her dower. With her were two high officials of her uncle's Court, his cousins George Palaeologus and Manuel Comnenus, who were empowered to discuss with Amalric the question of an alliance.[2]

Good relations between the Frankish princes and the Emperor had recently been endangered by the irresponsibility of another of Manuel's cousins, Andronicus Comnenus. This prince, the most brilliant and handsome of his family, had already been in disgrace for seducing one of his relatives, the Emperor's niece Eudocia, of whom gossip said that the Emperor himself was too fond. He had moreover proved himself an unwise governor of Cilicia in 1152. But in 1166 he was appointed again to this post. His predecessor, Alexius Axuch, who had been sent out when Coloman was captured, had failed to carry out the Emperor's orders to reconcile the Armenians; and it was hoped that Andronicus's personal charm, together with extensive subsidies, would be more successful with Thoros. But Andronicus, though already aged forty-six, was more interested in adventure than administration. He soon had occasion to visit Antioch. There he was struck by the beauty of the young Princess Philippa, Bohemond's sister.

[1] See Delaville Le Roulx, *op. cit.* pp. 74–6. Röhricht, *Regesta*, pp. 109 ff., gives frequent examples of grants to the Orders.
[2] William of Tyre, xx, 1, pp. 942–3; Ernoul, pp. 17–18; Cinnamus, p. 238.

Forgetful of his governmental duties he stayed on in Antioch wooing Philippa in a series of romantic serenades till she was dazzled and could refuse him nothing. Bohemond was furious and complained to his brother-in-law Manuel; who angrily recalled Andronicus and reinstalled Constantine Coloman in his place. Coloman was also ordered to proceed to Antioch and to try to capture Philippa's affection. But the Princess thought him plain and short and middle-aged in comparison with her splendid lover. Andronicus, however, whose motive had largely been to annoy the Empress whom he detested, found it prudent to abandon Antioch and his mistress. Taking with him a large share of the imperial revenues from Cilicia and Cyprus, he rode southward and offered his services to King Amalric. The deserted princess was married off hastily to an elderly widower, the Constable Humphrey II of Toron.

Amalric, charmed by Andronicus and impressed by his personal bravery, gave him the fief of Beirut which was then vacant. Soon afterwards Andronicus went to Acre, the dower of his cousin, the widowed Queen Theodora. She was now twenty-one and at the height of her beauty. It was a case of love on both sides. They were too closely related ever to marry; but the Queen shamelessly came to Beirut and lived there as his mistress. When Manuel heard of this new liaison, probably from the ambassadors that had escorted Queen Maria to Palestine, his rage was unbounded. His next ambassadors to Palestine secretly demanded the extradition of the culprit. Their instructions fell into Theodora's hands. As Amalric was known to be seeking Manuel's good-will, Andronicus thought it wise to depart. He gave out that he was returning home; and Theodora came once again from Acre to bid him good-bye. As soon as they were together they abandoned all their possessions and fled unattended over the frontier to Damascus. Nur ed-Din received them kindly; and they spent the next years wandering round the Moslem East, even visiting Baghdad, till at last a Moslem emir gave them a castle near the Paphlagonian border of the Empire, where Andronicus, excommunicated by the

Church, settled down happily to the life of a brigand. Amalric was not sorry to see them go; for it enabled him to take back his sister-in-law's rich dower of Acre.[1]

Amalric had apparently sent back to Manuel with George Palaeologus a proposition for the conquest of Egypt. Manuel's next embassy, led by two Italians, Alexander of Conversano, Count of Gravina, and Michael of Otranto, brought back his conditions, which were, it seems, a share in the spoils of Egypt and a completely free hand in Antioch, and perhaps the cession of other Frankish territory. The terms were high; and Amalric therefore sent the Archdeacon of Tyre, William, the future historian, to Constantinople, to resume discussions. When William arrived there he learnt that the Emperor was campaigning in Serbia. He followed him and met him at Monastir. Manuel received him with his usual lavish generosity and brought him back to his capital; where a treaty was made, by which the Emperor and the King would divide their conquests in Egypt. William returned to Palestine late in the autumn of 1168.[2]

Unfortunately, the barons of the kingdom would not wait for his return. News from Egypt emphasized the insecurity of Shawar's rule there. He was known to resent the Frankish garrison at Cairo, and he was late in paying his tribute. There were rumours, too, that his son Kamil was negotiating with Shirkuh and had asked for the hand of Saladin's sister. The arrival in Palestine in the late summer of Count William IV of Nevers with a fine company of knights encouraged those that wanted immediate action. The King summoned a council to Jerusalem. There the Grand Master of the Hospital, Gilbert of Assailly, urged vehemently that there should be no more delay; and the majority of the lay baronage agreed with him. The Count of Nevers and his men, who had come to fight for the Cross, added their support. The Templars flatly opposed any expedition and announced that

[1] William of Tyre, xx, 2, pp. 943–4; Cinnamus, pp. 250–1; Nicetas Choniates, pp. 180–6. For Andronicus's subsequent history, see below, pp. 427–9.
[2] William of Tyre, xx, 4, pp. 945–7.

they would not take part. Their opposition may have been due to jealousy of the Hospital, which had already decided to take Pelusium as its portion, as a counter to the Templar fortress of Gaza. But the Temple was also financially connected with the Moslems and with the Italian merchants, whose trade was now greater with Egypt than with Christian Syria. King Amalric agreed that some action would soon be needed, in view of Shawar's weakness and unreliability; but he wished to wait till the Emperor's help was available. He was overruled. Against the vigorous determination of the Hospitallers and his own vassals, who saw no reason why the Greeks should share in the spoils, he gave way. An expedition was planned for October.[1]

William of Tyre came back with his treaty from Constantinople to find the King already gone. Amalric had given out that he was to attack Homs, so as to deter Nur ed-Din from action; and indeed Nur ed-Din, who had troubles of his own in north-east Syria, was anxious to avoid a war with the Franks. Shawar also did not realize what was on foot till the Frankish army marched out from Ascalon on 20 October, to arrive ten days later before Bilbeis. He was horrified. He never expected Amalric so wantonly to break his treaty with him. His first ambassador, an emir named Bedran, met the King at Daron, on the frontier, but was bought over by him. The next ambassador, Shams al-Khilafa, found the King in the desert a few days out from Bilbeis. He reproached Amalric bitterly for his perfidy; to which the King replied that he was justified by the negotiations that Shawar's son Kamil was conducting with Shirkuh; and anyhow, he said, the Crusaders newly come from the West had determined to attack Egypt and he was there to restrain them. He might, he added, retire if he were paid another two millions of dinars. But Shawar now suspected the King's good faith. To Amalric's surprise he decided on resistance.

[1] William of Tyre, xx, 5, pp. 948–9 (he mentions the arrival of the Count of Nevers in the previous chapter); Michael the Syrian (III, pp. 332–3) and the Arab historians (Ibn al-Athir, pp. 553–4, and *Atabegs*, pp. 246–7, and Abu Shama, pp. 112–13) were aware that the King was overridden by his Council.

His son Taiy, who commanded the garrison at Bilbeis, refused to open his gates to the Franks. But his forces were small. After three days of desperate fighting, of which Amalric had not thought the Egyptians capable, the Frankish army entered the fortress on 4 November. There followed an appalling massacre of the inhabitants. The protagonists were probably the men from Nevers, ardent and lawless like most newcomers from the West. Their Count had died of fever in Palestine before the expedition started; and there was no one that could control them. Amalric tried to restore order; and when at last he succeeded he himself bought back from the soldiers the survivors that they had taken captive. But the harm was done. Many of the Egyptians who disliked Shawar had been ready to welcome the Franks as deliverers; and the Coptic communities, particularly numerous in the Delta cities, had hitherto worked with their fellow-Christians. But Copts as well as Moslems had perished in the slaughter. The whole Egyptian people was united in hatred of the Franks. A few days later a small Frankish fleet, manned mainly by westerners, which was to sail up the Tanitic mouth of the Nile, arrived in Lake Manzaleh and fell suddenly on the town of Tanis. The same scenes of horror followed; and it was the Copts above all that suffered.

Amalric delayed a few days at Bilbeis, no doubt to re-establish control over his army. He missed the chance of taking Cairo by surprise, and only appeared before the walls of Fostat, the old suburb at the south of the great city, on 13 November. Shawar, doubting his ability to hold Fostat, set fire to it, and sent his ambassador Shams once again to the King to say that sooner than let Cairo itself fall into Frankish hands he would burn it too to the ground with all its wealth. Amalric, whose fleet was held up in the Delta by barriers placed across the river-bed, saw that the expedition had gone wrong. On the advice of his Seneschal, Miles of Plancy, he let Shawar know that he could be bought off. Shawar played for time; he began to haggle over the sum that he could afford. He paid 100,000 dinars down to ransom his son Taiy and talked of further payments. Meanwhile the Frankish army

moved a few miles northwards and encamped at Mataria, by the
sycamore beneath whose shade the Virgin had halted on the
Flight into Egypt. They waited eight days there, when suddenly
the news came that Shirkuh was marching into Egypt on the
invitation of the Fatimid Caliph.[1]

Shawar had not wished to take so desperate a step; but his son
Kamil overruled him and forced his titular sovereign al-Adid to
write to Aleppo, offering Nur ed-Din a third of the land of Egypt
and fiefs for his generals. The young Caliph must have seen the
danger of calling on a protector in whose eyes he was a heretic
and a pretender. But he was powerless. When the invitation
reached him, Nur ed-Din sent to Homs where Shirkuh was
residing; but his messenger found Shirkuh already at the gates of
Aleppo. This time Nur ed-Din did not hesitate. He gave Shirkuh
eight thousand horsemen and a war-chest of 200,000 dinars to use
with the army of Damascus for the conquest of Egypt, and he
ordered Saladin to accompany him. Shawar, uncertain still where
his interests lay, warned Amalric, who moved with his army
towards the Isthmus, hoping to fall on Shirkuh as he emerged
from the desert. But Shirkuh slipped past him to the south. There
was no alternative now for the Franks but evacuation. Ordering
his fleet to return to Acre and summoning the garrison left
in Bilbeis to join him, Amalric began his retreat on 2 January
1169.[2]

Six days later Shirkuh entered Cairo. Leaving his army encamped at the Gate of el-Luq, he went to the Palace, where the
Caliph gave him ceremonial gifts and promised money and food
for his troops. Shawar greeted him cordially. For the next days
he visited him daily to discuss financial arrangements and a
partition of the vizierate. Shirkuh received these overtures

[1] William of Tyre, xx, 6–9, pp. 949–56; Abu Shama, pp. 114–15, 136–40,
quoting Imad ed-Din; Beha ed-Din, *P.P.T.S.* p. 52; Ibn al-Athir, pp. 554–6,
and *Atabegs*, pp. 247–50.
[2] Beha ed-Din, *P.P.T.S.* pp. 52–3; Ibn al-Athir, p. 563, and *Atabegs*, p. 250;
Abu Shama, p. 117. According to Beha ed-Din, repeated more fully by
Ibn al-Athir, Saladin was again very unwilling to join the expedition.

graciously; but his nephew Saladin, who was his chief adviser, insisted on further action. The Caliph was persuaded to come in disguise to Shirkuh's headquarters. Then, on 18 January, Shawar was invited to join Shirkuh on a little pilgrimage to the tomb of the holy as-Shafii. As he set out, Saladin and his emirs fell on him. His escort was disarmed and he himself taken prisoner. In less than an hour an order from the Caliph for his decapitation had been produced and his head was lying at the Caliph's feet. Then, to avoid any attempt against himself, Shirkuh announced that anyone who wished could pillage the late vizier's house. As the mob rushed there, he and the Caliph moved to the palace and quietly took over the government. Shawar's rule had been too unpopular and Shirkuh's regard for legitimacy too scrupulous for any of the provincial governors to oppose the new régime. Within a few weeks Shirkuh was master of all Egypt. His emirs took over the fiefs that had belonged to Shawar and his family; and he himself had the title of vizier and king.[1]

Shirkuh did not long survive his elevation. He died from over-eating on 23 March 1169. His fame in history has been outshone by those of his master Nur ed-Din and of his nephew Saladin. Yet it was he who saw, more clearly than any other Moslem, that the conquest of Egypt, with its strategic position and its boundless resources, was the necessary preliminary to the recovery of Palestine; and, in spite of the hesitations and scruples of Nur ed-Din, he had worked ceaselessly to this end. His nephew reaped the harvest of his persistence. His appearance was insignificant. He was short and stout, red-faced and blind in one eye; and his features revealed his low birth. But he was a soldier of genius; and few generals have been so devotedly loved by their men.[2]

[1] Beha ed-Din, *P.P.T.S.* pp. 53–5 (quoting Imad ed-Din); Ibn al-Athir, pp. 558–60 and *Atabegs*, pp. 251–3; Abu Shama, pp. 118–19, 142–5; William of Tyre, xx, 10, pp. 956–8.
[2] Beha ed-Din, *P.P.T.S.* p. 55; Ibn al-Athir, pp. 560–1; William of Tyre (xix, 5, p. 892) describes him in much the same terms as the Arabic writers. Beha ed-Din (pp. 50–1) describes his anxious determination to annex Egypt to his master's realm.

The Lure of Egypt

The fateful importance of Shirkuh's triumph was well realized by the Franks. While some of them blamed it on the greed of Miles of Plancy, who had made his King accept money rather than fight, others sought a scapegoat in the Master of the Hospital, who was forced to retire from his post and go home to the West. Amalric himself appealed to the West for a new Crusade. An impressive embassy, led by the Patriarch Amalric and the Archbishop of Caesarea, was dispatched early in 1169 with letters to the Emperor Frederick, to Louis VII of France, to Henry II of England, to Margaret, Queen Regent of Sicily, and to the Counts of Flanders, Blois and Troyes. But after two days at sea the ambassadors' ships ran into so severe a storm that they were driven back to Acre; and none of the passengers would consent to risk again the perils of the deep. A second embassy was sent out, led by Frederick, Archbishop of Tyre, accompanied by his suffragan, John, Bishop of Banyas, and Guibert, Preceptor of the Order of the Hospital. They reached Rome in July 1169; and Pope Alexander III gave them letters of recommendation to all his clerics. But none of their letters was of avail. King Louis kept them for many months at Paris, where the Bishop of Banyas died, while he explained to them his preoccupations with the Plantagenets. They went on to England where King Henry talked of his troubles with the Capetians. The quarrels between the Pope and the Emperor made a visit to Germany pointless. After two years of ineffectual begging they returned disconsolate to Palestine.[1]

An embassy to Constantinople was more successful. Manuel was well aware that the balance of power in the East had been dangerously upset. He offered Amalric the co-operation of the great Imperial fleet for his next campaign.[2] The King accepted gladly. Egypt might yet be recovered. Nur ed-Din seemed to be

[1] William of Tyre, xx, 12, pp. 960-1; letters of Amalric in R.H.F. vol. xvi, pp. 187-8; Ibn al-Athir, Atabegs, pp. 258-9. The Master of the Hospital was drowned in 1183 crossing from Dieppe to England. See Delaville Le Roulx, Les Hospitaliers, pp. 76 ff.
[2] William of Tyre, xx, 13, pp. 961-2.

384

fully occupied in the north. The death of Kara Arslan, the Ortoqid emir of Diarbekir in 1168, and the quarrels over the inheritance had embroiled him with his brother Qutb ed-Din of Mosul; and the revolt of Ghazi ibn Hassan, governor of Menbij, had followed soon afterwards and took several months to liquidate. Now Qutb ed-Din was dying, and the question of the succession to Mosul would soon arise.[1] In Egypt Shirkuh's titles and power had passed to his nephew Saladin. But Saladin was untried as a ruler. Others of Shirkuh's emirs had hoped for the succession; but the Caliph had chosen Saladin, trusting that his inexperience would force him to rely on Fatimid officials. Meanwhile al-Adid's chief eunuch, a Nubian called al-Mutamen, or the Confidential Adviser, wrote secretly to Jerusalem to promise help should the Franks invade Egypt. Unfortunately, one of Saladin's agents, puzzled by the shape of a pair of sandals worn by a court messenger, took them and unstitched them, and found the letter within. Saladin waited to take vengeance. But news of his insecurity encouraged the Christians.[2]

Amalric had urged haste on the Emperor; and on 10 July 1169, the Imperial armada set out from the Hellespont, under the command of the Grand Duke Andronicus Contostephanus. The main fleet sailed to Cyprus, capturing two Egyptian ships on the way; and a smaller squadron made straight for Acre, bringing money-subsidies for Amalric's soldiers. Amalric was asked to send to Cyprus as soon as he wished the fleet to sail on. But Amalric was not ready. The campaign of 1168 had disorganized his forces. The Hospitallers' losses had been very heavy. The Templars still refused to take part; and the barons, discouraged by their previous experience, were no longer as enthusiastic as before. It was only in late September that he summoned the fleet to Acre, where its

---

[1] Beha ed-Din, *P.P.T.S.* p. 52; Abu Shama, pp. 188–9; Ibn al-Athir, *Atabegs*, p. 264; Michael the Syrian, III, pp. 339–42; Qutb ed-Din died the following year (1170).

[2] Beha ed-Din, *P.P.T.S.* pp. 55–6; Ibn al-Athir, pp. 566–8; Abu Shama, p. 146. The diploma of Saladin's appointment by the Caliph exists in Berlin, 98 folios long.

splendid appearance thrilled the inhabitants; and it was only in mid-October that the whole expedition was ready to leave for Egypt. The delay was doubly unfortunate. Manuel, who was given to optimism, had counted on a short campaign and had provisioned his ships for three months only. The three months were nearly over. Cyprus, not yet recovered from Reynald's ravaging, had not been able to help in the revictualment; nor were provisions obtainable at Acre.[1] At the same time Saladin received ample warning of the expedition. To secure himself in Cairo, on 20 August 1169, he arrested and beheaded the eunuch al-Mutamen, then dismissed all the palace servants known to be faithful to the Caliph, replacing them by his own creatures. The dismissed officers, encouraged by the Caliph, incited the Nubian Palace Guard to revolt and attack Saladin's troops. Saladin's brother, Fakhr ed-Din, counter-attacked but could do nothing, till Saladin set fire to the Guards' barracks at Fostat. Knowing their wives and families to be there the Nubians fled to rescue them. Fakhr ed-Din then fell on them and slaughtered them almost to a man. The Caliph, who had been watching the battle, hastened to assure Saladin of his loyalty. His desertion of the Nubians completed their rout. The Armenian Guard, which had not taken part in the fighting, was burnt to death in the barracks. The opposition to Saladin in Cairo was silenced.[2]

The Christian army set out at last on 16 October. Andronicus Contostephanus, chafing at Amalric's delays, offered to convey the bulk of the soldiers by sea; but the Franks insisted on the land-route. On 25 October the army entered Egypt at Farama, near Pelusium. Saladin expected an attack on Bilbeis and concentrated his forces there; but the Franks, ferried over the eastern branches of the Nile by the Byzantine ships, who had kept pace with them along the coast, marched swiftly to Damietta, the rich fortress that commanded the main branch of the Nile, up which the fleet could sail towards Cairo. Saladin was taken by surprise. He dared not

[1] Nicetas Choniates, pp. 208–9; William of Tyre, *loc. cit.*
[2] Abu Shama, pp. 147–8; Ibn al-Athir, p. 568.

leave Cairo himself, for fear that the Fatimid supporters might be encouraged to revolt. But he sent reinforcements to Damietta, and wrote himself to Syria to beg for help from Nur ed-Din. The garrison at Damietta had thrown a great chain across the river. The Greek ships, already delayed by contrary winds, could not sail up past the city and intercept the troops and the provisions that came downstream from Cairo. A sudden assault might have captured the fortress; but though Contostephanus, anxious about his dwindling supplies, urged immediate action, Amalric was awed by the huge fortifications. He wished to construct more siege-towers. His first tower, by some error of judgement, had been placed against the strongest part of the walls. The Greeks, to the horror of local Christians and Moslems, used their engines to bombard a quarter sanctified by a chapel dedicated to the Virgin, who had halted there in her flight. Every day fresh troops arrived in the city. Every day the Greek sailors and their compatriots on shore had their rations reduced; and their Frankish allies, who were amply supplied, would give them no help. Every day Contostephanus pleaded with Amalric to risk a full-scale attack on the walls, and Amalric answered that the risk was too great; and his generals, always suspicious of the Greeks, whispered that Contostephanus's zeal was caused by a desire to have Damietta as part of the Imperial spoils. By the beginning of December it was clear that the expedition had failed. Without food the Greeks could go on no longer. A fire-boat launched by the defenders into the middle of the fleet had caused heavy losses, though Amalric's prompt intervention had restricted the damage. The fortress was now well manned and well supplied; and a Moslem army was said to be approaching from Syria. When the rains came early and turned the Christian camp into a morass, it was time to raise the siege. Whether Amalric or Contostephanus was the first to begin negotiations with the Saracens is uncertain; nor are the terms that were arranged known to us. A money-indemnity was probably given to the Christians; and Amalric certainly hoped that a show of friendship towards Saladin might detach him from

Nur ed-Din with whom his relations were suspected of lacking cordiality.

On 13 December the Christians burnt all their siege-machines to prevent them falling into Moslem hands, and moved from Damietta. The army reached Ascalon on the 24th. The fleet was less fortunate. As it sailed northward a great storm arose. The starving sailors could not control their ships, and many of them foundered. For days Greek corpses were washed ashore on the coast of Palestine. Contostephanus himself escaped and sailed to Cilicia and thence travelled overland to report to the Emperor. The remnants of the armada reached the Bosphorus early in the new year.[1]

The disastrous outcome of the expedition inevitably gave rise to recriminations. The Franks blamed the Greeks for their shortage of supplies; the Greeks, more reasonably, blamed the Franks for their endless delays. But both Amalric and the Emperor realized that the alliance must not be broken. For Saladin was now unquestioned master of Egypt.

Saladin was too wise to fall into the diplomatic trap prepared for him by Amalric. Nur ed-Din had trusted Shirkuh, but he was suspicious of the ambitions of the new ruler of Egypt. Saladin, however, behaved with perfect correctitude. In April 1170 his father, Najm ed-Din Ayub, was sent to him by Nur ed-Din with a company of Syrian troops, partly as a gesture of friendship, partly perhaps as a hint; for Ayub was devoted to his master. As a large number of Damascene merchants travelled with the convoy, eager to open up trade with Cairo, Nur ed-Din himself

[1] William of Tyre, xx, 14–17, pp. 962–71; Cinnamus, pp. 278–80. He says that after the campaign Saladin sent to offer Manuel a yearly tribute but Manuel refused it; Nicetas Choniates, pp. 209–19, implies on the other hand that Manuel made a peace with Egypt; Beha ed-Din, *P.P.T.S.* pp. 56–9; Abu Shama, pp. 151–3; Ibn al-Athir, pp. 668–70, and *Atabegs*, pp. 259–60. Michael the Syrian (iii, p. 335, and Armenian version, pp. 369–70) suggests that the Greeks were bribed by Saladin to give up the campaign. His evidence is so consistently anti-Greek as to be of little value. William of Tyre says that Contostephanus was the first to ask for an armistice, Nicetas that it was the King.

led a demonstration against Kerak, in order to allow the great caravan to pass safely through the territory of Oultrejourdain.[1] It was Nur ed-Din's only move against the Franks. During their Egyptian expedition he had left them in peace, and in January 1170 they had even been able to recover the castle of Akkar, on the south of the Buqaia, which had been lost probably in 1165. Amalric, as regent of Tripoli, assigned it together with the town of Arqa to the Hospitallers, who now controlled the whole valley.[2]

On 29 June 1170 Syria was visited by a terrible earthquake, as destructive as those of 1157; and for the next few months Christians and Moslems alike were busy repairing ruined fortresses. Aleppo, Shaizar, Hama and Homs were all severely damaged, as were Krak des Chevaliers, Tripoli and Jebail. At Antioch the damage was enormous; but the Franks saw divine justice in it. For the Greek Patriarch and his clergy were celebrating Mass in the Cathedral of St Peter, when the edifice collapsed on them. As Athanasius lay dying under the ruins, Prince Bohemond and his court hurried to Qosair, to his rival Aimery, to beg him to return to his see. The brief episode of Greek ecclesiastical rule was ended.[3]

The Emperor could not intervene, angry though he was at the news; for things were going badly in Cilicia. The Armenian prince Thoros died in 1168, leaving a child, Roupen II, to succeed him, under the regency of a Frankish lord called Thomas, whose mother had been Thoros's sister. But Thoros's brother Mleh disputed the succession. He had at one time taken vows as a Templar, then, after quarrelling with Thoros and attempting to assassinate him, he had fled to Nur ed-Din and become a Moslem. Early in 1170 Nur ed-Din lent him troops with which he was able

[1] Beha ed-Din, *P.P.T.S.* pp. 59–60; Abu Shama, pp. 153–4; Ibn al-Athir, *Atabegs*, pp. 260–1.
[2] Abu Shama, p. 149. The gift of Akkar and Arqa to the Hospital was made after the earthquake in June (Röhricht, *Regesta*, p. 125).
[3] Michael the Syrian, III, p. 339; Ibn al-Athir, *Atabegs*, p. 262; William of Tyre, xx, 18, pp. 971–3.

not only to dethrone his nephew but also to invade the Cilician plain and take Mamistra, Adana and Tarsus from their Greek garrisons. He then attacked the Templars at Baghras. Bohemond appealed to Amalric, who marched up into Cilicia and temporarily, it seems, restored Imperial rule. This friendly action may have reconciled Manuel to his loss of ecclesiastical control in Antioch. But Mleh was irrepressible. A year or so later he managed to capture Constantine Coloman and again overrun Cilicia.[1]

Nur ed-Din was meanwhile occupied farther east. His brother, Qutb ed-Din of Mosul died in the summer of 1170. His two sons, Saif ed-Din and Imad ed-Din disputed the inheritance; and some months passed before Nur ed-Din could settle the matter to his liking.[2] The respite was useful for the Franks. But the problem of Egypt remained unsolved. Amalric remained faithful to his policy of a close alliance with the Emperor and constant appeals to the West. In the spring of 1171 he decided to pay a personal visit to Constantinople.

His departure was delayed by a sudden offensive made by Saladin against his southern frontier. Early in December 1170 a great Egyptian army appeared before Daron, the southernmost Frankish fortress on the Mediterranean coast. Its defences were weak; and though Saladin had no siege-engines with him, its fall seemed imminent. Amalric, taking with him the Patriarch and the relic of the True Cross, hastened with a small but well-trained force to Ascalon, arriving there on 18 December and moving on to the Templars' fortress at Gaza, where he left Miles of Plancy in charge, as the Templar knights joined him in the march on Daron. He managed to break through the Egyptian army and enter Daron; whereupon Saladin raised the siege and marched on Gaza. The

[1] William of Tyre, xx, 26, pp. 991–2; Nicetas Choniates, p. 183; Michael the Syrian, III, pp. 331, 337; Sembat the Constable, pp. 622–5; Vahram, *Rhymed Chronicle*, pp. 508–9; the dating is impossible to disentangle. William of Tyre places it after Amalric's visit to Constantinople, Michael before the earthquake of 1170. Tarsus was still Greek when Henry the Lion returned from his Crusade in 1172 (Arnold of Lübeck, pp. 22–3).
[2] See references above, p. 385 n. 1, and below, p. 393.

lower town was taken, despite a futile resistance ordered by Miles; and its inhabitants were massacred. But the citadel was so formidable that Saladin did not venture to attack it. As suddenly as he had come he disappeared back to the Egyptian frontier. He then sent a squadron up the Gulf of Akaba, which captured the Frankish outpost of Aila, at the head of the Gulf, during the last days of the year.[1]

Amalric left Acre for Constantinople on 10 March, with a large staff, including the Bishop of Acre and the Marshal of the Court, Gerard of Pougi. The Master of the Temple, Philip of Milly, resigned his post in order to go ahead as ambassador. After calling in at Tripoli the King sailed on to the north. At Gallipoli he was met by his father-in-law, who, as the wind was contrary, took him overland to Heraclea. There he embarked again in order to enter the capital through the palace gate at the harbour of Bucoleon, an honour reserved for crowned heads alone.

Amalric's reception delighted him and his staff. Manuel liked westerners in general, and he found Amalric sympathetic. He showed his usual lavish generosity. His family, particularly the King's father-in-law, all joined in offering hospitality. There were endless religious ceremonies and festivities. There was a dancing display in the Hippodrome and a trip in a barge up and down the Bosphorus.[2] In the midst of it all the Emperor and the King discussed the future. A treaty was made and signed, but its terms are unrecorded. It seems that the King recognized in some vague way the Emperor's suzerainty over the native Christians; that Manuel promised naval and financial help whenever another expedition against Egypt should be planned; and that common action should be taken against Mleh of Armenia. There were probably clauses about the Greek Church in Antioch, and even perhaps in the kingdom, where Manuel had already in 1169 taken charge of the

[1] William of Tyre, xx, 19–20, pp. 973–7; Ibn al-Athir, pp. 577–8.
[2] William of Tyre, xx, 22–4, pp. 980–7; Cinnamus, p. 280 (a very brief account, in which he says that Amalric promised 'δουλείαν' to the Emperor). Michael the Syrian, III, p. 343.

The Lure of Egypt

redecoration of the Church of the Nativity at Bethlehem. An inscription on the mosaic attests that the artist Ephraim made them on the orders of the Emperor. He was also responsible for the repairs at the Holy Sepulchre.[1]

Whatever were the details of the treaty, the Franks were well satisfied by their visit and full of admiration for their host. They sailed homeward from Constantinople on 15 June, hopeful for the future.

The appeal to the West was less successful. Frederick of Tyre was still wandering ineffectually through the courts of France and England. About the end of 1170 Amalric wrote to him to invite Stephen of Champagne, Count of Sancerre, to Palestine, to marry the Princess Sibylla.[2] The suggestion was prompted by a tragedy that had befallen the royal family. Amalric's son Baldwin was now nine years old and had been sent with comrades of his own age to be instructed by William, Archdeacon of Tyre. He was a handsome, intelligent boy; but one day, when his pupils were testing their endurance by driving their nails into each other's

[1] De Vogue, Les Eglises de la Terre Sainte, pp. 99-103, gives the inscription on the mosaics of Bethlehem. The Greek traveller Phocas refers to them and tells of the repairs at the Holy Sepulchre (pp. 19, 31). La Monte, 'To what extent was the Byzantine Empire the suzerain of the Crusading States?' discusses the question of Imperial suzerainty, and decides that it was never admitted. But Manuel, like his predecessors before the Crusades, probably considered himself responsible for the welfare of the Orthodox in Palestine and his right to interfere on their behalf was admitted. See above, p. 321 n. 1, for the Patriarch of Jerusalem whom Manuel kept in reserve at Constantinople. It was probably due to Manuel's help that repairs were made about this time to Orthodox establishments in Palestine, such as the Lavra of Calamon (see Vailhé, 'Les Laures de Saint Gérasime et de Calamon', in Echos d'Orient, vol. II, p. 117), and the monastery of St Euthymius. (See Johns, 'The Crusaders' attempt to colonize Palestine and Syria', in Journal of the Royal Central Asian Society, vol. XXI, pp. 292-3.)

[2] William of Tyre, XX, 25, p. 988. Stephen was the grandson of the crusading Count of Blois and youngest son of Tibald, Count of Blois, Chartres and Troyes. He was born about 1130, and made a runaway marriage, in 1151, with Matilda of Douzy. (See Anselme, Hist. Généalogique de la France, II, p. 847). But as his wife is sometimes called Alix, sometimes Maria, it is probable that he was married more than once and was a widower in 1170.

392

arms, William noticed that the prince alone never flinched. He watched carefully and soon realized that the boy was insensitive to pain because he was a leper.[1] It was the judgment of God for the incestuous marriage of his parents, Amalric and Agnes; and it boded ill for the kingdom. Even if Baldwin grew up he could never carry on the dynasty. The young Greek Queen might yet bear a son; but meanwhile, for safety's sake, Amalric would be wise to marry his eldest child, Sibylla, to some rich experienced western prince who could act if need be as regent or even as king. Stephen accepted the invitation and landed with a party of knights in Palestine in the summer of 1171, a few days before Amalric arrived back from Constantinople. But he did not like the look of Palestine. He brusquely broke off the marriage negotiations and, after paying his vows at the Holy Places, left with his company for the north, intending to visit Constantinople. As he passed through Cilicia he was waylaid by Mleh of Armenia, who robbed him of all that he had with him.[2]

Next year an even more important visitor came to Jerusalem, Henry the Lion, Duke of Saxony and Bavaria, grandson of the Emperor Lothair and son-in-law of Henry II of England. But he, too, refused to fight for the Cross. He had come merely as a pilgrim and left as soon as possible for Germany.[3]

The indifference of the West was bitterly disappointing; but perhaps an expedition against Egypt was not needed at once. For Saladin's relations with Nur ed-Din seemed close to breaking-point. By January 1171 Nur ed-Din had installed a garrison of his own at Mosul, where his nephew Saif ed-Din ruled, and had annexed Nisibin and the Khabur valley for himself and Sinjar for his favourite nephew Imad ed-Din. Then, piously anxious for the triumph of orthodox Islam, he wrote to Saladin demanding

[1] William of Tyre, xxi, 1, pp. 1004-5.
[2] *Ibid.* xx, 25, p. 988.
[3] His Crusade is described at length by Joranson, 'The Crusade of Henry the Lion', in *Medieval Essays presented to G. W. Thompson.* The chief source is Arnold of Lübeck.

that prayers in the Egyptian mosques should no longer mention the Fatimid Caliph but the Caliph of Baghdad. Saladin did not wish to comply. After two centuries of Fatimid rule Shia influences were strong in Egypt. Moreover, though he might own Nur ed-Din as his master, his authority in Egypt came from the Fatimid Caliph. He prevaricated, till in August Nur ed-Din threatened to come himself to Egypt if he were not obeyed. After taking police precautions Saladin prepared for the change; but no one dared make the first move till on the first Friday of the Moslem year 567 a visiting divine from Mosul boldly stepped into the pulpit of the Great Mosque and prayed for the Caliph al-Mustadi. His lead was followed throughout Cairo. In the palace the Fatimid Caliph al-Adid lay dying. Saladin forbade his servants to tell him the news. 'If he recovers, he will learn soon enough', he said. 'If he is to die, let him die in peace.' But when the poor youth a few hours before his death asked to see Saladin his request was refused for fear of a plot. Saladin repented of his refusal when it was too late, and spoke of him with affection. With al-Adid the Fatimid dynasty perished. The remaining princes and princesses were rounded up, to spend the rest of their lives in luxury cut off from any contact with the world.[1]

A few days later Saladin set out to attack the castle of Montreal, south of the Dead Sea. He pressed the siege hard; and Amalric, owing to misinformation, left Jerusalem too late to come to its rescue. But, just as the garrison was preparing to capitulate, suddenly Nur ed-Din appeared on the road to Kerak; whereat Saladin raised the siege. He told Nur ed-Din that his brothers' wars in upper Egypt obliged him to return to Cairo. To Nur ed-Din his action seemed mere treachery that must be punished by force. Hearing of his anger Saladin was alarmed and summoned a council of his family and his chief generals. The younger members of the family counselled defiance. But Saladin's father, old Najm ed-Din Ayub, rose to say that he for one was loyal to

[1] Ibn al-Athir, pp. 575–80, and *Atabegs*, pp. 202–3; Kemal ad-Din, ed. Blochet, p. 551; Beha ed-Din, *P.P.T.S.* pp. 61–2.

his master and berated his son for his ambition, and scolded him again in private for letting his ambition be so obvious. Saladin took his advice and sent abject apologies to Nur ed-Din; who accepted them for the moment.[1]

In the summer of 1171 Nur ed-Din planned but gave up an expedition into Galilee. In the late autumn, angered by an act of piracy committed by Franks from Lattakieh on two Egyptian merchant ships, he devastated Antiochene and Tripolitan territory, destroying the castles of Safita and Araima, and had to be bought off with a heavy indemnity.[2] But in 1172 he kept the peace, partly because of his distrust of Saladin and partly because he wished to gain Seldjuk help for an attack on Antioch. But the Seldjuk Sultan, after a stern warning from Constantinople, rejected his advances and instead began a two years' war against the Danishmends. The Byzantine alliance, though it was to achieve little else, at least saved Antioch from a coalition between Aleppo and Konya.[3] About the same time Nur ed-Din at last consented to release Raymond of Tripoli for the sum of 80,000 dinars. The King and the Hospitallers together raised the bulk of the money; and Raymond was allowed to return home. He never paid some 30,000 dinars that remained owing to Nur ed-Din.[4]

War began again in 1173. Amalric felt secure enough to march north into Cilicia to punish Mleh for his outrage against Stephen of Champagne and to carry out his promise to the Emperor. The

[1] William of Tyre, xx, 27, pp. 992–4; Ibn al-Athir, pp. 581–3, and *Atabegs*, pp. 286–8; Kemal ad-Din, ed. Blochet, p. 552; Maqrisi, ed. Blochet, *Revue de l'Orient Latin*, vol. VIII, p. 506. Beha ed-Din, *P.P.T.S.* pp. 62–3, a tactfully vague account, mixing the expeditions of 1171 and 1173. He also makes Saladin say that he alone refused to consider opposition to Nur ed-Din (p. 65).

[2] Ibn al-Athir, *Atabegs*, p. 279; Kemal ad-Din, p. 584; Beha ed-Din, *P.P.T.S.* p. 62, says that Nur ed-Din captured Arga, a mistake for Aryma.

[3] Cinnamus, pp. 291–2; Imad ed-Din, pp. 159–60. Henry the Lion was hospitably received by Kilij Arslan when he passed through Anatolia on his return from Palestine.

[4] Abu Shama, p. 168; William of Tyre, xx, 28, p. 995. The circumstances of Raymond's release are obscure. See Baldwin, *Raymond III of Tripolis*, p. 11 and n. 23. The date was between September 1173 and April 1176.

campaign achieved nothing except to check Mleh's further expansion.[1] Nur ed-Din used the opportunity to invade Oultrejourdain, and summoned Saladin to come to his support. Saladin, faithful to his father's advice, came up with an army from Egypt and laid siege to Kerak. Meanwhile Nur ed-Din moved down from Damascus. On his approach Saladin raised the siege and returned to Egypt, saying, with truth, that his father was dangerously ill. But it was clear that he had no wish to destroy the Frankish buffer-state that lay between him and his imperious master. Nur ed-Din in his turn encamped before Kerak. The fief of Oultrejourdain, of which it was the capital, belonged to an heiress, Stephanie of Milly. Her first husband, Humphrey, heir of Toron, had died a few years before. Her second husband, Amalric's seneschal Miles of Plancy, was away with the King. It was her first father-in-law, the old Constable, Humphrey II of Toron, who came to her rescue. On the mobilization of the forces left in the kingdom, Nur ed-Din retired. His fury against Saladin was unbounded. When he heard of the death, in August, of Najm ed-Din Ayub, his most loyal servant in Cairo, he vowed to invade Egypt himself in the coming spring.[2]

This disunity in the Moslem world was consoling to the Franks; and in the autumn of 1173 they received overtures from another unexpected quarter. Little had been heard of the Assassins during the last decades, apart from their arbitrary murder of Raymond II of Tripoli in 1152. They had been quietly consolidating their territory in the Nosairi mountains. In general they showed no animosity towards the Franks. Their hated enemy was Nur ed-Din whose power restricted them on the east. But he had been unable to suppress them; and a dagger found on his pillow one night warned him not to go too far. Shia rather than Sunni in their sympathies, they had been shocked by the end of the Fatimid

[1] William of Tyre, xx, 26, pp. 991-2; see references above, p. 393 n. 1. William probably confused Amalric's two expeditions.

[2] Ibn al-Athir, pp. 587-93, and *Atabegs*, p. 293; Kemal ad-Din, ed. Blochet, p. 553; Maqrisi, ed. Blochet, *Revue de l'Orient Latin*, vol. vIII, pp. 509-11. Najm ed-Din Ayub died as the result of a fall when playing polo.

Caliphate. In 1169 the Assassin headquarters at Alamut in Persia sent a new governor for the Nosairi province, Rashid ed-Din Sinan of Basra. This formidable sheikh, who was to be known to the Franks as the Old Man of the Mountains, began a more active policy. He now sent to Amalric suggesting a close alliance against Nur ed-Din and hinting that he and all his flock were considering conversion to Christianity. In return he apparently asked that a tribute which the Templars at Tortosa had succeeded in imposing on various Assassin villages should be cancelled. Whether or not Amalric believed that the Assassins would ever become Christians, he was glad to encourage their friendship. The sheikh Sinan's envoys returned towards the mountains with the promise of a Frankish embassy to follow soon after. As they journeyed past Tripoli a Templar knight, Walter of Mesnil, acting with the connivance of his Grand Master, ambushed them and slew them all. King Amalric was horrified. His policy was ruined and his honour stained, just because the Order was too greedy to sacrifice a small portion of its revenues. He ordered the Grand Master, Odo of Saint-Amand, to hand over the culprit. Odo refused, merely offering to send Walter to be judged by the Pope, whose sole authority he recognized. But Amalric was too angry to trouble about the Order's constitution. He hurried with some troops to Sidon, where the Grand Master and the Chapter were staying, forced his way into their presence and kidnapped Walter, whom he cast into prison at Tyre. The Assassins were assured that justice had been done; and they accepted the King's apologies. Meanwhile Amalric planned to demand from Rome that the Order be dissolved.[1]

The year 1174 opened well for the Christians. The Assassins were friendly. The Byzantine alliance held good. The young King of Sicily, William II, promised naval help for the spring. The discord between Nur ed-Din and Saladin was reaching a crisis; and Saladin himself was none too secure in Egypt, where the Shia nobility was again intriguing against him and was in contact with

[1] William of Tyre, xx, 29–30, pp. 995–9.

the Franks. In 1173 he had sent his eldest brother, Turan Shah, to conquer the Sudan, so that it might serve as an asylum for the family, should the worst occur. Turan occupied the country as far as Ibrim, near Wady Halfa, where he slew the Coptic bishop and his flock, both his congregation and his seven hundred pigs. But he reported that the land was unsuitable as a refuge. Saladin then sent him to southern Arabia, which he preferred. He conquered it in his brother's name and ruled there as viceroy till 1176.[1]

But there was no need to flee from the wrath of Nur ed-Din. In the spring of 1174 the atabeg came to Damascus to plan his Egyptian campaign. As he rode out one morning with his friends through the orchards he talked to them of the uncertainty of human life. Nine days later, on 15 May, he died of a quinsy. He had been a great ruler and a good man, who had loved above all things justice. After his illness nineteen years before, something of his energy had left him; and more and more of his time was spent on pious exercises. But his piety, narrow though it was, won him the respect of his subjects and of his enemies. He was austere and smiled seldom. He lived simply and forced his family to do likewise, preferring to spend his vast revenues on works of charity. He was a careful and watchful administrator; and his wise government consolidated the realm that his sword had won. In particular he sought to curb the restlessness of his Turkish and Kurdish emirs by settling them on fiefs for which they paid the rent in soldiers, but his own law courts kept them strictly under control. This mitigated feudalism did much to restore the prosperity of Syria after nearly a century of the rule of nomads. In appearance he was tall and dark-skinned, almost beardless, with regular features and a gentle, sad expression. Polo-playing was his only recreation.[2]

Nur ed-Din's heir was his son, Malik as-Salih Ismail, a boy of eleven, who had been with him at Damascus. There the emir Ibn al-Muqaddam, backed by the boy's mother, seized the regency,

---

[1] Ibn al-Athir, pp. 599, 602–3, and *Atabegs*, p. 293; Beha ed-Din, *P.P.T.S.*, pp. 65–6.
[2] Ibn al-Athir, pp. 604–5; Beha ed-Din, *P.P.T.S.* p. 65.

while Gümüshtekin, governor of Aleppo, which had been Nur ed-Din's chief capital, proclaimed himself there as regent. The boy's cousin, Saif ed-Din of Mosul, intervened to annex Nisibin and all the Jezireh as far as Edessa. Saladin, as the governor of Nur ed-Din's richest province, wrote to Damascus to claim that the regency was his. But he was powerless at the moment to follow up his claim.[1] The collapse of Moslem unity offered the Franks a chance that Amalric was swift to take. In June he marched on Banyas. Al-Muqaddam came out from Damascus to meet him and, probably as Amalric intended, at once proposed to buy him off with the promise of a large sum of money, the release of all the Frankish prisoners at Damascus and an alliance in the future against Saladin.[2] Amalric, who was beginning to suffer from an attack of dysentery, accepted the proposals. After a pact was signed he rode back through Tiberias and Nablus to Jerusalem, refusing the comfort of a litter. He arrived there seriously ill. Greek and Syrian doctors were summoned to his bedside, and he told them to bleed him and give him a purge. They refused, for they thought him too weak to stand the strain. So he had recourse to his own Frankish doctor, who had no such scruples. The treatment seemed to do him good, but only for a day or two. On 11 July 1174, he died, at the age of thirty-eight.[3]

If history is only a matter of challenge and response, then the growth of Moslem unity under Zengi, Nur ed-Din and Saladin was the inevitable reaction to the First Crusade. But fate too often capriciously loads the dice. At the beginning of 1174 Saladin's star seemed to be setting. The death of Nur ed-Din and the death of Amalric, neither of them expected, saved him and opened the gateway for his victories to come. For the Franks of the East the death of Amalric, at such a moment, and the accidents that had befallen his family foreboded the end of their kingdom. Amalric was the last king of Christian Jerusalem worthy of his throne. He had made

[1] Ibn al-Athir, pp. 606–9; Kemal ad-Din, ed. Blochet, pp. 558–60.

[2] William of Tyre, xx, 31, p. 1000; Abu Shama, p. 162; Ibn al-Athir, p. 611.

[3] William of Tyre, xx, 31, pp. 1000–1. The Syrian doctor was probably Suleiman ibn Daoud. See above, p. 318 n. 1.

mistakes. He had been swayed by the enthusiasm of his nobles in 1168 and by their hesitations in 1169. He had been too ready to accept gifts of money, which his government needed for the moment, rather than carry out a policy far-sightedly. But his energy and his enterprise had been boundless. He had shown that neither his vassals nor the Orders could defy him unscathed. Had he lived longer he might have challenged the inevitability of the triumph of Islam.

BOOK V

THE TRIUMPH OF ISLAM

CHAPTER I

MOSLEM UNITY

'The wise shall inherit glory: but shame shall be the promotion
of fools.'   PROVERBS III, 35

To Saladin, watching anxiously in Cairo, King Amalric's death
came as a sign of God's favour. Shia intrigues against him had
come to a head in April when a plot to kill him was betrayed to
him. He struck at once and crucified the ring-leaders; but he
could not be sure that there were not others ready to conspire,
should a Christian army come to their aid. And in the meantime
Nur ed-Din's heritage might pass firmly into other hands.[1] Now,
with Amalric dead, there was no danger of an invasion by land.
A Sicilian fleet was, it is true, in the offing; for King William II
had heard neither of the collapse of the Shia conspiracy nor of
the death of Amalric. On 25 July 1174 the Sicilians, with two
hundred and eighty-four ships to convey their men, their beasts
and their provisions, under Tancred, Count of Lecce, appeared
suddenly before Alexandria. But they found themselves deprived
of the support on which they had counted; and they had already
refused to countenance any help from the Emperor, for William
had quarrelled with Manuel, who had offered him the hand of his
daughter Maria and then had withdrawn the offer; and anyhow
he wished to show that he could do better than the Byzantines in
1169. On their failure to surprise the city and on Saladin's
approach with an army, they took to their ships again and sailed
away on 1 August. Saladin was free now to march into Syria.[2]

---

[1] Ibn al-Athir, p. 600.
[2] Abu Shama (quoting Imad ed-Din), pp. 164–5; Beha ed-Din, *P.P.T.S.*
pp. 66–7, dating the arrival of the Sicilians 7 September; William of Tyre,
XXI, 3, p. 1007.

Ibn al-Muqaddam, governor at Damascus, was frightened and appealed to the Franks for help. His fear increased when the young as-Salih fled with his mother to Aleppo to the more vigorous guardianship of Gümüshtekin. Ibn al-Muqaddam next appealed to Saif ed-Din of Mosul to come to his rescue; but Saif ed-Din preferred to consolidate his gains in the Jezireh. The people of Damascus then insisted on their governor summoning Saladin. Saladin set out at once, with seven hundred picked horsemen. He rode swiftly through Oultrejourdain where the Franks made no attempt to stop him, and arrived at Damascus on 26 November. He was received there with joy. He spent the night at his father's old house. Next morning Ibn al-Muqaddam opened the citadel gates to him. He installed his brother Toghtekin as governor in as-Salih's name and, after delighting the Damascenes by generous gifts to them from as-Salih's treasury, marched on northward against Gumushtekin.[1]

King Amalric's death had left the Franks powerless to intervene. The only remaining prince of the royal house was the thirteen-year old leper, Baldwin. His sister Sibylla, a year older, was still unmarried. His step-mother, Queen Maria Comnena, had only given birth to daughters, of whom one had died and the other, Isabella, was aged two. The barons accepted Baldwin as their king without demur. Four days after his father's death he was crowned by the Patriarch. No regent was appointed. The Seneschal, Miles of Plancy, the late King's closest friend and lord in his wife's right of the great fief of Oultrejourdain, carried on the government. But Miles was unpopular, particularly amongst the locally-born aristocracy, with whose support Count Raymond of Tripoli claimed the regency. Next to the King's sisters Raymond was his closest relative on the royal side of the family. His mother, Hodierna of Jerusalem, had been Amalric's aunt. Though Bohemond of Antioch was descended from Hodierna's elder sister, Alice, he was a generation further away from the Crown.

[1] Beha ed-Din, *P.P.T.S.* pp. 67–70; Ibn al-Athir, pp. 614–16; Maqrisi, ed. Blochet, *Revue de l'Orient Latin*, vol. VIII, p. 517.

Moreover, he lived far off; whereas Raymond had recently married the second great heiress in the Kingdom, Eschiva of Bures, Princess of Galilee, widow of Walter of Saint-Omer. Raymond's supporters, led by the old Constable, Humphrey II of Toron, by the Ibelin family and by Reynald of Sidon, insisted on his rights being heard before the High Court. Miles prevaricated for as long as he could, but had to yield. Late in the autumn Raymond was installed as Regent. A few weeks later Miles, who had taken his fall from power with an ill grace, was assassinated one dark night in the streets of Acre.[1]

Raymond was now aged thirty-four, a tall, thin man, dark-haired and dark-skinned, his face dominated by a great nose, in character cold and self-controlled and a little ungenerous. There was nothing in him of the enthusiastic chivalry of the early Crusaders. During his long years in captivity he had read deeply, he had learnt Arabic and he had studied the ways of the Moslems. He saw the problems of the Frankish states from a local standpoint. He was interested in their survival, not in their role as the spearhead of aggressive Christendom. He was able and ably supported by his friends, but he was only regent and he had enemies.[2]

His regency began a cleavage within the kingdom. There had been factions before, especially in the days of Queen Melisende. But they had been short-lived. The Crown had kept control. Now two definite parties arose, the one composed of the native barons and the Hospitallers, following the leadership of Count Raymond, seeking an understanding with their foreign neighbours and unwilling to embark on risky adventures; the other composed of newcomers from the West and the Templars. This party was aggressive and militantly Christian; and it found its leaders in 1175, when at last Reynald of Châtillon was released from his Moslem prison, together with Joscelin of Edessa, a Count without a county, whom fate had turned into an adventurer.[3] Personal

[1] William of Tyre, XXI, 3-4, pp. 1007-9.
[2] William of Tyre, XXI, 5, pp. 1010-12.
[3] For the release of Reynald and Joscelin, see below, p. 408.

animosities were even stronger than differences in policy. Most of the nobles now were cousins of each other; and family quarrels are always the most bitter. The two wives of King Amalric hated each other. Agnes of Courtenay, Count Joscelin's sister, had married twice since her divorce. Her next husband, Hugh of Ibelin, had died a few years after the marriage; his successor, Reynald of Sidon, was glad to discover that he, like Amalric, was too closely related to his wife and secured an annulment.[1] While Agnes sided with her brother and the Templars, he joined the other party. Queen Maria Comnena was soon remarried, to Hugh of Ibelin's brother Balian, to whom she brought her dower-fief of Nablus. This marriage was happy; and the Dowager-Queen played a great role in her husband's party.[2] Reynald of Châtillon, a few months after his release, married the heiress of Oultre-jourdain, Stephanie, the widow of Miles of Plancy, who considered Count Raymond to be her husband's murderer.[3] Raymond's long quarrel with the Templars began on a personal question. A Flemish knight, Gerard of Ridfort, came to Tripoli in 1173 and took service under the Count, who promised him the hand of the first suitable heiress in his county. But when the lord of Botrun died a few months later, leaving his lands to his daughter Lucia, Raymond ignored Gerard's claim and gave her to a rich Pisan called Plivano, who ungallantly put the girl on to a weighing-machine and offered the Count her weight in gold. Gerard, angry and disappointed, joined the Order of the Temple and soon became its most influential member and its seneschal. He never forgave Raymond.[4]

[1] Hugh of Ibelin, who had been Amalric's commissioner in Cairo in 1167, died about 1169. He had been engaged to Agnes before she married Amalric (William of Tyre, XIX, 4, p. 890). William also tells of Reynald of Sidon's divorce. Reynald's father showed that he and Agnes were related. It was doubtless through her mother, Beatrice widow of William of Sahyun, whose maiden name is not recorded.
[2] William of Tyre, XXI, 18, p. 1035; Ernoul, p. 44. [3] Ernoul, pp. 30–1.
[4] Ernoul, p. 114; *Estoire d'Eracles*, pp. 51–2. Plivano paid 10,000 besants for his bride. If they were of full gold content her weight would have been about 10 stone.

The young King, precociously aware of the intrigues around him, tried to hold the balance between the parties. Raymond remained his regent for three years; but ties of kinship drew him closer to the Courtenays. He made his uncle Joscelin seneschal in 1176; and his mother, the Lady Agnes, returned to the Court. Her influence was disastrous. She was vicious and greedy, insatiable for men and for money. She had not been allowed to bring up her children. Baldwin had been given to the care of William of Tyre and Sibylla to that of her great-aunt, the Princess-Abbess Joveta of Bethany. But now she began to interfere in their lives. Baldwin listened to her, against his better judgment; and Sibylla fell under her domination.[1]

Raymond's first duty as regent was to curb the growth of Saladin's power. The Franks had been unable to prevent the union of Damascus with Cairo; but at least Aleppo was still separate. As soon as reinforcements came from Egypt Saladin had marched to Aleppo from Damascus. On 9 December 1174 he entered Homs and left troops to invest the castle, which held out against him. He passed on through Hama to Aleppo. When Gümüshtekin closed the gates in his face, he began a regular siege of the city, on 30 December. The citizens were half inclined to surrender to him; but the young as-Salih came down himself into their midst and pleaded with them to preserve him from the man who had filched his heritage. Touched by his plight the defenders never flagged. Meanwhile Gümüshtekin sent for help from the Assassins and from the Franks. A few days later some Assassins were found in the heart of Saladin's camp, at his very tent. They were slain after a desperate defence. On 1 February Count Raymond and a Frankish army appeared before Homs, and with the help of the castle garrison began to attack the city walls. This

---

[1] Joscelin is attested as Seneschal from 1177 onwards (Röhricht, *Regesta*, p. 147). He is always called 'Count Joscelin'. In charters Agnes is called Countess, having been Countess of Jaffa and Ascalon during her marriage to Amalric. She was never Queen and is never so called. William of Tyre, XXI, 2, p. 1006, for Sibylla's upbringing, and above, p. 392, for Baldwin's.

had the desired effect. Saladin raised the siege of Aleppo and came hurrying south. Raymond did not stay to meet him. For the next month Saladin was held up by the siege of the castle of Homs. By April he was master of all Syria as far north as Hama; but Aleppo was still independent. In gratitude to the Franks Gümüshtekin released Reynald of Châtillon and Joscelin of Courtenay and all the other Christian prisoners languishing in the dungeons of Aleppo.[1]

Saladin's successes roused Nur ed-Din's nephew, Saif ed-Din of Mosul, who sent his brother, Izz ed-Din, with a large army into Syria to join Gümüshtekin. Saladin, hoping perhaps to cause trouble between Aleppo and Mosul, offered to cede to Gümüshtekin Hama and Homs. The offer was rejected. But the allied army was caught in a ravine amongst the hills north of Hama and cut to pieces by Saladin's veterans. Saladin did not feel strong enough to follow up his victory. A truce was arranged, which allowed Saladin to occupy a few towns north of Hama but otherwise left things as they were.[2]

Saladin now threw off his alleged vassaldom to as-Salih. He had, he said, done his best to serve him loyally, but as-Salih had preferred other counsellors and rejected his help. He therefore took the title of King of Egypt and Syria and struck coins in his own name alone. The Caliph at Baghdad graciously approved and sent royal robes that reached him at Hama in May.[3]

The truce with the house of Zengi was short-lived. In March 1176 Saif ed-Din of Mosul himself crossed the Euphrates with a large army and joined with Gumushtekin's troops outside Aleppo. Saladin, whose army had been reinforced again from Egypt, went

[1] William of Tyre, xxi, 6, pp. 1012–13, 1023; Abu Shama, pp. 167–8; Ibn al-Athir, pp. 618–20; Kemal ad-Din, ed. Blochet, pp. 562–4.

[2] Beha ed-Din, *P.P.T.S.* pp. 70–1; Ibn al-Athir, pp. 621–2, calls the site of the battle the Horns of Hama; Kemal ad-Din, ed. Blochet, p. 564.

[3] The first of the coins bearing Saladin's royal title are dated A.M. 570 (1174–5). He never assumed the title of Sultan, but Arab writers, even his contemporaries, usually give it to him (e.g. Ibn Jubayr and Beha ed-Din). See Wiet, *op. cit.* pp. 335–6.

up to meet him. An eclipse of the sun on 11 April alarmed his men as they crossed the Orontes near Hama; and they were caught by surprise ten days later by Saif ed-Din, as they were watering their horses. But Saif ed-Din hesitated to attack at once. Next morning, when Saif ed-Din brought all his forces up to attack Saladin's camp on the Mound of the Sultan, some twenty miles south of Aleppo, it was too late. Their first onrush almost succeeded; but Saladin counter-charged at the head of his reserves and broke the enemy's lines. By evening he was master of the field. The treasure that Saif ed-Din had left in his camp on fleeing was all given by Saladin to reward his own men. The prisoners that were taken were well treated and soon sent back to their homes. His generosity and clemency made an excellent impression.[1]

Aleppo still refused to open its gates to Saladin; so he attacked and captured the fortresses between the city and the Euphrates, Biza'a and Menbij, then laid siege to Azaz, the great fortress that commanded the road to the north. There, once again, he nearly perished at the hands of one of the Assassins, who entered the tent where he was resting. Only the cap of mail that he wore under his turban saved him. Azaz capitulated on 21 June. On 24 June he appeared again before Aleppo. But now he agreed to come to terms. As-Salih and the Ortoqid princes of Hisn Kaifa and Mardin who had supported him agreed to cede to Saladin all the land that he had conquered; and they and Saladin swore solemnly to keep the peace. When the treaty had been signed on 29 July, as-Salih's little sister came out to visit Saladin's camp. He asked her kindly what gift she would like; and she answered: 'The Castle of Azaz.' Saladin thereupon gave it back to her brother.[2]

Though Aleppo was still unconquered, as-Salih and his cousins were cowed. Saladin could turn to deal with the Assassins and the

---

[1] Beha ed-Din, *P.P.T.S.* pp. 71–4; Ibn al-Athir, pp. 625–6. Beha ed-Din makes the battle take place at Tel es-Sultan and at the Horns of Hama.

[2] Beha ed-Din, *P.P.T.S.* pp. 74–5; Kemal ad-Din, ed. Blochet, pp. 146–7; Ibn al-Athir, *loc. cit.* According to Kemal ad-Din public opinion in Aleppo was against a treaty and strongly supported as-Salih.

Franks. He entered the Nosairi mountains to lay siege to Masyaf, the chief Assassin stronghold. Sheikh Sinan was away; and as he hurried home, Saladin's soldiers could have captured him had not some mysterious power restrained them. There was magic about. Saladin himself was troubled by terrible dreams. One night he woke suddenly to find on his bed some hot cakes of a type that only the Assassins baked, and with them a poisoned dagger and a piece of paper on which a threatening verse was written. Saladin believed that the Old Man of the Mountains had himself been in the tent. His nerves gave way. He sent a messenger to Sinan asking to be forgiven for his sins and promising, in return for a safe-conduct, henceforward to leave the Assassins undisturbed. The Old Man pardoned him, and the treaty between them was kept.[1]

With the Franks no such treaty could be made. There had been a truce in 1175, when Saladin, in order to be able to deal with Saif ed-Din, had released the Christian prisoners in his possession.[2] But next year the Franks broke the truce. While Saladin was besieging Aleppo, Raymond of Tripoli invaded the Beqa'a from the Buqaia, while the royal army under Humphrey of Toron and the fifteen-year old King came up from the south. Raymond seems to have suffered a slight defeat at the hands of Ibn al-Muqaddam, now governor of Baalbek; but the Christians made a junction and severely defeated Saladin's brother Turan Shah and the militia of Damascus. They retired again as soon as Saladin approached from the north. He did not follow after them. He was anxious to return to Egypt. Leaving Turan Shah in command of a strong army in Syria, he once more slipped through Oultrejourdain and arrived at Cairo at the end of September.[3]

[1] Abu Firas, ed. Guyard, *Journal Asiatique*, 7me série, vol. IX, 1877, Arabic text, pp. 455–9; Ibn al-Athir (*loc. cit.*) reports a threatening letter sent by Sinan to Saladin's maternal uncle, Shihab ed-Din.
[2] William of Tyre, XXI, 8, pp. 1017–19. He reproaches Humphrey of Toron, who was responsible for the truce, for missing an opportunity for striking at Saladin when he was embarrassed.
[3] William of Tyre, XXI, 11, pp. 1021–3; Ibn al-Athir, p. 627.

For a year there was a respite from fighting, for which both sides were thankful. While Saladin reorganized Egypt and rebuilt and refortified Cairo, the government at Jerusalem faced its main internal problem. In 1177 King Baldwin came of age, at sixteen, and Raymond gave up the regency. But the King's leprosy was growing worse; he surely could not live for many years. To provide for the succession the Princess Sibylla must be married. In 1175, probably at the suggestion of Louis VII of France, Baldwin had invited William Long-Sword, eldest son of the Marquis of Montferrat, to come to Palestine and accept Sibylla's hand. It was a good choice. William was well-connected. His father was the richest prince in northern Italy. He was cousin both of the Emperor Frederick Barbarossa and of King Louis. He himself, though no longer young, was gallant and handsome enough to please the gay Princess. He landed at Sidon in October 1176. On his marriage to Sibylla a few days later he was given the county of Ascalon and Jaffa and generally accepted as heir to the throne. But the hopes based on his vigour and his high connections were vain. Early in 1177 he fell ill of malaria. His illness dragged on for some months; and in June he died. His widow gave birth to a son in the late summer, an heir to the kingdom but one that made a regency inevitable. The King's envoys scoured Europe once more to find a second husband for the Princess.[1]

His envoys also scoured Europe to find allies against Saladin; for the lull in the war would certainly not last long. But the princes of the West were fully occupied in their own affairs; and even Constantinople could not provide the same help as before. The year 1176 was a turning-point in the history of Byzantium. The Seldjuk Sultan, Kilij Arslan II, had grown restive against the Emperor. While Nur ed-Din lived he had been kept under control; for Nur ed-Din had intervened in Anatolia in 1173, to

---

[1] William of Tyre, xxi, 13, pp. 1025–6; William's mother was half-sister to King Conrad and to Frederick Barbarossa's father. His father and King Louis's mother, Adelaide of Maurienne, were the children by two different marriages of Gisela of Burgundy.

prevent the Seldjuks from swallowing the lands of the Danish-mends. Nur ed-Din's general Abdalmassih, his brother Qutb ed-Din's former minister at Mosul, restored Caesarea-Mazacha to the Danishmend Dhu'l-Nun and himself remained with a garrison in Sivas. Kilij Arslan's brother Shahinshah was at the same time confirmed in the possession of Ankara, where the Emperor had installed him some years before. But Nur ed-Din's death removed this restraint on Kilij Arslan. By the end of 1174 Abdalmassih was back in Mosul, Dhu'l-Nun and Shahinshah were in exile at Constantinople, and Kilij Arslan was in possession of their lands. He then turned against Byzantium. In the summer of 1176 Manuel determined to deal once and for all with the Turks. Some slight successes the previous summer had encouraged him to write to the Pope to announce that the time was propitious for a new Crusade. Now he would make the road across Anatolia safe for ever. While an army under his cousin Andronicus Vatatses was sent through Paphlagonia to restore Dhu'l Nun to his territory, Manuel himself led the great Imperial army, swelled by all the reinforcements that he could muster, against the Sultan's capital at Konya. Kilij Arslan, hearing of the expedition, sent to ask for peace. But Manuel no longer had faith in his word.

Early in September the Paphlagonian expedition came to disaster before the walls of Niksar. The head of Vatatses was sent as a trophy to the Sultan. A few days later Manuel's army moved out of the Meander valley, past the fortress that he had built at Sublaeum the year before, and round the top of the Lake of Egridir into the hills that led up toward the great range of the Sultan Dagh. Heavy wagons containing siege-machinery and provender slowed its progress; and the Turks had devastated the land through which it must travel. The road led through a pass called Tzibritze by the Greeks, with the ruined fort of Myrio-cephalum standing at the far end. There the Turkish army was gathered visible on the bare hill-side. Manuel's more experienced generals warned him not to take his lumbering army through the difficult passage in face of the enemy; but the younger princes trusted in their prowess and were eager for glory. They persuaded him to march on. The Sultan had gathered troops from all his allies and vassals. His army was as large as Manuel's, less well-armed but more mobile. On 17 September 1176 the vanguard forced its way through the pass. The Turks yielded before them, to swing round into the hills and charge down the slopes into the pass as the main Imperial army pressed along the narrow road. The Emperor's brother-in-law, Baldwin of Antioch, at the head of a cavalry regiment, counter-charged up the hill into the enemy; but he and all his men were killed. The soldiers in the valley saw his defeat. They were so tightly packed together that they could scarcely move their hands. Brave leadership might still have saved the day. But Manuel's courage deserted him. He was the first to panic and fled back out of the pass. The whole army now tried to follow him. But in the chaos the transport wagons blocked the road. Few of the soldiers could escape. The Turks, waving the head of Vatatses before them, massacred as they pleased till darkness fell. Then the Sultan sent a herald to the Emperor as he tried to rally his troops in the plain, and offered him peace on condition that he retired at once and dismantled his two new fortresses of Sublaeum and Dorylaeum. Manuel gratefully accepted the terms. His unconquered vanguard came back safely through the pass, and joined up with the pathetic remnant that Manuel now led homewards, harassed by Turks who could not understand Kilij Arslan's forbearance. It is probable that the Sultan did not comprehend the completeness of his victory. His main interest was now in the East. He was not at the moment interested in expanding westward. All that he wanted there was security.[1]

Manuel, however, was well aware of the significance of the disaster, which he himself compared to that of Manzikert, just

[1] Nicetas Choniates, pp. 236–48; Michael the Syrian, III, pp. 369–72. See Chalandon, *Les Comnènes*, pp. 506–13, and Cahen, *La Syrie du Nord*, p. 417 n. 3, and for the battle itself, Ramsay, 'Preliminary report', in *History and Art of the Eastern Provinces of the Roman Empire*, pp. 235–8.

over a century before.[1] The great war-machine that his grandfather
and father had built up had suddenly been destroyed. It would
take many years to rebuild it; and indeed it was never rebuilt.
There were troops enough left to defend the frontiers and even to
win a few petty victories in the next three years. But nevermore
would the Emperor be able to march into Syria and dictate his
will at Antioch. Nor was there anything left of his great prestige
which had in the past deterred Nur ed-Din at the height of his
power from pressing too far against Christendom. For the Franks
the disaster at Myriocephalum was almost as fateful as for
Byzantium. Despite all the mutual mistrust and misunderstanding,
they knew that the existence of the mighty Empire was an ultimate safeguard against the triumph of Islam. At the moment,
when the ruler of northern Syria was the weak boy as-Salih, they
did not notice the importance of the battle. But when William
of Tyre visited Constantinople three years later and learnt fully
what had happened, he realized the dangers ahead.[2]

Though Manuel's army had perished, his fleet was still strong,
and he was ready to use it against Saladin. Once again, in 1177,
he promised to send it in support of a Frankish attack against
Egypt. During that summer there had been rumours of a new
Crusade from the West; both Louis VII and Henry II of England
were said to have taken the Cross.[3] But only one western potentate appeared in Palestine. In September, while King Baldwin was
recovering from a bad attack of malaria, Philip, Count of Flanders,
landed with a considerable following at Acre. He was the son of
Count Thierry and of Sibylla of Anjou; and the Franks, remem-

---

[1] Nicetas Choniates, p. 249. Manuel on the other hand tried to minimize
the disaster in his letter about it to Henry II of England (quoted in Roger of
Hoveden, *Chronica*, II, p. 101). The battle was noticed by many western
chroniclers, e.g. *Vita Alexandri*, in *Liber Pontificalis*, II, p. 435, and *Annales
S. Rudberti Salisburgensis*, p. 777.

[2] William of Tyre, XXI, 12, p. 1025.

[3] Henry II and Louis VII agreed in the Treaty of Ivry, 21 September 1177, to
go on a joint Crusade (Benedict of Peterborough, I, pp. 191-4). The scheme was
dropped soon afterwards.

bering his father's four Crusades and his mother's pious love of the Holy Land, hoped great things of him. The news of his coming brought four high-born ambassadors from the Emperor, offering money for an Egyptian expedition; and on their heels a Byzantine fleet of seventy well-fitted men-of-war arrived off Acre. King Baldwin, too ill to fight himself, hastened to offer him the regency if he would lead an expedition into Egypt. But Philip hesitated and prevaricated. He had come, he said first, merely for the pilgrimage, next that he could not assume such responsibilities alone; and when the King suggested that Reynald of Châtillon should be joint leader, he criticized Reynald's character. It was pointed out to him that the Byzantine fleet was there ready to co-operate. He merely asked why he should oblige the Greeks. At last he revealed that his only object in coming to Palestine had been to marry off his two cousins, the Princesses Sibylla and Isabella, to the two young sons of his favourite vassal, Robert of Béthune. This was more than the barons of Jerusalem could bear. 'We thought you had come to fight for the Cross and you merely talk of marriages', cried Baldwin of Ibelin when the Count made his demand before the Court. Thwarted and furious, Philip prepared to depart again. The wrangling had shocked the Emperor's ambassadors. It was clear that there was going to be no expedition to Egypt. They waited about a month, then disgustedly sailed away with the fleet, to give warning to their master of the incurable frivolity of the Franks.[1]

The Count of Flanders left Jerusalem for Tripoli at the end of October. Perhaps his conscience now troubled him, for he agreed to accompany Count Raymond on an expedition against Hama;

[1] William of Tyre, XXI, 14–18, pp. 1027–35. He suggests that Raymond of Tripoli and Bohemond of Antioch were both of them opposed to an Egyptian expedition and discouraged Philip. But the Ibelins were disgusted by Philip, and as they habitually worked in with Raymond, it is possible that William exaggerated. He was responsible for the Byzantine alliance and therefore upset by its abandonment, and Philip's willingness later to help both Raymond and Bohemond may have led him to suspect them. See also Ernoul, p. 33, who tells of Baldwin of Ibelin's taunt.

and King Baldwin provided troops from the kingdom to reinforce him. While a small contingent raided the territory of Homs, only to fall into an ambush and lose all the booty that it had collected, the two Counts laid siege to Hama, whose governor was seriously ill. But when troops came up from Damascus, they retired, having achieved nothing. From Tripoli Count Philip moved on to Antioch, and there agreed to help Prince Bohemond attack the town of Harenc. Harenc had belonged to as-Salih's former minister Gümüshtekin; but he had quarrelled with his master, who had put him to death. His vassals at Harenc had therefore revolted against as-Salih, but on the Franks' approach their mutiny ended. Bohemond and Philip half-heartedly laid siege to the town. Their mining operations were unsuccessful; and as-Salih was able to send a detachment through their lines to reinforce the garrison. When as-Salih sent envoys to point out to them that Saladin, the real enemy both of Aleppo and Antioch, was back in Syria, they agreed to raise the siege. Philip of Flanders returned to Jerusalem for Easter, then took a ship from Lattakieh for Constantinople.[1]

Saladin had crossed the frontier from Egypt on 18 November. His intelligence service was always excellent. He knew that the Franco-Byzantine alliance had collapsed and that the Count of Flanders was away in the north. He decided on a sudden counterattack up the coast into Palestine. The Templars summoned all the available knights of the Order to defend Gaza; but the Egyptian army marched straight on to Ascalon. The old Constable Humphrey of Toron was seriously ill, and the King had only recently risen from a sickbed. With the troops that he could muster, five hundred knights in all, and with the Bishop of Bethlehem bearing the True Cross, Baldwin hurried to Ascalon and entered the fortress just before the enemy came up. He had summoned every man of arms in the kingdom to join him there; but the first levies were intercepted by Saladin and taken prisoner. Leaving a small force

---

[1] William of Tyre, XXI, 19, 25, pp. 1036, 1047–9; Ernoul, p. 34; Michael the Syrian, III, pp. 75–6; Abu Shama, pp. 189–92; Beha ed-Din, *P.P.T.S.* pp. 76–7; Ibn al-Athir, pp. 630–3; Kemal ad-Din, ed. Blochet, pp. 148–53.

to contain the King in Ascalon, Saladin marched on towards Jerusalem. For once, Saladin was over-confident. There was no enemy left between him and the Christian capital; so he loosened the discipline of his troops and allowed them to wander round the countryside pillaging. With the courage of despair, Baldwin managed to send a message to the Templars telling them to abandon Gaza and join him. When they came near he broke out of Ascalon and rode with all his men up the coast to Ibelin and then swung inland. On 25 November the Egyptian army was crossing a ravine near the castle of Montgisard, a few miles south-east of Ramleh, when suddenly the Frankish knights fell on it coming from the north. It was a complete surprise. Some of Saladin's troops were absent foraging; and he had no time to regroup the remainder. Many of them fled before the first shock. Saladin himself was only saved by his personal Mameluke Guard. The regiments that held their ground were almost annihilated. Among the Christians the King was in the forefront. The bravery of the Ibelin brothers, Baldwin and Balian, and of Raymond's stepsons, Hugh and William of Galilee, helped on the victory; and Saint George himself was seen fighting by their side.

Within a few hours the Egyptian army was in full flight home-wards, abandoning all the booty and the prisoners that it had taken. The soldiers even threw away their weapons in order to flee the quicker. Saladin managed to restore some measure of order; but the crossing of the Sinai desert was painful, with Bedouins harassing the almost defenceless fugitives. From the Egyptian frontier Saladin sent messengers on dromedaries to Cairo to assure any would-be rebels that he was still alive; and his return to Cairo was announced by pigeon-post all over Egypt. But his prestige had suffered terribly.[1]

It had been a great victory and it had saved the kingdom for the

[1] William of Tyre, XXI, 20–24, pp. 1037–47; Ernoul, pp. 41–5; Michael the Syrian, III, p. 375; Beha ed-Din, *P.P.T.S.* pp. 75–6; Abu Shama, pp. 184–7; Ibn al-Athir, pp. 627–35.

moment. But it had not in the long run changed the situation. The resources of Egypt are limitless; whereas the Franks were still short of men. Had it been possible for King Baldwin to pursue the enemy into Egypt or to make a swift attack upon Damascus, he might have crushed Saladin's power, but without help from outside he could not risk his own small army on an offensive. Instead, he decided to erect strong fortifications along the Damascene frontier, where the loss of Banyas had upset the defensive system of the kingdom. While Humphrey of Toron fortified the hill of Hunin, on the road from Banyas to Toron, the King set about building a castle on the upper Jordan between Lake Huleh and the Sea of Galilee, to command the ford by which Jacob had wrestled with the angel, a ford known also as the Ford of Sorrows. The land on either side was inhabited by Moslem peasants and herdsmen, some owing allegiance to Damascus, some to the Christians. They passed to and fro freely across the frontier, which was marked only by a great oak tree; and the Franks had undertaken never to fortify the crossing. Baldwin had wished to abide by the treaty and build a castle elsewhere; but the Templars overruled him. The local Moslems complained of the breach of faith to Saladin, who offered Baldwin first 60,000, then 100,000 gold pieces to give up the work. On the King's refusal, he vowed to take action himself.[1]

After his disaster at Montgisard he had remained for several months in Egypt, till he was sure that everything was well under control. In the late spring of 1178 he returned to Syria and spent the rest of the year at Damascus. The only warfare of the year consisted of a few raids and counter-raids.[2] Farther north there was peace between Antioch and Aleppo, and an alliance between Antioch and Armenia, whose renegade Prince Mleh had been

[1] William of Tyre, XXI, 26, pp. 1050–1; Ernoul, pp. 51–2; Abu Shama, pp. 194–7; Ibn al-Athir, p. 634. Saladin was occupied at the time by a local revolt at Baalbek. Jacob's Ford is now crossed by a bridge known as the Bridge of the Daughters of Jacob.
[2] Ibn al-Athir, p. 633.

overthrown soon after Nur ed-Din's death by his nephew Roupen III. Roupen was a friend of the Franks, whom he had assisted at the ineffectual siege of Harenc.[1] Bohemond III also sought the friendship of the Emperor, and in 1177 married as his second wife a relative of Manuel's, called Theodora.[2]

In the spring of 1179, when the seasonal movement of flocks began, King Baldwin set out to round up the sheep that would be passing towards Banyas from the plains of Damascus. Saladin sent his nephew Faruk Shah to see what was happening. He was to inform his uncle by pigeon-post of the direction taken by the Franks. On 10 April Faruk-Shah suddenly came upon the enemy in a narrow valley in the forest of Banyas. The King was taken by surprise. He was only able to extricate his army owing to the heroism of the old Constable, Humphrey of Toron, who held up the Moslems with his bodyguard till the royal army had escaped. Humphrey was mortally wounded; he died at his new castle at Hunin on 22 April. Even the Moslems paid tribute to his character. His death was a terrible blow to the kingdom; for he had been its one universally respected elder statesman.

Saladin followed up the victory by laying siege to the castle at Jacob's Ford. But the defence was so vigorous that he retired after a few days to encamp before Banyas. From there he sent raiders into Galilee and through the Lebanon to destroy the harvests between Sidon and Beirut. King Baldwin gathered together the forces of the kingdom and summoned Raymond of Tripoli to join him. They marched up through Tiberias and Safed to Toron.

[1] Sembat the Constable, p. 624; Vahram, *Rhymed Chronicle*, p. 509. For Roupen's marriage, see below, p. 422.

[2] William of Tyre, xxii, 5, p. 1069. The date of this marriage and even the bride's name are disputed. The *Lignages* (v, p. 446) call her Irene and give her a daughter called Constance, otherwise unknown. It is unknown whether she was a Comnena or related to the Emperor through her mother. Rey, 'Histoire des Princes d'Antioche', *Revue de l'Orient Latin*, 1896, ii, pp. 379–82, believes her to have been Bohemond's first wife. It is more probable that his first wife was Orgillosa of Harenc, who appears on charters 1170–5 (Röhricht, *Regesta*, pp. 125, 139). William definitely says that Bohemond left Theodora to live with Sibylla.

There they learnt that Faruk-Shah and a party of raiders were coming back from the coast laden with booty. They moved north to intercept them in the valley of Marj Ayun, the Valley of Springs, between the Litani river and the upper Jordan. But Saladin had noticed from an observation post on a hill north of Banyas that the flocks on the opposite side of the Jordan were scattering in panic. He realized that the Frankish army was passing by and set out in pursuit. On 10 June 1179, while the royal army routed Faruk-Shah at Marj Ayun, Count Raymond and the Templars moved on a little ahead towards the Jordan. By the entrance of the valley they came on Saladin's army. The Templars joined battle at once; but Saladin's counter-attack drove them back in confusion on Baldwin's troops. These, too, were forced back; and before long the whole Christian army was in flight. The King and Count Raymond were able with part of their men to cross the Litani and shelter at the great castle of Beaufort, high above the western bank. All the men left beyond the river were massacred or later rounded up. Some of the fugitives did not stop at Beaufort but made straight for the coast. On the way they met Reynald of Sidon with his local troops. They told him that he was too late; so he turned back, though had he advanced to the Litani he might have saved many other fugitives.

Amongst Saladin's prisoners were Odo of Saint-Amand, Grand Master of the Temple, whose rashness had been the prime cause of the rout, Baldwin of Ibelin and Hugh of Galilee. Hugh was soon ransomed by his mother, the Countess of Tripoli, for 55,000 Tyrian dinars. For Baldwin of Ibelin Saladin demanded 150,000 dinars, a King's ransom, so highly did he rate Baldwin's importance. After a few months Baldwin was released on the return of a thousand Moslem prisoners and on his promise to find the money. It was proposed to exchange Odo for an important Moslem prisoner; but the Grand Master was too proud to admit that anyone could be of equal value to him. He remained in a dungeon at Damascus till his death the following year.

Saladin did not follow up his victory by an invasion of Palestine, perhaps because he had heard of the arrival there of a great company of knights from France, led by Henry II of Champagne, Peter of Courtenay and Philip, Bishop of Beauvais. Instead, he attacked Baldwin's castle at Jacob's Ford. After a siege of five days, from 24 to 29 August, he succeeded in mining the walls and forcing an entrance. The defenders were put to death and the castle rased to the ground. The French visitors would not go out to try to save the castle but soon returned home. Once more the Crusaders from the West had been utterly ineffectual.[1]

After the Egyptian fleet had carried out a successful raid in October on the shipping in the very port of Acre, and after a great Moslem foray into Galilee early in the new year, King Baldwin sent to ask Saladin for a truce. Saladin agreed. There had been a terrible drought throughout the winter and early spring; and the whole of Syria was faced with famine. No one desired raids that might damage the meagre harvests. And Saladin had probably decided that the conquest of Aleppo should precede the conquest of Jerusalem. A two-years' truce was fixed by a treaty signed by representatives of Baldwin and of Saladin in May 1180. Tripoli was excluded from the truce; but after the Egyptian navy had raided the port of Tortosa and Saladin had been checked in a raid on the Buqaia, he made a similar treaty with Raymond.[2] In the autumn he marched northwards to the Euphrates, where the Ortoqid prince, Nur ed-Din of Hisn Kaifa, who had become his ally, had quarrelled with Kilij Arslan the Seldjuk. Nur ed-Din had married the Sultan's daughter, but neglected her in favour of a dancing-girl. On 2 October 1180 Saladin held a congress near Samosata; the Ortoqid princes were there and envoys from

---

[1] William of Tyre, XXI, 27–30, pp. 1052–9; Ernoul, pp. 53–4; Abu Shama, pp. 194–202; Ibn al-Athir, pp. 635–6; Maqrisi, ed. Blochet, *Revue de l'Orient Latin*, vol. VIII, pp. 530–1. There is some doubt whether Odo of Saint-Amand was in fact killed, as a Bull of Pope Alexander III suggests that he lived on as a prisoner. See d'Albon, 'La Mort d'Odon de Saint-Amand' in *Revue de l'Orient Latin*, vol. XII, pp. 279–82.

[2] William of Tyre, XXII, 1–3, pp. 1053–6; Abu Shama, p. 211; Ibn al-Athir, p. 642.

Kilij Arslan, from Saif ed-din of Mosul and from Roupen of Armenia. They solemnly swore to keep peace with one another for two years to come.[1]

King Baldwin spent the respite in an attempt to build up a Christian front against Islam. William of Tyre, Archbishop since 1175, went to Rome to a Lateran council in 1179 and on his way back visited Constantinople during the last days of the year. The Emperor Manuel was as courteous and friendly as ever; but William could see that he was a dying man. He had never recovered from the shock of the battle of Myriocephalum. But he still showed great interest in Syria. William stayed there for seven months. He was present at the great ceremonies when Manuel's daughter Maria, a spinster of twenty-eight, married Rainier of Montferrat, Sibylla's brother-in-law, and Manuel's son, Alexius, aged ten, married the Princess Agnes of France, aged nine. He returned with Imperial envoys as far as Antioch.[2] The Armenian Prince Roupen was eager to strengthen his alliance with the Franks. Early in 1181 he came on a pilgrimage to Jerusalem, and there he married the Lady Isabella of Toron, the daughter of Stephanie of Oultrejourdain.[3] Even the Syrian Jacobites proclaimed their loyalty to the united Christian cause when their Patriarch, the historian Michael, visited Jerusalem and had a long interview with the King.[4]

There were hopes, too, of an ally from the Farther East. Since 1150 a letter purporting to be written by that great potentate Prester John to the Emperor Manuel had been circulating through western Europe. Though it was almost certainly the forgery of a German bishop, its account of the Priest-King's wealth and piety was too good not to be believed. In 1177 the Pope sent his doctor Philip with a message asking for information and for aid. It

[1] Ibn al-Athir, pp. 639–40.
[2] William of Tyre, XXII, 4, pp. 1066–8.
[3] Sembat the Constable, p. 627. Ernoul, p. 31, refers to the marriage, calling Roupen the son of Thoros. He also (pp. 25–30) tells of a visit of Thoros to Jerusalem, unrecorded elsewhere and probably mythical.
[4] Michael the Syrian, III, p. 379.

seems that Philip ended his journey in Abyssinia; but it had no concrete result.[1]

But still no powerful knight came from the West, not even to accept the offer of the hand of Princess Sibylla and the succession to the throne. Frederick of Tyre, when he was in Rome, had sent to Hugh III of Burgundy, of the royal Capetian line, to beg him to accept the candidature. Hugh agreed at first, but preferred to remain in France. Meanwhile, Sibylla herself had fallen in love with Baldwin of Ibelin. The family of Ibelin, though its origins had been modest, was now in the forefront of the Palestinian nobility. On the death of Balian the Old, the founder of the family, Ibelin itself was given to the Hospitallers; but Ramleh passed to his eldest son Hugh, and on Hugh's death to his brother Baldwin, who had married but repudiated, on the convenient excuse of kinship, the heiress of Beisan. The youngest brother, Balian, was now the husband of Queen Maria Comnena, and lord of her dower-town of Nablus. Baldwin and Balian were the most influential of all the local nobles; and despite his undistinguished pedigree Baldwin's marriage to Sibylla would have been popular throughout the land. Before any betrothal was arranged, Baldwin was captured at Marj Ayun. Sibylla wrote to him to his jail to assure him of her love. But when he was released she told him coldly that she could not contemplate marriage while he still owed a vast ransom. Her argument was reasonable, if discouraging; so Baldwin, not knowing how to raise the money, journeyed to Constantinople and begged it from the Emperor. Manuel, with his love of generous gestures, paid it all. Baldwin came back triumphant to Palestine in the early spring of 1180, only to find Sibylla betrothed to another man.[2]

The Lady Agnes never liked the relatives of her various

[1] Röhricht, *Regesta*, pp. 67, 145. For the Prester John Legend, see Marinescu, 'Le Prêtre Jean' in *Bulletin de la Section Historique de l'Académie Roumaine*, vol. x.

[2] The story of Baldwin of Ibelin's love affair is given only by Ernoul, pp. 48, 56–9. Ernoul was in the service of Baldwin's brother Balian and was therefore well informed about the family.

husbands and disapproved of the Ibelins. Some years before a knight from Poitou, Amalric, second son of the Count of Lusignan, had arrived in Palestine. He was a good soldier; and on Humphrey of Toron's death he was appointed Constable. About the same time he married Baldwin of Ibelin's daughter Eschiva. He was also Agnes's lover. He had in France a young brother called Guy. With Agnes's backing he began to tell Sibylla of the extraordinary good looks and charm of this youth till at last she begged him to bring him out to Palestine. While Baldwin was at Constantinople Amalric hurried home to fetch Guy, and to prepare him for the part that he was to play. Sibylla found him as handsome as she had been told and announced that she intended to marry him. The King, her brother, protested in vain; for Guy, as anyone could see, was a weak and foolish boy. The Palestinian barons were furious to realize that they might have as their future king this youngest son of a petty French noble whose only distinction was his descent from the water-fairy Melusine. But Agnes and Sibylla pestered the sick weary King till he gave his consent. At Easter 1180 Guy was married to Sibylla and was enfeoffed with the counties of Jaffa and Ascalon.[1]

For political as well as for personal reasons the Ibelins were disgusted, and the breach between them and the Courtenays, supported by Reynald of Châtillon, grew greater. In October 1180 the King tried to bring them together by betrothing his half-sister Isabella to Humphrey IV of Toron. Isabella was Balian of Ibelin's stepdaughter and Humphrey Reynald of Châtillon's stepson. Humphrey was, moreover, as grandson and heir of the great Constable and heir-apparent through his mother of the fief of Oultrejourdain, the most eligible of the local nobility, whom the marriage might be expected to gratify. Owing to the youth of the Princess, who was only eight, the actual ceremony was post-

---

[1] William of Tyre, xxii, 1, pp. 1064–5; Ernoul, pp. 59–60; Benedict of Peterborough, i, p. 343, who reports that Sibylla had already taken Guy as her lover. When the King discovered this, he wished to put Guy to death, but at the request of the Templars he spared him and allowed the marriage.

poned for three years.[1] But the betrothal did no good. A few days later the Courtenays showed their power in the appointment of a new Patriarch. The Patriarch Amalric died on 6 October. On 16 October the Chapter of Jerusalem, under pressure from the Lady Agnes, elected as his successor Heraclius, Archbishop of Caesarea. He was a barely literate priest from the Auvergne whose good looks Agnes had found irresistible; and her favour had procured his steady advancement. His present mistress was the wife of a draper at Nablus, Paschia de Riveri, who was soon to be known throughout the realm as Madame la Patriarchesse. William of Tyre came bustling from his diocese to try to prevent the election, but in vain. The electors named him as their second choice; but the King, at his mother's bidding, confirmed the appointment of Heraclius.[2]

Power was now firmly in the hands of the Courtenays and the Lusignans and their allies, Reynald of Châtillon and the new Patriarch. In April 1181 they struck at William of Tyre, who, as the King's old tutor, was dangerous to them. On a trivial excuse Heraclius excommunicated him. After fruitless attempts to heal the breach, William left in 1182 or 1183 for Rome, to plead his cause at the papal Court. He stayed on there; and there he died, poisoned, men said, by an emissary sent by the Patriarch.[3] Raymond of Tripoli was the next to be attacked. When early in

---

[1] William of Tyre, xxii, 5, pp. 1068–9; Ernoul, pp. 81–2. According to William, Humphrey ceded his lands in Galilee to the King in return for the engagement. Baldwin gave Toron to his mother. Ibn Jubayr, ed. Wright, p. 304, says that it belongs to the 'sow, the mother of the pig who is lord of Acre' and Hunin to his uncle Joscelin.

[2] William of Tyre, xxii, 4, p. 1068, a brief notice carefully omitting any question of his own candidature. Ernoul, pp. 82–4, specifically saying that Agnes insisted on Heraclius's election, because 'pour sa biauté l'ama'; she had already made him Archbishop of Caesarea. He adds that William warned the canons against electing him. *Estoire d'Eracles*, ii, pp. 57–9, saying that William prophesied that the Cross, recovered by a Heraclius, would be lost by a Heraclius.

[3] Ernoul, pp. 84–6: *Estoire d'Eracles*, ii, pp. 57–9, saying that William was poisoned by a doctor that Heraclius sent to Rome, and that Heraclius subsequently visited Rome himself. The dates of William's departure and death are

1182 he prepared to cross from his county into his wife's territory of Galilee, the King's officers forbade him to enter the kingdom; for Agnes and her brother Joscelin had persuaded Baldwin that he was plotting against the Crown. Only after furious protests from the barons of the kingdom would Baldwin relent. He reluctantly consented to see Raymond, who convinced him of his innocence.[1]

The intrigues round the dying leper King would have been less dangerous had not the foreign situation been critical. On 24 September 1180, the Franks lost their most powerful ally, when the Emperor Manuel died at Constantinople. He had genuinely liked them and had genuinely worked for their benefit, except when it had clashed with the interests of his Empire. He had been a brilliant and impressive man, but not a great Emperor; for his ambition to dominate Christendom had led him into adventures that the Empire could no longer afford. His troops had been sent into Italy and into Hungary when they were needed on the Anatolian frontier or in the Balkans. He had treated his treasure-chest as though it were inexhaustible. The disaster at Myriocephalum was a deadly blow to his over-strained army; and in a long series of commercial concessions made to the Italian cities in return for immediate diplomatic advantages he had sapped the economic life of his subjects; and in consequence the Imperial treasury would never be full again. The splendour of his Court had dazzled the world into the belief that the Empire was greater than in fact it had become; and, had he lived longer, his fleet and his gold might yet have been of value to the Franks. His personality had held the Empire together; but with his death its decline became evident. He had fought against death, determinedly clinging to prophecies

unknown. His history breaks off at 1183. Heraclius visited Rome in 1184 (see below, p. 444). On the other hand William is mentioned in a charter of Pope Urban III, dated 17 October, 1186, as an assessor in a law suit between the Hospital and the Bishop of Buluniyas. (Röhricht, *Regesta, Additamenta,* p. 44.) Röhricht therefore assumes that he had returned to the Holy Land (*Geschichte der Kreuzzugen,* p. 491 n. 5). It is more likely that the papal chancery made a mistake over the name. Josias was Archbishop of Tyre by 21 October 1186 (Röhricht, *Regesta,* p. 173). [1] William of Tyre, XXII, 9, pp. 1077-9.

that offered him fourteen more years of life, and he made no effort to arrange for the regency that his son would need.[1]

The new Emperor, Alexius II, was aged eleven. According to the old-established precedent the Empress-Mother took over the regency. But the Empress Maria was a Latin from Antioch, the first Latin to be ruler of the Empire, and as a Latin she was disliked by the people of Constantinople. Manuel's love for the Latins had long been resented. The long sequence of ecclesiastical wrangles at Antioch had added to the bitterness of the Byzantines. The tumultuous passage of the Crusaders through imperial territory had never been forgotten, and there were memories of the massacres of Cyprus, and massacres by Venetians, Pisans and Genoese. Most hated of all were the Italian merchants who strutted through Constantinople, complacent in their control of the Empire's trade, obtained, often, by attacks on peaceful citizens in the provinces. The Empress took as her adviser and, it was thought, as her lover, a nephew of her husband, the Protosebastus Alexius Comnenus, the uncle of Queen Maria of Jerusalem. He was unpopular and unwise. Together they leaned on the Latin element and especially on the Italian merchants. The opposition to the Empress was led by her stepdaughter, the Porphyrogennete Maria and her husband Rainier of Montferrat. Their plot to murder the favourite failed; but when they took refuge in the Church of St Sophia he further offended the populace by attempting to profane the sanctuary. The Empress was forced to pardon the conspirators; but in her insecurity she begged her brother-in-law, Bela III of Hungary, to come to her rescue. Her husband's cousin, Andronicus Comnenus, forgiven after his career of seduction in the East, was now living in retirement in Pontus. His compatriots remembered his gallantry and glamour; and when his friends put him forward as a national leader there was a ready response. In August 1182 he marched across Anatolia. The few troops that did not rally to him were easily defeated. Soon the Empress was left in Constantinople

---

[1] See Chalandon, *op. cit.* pp. 605–8. William of Tyre, XXII, 5, p. 1069, reports his death.

with only the Latins to support her. As Andronicus approached the Bosphorus the people of Constantinople suddenly fell on all the Latins in the city. Latin arrogance had provoked the massacre; but its horrible course shocked many of the most patriotic of the Byzantines. Only a few Italian merchants survived. They took to their ships and sailed westward, raiding the coasts that they passed. The road to Constantinople was open to Andronicus.

His first action was to eliminate his rivals. The Protosebastus was imprisoned and cruelly blinded. The Porphyrogennete Maria and her husband suffered mysterious deaths. Then the Empress was condemned to be strangled and her young son was forced himself to sign the warrant. Andronicus became joint-Emperor; then, two months later, in November 1182, the boy Alexius II himself was murdered, and Andronicus, at the age of sixty-two, married his widow, the twelve-year-old Agnes of France.

Apart from these murders Andronicus began his reign well. He purged the civil service of its corrupt and supernumerary members; he insisted on the strict administration of justice; he forced the rich to pay their taxes and he protected the poor against exploitation. Never for centuries had the provinces been so well governed. But Andronicus was frightened, with good cause. Many of his kin were jealous of him and the aristocracy resented his policy; and foreign affairs were menacing. He realized the dreadful impression made in the West by the massacre of 1182 and hastened not only to make a treaty with Venice in which he promised a yearly indemnity as compensation for Venetian losses, but he also sought to placate the Pope by building a church for the Latin rite in the capital; and he encouraged western merchants to return. But the main enemies of Byzantium were the Hohenstaufen Emperor and the King of Sicily; and in 1184 an ominous marriage took place between the Emperor Frederick's son Henry and William II's sister and heiress, Constance. Knowing that the Sicilians were certain to attack him soon, Andronicus wished to be sure of his eastern frontier. He saw that Saladin was in the ascendant there; so, entirely reversing Manuel's policy, he made a treaty with

Saladin, giving him a free hand against the Franks in return for his alliance against the Seldjuks. It seems that details of the divisions of future conquests and spheres of influence were planned. But the treaty came to nothing; for Andronicus, fearful for his position at Constantinople, began to take repressive measures that increased in ferocity till no one in the capital felt safe. Not only did he strike at the aristocracy, but even merchants and humble workmen were arrested by his police on the flimsiest suspicion of conspiracy, and were blinded or sent to the scaffold. When in August 1185 a Sicilian army landed in Epirus and marched on Thessalonica, Andronicus panicked. His wholesale arrests and executions drove the populace into revolt; which broke out when an elderly and inoffensive cousin of the Emperor's, Isaac Angelus, succeeded in escaping from his jailers to the altar of St Sophia and appealed from there for help. Even his own bodyguard deserted Andronicus. He tried in vain to flee across to Asia, but he was captured and paraded round the city on a mangy camel, then tortured and torn to death by the furious mob. Isaac Angelus was proclaimed Emperor. He restored some sort of order and made a humiliating peace with the King of Sicily. But he was utterly ineffectual as a ruler. The ancient Empire had become a third-rate power with little influence in world-politics.[1]

The decline of Byzantium upset the balance of power in the East. The Princes of Armenia and Antioch were delighted, and celebrated their relief by quarrelling with each other. On the news of Manuel's death Bohemond III repudiated his Greek wife in order to marry a loose lady of Antioch called Sibylla. The Patriarch Aimery had not liked the Greek marriage, but he was shocked by the adultery. He excommunicated Bohemond, put the city under an interdict, and retired once more to Qosair. The nobles of Antioch hated Sibylla, with reason; for she was a spy who received an income from Saladin in return for information

[1] For the reign of Andronicus, see Nicetas Choniates, pp. 356–463. William of Tyre, XXII, 10–13, pp. 1079–86, gives a fairly well-informed account of Andronicus's accession.

about the strength and movements of the Frankish armies.
They supported Aimery. A civil war was breaking out, when
King Baldwin sent an ecclesiastical deputation, headed by the
Patriarch Heraclius, to arbitrate. In return for financial compensa-
tion Aimery agreed to raise the interdict but not the excom-
munication, but Sibylla was recognized as Princess. Many of the
nobles were dissatisfied with the settlement and fled to Roupen's
court. Relations between the two Princes were further complicated at the end of 1182, when the Byzantine governor of Cilicia,
Isaac Comnenus, in revolt against Andronicus, sought help from
Bohemond against Roupen and admitted his troops into Tarsus.
Bohemond promptly changed his mind and sold Tarsus and the
governor to Roupen, then repented of it. The Templars ransomed
Isaac on the understanding that the Cypriots, who sympathized
with him, should pay them back. Isaac thereupon retired to
Cyprus, where he set himself up as an independent Emperor and
forgot about the debt. Roupen next alarmed his neighbours by
swallowing up the little Armenian principality of the Hethou-
mians, which had lasted on at Lampron in the north-west of
Cilicia under the patronage of Constantinople. His extension of
power alarmed Bohemond, who in 1185 invited him to a banquet
of reconciliation at Antioch and arrested him on his arrival. But
Roupen's brother Leo finished off the conquest of the Hethou-
mians and attacked Antioch. Roupen was released on ceding
Mamistra and Adana to Bohemond; but on his return to Cilicia
he soon recovered them and made himself master of the whole
province. Bohemond made various ineffectual raids but achieved
nothing more.[1]

These deplorable squabbles between the petty Christian rulers
were very convenient for Saladin. Neither Byzantium nor even

[1] William of Tyre, XXII, 6–7, pp. 1071–4; William of Tyre, *Latin Continuation*, p. 208; Ernoul, p. 9; Nicetas Choniates, pp. 376–7; Neophytus, *De Calamitatibus Cypri*, p. clxxxvii; Michael the Syrian, III, pp. 389–94; Sembat the
Constable, p. 628; Vahram, *Rhymed Chronicle*, pp. 508–10. For Sibylla's spying,
see Ibn al-Athir, pp. 729–30; Abu Shama, p. 374.

the Franks of northern Syria would impede his progress nor send help to the kingdom of Jerusalem. The only Christian state in the East that commanded respect amongst the Moslems was the distant kingdom of Georgia, at present engaged in growing at the expense of the Seldjuk princes of Iran, whose difficulties were very convenient to the Sultan.[1] Under these circumstances it was essential for the kingdom to keep the truce of 1180. But Reynald of Châtillon, lord now of Oultrejourdain, could not understand a policy that ran counter to his wishes. By the terms of the truce Christian and Moslem merchants could pass freely through each other's territory. It irked Reynald to see the rich Moslem caravans passing unscathed so close to him. In the summer of 1181 he yielded to temptation and led his local troops out eastward into Arabia, to Taima, near the road from Damascus to Mecca. Close to the oasis he fell upon a caravan that was travelling peacefully to Mecca and made off with all its goods. He seems even to have contemplated moving down to attack Medina; but Saladin, who was in Egypt, sent a hasty expedition under his nephew Faruk-Shah from Damascus into Oultrejourdain, which brought Reynald hurrying home. Saladin complained to King Baldwin of the breach of the treaty and demanded compensation. Baldwin admitted the justice of the claim; but in spite of his urgent representations, Reynald refused to make any amends. His friends at the Court supported him, till Baldwin weakly let the matter drop. But Saladin followed it up. A few months later a convoy of fifteen hundred pilgrims was forced by the weather to land in Egypt near Damietta, ignorant that the truce had been violated. Saladin threw them all into chains and sent to Baldwin offering to release them as soon as the merchandise pillaged by Reynald was returned. Once again Reynald refused to give anything back. War was now inevitable.[2]

---

[1] For Georgian history under King George III (1156–84), see *Georgian Chronicle*, pp. 231–7. He was succeeded by his daughter, the great Queen Thamar. See Allen, *History of the Georgian People*, pp. 102–4.

[2] William of Tyre, XXII, 14, p. 1087, omitting to tell why Saladin arrested the pilgrims; Ernoul, pp. 54–6; Abu Shama, pp. 214–18; Ibn al-Athir, pp. 647–50.

Moslem Unity

Reynald and his friends persuaded the King to concentrate the royal army in Oultrejourdain, to catch Saladin as he came up from Egypt. The Ibelins and Raymond vainly pointed out that this would expose Palestine to him should he get by. Saladin left Egypt on 11 May 1182. As he bade a ceremonious farewell to his ministers, a voice from the crowd shouted out a line of poetry whose meaning was that he would never see Cairo again. The prophecy came true. He took his army across the Sinai desert to Akaba, and moved northward without difficulty, well to the east of the Frankish army, destroying the crops as he went. When he arrived at Damascus he found that Faruk-Shah had already raided Galilee and sacked the villages on the slopes of Mount Tabor, taking twenty thousand head of cattle and one thousand prisoners. On his return Faruk-Shah attacked the fortress of Habis Jaldak, carved out of the rock above the river Yarmuk beyond the Jordan. A tunnel that he cut through the rock put it at his mercy; and the garrison, Christian Syrians with no great wish to die for the Franks, promptly surrendered. Saladin spent three weeks in Damascus, then with Faruk-Shah and a large army left on 11 July and crossed into Palestine round the south of the Sea of Galilee. The King, aware now of the folly of his previous strategy, had come back from Oultrejourdain and marched up the west bank of the river, bringing the Patriarch and the True Cross to bless his arms. The two armies met beneath the Hospitallers' castle of Belvoir. In the fierce battle that followed the Franks held their ground against Saladin's attacks, but their counter-attacks did not break the Moslem lines. At the end of the day each side retired, claiming the victory.[1]

It had been a check for Saladin as the invader, but only temporary. In August he once again crossed the frontier in a lightning march through the mountains to Beirut. At the same moment

___

[1] William of Tyre, xxii, 14–16, pp. 1087–95; Abu Shama, pp. 218–22; Ibn al-Athir, pp. 651–3. The verse sung at Saladin when he left Cairo ran, 'Enjoy the perfume of the ox-eyes of Nejd. After tonight there will be no more ox-eyes.'

0

his fleet, summoned from Egypt by the pigeon-post that operated between Damascus and Cairo, appeared off the coast. But Beirut was well fortified; and its bishop, Odo, organized a brave, vigorous defence. Baldwin, on the news, rushed his army up from Galilee, only pausing to collect the ships that lay in the harbours of Acre and Tyre. Failing to take the city by assault before the Franks arrived, Saladin withdrew.[1] It was time for him to deal with business that was more urgent.

Saif ed-Din of Mosul died on 29 June 1180, leaving only young children. The emirs of Mosul invited his brother, Izz ed-Din, to succeed him. Eighteen months later, on 4 December 1181, as-Salih of Aleppo died suddenly of a colic, universally attributed to poison. He was only eighteen, a bright, intelligent boy who might have been a great ruler. On his death-bed he begged his emirs to offer the succession to his cousin of Mosul, so as to unite the family lands against Saladin. Izz ed-Din arrived at Aleppo at the end of the year and was given an enthusiastic welcome. Messengers came from the emir of Hama to offer him allegiance. But the two years' truce with Saladin had not run out; and Izz ed-Din refused their offer, more from indolence than from honour. He had enough to worry him: for in February 1182 his brother Imad ed-Din of Sinjar claimed a share in the inheritance and intrigued with the commander of the army of Aleppo, Kukburi. In May Izz ed-Din returned to Mosul, and Imad ed-Din gave him Sinjar in return for Aleppo. Kukburi was rewarded with the emirate of Harran. From there he plotted with his Ortoqid neighbours, the princes of Hisn Kaifa and Birejik, against the princes of Aleppo and Mosul and the Ortoqid Qutb ed-Din of Mardin; and the conspirators called Saladin to their aid. The truce among the Moslem princes ended in September. The day that it was over Saladin crossed the frontier and after a feint attack on Aleppo he moved over the Euphrates at Birejik. The towns of the Jezireh fell before him, Edessa, Saruj, and Nisibin. He pressed on to Mosul and began

[1] William of Tyre, XXII, 17–18, pp. 1096–1101; Abu Shama, p. 223; Ibn al-Athir, pp. 653.

the siege of the city on 10 November. Once again he was thwarted by fortifications too strong to storm. His spiritual master, the Caliph an-Nasir, shocked at this war between fellow-Moslems, tried to negotiate a peace. The Seldjuk ruler of Persarmenia and the Prince of Mardin prepared to send a relieving force. So Saladin retired to Sinjar, which he took by storm after a fortnight's siege. For once he was unable to restrain his soldiers from pillaging the city; but he released the governor and sent him honourably attended to Mosul. Izz ed-Din and his allies marched out to meet him near Mardin, but sent ahead to suggest a truce. When Saladin answered truculently that he would meet them on the battlefield, they dispersed and fled to their homes. He did not pursue them, but went north to conquer Diarbekir, the richest and greatest fortress of the Jezireh, with the finest library in Islam. He gave the city to the Prince of Hisn Kaifa. After reorganizing the Jezireh, setting each city to be held as a fief under an emir that he trusted, he appeared again, on 21 May, before Aleppo.[1]

When Saladin moved against them, both Imad ed-Din and Izz ed-Din had sought help from the Franks. An embassy from Mosul promised them a yearly subsidy of 10,000 dinars, with the retrocession of Banyas and Habis Jaldak, and the release of any Christian prisoner that might be found in Saladin's possession, if they would make a diversion against Damascus. It was a hopeful moment; for a few days after Saladin invaded the Jezireh, his nephew Faruk-Shah, governor of Damascus, suddenly died. King Baldwin, accompanied by the Patriarch and the True Cross, thereupon led a raid through the Hauran, which sacked Ezra and reached Bosra, while Raymond of Tripoli recaptured Habis Jaldak. Early in December 1182 Raymond led a cavalry raid that again penetrated to Bosra; and a few days later the royal army set out against Damascus and encamped at Dareiya in the suburbs. It has a famous mosque, which Baldwin spared after receiving a delegation from the Christians of Damascus warning that

[1] Beha ed-Din, *P.P.T.S.* pp. 79–86; Kemal ad-Din, ed. Blochet, pp. 159–60; Ibn al-Athir, pp. 656–7.

reprisals would be taken against their churches should it be harmed. The King did not try to attack the city itself, and soon retired laden with booty, to spend Christmas at Tyre. He planned a further campaign for the spring, but early in the new year he fell desperately ill of a fever at Nazareth. For some weeks he lay between life and death; and his disease immobilized his army.[1] Farther north, Bohemond III was powerless to take any action against Saladin. He sent to his camp before Aleppo and concluded a four years' truce with him. It enabled him to repair the defences of his capital.[2]

At Aleppo Imad ed-Din made little effort to oppose Saladin. He was unpopular there; and when Saladin offered to give him his old home at Sinjar together with Nisibin, Saruj and Rakka, to hold as a fief, he gladly complied. On 12 June 1183 Saladin took possession of Aleppo. Five days later Imad ed-Din departed for Sinjar, honourably escorted, but mocked by the crowds of the city that he abandoned so lightly. On 18 June Saladin made his formal entry and rode up to the castle.[3]

On 24 August the Sultan returned to Damascus, which was to be his capital.[4] His Empire now stretched from Cyrenaica to the Tigris. For more than two centuries past there had not been so powerful a Moslem prince. He had the wealth of Egypt behind him. The great cities of Damascus and Aleppo were under his direct government. Around them and north-eastward as far as the walls of Mosul were military fiefs on whose rulers he could rely. The Caliph at Baghdad supported him. Izz ed-Din at Mosul was cowed by him. The Seldjuk Sultan in Anatolia sought his friendship, and the Seldjuk princes of the East were powerless to oppose him. The Christian Empire of Byzantium was no longer a danger to him. It only remained now to suppress the alien intruders whose possession of Palestine and the Syrian littoral was a lasting shame to Islam.

[1] William of Tyre, xxii, 20–22, 25, pp. 1102–16; Ibn al-Athir, pp. 155–9.
[2] Ibn al-Athir, p. 662.
[3] Beha ed-Din, *P.P.T.S.* pp. 86–8; Ibn al-Athir, pp. 662; Abu Shama, pp. 225–8; Kemal ad-Din, ed. Blochet, p. 167; William of Tyre, xxii, 24, pp. 1113–14, who well understood the significance of Saladin's conquest of Aleppo.   [4] Beha ed-Din, *P.P.T.S.* p. 89.

CHAPTER II

THE HORNS OF HATTIN

'Our end is near, our days are fulfilled; for our end is come.' LAMENTATIONS IV, 18

When King Baldwin rose from his sick-bed at Nazareth it was clear that he would no more be able to govern the country. His leprosy had been aggravated by his fever. He had lost the use of his arms and legs; and they were beginning to decay. His sight had almost gone. His mother, his sister Sibylla and the Patriarch Heraclius kept guard over him and persuaded him to hand the regency to Sibylla's husband, Guy of Lusignan. Guy was to be in complete control of the kingdom, except only the city of Jerusalem, which, with a revenue of 10,000 besants, the King reserved for himself. The barons of the realm reluctantly accepted the King's decision.[1]

Reynald of Châtillon was absent from these deliberations. When he heard of Saladin's departure to the north in the autumn of 1182, he set in motion a project that he had long had in mind, to launch a squadron on the Red Sea to raid the rich sea-caravans to Mecca and even to attack the Holy City of Islam itself. Towards the end of the year he marched down to Aila at the head of the Gulf of Akaba, bringing galleys that he built with timber from the forests of Moab and tried out on the waters of the Dead Sea. Aila, which had been held by the Moslems since 1170, fell to him; but the fortress on the island close by, the Ile de Graye of the Frankish historians, held out; and Reynald remained with two of his ships to blockade it. The rest of his fleet set gaily out, with local pirates to pilot them. They sailed down the African coast of the Red

[1] William of Tyre, XXII, 25, pp. 1116–17.

436

Sea, raiding the little coastal towns that they passed, and eventually attacked and sacked Aidib, the great Nubian port opposite to Mecca. There they captured richly laden merchantships from Aden and from India; and a landing-party pillaged a huge defence-less caravan that had come over the desert from the Nile valley. From Aidib the corsairs crossed over to the Arabian coast. They burnt the shipping at al-Hawra and Yambo, the ports of Medina, and penetrated to ar-Raghib, one of the ports of Mecca itself. Close by they sank a pilgrim-ship bound for Jedda. The whole Moslem world was horrified. Even the Princes of Aleppo and Mosul, who had called upon Frankish help, were ashamed to have allies that planned such an outrage on the Faith. Saladin's brother Malik al-Adil, governor of Egypt, took action. He sent the Egyptian admiral, Husam ed-Din Lulu, with a fleet manned by Maghrabi sailors from North Africa, in pursuit of the Franks. Lulu first relieved the castle of Graye and recaptured Aila, from which Reynald himself had already retired; then he caught up with the corsair fleet off al-Hawra, destroying it and capturing almost all the men on board. A few of them were sent to Mecca, to be ceremoniously executed at the Place of Sacrifice at Mina during the next Pilgrimage. The rest were taken to Cairo, and there they were beheaded. Saladin vowed solemnly that Reynald should never be forgiven for his attempted outrage.[1]

On 17 September 1183 Saladin left Damascus with a great army to invade Palestine. On the 29th he crossed the Jordan, just south of the Sea of Galilee and entered Beisan, whose inhabitants had all fled to the safety of the walls of Tiberias. On the news of his coming Guy of Lusignan summoned the full force of the kingdom, strengthened by two rich visiting Crusaders, God-frey III, Duke of Brabant, and the Aquitanian Ralph of Mauléon, and their men. With Guy were Raymond of Tripoli, the Grand

---

[1] Abu Shama, pp. 231–5; Ibn al-Athir, p. 658: Maqrisi, ed. Blochet, *Revue de l'Orient Latin*, vol. VIII, pp. 550–1. Ernoul (pp. 69–70), the only Frankish chronicler to mention the raid, speaks of it as a scientific expedition. Ibn Jubayr (ed. Wright, p. 49) saw the Frankish prisoners at Cairo.

Master of the Hospital, Reynald of Châtillon, the Ibelin brothers, Reynald of Sidon and Walter of Caesarea. Young Humphrey IV of Toron came to join them with his stepfather's forces from Oultrejourdain; but he was ambushed by the Moslems on the slopes of Mount Gilboa, and most of his men were slain. Saladin

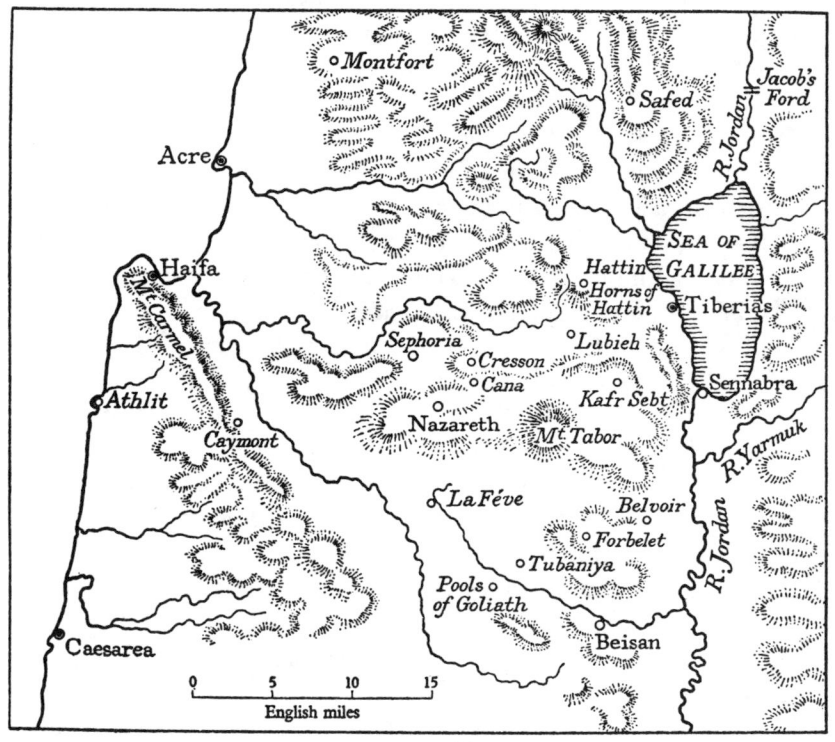

Map 6. Galilee.

then sent detachments to capture and destroy the little forts of the neighbourhood, while others sacked the Greek convent on Mount Tabor but failed to break through the strong walls of the Latin establishment on the summit of the hill. He himself encamped with his main army by the fountain of Tubaniya, on the site of the ancient city of Jezreel.

438

The Franks had assembled at Sephoria and marched on into the plain of Jezreel on 1 December. The advance-guard, under the Constable Amalric, was at once attacked by the Moslems, but the timely arrival of the Ibelins with their troops rescued it. The Christians encamped at the Pools of Goliath opposite to Saladin, who then extended his wings so as almost to encircle them. For five days the armies remained stationary. It was difficult for supplies to come through to the Christians. After a day or two the Italian mercenaries complained of hunger; and only the timely discovery of fish in the Pools of Goliath saved the army from starvation. Most of the soldiers, including the knights from France and the irrepressible Reynald, wished to attack the Moslems. Guy hesitated and dithered; but Raymond and the Ibelins firmly insisted that to provoke a fight against such superior numbers would be fatal. The army must remain on the defensive. They were right. Saladin many times tried to lure them out. When he failed he lifted his camp on 8 October and moved back behind the Jordan.[1]

Guy's behaviour had shocked both the soldiery who believed him to be a coward and the barons who knew him to be weak. On his return to Jerusalem he quarrelled with the King. Baldwin felt that the air of Tyre would be kinder to him than the windy heights of Jerusalem. He asked his brother-in-law to make an exchange of the two cities. Guy received the request rudely; whereupon Baldwin with an access of angry energy summoned his chief vassals and on their advice deposed Guy from the regency. Instead, on 23 March 1183, he proclaimed as his heir his nephew Baldwin, Sibylla's son by her first marriage, a child of six years, and tried to persuade his sister to have her marriage annulled. Meanwhile, though he could not move without help, and could no longer sign his name, he resumed the government himself. Guy's response was to retire to his county of Ascalon and Jaffa and there throw off his allegiance to the Crown. Baldwin

---

[1] William of Tyre, XXII, 26–7, pp. 1118–24; Ernoul, pp. 96–102; Beha ed-Din, *P.P.T.S.* pp. 90–1; Abu Shama, pp. 243–6.

seized Jaffa, which he put under the direct authority of the Crown, but Guy defied him in Ascalon. In vain the Patriarch Heraclius and the Grand Masters of the Temple and the Hospital interceded for the rebel. The King lost his temper with them and banished them from the Court. He had summoned them to order them to preach the Crusade in western Europe, but some months passed before they would now consent to go.[1]

The council of barons on whose advice the King deposed Guy was composed of Bohemond of Antioch, Raymond of Tripoli, the Lord of Caesarea, and the two Ibelins. The Lord of Oultre-jourdain was not present. The time had come for the marriage to take place between the Princess Isabella, now aged eleven, and Humphrey of Toron, aged about seventeen. Reynald determined that the ceremony should be celebrated with all the pomp at his disposal at his castle of Kerak, to which the bridegroom was heir. During the month of November guests began to arrive at the castle. Many of them, such as the bride's mother, Queen Maria Comnena, were Reynald's personal enemies; but they came in a last attempt to heal the breach between the warring factions. With the guests arrived entertainers, dancers, jugglers and musicians from all over the Christian East. Suddenly the festivities were interrupted by the terrible news that Saladin was approaching with his army.

The destruction of Kerak and its godless lord ranked high among Saladin's ambitions. So long as Reynald held his great castle he could intercept all the traffic that tried to pass between Syria and Egypt; and experience had shown that no treaty could restrain him. On 20 November Saladin was joined by reinforcements from Egypt and encamped before the walls. The farmers and shepherds of the countryside, Christian Syrians, drove their flocks for safety within the town, and many took refuge in the court-yards of the castle. Saladin at once attacked the lower town and forced an entrance. Reynald was only able to escape back into the

[1] William of Tyre, XXII, 29, pp. 1127–8. William says that Baldwin V was crowned on this occasion.

castle owing to the heroism of one of his knights, who single-handed defended the bridge over the fosse between the town and the citadel till it could be destroyed behind him. With a fine show of bravura the wedding-ceremonies were continued in the castle. While rocks were hurled at its walls, the singing and dancing went on within. The Lady Stephanie, mother of the bridegroom, herself prepared dishes from the bridal feast which she sent out to Saladin. He in return asked in which tower the young pair were housed and gave orders that it should not be bombarded by his siege-engines. But otherwise he did not relax his efforts. His nine great mangonels were in continuous action, and his workmen almost filled up the fosse.

Messengers had hurried to Jerusalem to beg the King for help. He summoned the royal army which he put under the command of Count Raymond; but he insisted on coming himself in his litter with his men. They hastened down past Jericho and up the road by Mount Nebo. On his approach Saladin, whose engines had made little effect on the strong walls of the fortress, lifted the siege and on 4 December moved back towards Damascus. The King was carried in triumph into Kerak; and the wedding-guests were free to go home.[1] Their experience had not ended their discord, from which the young bride suffered the most. Her mother-in-law, no doubt at Reynald's request, forbade her to see her mother; and her mother, deep in party intrigues that were dear to her Greek blood, regarded her as half a traitor. Only her husband was kind to her. Humphrey of Toron was a youth of extraordinary beauty and great learning, more fitted in his tastes to be a girl than

[1] William of Tyre, XXII, 28, 30, pp. 1124-7, 1129-30; Ernoul, pp. 102-6; he alone tells of the marriage feast at which, as Balian's squire, he may have been present. He believed that Saladin as a boy had been a hostage at Kerak, where the Lady Stephanie had dandled him on her knee. No other source mentions Saladin's early captivity. As Saladin was born in 1137 and Stephanie probably not before 1145—she married her first husband about 1162/3 and girls married young in Palestine—the story is improbable. Abu Shama, p. 248; Beha ed-Din, *P.P.T.S.* pp. 91-2; Maqrisi, ed. Blochet, *Revue de l'Orient Latin*, vol. IX, pp. 13-14.

a man. But he was gentle and considerate to his child-wife; and she loved him.[1]

Next autumn Saladin once again marched against Kerak, with an army to which his Ortoqid vassals sent contingents. Once again the huge fortifications were too much for him. He could not lure the defenders out to fight on the slopes below the town; and once again, when an army from Jerusalem approached, he retired into his own territory, only leaving a detachment to raid Galilee and to pillage the country as far south as Nablus. Saladin himself returned to Damascus. There was still much to be done in the reorganization of his Empire. The time had not quite come for the elimination of the Christians.[2]

In Jerusalem the leper-King kept the reins of the government in his decaying hands. Guy still held Ascalon, refusing to admit royal officers into the town. But his friends the Patriarch and the Grand Masters were away in Europe, trying vainly to impress the Emperor Frederick and King Louis and King Henry with the perils awaiting the Christian East. The western potentates received them with honour and discussed plans for a great Crusade. But they each made excuses why they could not themselves participate. All that came of the mission was that a few individual knights took the Cross.[3]

In the autumn of 1184 Guy once again infuriated his brother-in-law. Ever since the Christian capture of Ascalon the Bedouin of the district had been allowed, on the payment of a small tribute to the King, to move as they pleased to pasture their flocks. Guy,

---

[1] See below, p. 448. The later history of the marriage belongs to the story of the Third Crusade. The author of the *Itinerarium Regis Ricardi* (p. 120) describes Humphrey as 'Vir feminae quam viro proprior, gestu mollis, sermone fructus'. Beha ed-Din (*P.P.T.S.* p. 288) reports of his beauty and says that he spoke Arabic well. *Estoire d'Eracles*, II, p. 152, tells of Isabella being forbidden to see her mother.

[2] Beha ed-Din, *P.P.T.S.* pp. 95-8; Abu Shama, pp. 249-56; letter of Baldwin IV to Heraclius, in Radulph of Diceto, II, pp. 27-8.

[3] For the mission, see Benedict of Peterborough, I, p. 338; Radulph of Diceto, II, pp. 32-3. Henry II consulted his council which told him not to go crusading.

annoyed because the tribute went to the King and not to himself,
fell on them one day and massacred them and annexed their
flocks.[1]

Baldwin was now bedridden and was never to rise again. He
saw how fatal had been the influence of his mother and her friends,
and sent for his cousin Raymond of Tripoli to take over the
administration. Meanwhile he prepared for his death. Before an
assembly of the barons, early in 1185, he announced his will. His
little nephew was to succeed to the throne. At the express wish
of the assembly Guy was not to have the regency, which was to go
to Raymond of Tripoli, who was to hold Beirut as payment for
his services. But Raymond refused the personal guardianship of
the little King, lest the boy, who seemed delicate, should die
young and he be accused of hastening his death. In view of the
boy's health the barons further swore that, should he die before he
reached the age of ten, Count Raymond should keep the regency
till the four great rulers of the West, the Pope, the Western
Emperor and the Kings of France and England, should arbitrate
between the claims of the Princesses Sibylla and Isabella. Meanwhile, in a last attempt to bring the factions together, the personal
guardianship of the boy was given to his great-uncle, Joscelin of
Courtenay, who now began to profess a cordial friendship
towards Raymond.[2]

[1] *Estoire d'Eracles*, II, p. 3.
[2] *Estoire d'Eracles*, II, p. 7; Ernoul, pp. 115–19 (the fullest account). He
places it after Saladin's second siege of Kerak (September 1184) and says that
Baldwin IV died soon afterwards. But William of Tyre (see above, p. 440
n. 1) tells of Baldwin V's coronation, giving the date of 20 November 1183.
As William probably died before the end of 1184, but wrote his last pages in
Rome, he may have known of Baldwin's decision to crown his nephew, ever
since Guy's disgrace in 1183, but have been mistaken in thinking that an actual
coronation had taken place. The legal rights of Sibylla and Isabella raised
a problem. An assize passed by Amalric I in 1171 allowed sisters to share fiefs,
according to the usual feudal custom in western Europe. Grandclaude, *op. cit.*
p. 340, believes that it concerned the succession to the throne. Queen Maria
had probably just given birth to her elder daughter. On the other hand the
children of a first marriage male and female were specifically given precedence
over those of a second marriage. (See La Monte, *Feudal Monarchy*, p. 36.) But

All the assembled barons swore to carry out the King's wishes. Among them was the Patriarch Heraclius, just back from the West, with the Grand Master of the Hospital, Roger of Les Moulins. The Grand Master of the Temple, Arnold of Toroga, had died during the journey. As his successor the Order had elected, after a stormy debate, Raymond's old enemy Gerard of Ridfort. Gerard also gave his assent to the King's will. The child was taken to the Church of the Holy Sepulchre and there, held in Balian of Ibelin's arms, he was crowned by the Patriarch.[1]

A few weeks later, in March 1185, King Baldwin IV was released by death from the agonies of his long disease. He was only twenty-four. Of all the Kings of Jerusalem he was the most unhappy. His ability was undoubted and his courage was superb. But from his sickbed he was powerless to control the intrigues around him and too often had yielded to the nagging influence of his evil mother and his foolish sister. At least he was spared the final humiliations that were to come to the kingdom.[2]

When the King's pathetic corpse had been buried in the Church of the Holy Sepulchre, Raymond as regent summoned the barons once more to ask them what policy he should follow. The winter rains had failed and there was a threat of famine. The only Crusader to come eastward was the old Marquis William of Montferrat, grandfather of the child-King; and he, after satisfying himself that all was well with his grandchild, settled down quietly in a fief in Galilee. His son Conrad, the King's uncle, set out to follow him but stopped on the way at Constantinople, where his brother Rainier had perished a few years before. There he offered his help to Rainier's avenger, the Emperor Isaac Angelus, whose

did the issue of the annulled marriage to Agnes take precedence over that of the imperial marriage to Maria? It is clear from the events of 1186 that public opinion supported Sibylla's claims (see below, p. 447). But the case was obscure enough to need mediation.

[1] *Estoire d'Eracles*, II, pp. 7-9; Ernoul, pp. 114, 118.

[2] Ernoul, pp. 118-19; *Estoire d'Eracles*, II, p. 9. Imad ed-Din (Abu Shama, p. 258) pays a tribute to Baldwin IV's memory.

sister he married. He forgot about his nephew and Palestine. It was clear to all the barons assembled in Jerusalem that till a large new Crusade could come the starving country could not face a war. They approved of Raymond's suggestion that a four-years' truce should be sought from Saladin.

Saladin on his side was willing. There had been a quarrel amongst his relatives in Egypt that needed a settlement; and he had heard that Izz ed-Din of Mosul was restive once more. The treaty was signed. Commerce was renewed between the Frankish states and their neighbours; and a flow of corn from the east saved the Christians from starvation.[1]

In April 1185 Saladin marched northward, crossing the Euphrates at Birejik on the 15th. There he was joined by Kukburi of Harran and by envoys from Izz ed-Din's vassals, the lords of Jezireh and Irbil. Izz ed-Din sent embassies to the Seldjuk rulers of Konya and of Persarmenia. The latter sent some troops to his aid; the former sent a threatening message to Saladin, but took no action. In June Saladin was before Mosul, refusing all Izz ed-Din's offers of peace, even when the Prince's aged mother came herself to plead with him. But Mosul was still too formidable a fortress. His troops began to sicken in the summer heat. When in August the Seldjuk Sultan of Persarmenia, Soqman II, suddenly died, Saladin moved northward to capture the Sultan's vassal cities of Diarbekir and Mayyafaraqin and to rest his men in the cooler air of the uplands. There he fell ill himself and rode, almost dying, to his friend Kukburi's castle at Harran. His brother, al-Adil, now governor of Aleppo, hastened to come with the best doctors of the East; but they could do nothing. Believing his end to be near and knowing that all his kinsmen were plotting for the inheritance, he made his emirs swear allegiance to his sons. Then, unexpectedly he began to mend. By January 1186 he was out of danger. At the end of February he received an embassy from Izz ed-Din and agreed to make peace. In a treaty signed by the ambassadors on

[1] Ernoul, pp. 121-8; *Estoire d'Eracles*, II, pp. 12-13; Beha ed-Din, *P.P.T.S.* pp. 104-5.

3 March Izz ed-Din became Saladin's vassal and was confirmed in his own possessions; but the lands across the Tigris south of Mosul, including Arbil and Shahrzur were put under emirs appointed by Saladin and owing him direct allegiance. Their presence guaranteed Izz ed-Din's loyalty.[1] Saladin himself was then at Homs, where Nasr ed-Din, Shirkuh's son and his own son-in-law, was emir. Nasr ed-Din had plotted for the throne of Syria during Saladin's illness. No one therefore was surprised when he was found dead in his bed on 5 March, after celebrating the Feast of Victims. The victim's child, Shirkuh II, a boy of twelve, was given the succession to Homs. Saladin confiscated much of his money, but the boy aptly quoted a passage from the Koran threatening torment to those that despoiled orphans and had it restored to him. In April Saladin was back in Damascus. His empire now stretched securely to the borders of Persia.[2]

The truce between the Christians and the Moslems was bringing back some prosperity to Palestine. Trade between the interior and the ports of Acre and Tyre was eagerly renewed, to the advantage of merchants of both religions. If peace could be maintained till some great Crusade could arrive from the West, then there might still be a future for the Kingdom. But fate was once more unkind to the Christians. About the end of August 1186 King Baldwin V died at Acre, not yet nine years old.[3]

The Regent Raymond and the Seneschal Joscelin were present at the death-bed. Professing himself anxious to work in with Raymond, Joscelin persuaded him to go to Tiberias and to invite the barons of the realm to meet him there, in security from the plots of the Patriarch, in order that the terms of Baldwin IV's will should be carried out. He himself would convey the little corpse

---

[1] Beha ed-Din, *P.P.T.S.* pp. 98–103; Kemal ad-Din, ed. Blochet, pp. 123–6; Abu Shama, p. 288; *Bustan*, p. 581.

[2] Abu'l Feda, p. 55. See Lane Poole, *Saladin*, pp. 194–5 (Shirkuh II quoted the verse, Koran, iv, 9); Beha ed-Din, *P.P.T.S.* pp. 103–4.

[3] Ernoul, p. 129; *Estoire d'Eracles*, II, p. 25.

to Jerusalem for burial. Raymond fell into the trap and went off in good faith. As soon as he was gone Joscelin sent troops that he could trust to occupy Tyre and Beirut and remained himself in Acre, where he proclaimed Sibylla as Queen. He dispatched the royal body to Jerusalem in charge of the Templars. His messengers summoned Sibylla and Guy from Ascalon to attend the funeral; and Reynald of Châtillon hurried to join them from Kerak.

Raymond discovered that he had been tricked. He rode down to Nablus, to Balian of Ibelin's castle, and, as lawful Regent of the realm, summoned the High Court of the barons. All his supporters hurried to join him. With Balian and his wife, Queen Maria, were her daughter Isabella with Humphrey of Toron, Baldwin of Ramleh, Walter of Caesarea, Reynald of Sidon, and all the tenants-in-chief of the Crown, with the exception of Reynald of Châtillon. There they received an invitation from Sibylla to attend her coronation. They replied by sending two Cistercian monks as envoys to Jerusalem, to remind the conspirators of the oath sworn to King Baldwin IV and to forbid any action to be taken till the Court had held its deliberations.

But Sibylla held Jerusalem and the seaports. The troops of the Seneschal Joscelin and the Constable Amalric, Guy's brother, were on her side, and Reynald had brought his men from Oultrejourdain. The Patriarch Heraclius, her mother's old lover, assured her of the support of the Church organization. The Grand Master of the Temple, Gerard of Ridfort, would do anything to spite his old enemy Raymond. Alone in Jerusalem the Grand Master of the Hospital was true to the oath that had been sworn. Amongst the people of Jerusalem there was much sympathy for Sibylla. She represented hereditary right; and though the throne was still nominally elective the claims of the heir could not be easily ignored. At the time of her mother's divorce Sibylla's legitimacy had been confirmed. Her brother had been King, and her son. Her one disadvantage was that her husband was disliked and despised.

The Patriarch and the Templars closed the gates of Jerusalem and posted guards, to prevent any attack from the barons at Nablus. They then made arrangements for the coronation. The royal insignia was kept in a coffer with three locks whose keys were in the care of the Patriarch and the two Grand Masters, each holding one. Roger of the Hospital refused to surrender his key for a purpose that he considered contrary to his oath; but at last, with a gesture of disgust, he threw it from his window. Neither he nor any of his knights would take part in the ceremony; which was held as soon as everything could be made ready. In view of Guy's unpopularity the Patriarch crowned Sibylla alone. But a second crown was placed by her side; and Heraclius after crowning her bade her use it to crown whatever man she thought worthy to govern the realm. She summoned Guy to approach her and kneel before her and placed the crown on his head. The assembled company then did homage to their new King and Queen. As he passed out of the church Gerard of Ridfort cried out aloud that this crown paid back the marriage of Botrun.

Against the fact of the coronation the High Court at Nablus could do little. Baldwin of Ibelin rose in the assembly to say that he for one would not stay in a country to be ruled by such a king and he advised all the barons to do likewise. But Raymond answered that all was not yet lost. They had with them, he said, the Princess Isabella and her husband Humphrey of Toron. Let them be crowned and brought to Jerusalem. Their rivals could not stand up against the united armies of all the barons, save only Reynald of Châtillon, and the sympathy of the Hospital. Raymond added that so long as he was Regent he could guarantee that Saladin would keep the truce. The barons agreed with him and swore to support him, even though it might mean civil war. But they counted without one of the principal actors. Humphrey was terrified at the fate in store for him; he had no wish to be king. He slipped away at once from Nablus and rode to Jerusalem. There he asked to see Sibylla. She spurned him at first, but as he stood sheepishly before her, scratching his head, she relented and

let him pour out his story. She listened graciously and herself took
him to see Guy, to whom he paid homage.[1]

Humphrey's defection defeated the barons. Raymond released
them from their oath, and one by one they went to Jerusalem and
offered their submission to Guy. Even Balian of Ibelin, the most
respected of them all, saw that nothing else could now be done.
But his brother Baldwin repeated his decision to abandon the
realm rather than accept Guy; and Raymond of Tripoli retired to
his wife's lands in Galilee, vowing that he, too, would never pay
homage to the new King. He would have loyally accepted
Isabella as Queen; but Humphrey's cowardice convinced him that
he himself was now the only worthy candidate for the throne.[2]

Soon afterwards King Guy held his first assembly of barons at
Acre. Raymond did not appear; and Guy announced that Beirut,
which Raymond had held as regent, was taken from him, and he
sent to tell him to render accounts for public money that he had
spent during his regency. Baldwin of Ibelin, who was present,
was summoned to pay homage by Reynald of Châtillon standing
at the King's side. He merely gave the King a formal salute,
telling him that he left his lands of Ramleh for his son Thomas who
would pay homage when he was old enough; he himself would
never do so. He left the kingdom a few days later and took service

---

[1] Ernoul, pp. 129–36, the fullest and most graphic account; *Estoire d'Eracles*,
II, pp. 25–31; Radulph of Diceto, II, p. 47; Arnold of Lübeck, pp. 116–17. The
first two sources (the more reliable) date the coronation September, Radulph
August and Arnold 20 July. Guy's first charter is dated October, Röhricht,
Regesta, p. 873.

[2] It is clear that Raymond considered himself as a candidate for the throne.
Ibn Jubayr reports rumours of his ambition as early as 1183 (Ibn Jubayr, p. 304).
Abu Shama (pp. 257–8) quotes Imad ed-Din's report that he was ready to turn
Moslem to achieve it, and Ibn al-Athir (p. 674) says that he counted on
Saladin's help. The late *Historia Regni Hierosolymitani* (pp. 51–2) says that he
claimed the crown because his mother (here called Dolcis) was born after her
father's coronation, whereas Melisende was born before. As only the youngest
of Baldwin II's daughters, the Abbess Joveta, was born in the purple, he cannot
have used this argument. Perhaps he put forward a similar argument to justify
the barons at Nablus in choosing Isabella rather than Sibylla, and the chronicler
muddled the story.

under Bohemond of Antioch, who welcomed him gladly and gave him a fief larger than that which he had left. Other lesser lords joined him there; for Bohemond made no secret of his sympathy with Raymond and his party.[1]

With the kingdom so torn into embittered factions it was as well that the truce with the Saracens held firm. Guy would have maintained it; but he reckoned without his friend Reynald of Châtillon. Protected by the truce the great caravans that travelled between Damascus and Egypt had been passing again without hindrance through Frankish lands. At the end of 1186 an enormous caravan was journeying up from Cairo, with a small convoy of Egyptian troops to protect it from Bedouin raiders. As it moved into Moab Reynald suddenly fell on it, slaying the soldiers and taking the merchants and their families with all their possessions to his castle of Kerak. The booty was larger than he had ever taken before. News soon reached Saladin of the outrage. Respectful of the treaty, he sent to Reynald to demand the release of the prisoners and compensation for their losses. Reynald refused to receive the envoys; who went on to Jerusalem to complain to King Guy. Guy listened sympathetically and ordered Reynald to make reparations. But Reynald, knowing that it was to his support that Guy owed and kept his throne, paid no attention to his order; and Guy could not or would not force his obedience.[2]

So shameless a breach of the truce made war inevitable, a war which the divided country was ill-fitted to face. Bohemond of Antioch hastened to renew his truce with Saladin.[3] Raymond of Tripoli made a truce for his county and extended it to cover his wife's principality of Galilee, even though its suzerain the King might be at war with the Moslems. At the same time he secured

[1] Ernoul, pp. 137–9; *Estoire d'Eracles*, II, p. 33; *Les Gestes des Chiprois* (p. 659) says that Guy would have struck Baldwin had it not been for his high birth.

[2] *Estoire d'Eracles*, II, p. 34. He says that Saladin's sister was captured in the caravan. Actually she was travelling back from Mecca in a subsequent caravan (see below, p. 454); Abu Shama, pp. 259-11.

[3] Beha ed-Din, *P.P.T.S.* p. 109.

Saladin's sympathy and promise of support in his aim of making himself king. Wise though Raymond's policy may have been it was undoubtedly treasonable. Encouraged by Gerard of the Temple, Guy summoned his loyal vassals and marched north to Nazareth, to reduce Galilee to submission before the Moslem attack should begin. Civil war was only averted by the intervention of Balian of Ibelin, who when he arrived at the camp roughly asked the King what he was doing. When Guy replied that he was going to besiege Tiberias, Balian pointed out the folly of the plan; for Raymond, with the Saracen help on which he could call, would have stronger forces than the King. Balian asked that instead he should be sent to talk to Raymond. But his appeal for unity had no effect on the Count, who would only submit to Guy if Beirut was returned to him. It was a price that Guy thought too dear.[1] But as news came of Saladin's preparations for the coming war, Balian pleaded once again with the King for reconciliation with Raymond. 'You have lost your best knight in Baldwin of Ramleh,' he said, mentioning his brother with pride. 'If you lose the help and counsel of Count Raymond too, you are finished.' Guy, usually ready to agree with anyone that spoke firmly to him, allowed Balian to go on a new embassy to Tiberias, together with Josias, Archbishop of Tyre, and the Grand Masters of the Hospital and Temple. It was essential that the latter, Raymond's bitterest enemy, should be involved in any peaceful settlement that was made.[2]

The delegates, escorted by ten Hospitallers, set out from Jerusalem on 29 April 1187. They spent that night at Balian's castle of Nablus. There Balian had business to transact; so he told the Grand Masters and the Archbishop to ride ahead; he would pass the day there and overtake them on the morrow at the Castle of La Fève, in the Plain of Esdraelon. Late in the evening of the

---

[1] Ernoul, pp. 141–2; *Estoire d'Eracles*, II, pp. 31–5. Ernoul says that Raymond actually received reinforcements from Saladin.

[2] Ernoul, pp. 142–3. Reynald of Sidon was to have joined the delegation, but set out independently.

30th Balian left Nablus with a few attendants intending to ride on through the night. But he suddenly remembered that it was the eve of Saint Philip and Saint James. So he turned aside from the road at Sebastea, the Samaria of the ancients, and knocked at the door of the Bishop's palace. The Bishop was awakened and admitted him; and they sat talking through the night till the dawn came and mass could be celebrated. He then said good-bye to his host and rode on his way.

On 30 April, while Balian was discussing business with his stewards, and the Grand Masters were riding over the hills to La Fève, Count Raymond at Tiberias received an envoy from the Moslems at Banyas. Saladin's young son al-Afdal, commandant of the camp there, was told by his father to send a reconnaissance into Palestine and very correctly asked permission for his men to traverse the Count's territory in Galilee. Raymond, bound by his private treaty with Saladin, could not refuse the embarrassing request. He only stipulated that the Moslems should cross the frontier after daybreak on the morrow and return before dark and that they should do no harm to any town or village in the land. He then sent messengers round all his fief to tell the people to keep themselves and their flocks within their walls for the whole day and to have no fear. At that moment he heard of the coming of the delegation from Jerusalem. Another message was sent out to give it the same warning. Early in the morning on 1 May Raymond watched from his castle the Emir Kukburi and seven thousand mamelukes ride gaily by.

About the middle of that morning Balian and his company arrived at La Fève. From afar they had seen tents of the Templars dressed below the walls; but when they drew near they found that they were empty; and in the castle itself there was silence. Balian's groom Ernoul entered the building and wandered from room to room. There was no one there, except two soldiers lying in one of the upper galleries, sick to death and unable to speak. Balian was perplexed and worried. He waited for an hour or two, uncertain what to do, then set out again along the road to Nazareth.

Suddenly a Templar knight galloped up dishevelled and bleeding, shouting out of a great disaster.

At the same hour Raymond at Tiberias watched the mamelukes ride home. They kept to the pact. It was well before nightfall, and they had not harmed a building in the province. But on the lances of the vanguard were fixed the heads of Templar knights.

Raymond's message had reached the Grand Masters at La Fève on the evening of the 30th. Though Roger of the Hospital protested, Gerard of the Temple at once summoned the Templars from the neighbourhood to join him there. The Marshal of the Temple, James of Mailly, was at the village of Kakun, five miles away, with ninety knights. He came and spent the night before the castle. Next morning the cavalcade rode to Nazareth, where forty secular knights joined them. The Archbishop of Tyre remained there; but Gerard paused only to shout to the townsfolk that there would be a battle soon and they must come to collect the booty. As the knights passed over the hill behind Nazareth they found the Moslems watering their horses at the Springs of Cresson in the valley below. At the sight of such numbers both Roger and James of Mailly advised retreat. Gerard was furious. He turned scornfully from his fellow Grand Master and taunted his Marshal. 'You love your blond head too well to want to lose it', he said. James proudly replied; 'I shall die in battle like a brave man. It is you that will flee as a traitor.' Fired by Gerard's insults the company charged down into the mamelukes. It was a massacre rather than a battle. James's blond head was one of the last to fall; and the Grand Master of the Hospital fell by his side. Very soon every Templar knight was slain except three, of whom Gerard was one. They galloped back wounded to Nazareth. It was one of them that rode on to find Balian. The secular knights were taken alive. Some of the greedy citizens of Nazareth had gone out to the battlefield to find the booty that Gerard had promised. They were rounded up and taken off as prisoners.

After sending to his wife to urge her to collect all her knights, Balian joined Gerard at Nazareth and tried to persuade him to come to Tiberias. Gerard pleaded that his wounds were too bad, so Balian went on with the Archbishop. They found Raymond aghast at the tragedy, for which he felt that his policy had been to blame. He gladly accepted Balian's mediation and, annulling his treaty with Saladin, he rode south to Jerusalem and made his submission to the King. Guy, for all his faults, was not vindictive. He gave Raymond a cordial welcome and even apologized for the manner of his coronation. At last the kingdom seemed to be united again.[1]

It was as well. For Saladin was known to be gathering a great army across the frontier in the Hauran. In May, while the host was assembling from all over his empire, he had made a journey down the road towards Mecca to escort a pilgrim-caravan in which his sister and her son were returning from the Holy City, to be sure that Reynald would not try another of his bandit raids. Meanwhile troops poured in from Aleppo and Mosul and Mardin till his army was the largest that he had ever commanded. Across the Jordan King Guy summoned all his tenants-in-chief and their tenants to bring their men to meet him at Acre. The Orders of the Hospital and the Temple, eager to avenge the massacre at Cresson, brought all their available knights, leaving only small garrisons to defend the castles under their care. The Templars gave further aid in handing to the King their share of the money sent recently to the Orders by King Henry II in expiation of the murder of Thomas Becket. They had been told to bank it against the Crusade that Henry had sworn to undertake, but the present need was too urgent. The soldiers that it served to equip carried with them a banner with Henry's arms. Moved by an appeal from

[1] The story is reported very fully by Ernoul, who was with Balian as his squire (pp. 143–54). *Estoire d'Eracles*, II, pp. 37–44; Imad ed-Din, in Abu Shama, p. 262; Ibn al-Athir (p. 678) says that al-Afdal sent Kukburi in command of the expedition and gives the number of horsemen as 7000. The *De Expugnatione* (pp. 210–11) gives the same number but its short account denies that Raymond insisted on no damage being done to property and tries to whitewash the Templars. La Fève is the Arab village of el-Fuleh (both names mean The Bean) half-way between Jenin and Nazareth.

Raymond and Balian, Bohemond of Antioch promised a contingent under Baldwin of Ibelin, and sent his son Raymond to join the Count of Tripoli who was his godfather. By the end of June 1200 fully armed knights, a larger number of light native cavalry, half-caste Turcopoles and nearly ten thousand infantrymen were gathered at the camp before Acre. The Patriarch Heraclius was asked to come with the True Cross. But he said that he was unwell, and entrusted the relic to the Prior of the Holy Sepulchre to give to the Bishop of Acre. He preferred, his enemies said, to remain with his beloved Paschia.

On Friday, 26 June, Saladin reviewed his troops at Ashtera, in the Hauran. He himself commanded the centre, his nephew Taki ed-Din the right wing and Kukburi the left. The army marched out in battle formation to Khisfin and on to the southern tip of the Sea of Galilee. There he waited for five days, while his scouts collected information about the Christian forces. On 1 July he crossed the Jordan at Sennabra, and on the second he encamped with half his army at Kafr Sebt, in the hills five miles west of the lake, while his other troops attacked Tiberias. The town fell into their hands after an hour of fighting. Raymond and his stepsons were with the King's army; but the Countess Eschiva, after sending a messenger to tell her husband what was happening, held out with her small garrison in the castle.

When news came that Saladin had crossed the Jordan, King Guy held counsel with his barons at Acre. Count Raymond spoke first. He pointed out that in tremendous summer heat the army that attacked was at a disadvantage. Their own strategy should be purely defensive. With the Christian army undefeated Saladin would not be able to maintain his great forces for long in the parched country. After a while he would have to retire. In the meantime the reinforcements from Antioch would arrive. Most of the knights inclined to follow this advice; but both Reynald of Châtillon and the Grand Master Gerard accused Raymond of being a coward and sold to the Saracens. King Guy was always convinced by the last speaker and gave orders for the army to move out towards Tiberias.

On the afternoon of 2 July the Christians encamped at Sephoria. It was an excellent site for a camp, with ample water and good pasturage for the horses. Were they to remain there, as they had remained by the Pools of Goliath four years before, Saladin would never risk attacking them. Their army was nearly as large as his own, and they had the advantage of the terrain. But that evening the messenger from the Countess of Tripoli arrived. Once again Guy held a council in his tent. The chivalry of the knights was moved to think of the gallant lady holding out desperately by the lake. Her sons with tears in their eyes begged that their mother should be rescued. Others followed to support their plea. Then Raymond rose. He repeated the speech that he had made at Acre but with more desperate emphasis. He showed the folly of leaving the present strong position and making a hazardous march in the July heat over the barren hillside. Tiberias was his city, he said, and its defender his wife. But he would rather that Tiberias and all within it were lost than that the kingdom was lost. His words carried conviction. The council broke up at midnight, resolved to remain at Sephoria.

When the barons had retired to their quarters the Grand Master of the Temple crept back to the royal tent. 'Sire,' he said, 'are you going to trust a traitor?' It was shameful to let a city be lost that was only six leagues away. The Templars, he declared, would sooner abandon their Order than abandon their chance of vengeance on the infidel. Guy, who had been sincerely persuaded by Raymond an hour before, vacillated and let Gerard over-persuade him. He sent his heralds through the camp to announce that the army would march at dawn for Tiberias.

The best road from Sephoria to Tiberias went slightly north of east across the Galilean hills and came down to the lake a mile north of the town. The alternative road ran to the bridge at Sennabra, where a branch followed the shore of the lake northward. Saladin's camp at Kafr Sebt lay across the Sennabra road, by which he had come from over the river. It is possible that traitors from the Christian camp went to tell him that Guy was

moving out from Sephoria along the northern road. He therefore
led his army for some five miles across the hills to Hattin, where
the road began to descend towards the lake. It was a village with
broad pastures and abundant water. He was joined there by most
of his troops from Tiberias, where only those needed to blockade
the castle remained.

The morning of Friday, 3 July, was hot and airless, as the
Christian army left the green gardens of Sephoria to march over
the treeless hills. Raymond of Tripoli as lord of the fief had the
right by feudal custom to command the van. The King commanded the centre, and Reynald with the Orders and Balian of
Ibelin brought up the rear. There was no water along the road.
Soon men and horses alike were suffering bitterly from thirst.
Their agony slowed up the pace of the march. Moslem skirmishers
continuously attacked both the vanguard and the rearguard,
pouring arrows into their midst and riding away before any
counter-attack could be made. By the afternoon the Franks had
reached the plateau immediately above Hattin. Ahead of them
a rocky hill with two summits rose about a hundred feet, and
beyond it the ground fell steeply to the village and on to the lake.
It was called the Horns of Hattin. The Templars sent to the King
to say that they could go no farther that day. Some of the barons
begged him to order the army to press on and fight its way
through to the lake. But Guy, moved by the weariness of his men,
decided to halt for the night. On the news Raymond rode in from
the front crying: 'Ah, Lord God, the war is over; we are dead men;
the kingdom is finished.' On his advice Guy set up his camp just
beyond Lubieh, toward the slope of the Horns, where there was
a well, and the whole army grouped itself around him. But the
site was ill-chosen, for the well was dry.

Saladin, waiting with all his men in the verdant valley below,
could hardly restrain his joy. His opportunity had come at last.

The Christians passed the night in misery, listening to the
prayers and songs that came from the Moslem tents below. A few
soldiers broke out of the camp in a vain search for water, only to

be killed by the enemy. To make their sufferings worse, the Moslems set fire to the dry scrub that covered the hill, and hot smoke poured in over the camp. Under cover of the darkness Saladin moved up his men. When the dawn broke on Saturday, 4 July, the royal army was encircled. Not a cat, says the chronicler, could have slipped through the net.

The Moslem attack began soon after daybreak. The Christian infantry had only one thought, water. In a surging mass they tried to break through down the slope towards the lake gleaming far below. They were driven up a hillock, hemmed in by the flames and by the enemy. Many of them were slaughtered at once, many others were taken prisoner; and the sight of them as they lay wounded and swollen-mouthed was so painful that five of Raymond's knights went to the Moslem leaders to beg that they might all be slain, to end their misery. The horsemen on the hill fought with superb and desperate courage. Charge after charge of the Moslem cavalry was driven back with losses; but their own numbers were dwindling. Enfeebled by thirst, their strength began to fail them. Before it was too late, at the King's request, Raymond led his knights in an attempt to burst through the Moslem lines. With all his men he bore down on the regiments commanded by Taki ed-Din. But Taki opened his ranks to let them through, and then closed up again behind them. They could not make their way back again to their comrades so, miserably, they rode from the battlefield, away to Tripoli. A little later Balian of Ibelin and Reynald of Sidon broke their way out. They were the last to escape.

There was no hope left now for the Christians; but they still fought on, retiring up the hill to the Horns. The King's red tent was moved to the summit, and his knights gathered round him. Saladin's young son al-Afdal was at his father's side witnessing his first battle. Many years afterwards he paid tribute to the courage of the Franks. 'When the Frankish King had withdrawn to the hill-top,' he said, 'his knights made a gallant charge and drove the Moslems back upon my father. I watched his dismay.

He changed colour and pulled at his beard, then rushed forward crying: "Give the devil the lie." So our men fell on the enemy who retreated up the hill. When I saw the Franks flying I cried out with glee: "We have routed them." But they charged again and drove our men back again to where my father stood. Again he urged our men forward and again they drove the enemy up the hill. Again I cried out: "We have routed them." But my father turned to me and said: "Be quiet. We have not beaten them so long as that tent stands there." At that moment the tent was overturned. Then my father dismounted and bowed to the ground, giving thanks to God, with tears of joy.'

The Bishop of Acre had been killed. The Holy Cross which he had borne into the battle was in the hands of an infidel. Few of the knights' horses survived. When the victors reached the hill-top, the knights themselves, the King amongst them, were lying on the ground, too weary to fight any more, with hardly the strength to hand their swords over in surrender. Their leaders were taken off to the tent that was erected on the battlefield for the Sultan.[1]

There Saladin received King Guy and his brother the Constable Amalric, Reynald of Châtillon and his stepson Humphrey of Toron, the Grand Master of the Temple, the aged Marquis of Montferrat, the lords of Jebail and Botrun, and many of the lesser barons of the realm. He greeted them graciously. He seated the King next to him and, seeing his thirst, handed him a goblet of rose-water, iced with the snows of Hermon. Guy drank from it and handed it on to Reynald who was at his side. By the laws of Arab hospitality to give food or drink to a captive meant that his life was safe; so Saladin said quickly to the interpreter: 'Tell the King that he gave that man drink, not I.' He then turned on Reynald whose impious brigandage he could not forgive and reminded him of his crimes, of his treachery, his blasphemy and his greed. When Reynald answered truculently, Saladin himself

[1] For the complicated and contradictory evidence about the Hattin campaign, see below, Appendix II.

took a sword and struck off his head. Guy trembled, thinking that his turn would come next. But Saladin reassured him. 'A king does not kill a king', he said, 'but that man's perfidy and insolence went too far.' He then gave orders that none of the lay barons was to be harmed but that all were to be treated with courtesy and respect during their captivity. But he would not spare the knights of the Military Orders, save only the Grand Master of the Temple. A band of fanatical Moslem *sufis* had joined his troops. To them he gave the task of slaying his Templar and Hospitaller prisoners. They performed it with relish. When this was done he moved his army away from Hattin; and the bodies on the battlefield were left to the jackals and the hyenas.

The prisoners were sent to Damascus, where the barons were lodged in comfort and the poorer folk were sold in the slave-market. So many were there that the price of a single prisoner fell to three dinars, and you could buy a whole healthy family, a man, his wife, his three sons and his two daughters, for eighty dinars the lot. One Moslem even thought it a good bargain to exchange a prisoner for a pair of sandals.[1]

The Christians of the East had suffered disasters before. Their Kings and Princes had been captured before; but their captors then had been petty lordlings, out for some petty advantage. On the Horns of Hattin the greatest army that the kingdom had ever assembled was annihilated. The Holy Cross was lost. And the victor was lord of the whole Moslem world.

With his enemies destroyed, it only remained for Saladin to occupy the fortresses of the Holy Land. On 5 July, knowing that no help could come to her, the Countess of Tripoli surrendered Tiberias to him. He treated her with the honour that she deserved and allowed her to go with all her household to Tripoli.[2] Then he moved the bulk of his army down to Acre. The Seneschal Joscelin

---

[1] Beha ed-Din, *P.P.T.S.* pp. 114–15; Kemal ad-Din (ed. Blochet, pp. 180–1) gives a slightly different version but with the same sense; Ernoul (pp. 172–4) tells roughly the same story.

[2] Ernoul, p. 171; *Estoire d'Eracles*, II, p. 69; Abu Shama, pp. 266–7.

of Courtenay, who commanded the city, thought only of his own safety. He sent a citizen called Peter Brice to meet Saladin when he arrived before the walls on the 8th, offering its surrender if the lives and possessions of the inhabitants were guaranteed. To many in the city this tame capitulation seemed shameful. There was a short riot in which several houses were burnt; but order was restored before Saladin took formal possession of Acre on the 10th. He had hoped to persuade most of the Christian merchants to stay there. But they feared for the future and emigrated with all their movable possessions. The immense stores of merchandize, silks and metals, jewels and arms, that were abandoned were distributed by the conquerors, particularly by Saladin's young son al-Afdal, to whom the city was given, amongst their soldiers and comrades. The great sugar-factory was pillaged by Taki ed-Din, to Saladin's annoyance.[1] While Saladin remained at Acre, detachments of his army received the submission of the towns and castles of Galilee and Samaria. At Nablus Balian's garrison held out for a few days and obtained honourable terms when it surrendered; and the castle of Toron resisted for a fortnight before its garrison capitulated. There was little other resistance.[2] Meanwhile Saladin's brother al-Adil came up from Egypt and laid siege to Jaffa. The town would not yield to him; so he took it by storm and sent all the inhabitants, men, women and children, into captivity. Most of them found their way to the slave-markets and harems of Aleppo.[3]

When Galilee was conquered Saladin moved up the Phoenician coast. Most of the survivors from Hattin had fled with Balian to Tyre. It was well garrisoned and the great walls that guarded it from the land were too formidable. When his first attack failed he

[1] Ernoul, *loc. cit.*; *Estoire d'Eracles*, II, pp. 70–1; Abu Shama, pp. 295–7; Beha ed-Din, *P.P.T.S.* p. 116; Ibn al-Athir, pp. 688–90.

[2] *Estoire d'Eracles*, II, p. 68; *De Expugnatione*, pp. 31–4; Beha ed-Din, *loc. cit.* (only mentioning Toron); Abu Shama, pp. 300–6; Ibn al-Athir, *loc. cit.*

[3] Ibn al-Athir, pp. 690–1. He himself bought a slave in the Aleppo market, a young girl who had lost a husband and six babies (p. 691); *De Expugnatione*, p. 229.

The Horns of Hattin

passed on. Sidon surrendered without a blow on 29 July. Its lord, Reynald, fled to his impregnable inland castle of Beaufort. Beirut attempted to defend itself but capitulated on 6 August. Jebail surrendered a few days later, on the orders of its lord, Hugh Ebriaco, whom Saladin released on that condition. By the end of August there only remained to the Christians south of Tripoli itself Tyre, Ascalon, Gaza, a few isolated castles and the Holy City of Jerusalem.[1]

In September Saladin appeared before Ascalon, bringing with him his two chief captives, King Guy and the Grand Master Gerard. Guy had been told that his liberty could be bought by the surrender of Ascalon; and on his arrival before the walls he harangued the citizens telling them to give up the struggle. Gerard joined his plea to Guy's; but they answered them both with insults. Ascalon was bravely defended. The siege cost Saladin the life of two of his emirs. But on 4 September the garrison was forced to capitulate. The citizens were allowed to leave with all their portable belongings. They were escorted by Saladin's soldiers to Egypt and housed in comfort at Alexandria, till they could be repatriated to Christian lands.[2] At Gaza, whose Templar garrison was obliged by the laws of the Order to obey the Grand Master, Gerard's command that it should surrender was carried out at once. In return for the fortress he obtained his liberty.[3] But King Guy was kept for some months longer in prison, first at Nablus and later at Lattakieh. Queen Sibylla was allowed to come from Jerusalem to join him. As Saladin doubtless expected, their release next spring added to the embarrassment of the Christians.[4]

[1] Beha ed-Din, *P.P.T.S.* pp. 116–17; Abu Shama, pp. 306–10; Ibn al-Athir, pp. 692–3; *De Expugnatione*, p. 236.
[2] Ernoul, p. 184; *Estoire d'Eracles*, II, pp. 78–9; *De Expugnatione*, pp. 236–8; Beha ed-Din, *P.P.T.S.* p. 117; Ibn al-Athir, pp. 696–7.
[3] Abu Shama, pp. 312–13; Beha ed-Din, *loc. cit.*; Ibn al-Athir, p. 697.
[4] According to Ernoul (pp. 175, 185) Sibylla was at Jerusalem up to the eve of the siege and was allowed then to go to Nablus (p. 185). Ibn al-Athir, p. 703; *Estoire d'Eracles*, II, p. 79, and the *Itinerarium Regis Ricardi*, pp. 21–3, say

The day that Saladin's troops entered Ascalon there was an eclipse of the sun; and in the darkness Saladin received a delegation from the citizens of Jerusalem, which he had summoned to discuss terms for the Holy City's surrender. But there was no discussion. The delegates refused to hand over the city where their God had died for them. They returned proudly to Jerusalem; and Saladin swore to take it by the sword. In Jerusalem an unexpected helper had arrived. Balian of Ibelin, who was with the Frankish refugees at Tyre, sent to ask Saladin for a safe-conduct to Jerusalem. His wife, Queen Maria, had retired there with her children from Nablus, and he wished to bring them down to Tyre. Saladin granted his request on condition that he only spent one night in the city and did not bear arms. When he came there, Balian found the Patriarch Heraclius and the officials of the Orders trying to prepare the city's defence; but there was no leader whom the people trusted. They all clamoured that Balian should stay and lead them and would not let him go. Deeply embarrassed, Balian wrote to Saladin to explain the violation of his oath. Saladin was always courteous to an enemy that he respected. He not only forgave Balian but himself sent an escort to convey Queen Maria, with her children, her household and all her possessions, down to Tyre.[1] With her went Balian's young nephew Thomas of Ibelin, and the young son of Hugh of Jebail. Saladin wept to see these children, heirs to vanished grandeur, pass through his camp into exile.

In Jerusalem Balian did what he could. The population was swollen by refugees from all the neighbouring districts, few of

that Sibylla was in Jerusalem throughout the siege and then went to Nablus only for a short interview. Beha ed-Din (*P.P.T.S.* p. 143) says that Guy was taken to Tortosa by Saladin and released there while Saladin was besieging Krak des Chevaliers. That was in July 1188, a few days before Saladin took Tortosa. Possibly Tortosa (Antartus) is a mistake of Beha ed-Din's for Tripoli, but the release is dated definitely July 1188. Ernoul, however (p. 185), says that Guy was released in March 1188, but (p. 252) dates it when Saladin was besieging Tripoli (July 1188). The *Itinerarium* says that Guy was released at Tortosa, where Sibylla eventually joined him (p. 25).

[1] Ernoul, pp. 174–5, 185–7; *Estoire d'Eracles*, II, pp. 81–4; *De Expugnatione*, p. 238.

them of use as fighters. For every man there were fifty women and children. There were only two knights in the city; so Balian knighted every boy over sixteen that was born of a noble family and thirty men of the bourgeoisie. He dispatched parties to collect all the food that could be found before the Moslem armies closed round. He took over the royal treasury and the money that Henry II had sent to the Hospital. He even stripped the silver from the roof of the Holy Sepulchre. Arms were given to every man that could bear them.

On 20 September Saladin encamped before the city and began to attack the north and north-west walls. But the sun was in his soldiers' eyes and the defences there were strong. After five days he moved his camp. For a short moment the defenders believed that he had lifted the siege; but on the morning of 26 September his army was established on the Mount of Olives and his sappers, flanked by his horsemen, were mining the wall near the Gate of the Column, not far from the spot where Godfrey of Lorraine had broken into the city eighty-eight years before. By the 29th there was a great breach in the wall. The defenders manned it as best they could and fought furiously; but they were too few to hold it for long against the hordes of the enemy. The Frankish soldiers wished to make one tremendous sortie and if need be die. But the Patriarch Heraclius had no mind to be a martyr. If they did so, he said, they would leave their women and children to inevitable slavery and he could not give his blessing to so impious an action. Balian supported him; he saw the folly of wasting more lives. On 30 September he went himself to the enemy camp to ask Saladin for terms.

Saladin had the city at his mercy. He could storm it when he wished; and within the city he had many potential friends. The pride of the Latin Church had always been resented by the Orthodox Christians who formed the majority of the humbler folk in the city. There had been no definite schism. The royal family and the lay nobility, except in Antioch, had shown friendliness and respect to the Orthodox clergy. But the upper hierarchy had been exclusively Latin. In the great shrines of their faith the native Christians had been made to attend ceremonies whose language and ritual were alien to them. They looked back longingly to the days when under just Moslem rulers they had been able to worship as they pleased. Saladin's confidential adviser for his dealings with the Christian princes was an Orthodox scholar from Jerusalem, called Joseph Batit. He now made contact with the Orthodox communities in the city; and they promised to open the gates to Saladin.

Their intervention was not needed. When Balian came before his tent Saladin declared that he had sworn to take Jerusalem by the sword and only unconditional surrender would absolve him from that oath. He reminded Balian of the massacres committed by the Christians in 1099. Was he to act differently? The battle raged as they spoke; and Saladin showed that his standard had now been raised on the city wall. But at the next moment his men were driven back; and Balian warned Saladin that unless he gave honourable terms the defenders in desperation before they died would destroy everything in the city, including the buildings in the Temple area sacred to the Moslems, and they would slaughter the Moslem prisoners that they held. Saladin, so long as his power was recognized, was ready to be generous, and he wished Jerusalem to suffer as little as possible. He consented to make terms and offered that every Christian should be able to redeem himself at the rate of ten dinars a man, five a woman and one a child. Balian then pointed out that there were twenty thousand poor folk in the city who could never afford such a sum. Could a lump-sum be given by the Christian authorities that would free them all? Saladin was willing to accept 100,000 dinars for the whole twenty thousand. But Balian knew that so much money could not be raised. It was arranged that for 30,000 dinars seven thousand should be freed. On Balian's orders the garrison laid down its arms; and on Friday, 2 October, Saladin entered Jerusalem. It was the 27th day of Rajab, the anniversary of the day when the Prophet in his sleep had visited Jerusalem and been wafted thence to Heaven.

The victors were correct and humane. Where the Franks, eighty-eight years before, had waded through the blood of their victims, not a building now was looted, not a person injured. By Saladin's orders guards patrolled the streets and the gates, preventing any outrage on the Christians. Meanwhile each Christian strove to find the money for his ransom and Balian emptied the treasury to raise the promised 30,000 dinars. It was with difficulty that the Hospital and the Temple could be made to disgorge their riches; and the Patriarch and his Chapter looked after themselves alone. It shocked the Moslems to see Heraclius paying his ten dinars for his ransom and leaving the city bowed by the weight of the gold that he was carrying, followed by carts laden with carpets and plate. Thanks to the remains of Henry II's donation, the seven thousand poor were freed; but many thousands could have been spared slavery if only the Orders and the Church had been more generous. Soon two streams of Christians poured out through the gates, the one of those whose ransoms had been paid by themselves or by Balian's efforts, the other of those who could afford no ransom and were going into captivity. So pathetic was the sight that al-Adil turned to his brother and asked for a thousand of them as a reward for his services. They were granted to him and he at once set them free. The Patriarch Heraclius, delighted to find so cheap a way of doing good, then asked that he might have some slaves to liberate. He was granted seven hundred; and five hundred were given to Balian. Then Saladin himself announced that he would liberate every aged man and woman. When the Frankish ladies who had ransomed themselves came in tears to ask him where they should go, for their husbands or fathers were slain or captive, he answered by promising to release every captive husband, and to the widows and orphans he gave gifts from his own treasury, to each according to her estate. His mercy and kindness were in strange contrast to the deeds of the Christian conquerors of the First Crusade.

Some of his emirs and soldiers were less kindly. There were tales of Christians being smuggled out in disguise by Moslems

who then blackmailed them of all that they possessed. Other
Moslem lords professed to recognize escaped slaves and charged
high ransoms privately to let their victims go. But wherever
Saladin found such practices, his punishment was sharp.[1]

The long line of refugees moved slowly down to the coast,
unmolested by the Moslems. They travelled in three convoys, the
first led by the Templars, the second by the Hospitallers, and the
third by Balian and the Patriarch. At Tyre, already overcrowded
with other refugees, only fighting men could be admitted. Near
Botrun a local baron, Raymond of Niphin, robbed them of many
of their goods. They moved on to Tripoli. There, too, earlier
refugees filled the city, and the authorities, short of food, would
admit no more and closed the gates against them. It was not till
they reached Antioch that they found any resting-place, and even
there they were not allowed willingly into the city. The refugees
from Ascalon were more fortunate. When Italian merchant
captains refused to take them on to Christian ports without heavy
fees, the Egyptian government refused to allow the ships to sail
till they accepted them free.[2]

The Orthodox Christians and the Jacobites remained in
Jerusalem. Each had officially to pay a capitation-tax in addition
to his ransom, though many of the poorer classes were excused
the payment. The rich amongst them bought up much of the
property left vacant by the Franks' departure. The rest was bought
by Moslems and by Jews whom Saladin encouraged to settle in
the city. When the news of Saladin's victory reached Constantinople the Emperor Isaac Angelus sent an embassy to Saladin to

[1] Ernoul, pp. 174-5, 211-30, the fullest and most authentic account. Ernoul
was with Balian in Jerusalem; *Estoire d'Eracles*, II, 81-99; *De Expugnatione*,
pp. 241-51, an account supplied by an eye-witness who was wounded during
the siege and who disapproved of the surrender; Abu Shama, pp. 320-40;
Beha ed-Din, *P.P.T.S.* pp. 118-20; Ibn al-Athir, pp. 699-703. The story of
Joseph Batit is told in *The History of the Patriarchs of Alexandria*, p. 207, a hostile
Coptic source. The author adds that the Orthodox Christians regretted the
capitulation, as they would have liked to massacre the Franks.
[2] Ernoul, pp. 320-4; *Estoire d'Eracles*, II, pp. 100-3.

congratulate him and to ask that the Christian Holy Places should revert to the Orthodox Church. After a little delay his request was granted. Many of Saladin's friends had urged him to destroy the Church of the Holy Sepulchre. But he pointed out that it was the site, not the building, that the Christians venerated; they would still wish to make pilgrimages there. Nor did he want to discourage that. In fact the Church was only closed for three days. Then Frankish pilgrims were admitted on payment of a fee.[1]

The Christian refugees had not left the city before the Cross over the Dome of the Rock was taken down and all signs of Christian worship removed, and the Mosque al-Aqsa cleaned of all traces of the occupation of the Templars. Both buildings were sprinkled with rose-water and dedicated once more to the service of Islam. On Friday, 9 October, Saladin was present with a vast congregation to give thanks to his God in the Mosque.[2]

With the recovery of Jerusalem Saladin's chief duty to his faith had been performed. But there were still some Frankish fortresses to be reduced. The Lady Stephanie of Oultrejourdain had been among the ransomed captives at Jerusalem, and she had asked Saladin for the release of her son Humphrey of Toron. He agreed on condition that her two great castles were surrendered to him. Humphrey was sent from his prison to join her; but neither at Kerak nor at Montreal would the garrison obey her order to give themselves up. As she had failed in her bargain she sent her son back into captivity. Her honourable action pleased Saladin, who gave Humphrey his liberty a few months later. Meanwhile al-Adil and the Egyptian army laid siege to Kerak. The siege lasted

[1] For the native Christians' fate, see Bar-Hebraeus, trans. Budge, pp. 326–7; Beha ed-Din, *P.P.T.S.* pp. 198–201, reports the exchange of embassies between Saladin and the Emperor. Maqrisi, ed. Blochet, *Revue de l'Orient Latin*, vol. IX, p. 33, reports the temporary closing of the Holy Sepulchre. For the Jews, see Schwab, 'Al-Harizi', in *Archives de l'Orient Latin*, I, p. 236.

[2] Beha ed-Din, *P.P.T.S.* p. 120; Ibn al-Athir, pp. 704–5; *Estoire d'Eracles*, II, p. 104; Ernoul, pp. 234–5; *De Expugnatione*, pp. 250–1; Ibn Khallikan, II, pp. 634–41, reports the uplifting sermon preached by the chief *cadi* of Aleppo at the first service in the Mosque al-Aqsa.

for more than a year. For many months the defenders were near to starvation. Their women and children were turned out to fend for themselves; some indeed were sold by their men-folk to the Bedouin in return for food. Only when the last horse in the fortress had been eaten did the castle surrender, at the end of 1188. Montreal, less closely pressed, held out for some months longer.[1]

Farther north the Templar castle of Safed surrendered on 6 December 1188, after a month's heavy bombardment, and the Hospitallers at Belvoir, high over the Jordan valley, followed suit a month later. The Château Neuf at Hunin had been occupied some time before. Beaufort, where Reynald of Sidon had taken refuge, was saved by his diplomacy. He was a learned man, with a passionate interest in Arabic literature. He came to Saladin's tent professing himself willing to surrender his castle and retire to Damascus, if he were allowed three months to settle his affairs. He even hinted that he might embrace Islam. So charming was his conversation that Saladin was convinced of his good faith, only to find out too late that the truce that he had granted had been used to strengthen the castle defences. In the meantime Saladin had moved into the territory of Tripoli and Antioch.[2]

Raymond of Tripoli died about the end of 1187. Soon after his escape from Hattin he had fallen ill of pleurisy, though men thought that his sickness was due to melancholy and shame. Many of his contemporaries considered him a traitor whose selfishness helped to ruin the kingdom; but William of Tyre and Balian of Ibelin both were his friends and defenders. His real tragedy was the tragedy of all the Frankish colonists of the second and third generation, who by temperament and from policy were ready to become part of the Oriental world but were forced by the fanaticism of their newly-come western cousins to take sides;

---

[1] Ernoul, p. 187; *Estoire d'Eracles*, II, p. 122; Abu Shama, p. 382; Beha ed-Din, *P.P.T.S.* pp. 139, 143.

[2] Beha ed-Din, *P.P.T.S.* pp. 122–3, 138–41, 142–3. He met Reynald and found him charming; Abu Shama, pp. 395–400; Kemal ad-Din, ed. Blochet, p. 191.

and in the end they could not but take sides with fellow-Christians. He had no children; so he bequeathed his county to his godson Raymond, son of his nearest male relative, Prince Bohemond of Antioch; but he stipulated that should a member of the house of Toulouse come to the East the county must be his. Bohemond accepted the inheritance for his son, then substituted the boy's younger brother, Bohemond, for fear that Antioch and Tripoli together might be more than one man could defend.[1]

Indeed, there was soon little left of the inheritance. On 1 July 1188 Saladin swept through the Buqaia, with reinforcements newly come from Sinjar. He passed by the Hospitaller fortress at Krak, which he thought too strong to attack. He moved towards Tripoli; but the arrival there of the King of Sicily's fleet deterred him. He turned north. At Tortosa he stormed the town, but the Templars' castle held out against him. He pressed on, under the walls of Marqab, where the Hospitallers tried to dispute his passage. Jabala surrendered on Friday, 15 July, Lattakieh on Friday the 22nd. Lattakieh had been a lovely city, with its churches and palaces dating from Byzantine times. The Moslem chronicler, Imad ed-Din, who was with the army, wept to see it pillaged and ruined. From Lattakieh Saladin turned inland to Sahyun. The vast castle of the Hospitallers was thought to be impregnable; but after a few days of fierce fighting it was taken by assault on Friday, 29 July. On Friday, 12 August, the garrison of Bakas-Shoqr, well protected though their castle was by stupendous ravines, surrendered when no help was forthcoming from Antioch. On Friday the 19th the town of Sarminya fell. A few days later, on the 23rd, Burzey, the southernmost of the Orontes castles, capitulated. Its commander was married to the sister of Saladin's secret agent, the Princess of Antioch. He and his wife were allowed their liberty. On 16 September the Templar

---

[1] Raymond's death is reported, without an exact date, by *Estoire d'Eracles*, p. 72, where the arrangements for the succession are given, by Imad ed-Din (in Abu Shama, p. 284) and by Beha ed-Din, *P.P.T.S.* p. 114. The Arab authors say that he died of pleurisy. For his conduct at Hattin, see below, Appendix II. Benedict of Peterborough says that he was found dead in his bed (ii, p. 21).

fort of Darbsaq in the Amanus mountains surrendered, and on the 26th the castle of Baghras, which commanded the road from Antioch into Cilicia.[1] But Saladin's army now was weary, and the troops from Sinjar wished to go home. When Prince Bohemond begged for a truce which recognized all the Moslem conquests, Saladin granted it to him. He could, he thought, finish off the task whenever he chose. For all that was left to Bohemond and his sons were their two capitals of Antioch and Tripoli and the port of Saint Symeon, while the Hospitallers kept Marqab and Krak and the Templars Tortosa.[2]

But farther south there was one other city that Saladin had not taken; and therein he made his great mistake. The refugee barons of Palestine were crowded now in Tyre, the strongest city of the coast, joined to the mainland only by a narrow sandy peninsula, across which a great wall was built. Had Saladin pressed an attack on Tyre as soon as Acre was his, even this wall could not have arrested him. But he delayed just too long. Reynald of Sidon, who then commanded the city, was negotiating the surrender; and Saladin had even sent two of his banners to be displayed on the citadel, when on 14 July 1187, ten days after the battle of Hattin, a ship sailed into the harbour. On board was Conrad, son of the old Marquis of Montferrat and brother of Queen Sibylla's first husband. He had been living at Constantinople but had been involved in a murder there; so he sailed secretly away with a company of Frankish knights to pay a pilgrimage to the Holy Places. He knew nothing of the disasters in Palestine and made for Acre. When his ship arrived off the port the captain was surprised not to hear the bell that was rung whenever a sail was sighted. He felt that something was wrong so did not cast anchor. Soon a sloop with a Moslem port-official aboard

---

[1] Ernoul, pp. 252–3; *Estoire d'Eracles*, II, p. 122; Abu Shama, pp. 356–76; Beha ed-Din, *P.P.T.S.* pp. 125–38; Kemal ad-Din, ed. Blochet, pp. 187–90; Ibn al-Athir, pp. 726–9; Abu Shama, pp. 361–2, quotes Imad ed-Din's description of Lattakieh and its sack.

[2] Ibn al-Athir, pp. 732–3; Beha ed-Din, *P.P.T.S.* p. 137. The truce was to last seven months.

came alongside; and Conrad, pretending to be a merchant, asked what was happening, and was told that Saladin had taken the city four days before. His horror at the news aroused the Moslem's suspicion; but before he could raise an alarm Conrad had sailed away up the coast to Tyre. There he was welcomed as a deliverer and put in charge of the defence of the city. Saladin's peace-terms were rejected, and his banners cast into the moat. Conrad was vigorous, ruthless and brave. He saw that the city could be held till help came from the West, and he was confident that on the news of the fall of Jerusalem help would surely come. When Saladin appeared a few days later before Tyre, the vigour of the defence was too much for him. He brought down the Marquis of Montferrat from Damascus and paraded him before the walls threatening his death were the city not given up to him; but Conrad's filial piety was not strong enough to deflect him from his duty as a Christian warrior. He was unmoved; and Saladin, with his usual kindliness, spared the old man's life. He raised the siege to march against Ascalon. When next he appeared before Tyre, in November 1187, its fortifications had been strengthened, some naval and military reinforcements had arrived, and the narrow terrain prevented him from using his men and mangonels to advantage. Ten Moslem ships were brought up from Acre; but on 29 December five of them were captured by the Christians; and a simultaneous attack on the walls was driven back. At a council of war Saladin listened to those of his emirs who pointed out that his troops needed a rest. The winter was wet and cold, and there was illness in the camp. On New Year's Day 1188, Saladin disbanded half his army and retired to conquer the inland castles. Conrad's energy and confidence had saved the city and with it the continuance of the Christian kingdom.[1]

Saladin was later to regret very bitterly his failure to capture Tyre. But his achievements had already been tremendous.

[1] Ernoul, pp. 179–83, 240–4; *Estoire d'Eracles*, II, pp. 74–8, 104–10; *Itinerarium Regis Ricardi*, pp. 18–19; Beha ed-Din, *P.P.T.S.* pp. 120–2; Ibn al-Athir, pp. 694–6, 707–12.

Whether his triumphs were due to the inevitable response of Islam to the challenge of the intruder Franks, or to the far-sighted policy of his great predecessors, or to the quarrels and the follies of the Franks themselves, or to his own personality, he had given proof of the force and the spirit of the East. At the Horns of Hattin and the gates of Jerusalem he had avenged the humiliation of the First Crusade, and he had shown how a man of honour celebrates his victory.

PRINCIPAL SOURCES FOR THE HISTORY OF THE LATIN EAST, 1100–1187

1. GREEK

The Greek historians only deal with the Latins in the East when they come into direct contact with Byzantium. Till 1118 ANNA COMNENA's *Alexiad* is still the most important Greek source, though the sequence of events in her account of Frankish affairs is rather confused.[1] For the reigns of John and Manuel Comnenus the two essential sources are the histories of JOHN CINNAMUS and NICETAS ACOMINATUS, or CHONIATES. The former was the secretary of Manuel Comnenus and wrote his work just after Manuel's death. His account of John's reign is a little perfunctory; but he deals carefully and authoritatively with Manuel's. Apart from mild patriotic prejudices he is a sober historian on whom reliance can be placed.[2] NICETAS wrote early in the thirteenth century, and covers the period from John's reign till after the Latin capture of Constantinople. His history is quite independent of that of Cinnamus. From the latter half of Manuel's reign onward he is describing events of which he had personal knowledge; and, in spite of an over-rhetorical style and a tendency to moralize, he is accurate and reliable.[3] No other Greek source is of major importance,[4] except for an interesting but rather vague account of a pilgrimage to Palestine in 1178 by a certain JOHN PHOCAS.[5]

[1] See above, vol. I, pp. 327–8.
[2] Published in the Bonn *Corpus*.
[3] Published in the Bonn *Corpus*.
[4] Zonaras is still useful for the first years of the century. See above, vol. I, p. 328. The verse chronicle of Manasses provides a little unimportant material (published in the Bonn *Corpus*). The relevant poems of Prodromus are published in the *Recueil des Historiens des Croisades*.
[5] Translated in the *Palestine Pilgrims' Text Society*, vol. v.

Appendix I

2. LATIN

For the early history of the Crusading states our main sources are historians of the First Crusade, notably FULCHER OF CHARTRES[1] and ALBERT OF AIX[2] and, to a lesser degree, RADULPH OF CAEN,[3] EKKEHARD OF AURA[4] and CAFFARO.[5] I have discussed these in the first volume of this history. It should be added that for the period 1100 to 1119, when it comes to an end, Albert's history can be regarded as a thoroughly reliable source. Where he obtained his information is unknown, but whenever it can be checked from Syrian sources it is confirmed by them.

Antiochene history for the period 1115 to 1122 is covered by a short work called *De Bello Antiochene*, by WALTER THE CHANCELLOR, who was probably the Chancellor to Prince Roger. It is an unpretentious work, full of useful information about the history and institutions of Antioch at the time.[6]

From 1127, when Fulcher ends his work, till the last decade before Saladin's conquest of Jerusalem our only important Latin source is WILLIAM OF TYRE's *Historia Rerum in Partibus Transmarinis Gestarum*, which covers the period 1095 to 1184.[7] William was born in the East shortly before 1130. He probably learnt Arabic and Greek as a child, then went to France to finish his education. Soon after his return to Palestine, in about 1160, he became Archdeacon of Tyre and Chancellor of the Kingdom from 1170 to 1174. He was also tutor of the future Baldwin IV. In 1175 he became Archbishop of Tyre. In 1183, after his failure to secure the Patriarchate, he retired to Rome, where he died before 1187. He began writing his history in 1169 and had finished the first thirteen books by 1173. He took the whole work with him to Rome and was still working on it at the time of his death. For his account of the First Crusade William relied mainly on Albert and to a lesser extent on Raymond of Aguilers, Baudri's version of the *Gesta*, and Fulcher. From 1100 to 1127 Fulcher is his main source,

[1] See above, vol. I, p. 329.   [2] See above, vol. I, p. 331.
[3] See above, vol. I, p. 331.   [4] See above, vol. I, p. 330.
[5] See above, vol. I, p. 332.   [6] Ed. in the *Recueil*.
[7] Ed. in the *Recueil*. See above, vol. I, pp. 321-2. For William's chronology, see Stevenson, *Crusaders in the East*, pp. 361-71, a full and authoritative discussion.

though he also used Walter the Chancellor. His only additions to them are personal anecdotes about the Kings and information about the Eastern Churches and about Tyre. For the period 1127 till his return to the East, he depended on the archives of the Kingdom and on a lost skeleton chronicle of the Kings. In consequence his information about northern Syria is sometimes unreliable. From the 1160's onward he had an intimate and shrewd personal knowledge of the events and actors that he described. His dates are confused and at times demonstrably wrong. It is probable that they were added to his manuscript by an early transcriber. William is one of the greatest of medieval historians. He had his prejudices, such as his dislike of lay-control of the Church, but he is temperate in his words about his personal enemies, such as the Patriarch Heraclius and Agnes of Courtenay, who both deserved his censure. He makes mistakes where his information was inadequate. But he had a broad vision; he understood the significance of the great events of his time and the sequence of cause and effect in history. His style is straightforward and not without humour. His work leaves the impression that he was himself a wise, honourable and likeable man. His other chief work, a History of the East, based on the Arabic history of Said ibn Bitriq, is unfortunately lost though it was used by historians of the following century, such as Jacques of Vitry

A Latin *Continuation* of William of Tyre's history was written in the West in 1194, with later additions.[1] It is a sober, objective work, probably based on a lost work which also is the base of the first book of the *Itinerarium Regis Ricardi*, which covers the years from 1184 till the Third Crusade.[2] The continuations in Old French present a greater problem. Towards the middle of the thirteenth century William's *History* was translated by a subject of the French King. He paraphrased some passages and included comments of doubtful value. To it he added a continuation which extended well into the thirteenth century. From its opening words this work is usually known as the *Estoire d'Eracles*. About the same time a certain Bernard the Treasurer brought out in the East a continuation to the year 1129 attributed to Ernoul, who was a squire of Balian of Ibelin. These two translations are closely related and are found in a large number of manuscripts, which, however, contain variations that can be divided into three groups for the

[1] Ed. by M. Salloch.
[2] The *Itinerarium* is published in the Rolls Series, edited by Stubbs.

period 1184 to 1198. It is impossible to say which is the original manuscript, as each group contains episodes not found in either of the others. The most likely solution is that they all depend for this period on a lost work by Ernoul himself. Ernoul certainly supplied the first-hand account of the events of 1 May 1187, found in Bernard's Ernoul; and the whole group shows an interest in the Ibelins and gives many eyewitness descriptions that would fit in with authorship by one of the Ibelin household. These continuations are on the whole reliable sources, though not objective. Ernoul seems to have been a careful recorder in so far as his party bias in favour of the Ibelins allowed. The chrono-logical order of the earlier passages is haphazard. They seem to consist of disjointed observations and memories.[1]

Saladin's conquest of Palestine is also described in a short *Libellus de Expugnatione Terrae Sanctae per Saladinum*, sometimes attributed to Ralph of Coggeshall and almost certainly written by an Englishman, a few years after the event that it describes. The author shows admiration for the Military Orders, particularly for the Temple, of whose misdeeds he is tactfully silent, but at the same time he is friendly to Raymond of Tripoli. He includes an eyewitness account of the siege of Jerusalem itself supplied by a soldier who was wounded there.[2]

There are some later histories of the Kingdom which give further information, notably the HISTORIA REGNI HIEROSOLYMITANI, a con-tinuation of Caffaro, the ANNALES DE LA TERRE SAINTE and a brief HISTORIA REGUM HIEROSOLYMITANORUM.[3] The history of the Second Crusade is treated fully in the *De Ludovici VII profectione in Orientum* of Odo of Deuil, a vivid and highly prejudiced account by a participant of Louis's journey as far as Attalia, and more briefly in the *Gesta Friderici* of Otto of Freisingen, himself also a participant; and the *Life of Louis VII* by SUGER.[4] AMBROISE's poem, *L'Estoire de la Guerre Sainte*,

---

[1] The *Estoire d'Eracles* is edited in the *Recueil*. Ernoul is edited by Mas Latrie. For a discussion of the whole problem, see Mas Latrie's introduction to Ernoul and Cahen, *La Syrie du Nord*, pp. 21-4.

[2] Ed. by J. Stevenson in the Rolls Series.

[3] The *Historia Regni Hier.* is published in *M.G.H.Ss.*, the *Annales de la Terre Sainte*, edited by Röhricht, in the *Archives de l'Orient Latin* and the *Historia Regum* in Kohler, *Mélanges*.

[4] Odo, or Eudes, of Deuil's book has recently been edited by Waquet, and Otto of Freisingen's *Gesta* by Hofmeister in *M.G.H.Ss.*, new series. There is no good edition of Suger's work.

Appendix I

as well as the *Itinerarium Regis Ricardi*, though dealing with the Third Crusade, gives retrospective information.[1]

Many western chroniclers contain passages of relevance to the Latin East, such as the Englishman William of Malmesbury, Benedict of Peterborough and the historians concerned with the Third Crusade; the Frenchman Sigebert of Gembloux and his continuators and Robert of Torigny; the Italians Romuald and Sicard of Cremona; and others.[2] The most important is the Norman Orderic Vitalis, whose chronicle, which ends in 1138, is full of information about Outremer, in particular about northern Syria. It is probable that Orderic had friends or relatives amongst the Normans of Antioch. Many of his stories are obvious legends, but much of his matter is convincing and is not found elsewhere.[3]

Of the relevant contemporary letters the most important group is contained in the papal correspondence. The correspondence of Louis VII and Conrad III throws light on the Second Crusade.[4] A few letters written by distinguished Latins in the East have survived.[5] The archives of three ecclasiastical establishments in the East have survived, those of the Holy Sepulchre and of the Abbeys of Saint Mary Josaphat and of Saint Lazarus. The archives of the Order of the Hospital are almost complete, but those of the Temple are only known by rare and indirect references. There are also a certain number of lay records dealing with the transfer of land in the Frankish States.[6] The papal archives give some additional information; and information on commercial affairs can be extracted from those of Pisa, Venice and Genoa.[7] The *Assises* of Jerusalem, which were written later, contain specific *assises* dating from the twelfth century.[8]

[1] Ambroise is edited by G. Paris. There is an English translation with useful notes by Hubert and La Monte.

[2] For editions of these chroniclers, see Bibliography, below, pp. 493–5.

[3] The best edition of Orderic is still that of Le Prévost.

[4] Published in *R.H.F.* and in *Wibaldi Epistolae* (Jaffé, *Bibliotheca*), respectively.

[5] Most are published in *R.H.F.* Others are found in various chronicles.

[6] See Bibliography, below, p. 494, for the *Cartulaires*. Most of them are summarized in Röhricht's *Regesta*.

[7] The Papal letters are to be found in *M.P.L.* The Italian archives have not been completely published. For a summary of existing publications, see Cahen, *op. cit.* pp. 3–4.

[8] The *Assises* are published in the *Recueil*. For a discussion, see La Monte, *Feudal Monarchy*, pp. 97–100, and Grandclaude, *op. cit., passim.*

Appendix I

Two travellers to Palestine during the twelfth century, SAEWULF, who was probably an Englishman who visited the country in 1101, and the German JOHN OF WURZBURG, who came in about 1175, both left records of interest.[1]

3. ARABIC

As the twelfth century advances the contemporary Arabic sources grow in number. For the first part of the century we are dependent on IBN AL-QALANISI[2] for Damascene affairs, on AL-AZIMI[3] for northern Syria and on the somewhat muddled work of IBN AL-AZRAQ[4] for the Jezireh, apart from citations from lost chronicles given by later writers. We have, however, the invaluable memoirs of USAMA IBN MUNQIDH.[5] Usama was a prince of Shaizar, born in 1095. He was exiled forty-three years later, as the result of a family intrigue, and spent the rest of his ninety-three years of life mainly in Damascus, with sojourns in Egypt and at Diarbekir. Though an utter intriguer to whom personal loyalty meant nothing, he was a man of great charm and intelligence, a soldier, a sportsman and a man of letters. His reminiscences, called *Instruction by Examples*, have no chronological order and are the unverified recollections of an old man, but they give an extraordinarily vivid picture of life amongst the Arab and Frankish aristocrats of his time. Almost as vivid are the *Travels* of the Spaniard IBN JUBAYR, who passed through the Kingdom of Jerusalem in 1181.[6]

Saladin's career inspired a whole crop of writers, of whom the most important are IMAD ED-DIN[7] of Isfahan, BEHA ED-DIN IBN SHEDAD,[8]

[1] Ed. and translated into English in *P.P.T.S.* vols IV and V.
[2] See above, vol. I, pp. 333-4.   [3] See above, vol. I, p. 334.
[4] Not fully published. Relevant extracts are analysed by Cahen, in *Journal Asiatique*, 1935.
[5] For Usama I use the translation by Hitti (*An Arab-Syrian Gentleman*) which is based on a more careful study of the original text than that of Derenbourg, published in 1895. The English translation by Potter is based on Derenbourg's version.
[6] The full text of Ibn Jubayr, edited by Wright, was published nearly 100 years ago at Leyden. A translation into French by Gaudefroy-Demonbynes is in process of publication, and a translation into English by R. Broadhurst is to be published shortly. Extracts are given in the *Recueil*.
[7] For Imad ed-Din's works, see Cahen, *La Syrie du Nord*, pp. 50-2. Abu Shama (see below), p. 482, gives long extracts from his works.
[8] The Arabic text is edited by Schultens, and in the *Recueil*. I refer in the footnotes above to the English translation published in the *P.P.T.S.*, which is made from a correlation of the two editions.

and the anonymous author of the *Bustan*, the *General Garden of all the Histories of the Ages*.[1] Imad ed-Din had been a Seldjuk functionary in Iraq who passed into Nur ed-Din's service and was Saladin's secretary from 1173 onwards. He wrote a number of works, including a History of the Seldjuks and an account of Saladin's wars. The latter was reproduced almost in its entirety by Abu Shama and is the most authoritative source for Saladin's biography. His language is peculiarly ornate, complex and difficult. Beha ed-Din was also a member of Saladin's entourage, which he joined in 1188. His Life of Saladin, written in a simple, concise style, depends mainly on hearsay and some reminiscences of Saladin himself till that date. Thenceforward he is as authoritative as Imad ed-Din. The *Bustan* was written at Aleppo in 1196/7. It is a rather bare and summary history of Islam, dealing mainly with Aleppo and Egypt, but contains information only found otherwise in the later and fuller history of Ibn abi Tayyi. Both may depend on a lost Shia source. The other contemporary chroniclers AL-FADIL, As-SHAIBANI and IBN AD-DAHHAN, are known only from quotations.[2]

The greatest historical writer of the thirteenth century is IBN AL-ATHIR of Mosul, who was born in 1160 and died in 1233. His *Kamil at-Tawarikh*, or *Historical Compendium*, is a history of the Moslem world, for which he made careful and critical selections from earlier and contemporary writers. For the First Crusade and the beginning of the twelfth century his entries are rather brief. For the end of the century he is mainly dependent on the writers of Saladin's entourage, though he adds a few personal reminiscences. For the middle of the century, which is covered by no important Moslem historian, he seems to have used original material. His chronology is deficient; he does not name his sources and often transforms their accounts, particularly to suit his pro-Zengid prejudices. But like William of Tyre, he is a real historian who tried to understand the broad significance of the events that he described. His second work, the *History of the Atabegs of Mosul*, is an inferior piece of writing, a somewhat uncritical panegryric, which, however, contains some information not found elsewhere.[3]

The *Mines of Gold* of IBN ABI TAYYI of Aleppo, the only great Shia chronicler, born in 1180, is known to us only from the copious if

[1] Ed. by Cahen in the *Bulletin de l'Institut Oriental à Damas*.
[2] See Cahen, *La Syrie du Nord*, pp. 52-4.
[3] For editions, see above, vol. I, p. 334 n. 2.

rather self-conscious use made of it by Sunni chroniclers. It was clearly a work of great importance, covering all Moslem history, with special reference to Aleppo; and from the surviving quotations it must have made a more detailed use of the same source as the *Bustan*.[1] KEMAL AD-DIN of Aleppo who lived from 1191 to 1262, the author of a probably unfinished biographical encyclopaedia, wrote before 1243 a *Chronicle of Aleppo*, a long, clearly and simply written work, largely dependent on al-Azimi, Ibn al-Qalanisi and the contemporaries of Saladin, as well as oral traditions and information. Kemal is not very careful in correlating his sources and he is prejudiced against the Shia.[2] SIBT IBN AL-DJAUZI, born at Baghdad in 1186, wrote one of the longest of Moslem chronicles, the *Mirror of the Times*; but as regards the twelfth century he merely reproduced information given by earlier writers.[3] ABU SHAMA, born at Damascus in 1203, completed in 1251 a history of the reigns of Nur ed-Din and Saladin, called the *Book of the Two Gardens*.[4] It consists largely of transcripts from Ibn al-Qalanisi, Beha ed-Din, Ibn al-Athir's *Atabegs*, Ibn abi Tayyi, al-Fadil and, above all, Imad ed-Din, to whose style, however, he gave a very welcome pruning.

Of later historians, ABU'L FEDA, Prince of Hama in the early fourteenth century, wrote a history which is nothing more than a useful summary of earlier historians but which enjoyed enormous popularity and is often quoted.[5] IBN KHALDUN, who wrote at the end of the fourteenth century, summarized Ibn al-Athir for Syrian affairs, but used for Egyptian history the lost chronicle of IBN AT-TUWAIR, written in Saladin's time.[6] MAQRISI, writing in the early fifteenth century, contains information about Egypt not found elsewhere.[7]

The biographical dictionary of IBN KHALLIKAN, compiled in the thirteenth century, contains a few unique pieces of historical information.[8]

[1] See Cahen, *op. cit.* pp. 55–7.
[2] See above, vol. I, p. 334 n. 3. His chapters covering the later twelfth century are translated by Blochet and published in the *Revue de l'Orient Latin*.
[3] A few extracts are published in the *Recueil*. A facsimile edition of another rather different MS. is published by Jewett (Chicago, 1907).
[4] An edition was published at Bulaq in 1871 and 1875. My references are to extracts published in the *Recueil*.
[5] Ed. in the *Recueil*.   [6] Ed. at Bulaq in 7 vols. in 1868.
[7] Extracts are translated by Blochet in *Revue de l'Orient Latin*.
[8] Translated into French by de Slane.

Appendix I

There are no sources dealing directly with the Anatolian Turks. Indeed, the thirteenth century IBN BIBI informs us that he could not start his history of the Seldjuks before the year 1192, the death of Kilij Arslan II, owing to the lack of material.[1] Nor are there any relevant sources in Persian.

4. ARMENIAN

The main Armenian source for the first decades of the twelfth century is, as for the First Crusade, MATTHEW OF EDESSA, who died in 1136.[2] His work was continued, in the same nationalistic and anti-Byzantine spirit, by GREGORY THE PRIEST, of Kaisun, up to the year 1162.[3] His contemporary, Saint NERSES SHNORHAL I, Catholicus from 1166 to 1172, wrote a long poem on the fall of Edessa, somewhat lacking in both poetical and historical interest.[4] Nor is the poem by his successor, the Catholicus GREGORY IV DGHA, on the fall of Jerusalem much more impressive.[5] Better, poetically, is the elegy written by a priest called BASIL THE DOCTOR on Baldwin of Marash, whose chaplain he was.[6] The Annals of SAMUEL OF ANI, written in Great Armenia and reaching the year 1177, are more important.[7] They depend partly on Matthew and partly on the lost histories of JOHN THE DEACON and a certain SARCAVAG. The next batch of Armenian historians, writing in Great Armenia in the late thirteenth century, such as MEKHITAR OF AIRAVANK, VARTAN and KIRAKOS, are not very reliable when they deal with Frankish affairs, though they are important for the Moslem background.[8] The historians of Lesser Armenia (Cilicia) begin with an anonymous writer who in about 1230 translated the Chronicle of Michael the Syrian, freely adapting it to suit his passionate patriotism.[9] About 1275 the Constable SEMBAT, translator of the *Assises* of Antioch, wrote a chronicle which depends for the twelfth century on Matthew and Gregory but adds a little information derived from the state archives.[10] A few years later the so-called 'ROYAL HISTORIAN'

[1] Ibn Bibi's comments are to be found at the beginning of vol. III of Houtsma, *Textes Relatifs à l'Histoire des Seldjoukides* (Old Turkish translation of Ibn Bibi).
[2] See above, vol. I, pp. 334–5.
[3] Ed. in the *Recueil* (to which I refer in footnotes). It is also translated by Dulaurier at the end of his edition of Matthew.
[4] Ed. in the *Recueil*.   [5] Ed. in the *Recueil*.   [6] Ed. in the *Recueil*.
[7] Ed. in the *Recueil*.   [8] Extracts in the *Recueil*.
[9] Ed. in the *Recueil*.   [10] Ed. in the *Recueil*.

Appendix I

wrote a chronicle which has never yet been published.[1] Early in
the fourteenth century the Chancellor VAHRAM OF EDESSA wrote a
Rhymed Chronicle, largely dependent on Matthew but containing
much information whose source is unknown.[2]

5. SYRIAC

Of the Syrian sources the World History of MICHAEL THE SYRIAN is
the most important.[3] He was a careful and conscientious historian,
whose only strong prejudice was against the Byzantines. He mentions
the Syrian sources, all now lost, which he used; and he also knew of an
unidentifiable Arabic source for the years 1107 to 1119, which also seems
to have been known to Ibn al-Athir.

An anonymous Syriac chronicle, written by an obscure priest at
Edessa in about 1240, contains valuable information about Edessa,
apart from information clearly derived from Michael.[4] Towards the
end of the thirteenth century Gregory Abu'l-Faraj, better known as
BAR-HEBRAEUS, wrote a world-history, based for the twelfth century
mainly on Michael and Ibn al-Athir, but with a certain amount of
information derived from Persian or other sources.[5]

6. OTHER SOURCES

The only Hebrew source of importance for this period is the Voyage of
BENJAMIN OF TUDELA, who gives a careful account of the Jewish
colonies in Syria at the time of his journey round the Mediterranean
in 1166 to 1170.[6]

Georgian sources, of value only for the history of Georgia and the
neighbouring lands, were collected together in the composite *Georgian
Chronicle*, edited in the eighteenth century.[7]

[1] The MS. is at Venice at the Mekhitarist Library.
[2] Ed. in the *Recueil*.
[3] Ed. and translated into French by Chabot.
[4] The earlier portion of this chronicle has been published in an English
translation by Tritton (*Journal of the Royal Asiatic Society*; see above, vol. I,
p. 349). The full text in Syriac is published by Chabot in the *Corpus Scriptorum
Orientalium*.
[5] Ed. and translated into English by Wallis Budge.
[6] Ed. Adler.   [7] Ed. Brosset.

484

Appendix I

In Old Slavonic there is the *Pilgrimage of* Daniel the Higumene who visited Palestine in 1104.[1]

Certain Norse sagas, notably those dealing with the Crusade of King Sigurd, contain pieces of interesting historical information in the midst of legendary details.[2]

[1] Translated into French by Mme de Khitrowo. I have not been able to see the Slavonic text. She has also translated the brief *Pilgrimage of the Abbess Euphrosyne* from the Slavonic.

[2] These are summarized in Riant, *Les Expéditions des Scandinaves.*

THE BATTLE OF HATTIN

The battle of Hattin is described at some length by the Latin and Arabic sources, but their stories are not always in harmony. I have attempted above on pp. 455–60 to give a consistent and probable account of the battle, but the divergences need to be recorded. It is unfortunate that the only writers who appear to have been present at the battle, apart from the Templar Terence (or Terricus) who wrote a brief letter about it, and some Moslems whose letters are quoted by Abu Shama, are Ernoul, who as Balian of Ibelin's squire presumably accompanied his master and escaped with him, and Imad ed-Din who was in Saladin's entourage. But Ernoul's original account has been tampered with by Bernard the Treasurer and the other continuators of William of Tyre; and Imad ed-Din's account, though vivid at times, is apt to be rhetorical rather than precise. The account of the crisis of the battle given by Saladin's son, al-Afdal, to Ibn al-Athir is vivid but very short.

The *Estoire d'Eracles* is the only source to make it clear that King Guy held two separate councils before the battle, one at Acre, probably on 1 July and one at Sephoria on the evening of 2 July. Raymond of Tripoli spoke on both occasions, and the two separate speeches quoted in the *Estoire* no doubt give the gist of his actual words. But the *Estoire* must be wrong in saying that the council at Acre was called after the Countess of Tripoli had sent to announce Saladin's capture of the town of Tiberias, as Saladin entered Tiberias on the morning of the 2nd; and Raymond does not mention Tiberias in his speech at Acre but merely advises a defensive strategy. Ernoul, as edited by Bernard the Treasurer, ignores the first council. Bernard probably took it upon himself to decide that Raymond's two speeches were made on the same occasion. The *De Expugnatione* also only mentions the second council. Raymond's second speech was known to Ibn al-Athir, who gives it in almost the same words as the *Estoire d'Eracles*, Ernoul and the *De Expugnatione*. Raymond's advice is therefore certain, though Imad ed-Din believed that he had urged the attack, and later writers of Richard Cœur de Lion's entourage who favoured Guy of Lusignan accuse him of treachery. Ambroise and the *Itinerarium Regis Ricardi* both suggest that Raymond lured the army on because of an agreement with Saladin, and the same charge is made in the letter of the Genoese to the Pope, and later by the Syriac Bar-Hebraeus.

Imad ed-Din says that the Countess of Tripoli had her children with her at Tiberias. But Ernoul says that Raymond's four stepsons escaped with him from the battle, and the letter of the Genoese reports their anxiety to rescue their mother at the council before the battle.

King Guy decided to move from Sephoria at Gerard of the Temple's request. This is clearly stated by the *Estoire* and Ernoul but glossed over by the author of *De Expugnatione*, who for some reason never wished to blame the Templars, to judge from his moments of reticence. Raymond, as lord of the territory, was required to advise on the route to be followed and chose the route through Hattin. This advice, which proved disastrous, was the excuse for Raymond's enemies to denounce him as a traitor. We are told in the letter of the Genoese and in the Hospitallers' circular letter on the battle of six traitors, who were apparently Raymond's knights—one was called Laodiceus or Leucius of Tiberias—and who told Saladin of the state of the Christian army. It is, I think, probable that their treachery took place at this juncture and lay in telling Saladin of the route chosen by the Christians. It is difficult to see what useful information they could later have given him. Both the *Estoire* and Ernoul blame Raymond for choosing the camping ground before Hattin. He believed that there was water there, but the spring was dry. The author of the *De Expugnatione* gives a fuller story. He says that Raymond, in the van, recommended hurrying on to the lake, but the Templars, in the rearguard, could go no farther. Raymond was appalled at the King's decision to encamp and cried out 'We are lost!'; but as the decision was made he presumably chose the camping site on the mistaken belief that there was water there. Imad ed-Din reports Saladin's joy at the Christian army's movements.

The actual site of the camp is uncertain. The *De Expugnatione*, the *Itinerarium* and Ambroise call it the village of Marescalcia or Marescallia—perhaps the Khan of Meskeneh preserves the name?—while Imad ed-Din and Beha ed-Din call it the village of Lubieh, which lies on the present road, two miles southwest of the Horns of Hattin. The Arab authors call the battle the battle of Hattin (or Hittin) and make it clear that the final scenes were enacted on the Horns of Hattin. The *Annales de la Terre Sainte* calls the battle Karneatin (i.e. Qarnei Hattin, the Horns of Hattin).[1] Ernoul says that the battle was fought at two leagues' distance from Tiberias. The Horns are in fact about five miles from Tiberias as the crow flies and about nine by road.

Imad ed-Din says that the Saracen archers began to fire arrows at the Christians on the march and complicates the story by saying that it was on the Thursday, because he wanted the battle to have taken place on a Friday. Ernoul and the *Estoire* refer to heavy losses suffered by the Christians on the march. It is uncertain when the ground was set on fire. Ibn al-Athir implies that the fire was started by accident by a Moslem volunteer, and both he and Imad ed-Din make it clear that the fire was raging when the battle began on the morning of 4 July. Imad ed-Din gives a vivid picture of the prayers and songs in the Arab camp during the night.

On the morning of the battle the Frankish infantry tried, according to Ibn al-Athir, to rush towards water. Imad ed-Din says that owing to the flames they could not advance towards the water. The *De Expugnatione* says that the infantrymen made off at once in a solid mass up a hill away from the knights and refused to come back at the King's orders, saying that they were dying of thirst. There they were all slaughtered. Ernoul, on the other hand, says that they surrendered, though five of Raymond's knights went to Saladin to beg him to kill them all. It may be this action was considered to be the treachery referred to by the Hospitallers (see above), though as Ernoul puts it, it might as well be a plea for a quick death for mercy's sake. Beha ed-Din merely says that the Christian army was separated into two parts, one of which, presumably the infantry, hemmed in by fire, was all killed, while the other, the knights round the King, was captured. The Moslem authorities all say that before the attack on the Frankish knights opened there was a single combat between a mameluk and a Christian knight, in which the former, wrongly believed by the Christians to be the Sultan's son, was slain.

According to Ernoul, when the King saw the slaughter of the infantry, he told Raymond to lead a charge against the Saracens.

[1] Qarnei is the dual of Qarn, a horn.

Raymond as lord of the district was the proper person to do so, and such a charge offered the only chance for the army to extricate itself. There seems therefore to be no ground for the accusation of treachery levelled at Raymond by later Christian writers, the Genoese and the King's friends, nor for the accusation of cowardice levelled at him by the Moslems. But Taki's clever manœuvre in opening his ranks to let Raymond through seemed to support the former accusation, though Imad ed-Din says that Raymond's men suffered heavy losses. Ernoul says that Raymond only fled from the battlefield when he saw that the King's position was hopeless and there was no chance of rescuing him. The *De Expugnatione* says that Balian and Reynald of Sidon fled with Raymond, without giving details, as does Imad ed-Din. But Ernoul implies that they escaped separately, which is more probable, as they were in a different part of the army. They must have broken through with the few Templars whose escape is reported by Terence. The *De Expugnatione*'s detailed account of the battle stops with Raymond's escape. Probably the author's informant was one of Raymond's men.

Imad ed-Din says that after Raymond's escape the King and his knights began to retire up the hill of Hattin, leaving their horses (which presumably had been wounded and were useless). He remarks how powerless Christian knights are without their horses. Ibn al-Athir says that they attempted to set up their tents on the summit but only had time to dress the King's. The knights were dismounted and exhausted when they were taken. Both say that the Cross was captured by Taki. Al-Afdal's account gives the story of the last moments of the Christian army; while Ibn el-Kadesi gives the detail that a strong wind arose at midday when the Moslems made their final attack.

The incidents in Saladin's tent after the battle are told in almost the same language by Ernoul and the *Estoire* and by Imad ed-Din and Ibn al-Athir. There is no need to doubt the story of the drink given to King Guy nor of Reynald of Châtillon's death at Saladin's own hands.

The size of the Christian army is given by the *Historia Regni Hierosolymitani* as 1000 knights of the Kingdom with an extra 1200 paid for by King Henry II, 4000 Turcopoles and 32,000 infantrymen, 7000 of which were paid for by Henry. This number is clearly exaggerated. The *Itinerarium* talks of a total of 20,000, which is still probably too high. The true figure for the knights may be 1000, with 200 more

equipped by Henry, that is, 1200 in all. The *Estoire d'Eracles* gives the
whole army as 9000 in one MS. and 40,000 in another. The Hospitaller's
letter talks of 1000 knights being killed or captured at the battle and
200 escaping. Ernoul says that Raymond of Antioch brought 50 or
60 knights (the MS. readings vary). Terence says that 260 Templars
were slain at the battle and hardly anyone escaped—he says 'nos' which
may mean only himself. The Hospitallers' letter puts the survivors at
200. The infantry cannot have outnumbered the cavalry by as much
as ten to one, and probably numbered considerably less than 10,000.
The Turcopole light cavalry may have numbered 4000, but it seems
to have played no special role in the battle and was probably smaller.
Saladin's army was probably slightly larger, but no reliable figures are
given. The figure of 12,000 horsemen and numerous volunteers given
by Imad ed-Din is certainly exaggerated, though not as exaggerated
as the figure of 50,000 that he gives for the Christian army. (Beha
ed-Din, however, goes further, saying that 30,000 Christians were killed
and 30,000 captured.) We may perhaps assume that Saladin's total
regular army numbered about 12,000 but that it was swelled by
volunteers and contingents from allies to about 18,000. The armies seem
to have been amongst the largest put in the field up to that date by
either the Crusaders or their enemies; but 15,000 on the Christian side
and 18,000 on the Moslem must be regarded as the maximum figure.
The Christian knights were better armed than any Moslem soldiers,
but the Moslem light cavalry was probably better armed than the
Turcopoles and the infantry as well or better than the Christian.

NOTES

The main sources for the battle are as follows:

Frankish. Ernoul, pp. 155–74; *Estoire d'Eracles*, II, pp. 46–49; *De Expugnatione*,
   pp. 218–28; *Itinerarium Regis Ricardi*, pp. 12–17; Benedict of Peterborough,
   II, pp. 10–14, incorporating the letter of the Genoese to the Pope and the
   letter of the Templar Terence; Ambroise, ed. Paris, cols. 67–70; Ansbert,
   Gesta Frederici, containing letter of the Hospitallers to Archimbald;
   Historia Regni Hierosolymitani, pp. 52–3; *Annales de la Terre Sainte*, p. 218.
Arabic. Beha ed-Din, *P.P.T.S.* pp. 110–16; Ibn al-Athir, pp. 679–88, including
   al-Afdal's description of the battle; Abu Shama, pp. 262–89, incorporating
   Imad ed-Din's whole account of the battle and extracts from Beha ed-Din
   and Mohammed ibn el-Kadesi.

Appendix II

There is a brief account of the battle in Michael the Syrian, III, p. 404, and a longer and inaccurate one in Bar-Hebraeus, trans. Budge, pp. 322–4, in which he mixes up Queen Sibylla with the Countess Eschiva of Tripoli. The Armenian version of Michael the Syrian (pp. 396–8) and Kirakos of Gantzag (pp. 420–1) give inaccurate accounts. The Syriac and Armenian accounts all report Raymond as a traitor.

There is a valuable discussion of the sources and of Raymond's role in Baldwin, *Raymond III of Tripolis*, pp. 151–60.

APPENDIX III: GENEALOGICAL TREES

1. ROYAL HOUSE OF JERUSALEM: COUNTS OF EDESSA: LORDS OF SIDON AND CAESAREA

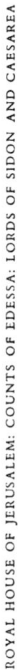

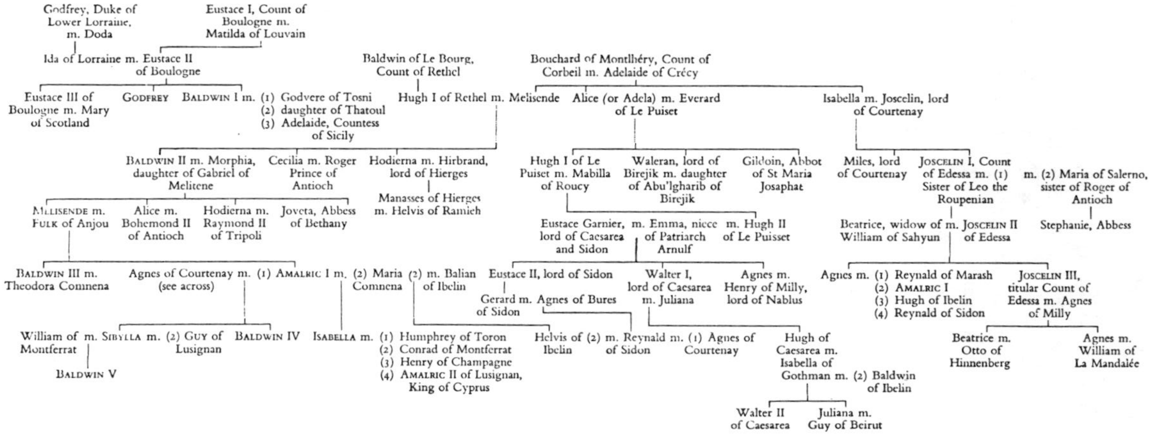

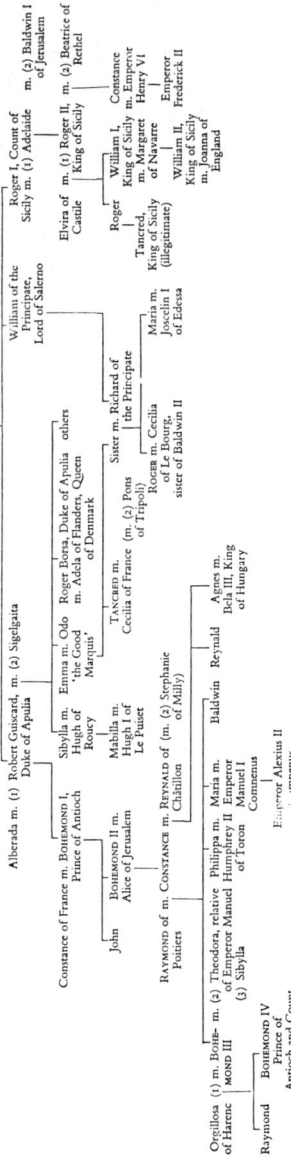

2. PRINCES OF ANTIOCH AND KINGS OF SICILY

3. COUNTS OF TRIPOLI AND PRINCES OF GALILEE

Elvira of Aragon m. RAYMOND I, Count of Toulouse, Marquis of Provence, Count of Saint Gilles

Alfonso-Jordan, Count | Helen m. BERTRAND, Count of Tripoli
of Toulouse

Bertrand
(illegitimate)

Cecilia of France m. Pons
widow of
Tancred of
Antioch

Agnes m. Reynald II
Mazoir of Marqab

RAYMOND II m. Hodierna
of Jerusalem

Hugh Falconberg
of Saint-Omer, Prince
of Galilee

Agnes m. William I of Bures, m. ? (2) Eschiva of
Prince of Galilee | Saint-Omer

? Ermengarde m. Gerard
of Ibelin | Agnes m. Gerard
of Sidon

William II, | ? Elinand of Bures, m. ? Eschiva of
Prince of Galilee | Prince of Galilee

RAYMOND III (2) m. Eschiva of Bures, Princess of Galilee, lady of Tiberias m. (1) Walter Falconberg of
Saint-Omer, probably
grandson of Hugh of
Saint-Omer, Prince of
Galilee

Melisende

Margaret of | Otto m. Euphemia | Ralph m.
Ibelin m. Hugh | of Sidon | Agnes of Sidon

Maria of Beirut, m. William
widow of
Baldwin of Ibelin

Note. The genealogy of the Princes of Galilee is very uncertain. See Ducange, *Familles d'Outremer*, ed. Rey, pp. 447–55, and Grousset, *Histoire des Croisades*, II, pp. 840–50.

4. LORDS OF TORON, OULTREJOURDAIN, NABLUS AND RAMLEH (HOUSE OF IBELIN)

Roman of Le Puy

Pagan, lord of
Oultrejourdain

×

Maurice, lord of
Oultrejourdain

Isabella m. Philip of Milly,
lord of Nablus

Guy of Milly, m. Stephanie m. Baldwin, lord
Lord of Nablus | of Nablus

Guy | Agnes m. Henry the
Garnier | Buffalo

Helvis | Agnes m.
m. Adan | Joscin III
of Beisan | of Edessa

Philip of Milly,
lord of Nablus

Stephanie m. (1) William Dorel,
lord of Botrun
(2) Reynald II Em-
briaco, lord of
Jebail

Manasses of (2) m. Helvis, heiress m. (1) Balian the Old,
Hierges | of Ramleh | lord of Ibelin

Hugh of | Richelda of m. Baldwin of m. (2) Isabella of
Ramleh m. | Beisan | Ramleh | Gothman, widow
Agnes of | | | of Walter I of
Courtenay | | | Caesarea
| | | (3) Maria of Nablus

Balian m.
Maria Comnena,
widow of
Amalric I,
lady of Nablus

Ermengarde m.
Prince of Galilee
? Elinand

Richelda
(see above)

Plivano of m. Lucia heiress
Genoa | of Botrun

Thomas

Eschiva m. Amalric II
(of Lusignan), King of
Cyprus and later
of Jerusalem

Stephanie
m. Amalric,
Viscount of
Nablus

John,
later lord
of Beirut

Philip | Helvis m.
Reynald of
Sidon

Margaret m.
(1) Hugh of
Tiberias
(2) Walter III
of Caesarea

Humphrey I,
lord of Toron

heiress of m. Humphrey II of
Banyas | Toron, Constable

m. (2) Philippa
of Antioch

Humphrey III m. Stephanie, m. (2) Miles of
heiress of | Plancy
Oultre- | (1) Reynald of
jourdain | Châtillon

Helen m.
Walter III
of Beirut

Isabella m.
Roupen III,
Prince of Armenia

Humphrey IV
m. Isabella
of Jerusalem

5. ORTOQID PRINCES

Ortoq

Ilghazi of Mardin

Bahram

Abd-al-Jabbar

Suleiman m.
Mayyafaraqin

Timurtash of
Mardin
(lord of Mardin
1122–1152)

Balak
(lord of Harran,
later of Kharput
and Aleppo)

Suleiman
Said ed-Daulah
(lord of Aleppo
1121–1122)

Alp of Mardin
1153–1176

Qutb ed-Din Ilghazi of Mardin
(lord of Mardin, 1176–1184)

Soqman of Hisn Kaifa

Ibrahim of | Dawud | Ayaz
Hisn Kaifa

Kara Arslan

Abu Bakr of | Nur ed-Din
Kharput | Mohammed
of Hisn Kaifa

Soqman II

6. HOUSE OF ZENGI

Aqsonqor

Imad ed-Din Zengi,
Atabeg of Mosul

Saif ed-Din Ghazi I,
atabeg of Mosul

Nur ed-Din Mahmud,
atabeg, later
King of Syria

Qutb ed-Din Mawdud,
atabeg of Mosul

Nasr ed-Din

As-Salih Ismail

Saif ed-Din
Ghazi II,
atabeg of
Mosul

Izz ed-Din
Masud,
atabeg of
Mosul

Imad ed-Din
Zengi,
atabeg of
Sinjar

BIBLIOGRAPHY

[NOTE. This bibliography is supplementary to the bibliography in vol. I of this *History*, and does not include works already mentioned there. The same abbreviations are employed.]

I. ORIGINAL SOURCES

1. COLLECTIONS OF SOURCES

BORGO, F. DAL. *Diplomata Pisana*. Pisa, 1765.

DEMETRACOPOULOS, A. K. *Bibliotheca Ecclesiastica*. Leipzig, 1866.

Fornmanna Sögur, 12 vols. Copenhagen, 1825–37.

HALPHEN, L. and POUPARDIN, R. *Chroniques des Comtes d'Anjou*. Paris, 1913.

Liber Jurium Reipublicae Genuensis (ed. Ricotti), 3 vols., in *Monumenta Historiae Patriae*. Turin, 1854–7.

MARCHEGAY, P. and MABILLE, E. *Chronique des Eglises d'Anjou*. Paris, 1869.

MURATORI, L. A. *Antiquitates Italicae*, 6 vols. Milan, 1738–42.

Recueil des Historiens des Croisades, Lois, 2 vols. Paris 1841–3, including the *Assises* and *Lignages* of Jerusalem (*R.H.C. Lois*).

REINAUD, M. *Extraits des Historiens Arabes*, in Michaud, *Bibliothèque des Croisades*, vol. II. Paris, 1829.

TAFEL, G. L. F. and THOMAS, G. M. *Urkunden zur ältern Handels und Staatsgeschichte der Republik Venedig*, 3 vols. Vienna, 1856–7.

2. LATIN AND OLD FRENCH SOURCES

Ambroise. *L'Estoire de la Guerre Sainte* (ed. Paris). Paris, 1897.

Annales Barenses, in *M.G.H.Ss.* vol. V.

Annales Beneventani, in *M.G.H.Ss.* vol. III.

Annales Herbipolenses, in *M.G.H.Ss.* vol. XVI.

Annales Palidenses, in *M.G.H.Ss.* vol. XVI.

Annales Romani, in *M.G.H.Ss.* vol. V.

Annales S. Rudberti Salisburgensis, in *M.G.H.Ss.* vol. IX.

Annales de Terre Sainte (ed. Röhricht), in *Archives de l'Orient Latin*, vol. II. Paris, 1884.

Ansbert. *Gesta Frederici Imperatoris in Expeditione Sacra*, in *M.G.H.Ss.*, *in usum scholarum*, 1892.

Arnold of Lübeck. *Chronica Slavorum, M.G.H.Ss.*, *in usum scholarum*, 1868.

Benedict of Peterborough. *Gesta Regis Henrici II* (ed. Stubbs), 2 vols., Rolls Series. London, 1867.

Bernard, St, Abbot of Clairvaux. *Epistolae, M.P.L.*, vol. CLXXXII.

Burchard of Mount Sion. *Description of the Holy Land* (trans. Stewart), *P.P.T.S.* vol. XII. London, 1896.

Bibliography

Caesarius of Heisterbach. *Dialogus Miraculorum* (ed. Strange), 2 vols. Cologne, 1851.

Cartulaire de Notre Dame de Chartres (ed. L'Epinois and Merlet), 3 vols. Chartres, 1852–5.

Cartulaire de Sainte Marie Josaphat (ed. Kohler). *Revue de l'Orient Latin*, vol. VII. Geneva, 1899.

Cartulaire du Saint Sépulcre (ed. Rozière). Paris, 1849.

Cartulaire Général de l'Ordre des Hospitaliers (ed. Delaville Le Roulx), 4 vols. Paris, 1894–1904.

Cartulaire Général de l'Ordre du Temple (ed. D'Albon). Paris, 1913.

Chronicon Mauriniacense, in *R.H.F.* vol. XII.

Chronicon Sancti Maxentii, in Marchegay and Mabille, *op. cit.*

Chronicon Vindocinense, in Marchegay and Mabille, *op. cit.*

Dandolo. *Chronicon Venetum*, in Muratori, *Rerum Italicarum Scriptores*, vol. XII.

De Expugnatione Terrae Sanctae per Saladinum Libellus (ed. Stubbs), Rolls Series. London, 1875.

Ernoul. *Chronique d'Ernoul et de Bernard le Trésorier* (ed. Mas Latrie). Paris, 1871.

Estoire d'Eracles, *R.H.C.Occ.* vols. I and II.

Eudes, *see* Odo.

Gesta Ambaziencium Dominorum, in Halphen and Poupardin, *op. cit.*

Gesta Consulum Andegavorum, in Halphen and Poupardin, *op. cit.*

Gestes des Chiprois, *R.H.C.Arm.* vol. II.

Historia Ducum Veneticorum, in *M.G.H.Ss.* vol. XIV.

Historia Regni Hierosolymitani, in *M.G.H.Ss.* vol. XVIII.

Historia Regum Hierusalem Latinorum, ed. in Kohler, *Mélanges pour servir à l'histoire de l'Orient Latin*, vol. I. Paris, 1906.

Historia Welforum Weingartensis, in *M.G.H.Ss.* vol. XXI.

Ibelin. *Le Livre de Jean d'Ibelin*, in *R.H.C. Lois*, vol. I.

Itinerarium Peregrinorum et Gesta Regis Ricardi (ed. Stubbs), Rolls Series. London, 1864.

John of Salisbury. *Historiae Pontificalis quae Supersunt* (ed. Lane Poole). Oxford, 1927.

John of Wurzburg. *Description of the Holy Land* (trans. Stewart), *P.P.T.S.* vol. V. London, 1896.

Landolph Junior. *Historia Mediolanensis*, in Muratori, *Rerum Italicarum Scriptores*, vol. V.

Letters of King Amalric, Masters of the Temple, officials of the Temple and other officials of Outremer, in *R.H.F.* vols. XV and XVI.

Lignages d'Outremer, in *R.H.C. Lois*, vol. II.

Louis VII, King of France, letters, in *R.H.F.* vols. XV and XVI.

Miracula Sancti Leonardi, Aa. Ss. (Nov.), vol. III.

Bibliography

Necrologia Panormitana (ed. Winkelmann), in *Forschungen zur deutschen Geschichte*, vol. XVIII. Göttingen, 1878.

Odo (Eudes) of Deuil. *De Profectione Ludovici VII in Orientem* (ed. Waquet). Paris, 1949.

Osborn. *De Expugnatione Lyxbonensi*, in Stubbs, *Memorials of the Reign of Richard I*, Rolls Series. London, 1864.

Otto, Bishop of Freisingen. *Chronica* (ed. Hofmeister), *M.G.H.Ss.*, *in usum scholarum*, 1912.

Otto, Bishop of Freisingen. *Gesta Friderici Imperatoris* (ed. Simson), *M.G.H.Ss.*, *in usum scholarum*, 1912.

Otto of Saint Blaise. *Chronica* (ed. Hofmeister), *M.G.H.Ss.*, *in usum scholarum*, 1912.

Paschal II, Pope. *Epistolae*, in *M.P.L.* vol. CLXIII.

Passiones Sancti Thiemonis, in *R.H.C.Occ.* vol. V.

Peter Diaconus. *Chronica* (ed. Wattenbach), *M.G.H.Ss.* vol. VII.

Pilgrimage of Saewulf to Jerusalem (trans. Bishop of Clifton), *P.P.T.S.* vol. IV. London, 1896.

Radulph of Diceto. *Opera Historica* (ed. Stubbs), Rolls Series. London, 1876.

Ralph of Coggeshall. *Chronicon Anglicanum* (ed. Stevenson), Rolls Series. London, 1875.

Robert of Torigny. *Chronique* (ed. Delisle), 2 vols. Rouen, 1872-3.

Roger of Hoveden. *Chronica* (ed. Stubbs), 4 vols., Rolls Series. London, 1868-71.

Romuald of Salerno. *Chronicon* (ed. Arndt). *M.G.H.Ss.* vol. XIX.

Suger, Abbot of Saint-Denis. *Gesta Ludovici cognomine Grossi* and *Historia gloriosi regis Ludovici VII* (ed. Molinier). Paris, 1887.

Suger, Abbot of Saint-Denis. *Opera* (ed. de la Marche). Paris, 1867.

Vita Alexandri III, in *Liber Pontificalis*, vol. II.

Vita Sancti Bernardi, in *M.P.L.* vol. CLXXXV.

Walter the Chancellor, *Bella Antiochena* in *R.H.C.Occ.* vol. V.

Wibald, *Wibaldi Epistolae*, in Jaffé, *Bibliotheca Rerum Germanicarum*, vol. I.

William the Monk. *Dialogus Apologeticus* (ed. Wilmart), in *Revue Mabillon*. Paris, 1942.

William the Monk. *Vita Sugerii*, in Suger, *Opera* (*see* above).

William of Nangis. *Gesta Ludovici VII*, in *R.H.F.* vol. XX.

William of Tyre. *Die lateinische Fortsetzung* (*Latin Continuation*) (ed. Salloch). Leipzig, 1934.

3. GREEK SOURCES

Chrysolan, Peter, Archbishop of Milan. *De Sancto Spiritu* in *M.P.G.* vol. CXXVII.

Cinnamus, John. *Epitome Historiarum*, *C.S.H.B.* Bonn, 1836.

Eustratius, Archbishop of Nicaea. *On the Holy Ghost*, in Demetracopoulos, *Bibliotheca Ecclesiastica*, vol. I.

Bibliography

Nicetas Choniates (Acominatus). *Historia, C.S.H.B.* Bonn, 1835.

Neophytus. *De Calamitatibus Cypri* (ed. Stubbs), Rolls Series. London, 1864. (In preface to *Itinerarium Regis Ricardi.*)

Phocas, John. *A Brief Description* (trans. Stewart), *P.P.T.S.* vol. v. London, 1896.

Prodromus, Theodore. *Poemata*, selections in *M.P.G.* vol. cxxxiii and *R.H.C.G.* vol. ii.

4. Arabic Sources[1]

Abu Firas. *Noble Word*, ed. in Guyard, 'Un Grand Maître des Assassins' in *Journal Asiatique*, 7me série, vol. ix, Paris, 1877.

Abu'l Mahâsin. Extracts in *R.H.C.Or.* vol. iii.

Abu Shama. *Book of the Two Gardens.* Extracts in *R.H.C.Or.* vols. iv and v; full edition. Cairo, 1870–1. (Except when otherwise stated references are to the *R.H.C.* edition.)

Al-Azimi. *Abrégé* (ed. Cahen), in *Journal Asiatique*, vol. ccxxxii. Paris, 1940.

Beha ed-Din ibn Shedad. *Life of Saladin* (trans. Conder), in *P.P.T.S.* vol. xiii. London, 1897.

Bustan al-Djami li Djami Tawarikhi z-Zaman (ed. Cahen), in *Bulletin d'Etudes Orientales de l'Institut de Damas*, vols. vii and viii. Damascus, 1938.

Ibn Jubayr. *Voyage* (Arabic text ed. Wright). Leyden, 1852.

Ibn Moyessar. Extracts in *R.H.C.Or.* vol. iii.

Ibn at-Tiqtaqa. *Al-Fakhri* (*History of Musulman Dynasties*); trad. Amar. Paris, 1910.

Imad ed-Din. *Al Fath al Qussi fi'l Fath al Qudsi* (ed. de Landsberg). Leyden, 1888. Extracts quoted by Abu Shama, *op. cit.*

Kemal ad-Din. *Chronicle of Aleppo* (later portions trans. Blochet) in *Revue de l'Orient Latin*, vols. iii and vi. Paris, 1895–8.

Maqrisi. *History of Egypt* (trans. Blochet). *Revue de l'Orient Latin*, vols. viii–x. Paris, 1900–2.

Sibt ibn al-Djauzi. Extracts in *R.H.C.Or.* vol. iii.

Usama ibn Munqidh. *Autobiography* (ed. Hitti). *An Arab-Syrian Gentleman of the Crusades.* New York, 1929.

Zettersteen Chronicle. Anonymous chronicle (ed. K.V. Zettersteen). Leyden, 1919.

5. Armenian, Syriac, Georgian and Hebrew Sources

Basil the Doctor. *Funeral Elegy of Baldwin of Marash, R.H.C.Arm.* vol. i.

Gregory the Priest. *Continuation of Matthew of Edessa's Chronicle, R.H.C.Arm.* vol. i.

Gregory IV Dgha, Catholicus. *Elegy on the Fall of Jerusalem, R.H.C.Arm.* vol. i.

Nerses Shnorhali, Catholicus. *Elegy on the Fall of Edessa, R.H.C.Arm.* vol. i.

---

[1] References to Ibn al-Athir are to his *Sum of World History* (*Kamil at-Tawarikh*), except when otherwise stated.

Bibliography

Anonymous Syriac Chronicle (full text ed. Chabot). *C.S.C.O.* vol. III. (Quoted as *Chron. Anon. Syr.*) References are to Tritton's translation—see above, vol. I, Bibliography, p. 349—except where otherwise stated.

Georgian Chronicle, in Brosset, *Histoire de la Géorgie.*

Benjamin of Tudela. *Voyages* (ed. Adler). London, 1907.

Joseph ben Joshua ben Meir. *Chronicle* (trans. Biellablotzky), 2 vols. London, 1835.

6. SLAVONIC AND NORSE SOURCES

Daniel the Higumene. *Vie et Pèlerinage de Daniel, Hégoumène Russe* (trans. de Khitrowo). *Itinér. Russes en Orient, Société de l'Orient Latin.* Geneva, 1889.

'Pèlerinage en Palestine de l'Abbesse Euphrosyne, Princesse de Polotsk' (trans. de Khitrowo), in *Revue de l'Orient Latin*, vol. III. Paris, 1896.

Agrip of Noregs Konungasögum (ed. Munch), in *Samlinger til det Norske Folks Sprog og Historie*, vol. II. Oslo, 1834.

Sigurdar Saga Jorsalafara ok brœdra hans in Fornmanna Sögur, vol. VII.

II. MODERN WORKS

ABEL, F. M. *Géographie de la Palestine*, 2 vols. Paris, 1933–8.

ALLEN, W. E. D. *History of the Georgian People.* London, 1932.

ALMEIDA, F. DE. *Historia de Portugal*, 4 vols. Coimbra, 1922–6.

ANSELME DE LA VIERGE MARIE (P. DE GUIBOURS). *Histoire Généalogique et Chronologique de la France*, 9 vols. Paris, 1726–33.

BALDWIN, M. W. *Raymond III of Tripolis and the Fall of Jerusalem.* Princeton, 1936.

BEL, A. Article 'Almohads', in *Encyclopaedia of Islam.*

BERNHARDI, W. VON. *Konrad III.* Leipzig, 1883.

BROSSET, M. F. *Histoire de la Géorgie.* St Petersburg, 1849.

BROWNE, E. G. *Literary History of Persia*, 4 vols. London, 1906–30.

CAHEN, C. 'Indigènes et Croisés', in *Syria*, vol. XV. Paris, 1934.

CAHEN, C. 'Notes sur l'histoire des Croisades et de l'Orient latin', in *Bulletin de la Faculté des Lettres de Strasbourg*, 1951.

CASPAR, E. 'Die Kreuzzugsbullen Eugens III', in *Neues Archiv der Gesellschaft*, vol. XLV. Hanover, 1924.

CATE, J. L. 'A Gay Crusader', in *Byzantion*, vol. XVI, 2. New York, 1943.

CODERA, F. *Decadencia y Desaparición de los Almoravides en España.* Saragossa, 1899.

COSACK, H. 'Konrad III's Entschluss zum Kreuzzug', in *Mitteilungen des Instituts für österreichische Geschichtsforschung*, vol. XXXV. Vienna, 1914.

CUISSARD, C. *Les Seigneurs du Puiset.* Orleans, 1881.

Bibliography

Curzon, H. de. *La Règle du Temple.* Paris, 1886.

D'Albon, G. A. M. J. A. 'La Mort d'Odon de Saint-Amand', in *Revue de l'Orient Latin,* vol. xii. Paris, 1904.

Delaville Le Roulx, G. *Les Hospitaliers en Terre Sainte et à Chypre.* Paris, 1904.

Delisle, L. *Mémoire sur les Opérations Financières des Templiers.* Paris, 1889.

Dib, P. Article 'Maronites', in Vacant et Mangenot, *Dictionnaire de Théologie Catholique.*

Dodu, G. *Histoire des Institutions Monarchiques dans le Royaume Latin de Jérusalem.* Paris, 1894.

Dositheus, Patriarch of Jerusalem. Ἱστορία περὶ τῶν ἐν Ἱεροσολύμοις Πατριαρχευσάντων. Bucharest, 1715.

Erdmann, K. 'Der Kreuzzugsgedankes in Portugal', in *Historische Zeitschrift,* vol. cxli. Munich, 1930.

Gerulli, E. *Etiopi in Palestina.* Rome, 1943.

Gleber, H. *Papst Eugen III.* Jena, 1936.

Grandclaude, M. 'Liste d'Assises remontant au premier Royaume de Jérusalem', in *Mélanges Paul Fournier.* Paris, 1929.

Hagenmeyer, H. *Chronologie du Royaume de Jérusalem.* Paris, 1901.

Hammer, J. von. *Histoire de l'Ordre des Assassins* (French trans.). Paris, 1833.

Hertzog, E. *Die Frauen auf den Fürstentronen der Kreuzfahrerstaaten.* Zürich, 1915.

Johns, C. N. 'The Crusaders' attempt to colonize Palestine and Syria', in *Journal of the Royal Central Asian Society,* vol. xxi. London, 1934.

Joranson, E. 'The Crusade of Henry the Lion', in *Medieval Essays presented to G. W. Thompson.* Chicago, 1938.

Kohler, C. 'Un nouveau récit de l'invention des Patriarches Abraham, Isaac et Jacob à Hébron', in *Revue de l'Orient Latin,* vol. iv. Paris, 1896.

Kügler, B. *Studien zur Geschichte des zweiten Kreuzzuges.* Stuttgart, 1866.

La Monte, J. L. 'The Lords of Caesarea in the period of the Crusades', in *Speculum,* vol. xxii. Cambridge, Mass., 1947.

La Monte, J. L. 'The Lord of Le Puiset on the Crusades', in *Speculum,* vol. xvii. Cambridge, Mass., 1942.

La Monte, J. L. 'The Lords of Sidon', in *Byzantion,* vol. xvii. New York, 1944.

La Monte, J. L. 'To what extent was the Byzantine Empire the suzerain of the Crusading States?' *Byzantion,* vol. vii. Brussels, 1932.

Lane Poole, S. *Saladin.* London, 1898.

Le Quien, M. *Oriens Christianus,* 3 vols. Paris, 1740.

Luchaire, A. *Louis VI le Gros.* Paris, 1890.

Marinescu, C. 'Le Prêtre Jean', in *Bulletin de la Section Historique de l'Académie Roumaine,* vol. x. Bucharest, 1923.

Bibliography

MARTIN, ABBÉ. 'Les premiers princes croisés et les Syriens jacobites de Jérusalem', in *Journal Asiatique* (8me série), vols. XII and XIII. Paris, 1888–9.

MELVILLE, M. *La Vie des Templiers*. Paris, 1951.

MUSIL, A. Article 'Aila', in *Encyclopaedia of Islam*.

NAU, F. 'Le croisé lorrain, Godefroy de Ascha', in *Journal Asiatique* (9me série), vol. XIV. Paris, 1899.

NEUMANN, C. *Bernhard von Clairvaux und die Anfänge des zweiten Kreuzzuges.* Heidelberg, 1882.

RAMSAY, W. M. 'Preliminary report on exploration in Phrygia and Lycaonia' and 'War of Moslem and Christian for the posession of Asia Minor', in *Studies in the History and Art of the Eastern Provinces of the Roman Empire.* Aberdeen, 1906.

REY, E. G. 'Les Seigneurs de Giblet', in *Revue de l'Orient Latin*, vol. III. Paris, 1895.

REY, E. G. 'Les Seigneurs de Barut' and 'Les Seigneurs de Montréal et la Terre d'Oultrejourdain', in *Revue de l'Orient Latin*, vol. IV. Paris, 1896.

REY, E. G. 'Résumé de l'Histoire des Princes d'Antioche', in *Revue de l'Orient Latin*, vol. IV. Paris, 1896.

RICHARD, J. *Le Comté de Tripoli sous la dynastie Toulousaine*. Paris, 1945.

SCHLUMBERGER, G. *Campagnes du roi Amaury de Jérusalem en Egypte.* Paris, 1906.

SCHLUMBERGER, G. *La Numismatique de l'Orient Latin.* Paris, 1878.

SCHLUMBERGER, G. *Les Principautés Franques du Levant.* Paris, 1877.

SCHLUMBERGER, G. *Renaud de Châtillon.* Paris, 1923.

SCHWAB, M. 'Al-Harizi et ses pérégrinations en Terre Sainte', in *Archives de l'Orient Latin.* vol. I. Paris, 1881.

VACANDARD, E. *Vie de Saint Bernard, Abbé de Clairvaux*, 2 vols. Paris, 1895.

VAILHÉ, S. 'Les Laures de Saint Gérasime et de Calamon', in *Echos d'Orient*, vol. II. Paris, 1899.

VOGUE, C. J. M. DE. *Les Eglises de la Terre Sainte.* Paris, 1860.

WALKER, C. H. 'Eleanor of Aquitaine and the disaster at Cadmos Mountain', in *American Historical Review*, vol. LV. New York, 1950.

INDEX

Note. Names of peoples, such as Arabs, Greeks, Turks, Franks, Frenchmen, Italians, Germans, Egyptians, or of their countries, or countries such as Syria or Palestine, or of states such as Byzantium or the Caliphate or the four Crusader states, Jerusalem, Antioch, Tripoli and Edessa, or of their capitals, are not included in this index.

Index

Alberic of Beauvais, Bishop of Ostia, 221, 228
Albert, Count of Biandrate, 18–24, 31
Albert of Aix, historian, 19, 476
Albert of Namur, lord of Jaffa, 191
Albistan, 40, 45–6, 122, 356
Albu ibn Arslantash, lord of Sinjar, 108–10
Aleppo, 9, 11, 39–40, 44, 52–3, 113, 121, 127–8, 131–3, 134, 147–51, 154–5, 158, 160, 162–3, 165, 171–5, 179–80, 182–3, 185, 195, 213, 215–16, 227, 234, 238, 242, 278, 281, 325, 328, 336, 341, 343–4, 354, 357, 369, 372, 382, 389, 395, 398, 404, 407–9, 416, 418, 421, 433–5, 437, 445, 454, 481–2
Alexander the Great, King of Macedon, 189
Alexander III, Pope, 422
Alexander of Conversano, Count of Gravina, 260, 379
Alexandretta, 9, 212, 328, 346
Alexandria, 12, 374–5, 403, 462
Alexius I, Comnenus, Emperor, relations with Frankish kingdom, 8–9, 14–16; and Crusades of 1101, 19–22, 25–8; and Bohemond, 38, 40, 46–51; and Tancred, 53–5, 119, 121, 138; and County of Tripoli, 56, 62, 65–6, 69–70; relations with Papacy, 35, 136–7; death, 105, 206–7. Other references, 240, 260, 308–9
Alexius II, Comnenus, Emperor, 422, 427–8
Alexius, see Axuch, Bela
Alfonso I, King of Aragon, 250
Alfonso VII, King of Castile, 250
Alfonso-Henry, Count of Portugal, 258
Alfonso-Jordan, Count of Toulouse, 61, 65, 253, 280, 281
Ali ibn Wafa, Assassin, 325–6
Alice of Jerusalem, Princess of Antioch, marriage, 176–7; plots for regency, 183–4, 188–90, 198–200. Other references, 202, 213, 231, 305, 404
Alice of Montlhéry, lady of Le Puiset, 190 n.
Almohads, 250
Almoravids, 250–1, 258
Almyro (Halmyrus), 65
Alp Arslan, Seldjuk prince, 181–2, 237, 239
Alp Arslan, prince of Aleppo, 127–8
Alps, 248, 257

Altuntash, governor of Bosra, 241–3
Alvisus, Bishop of Arras, 254
Amadeus, Count of Savoy, 254
Amalfi, Amalfitans, 156, 294
Amalric I, King of Jerusalem, accession and description, 362–5; reign, 367–99; legal activities, 301–2, 364. Other references, 233, 299, 305, 309, 315, 318 n., 334, 340, 353, 403, 404, 443 n.
Amalric of Lusignan, later Amalric II, King of Jerusalem, 424, 439, 447, 459
Amalric of Nesle, Patriarch of Jerusalem, 360–1, 377, 384, 390, 404
Amanus mountains, 9, 54, 201, 222
Amasea, 22–3
Ambroise, historian, 478–9, 487
al-Amir, Caliph, 13, 168–9, 337
Amir ibn Sallah, vizier of Egypt, 337–8
Amman, 372
Ammar, Banū, 8, 11, 12, 34, 54, 57–8, 60, 69, 115; see Abu'l Manaqib, Fakhr el-Mulk
Amrun, Banū, 11
Anacletus, II, Anti-Pope, 252
Anatolia, 13–15, 21, 28, 29, 44, 108, 111, 118–19, 135, 207, 216, 222, 224, 238, 264, 266–7, 274–6, 282, 285, 315, 321, 355, 411–12, 426, 427
Anazarbus, 182–3, 201, 212, 351, 364
Andronicus I, Comnenus, Emperor, 332, 364, 377–9, 427–9, 430
Andronicus, see Comnenus, Contostephanus, Vatatses
Angelus, see Isaac
Angoulême, see Fulcher, Geoffrey
Ani, 159; see Samuel
Anjou, 177–8; see Fulk, Geoffrey, Sibylla
Ankara, 22, 26, 28, 139, 210, 412
Anna, see Comnena
Annales de la Terre Sainte, 478, 488
Anne, St, convent of, 102, 231
Anselm of Buis, Archbishop of Milan, 18–21
Anselm, Bishop of Bethlehem, 223–4
Anterius, Bishop of Buluniyas, 425 n.
Antioch, Pisidian, 271
Anti-Taurus mountians, 8, 14, 119, 356
Apamea, 11, 52–3, 120, 122, 131, 148, 153, 328, 343, 349; Archbishops of, see Peter, Serlon; see also Enguerrand
Apulia, 49, 51, 143, 191

Index

Index

Baldwin II, of Le Bourg, King of Jerusalem, as Count of Edessa, 10, 36–9, 41–3; first captivity, 43–7, 55, 107, 111–12; as Count again, 67–8,.79–80, 96, 112–18, 122–5, 129, 132, 135; reign, 143–9, 151–85. Other references, 187–8, 190–1, 233, 234, 292, 297, 305–6, 323, 449 n., 451

Baldwin III, King of Jerusalem, early reign, 233–4, 241–3, 328–9; and Second Crusade, 279–84; regent of Antioch, 331–3; regent of Tripoli, 333; displaces his mother, 334–5; government, 336–43, 345, 347–8; relations with Byzantium, 349–50, 353–4; later years, 357–61. Other references, 185, 232 n., 300, 309, 362, 367

Baldwin IV, King of Jerusalem, his leprosy, 299, 392–3; reign, 404–7, 410–1, 414–22, 424–6, 430–5, 439–44; his will, 443, 446–7. Other reference, 362

Baldwin V, King of Jerusalem, 300, 411, 439, 443–4, 446

Baldwin, Archbishop of Caesarea, 83

Baldwin, Archbishop of Nazareth, 280, 328

Baldwin of Antioch, 365, 413

Baldwin, lord of Grandpré, 20

Baldwin, lord of Marash, 201–2, 214, 240, 483

Baldwin of Ibelin, lord of Ramleh, 415, 417, 420, 423–4, 438, 440, 447–50, 451

Balian I, lord of Ibelin, 192, 229, 233, 249, 423

Balearic Islands, 92

Balian II of Ibelin, marries Queen Maria, 406, 423, 424; intermediary between Guy and Raymond, 451–4; at Hattin, 457–8; defends Jerusalem, 463–7. Other references, 417, 438, 440, 444, 447–9, 461, 469, 478, 486, 489

Balikesri, 270

Balikh, 42

Balis, 113, 127, 134, 149, 341

Balkan peninsula, 19, 27, 111, 206, 263, 266, 276, 426

Banyas, 95, 170, 179–80, 192, 196, 197, 227–8, 281, 295, 336, 342–3, 370–1, 399, 418, 419, 420, 434, 452; Bishops of, see Adam, James

Barac, doctor, 361

Barada, river, 282

Barcelona, 35 n., 250, 294; Bishop of, see Berengar

Bar-Hebraeus, Abu'l Faraj, historian, 484, 487

Barkiyarok, Sultan, 13, 40, 108, 130

Barre, see Everard

Bar-Sabuni, Jacobite Bishop, 135–6

Barsauma, Jacobite priest, 236

Barsauma, Mar, monastery of, 136

Barsauma, Saint, 323, 371

Barzenona, 35 n.

Basarfut, 40, 243

Basil, Jacobite Bishop of Edessa, 235, 237, 240

Basil, Prince of Gargar, 327

Basil the Doctor, Armenian poet, 483

Basil, Armenian lord, 201

Basle, 255

Basoches, see Gervase

Basra, 396

Bathys, river, 268

Batit, Joseph, 465

Baudri, Archbishop of Dol, 476

Bavaria, 256 n.; see Henry, Welf

Bazawash, mameluk, 202–3, 204

Beatrice, Countess of Edessa, 190, 309, 328–9, 330, 331, 362 n.

Beaufort, 364, 420, 462, 469

Beauvais, see Alberic, Philip

Becket, see Thomas

Bedouins, 5, 97–8, 113, 230, 295, 319, 442–3, 450

Bedran, emir, 380

Beersheba, 99, 229

Beha ed-Din ibn Shedad, historiar, 480–2, 486–90

Behesni, 330

Beirut, 11, 57, 76, 91–2, 99, 101–2, 118, 175, 190, 294, 311, 316, 335 n., 361, 378, 419, 432–3, 443, 447, 449, 451; Bishop of see Odo; see also Guy

Beisan, 4, 437

Beit Nuba, 231

Bekaa, 410

Bela III (Alexius), King of Hungary, 365 n., 427

Belgrade, 19, 27

Belin (La Mahomerie), 170

Bellesme, see John

Belvoir, 376, 432, 469

Bena Zahr, see al-Juyushi

Index

Burgundy, 254; *see* Hugh III, Stephen
Buri, Taj al-Mulk, 34, 46, 57 n., 63, 95, 179–80, 182, 196
Bursuk, Turk, 234
Bursuq ibn Bursuq of Hamadan, 121, 123, 130, 131–3
Burzey, 470
Butaiha, 351
Butumites, Manuel, 40, 93–4, 137–8

Caen, *see* Radulph
Caesarea, 5, 7, 72, 73–4, 93, 191–2, 280, 294, 296 n., 297, 310; Archbishops of, *see* Baldwin, Evremar, Heraclius, Hernes; *see also* Eustace, Hugh, Walter
Caesarea-Mazacha, 26, 264, 342, 412
Caffaro, historian, 476
Cairo, 12, 168–9, 320, 348, 366, 368, 372–6, 381–2, 396, 407, 410–11, 417, 432, 433, 437, 450
Calabria, 286
Calamon, 391 n.
Calixtus II, Pope, 166
Calvary, 164, 184
Camaterus, John, Prefect of Constantinople, 360
Cambrai, *see* Lithard
Cantacuzenus, admiral, 46, 53
Capetian dynasty, 357
Cappadocia, 138
Caramania, 273
Carmel, Mount, 5, 7, 87
Carniola, 19
Carpenel, Geldemar, lord of Haifa, 74–5
Carrhae, 42
Castile, 92, 250; *see* Alfonso VII, Urraca
Catalonia, 250
Cathars, 253
Catherine, St, monastery of, 319
Cecilia of France, Princess of Antioch, later Countess of Tripoli, 48–9, 124–6, 134 n., 152, 188, 195
Cecilia of Rethel, Princess of Antioch, 126, 152, 154, 182
Cerdagne, 61; *see* William-Jordan
Cerularius, Michael, Patriarch of Constantinople, 48
Chalcedon, 267, 269
Chamelle, La, 57, 66, 70
Champagne, 48; *see* Henry, Stephen
Chartres, 176, 229; *see* Fulcher, Tibald

Chastel Arnaud, 90–1
Chastel Ernant, 231
Chastel Rouge, 132, 134 n., 188, 190
Château-Neuf, *see* Hunin
Châtillon-sur-Loing, 345; *see* Reynald
Cheravas, 261
Christopher the Chancellor, 356
Chrysolan, Peter, Archbishop of Milan, 137
Cilicia, 9, 33, 40, 46, 50, 53–4, 66, 113, 119, 122, 182, 200–2, 206, 212, 214, 217, 219, 222–3, 234, 247, 267, 274, 276, 294 n., 295, 332, 346, 351, 356, 364, 377–8, 389–90, 393, 395, 430
Cinnamus, John, historian, 270, 475
Cistercian order, 252
Clairvaux, 248, 254, 255, 256, 257
Cleopatra, Queen of Egypt, 103
Cluny, 254; *see* Peter
Cologne, 254
Coloman, King of Hungary, 19
Coloman, Constantine, governor of Cilicia, 364, 367, 369–70, 377–8, 390
Comnena, Anna, historian, 50, 208–9, 475
Comnena, Eudocia, 377
Comnena, Maria, Caesarissa, 265, 332
Comnena, Maria, Porphyrogennete, 403, 422, 427–8
Comnena, *see* Maria, Theodora
Comnenus, Alexius, Porphyrogennete, 222
Comnenus, Alexius, Protosebastus, 427–8
Comnenus, Alexius Bryennius, Grand-Duke, 360
Comnenus, Andronicus, Porphyrogennete, 222
Comnenus, Isaac, Porphyrogennete, 222, 224
Comnenus, Isaac, Sebastocrator, 211, 219
Comnenus, John, renegade, 219
Comnenus, Manuel, Sebastus, 377
Comnenus, *see* Alexius, I, Alexius II, Andronicus I, Isaac, John II, Manuel I
Conrad III, King of Germany, and Second Crusade, 255–6, 257, 259–63, 266–71, 274, 276, 279–88. Other references, 222, 248, 354, 411 n., 479
Conrad of Montferrat, lord of Tyre, 444, 471–2
Conrad, Constable of Germany, 20–4, 31, 76–8

506

Index

Constance, Princess-regnant of Antioch, minority, 183–4, 188, 198, 305; first marriage, 199–200; question of remarriage, 306, 309, 330–2, 333; remarries, 345–6; marries daughter to Manuel, 358–60; falls from power, 364–5, 371

Constance of France, Princess of Antioch, 48–9, 176

Constance of Sicily, later Empress, 428

Constance of Antioch, daughter of Bohemond III, 419 n.

Constance, city, 255

Constantine the Great, Emperor, 15

Constantine I, Roupenian prince, 182

Constantine II, Roupenian prince, 202, 214

Constantine, see Coloman, Ducas, Gabras

Constantinople, 19–21, 24–7, 30, 40, 55, 65–6, 102, 105, 121, 130, 188, 198, 210–11, 214, 217, 219, 220, 224, 234, 238, 261, 263–4, 266, 268, 270–1, 276, 280, 285–6, 309, 331, 333, 346, 348–51, 355–8, 360, 365, 377, 379, 384, 390–3, 395, 411, 414, 423–4, 426–9, 444, 467, 471, 475

Contostephanus, Andronicus, Grand-Duke, 234, 385–8

Contostephanus, John, 234, 356, 359

Copts, 295, 381

Cordova, 250

Corfu, 166–7, 275

Corinth, 275

Corycus, 46

Cotyaeum, 139

Courtenay family, 37–8, 237, 323, 424–5; see Agnes, Isabella, Joscelin I, II and III, Peter, Stephanie

Crassus, Roman general, 42

Cremona, see Sicard

Cresson, springs of, 453, 454

Cydnus, river, 103, 351

Cyprus, 9, 34, 46, 60, 62, 92, 222 n., 346–8, 349, 360, 378, 385–6, 427, 430

Cyrenaica, 435

Dadjik, 351

Daimarg, battle, 195

Daimbert of Pisa, Patriarch of Jerusalem, 35–6, 41, 71, 72, 81–4, 177, 310, 321

Damascus, 11, 34, 58, 63, 69, 88–9, 95, 97–8, 126–8, 131, 133, 138, 146–8, 158, 167, 170–4, 178–80, 192, 195–7, 202–4, 220, 225–8, 234, 238, 241–4, 281–4, 319, 320, 325, 335, 338, 343, 350, 366, 372,

378, 398, 410, 416, 418, 420, 431–5, 437, 441–2, 450, 460, 472, 480, 482

Damietta, 386–8, 431

Danes, Denmark, 91, 249

Daniel the Higumene, 86 n., 321, 485

Danishmend dynasty, 8, 9, 13–14, 21–4, 30, 38–9, 40, 108, 119, 126 n., 148, 172, 183, 200, 207–8, 210–11, 216, 219, 222, 264, 342, 356, 395, 412; see Ain ed-Daulat, Dhu'l-Nun, Ghazi, Mohammed, Yakub Sangur, Yighi-Siyan

Danube, river, 27, 206, 211, 260, 263

Daphne, 316

Darbsaq, 471

Dareiya, 350, 434

Daron, 297, 380, 390

David II, King of Georgia, 159–60

David, Tower of, at Jerusalem, 91

Dawud, Seldjuk Sultan, 194–5

Dawud, Ortoqid, 216

Dead Sea, 5, 72, 97, 98, 176, 223, 229–30, 394, 437

De Expugnatione Terrae Sanctae Libellus, 478, 486–9

Delta, 12, 18, 373, 381

Demetrius, see Branus, Macrembolites

Deraa, 146–7, 242

Deuil, see Odo

Devol, river, 50; Treaty of, 50–1, 136, 214, 218, 308

Dhahak, emir of Baalbek, 341

Dhu'l Nun, Danishmend prince, 264, 342, 412

Dhu'l Qarnain, Danishmend prince, 342

Dhirgam, vizier of Egypt, 367

Diarbekir, 41, 235, 239, 369, 434, 445, 480

Diert, 369

Dijon, 257

Diogenes, see Romanus

Dog River, 71, 72

Dome of the Rock, at Jerusalem, 468

Domenico, see Michiel

Domfront, see Radulph

Dorylaeum, 13, 21, 28, 29, 139, 265, 268, 276, 413

Douro, river, 258

Douzy, see Matilda

Dreux, see Robert

Druzes, 12

Dubais ibn Sadaqa, Bedouin, 171–3, 181, 194

Ducas, Constantine, co-Emperor, 208

507

Index

Index

Index

Izz al-Mulk, governor of Tyre, 93–4
Izz ed-Din, Zengid prince, 408, 433–4, 445–6
Izz ed-Din, *see* Mas'ud

Jabala, 11, 33–4, 54, 57, 64, 66, 115, 134 n., 184, 307, 311, 365 n.; 470; Bishop, *see* Hugh
Jacob, patriarch, 319, 418; Jacob's Ford, 418–19, 421
Jacobite church, 9, 10, 12, 36, 86, 135–6, 232, 295, 322–3, 327, 329, 371, 422, 467; Patriarchs, *see* Athanasius, John Michael; Bishop of, *see* Basil
Jacques of Vitry, historian, 477
Jaffa, 5, 7, 74–9, 82, 89–90, 99, 166, 190–2, 229, 231–2, 294, 297, 334, 424, 439–40
James, Bishop of Banyas, 384
James of Mailly, Marshal of the Temple, 453
Jamnia, 229
Janah ed-Daulah, emir of Homs, 11, 57–9, 120
Jasr, 171
Jaulan, 6, 159, 242
Jawali, governor of Harran, 41
Jawali Saqawa, governor of Mosul, 64, 110–14
Jebail, 60, 69, 88, 294, 306, 372 n., 389, 462; *see* Embriaco
Jebarre, Gerald, Hospitaller, 199
Jekermish, atabeg of Mosul, 41–5, 107–10
Jemal ed-Din, *see* Mohammed
Jerash, 159
Jerba, 251
Jericho, 4, 85, 231, 311, 441
Jews, 4, 101, 239, 254, 295–6, 467
Jezireh, 10, 11, 40–1, 54, 107–8, 117, 121, 131–3, 155, 159, 171, 210, 216, 327, 398, 404, 433–4
Jezreel, 4, 438–9
Jihan, river, 54, 183, 210
John, Saint, Evangelist, 157
John, Saint, the Almsgiver, 156–7
John II, Comnenus, Emperor, 50, 166, 183 n., 206–20, 222–4, 234, 238, 247, 309, 475
John, Prester, Christian king, 247, 422
John the Oxite, Patriarch of Antioch, 33, 35
John, Patriarch of Jerusalem, 322 n.
John, Jacobite Patriarch, 185

John, Armenian Archbishop of Edessa, 235
John of Bellesme, Chamberlain, 304
John the Deacon, historian, 483
John of Wurzburg, pilgrim, 294, 480
John, *see* Camaterus, Cinnamus, Contostephanus, Phocas
John, St, church at Edessa, 114
John Roger, Caesar, 265, 332
Jordan, river, 4, 6, 57, 126, 146, 159, 170, 242, 243, 337, 343, 351, 376, 418, 420, 432, 436, 438, 454, 455
Joscelin I, of Courtenay, Count of Edessa, comes to East, 37–8; lord of Turbessel, 39–40, 41–3, 113–15, 122–3; first captivity, 43, 67–8, 107; released, 111–12; banished, 96, 124; supports Baldwin II, 143–4; Count of Edessa, 144, 152, 154, 159; second captivity, 161–3; escape, 163–5; government in Edessa, 171, 175, 180–1, 184–5. Other references, 125–6, 187–8, 292, 305, 362 n.
Joscelin II, of Courtenay, Count of Edessa, accession, 193; early wars, 201–2, 204; relations with Byzantium, 212, 214–18, 222; loss of Edessa, 234–7; at Turbessel, 278–80, 325; capture and death, 327–8. Other references, 171, 173, 185–6, 188, 221, 228, 362
Joscelin III, of Courtenay, titular Count of Edessa, 330, 358, 405–7, 408, 426, 443, 446–7, 460–1
Joseph, an Armenian, 151
Joseph, *see* Batit
Josias, Archbishop of Tyre, 425 n., 451–4
Joveta (Yvette), of Jerusalem, Abbess of Bethany, 171–2, 173, 174, 177, 231–2, 311, 407, 449 n.
Judaea, 80, 100, 167, 230, 321, 334
Juyush-beg, governor of Mosul, 130
al-Juyushi, Bena Zahr ad-Daulah, mameluk, 88

Kafarlata, 40, 52, 243
Kafartab, 45, 53, 131–2, 171, 173, 174, 176, 197, 215, 219
Kafr Sebt, 455–6
Kahf, 200
Kaisun, 112, 123–4, 129, 185, 201, 330, 483
Kakun, 453
Kamil ibn Shawar, 373–4, 379–80, 382

Index

Index

Mahmud, Seldjuk Sultan, 147–8, 181–2, 194
Mahmud, Shihab ed-Din, atabeg of Damascus, 197, 202, 226
Mailly, see James
Mainz, 254
Majd ed-Din, governor of Aleppo, 357
Malagina, 265
Malik Ghazi Gümüshtekin, Danishmend emir, 13, 22–8, 30, 32, 108, 138
Malik Shah, Seldjuk Sultan, 13, 41
Malik Shah ibn Kilij Arslan, Seldjuk Sultan of Rum, 118–19, 138–9
Malmesbury, see William
Malta, 251
Mamistra, 33, 46, 54, 66, 122, 130, 182, 200, 212, 311, 332, 352, 364, 389, 430; Bishop of, see Radulph
Manakil al-Asakir, 282
Manalugh, Seldjuk general, 139
Manasses, Bishop, 35, 48, 76
Manasses of Hierges, Constable, 165 n., 233–4, 249, 334–5
Manfred, Marquis, 103 n.
Manuel I, Comnenus, Emperor, accession, 224, 234; receives Raymond of Antioch, 238; and Second Crusade, 260–1, 262–3, 266–72, 274–7, 285–6, 288; wars with Turks, 264–5, 412–15; negotiations with Constance of Antioch, 309, 331, 358–60; annexes Edessene territory, 329–30; alliance with Amalric, 321, 370, 379–80, 384–6, 388; death, 426–7. Other references, 198, 222, 371, 377–8, 403, 419, 422–3, 429, 475
Manuel, see Comnenus
Manzikert, battle, 217, 413
Maqrisi, historian, 482
Maraclea, 57
Maragha, 121
Marash, 14, 40, 50, 102, 130, 153 n., 201, 325, 327; see Baldwin, Geoffrey, Reynald, Richard
Mardin, 37, 41, 63, 107, 111, 128, 131, 155, 159, 162, 172, 369, 409, 433–4, 454
Marescalcia, 487
Margaret of Navarre, Queen of Sicily, 384
Maria of Antioch, Empress, 359–60, 371, 427–8
Maria Comnena, Queen of Jerusalem, 292, 377, 378, 393, 404, 406, 423, 440–1, 443 n., 447, 453, 463

Maria of Salerno, Countess of Edessa, 126, 161 n., 181, 362 n.
Maria of Milly, lady of Oultrejourdain, 335 n.
Mary Josaphat, St, Abbey, 190, 311, 479
Marj Ayun, 420, 423
Mark Antony, 103
Maronites, 12, 294, 322
Marqab, 11, 54, 134, 190, 470; see Mazoir
Marseilles, 232, 294, 315
Martin, governor of Lattakieh, 122
Mary of Scotland, Countess of Boulogne, 143 n.
Mas'ud ibn Kilij Arslan, Seldjuk Sultan or Rum, 119, 139, 207–8, 211, 219, 264–6, 325, 327–8, 330, 342
Mas'ud ibn Mohammed, Seldjuk prince, 121, 128, 130, 194–5, 225, 237
Mas'ud, Izz ed-Din, governor of Aleppo, 175
Mas'ud, governor of Tyre, 168–9
Masyaf, 410
Mataria, 382
Matilda of England, Western Empress, 178
Matilda of Douzy, Countess of Sancerre, 392 n.
Matthew of Edessa, historian, 36, 126, 483, 484
Mauléon, see Ralph, lord of
Maurice, Cardinal of Porto, 33 n., 73, 81–2
Maurice, lord of Oultrejourdain, 335 n.
Maurus, ambassador, 262
Mawdud, mameluk, 111–12, 115–18, 121–4, 126–7, 129
Mayyafaraqin, 115, 121, 162, 172, 445
al-Mazdaghani, vizier of Egypt, 179
Mazoir, Reynald, lord of Marqab, 150–1, 190, 195, 200
Mazyad, Banū, 113; see Sadaqa
Meander, river, 208, 265, 356, 412
Mecca, 133, 361, 431, 436–7, 454
Medina, 431, 437
Mekhitar of Airavanq, historian, 483
Melaz, Danishmend princess, 126 n.
Melisende, Queen of Jerusalem, marriage, 177–8; accession, 185, 187; and Hugh of Le Puiset, 191–3; religious interests, 231–2, 311, 321, 360–1; government, 233–4, 236, 241, 247; and Second Crusade, 279–80, 283, 287; falls from power, 333–5, 337; death, 361. Other

514

Index

references, 198, 203, 253, 297, 300, 306, 332, 347, 358, 359, 405, 449 n.
Melisende of Tripoli, 332, 359–60
Melisende of Montlhéry, Countess of Rethel, 190 n.
Melitene, 14, 36, 39, 108, 110, 118–19, 122, 172, 207–8, 210, 264, 342
Melusine, water-fairy, 424
Menbij, 113, 165, 170, 312, 330, 385, 409
Merle, see Ralph
Mersin, 212
Mersivan, 23, 31, 33
Meskeneh, 487
Mesnil, see Walter
Mesopotamia, 9, 40, 155
Messina, 84
Messines, see William
Metz, 259, 261
Michael VII, Emperor, 15
Michael, Jacobite Patriarch, 323, 371, 422, 483, 484
Michael, Prince of Gargar, 201
Michael of Otranto, 379
Michael, see Branas, Italicus, Palaeologus
Michiel, Domenico, Doge of Venice, 166-7, 170
Milan, 18; Archbishops of, see Anselm, Chrysolan
Miles of Plancy, Seneschal, 381, 384, 390, 393, 404–5
Military Orders, see Hospital, Temple
Milly, see Maria, Philip, Stephanie
Mina, 437
al-Mina, 57, 59
Minya, 374
Mirabel, 334
Misrin, 45
al-Mizza, 282
Mleh, Roupenian Prince of Armenia, 214, 331, 369, 389–90, 391, 393, 395, 418–19
Moab, 6, 230, 436; see Kerak, Rabboth
Mohammed ibn Malik-Shah, Seldjuk Sultan, 13, 41, 63–4, 105, 108, 110–11, 118–19, 121, 130, 133, 147
Mohammed ibn Ghazi, Danishmend prince, 202, 211, 219, 220, 264
Mohammed of Isfahan, governor of Harran, 41
Mohammed, Jemal ed-Din, governor of Baalbek, 226
Monastir, 379

Monastras, general, 46, 53
Mongols, 348
Monotheletes, 12, 294, 322
Montebello, see Hugh
Montferrat, see Conrad, Rainier, William
Montfort, see Bertrada
Montgisard, 417–18
Montlhéry, see Alice, Isabella, Melisende
Montreal, 98, 229–30, 366, 394, 468–9
Moqtafi, Caliph, 195
Morocco, 251
Morphia of Melitene, Queen of Jerusalem, 36, 144, 146, 154–5, 165 n., 171, 172 n., 177, 321
Mosul, 40–1, 64, 107, 108, 110–12, 123, 128–9, 130, 172–4, 175, 181–2, 194, 197, 225, 237, 244, 325, 336, 369, 393, 396, 408, 412, 433–5, 437, 445–6, 454, 481
Mount Sion, Abbey, 311
Muhris, Banū, 11
Mujir ed-Din Abaq, Burid prince of Damascus, 226, 335–7, 340–1, 342
Munietra, 372 n.
Munqidhite dynasty, 8, 11, 57, 118, 131–3, 148, 172–4, 215–16, 319–20, 343, 348; see Shaizar, Murshid Sultan, Usama
Murad, Fountain of, 326
Murshid, Munqidhite prince, 67
Musa, Wadi, 97, 230 n.
Musbih ibn Mula'ib of Apamea, 53
Muslimiye, 39
al-Mustadi, Caliph, 394
al-Mustarshid, Caliph, 181, 194-5
al-Mustazhir, Caliph, 13, 105, 121, 130, 181
al-Mutamen, eunuch, 385–6
Muwaffaq of Nishapur, 120
Myriocephalum, battle, 412-14, 422, 426

Nablus, 4, 156, 204, 228, 295, 297, 317, 334–5, 337, 372, 399, 406, 425, 442, 447–9, 451–2, 461, 462; see Philip, Raourt
Najm ed-Din, see Ayub
Namur, see Albert
Naqura, 118
an-Nasir, Caliph, 434–5
Nasr ibn Abbas, 365–6
Nasr ed-Din, Zengid prince, 244, 343, 344
Nasr ed-Din, emir of Homs, 446
Nativity, church at Bethlehem, 321, 391

515

Index

Index

Paschia, *see* Riveri

Paul, St, Cathedral at Tarsus, 29

Paul, St, monastery, 312

Payens, *see* Hugh

Pelusium, 99, 367, 368, 380, 386

Pergamum, 139, 270

Persarmenia, 445

Persia, Persians, 5, 110, 111, 114, 128, 165 n., 179, 247, 268, 446

Petchenegs, 15, 21, 26, 113

Peter, Bishop of Albara, Archbishop of Apamea, 149–50

Peter, Archbishop of Lyons, 221

Peter, Archbishop of Tyre, 338

Peter the Venerable, Abbot of Cluny, 254, 286

Peter of Courtenay, 421

Peter the Hermit, 3, 19

Peter the Latin, monk, 184

Peter, *see* Brice, Chrysolan

Peter, St, cathedral at Antioch, 125–6, 136, 152

Peter, St, church at Rome, 220

Peterborough, *see* Benedict

Petra, 72, 97, 230

Petra Deserti, *see* Kerak

Petronilla, Queen of Aragon, 250

Petzeas, governor of Lattakieh, 54

Phanar, quarter at Constantinople, 266

Philadelphia, 138, 270

Philip I, King of France, 48–9, 176, 177

Philip of Alsace, Count of Flanders, 414–16

Philip, Bishop of Beauvais, 421

Philip of Milly, lord of Nablus, lord of Oultrejourdain, Grand Master of the Temple, 236, 335 n., 359 n., 391

Philip, doctor, 422–3

Philippa of Toulouse, Duchess of Aquitaine, 27

Philippa of Antioch, lady of Toron, 377–8

Philippopolis, 19, 260–1; Archbishop of, *see* Italicus

Philocales, Eumathius governor of Cyprus, 62, 138

Philomelium, 28, 29 n., 139, 208, 265

Philopatium, palace near Constantinople, 209, 266, 269

Phocas, John, pilgrim, 321, 392 n., 475

Phrygia, 208, 210

Piacenza, Bishop of, 83

Picquigny, *see* Gormond

Picridium, palace near Constantinople, 266

Pilgrim, Mount, 60–1, 66, 68

Piriska, *see* Irene

Pisa, Pisans, 15–16, 54, 65 n., 73, 206, 211, 294, 315, 427, 479

Plancy, *see* Miles

Plantagenet dynasty, 357

Plivano, lord of Botrun, 406, 459

Poemamenum, 138

Poitiers, *see* Raymond

Pol, *see* Stephen

Poland, *see* Boleslav

Polovtsians, 206–7, 276

Pomerania, 255

Pons, Count of Tripoli, 65, 124–6, 131–2, 134 n., 137–8, 144, 148, 152–4, 160, 169–70, 174, 187–90, 195, 202–3, 305

Pons, lord of Tel-Mannas, 122

Pontus, 327

Poree, *see* Gilbert

Porto, *see* Maurice, Theodwin

Portugal, 92, 258–9

Pougi, *see* Gerard

Pracana, 265–6

Prester, *see* John

Prosuch, general, 261

Provence, Provençals, 24, 33, 65, 69, 314–15

Qadmus, 11, 200

Qalat al-Hosn, 59; *see* Krak

Qalat Jabar, 112, 239

Qalat Sanjil, 60

Qaraja, governor of Harran, 41

Qaraja, eunuch, 134

Qinnasrin, 39 n., 149, 196

Qolaia, 127

Qosair, 371, 389, 429

al-Qubba, 133

Qutb ed-Din, Zengid prince, 244, 336, 385, 390, 412

Qutb ed-Din, Ortoqid prince, 433

Raban, 112, 129; *see* Simon

Rabboth-Moab, 310

Rabwa, 282

Radulph of Domfront, Patriarch of Antioch, 198–200, 217–19, 220–2, 235

Radulph of Caen, historian, 125, 476

Rafaniya, 63, 128, 174

ar-Raghib, 437

517

Index

ar-Rahba, 90, 134
ar-Rahub, 243
Rainfred, knight, 93
Rainier of Montferrat, Caesar, 422, 427–8, 444
Rainier of Brus, governor of Banyas, 228
Rakka, 435
Ralph, Bishop of Bethlehem, 338, 361
Ralph, lord of Mauléon, 437
Ralph of Merle, 331, 333
Ralph, Chancellor, 347
Ralph of Coggeshall, historian, 478
Ramiro, King of Aragon, 250
Ramleh, 5, 229, 417, 432, 469; first battle, 74–5; second battle, 36, 76–8, 80, 136; third battle, 89–90; Bishop of, *see* Robert; *see also* Baldwin, Hugh, Thomas
Rancon, *see* Geoffrey
Ranculat, *see* Rum Kalaat
Raourt of Nablus, 193
Rashid, Caliph, 195
Ratisbon, 259, 262
Ravendel, 10, 114, 329–30
Raymond of Poitiers, Prince of Antioch, marries Princess Constance, 199–200; early wars, 201–2, 204; relations with Byzantium, 206, 212–13, 215–18, 223–4, 234, 238; quarrel with Patriarch 220–1; and Second Crusade, 275, 278–80, 285; death, 325–6, 328, 330. Other references, 184, 228, 235–6, 240, 331, 347
Raymond VI of Saint-Gilles, Count of Toulouse, and Crusades of 1101, 20–5; imprisoned by Tancred, 30–1, 33–4; founds county in Lebanon, 56–61. Other references, 7, 8, 9, 46, 88, 138, 260, 280, 309, 311
Raymond II, Count of Tripoli, 126 n., 203–5, 280, 287, 309, 332–3, 359, 396
Raymond III, Count of Tripoli, Prince of Galilee, minority, 305, 333; relations with Byzantium, 309, 359–60, 367; captivity, 369–70, 395; regent of Jerusalem, 404–8, 410–11; wars with Saracens, 415–16, 419–21, 432, 434, 437–9; leads baronial party in Jerusalem, 425–6, 440–2; regent again, 443–6; and King Guy, 447–54; and Hattin campaign, 455–8, 486–9, 491; death, 469–70. Other reference, 319 n.
Raymond, heir to Antioch, 455, 470, 490

Raymond of Le Puy, Grand Master of the Hospital, 338–9
Raymond, lord of Niphin, 467
Raymond of Aguilers, historian, 476
Raymond-Berenger III, Count of Barcelona, 250
Raymond-Berenger IV, Count of Barcelona, 250
Red Sea, 12, 98, 436–7
Rethel, *see* Hugh, Cecilia, Hodierna
Reynald of Châtillon, Prince of Antioch, lord of Oultrejourdain, marries Princess Constance, 345–6; persecutes Patriarch, 346–7; ravages Cyprus, 347–8; submits to Manuel, 348–54; in captivity, 357–8, 370; released, 405–6, 408; marries heiress of Oultrejourdain, 406; raids, 431, 436–9; besieged at Kerak, 440–1; supports Guy, 447–50; and Hattin campaign, 454–5, 457, 459–60, 489. Other references, 186, 306, 319, 365, 386, 415, 425
Reynald, lord of Marash, 326–7, 362
Reynald Garnier, lord of Sidon and Beaufort, 319, 405–6, 420, 438, 447–8, 458, 462, 469, 471, 489
Reynald of Saint-Valery, knight, 349, 369
Reynald, *see* Mazoir
Rhine, river, 262
Rhodes, 356
Richard of Salerno, of the Principate, 38 n., 47, 110, 112–13, 114, 124
Richard, lord of Marash, 122
Ridwan, ruler of Aleppo, 11, 45–6, 52–3, 59, 89, 107–10, 113, 117–18, 120, 121–2, 127, 128, 133, 175
Ridwan ibn al-Walakshi, vizier of Egypt, 204
Risberg, *see* Otto
Riveri, Paschia de, draper's wife, 317, 425, 455
Roard, castellan of Jerusalem, 223–4
Robert II, Curthose, Duke of Normandy, 97
Robert Guiscard, Duke of Apulia, 190 n.
Robert of Paris, Cardinal, 83
Robert, Count of Béthune, 415
Robert, Count of Dreux, 253, 281
Robert, Bishop of Ramleh, 83, 106
Robert the Leper, lord of Zerdana, 153–4
Robert of Sourdeval, 329
Robert, governor of Suadieh, 122

Index

Robert of Vieux-Ponts, 149–50
Rodosto, 19
Roger II, King of Sicily, 102–3, 175, 193, 199, 207, 211, 220, 222, 248, 251–2, 254, 259, 266, 267, 275–6, 285–6
Roger of Salerno, Prince of Antioch, 125–6, 130–6, 144, 147–50, 181, 295, 476
Roger of Les Moulins, Grand Master of the Hospital, 438, 440, 442, 444, 447–8, 451–3
Roger, lord of Hab, 122
Roger of Haifa, governor of Arsuf, 79
Roger of Rozoy, 77–8, 90
Roman of Le Puy, lord of Oultrejourdain, 191, 230
Romanus IV, Diogenes, Emperor, 217
Rome, 47, 84, 105, 220, 221, 247, 257, 422, 425, 476
Romuald, historian, 479
Roucy, see Hugh, Mabilla
Roupen II, Roupenian prince of Armenia, 389
Roupen III, Roupenian prince of Armenia, 419, 422, 430
Roupen, Roupenian prince, 214
Roupenian dynasty, 14, 30, 51, 119, 122, 130, 135, 182, 201–2, 214; see Constantine, Leo, Mleh, Roupen, Stephen, Thoros
'Royal Historian', 483–4
Rozoy, see Roger
Rudolf, Cistercian, 254
Rum, 121, 135, 148
Rum Kalaat, 329
Russia, 276

Sa'ad ed-Daulah al-Qawasi, mameluk, 74
Sabas, St, monastery, 232, 321
Sabawa, general, 52, 89–90, 108
Sadaqa, emir of the Banū Mazyad, 113
Saewulf, pilgrim, 5, 7, 87, 480
Safed, 4, 297, 343, 376, 469
Safita, 395
Sahyun, 188, 470
Said ibn Bitriq, historian, 477
Saif ed-Din Ghazi I, Zengid, 239, 241, 243–4, 325, 336
Saif ed-Din Ghazi II, Zengid, 390, 393, 398, 404, 408–9, 410, 421–2, 433
Saif ed-Din ibn Amrun, emir of Kahf, 200
Saif ed-Din, see al-Adil
Saint Abraham, see Hebron

Saint-Amand, see Odo
Saint-Denis, 257, 261; see Suger
Saint-Jean-en-Vallée, Abbey, 176
Saint-Omer, see Gerard, Hugh, Walter, William
Saint-Pol, see Hugh
Saint Symeon, 9, 31, 47, 50, 66, 151, 176, 190, 221, 273, 278, 294, 316, 327; monastery, 312
Saint-Valery, see Reynald
Saladin (Salah ed-Din Yusuf), Sultan, expeditions to Egypt, 368, 372, 375–6, 379, 382–3; vizier of Egypt, 385–8, 390–1; relations with Nur ed-Din, 393–9; takes over Damascus, 403–4; in northern Syria, 407–10; defeat at Mont-gisard, 416–7; wars against Franks, 417–21, 430–3; truce in Syria, 421–2; takes Aleppo, 433–5; invades Galilee, 438–9; attacks Kerak, 440–2; illness, 445–6; reconquers Palestine, 450–72, 486–90. Other references, 317 n., 319, 321, 411, 414, 436–7, 449 n., 478, 481–2
Salerno, see Maria, Richard, Roger
as-Salih Ismail, King, 287 n., 398, 404, 407–9, 414, 416, 433
Salkhad, 241–2
Salona, see Adelaide, Boniface
Salzburg, Archbishop of, see Thiemo
Samaria, 5, 334, 452, 461
Samaritans, 296
Samosata, 117, 129, 240, 329–30, 342, 421–2
Samuel of Ani, chronicler, 483
Sancerre, see Stephen
Sangarius, river, 207, 219
Sangur, Danishmend prince, 108
Sanjar, Seldjuk Sultan, 13, 147–8, 194
Santarem, 258
Sarcavag, historian, 483
Sardenay, 319
Sarkhak, emir of Bosra, 336
Sarmeda, 122, 149–50
Sarmin, 45, 132, 344, 470
Saruj, 10, 37, 113, 117, 160, 433, 435
Sarventikar, 31 n., 201
Save, river, 19
Savoy, see Amadeus
Sawad, 96
Sawar, governor of Aleppo, 195–6, 197, 201, 215, 220, 234
Sawinj, Burid prince, 196

519

Index

Index

Index

Thoros II, Roupenian prince of Armenia, 214, 299, 331-2, 346, 347-8, 351-3, 356, 358 n., 364, 369-70, 371, 377, 389
Thrace, 261
Tibald, Count of Blois, Chartres and Troyes, 392 n.
Tiberias, 4, 96, 127, 147, 168, 227, 228, 317, 371, 399, 419, 437, 446, 451, 452-7, 460, 486-7
Tibnin, see Toron
Tiflis, 159
Tigris, river, 194, 236, 435, 446
Timurtash, Ortoqid prince, 162, 165, 171-2, 330, 337
Tivoli, 286
Tizin, 52
Toghrul, Seldjuk prince, governor of Arran, 159-60
Toghrul Arslan, Seldjuk prince, 118-19, 122, 207-8, 210
Toghtekin, atabeg of Damascus, 11, 34, 62-4, 67, 89, 91, 93-7, 122-3, 126-8, 131-5, 146-9, 158-9, 161, 168-70, 173-4, 178-9, 335
Toghtekin, Ayubite, 404
Toroga, see Arnold
Toron, 95, 96, 99, 418, 419, 461; see Humphrey, Isabella
Tortosa, 11, 34 n., 57-60, 64, 66, 68, 287, 311, 333, 376, 397, 421, 462 n., 470
Toul, Bishop of, see Henry
Toulouse, 61, 64-5; see Alfonso-Jordan, Bertrand, Raymond
Transjordan, 7, 72, 77, 89, 97, 147, 227
Trebizond, 139, 210, 219
Tripoli, in Africa, 251
Troyes, see Tibald
True Cross, relic, 74-5, 79, 89, 132, 148, 153-4, 158, 161, 166, 204, 338-9, 374, 390, 416, 432, 434, 455, 459, 460, 489
Tsitas, general, 21
Tuban, 59
Tubaniya, 438-9
Tudela, see Benjamin
Tughril, Seldjuk prince, 194
Tuman, governor of Aleppo, 175
Turan, Shah, Ayubite, 397-8, 410
Turbessel, 38, 52, 68, 111-14, 121, 164-5, 195, 197, 201, 222, 235, 238, 278, 280, 312, 327, 328, 329-30

Tutush, Seldjuk prince, 8
Tutush II, Seldjuk prince, 89
Tyre, 11, 72, 87, 91-9, 165, 167-71. 294. 298, 310-11, 315-16, 377, 433, 439, 446, 447, 461-2, 467, 471-2, 477; Archbishops of, see Frederick, William
Tzibritze, 412

Ulaim, Banū, 40
Unur, regent of Damascus, 203, 225-8, 239, 241-4, 281-3, 287, 325, 335
Urban II, Pope, 18, 20, 35, 83, 248
Urraca, Queen of Castile, 250
Usama, Munqidhite prince, 216, 227-8, 318 n., 319-20, 338, 343-4, 365-6, 480

Vacher, Bernard, knight, 241-2
Vahka, 219, 331, 364
Vahram, vizier of Egypt, 196, 204, 337
Vahram of Edessa, chronicler, 484
Varangian Guard, 267, 353
Vartan, historian, 483
Vasil Dgha, prince of Kaisun, 124, 129
Vatatzes, Theodore, 351
Vendôme, see Geoffrey
Venice, Venetians, 15-16, 92-3, 166-70, 206, 211, 294, 300, 314-15, 427-8, 479; Doges, see Falieri, Michiel
Vermandois, see Hugh
Vézélay, 252-3, 262, 265
Vienna, 276
Vieux-Ponts, see Robert
Vitalis, see Orderic
Viterbo, 247, 257
Vitry, see Jacques, Matilda
Vladislav I, King of Bohemia, 259
Volo, Gulf of, 65

Wadi Halfa, 397
Waleran of Le Puiset, lord of Birejik, 129-30, 146, 161, 165, 172 n., 190, 292
Walter Falconberg of St-Omer, Prince of Galilee, 405
Walter III, Brisebarre, lord of Beirut and Oultrejourdain, 335 n.
Walter I, Garnier, lord of Caesarea, 191 n.
Walter II, Garnier, lord of Caesarea, 438, 440, 447
Walter, lord of Hebron, 122
Walter the Chancellor, historian, 476
Walter of Mesnil, Templar, 397

Index